THE NEW MIDDLE A

BONNIE WHEELER, *SERIES EDITC*

The New Middle Ages *is a series dedicated to transdiscipli-nary studies of medieval cultures, with particular emphasis on recuper... ...women's history and on femin... ...and gender analy... This peer-reviewed series includ... ...th scholarly mon... hs and essay collections.*

PUBLISHED BY PALGRAVE

ELEANOR OF AQUITAINE
LORD AND LADY

Edited by

Bonnie Wheeler and John Carmi Parsons

ELEANOR OF AQUITAINE
© John Carmi Parsons and Bonnie Wheeler, 2003, 2008.
All rights reserved.

First published in hardcover in 2002 by
PALGRAVE MACMILLAN™
175 Fifth Avenue, New York, N.Y. 10010 and
Houndmills, Basingstoke, Hampshire, England RG21 6XS.
Companies and representatives throughout the world.

PALGRAVE MACMILLAN IS THE GLOBAL ACADEMIC IMPRINT OF THE
PALGRAVE MACMILLAN
division of St. Martin's Press, LLC and of Palgrave Macmillan Ltd.
Macmillan® is a registered trademark in the United States, United
Kingdom and other countries. Palgrave is a registered trademark in the
European Union and other countries.

ISBN-13: 978-0-230-60236-6

Library of Congress Cataloging-in-Publication Data
Eleanor of Aquitaine : lord and lady / edited by John Carmi Parsons and
Bonnie Wheeler.
    p.   cm.—(The new Middle Ages series)
    Includes bibliographical references and index.
    ISBN 0-312-29582-0 (hc)
    ISBN 0-230-60236-3 (pbk)
    1. Eleanor, of Aquitaine, Queen, consort of Henry II, King of England,
1122?–1204.   2. Great Britain—History—Henry II, 1154–1189.
3. France—History—Louis VII, 1137–1180.   4. Queens—Great
Britain—Biography.   5. Queens—France—Biography.   I. Parsons, John
Carmi, 1947-   II. Wheeler, Bonnie, 1944-   III. New Middles Ages
(Palgrave (Firm))

DA209.E6 E427   2002
942.03'1'09-dc21

                                                                    [B]
                                                          2002022036

A catalogue record for this book is available from the British Library.

Design by Letra Libre, Inc.

First PALGRAVE MACMILLAN paperback edition: June 2008
10 9 8 7 6 5 4 3 2 1

Printed in the United States of America.

Transferred to Digital Printing in 2008

PERMISSIONS

Grateful acknowledgment is made to publishers and individuals for permission to reprint from the following materials:

The Eleanor Vase. Photograph reprinted by permission of George T. Beech.

Fontevraud Abbey, Interior of Nave and Choir from West. Reprinted by permission of Editions Gaud.

Fontevraud Abbey, Tombs of Henry II and Eleanor of Aquitaine. Reprinted by permission of Kathleen Nolan.

Fontevraud Abbey, Tomb of Eleanor of Aquitaine. Reprinted by permission of Art Resource.

Fontevraud Tombs, Tomb of Eleanor of Aquitaine, detail of head and torso. Reprinted by permission of Editions Gaud.

Tomb Plaque of Geoffrey of Anjou, Le Mans, Musée de Tessé. Reprinted by permission of Art Resource.

Sarcophagus of Blanca of Navarre, Santa Maria del Real, Nájera, detail of front. Reprinted by permission of C. and E. del Alamo.

Seal of Eleanor of Aquitaine (1152), drawing of. Courtesy of the Bibliothèque nationale de France. Photograph reprinted by permission of E.A.R. Brown.

Seal of Eleanor of Aquitaine (1153–54), drawing of. Courtesy of the Bibliothèque nationale de France. Photograph reprinted by permission of E.A.R. Brown.

The third seal of Eleanor of Aquitaine, casts and drwings of the obverse and reverse. Courtesy of the Bibliothèque nationale de France. Photograph reprinted by permission of E.A.R. Brown

Tomb Slab of Adelaide of Maurienne, Saint-Pierre-de-Montmartre, Paris. Reprinted by permission of Arch. Phot. Paris/CNMHS.

CONTENTS

SERIES EDITOR'S FOREWORD

The New Middle Ages contributes to lively transdisciplinary conversations in medieval cultural studies through its scholarly monographs and essay collections. This series provides focused research in a contemporary idiom about specific but diverse practices, expressions, and ideologies in the Middle Ages. The 800th anniversary of Eleanor of Aquitaine's death (†1204) is approaching, and we thought it was time for a reassessment of the life and significance of this medieval queen. *Eleanor of Aquitaine, Lord and Lady* is the first collection of scholarly essays concerned with this pivotal medieval woman in a generation. We are interested in seeing what the new tools and insights of the past generation might reveal about Eleanor. The new historical studies in this volume represent a reassessment of archival and sigillographic materials as well as of the most famous object connected to the queen, the Eleanor Vase. Other studies in the volume benefit from this past generation's sharp focus on women and gender studies. Yet others are concerned with Eleanor as a figure in literary and popular traditions. Here historians rake through the records to determine what we can now say with authority about this duchess and queen, and they point out how myth (and even prejudice) has sometimes occluded our view. Other scholars consider Eleanor's vast after-life as a cultural icon, a touchstone for troubled cultural preoccupations about women, sexuality, and power. All of us who work on Eleanor remain fascinated by what we don't know. This is a woman whose power seemed matched by her discretion, though what we call "discretion" may be only another word for suppressed narratives. What we know now, and what remains amazing, is the travelogue of a woman whose long life was in large measure dedicated to amplifying the power of her kin-groups. Her physical fortitude was prodigious. Her body inscribes Europe; no wonder we are so tantalized to know more of her spirit.

Bonnie Wheeler
Southern Methodist University

PROLOGUE

LADY AND LORD: ELEANOR OF AQUITAINE

John Carmi Parsons and Bonnie Wheeler

Rarely in the course of historical endeavor has so much been written, over so many centuries, about one woman of whom so little is really known. It is bewilderingly futile to disentangle fact and legend within the parameters of Eleanor of Aquitaine's life as they are often represented. She is identified as the greatest heiress in Christendom, marrying and being crowned queen of France at thirteen; bemoaning an unexciting marriage to Louis VII; riding bare-breasted to the Crusades; dallying scandalously with her uncle at Antioch; returning to France to divorce Louis; fighting endlessly with her second husband Henry II of England; poisoning his mistress Rosamund Clifford; presiding as his lieutenant in Aquitaine and holding "courts of love" to encourage and engage in amatory liaisons; enduring imprisonment as a rebellious (and perhaps cross-dressing) queen; dominating her sons and their politics almost to her last breath. Hardly surprising that such a woman consistently attracts legends of lust and letters, but where does historical narrative end and legend begin? As Elizabeth A.R. Brown remarks, this ambiguity has invited many to project personal prejudices onto depictions of this queen. A rich mixture of traditions about this woman has inevitably resulted, and it was perhaps with relief that Henry II's biographer W.L. Warren excused himself from unsnarling them by situating Eleanor as "a creature of legend and romance, but not of history."[1] Again to paraphrase Winston Churchill, Eleanor of Aquitaine remains a mysterious and enigmatic riddle.

Several essays in this book offer a common thread, apposite to these introductory pages, by quoting a remark about Eleanor in H.G. Richardson and G.O. Sayles's *The Governance of Medieval England:* "It may be that she was cursed by fate in being born a woman." The British historians' statement rested on an assumption that medieval society was as inflexibly male-oriented in practice as it may appear to have been in theory. Feminist scholarship on the Middle Ages has consistently taken issue with such beliefs. Medieval Europe's monarchies operated from royal courts that were really households writ large, a domestic and personal arena in which royal women could play pivotal roles. Historians acknowledge today that medieval lineal systems of property inheritance preferred male heirs to safeguard family estates and continue the lineage's wonted liberality to the religious houses whose chroniclers recorded earlier generations' great deeds.[2] But a preference for male heirs never attenuated the importance of kinship ties through female lines. Nor did it deny women's inheritance rights in the absence of sons or brothers, though custom usually entailed an heiress's marriage to a husband who could perform the duties appropriate to her male predecessors and, ideally, to her male descendants.[3]

Such insights underlie this volume's subtitle, "Lord and Lady." Eleanor's patrilineal descent, from a lineage already prestigious enough to have produced an empress in the eleventh century,[4] gave her the lordship of Aquitaine. But marriage reemphasized her sex which, in the medieval scheme of gender-power relations, relegated her to the position of Lady in relation to her Lordly husbands. With or without Eleanor's ready assent, marriage thus transferred to Louis VII and Henry II crucial aspects of her lordship. Yet as the wife and mother of kings, her wealth and influence afforded her fields of action by no means insignificant to her husbands' governments, as shown by Henry II's decision to keep her closely guarded in England, far from Aquitaine, for the last fifteen years of his life. Eleanor's unquestioned importance in the governments of her sons Richard I and John demonstrates that her influence and political reach were recognized during her widowhood as well.

This collection does not claim to offer resolution of these or other aspects of Eleanor's long and eventful life. We have assembled essays by authorities in various fields to suggest fresh nuances to a wide variety of topics, to provide a context for her life, and to further an evolving understanding of Eleanor's multifaceted career. These chapters confirm that this woman did not enjoy fame (or infamy) merely because she was the greatest heiress of her day or because she divorced one king to marry another—unusual as that scenario admittedly was for the European Middle Ages. Stripped of legendary accretions, the outlines of Eleanor of Aquitaine's life confirm that she was a pivotal figure in the history of the twelfth century by reason of her personal inheritance as well as the eminence and political and diplomatic scope her marital rank afforded her. Her inheritance made her a highly desirable consort for Louis VII, who clearly had to respect her rights and status in Aquitaine even as he sought to incorporate the government of her domains within his regal prerogatives. Divorce from

Louis in 1152 reintroduced Eleanor to the matrimonial politics of the twelfth century and led to her swift second marriage to Henry of Anjou, himself the son of an emperor's wife, already duke of Normandy and soon to become King Henry II of England. She supported her sons by Henry in a revolt against him that forced the king to devise a more definitive redistribution of wealth and power among the sons, but won Eleanor fifteen years of obscure confinement in England. As an aging widow, she vigorously assured the Angevin domains' continuity. She preserved her lordship in Aquitaine, supervised collection of the ransom Emperor Henry VI demanded for Richard I's release in 1194, and in 1199 sprang to support her son John's claim to the English throne and the other Angevin domains. Before or after Eleanor's time, few women in medieval Europe exerted such decisive influence over so wide and disparate an assemblage of territories.

An obvious question arises: why do we still await a satisfying study of this woman's life?[5] One reason is the state and nature of the surviving evidence and the selective attention scholars have given it. In a 1959 article that remains a point of reference for work on Eleanor of Aquitaine, H.G. Richardson doubted if her charters and letters would ever be collected.[6] Undeniably, however, the lack of such an edition until the present day has had a negative impact on scholarship concerning Eleanor. The resulting dependence on, indeed preference for, the narrative sources that have been plentifully edited have skewed our view of this woman. This aspect of the problem is due to the nature of these sources. French narratives favorable to the Capetian house and Louis VII, such as Odo of Deuil's *De Profectione Ludovici VII in Orientem,* appear to have been edited after their initial composition to delete references to the divorced queen.[7] It was only after Eleanor's death, however, that writers freely circulated rumors of an intimate liaison with her uncle, Raymond of Poitiers, at Antioch during the Second Crusade.[8] Perhaps such writers hoped to discredit Eleanor's sexual behavior to cast doubt on the paternity of the sons she so rapidly produced after she married Henry of Anjou. But these later chroniclers' eructations contrast impossibly with contemporary exordia of Eleanor, as for example Richard of Devizes's "incomparable woman, beautiful yet virtuous, powerful yet gentle, humble yet keen-witted, qualities which are most rarely found in a woman . . .still tireless in all labours, at whose ability her age might marvel." Or the Fontevraud necrology's queen who "graced the nobility of her birth with the honesty of her life, enriched it with her moral excellence, adorned it with the flowers of her virtues and, by her renown for unmatched goodness, surpassed almost all the queens of this world."[9] By interrogating Eleanor's historical and literary reception by near-contemporary and later authors, several contributions to this volume, especially chapters 1 and 11–16, respectively by Elizabeth A.R. Brown,

Evelyn Mullally, Peggy McCracken, John Carmi Parsons, Tamara O'-Callaghan, Fiona Tolhurst, and Margaret Aziza Pappano, address this contrast and make it a theme of the collection.

Later writers found congenial the salacious implications of Eleanor's detractors and, expanding on them, enabled the formation of the unenviable reputation that continues to shadow her, especially in modern popularizing works. In the mid-thirteenth century, the English chronicler Matthew Paris's remark that Eleanor's beauty led to the ruin of nations was possibly a veiled comment on the Queen Eleanor of his own day, the beautiful and politically controversial Eleanor of Provence (d. 1291), wife of Henry III (r. 1216–71). Matthew consistently criticized this Henry's susceptibility to his wife's influence.[10] Later medieval ballads, such as "Queen Eleanor's Confession," drew on the tales that Eleanor poisoned Henry II's inamorata Rosamund Clifford and that the queen herself was an habitual adulteress. A variant of this ballad makes her eldest son the fruit of an illicit liaison with William Marshal, and another has one of her Angevin daughters fathered by a French friar.[11] In the sixteenth century, debate over female power sharpened in the reigns of Mary and Elizabeth Tudor in England and Mary Stuart in Scotland, and Eleanor of Aquitaine's reputation suffered further: she now appeared as a wife who rebelled against her husband's just authority. Shakespeare's *King John* portrays her as a "canker'd grandam" who helps John plan Arthur of Brittany's death.[12] By the mid-nineteenth century, Agnes Strickland could speak confidently of Eleanor's "disgusting levity," and later editors of medieval sources echoed such sentiments. In the preface to a collection of medieval sermon *exempla*, the French medievalist Lecoy de la Marche unhesitatingly identified Eleanor as the unnamed French queen in one such story, merely on the grounds that its details appeared consonant with Eleanor's "galanteries." The English ballad collector Francis Child sourly noted in 1889 that the murder and adultery ascribed to Edward I's wife in another ballad tradition, "The Lamentable Fall of Quene Elnor," were better suited to Eleanor of Aquitaine than to what was then believed of her later namesake.[13]

The most influential full-scale studies of Eleanor published in the twentieth century have been Amy Kelly's *Eleanor of Aquitaine and the Four Kings* (1950), Marion Facinger Meade's *Eleanor of Aquitaine: A Biography* (1977), D.D.R. Owen's *Eleanor of Aquitaine: Queen and Legend* (1993), and the prolific popular writer Alison Weir's *Eleanor of Aquitaine: By the Wrath of God, Queen of England* (1999).[14] Kelly was a literary scholar; her Eleanor often disappears behind the four kings whose deeds were more thoroughly discussed by contemporary narrative writers, Kelly's chief sources. Fueled by intimate familiarity with medieval literature, however, Kelly inventively filled in the factual gaps in Eleanor's life. It was perhaps inevitable that the early evolution of post–World War II feminism would concentrate initially on the lives of the most visible women of the past. Thanks to the indelible image of Eleanor that Katharine Hepburn created in the film version of *The Lion in Winter* (1968), this queen was often among those singled out for attention by the first generation of feminist historians. Thus Marion Meade argued that misogynistic clerical writers unfairly blamed Eleanor (her sexuality, beauty, ambition, and/or lust) for her husbands' problems with her inheritance and her natural desire to control it, an interpretation consonant with similar studies of male demonization of women who seek to exercise power over men.[15] (Meade's publicity rather overstated her position among those who published on Eleanor, however, by implying that her book offered the first woman's view of Eleanor, neatly ignoring the fact that Agnes Strickland and Amy Kelly were women.) D.D.R. Owen, another literary specialist, discounted a "galante" Eleanor. Following the lead Elizabeth A.R. Brown established in her ground-breaking 1977 article discussed below, Owen dismantled several legends that still surround Eleanor—for example the story in which she is an "amazon" who rode bare-breasted to the Crusade, a fanciful tale Owen traced to the pages of Agnes Strickland. But Owen could not entirely avoid the lure of tradition and, though he accepted that Eleanor's "courts of love" at Poitiers had no basis in fact, tried to identify Eleanor's influence and image in the pages of twelfth-century romances. Weir draws heavily on the romantic legends that have shadowed Eleanor for centuries and manipulates them to weave a lush tapestry of courtly intrigue and infamy. And indeed, the creation of Eleanor's legendary is not yet finished. As Elizabeth A.R. Brown points out in chapter 1 of this volume, new legends about Eleanor have arisen as recently as 1977, and have already furnished new material for scholarly discussion.[16]

In their conspicuous bibliographical omissions and inability to extricate themselves fully from the grip of tradition, Meade's and Weir's works fall short of providing convincing overviews of Eleanor's life.[17] Owen's effort to explicate legends about Eleanor's personal life makes his study the most inclusive of the four, but it does not provide a substantive and authoritative account of Eleanor's career. The lack of a comprehensive view of her career based on the full range of record evidence as well as narrative sources means that modern scholarship on these matters has tended, at its most successful, to concentrate on fine points rather than broadly revisionist overviews. Shorter essays and articles have contributed more positively to an evolving revision of Eleanor's image than the monographs noted above. Examples are studies of her alleged liaison with Geoffrey de Rançon and its role in the military disaster at Mount Cadmos on the Second Crusade;[18] and the ongoing discussion of her supposedly unparalleled role as a literary patron and her associated share in the creation, or furtherance, of the literary phenomenon commonly called "courtly love," which naturally blended with the adultery rumors to create a yet more luxurious and seductive queen.[19] Here we must include Edmond-René Labande's 1952 article, "Pour une image véridique d'Aliénor d'Aquitaine," and the 1977 anthology *Eleanor of Aquitaine: Patron and Politician,* edited by William W. Kibler, a collection of articles addressing various aspects of Eleanor's life and society. Jane Martindale's "Eleanor of Aquitaine," her contribution to the proceedings of a 1989 symposium on Richard I at King's College London, published in 1992, has focused attention on Eleanor's career in the specific context of her Aquitanian domains. Martindale's "Eleanor of Aquitaine: The Last Years," published in a 1999 collection of articles on the reign of Eleanor's son King John, importantly drew attention to the dowager queen's role in assuring John's succession to the Angevin domains.[20]

Of all these earlier articles, the most valuable, and the most accessible to English-speaking readers, is surely Elizabeth A.R. Brown's "Eleanor of Aquitaine: Parent, Queen and Duchess," her contribution to the proceedings of a 1977 University of Texas symposium edited by William W. Kibler. We are greatly indebted to Professor Brown for rethinking, radically revising, and updating that article for the present collection, in which it appears as chapter 1. Brown emphasizes Eleanor's sense of her paternal lineage, in particular the influence of the life of her grandfather, William IX of Aquitaine. It is with this grandfather that Brown associates Eleanor's participation in the Second Crusade, her desire to vindicate the claims to the county of Toulouse that derived from William IX's marriage to a lady of that family, and her patronage of Fontevraud Abbey,[21] in whose foundation William IX had participated. In other words, Brown presents Eleanor as the heir of the long line of Aquitaine's dukes—as a Lord. Intriguingly, Brown finds that many traditions linking Eleanor to behaviors conventionally associated with the medieval Lady, such as her alleged literary or artistic patronage, rest on little or no historical foundation.

In chapters 2 and 3, Marie Hivergneaux and Ralph Turner focus on charter evidence to shape convincing new arguments for Eleanor's political role during two marriages and her widowhood. Here we squarely confront the anomaly of heiress and wife, Lord and Lady. Hivergneaux discusses the many documentary sources that attest to Eleanor's role in the administration of Aquitaine during her marriages, a body of evidence until recently unexplored as a whole. These documents reveal that Louis and Henry found it expedient to associate Eleanor closely with the administration of Aquitaine at some times and to distance her from it at others, but Hivergneaux stresses the apprenticeship any administrative association would have given Eleanor in the conduct of government. We thus have here a ready explanation for the evident absorption of administrative methods that enabled Eleanor's sudden and most remarkable reemergence into political life as a widow, aged sixty-five. Compared with the lives of other aristocratic widows, such as the Anglo-Norman countesses RàGena DeAragon discusses in chapter 4, Eleanor's energetic widowhood, as Turner discusses it, offers fruitful ground for speculation about the degree to which such women shared in their husbands' official or administrative lives. Does the absence of their names from official witness lists prove their exclusion from counsel and administration, or were they more closely acquainted with such matters than we often assume? There is an important contrast here between Louis VII's acts for Aquitaine in the South and those for the Capetian domain in the North. As Marion Facinger (Meade) noted, Eleanor is rarely named in the king's acts for the Capetian domain, where her mother-in-law the dowager Queen Adelaide of Maurienne evidently eclipsed her in administrative matters. In this sense it is significant that Eleanor became Henry II's lieutenant in Poitou only after the death in 1167 of his mother (who had governed primarily in Normandy, of which she was heiress, as Eleanor was heiress of Poitou) and the cessation of Eleanor's childbearing after 1166.[22]

In many respects, Eleanor's politically active old age must be ascribed to the simple fact that she outlived Henry II, ironically perhaps because of the years of quiet confinement to which he had relegated her. But Turner's examination of her years as widow and queen-mother echoes studies by Charles T. Wood and John Carmi Parsons on the influential roles mature, experienced queens-mother could play in contrast to younger, unseasoned queens-consort. It is worth noting how readily Eleanor of Aquitaine eclipsed the wives of her sons Richard I and John, just as Eleanor's mothers-in-law had eclipsed her in royal affairs during her marriages.[23] Turner notes that Eleanor ably manipulated her maternal role in tandem with her lordship of Aquitaine to safeguard the duchy from Philip Augustus in 1200, by first swearing homage to Philip and then establishing herself in joint tenure of the duchy with John. It is not implausible to suggest that this remarkable woman's physical survival alone was a major element in halting Philip's southward advance into her share of the Plantagenet domains.

By offering major correctives to such biological parameters of Eleanor's life, Andrew Lewis, in chapter 7, furthers our understanding of Eleanor's roles as Lord and Lady. Born in or about 1124 (not 1122), she was younger than generally assumed when she had her last child in 1166 (not 1167). That she evidently bore nine (not eight) children between 1153 and 1166 strengthens the idea that frequent pregnancies restricted her official activities in those years. With particular reference to John's childhood, Lewis turns attention to a question that has long dominated discussion of Eleanor's performance of her queenly duties—the impact that her maternal feelings might have had on the destinies of her inheritance and lordship. James Goldman's play *The Lion in Winter,* and the film based upon it, focused perhaps undue attention on this point through its vivid portrayal of John as Henry II's favored pet who resented Eleanor's absence from his early life. The role her behavior may have played on the character formation of "bad" King John has elicited much discussion, including earlier contributions by Ralph Turner, Lois L. Huneycutt and John Carmi Parsons.[24] Scrutiny of the conflicting statements that have come down to us about John's early years leads Lewis to conclude that this last-born son was indeed neglected during the years Eleanor spent as Henry II's lieutenant in Aquitaine (1168–74), when she was distracted by the demands of lordship. Such neglect, Lewis argues, stands in contrast to John's older brothers, with whom Eleanor was able to maintain more regular contact in their early years. Here Eleanor's political ambitions as Lord appear in conflict with her maternal duties as Lady; evidently the nursery was an arena in which she found it difficult to be both Lord and Lady at once. If the proof lies in the pudding, however, we must also recall that, as Brown and Turner note, Eleanor in 1199 unhesitatingly supported John as the only viable heir to Plantagenet authority upon Richard I's death, to the exclusion of her youthful grandson Arthur of Brittany. John actively responded to her support; indeed, as Turner notes, John's rapid march to his mother's assistance when Arthur trapped her at Mirebeau in 1202 was that beleaguered king's only decisive and successful military action. If political life shaped a Lady's mothering, it could also shape her effective functioning as Lord and parent.[25]

Developing a suggestion in Elizabeth A.R. Brown's 1976 article, Constance Berman and Miriam Shadis examine in chapter 8 the careers of four of Eleanor's daughters and their female issue. Eleanor was parted from her daughters by Louis VII after the divorce; if she did see them again, it was only years later. Likewise she had to part from her daughters by Henry II because the king needed to marry them well, and soon, to establish his new dynasty among the older royal lines of Europe. Yet in their adult behavior all five women—and many of their female descendants—demonstrated an ability to exercise power shrewdly which (though we cannot claim it was genetically inherited) may well have derived from a consciousness of, and identity with, an exceptional ancestor. Berman and Shadis interrogate many aspects of accepted chronologies of women's access to power in medieval Europe and demonstrate from the careers of Eleanor's female descendants that as patrons and regents, aristocratic women continued to function effectively to the end of the Middle Ages. Eleanor of Aquitaine is an extreme case, by reason of the vast inheritance that afforded her the scope for Lordly activities. But Ladies of the medieval aristocracy had to be prepared to step into husbands' or fathers' shoes should the need arise, and the careers of Eleanor's descendants show that women did so competently and productively.

The essays in this collection generally focus on Eleanor as duchess of Aquitaine, but in chapters 5 and 6, Lois Huneycutt and Heather Tanner offer new approaches by reconsidering Eleanor's life in the contexts of the careers of her predecessors as queens-consort of England from perspectives suggested by recent investigations into the positions and methods of medieval queenship. Huneycutt and Tanner thus open newly spacious parameters in which to assess Eleanor's political behavior as queen and as duchess. Activist traditions of queenly involvement in English royal government established by Matilda of Scotland (d. 1118) and Matilda of Boulogne (d. 1151), wives of Henry II's predecessors Henry I (r. 1100–35) and Stephen (r. 1135–54), may have provided further impetus to Eleanor's drive to wield power in her own name.[26] This may be especially true for Matilda of Boulogne, like Eleanor an heiress who used her resources to support Stephen (though not her sons against him) and to establish her own position through judicious patronage in the secular and religious spheres. This last point suggests one approach to Eleanor of Aquitaine's career that the essays in this volume do not directly address: the directions and rhythms of her religious patronage in England. Several contributors to this volume discuss Eleanor's religious patronage only in the contexts of her domains on the Continent. DeAragon in particular confirms that Eleanor's religious life was unusual, in that the majority of widows of the higher Anglo-Norman aristocracy in the late twelfth and early thirteenth centuries did not retire to monasteries as Eleanor did—at Fontevraud, not in England. Evidence that Eleanor did not actively support new foundations in England, nor patronize existing houses there, might strengthen our understanding of the degree to which her Aquitanian origins shaped both her religious life and her political reach. Together, the essays by Huneycutt, Tanner, and DeAragon emphasize the extent to which twelfth-century European queenship retained a fluidity of gesture assured by the lack of a well-developed theoretical framework to define such an office. Like other powerful aristocratic women, queens could thus adopt a rich variety of political, religious, or other strategies as the occasion warranted.

A special feature of this collection is chapters 9 and 10 by James Brundage and Constance Brittain Bouchard, who examine aspects of Eleanor's divorce from Louis VII. Brundage examines the formation of canon law governing divorce in the twelfth century and its procedural application in Eleanor's case, while Bouchard focuses on the social contexts of consanguinity in noble marriages and the aristocracy's exploitation of the potential for divorce that consanguinity afforded. Churchmen were aware as early as 1143 that Louis and Eleanor were related within the forbidden degrees of kinship, but husband and wife apparently did not find it disturbing until 1148, when Eleanor brought it up during their quarrel at Antioch. That quarrel led to a period of growing strain in their marriage but in the end, their blood kinship had little to do with the divorce of 1152. Brundage and Bouchard agree that the real reason for the divorce was the queen's failure to bear Louis a son. As Bouchard points out, even the pope had urged the couple to stay together and forbade debate on their kinship. By the mid-twelfth century, the Church had strengthened its position on the indissolubility of marriage and preferred to see a marriage continue rather than annul it on the grounds of consanguinity. But many aristocratic couples found the "revelation" of blood kinship a convenient excuse to end their marriages if it suited them, and in the case of Louis and Eleanor, the tactic worked. That consanguinity was only a surface excuse for their divorce became evident when both of them swiftly took second spouses to whom they were more closely related than they were to each other. Here, then, Eleanor used a Lordly strategy only to rush into a second marriage and again relegate herself to the Lady's position.

The essays in this volume examine the historical record of Eleanor of Aquitaine's life as well as her legendary history (or rather, the history of her legendary). Evelyn Mullally, Peggy McCracken and John Carmi Parsons consider the contexts of Eleanor's reputation in literary and narrative sources. Mullally in chapter 11 examines Eleanor's portrayal in the *Histoire de Guillaume le Maréchal,* a secular verse biography of a renowned knight and politically astute contemporary of Eleanor's whose recollections, passed on to family members and followers, form the work's core. On the basis of his experience of Eleanor, Marshal saw her in a distinctly positive light, as a wise and generous queen who rewards loyalty and has the interests of the kingdom at heart.[27] If the *Histoire* presents Eleanor not as a powerful Lord but as a gracious Lady, it offers a significant corrective to the less attractive writings of monastic annalists and authors of romance such as those McCracken and Parsons consider. The *Histoire* stands as one of our most important witnesses to Eleanor's reception close to her own lifetime, as an account of how a sagacious and steadfast Angevin champion knew her.

In chapter 12, McCracken acknowledges the historical unreliability of the evolution of the tale of Eleanor's adultery with her uncle. But the portrayal and scandalizing of her desire may convey contemporary ideas on the institution of queenship, including male anxieties about sexuality and sovereignty that affected definitions of queenship. Chief among these were the insistence on legitimate births in the king's family, the fraught

question of the queen's access to authority, and the uncomfortable realization that she could successfully base her influence and power on her
role as the king's sexual partner. McCracken finds all these apprehensions
embodied and reflected in successive versions of the tale of Eleanor's relationship with her uncle. In chapter 13, Parsons compares allegations of
Eleanor's adultery and incest with those against another queen of France,
Marie-Antoinette, in the 1770s and 1780s. Both queens reportedly disparaged their husbands' sexual abilities and were accused of polluting the
body politic through adultery and incest. According to Parsons, these tales
about Eleanor rest on no reliable basis; he finds a common ground for
such markedly similar rumors about the two queens in the charged relationship between women's bodies and the body politic, especially in the
anxieties characteristic of the twelfth and eighteenth centuries for female
participation in the official sphere. Eleanor's Lordly inheritance sharpened
these anxieties by allowing her to transgress limits that male-created
sources were imposing on the Lady and, as can be seen in the events of
1173–74, to challenge the king's authority.

This collection turns attention less to Eleanor's personal involvement in
the literary works so long associated with her patronage than to representations of her. As our contributors agree, most evidence linking Eleanor personally with the authors of these works, or with their composition, is
unreliable. This does not mean, however, that authors of her day did not appeal to her image and use it to enunciate ideas about gender, power, and love
(Andreas Capellanus in particular). Tamara O'Callaghan and Margaret Pappano accordingly argue, in chapters 14 and 16 respectively, that the *Roman
de Troie* and Marie de France's *Lanval* refer to Eleanor who, though she commissioned neither work, may have been an intended or hoped-for reader.
O'Callaghan sees Benoit de Sainte-Maure's invention of Briseida in the
Roman de Troie as a means to contrast Briseida's fickleness with Helen's noble
love for Paris, and emphasizes that Benoit constructs Helen's love affair with
Paris so as to avoid, as much as possible, any hint of sexual scandal. Eleanor
too had left one husband to marry a second soon after her divorce; Benoit's
displacement on to Briseida of criticism for her inconstancy allows him to
praise the queen, his anticipated audience, for the excellence that, he implies,
was potent enough to eradicate the faults of other women.

Pappano's examination of Marie de France's *Lanval* suggests a reading
of Marie's Guenevere and "fairy lady" as characters who reflect two aspects
of queenship Eleanor herself represented, aspects directly related to the
subtitle of this volume. For Pappano, Marie's Guenevere figures a queen-
consort's passive role, her position at court settled by the workings of males
(as in Arthur's regulation of gifts to his knights), and her desires unable to
be as openly or straightforwardly expressed as can the king's. In this sense,

Marie's Guenevere represents Eleanor as subject to the authority of her male partners. In contrast, the fairy lady rules her own domains, as Eleanor ruled Aquitaine, and can bestow her own gifts upon Lanval, who leaves Arthur's Camelot to accompany the fairy lady to her realm at Avalon. Pappano concludes that Marie's romance offers a unique female perspective on Eleanor's status and reign.

Medieval literature offers many other highly suggestive attestations to Eleanor's reception. Middle English romances often celebrated her son Richard the Lionheart as a crusading hero, though few of them mention Eleanor or any maternal figure. One of the most gripping and blood-thirsty of the Richard romances to invoke a mother is *Richard Coeur de Lion,* whose hero's Christian majesty is strangely validated by his intensely violent delight in mayhem. His barbaric habits seem to derive from his odd mother, here named Cassodorien rather than Eleanor, to whom another old tale of fear of Christian rituals is adapted. When her husband King Henry one day requires the queen to stay in church during Mass, she reacts by seizing her daughter and her son John during the "sakeryng" of the sacrament and bolting upward through the roof of the church. Nether she or her daughter ever return, though the literary characterization of poor John is reinforced when she drops him from the sky and he breaks his thigh.[28]

This unnatural if not demonic aspect of Richard's maternal figure is familiar from the many medieval stories about the fairy (or demon) Mélusine, which we see here attaching itself to Eleanor (or rather, to Richard's mother). Indeed, many of the literary scenarios with which Eleanor has been associated, especially Arthurian romance, also suggest resonances of her reception. As O'Callaghan argues, some of these works embody elements that suggest an assault on the legitimate continuity of lineage, a threat that can well be understood to have been widely associated with Eleanor's career. In a society whose order was predicated upon the inheritance of land and power by legitimate heirs, adultery and incest were bound to cause anxieties. These were perhaps sharpened by the Church's tightening of its controls over marriage, especially the growing prominence of the strictures of consanguinity, which could make incest—however unintentional—very hard to avoid. It need hardly be said, moreover, that generational conflict with patriarchal lords was common in the Middle Ages. With adultery, incest, and generational conflict very much in the air, Mordred's jealousy of Arthur could echo in the Arthurian context that of Richard, Geoffrey, and John against Henry II, in the general sense of familial conflict with a patriarchal king.[29] And whether Mordred appears as Arthur's nephew or son, Guenevere's involvement with him is incestuous, echoing the rumors about Eleanor's incestuous adulteries as (in some works) does Arthur's with his sister, Mordred's mother. It is not entirely surprising that a queen whose life, in its twelfth-century contexts, assumed truly spectacular proportions would attract stories that incorporated such elements as these. The majestic extent of Henry II's domains and the dramatic reach of his life, not to mention Eleanor's, would unavoidably have drawn attention and literary comment. Some of this comment was narrowly historical, as in chronicles, or combined event and legend in the *historie* noted by Fiona Tolhurst in chapter 15; or it could appear imaginative and appealing in the hands of such poets as Wace and Lawman, whose works Tolhurst also examines.

In chapter 17, George Beech also addresses the Lord-Lady dichotomy by examining the queen's active involvement in the transmission of luxury items. She originally came into possession of the sumptuous object known as the Eleanor vase not by purchase, but as a gift or heirloom from her grandfather William IX of Aquitaine. Thus an artefact originally conferred as a token of esteem between male rulers—the Muslim Mitadolus and Eleanor's grandfather—came to her as part of her Lordly lineal inheritance. By giving the vase to Louis VII in the early days of their marriage, however, she made it a token of her conjugal bond which, as Hivergneaux notes, transferred to Louis significant aspects of his wife's inherited power and authority and left Eleanor herself in the position of Lady. We would like to know more about her reactions when Louis gave the vase to Abbot Suger. Was she glad to see this Lordly object, which she herself had (unwittingly?) made into a token of her subjection, pass out of royal possession? Or did she understand its transfer to the royal abbey as a kind of perpetual confirmation of that subjection?

Chapters 18 and 19 in this volume address the most famous physical monument to Eleanor's career, the royal (or, as Charles Wood suggests here, ducal) cemetery in Fontevraud Abbey, on the borders between Eleanor's Poitevin patrimony and Henry II's Angevin domains. These chapters, by Wood and Kathleen Nolan, cogently argue that Eleanor of Aquitaine was responsible for the first three royal effigies at Fontevraud, those of Henry II, Richard I, and herself. These effigies appropriated Fontevraud's geopolitically liminal space between Henry II's ancestral sphere in Anjou and Eleanor's in Poitou to monumentalize images of royal marriage and succession. Just as the Eleanor vase visualizes a transfer of power within Eleanor's marriage to Louis VII, the Fontevraud effigies realize the conjugal space between Eleanor and Henry II. As Eleanor's sponsored creations, the effigies allow Wood and Nolan to consider her motives in commissioning them. Nolan elucidates the ways in which Eleanor blended the traditions of royal burial she had observed throughout her life, a classic example of a royal woman's ability to integrate and transform. If, as Wood suggests, the effigies commemorated Eleanor's ancestral lineage, the queen's statement becomes all the stronger, and makes it correspondingly harder to distinguish the Lord's actions from those of the Lady, whose place it was to remember and commemorate ancestral dead.

Nolan sees the Fontevraud effigies as an Angevin, not an Aquitanian, necropolis, but Eleanor's immediate intent may be less significant than its later results. David Carpenter has recently suggested that in the end, Eleanor's wish to commemorate her family may have reached far beyond Fontevraud. Carpenter argues that close affinities exist between Richard I's effigy and the burial of Eleanor's grandson, Henry III, in Westminster Abbey. Henry III certainly had great affection for Fontevraud and often had masses celebrated there for the souls of his ancestors.[30] As Wood notes, Henry in 1255 ordered his mother's body moved into the abbey church from the chapter house, where she had been buried at her death in 1246, and commissioned her effigy which, as Nolan notes, was executed in the then-archaic style of the earlier gisants. It is debated whether Henry III patterned Westminster on Fontevraud as a royal necropolis.[31] But whatever Henry III's plans for Westminster may have been, it can well be said that Eleanor of Aquitaine initiated at Fontevraud traditions of monumentalized royal burial and handed them on to the Plantagenets and the Capetians, who developed them at Saint-Denis as the Plantagenets did at Westminster. Whether we regard the Fontevraud effigies as Eleanor's creations as Lord of Aquitaine or as Henry II's Lady, they stand liminally in time as well as space, linking earlier and later royal traditions that had a powerful impact on the face of the royal office in both kingdoms. Here, then, while Eleanor was acting in the long tradition of the royal Lady as a commemorator of the dead, she ultimately reshaped Lordly official images of male rulership.[32]

Jane Martindale's epilogue rounds off the collection with a look back at many of the topics discussed by the essays in this volume. Her thoughtful discussion of the "queenly court" over which one chronicler stated Eleanor presided in England after Richard's accession in 1199 also addresses the Lord-Lady anomaly in Eleanor's career, interrogating the nature and extent of the regal power this woman exercised. Martindale intriguingly forecasts the scope of her forthcoming monograph on Eleanor by offering useful and provocative suggestions for future directions in which research on Eleanor of Aquitaine might turn.

We fittingly close this introduction with reference to the various interpretations our contributors offer of the book that appears in the hands of Eleanor's Fontevraud effigy. Many across the centuries have seen this book as a copy of the romances thought to have been central to Eleanor's enjoyment of life, but this facile suggestion has long since fallen out of favor.

Elizabeth A.R. Brown suggests it may be the Book of Kings, consonant with this queen's taste for power and Lordly matters. In much the same vein, while Charles Wood does not offer a specific identity for the book, he suggests that Eleanor ponders dynastic immortality as she reads it. Nolan sees the book as a Psalter or (very early) Book of Hours, tokens of piety suitable to a Lady and, at the same time, symbols of the final Christian victory to which Eleanor could aspire without reference to the males in her life. While this most concrete of her images may represent a queen's wish to fix her own image for all time, then, its outlines blur and defy interrogation even as we contemplate it. This queen keeps her counsel, and her secrets.

Notes

1. Elizabeth A.R. Brown, chapter 1 in this volume; Warren, *Henry II*, p. 121.
2. For new understandings of how the sustained privileging of the male line of descent in medieval France simultaneously supported the power of women within the family group, see Bouchard, *Those of My Blood*.
3. In recent decades, Georges Duby most consistently upheld the older view. On Duby's contested views of medieval women, see Stuard, "Fashion's Captives," pp. 73–74; Kimberley LoPrete's review of Duby's *Love and Marriage in the Middle Ages*, *Speculum* 70 (1995):607–09, and the essays in *Aristocratic Women in Medieval France*, ed. Evergates.
4. Agnes (1024?–1077, daughter of Duke William V of Aquitaine [d. 1030] and his third wife Agnes [d. 1068], daughter of Count Otto-William of Burgundy), in 1043 married, as his second wife, Emperor Henry III (1017–56) (Brandenburg, *Die Nachkommen Karls des Grossen*, tables 2, 10). The politics of this marriage have been little discussed. It was politically less important than Henry III's first marriage, to a daughter of King Canute of England and Denmark by Aelfgifu-Emma of Normandy, widow of Aethelred II of England. But it allied the emperor with the Aquitanian lineage that had supported the foundation of Cluny in Burgundy and the propagation of Cluniac spirituality, congenial to Henry III's reforming spirit. Agnes was descended from the Carolingians on both sides, and her maternal descent from the house of the counts of Burgundy and the last Italian kings of the house of Ivrea may also have made her attractive to Henry. The vanished kingdom of Burgundy had only recently been claimed for the Empire, and Henry had been careful early in his reign to have the magnates there swear homage to him (Fuhrmann, *Germany in the High Middle Ages*, pp. 40–41). Associations with Cluniac spirituality have also been argued as deciding Henry I of France's choice of a bride in 1051 from the remote principality of Kiev (Poulet, "Capetian Women and the Regency" p. 101; Dunbabin, "What's in a Name?" does not address this hypothesis in theorizing Henry I's Kievan marriage).

5. Jane Martindale's monograph on Queen Eleanor, now in preparation, will redress this situation.

6. Richardson, "Letters and Charters."

7. Odo of Deuil, *De Profectione Ludovici VII*, pp. xxiii and n67.

8. Archbishop William of Tyre (d. 1186) wrote his chronicle between 1170 and 1184, twenty to thirty years after Eleanor and Louis were in Antioch, though still during her lifetime and those of Louis VII and Henry II. William was more explicit on her sexual behavior there than John of Salisbury, who wrote his account of the calamitous stay in Antioch about fifteen years after the event. For the chronology of these accounts see Peggy McCracken, chapter 12 in this volume.

9. Both quoted in Owen, *Eleanor: Queen and Legend*, p. 102.

10. On Matthew Paris's attitude toward Eleanor of Provence see Howell, *Eleanor of Provence*, index at p. 343 s.v. "Paris, Matthew," and Parsons, "'Loved Him—Hated Her.'"

11. Percy, *Reliques of Ancient English Poetry*, 2:145; variants of the text are printed in Child, *Ballads*, 6:257–64. For discussion of this ballad see Owen, *Eleanor: Queen and Legend*, pp. 158–60; Chambers, "Some Legends Concerning Eleanor"; and the article by Elizabeth Carney, "Fact and Fiction in 'Queen Eleanor's Confession.'"

12. Carole Levin, "John Foxe and the Responsibilities of Queenship," in *Women in the Middle Ages and the Renaissance*, ed. Rose, pp. 113–34 at 118 and n20; William Shakespeare, *The History of King John*, act 2 scene 1, and act 3 scene 2.

13. Child, *Ballads*, 6:257. See also, e.g., *Anecdotes historiques*, p. 212.

14. Full publication information for these works may be found in the compiled bibliography at the end of this volume.

15. An intriguing study of non-Western material is Lassner, *Demonizing the Queen of Sheba*.

16. Brown, chapter one in this volume.

17. Weir's bibliography includes neither Labande's important 1952 article, "Pour une image véridique" nor Brown's thoughtful and informative 1977 article, "Eleanor of Aquitaine: Parent, Queen, and Duchess." Meade's book appeared at almost the same time as Brown's article and Meade was probably unable to incorporate it, but she also ignores Labande. In *Eleanor: Queen and Legend* Owen includes only Labande's later article "Filles," omitting bibliographical reference to Brown. To our regret (but as a crucial space-saving requirement) citations in this volume are provided in short titles; for full publishing information, see the compiled primary and secondary bibliography at the end of this volume.

18. Walker, "Eleanor and the Disaster of Cadmos Mountain."

19. For persistent association between Eleanor of Aquitaine and literary works traditionally linked with her, see Owen, *Eleanor: Queen and Legend*, and Ferrante, *To the Glory of Her Sex;* but compare the close consideration of original sources by Broadhurst, "Henry II and Eleanor of Aquitaine," and

discussion in Brown in this volume. Also in this volume, Peggy Mc-
Cracken, Tamara O'Callaghan, and Margaret Pappano all suggest important new approaches to Eleanor of Aquitaine's association with the literary
texts of her day.

20. For full publication information on these articles, see the compiled bibliography at the end of this volume.

21. Throughout this volume, we adopt Elizabeth A.R. Brown's preferred
spelling "Fontevraud" except, obviously, when bibliographical citations require otherwise.

22. Facinger, "Medieval Queenship."

23. Wood, "The First Two Queens Elizabeth," p. 122; Parsons, "Intercessionary
Patronage," pp. 149–50. On Richard's wife Berengaria of Navarre, see
Trindade, *Berengaria;* for John's wife Isabelle of Angoulême, see Jordan, "Is-
abelle d'Angoulême" and Vincent, "Isabella of Angoulême."

24. Turner, "Eleanor and Her Children," pp. 325–26; Huneycutt, "Public Lives,
Private Ties"; Parsons, "Impact of Childhood Caregivers."

25. For theoretical orientation to mothering, see the introduction to *Medieval
Mothering,* ed. Parsons and Wheeler, pp. ix-xvii. For an earlier period, see
Dockray-Miller, *Mothering and Motherhood in Anglo-Saxon England.*

26. On Henry I's second wife see Wertheimer, "Adeliza of Louvain."

27. Elizabeth Carney, "Fact and Fiction in 'Queen Eleanor's Confession.'"

28. *Richard Coeur de Lion,* ed. Brunner, lines 167–240. We are indebted to
Carol F. Heffernan for this reference.

29. Jane Beitscher, "'As the Twig is Bent . . .'"

30. Carpenter, "Burial of King Henry III"; see also Martindale, "The Sword
on the Stone,"226–30, and Boase, "Fontevrault and the Plantagenets."

31. Binski, *Westminster Abbey,* pp. 91–93; Parsons, "The Year of Eleanor of
Castile's Birth,"258–59, and Parsons, "Burials and Posthumous Commemorations of English Queens," pp. 326–27.

32. Brown, "Burying and Unburying."

CHAPTER 1

ELEANOR OF AQUITAINE RECONSIDERED: THE WOMAN AND HER SEASONS

Elizabeth A.R. Brown

> *In this chapter, Elizabeth A.R. Brown revises conclusions she presented in a study of Eleanor of Aquitaine as parent, patron, and politician which was published in 1976. She focuses on the myths that Eleanor has inspired and examines the artistic, sigillographic, and numismatic evidence that can legitimately be linked with Eleanor.*

Eleanor of Aquitaine is a woman who, over the centuries, has seen many seasons. Born in 1124 in the south of France, in or near Poitiers, she lived for eighty years, dying at the end of March 1204 and being buried at the abbey of Fontevraud where she had lived for a decade.[1] Since her death, for almost 800 years, she has proved perpetually fascinating and has been many things to many people. She has intrigued historians of literature, culture, art, politics, and institutions; novelists, cinemasts, and playwrights; and a horde of people who know little more about the Middle Ages than that she (and Joan of Arc) lived then. Despite (and in part because of) the wealth of books and articles dedicated to her, she herself remains elusive. Her contemporaries and near-contemporaries are less informative about her than they are about her husbands, Louis VII of France (1120–80; r. 1137–80) and Henry II of England (1133–89; r. 1154–89). Still, "the not inconsiderable bulk of record material" has cast light on many aspects of her numerous activities and interests, and will, in future, yield more information about her patronage of religious foundations and the people, both French and English, who served in her household.[2]

The search for the "true" Eleanor has been hampered by the legends that, since her own time, she has inspired.[3] In 1941, Frank McMinn Chambers made a commendable attempt to dismantle the mythic scaffolding that has encased her for centuries.[4] However, his pathbreaking article has attracted little attention, doubtless because so much of Eleanor's fascination stems from her legend. In 1993, D.D.R. Owen determined to dispel the myths by showing how they came into being.[5] His endeavor was well-intended, but he did not himself escape the stories' power. His book, after all, is aimed at a popular audience. He could not bring himself to reject out of hand the cherished but nonetheless fallacious tradition of Eleanor as queen of the courts of love,[6] which has no basis in fact and rests on the testimony of a mordantly humorous and ironic work of satire, the *De amore* of Andreas Capellanus.[7] The judgments concerning love that the book associates with Eleanor are poignantly barbed reminders of her own amatory errors, more likely to provoke laughter at the court of France than among Eleanor's friends and family or from Eleanor herself.[8] Nonetheless, popularized by Amy Kelly,[9] the myth of Eleanor as Queen of the Troubadours and Queen of the Courts of Love has had remarkable resilience. In contributing to its continued propagation, Owen is not alone,[10] although others, including John Gillingham and Eleanor's most recent biographer, Alison Weir, have flatly repudiated it.[11]

Nor is Owen alone in publishing—and thus implicitly endorsing—two images that have been associated with Eleanor but that have no proven relevance to her. The first, on the cover of his book, is a portion of a fragmentary wall painting from the chapel of Sainte-Radegonde at Chinon, painted around 1200, which depicts two crowned men and a young woman with flowing hair, all on horseback, attended by falconers.[12] It has been interpreted in a variety of fashions, all of them speculative. Owen, following Desmond Seward, reproduces the central portion of the painting, which shows the young woman and the crowned figure before whom she rides. Both Owen and Seward associate Eleanor with the crowned individual and identify the young woman as her daughter-in-law Isabelle of Angoulême, whom Eleanor's youngest son John married in August 1200. Alison Weir likewise suggests that this crowned figure is Eleanor but identifies the young woman as her daughter Jeanne. Taking a different tack, Martin Aurell declares that the first crowned figure is Henry II, the second Eleanor. Aurell believes that Henry is shown taking Eleanor into captivity and that she is bidding farewell to her son Richard, identified as the fourth figure, uncrowned and holding out to Eleanor a falcon, his favorite bird. Most recently, Jean Flori has proposed that Eleanor commissioned the painting after her liberation, "perhaps in 1193, when Richard was captured." Like Aurell, he thinks the painting commemorates the moment when she was being taken, captive, to England, and turns "one last time" toward her sons Henry and "especially Richard, to whom she has just given a falcon as the symbol of lordly power."[13] The second questionable image Owen offers is a capital from the church of Langon near Bordeaux that he believes represents Eleanor and Henry II in 1152[14] (a likeness similarly endorsed by Amy Kelly and Alison Weir).[15] This identification is as groundless as the first.

The relative sparseness of evidence regarding Eleanor and the mythical status she has acquired go far to explain why historians have linked her with movements and events in which she played no part.[16] For the same reasons, she has been an irresistible target for wish-fulfillment and projection. To her have been linked ideas about what women might have been in the twelfth century: patronesses of literature,[17] architecture, and art;[18] idealized and idolized love-objects; prototypical leaders and advocates of women's liberation.[19] Reflecting assumptions and prejudices that are still powerful, recent popular books have presented her as a woman whose amatory, sexual, domestic, and cultural interests overbalanced her other concerns. My research on this point has not been absolutely exhaustive: I have searched in vain on two continents for a book dealing with what its title calls her "Vie ardente."[20] Nonetheless, I can offer numerous examples of these perspectives. An ostensibly scholarly book depicts Eleanor breathlessly awaiting her daughter Marie's reactions to the decorations with which she, the anxious mother, had adorned her daughter's apartment.[21] Another author has Eleanor designing costumes and establishing an equestrian school for female crusaders in 1146, a variation on the legend of Eleanor the Amazon advanced by Agnes Strickland, the Victorian lady historian of the queens of England.[22] A fellow-Victorian, Mary Anne Everett Green, focused on Eleanor's role as parent, concluding that she was a bad mother who spoiled her children and judging her daughters more fortunate than her sons in "escap[ing] uninjured from such injudicious treatment, perhaps from their having left home when quite young."[23] Bishop Stubbs considered her something of a shrew, who "long retarded the reforming schemes of [Henry II's] great administrative genius." Admitting that "her faults have [probably] been exaggerated," he nonetheless concluded that "she can hardly be said to shine as a virtuous woman or a good wife."[24]

Typical of the flights of imaginative fancy Eleanor has inspired in more recent times, a book published in 1967, subtitled *The Two Marriages of a Queen*, aims to make Eleanor a thoroughly romantic heroine. Its author (who also wrote *Courtesan of Paradise, The Pompadour, Why So Pale?, The Reluctant Abbess,* and *The Passion of Peter Abelard*) divides her book into two sections: *The Inadequate Husband* and *The Lecherous Husband*. Having accounted for Eleanor's dramatic deeds by invoking her "Gothic blood," the author ends her book not with the dramatic scene in which Eleanor falls dead in the arms of a faithful attendant when a messenger reports the capitulation of Château-Gaillard but rather with a description of the sympathetic withering of two roses Eleanor is said to have planted in the garden of Fontevraud to honor Tristan and Isolde.[25]

Eleanor needs no such dramatic embellishment. Her authentic activities and accomplishments are impressive and interesting. She lived for some eighty years at a time when many women died in childbirth in their twenties or thirties. She possessed enormous landed wealth, having inherited from her father, William X of Aquitaine, vast tracts of land with a proud history of independence. She was a crusader. Divorced from one king, she married another ruler with startling speed. For sixty-seven years (three more than Queen Victoria) she was sovereign ruler of Aquitaine, and she was sporadically queen, first of France and then of the English dominions. She was the mother of three kings. She had at least eight other children— three other boys and five girls (two by Louis VII). The lives and marriages of those who survived to adulthood[26] affected the fortunes of France, Champagne, Brittany, Toulouse, Spain, the Empire, and Sicily. She knew the most important people of her age: the small but mighty Suger of Saint-Denis, the dour and daunting Bernard of Clairvaux, the stubborn and proud seeker-after-martyrdom, Thomas Becket of Canterbury. As duchess and queen she presided over a court visited by the great and near-great. And she lived during a period, the twelfth century, whose vitality and creativity historians have long sought to comprehend.

In this essay I shall present a brief account of what, in my judgment, can be known of Eleanor and her life. I start with a narrative of her life, based on her acts and the writings of contemporaries, with any elaboration being, I hope, inferentially responsible. I shall then discuss the artistic, sigillographic, and numismatic evidence associated with Eleanor and offer a few deductions regarding Eleanor that this testimony suggests.

Eleanor's Life

Eleanor's life divides readily into five distinct periods. The first, her childhood and adolescence, extends from her birth in 1124 to her marriage at thirteen (in 1137) to Louis VII of France, who was then seventeen. The second is the French crusading period, extending from 1137, the year of her marriage, to 1152, when she was twenty-eight. In that year she left her husband Louis and their two daughters and wedded Henry of Anjou (soon to be Henry II of England), who was then nineteen, nine years her junior. The next period is a longer one, extending from 1152 to 1173. During these twenty-one years she had at least nine children, the first when she was twenty-nine, the last at forty-four. These were her active, childbearing years, which at the end became pervertedly maternal as she plotted with her sons against their father. The fourth period extends from 1173 to 1189, the year of Henry's death. This was a time of forced withdrawal from active life, as, kept a prisoner by Henry, she passed the years from fifty-one to sixty-seven—doubtless impatiently awaiting Henry's passing and her own release. Then, finally came the fifth period, the period of her triumph, from 1189 to 1204, when for a decade and a half she demonstrated what energy, constructive and destructive, she had stored up during her fallow years.

Eleanor's background and the few facts that are known of her childhood provide a perspective for understanding her interests and aims as an adult. She was the first daughter and second child of William X of Aquitaine and his first wife, Anor (or Ænor) of Châtellerault.[27] The form of her name, Alienor, shows that she was named, after her mother, another ("alia") Anor. She was the granddaughter of William IX of Aquitaine, the mocking, cynical, womanizing duke-poet and crusader, at least one of whose wives took refuge from him in the house of Fontevraud, where abbesses directed the community of men and women assembled there to serve God. After this, he had a notorious affair with the *vicomtesse* of Châtellerault, whose daughter he married to his son.[28] William IX's exploits with and writings about women gained him considerable renown. A fourteenth-century troubadour's *Vida* called him "one of the world's great courtiers and beguilers of women, who traveled far and wide to deceive them."[29] In one poem William wrote of the distant and adored love, never seen, with whom he could easily dispense because of the nicer, prettier, and worthier one next door.[30] William's writings suggest that he thought women should be on a pedestal or bed, but never in the council chamber.[31] He may actually have established at Niort the "abbey" of courtesans modeled on Fontevraud, about which he wrote.[32] In short, he seems to have had little respect for either women or the church.

As a child Eleanor must have known her grandfather, since he did not die until 1127, when she was three. She may not have remembered him, but she surely heard talk of him and his exploits, and she, her parents, and her elder brother William were under his authority at the beginning of her life. William X, Eleanor's father, was less flamboyant than his own father and was known chiefly for his enormous appetite. As this suggests, he was no ascetic; he had two bastard sons, and after the death of his first wife in 1130 married again. Nonetheless, he was remembered not for his pursuit of women but rather as a faithful son of the church, cowed and humbled by Bernard of Clairvaux in 1125, and on Good Friday, April 9, 1137, dying on pilgrimage to Santiago of Compostella, where he was buried before the church's main altar.[33]

Eleanor and her sister Alice Petronilla were left orphans and alone, for their elder brother had died in the same year as their mother in 1130.[34] Before departing for Spain, however, their father had provided his daughters and his lands with a powerful guardian, Louis VI, king of France (ca. 1077–1137, r. 1108–37).[35] Louis VI shrewdly decided that his son, namesake, and heir (who had been crowned in 1131 at Reims) should marry Eleanor. From this decision unfolded the chain of events that led, proximately, to the subordination of Aquitaine to France and then to England, and, finally, to the long wars of the fourteenth and fifteenth centuries that resulted in 1453 in the fall of Bordeaux and the territory's definitive incorporation into the kingdom of France. In the short run, the move was advantageous to both Eleanor and Louis. The marriage brought to Eleanor, who was then just thirteen, assurance of support against the restless lords of Aquitaine, whereas Louis gained authority in a rich region that had been exempt from French control and also the prospect of the territory's eventual incorporation into the realm of France.[36]

Leaving his father ill in Paris, the young Louis, then seventeen, proceeded southward with Abbot Suger of Saint-Denis and a host of other "heroes."[37] In late July he and Eleanor were married at Bordeaux. With him, she was crowned with the royal diadem in a ceremony in which a novel coronation *ordo* emphasized the subordination of Aquitaine as well as Burgundy to the king of France.[38] On August 1, Louis VI died, and the news of his death was rapidly transmitted to the South. On August 8, another ceremony was held at Poitiers, where a second coronation rite was performed. Orderic Vitalis reports that by this coronation "Louis obtained the kingdom of the Franks and the duchy of Aquitaine, which none of his ancestors had held."[39] Thus the ceremony may have been regarded as a reaffirmation of the earlier rituals at Reims and Bordeaux. Eleanor brought Louis the sweeping lands he now ruled as duke, the status that prompted him to begin using an impressive equestrian counterseal. Largely owing to his marriage to Eleanor, Louis had, as king, the prospect of exercising far more authority and enjoying far more wealth than had his father. Promoting and defending his wife's interests, Louis led expeditions against Poitiers and Toulouse.[40]

By all reports, Louis VII doted on Eleanor. For her, however, the next eight years were unhappy. She hated the eunuch Thierry Galeran, an adviser Louis inherited from his father. The mockery she visited on him may have been prompted not only by resentment at his influence over Louis, but also by frustration at her own barrenness.[41] Louis's campaigns in the south failed to make good the claim to Toulouse that Eleanor had inherited from her grandmother Philippa, daughter of Count William of Toulouse and Emma of Mortain.[42] The marriage of Eleanor's sister to her husband's seneschal, Count Raoul of Vermandois, was scandalous because of Raoul's existing union to a noblewoman of the house of Champagne, and it brought the church's wrath down upon the couple. This marriage led to Louis's involvement in a tragic war with Champagne that culminated in an awful holocaust at Vitry. The conflict finally ended in 1144. The consecration of Suger's new chevet at Saint-Denis was the occasion for the conclusion of peace among king, church, and count. Equally important, it brought Eleanor into contact with Bernard of Clairvaux, who promised that if she worked for peace, she would bear a child. The prophecy was fulfilled, and within a year she produced an infant. The baby seemed a miraculous response to the prayers of Bernard and Eleanor (doubtless directed, as the child's name indicates, to the mother of God), but it was nonetheless a disappointment, since Eleanor did not have a boy who could succeed his father, but rather a girl, Marie.[43]

In 1145 Eleanor's life changed dramatically. In that year her husband determined to take the Cross, and in all likelihood he encouraged her to join the expedition.[44] Bernard of Clairvaux preached the Crusade at Vézelay in the spring of 1146, and in the summer of 1147 the couple set forth. For two years Eleanor traveled and saw the wonders of the East: the splendors of Constantinople, the court of her uncle Raymond in Antioch (which she quit with great reluctance), the holy places of Jerusalem. The expedition changed her ideas. She was still young, and at twenty-three or twenty-four she may well have become infatuated with her cultivated and handsome uncle Raymond, who was not much her senior.

In the course of the Crusade clear signs of a breach between Eleanor and Louis materialized. According to John of Salisbury,[45] a well-informed source, it was Eleanor who first raised the issue of consanguinity, the grounds on which the marriage was eventually dissolved. Louis, tender of conscience as Eleanor doubtless knew him to be, was willing to move at once to divorce. He was, however, dissuaded by his counselor Thierry Galeran, who told him it would be "a lasting shame to the kingdom of the Franks if, in addition to his other misfortunes"—a clear allusion to the disappointing progress of the Crusade—"the king was said to have been despoiled of his wife or to have been abandoned by her."[46]

When Louis and Eleanor were returning home in 1149, they laid their problems before the pope, Eugenius III. He would hear no word of divorce. Confirming their marriage "by word and writing, he prohibited under pain of anathema that anyone should speak against it and that it should, under any pretext whatsoever, be dissolved."[47] As John of Salisbury reports, this decision (*constitutio*) pleased the king greatly, since "he vehemently loved the queen, in an almost boyish fashion."[48] John says that the pope made the king and queen sleep in the same bed, which he ordered adorned with his own precious hangings, and that he chatted with them in an attempt to restore their love (*caritas*). According to John, at their departure the pope blessed both them and the realm of the Franks. There seems no reason to doubt John's words, which suggest that Eugenius was concerned for the kingdom as well as the king, and was anxious to spare France the ignominy and troubles a royal divorce would occasion.[49]

Eugenius's strategies were, for a time, successful. They resulted in the birth of a second child, another girl, Alice.[50] Then, for two years, all is silence as regards Eleanor. During this time Geoffrey of Anjou and his son Henry approached Louis to ask his aid in recovering the kingdom of England and the duchy of Normandy. They were seeking these lands by right of Geoffrey's wife, Matilda, sole direct heiress of Henry I of England, whose claims to England had been overridden at her father's death by her cousin, Henry's nephew, Stephen of Blois (ca. 1100–54; r. 1135–54). Like Matilda, Stephen was the offspring of a child of William the Conqueror— Stephen of William's daughter Adela, and Matilda of Henry I. But it was Stephen who gained the throne of England, and the marriage of his son Eustace to Louis VII's sister Constance strengthened the ties between Stephen and the French king. In 1150, however, Suger took the side of Stephen's adversaries and encouraged Geoffrey of Anjou and Matilda to make peace with Louis VII (and also persuaded them to promise to protect the Norman lands of Saint-Denis if war broke out). Thus Suger can in some measure be held responsible for the encounter between the seventeen-year-old Henry and Eleanor (then twenty-six) that led, in less than three years, to their marriage.[51] Louis went to war on behalf of the Angevins, helped them conquer Normandy, and bestowed the duchy on Henry. As his reward Louis received not only Henry's liege homage, but also precious Norman territories bordering his own lands, near the site where, within fifty years, Richard I of England, the son of Eleanor and Henry, would build Château-Gaillard.[52]

This success did not eclipse the serious problems Louis faced. His reputation had been tarnished by the failure of the crusade, and his campaign on the Angevins' behalf hardly served his own long-term interests. Whether motivated by guilt prompted by the crusade's outcome, or whether simply worn out by Eleanor, Louis VII was in 1152 ready for separation from a woman who had brought him only daughters and distress. Had Suger not died in January 1151, he might have dissuaded the king and queen from separating. As it was, Louis arranged for his relatives to "inform him" of the same consanguineous impediment to his marriage with which Eleanor had confronted him at Antioch. At this point Louis was doubtless eager to rid himself of his wife, and a final breach ensued—despite Eugenius's *constitutio*. Louis's kin took solemn oaths testifying to the closeness of his blood ties to Eleanor, and the chief prelates of France pronounced their divorce on March 21, 1152.[53] Eleanor departed for Poitiers at once, leaving her husband of fifteen years and her two daughters, who were, respectively, seven years and eighteen months old. A curious amalgam of impulsiveness and calculated shrewdness, she seems to have known precisely what she would do when her divorce from Louis was accomplished.[54]

Eleanor demanded the return of her duchy, but Louis VII balked.[55] Not until August 1154 did he cease entitling himself duke of Aquitaine and using the counterseal he had employed since his marriage to Eleanor.[56] Louis's reluctance to restore Eleanor's lands to her cannot be explained solely by his desire to guard the interests of their daughters. His jealousy must have been piqued by Eleanor's adventures after she left him. First Thibaud of Blois (who would later marry Alice, the younger daughter of Eleanor and Louis) and then Geoffrey of Anjou (Henry's younger brother and their father's namesake) attempted to waylay Eleanor as she journeyed to Aquitaine, and each was apparently intent on making her his own.[57] Then, on May 18, 1152, within two months of the divorce, Eleanor married Henry, who had become count of Anjou on his father's death the preceding September.[58] Louis continued to call himself duke of Aquitaine and also summoned Henry to his court, confiscated his lands when he failed to appear, and captured two of his most important Norman castles. For his part, Henry moved cautiously, refraining from assuming the title of duke of Aquitaine until early 1153.[59] As to Eleanor, Henry does not seem to have delayed in asserting his authority over her. He apparently introduced his former tutor into her household as chancellor before the end of 1152. From the beginning Henry controlled her retinue, as he would later the household of their eldest son.[60] Leaving Eleanor pregnant on the Continent, Henry departed for England, where he succeeded in vanquishing King Stephen. Military success bolstered his self-assurance, as did the birth on August 17, 1153 of a son, named William after both his and Eleanor's ancestors.[61]

Physical attraction and love of power seem to have drawn Eleanor and Henry together. Eleanor's prestige and lands offered Henry assets he needed to conquer England, a goal he had cherished for a decade, since he was nine.[62] For Eleanor, the union meant that, unless Henry's plans failed, she would be exchanging one royal title for another. Further, Aquitaine would be disengaged from Capetian control and would again be independent. Did she hope to be able to dominate Henry? Perhaps. She would have been well advised, however, to consider Henry's background. His line was alleged to descend from Satan, but that was not the worst of it.[63] The similarities between the marriage of Henry's mother and father, on the one hand, and the union of Henry and Eleanor, on the other, were striking and did not bode well for Eleanor's future. Henry's mother, Matilda (ca. 1102/03–67), was the daughter and heiress of Henry I of England and the widow (in 1125) of Emperor Henry V. She was some ten years older than his father, Geoffrey (1113–51), who was fifteen or sixteen when they were married in 1128 or 1129.[64] Although his wife was his senior and her status superior to his, Geoffrey immediately revealed his intention to dominate her. Having dispatched her to Rouen, he received her back only when pressed to do so by the barons of England.[65] From that point on Matilda was subordinated to her husband, with whom she had three sons. Still, as would later be true of Eleanor, she emerged from subservience to advise her son Henry during the sixteen years she lived after her husband's death.[66]

Whatever difficulties lay ahead, the good fortune of Henry and Eleanor seemed assured in the last months of 1153. Within a week of the birth of their first son in mid-August, King Stephen's son Eustace of Blois died. Thus, the chief impediment to Henry's accession to the English throne was removed. In November 1153, the Treaty of Winchester guaranteed that Henry would one day be king of England, and in January he received the homage of the English barons.[67] At Easter 1154, Henry brought Eleanor from Poitiers to Normandy.[68] The move northward signified a shift in the balance of power between husband and wife. The balance altered even more perceptibly when, after the death of King Stephen on October 25, 1154, Henry and Eleanor were crowned king and queen of England in December.

At this point there was no question that Eleanor had chosen well. As to her abandoned husband, Louis soon freed himself from her spell. Late in 1153 he was engaged and quickly married to Constance, daughter of Alfonso VII of Castile (whose relationship to him was closer than Eleanor's). Safely joined to a woman of impeccable lineage, confronted by a rival whose authority was now established, Louis made peace with Henry of Anjou and England in August 1154 and ceased employing his Aquitanian titles and paraphernalia. Louis fixed on other means, independent of Eleanor, to manifest his piety and power. His moves suggest an impulse to vie with Eleanor and her ancestors and demonstrate that he was fully their equal—and indeed superior to them.[69]

In the fall of 1154 Louis departed on a lengthy pilgrimage through Spain to Santiago—where his former father-in-law, William X of Aquitaine, had died on a similar journey seventeen years before. In Toledo, splendidly welcomed by Alfonso VII of Castile, he received from him a magnificent jewel that the Moorish king Jafadola had given to one of Alfonso's ancestors. This jewel he subsequently offered to the reliquary of the crown of thorns at Saint-Denis, as earlier he had presented to Suger a vase that William of Aquitaine had received from the Arab king Mitadolus, which Eleanor had given him.[70] To strengthen the ties between the Spanish kingdoms and France, Louis is likely to have played some part in the transfer of the arm of Saint Eugenius, the alleged first bishop of Toledo, from Saint-Denis to Toledo. Finally, the king soon began planning a crusade that he hoped to wage with Henry of Anjou, by then Henry II of England, against the Saracens of Spain. On his return journey, as if to assert his sovereign superiority and compensate for his now truncated title, Louis VII on one occasion declared himself *imperator augustus* rather than simply "king" of all the Franks, thus adopting the imperial title borne by his new father-in-law Alfonso and perhaps challenging pretensions cherished by Henry II, who in 1152, shortly after his marriage to Eleanor, was said in one of her charters to be ruler of "the empire of the Poitevins and Angevins."[71]

While Louis was on pilgrimage to Compostella, Eleanor and Henry traveled to England. There, on December 19, 1154, they were crowned at Westminster Abbey. The next years were challenging for Henry, who was engaged in campaigns on the Continent and, in England, conflict with Thomas Becket. For Eleanor, they were relatively good times, despite the death of their first son William in 1156. In ten years she had six children who survived to adulthood—Matilda in 1156, Richard the next year, Geoffrey the next, Eleanor in 1161, Jeanne (or Joanna) in 1165, and John a year later. Until 1163 she acted as formal regent of England during Henry's frequent absences abroad. These official duties did not mean that Eleanor neglected her offspring. On her frequent journeys, selected children, generally the eldest, often traveled with her.[72] It is true that Jeanne and John were both sent to be raised at Fontevraud, and that John spent five years there. This was, in a sense, fitting, since both were named after the patron saint of the male establishment there.[73] Nonetheless, as I hypothesized in 1976 and continue to believe today, this was probably an unsettling experience for the two children, especially for John, and may have affected his sense of self-confidence and trust.[74] As Andrew Lewis points out,[75] at Fontevraud the children were near their first cousin once removed. Matilda, daughter of their paternal grandfather's sister Sibylle and Thierry of Alsace, would later be abbess of the house,[76] but it is unclear how much comfort she could have given them. Eleanor alone cannot be held responsible for sending the children to Fontevraud or for the consequences of this step, and John's epitaph at Fontevraud indeed attributes to Henry alone the decision to dispatch his son to the abbey. Henry (like his ancestors) was devoted to Fontevraud, and his aunt Matilda (his father's sister) had been abbess from 1149 or 1150 to 1155. According to Henry's epitaph, it was she (and God) who had fostered his dedication to the house, and in 1152 she had welcomed Eleanor to Fontevraud shortly after Eleanor married Henry.[77]

Eleanor's involvement with her children was balanced by, and perhaps subordinate in importance to, her commitment to politics and governance. During her childbearing years she was, as regent, formally engaged in the administration of the realm, at least until 1163.[78] She was doubtless the motive force behind the campaign against Toulouse that Henry II undertook in 1159, repeating the similar move made earlier by Louis VII, with similar lack of success. The resentment aroused by the expedition doubtless made Henry regret his attempt to further Eleanor's ambitions. Between 1163 and 1170, Henry, then in his thirties, was in his prime. Involved in his contest with Becket, he aggressively controlled the affairs of the kingdom as Eleanor was relegated to traveling, appearing at Christmas courts, and producing her last children.[79]

A striking change occurred in 1168, when Eleanor assumed, at Henry's wish, control of the duchy of Aquitaine. The fact that Henry set Eleanor over Aquitaine after the death of his mother Matilda in the fall of 1167 suggests an impulse on his part to free himself from the control (and perhaps annoyance) of powerful women.[80] With his mother removed by death, his wife could be sent off to the Continent. This step served his immediate interests. He was thirty-five, and with his forty-four-year-old wife occupied in Aquitaine, he could indulge his appetites and rule his lands as he wished.

Had Henry foreseen the long-term consequences of dispatching Eleanor to Aquitaine, he might have decided to keep her at his side. From this time on, Eleanor's ambitions were centered on her children and their fortunes. She was not primarily concerned with fostering their development but was most interested in using them in her struggle against Henry.

Assigning Aquitaine to Eleanor's governance was only the first of a number of tactical errors and setbacks that Henry made and suffered between 1168 and 1172. First, the treaty of Montmirail, concluded with Louis VII in 1169, provided for the fateful (and foolish) division of Henry's continental lands among his sons, and brought into his household Alice, Louis's daughter by his third wife, Adela of Champagne, and the intended wife of Henry's son Richard. Second, in June 1170 the young Henry was crowned, and the ceremony was performed by the Archbishop of York rather than by Thomas Becket of Canterbury.[81] Third, six months later, on December 29, 1170, Becket was murdered at Canterbury. Fourth, in June 1172 Henry's fifteen-year-old son Richard was, in Eleanor's presence, solemnly installed at Poitiers as duke of Aquitaine and was invested with the ducal regalia—including the ring of Saint Valérie—in a special ceremony at Limoges.[82] Fifth, the young Henry was crowned a second time in the fall of 1172.[83] Sixth and finally, Thomas Becket was canonized on February 21, 1173.

In these years, Henry gave his sons the trappings without the reality of power and inadvertently strengthened the ties that bound them all to France. By raising his son and namesake to the kingship, following Capetian rather than English practice, Henry created a jealous rival and at least one potential ally for his disaffected and now independent wife, who acquired a virtual consort when their son Richard became duke of Aquitaine. Further, through his part in the Becket affair, Henry advanced the decline of his own authority and popularity.

Trouble was brewing. It erupted shortly after Raymond of Toulouse did homage to Henry and to Richard (as count of Poitou)—note, not to Eleanor—in February 1173 at Limoges.[84] Eleanor may have been disturbed at being excluded from the ceremony. If she was, she did not have to wait long for revenge. As Raymond is said to have informed Henry, the English king's family was conspiring against him, and battle was soon joined. Eleanor played an essential part in her sons' rebellion and may have inspired it.[85] Understandably, Henry had her seized. For the rest of his life she was secluded and closely watched wherever she was, in England or on the Continent.[86] For fifteen years Henry used her as he struggled with his sons. Her sequestration did not bring peace, and a period of intense conflict culminated in the death of the young Henry on July 11, 1183.[87] The young king's dying wish may have been for his mother's freedom, but if it was, it was not fulfilled. After young Henry's death, Eleanor was allowed to visit her dower lands, but she was immediately confined thereafter, suggesting that the tour was staged by Henry as part of his effort to parry French claims to the dower rights of young Henry's widow, the sister of Philip Augustus.[88] In 1184 Eleanor appeared at court, to visit her daughter Matilda, in exile in England with her husband Henry the Lion of Saxony. But she was not free to travel as she wished.[89] She was paraded abroad when it suited Henry and confined when it did not.

In 1185, two years after the death of the young Henry, Eleanor's control over the duchy of Aquitaine was restored in order to bring the restive Richard to heel. Henry forced his son to surrender the county of Poitou to his mother, and warned him that if he delayed, "the queen his mother would lay waste all his lands with a great army."[90] Eleanor acquired authority in her lands, but Richard apparently lost none of the power he had possessed, which suggests that the surrender was nominal. Still, Eleanor's position was far more favorable than before.[91] She did not return to England until 1186. She continued to influence her sons, and in 1188, Richard took up her vendetta against Toulouse.[92]

Henry's maneuvers did not produce peace. His domestic difficulties were mercilessly exploited by a vigorous and wily opponent, Philip Augustus of

France, who in 1180, at the age of fifteen, succeeded his father Louis VII.[93] Philip Augustus's policies towards Eleanor and Henry II more than atoned for whatever suffering Eleanor's divorce and remarriage had inflicted on her children, Philip's half-sisters, Marie and Alice, whom Louis VII had married to Henri, count of Troyes, and Thibaud the Good, count of Blois, the brothers of his third wife, Philip's mother, Alice of Champagne.[94] In May 1189, Philip joined forces with Henry and Eleanor's sons Richard and John—an unlikely and unholy alliance—to attack Henry. On July 4, the English king capitulated. Two days later, deserted by his sons, he died.[95] He was buried at Fontevraud, although he had wished to be interred at Grandmont, a house he particularly favored. Giraldus Cambrensis (Gerald de Barri) judged Fontevraud "obscure and by no means suited to such great majesty," but since Henry's advisers had earlier declared that his burial at Grandmont would be "against the dignity of his kingdom," the complaint may stem from the conviction that kings of England should be buried in a grander church in the kingdom they ruled, rather than from any particular opposition to Fontevraud—or Grandmont.[96] Henry had been devoted to Fontevraud and its daughter houses, and the decision that he should be interred at the abbey was made by William Marshal, who was devoted to Henry. As a result Henry's became the first of a series of burials that would make Fontevraud a family mausoleum.[97]

With Henry's death and Richard's accession to the throne, the fortunes of Eleanor of Aquitaine changed radically. When William Marshal visited her in England, he found her "delivered" and in better spirits and state than she had been for some time.[98] Released from confinement, she set off on a perambulation of England and ordered the release of many whom her husband had imprisoned, thus sharing with other unfortunates the liberty she had gained. To guarantee loyalty to her son, she ordered all free men of the kingdom to pledge their fidelity to him, and it was she who administered the realm until Richard's return to England.[99] In gratitude, Richard confirmed her possession of her dower lands, and also promised to discharge his brother John from his promise not to return to England for three years after Richard left on crusade.[100] For her part, Eleanor set aside Richard's long-term engagement to Philip Augustus's sister Alice (whom she nonetheless succeeded in detaining at the English court until 1195),[101] and she arranged Richard's marriage to Berengaria, daughter of the king of Navarre. These moves may have been motivated in part by disgust and anger, if Henry II had actually dallied with Alice (as he was rumored to have done).[102] The choice of Berengaria (whom Richard of Devizes called "more sensible than stunning")[103] also had the advantage of ensuring that Richard would have a wife who would not challenge Eleanor's authority or influence over her son. The rejection of Alice of

France also put Philip Augustus on notice that Eleanor and Richard were people to be reckoned with.

In the winter of 1190–91 Eleanor accompanied Berengaria to Sicily, where Richard and Philip Augustus stayed before their departure for the Holy Land.[104] Lengthy negotiations were necessary before Philip Augustus agreed to Richard's abandonment of his half-sister Alice, and Richard set sail before Berengaria arrived in Sicily. Eleanor deposited her and returned at once to Normandy.[105] In the two years since Henry's death, Eleanor's actions established her as a formidable political figure. She had spent her fifties and early sixties in an involuntary moratorium, for which she compensated in the next decade, in a burst of hypergenerativity.

While Richard was crusading in the Holy Land, and later, while he was imprisoned in the Empire in 1193 and 1194, Eleanor governed strongly and justly. She defended Richard's interests in England and on the continent against his younger brother John and against Philip Augustus, who had deserted the Holy Land in August 1191 to return to France.[106] In February 1192, she acted speedily and decisively to bring John to heel. She and the justiciar informed him that if he went to France (where he would surely have conspired with Philip Augustus) they would "seize his lands and fortresses and take them into the king's hand."[107] It was Eleanor who raised the ransom of 100,000 marks required for Richard's release, and she traveled to Mainz to see him freed.[108] There, on February 4, 1194, and apparently on Eleanor' advice, Richard did homage to the emperor Henry VI, thus gaining a sure ally against Philip Augustus and John, who had tried to persuade Henry to keep Richard imprisoned.[109] After Richard and Eleanor returned triumphant to England it was Eleanor, not Berengaria, who presided as queen, sitting opposite Richard when, on April 17, 1194, he ceremoniously wore his crown at Winchester.[110] Eleanor's status was also witnessed by her continuing receipt of the Queen's Gold, even as her sons' wives came and went.[111]

Eleanor arranged a short-lived truce between Richard and John in the summer of 1194,[112] but then retired to Fontevraud. She played no active part in Richard's campaigns against Philip Augustus, John, and assorted rebels on the Continent, which culminated, between 1196 and 1198, in Richard's construction of the monumental Château-Gaillard in the Vexin.[113]

While Richard was warring and building, Eleanor was in honorable retreat at Fontevraud. She showered the house with gifts, having walls constructed to protect it, providing an endowment for the habits of the religious, and donating a gold processional cross adorned with jewels, and many gold and silver vessels and silken cloths.[114] She doubtless rejoiced in 1196 at the marriage of her daughter Jeanne to Raymond VI of Toulouse, which finally brought the count of Toulouse within Aquitaine's orbit, since

Raymond promised that he and his heirs would hold certain lands as vassals of the dukes of Aquitaine.[115] In the same year Eleanor's grandson, Otto of Brunswick, son of her daughter Matilda and Henry the Lion, was invested with the county of Poitou, and in July 1198, through Richard's efforts, Otto was crowned emperor. Thus a grandson, ruler of Poitou, the land Eleanor had inherited from her ancestors, became the first Angevin to occupy the imperial throne Henry II had coveted for himself.[116]

By the beginning of 1199, Eleanor had lost all but four of her children. Her two daughters by Louis VII were gone, Alice apparently shortly after 1183[117] and Marie in 1198 (after having become a nun at Fontaines-les-Nones, a priory of Fontevraud near Meaux).[118] Of her children by Henry, only Richard, Eleanor (married to Alfonso VIII of Castile), Jeanne, and John survived. Then, on April 6, 1199, Richard died in besieging the castle of Châlus-Chabrol in the Limousin. After being wounded, he summoned his mother to him, and she was with him at the end. She accompanied his body to Fontevraud to be interred near his father, on Palm Sunday.[119] Her son's death roused her once again to action, to defend the rights of her last son, John, to the throne of England.

The months after Richard died witnessed a flurry of activity. Eleanor issued numerous charters, which, as H.G. Richardson declared, "are as authoritative and binding as the charters of any English king."[120] Nor did she simply give written orders and commands. She herself led the mercenaries Richard had been commanding north to Anjou, where they vanquished the supporters of her grandson Arthur of Brittany (son of Geoffrey and Constance of Brittany), who was claiming the throne of England.[121] Next she traveled through Poitou and Gascony to affirm the regions' loyalty.[122] Having in July 1199 formally recognized Philip Augustus's overlordship of Poitou (although not of Aquitaine, which she held independently),[123] she and her son John entered into an arrangement that made them corulers of Poitou and Aquitaine. The acts confirming the agreement are curious. Ordering that all homages, acts of fidelity, and services be rendered to him as liege lord, Eleanor bestowed on John, "her dearest son" and "rightful heir," all of Poitou and received his homage for it. In turn, John acknowledged his homage to his mother for Poitou and declared that during her lifetime his mother should have and hold Poitou as *domina,* and that neither he nor she would make any alienation without the other's consent, except for appropriate donations for the benefit of their souls.[124] Perhaps the phraseology of Eleanor's charter, doubtless carefully chosen, was intended to suggest her endorsement of the rightfulness of John's claim to the kingdom of England.

In September 1199, Eleanor lost her daughter Jeanne. Eleanor was with her when she died in Rouen after taking the veil as a nun of Fontevraud, by special permission of Hubert Walter, archbishop of Canterbury. Jeanne's body was taken for burial to Fontevraud, presumably by Eleanor, and there, fifty years later, her body was joined by that of her son Raymond VII of Toulouse.[125] In 1200, after John and Philip Augustus concluded a peace that was to be sealed by the marriage of Philip's son Louis and one of Eleanor's granddaughters, Eleanor set forth for the court of her daughter and son-in-law, Eleanor and Alfonso VIII of Castile.[126] There, the chroniclers report, she selected as Louis's bride her granddaughter Blanche, and the couple was married on May 23.[127] This marriage would finally, for a time, ensure the peace between England and France that she and her children had long disrupted.

Eleanor continued to be interested and involved in the affairs of her sole surviving son, John. He badly needed her assistance because of his reckless, ill-advised marriage to Isabelle of Angoulême on August 24, 1200. This union brought him and Philip Augustus into conflict yet again.[128] Early in 1201 Eleanor intervened from her sickbed to help John retain the allegiance of a powerful Poitevin lord.[129] After John's formal condemnation by the court of France on April 28, 1202, Philip Augustus invaded his lands. Eleanor, then seventy-eight, again went to her son's aid, and her presence in the field resulted in one of John's few victories. In the summer of 1202, she was besieged in the castle of Mirebeau by her grandson Arthur of Brittany, and freed when John came to her rescue in a spectacular display of strength.[130] This time Eleanor's return to Fontevraud was definitive. There she learned of Philip Augustus's triumphs over John and, in the spring of 1203, of the disappearance of her grandson Arthur—and perhaps of the rumors linking John with his death.[131] There she heard of Philip Augustus's attacks on Normandy, his siege of Château-Gaillard, and, finally, its capitulation on March 6, 1204.[132] Three weeks later Eleanor died and, like her husband Henry, her son Richard, and her daughter Jeanne, was buried at Fontevraud, where she had long lived. Like Jeanne, she became a nun of Fontevraud before her death, and in the abbey's necrology she was remembered as "our dearest mother."[133]

This, then, is one reading of the written sources regarding the Eleanor who lived and ruled 900 years ago. The sources suggest a life of turbulence and strategem in which periods of inactivity were never spent in calm tranquility but always in suspenseful waiting for the crises that inevitably materialized. Eleanor derived great pleasure from political maneuvering and the exercise of power, games she played exceedingly well. She was a stubborn, indomitable fighter, whose ambitions sometimes overpowered her reason. Her compulsive pursuit of her grandfather's dream of annexing Toulouse was misguided, and in the end unsuccessful. Her determination and tenacity could be counterproductive, and yet, had she not possessed those qualities, she might not have surmounted the challenges her two husbands posed and succeeded in outliving and triumphing over them both. She was more inclined to stir up troubles than to settle them, perhaps because for long stretches of time she was prevented from exercising authority over lands that were rightfully hers. In her pursuit of power and advantage her children often served as her pawns. The fruits of her struggles, it is true, accrued to them. Nonetheless, she seems to have been more interested in the excitement of the fray than in ensuring their long-term welfare. To the end of her life, Eleanor's penchant for intrigue and her political impulses were more pronounced than her maternal inclinations.

In addition to the documentary and chronicle evidence, a few objects and monuments connected with Eleanor survive. Once divorced from the images and artifacts that overzealous mythologizers have misleadingly associated with Eleanor, the authentic material evidence that remains is sparse. Mute as it is, it must be treated with prudence and restraint. Still, like the chronicles and charters, the tangible remains invite analysis and interpretation for the light they can shed on Eleanor as woman, duchess, and queen.

Eleanor and Saint Valérie's Ring and Relics

Although they are not unquestionably linked with Eleanor, two twelfth-century reliquaries created to honor Saint Valérie prompt reflections on Eleanor's likely connection with the saint's cult, and the aspects of the saint's life that might have attracted Eleanor's attention and admiration. The two extant reliquaries dedicated to Saint Valérie that were crafted during Eleanor's lifetime are unlikely to be the only ones produced in homage to a saint who was becoming especially cherished by the people of the Limousin. Fashioned in Limoges, probably between 1175 and 1185, they witness the growth of the cult of Saint Valérie in the Limousin.[134]

The importance of Saint Valérie was witnessed in 1172, when, in Eleanor's presence, her son Richard was made duke and *princeps* of Aquitaine at Limoges. At this ceremony, he was solemnly invested with the ring of Valérie, "so that," as the *ordo* says, "he may be fortunate in deed, abundant in faith, and finally come to glory with the Lord of Lords."[135] If Richard's investiture followed the ritual prescribed in the first surviving *ordo* (recorded in the first quarter of the thirteenth century), the ring was the first of the regalia the bishop of Limoges bestowed on the new duke. He received it outside the church, after the bishop had aspersed him and clad him in a silken cloak, and before receiving the golden circlet crown and ducal banner, and then, inside the church, the ducal sword (all of which were offered back to the church at the end of the ceremony). Of the regalia, it was the ring that represented the *dignitas* of the duchy, and the ring was Saint Valérie's.[136]

Eleanor would have found in the story of Saint Valérie distant similarities to her own life. Valérie had been by hereditary right lady of Limoges and duchess of Aquitaine, lands she had inherited from her father. Engaged to her father's successor as governor, she was in his absence converted to Christianity by Saint Martial. Having refused to marry and taken a vow of chastity, she was decapitated by order of her fiancé, who too late perceived the error of his ways and was converted himself. After her troubles with Louis VII and Henry II, Eleanor might well have found Valérie's steadfastness inspiring and enviable. As regards the saint's cult, she might have seen in the bestowal of Valérie's ring on Richard in 1172 a symbol of the ties that linked him not only to the saint but also to herself.

The history of the veneration of Saint Valérie at Saint-Martial of Limoges and in the Limousin is only beginning to be known, but Daniel Callahan's work with the liturgical books of the house suggests that it was being deliberately fostered in the middle of the twelfth century. As Marie-Madeleine Gauthier has shown, the appearance of the ring at Richard's coronation in 1172, its first known use, and the fabrication of the two chasses are early, tangible evidence of the saint's popularity.[137] Given Eleanor's and Richard's control of Aquitaine in these years, and the use of Valérie's ring at Richard's installation, they seem likely promoters of the saint's cult. This, however, is speculation. Let us turn from conjectural associations between Eleanor and the relics of Saint Valérie to an object known to have belonged to Eleanor, the splendid crystal vase now in the Louvre.

Eleanor and the Rock Crystal Vase of Saint-Denis

George Beech has revolutionized understanding of the rock crystal vase of Saint-Denis by establishing the provenance of its core and elucidating the circumstances by which it came into Eleanor's hands and then passed from her to Louis VII, and from him to Abbot Suger and Saint-Denis.[138] Although the vase itself provides no immediate access to Eleanor, some features of its history and the inscription on its base are suggestive regarding the name by which Eleanor was known, her relationship to her first husband, Louis VII, and that king's feelings for her.

The inscription, composed by Abbot Suger, declares, "This vase Anor as bride gave to King Louis, Mitadolus to her grandfather, the king to me, and Suger to the saints."[139] That Eleanor should have given the vessel to Louis VII as a wedding gift is not surprising and suggests her willingness, at the beginning of their union, to pass on to him—or at least share fully with him—her Aquitanian heritage. It is interesting that the inscription identifies her by the name her mother had borne, rather than by the diminutive that was her own. From time to time Eleanor may well have used the more formal name, perhaps seeking stature and authority, perhaps out of nostalgia for the mother she had lost.

As to the gift itself, it is remarkable that Louis VII alone—not Eleanor and he—presented the vase to Suger (possibly when the chevet of Saint-Denis was dedicated, in 1144). Consider the gift: a precious object his wife had inherited from her grandfather, which she had given to her husband early in their marriage. Why did he, and he alone, decide to dispose of it? Did he do so because he no longer wanted an object that was linked with her, a reminder of their marriage, which was fruitless in 1144? Did he do so in hopes that the proffer to the saints of an object linked directly with her family might bring her the favor of God and them both a child? No more than Louis's motivations can Eleanor's reactions to his gift be known. Still, it seems more than likely that if Louis presented the vase to Suger in 1144, Eleanor, then twenty and still childless, would have been saddened to see him part with a rare object she had received from her grandfather and in all likelihood treasured as a keepsake and reminder of him and his exploits. Whatever Louis's motivations, she might well have perceived the gift to Suger as a rejection of her. Suger reports that Louis offered it to him "in magno amoris munere"—"as a great gift of love,"[140] and Eleanor might well have wished that the *amor* her husband thus witnessed for Suger and Saint-Denis was directed at herself.

Eleanor's Seals and Coins

Eleanor's authentic seals provide less ambiguous evidence than do the reliquaries of Saint Valérie or the rock crystal vase, although, as is true of all mute objects, the seals' significance is not easy to assess. Probably because of their legibility, two seals of Eleanor of Provence (wife of Henry III of England) have been fallaciously assigned to Eleanor of Aquitaine,[141] and they are indeed more impressive than the fragmentary surviving remains of two impressions of one of her seals (Fig. 1.1). However, drawings made for the antiquarian Roger de Gaignières (1642–1715) preserve the images of this seal and two earlier ones, showing them as they existed 300 years ago, and thus facilitating analysis of their iconography.[142]

Although Eleanor sealed acts as queen of France, neither the instrument she used nor any image of it is extant.[143] The first of her seals whose likeness survives (Fig. 1.2) was appended to an unusual act of 1152, which she issued simply as countess of the Poitevins, shortly after her divorce from Louis VII and her marriage to Henry of Anjou, both of which events the

Fig. 1.1. Casts of the obverse and reverse of the third seal of Eleanor of Aquitaine. In the center, the seal attached to AN, J628, no. 5; to the sides, the seal in the Collection du Poitou at the AN; below, the drawing made for Gaignières, Paris, BnF, lat. 5480, p. 265.

charter mentions. Interestingly, Eleanor did not designate herself as duchess of the Aquitanians (a title found on her seal, as will be seen). Nor did she call herself countess of the Angevins, the additional title her marriage to Henry had brought her. In the act, issued at Fontevraud in the presence of Henry's aunt Matilda, abbess of the monastery, Eleanor declared that she had come to the house by God's inspiration, and with the aid of divine grace had been able to carry out the plans she had conceived. There, while attending the nuns' chapter, she was stricken by conscience and confirmed her ancestors' donations to the house, as well as a grant she and Louis VII had made during their marriage.[144] These declarations are moving, dramatic, and unconventional. The emphasis Eleanor lays on God's role in motivating her act is especially noteworthy. The dating clause is similarly unusual and may reflect the loftiness of Eleanor's ambitions. There, after references to King Louis of France and Bishop Gislebert of Poitiers, her husband Henry (earlier termed "consul of the Angevins") is declared to be "governing the *empire* of the Poitevins and the Angevins."[145] The document

Fig. 1.2. Drawing of a seal of Eleanor of Aquitaine (1152), made for Roger de Gaignières, Paris, BnF, lat. 5480, p. 486.

does not announce the presence of the seal with which Eleanor validated the act, and on first inspection the seal seems modest and unpretentious. However, one feature—the dove perched on Eleanor's right hand—is suggestive and deserves comment.[146]

The lozenge-shaped seal, said to have been in green wax and attached by a white cord, depicts a bare-headed, willowy woman, wearing a sinuous long-sleeved dress with trailing sleeves,[147] standing and holding a fleur-de-lis in her right hand, with a dove poised on her extended left hand. The legend, more than half destroyed, declares Eleanor duchess of the Aquitanians, and the remainder may have designated her as countess of the Poitevins. If this is so, the seal may be one she used in these capacities after her divorce from Louis VII and before her marriage to Henry of Anjou.[148] If the drawing was made to scale (as seems likely), the seal was relatively small, measuring 45 mm. by 73 mm.[149] No counterseal was drawn, perhaps because there was none.

The fleur-de-lis in Eleanor's hand recalls the symbol that her successors as queens of France carried on their seals, but fleurs-de-lis were widely used on seals, and it would be rash to assume that Eleanor had consciously retained this symbol from a seal she had used as Louis VII's queen, as an allusion to her former status.[150] Far more unusual and arresting is the dove poised on her right hand. Its significance seems clear. The dove was the most common form in which the Holy Spirit was represented, and the presence of the dove in depictions of saints and rulers and on regalia signified the wisdom and intelligence the Holy Spirit was believed to impart.[151] Doves appeared on imperial scepters from the eleventh century, and, doubtless as a result of the iconographical cross-fertilization that took place among the elite, Edward the Confessor (r. 1042–66) had himself depicted on his great seal with a scepter surmounted by a dove in his right hand, an orb, also evocative of imperial practice, in his left.[152] These symbols became part of the English royal iconographic vocabulary, and the two queens of Henry I of England (r. 1100–35) were depicted on their seals with a scepter surmounted by a dove in their right hands, and an orb in their left.[153] More important, on their great seals both Henry I and Stephen (r. 1135–54) held in their left hands an orb surmounted by cross and dove, and in their right a sword—the orb and cross signifying their power, the dove their wisdom, and the sword their ability to execute justice.[154] Thus the bird on Eleanor's seal may suggest not only the intelligence and wisdom bestowed on her as a gift of the Holy Spirit but also her ambition to possess as her own the English sigillographic dove employed by her new husband's ancestors. The presence of the dove of the Holy Spirit is especially appropriate to an act recording steps Eleanor presented herself as taking by divine inspiration.

A second seal of Eleanor that was reproduced for Gaignières (Fig. 1.3) was attached to an undated charter that was executed between the birth of her son William on August 17, 1153 and her coronation as queen of England on December 19, 1154. The act was a gift to La Trinité of Vendôme, which Henry's forebears Geoffrey of Anjou and Agnes of Burgundy had founded in 1034. Entitling herself duchess of the Aquitanians and the Normans and countess of the Angevins and acknowledging the counsel of the venerable men of Poitou and Anjou and the petitions of the abbot and monks of La Trinité, Eleanor relinquished certain rights to the abbey for the souls of her father and mother and for "the prosperity of [her] husband Duke Henry, and the promotion of the safety and the honor of Henry and [her] son William."[155] The badly damaged legend identifies her as duchess of the Normans and countess of Anjou, and the effaced part presumably bore her title as duchess of the Aquitanians. Again, no counterseal is depicted. If the seal is drawn to scale, it measured 55 mm. by 85 mm., and was slightly larger than the seal Eleanor used in 1152. The later seal, said to have been executed in red wax and attached by a leather thong, resembles Eleanor's earlier one.[156] Here, however, her head, rather than being bare, is

Fig. 1.3. Drawing of a seal of Eleanor of Aquitaine (1153–54), made for Roger de Gaignières, Paris, BnF, lat. 5419, p. 80.

veiled, and the veil (or possibly a cape) falls behind her, to her feet. On this seal she holds no fleur-de-lis. Rather, her empty right hand is outstretched, palm forward. Does the absence of the fleur-de-lis provide evidence that its presence on the earlier seal recalled Eleanor's ties with France, and that two years later she had determined to banish any such symbol from her seal? Perhaps, but, in view of the ubiquity of fleurs-de-lis on women's seals, this seems unlikely. Whatever Eleanor's motivation in deciding against using the symbol on this seal, its absence elevates the prominence—and, arguably, the significance—of the dove on Eleanor's left hand. As before, the inclusion of the dove suggests that she wished to link herself with the gifts of the Holy Spirit and the symbol cherished by English royalty.

Two impressions of the seal Eleanor employed in 1199 and 1200 survive, badly damaged (Fig. 1.1). One, in green wax and appended on a cord of white laces, was attached to a donation (undated) she made to

Fontevraud.[157] The other, in natural wax and appended by a cord woven of blue, brown, and natural laces, validated Eleanor's gift of the "feodum de sancta Severa" to André de Chauvigny (described as "dearest friend and relative"). The gift was made in 1199 at Val-de-Reuil near Rouen, and one of the witnesses was William Marshal.[158] Although the fragments are difficult to read, they (and their dimensions) are consistent with the depictions of a seal and counterseal appended to an act issued by Eleanor at Fontevraud in 1200, which were made for Gaignières, and which measure 54 mm. by 96 mm. (Fig. 1.1). In the act of 1200 (a gift to one of her servants of the "terram de Hobriteby et de Harfineby" that Richard had conferred on her) Eleanor entitled herself queen of the English, duchess of the Normans and Aquitanians, and countess of the Angevins; the donation is said to have been sealed in green wax on a brown silken cord. The obverse and reverse are, apart from their legends, remarkably similar. The images resemble in some respects those on the seals Eleanor used earlier, but here her attributes are significantly different. Her head is missing in the surviving fragments, but the drawing made for Gaignières shows her wimpled and wearing an impressive crown of three points fleury. In her right hand she carries a branchlike scepter and in her left a globe surmounted by a cross on which a bird is balanced. No longer is the bird perched on her hand. Rather it here stands on top of the cross affixed to the orb that Eleanor holds. The legend on the obverse declares her "Eleanor by grace of God queen of the English and duchess of the Normans." On the reverse she is depicted in a similar pose, with similar attributes, but here she is identified as "Eleanor duchess of the Aquitanians and countess of the Angevins."[159] Several aspects of this seal deserve comment. First, the seal depicts Eleanor in female regal majesty, the branchlike scepter topped with fleur de lis far more impressive than the single fleur-de-lis she (like the queens of France) held on her seal of 1152. Even more important, in her left hand she holds precisely the same symbol of rulership that her husband bears on his great seal: an orb surmounted with cross and dove. Similarly, her crown with three points fleury is a duplicate of the one he wears on his seal. Further, the phrase "by grace of God" in the legend on the obverse echoes the similar words on the seal of Adele of Champagne (d. 1206), whom Louis VII married in 1160, whose seal, unlike that of her predecessor Constance of Castile, proclaimed her ruler "Dei gratia."[160]

Despite these features, the seal Eleanor used in 1199 and 1200 lacks the majestic form of those employed by two women whose status was similar to hers. Consider the impressive round seal of Eleanor's mother-in-law Matilda. As wife of Emperor Henry V, Matilda had been empress of Germany until Henry V's death in 1125, and her striking seal identified her as Empress of the Romans. She continued to use the seal after Henry V died and after she married Geoffrey of Anjou and was struggling to realize her claim to the throne of England. She evidently considered it hers by right. Like male sovereigns, Matilda is portrayed crowned and seated, and like the seals of males, her seal is round, not lozenge-shaped. In her right hand she holds a scepter, her left hand clasped against her chest.[161]

The second extraordinary seal is that of Constance, daughter of Louis VI and Adelaide of Maurienne. She employed her round seal as duchess of Narbonne, marchioness (of Provence), and countess of Toulouse. Pressing a cross to her chest with her right hand, she holds in her left an orb adorned with fleur-de-lis, a feature linking her seal with those of kings and emperors. She wears no crown, but the straight-backed throne on which she sits is more impressive than Matilda's, and her image is flanked by the regal symbols of radiant orb (sun or star) and crescent. How did Constance come to possess such a seal? Like Matilda, she acquired it through her first marriage. Her first husband was Eustace of Blois, son of Matilda's adversary Stephen of England, and Eustace was recognized as heir to the realm of England (and king) in 1151. After Eustace's death in 1152 she married Raymond V of Toulouse in a move her brother Louis VII clearly devised in order to ensure French influence in the region Eleanor of Aquitaine aimed to dominate and possess. The legends identify her (on the obverse) as duchess of Narbonne and marchioness and (on the reverse, where she is shown on horseback) as countess of Toulouse.[162] Constance may have adopted the form she used in imitation of Matilda, and the "royal lineage" with which her seal's shape proclaimed affiliation was surely English, not French. In the case of both Matilda and Constance, their sigillographic status seems to have derived from their first marriages and to have been unaffected by their later unions.[163]

Through their shapes and the seated positions of the rulers, these two seals convey, as Eleanor's seals do not, an immediate impression of and claim to royal dignity and authority. Nor was Eleanor among those noble women who, beginning in the last quarter of the twelfth century, were asserting their identities by having their own arms included on their seals.[164] Eleanor's failure to employ such distinctive sigillographic devices is initially surprising. On the other hand, the constant and distinctive presence of a dove on her seals clearly suggested that the Holy Spirit was bringing her wisdom and intelligence. Further, despite its lozenge-shaped form, her last seal endowed her with attributes like those that adorned her husband Henry's seal. On it, her dove surmounted an orb with a cross, an unmistakable token of imperial power and authority.

The coins issued while Eleanor was countess of Poitou and duchess of Aquitaine are far less assertive than her seals. Numismatically, Poitou is less significant than Aquitaine, since in Poitou the coinage was immobilized and continued to display legends dating from the Carolingian period—the name of Charles the Bald—or designating the important center of production at Melle. On the other hand, after Eleanor's son Richard became count, he issued coins bearing his own name. After his death, these coins as well as those modeled on more antique prototypes continued to be minted.[165] None bore Eleanor's name. As to Aquitaine, coins there were regularly issued under the names of rulers of the duchy. Thus it is all the more intriguing that the coins minted while Eleanor was duchess bore not her name but those of her husbands and her son Richard.[166] A coin with Eleanor's name on the obverse and her husband Louis's on the reverse seems doubtless to be, as Poey d'Avant put it, "une monnaie inventée à plaisir"[167]—yet another legendary fabrication. Presumably Eleanor of Aquitaine could have had coins minted that manifested her authority over her duchy. Matilda of England issued some crude coins as "imperatrix" and "comitissa." Similarly, other contemporary female rulers issued coins under their own names: Urraca of Castile, Eleanor of Vermandois, Jeanne of Constantinople at Saint-Omer, Ermengard of Narbonne, and Clemence of Burgundy.[168] In this company, Eleanor appears distinctly unaspiring and retiring. Numismatically at least, Eleanor was overshadowed by her husbands and sons.

Eleanor's Images at Poitiers and Fontevraud

Another stylized depiction of Eleanor survives, which is even more conventional than her sigillographic images. In the cathedral of Poitiers, at the base of the splendid Crucifixion window, Eleanor appears as a kneeling queen opposite a similarly devout king, each holding an edge of a miniature window they are offering to the church. Here Eleanor is depicted as a generic queen, the small size of her figure precluding any distinctiveness of feature. The inclusion of both rulers suggests that Eleanor and Henry participated jointly in the donation, which seems to have been made between 1165/70 and Henry's death in 1189. Given the tenseness of the couple's relations after 1166, their appearance together as donors of the glass is curious. If Eleanor was primarily responsible for the gift, it suggests the close ties, political and patronal if not emotional, that bound her to Henry, however badly he was treating her. If, on the other hand, the initiative was Henry's, Eleanor's presence in the window witnesses the importance of her authority in the lands her ancestors had long ruled.[169]

Another representation of Eleanor, apparently created soon after her death, may preserve the image that she herself wished remembered. This is her gisant at Fontevraud, whose form she may have determined.[170] It shows her not as the eighty-year-old woman she was when she died, but rather as much younger. Thus, the image cannot be a portrait, although it may preserve hints of her features. The effigy's most unusual characteristic is the book the queen holds. This feature may have been selected because of Eleanor's interest in things of the mind. The tilt of the effigy's head and eyes shows that the gisant is not reading but is engaged in contemplation, perhaps calculation, cerebral occupations consistent with the gifts the Holy Ghost conveys.[171] Like the dove on her seals, the ensemble suggests the importance of intelligence and wisdom to a woman who was richly endowed with both.

Owing to the twists of fortune experienced by Fontevraud, Eleanor's gisant at one time lost its book, and the object Eleanor holds today cannot be the one her effigy originally clasped. Over the centuries her gisant and those of her relatives suffered at the hands of Huguenots, overenthusiastic reformers, revolutionaries, and prisoners who were incarcerated at Fontevraud between 1804 and 1963. Painted and repainted, the monuments were in 1638 grouped together as an ensemble, apart from the remains they were designed to shelter.[172] When Charles Alfred Stothard saw (and drew) Eleanor's effigy in 1816, it was in a cellar, and Eleanor's book, as well as her left hand, were missing.[173] However, the drawings of her tomb made before the Revolution enabled mid-nineteenth-century restorers to remedy these losses and return to the queen the hand and the book she had lost.

Eleanor's funerary image is appropriate to the life she lived. It reposes with the monuments of members of her family, her husband and son representing her other children and relatives, whose lives she profoundly affected. No more splendid than the other gisants that lie near it, her effigy lacks the grandeur of royal and noble funerary monuments created for her contemporaries—Louis VI's wife Adelaide de Maurienne, Louis VII, the counts of Champagne—as well as, retrospectively, the Merovingian rulers, Childebert, Childeric, and Fredegonde.[174] The simplicity of her tomb recalls the modesty of her seals and, even more, the coins issued while she ruled. If Eleanor herself had a hand in determining the style of these objects, she may have elected the forms she did not out of feelings of diffidence but rather because, wishing to be recognized for her actual achievements, she had little use for empty symbols and ostentatious displays of the trappings of status and rank. The dove on her seals symbolized the qualities of mind that she particularly cherished.

The restraint of Eleanor's gisant, her seals, and her coins suggests that she would not wish to be remembered as her mythologizers have fashioned her, for sensational and dramatic deeds and accomplishments that are not hers. She should, rather, be appreciated for what she was: a long-lived woman of great energy, cunning, and administrative ability; a forthright lady;[175] a restless woman who resorted, out of inclination and sometimes necessity, to manipulation and scheming to achieve her aims; a woman who could bend anyone to her will;[176] a woman who knew her own mind and kept her own counsel. Is this the real Eleanor? Perhaps. In the end, however, she escapes our grasp, frustrating our desire to understand her fully. She remains, sphinx-like and iconic, a loadstar destined to elicit, for years to come, speculation about and imaginings of the seasons of her life.

Notes

1. This article revises, corrects, and expands on my study, "Eleanor of Aquitaine: Parent, Queen, and Duchess," in *Eleanor of Aquitaine: Patron and Politician,* ed. Kibler, pp. 9–34. It includes material I presented in the Edna V. Moffatt Lecture at Wellesley College in 1982, and in talks I gave at the Fifth Pennsylvania Symposium on Medieval and Renaissance Studies at the University of Pittsburgh on October 25, 1991, and at the Metropolitan Museum of Art on April 19, 1996. I profited from the questions and comments I received on each of these occasions, and am grateful as well for the many suggestions I have received from the late John F. Benton and from Andrew W. Lewis, and for the help and counsel of John Gillingham, Patricia Danz Stirnemann, and Charles T. Wood. Conversations with the late William Goldman and Katharine Hepburn were as illuminating as they were enjoyable. I extend thanks, as always, to the staffs of the Archives nationales, the Bibliothèque nationale de France, and the Bibliothèque de l'Arsenal in Paris and, in New York, the library of Columbia University and the New York Public Library.

   I rely throughout on the fundamental studies by Richardson, "Letters and Charters," 193–213, and Labande, "Pour une image véridique," 175–234. For the spelling of Fontevraud, I observe current practice, which is closer to what René Crozet considers preferable usage ("Fontevrauld") than is "Fontevrault," the spelling that was long favored: Crozet, "Fontevrault," 427 n1. See also Martindale, "Eleanor of Aquitaine," p. 20 n7. Bienvenu presents valuable evidence concerning the relations of Eleanor and her family with the house, in "Aliénor et Fontevraud." For the date of Eleanor's birth, see Lewis, chapter 7 in this volume; Duby endorses this date in his reflective, interpretative essay on Eleanor, in *Dames du XIIᵉ siècle* 1:14. For the date of her death, see Labande, "Pour une image véridique," 233 (citing evidence for March 31 and April 1); Anselme *Histoire généalogique* 2:521 (March 31, 1204); and her entry in the third martyrology of Fontevraud, under the date 3 Kal. Aprilis (March 30), in Pavillon, *La vie dv Bien-hevrevx Robert d'Arbrissel;* p. 577 ("Ex 3. Martyrol. Abbatiæ FE"; although note the date 6 Kal. Julii, June 26, that Pavillon, curiously, gives with her epitaph, no. 97 at p. 589). This obituary states that Eleanor, "[a]d ultimum," took the veil of the order of Fontevraud and elected burial at the abbey, which suggests that she died there.

I use the following abbreviations: AN—Paris, Archives nationales; BnF—
Bibliothèque nationale de France.

2. In 1959 Richardson ("Letters and Charters," 208 n3) pointed out the rich
sources for her household, which Vincent employs in "Isabella of Angoulême," p. 199; see also Marie Hivergneaux's analysis of Eleanor's charters in chapter 2 in this volume, and Martindale's "Eleanor of Aquitaine:
The Last Years," esp. 149–52, 155–63. Both Hivergneaux and Martindale
utilize the collection of Eleanor's acts that Nicholas Vincent has amassed.
Richardson ("Letters and Charters," 193 n1) regretted that charter evidence was used by neither Kelly, *Eleanor and the Four Kings,* nor Labande,
"Pour une image véridique." As regards Labande's article, this assessment
seems to me overly harsh. Although largely dependent on chronicles, Labande's long, detailed, and well-documented article is far more reliable
than the study by Kelly, whom Ralph V. Turner terms "a biographer with
a colorful imagination": see Turner, chapter 3 of this volume. I discuss
Kelly's work at greater length below. In her recent *Eleanor of Aquitaine,* Alison Weir makes interesting use of Charter, Liberate, and Pipe Rolls, although her notes, which are generally sparse and incomplete, do not give
precise references to the entries on which she draws. Martindale uses many
charters in her study, "Eleanor of Aquitaine," which focuses on the duchy;
e.g., pp. 36–37, where Martindale quotes the same passages from Richardson and comments on Kelly's book and others; see her p. 46 for her use of
material from the Pipe Rolls.

3. Duby comments on the speed with which legends were fabricated about
Eleanor, in *Dames* 1:15–18, 30, 33–37. Daniela Laube examines the sources
for Eleanor's life and the development of her reputation through the centuries, in *Zehn Kapitel,* esp. pp. 3–24, 102–32, 142–57.

4. Chambers, "Some Legends Concerning Eleanor," 459–68.

5. Owen, *Eleanor of Aquitaine: Queen and Legend,* pp. 103–61, where Owen
traverses the same ground covered by Chambers but quotes more extensively from the sources. No reference to Chambers's article appears in
Owen's bibliography or notes.

6. Owen, *Eleanor of Aquitaine,* p. 65 ("We often read of her presiding over her
flourishing court at Poitiers, surrounded by poet-musicians, convening with
her daughter Marie and other noble ladies those so-called courts of love,"
though later, "Unfortunately there is no evidence for Marie's presence at
Poitiers; and whatever grains of truth there may be in the romantic picture
of Eleanor's court as a centre of civilized dalliance, we may be sure she had
not lost her devotion to more serious matters"); and cf. 152–56, where he
directly attacks the legend. Owen apparently did not consult McCash,
"Marie de Champagne and Eleanor," 698–711, in which McCash tries (unsuccessfully, in my view) to revive the notion that Marie and Eleanor had
"a friendly relationship" and that there was contact between them. Labande
is critical of McCash's work, referring to her suggestion that Eleanor saw
Marie when she was traveling to Germany to ransom Richard as "Possibil-

ité certes, mais néanmoins hypothèse" ("Filles,"102–103); see also 104,
where Labande denounces the legend of the courts of love and declares that
"on franchit les limites de la prudence historique" in presenting Marie of
Champagne as a patroness of troubadours. In contrast, Theodore Evergates
seems to be persuaded by McCash's logic, although he acknowledges "the
absence of firm evidence": "Aristocratic Women in Champagne," pp. 79 and
208 n13. Evergates, pp. 77–79 and 209 n14, leaves open the question
whether Marie of Champagne held "mock courts to entertain her women
friends and relatives," but endorses the case for Marie's literary patronage
that Rita Lejeune made in "Rôle littéraire de la famille d'Aliénor," 324–28;
see also Lejeune, "Rôle littéraire d'Aliénor," 5–57 (note the useful itinerary
at 50–57). In this latter article (at 42), Lejeune says that Andreas Capellanus
"rapporte très fidèlement l'esprit et les sentences de ces assises féminines
dont Aliénor était, au propre et au figuré, la souveraine." I have grave reservations about Lejeune's work on the literary patronage of Eleanor and her
family, which John F. Benton shared; see his "The Court of Champagne"
551–91, see also n10 below.

7. Particularly important is Robertson, "The Subject of the *De Amore,*"
   145–61; see Kertesz, "The *De Arte (Honeste) Amandi,*" 5–16. In 1961 Benton declared that "[t]he weightiest evidence places [Andreas] at the royal
   court of France" ("Court of Champagne," 578). In 1978, Alfred Karnein
   supported this position, arguing persuasively that Andreas worked in the
   chancery of Philip Augustus, and was possibly the king's chamberlain ("Auf
   der Suche nach einem Autor"). Bourgain, "Aliénor d'Aquitaine et Marie de
   Champagne," 32 n12, emphasizes "le caractère plaisant ou légèrement par-
   odique" of Andreas Capellanus's book and summarizes Karnein's hypothesis concerning Andreas Capellanus, which, Bourgain says, "expliquerait bien
   des choses" (30). As I noted in 1976 (Brown, "Eleanor of Aquitaine: Parent,
   Queen, and Duchess," p. 29 n76), twenty years earlier Paul Rémy had presented a balanced and judicious assessment of the question in "Les 'cours
   d'amour.'" Joan M. Ferrante has demonstrated that, whatever the nature of
   Andreas's work, the notion of courtly love existed in medieval texts and was
   not an invention of Gaston Paris ("*Cortes'Amor*").

8. See Benton, "Court of Champagne," 581–82; Brown, "Eleanor of
   Aquitaine: Parent, Queen, and Duchess" pp. 18–19; and Weir, *Eleanor,* p.
   182 (who comments on some of the same judgments I discussed in 1976).
   Duby terms "les sentences ridicules" and says that Andreas, "lui aussi bur-
   lesque," featured Eleanor as "législatrice imaginaire et risible," "par mo-
   querie" (*Dames* 1:16, 37).

9. Amy Kelly has done more than any other author to confirm the notion of
   Eleanor's association with courts of love; her more florid passages on the
   courts are found in *Eleanor and the Four Kings,* pp. 85, 161, 167. Her biases
   were clear in the article she published thirteen years before the book,
   "Eleanor of Aquitaine and Her Courts of Love," 3–19, which is no#wor-
   thy for the sparseness of evidence cited. In 1941, Chambers seriously ques-

tioned ("Some Legends," 465) Kelly's interpretation, but this did not deter her from including most of the material she presented in the article in ch. 15 of her book: *Eleanor and the Four Kings*, pp. 157–67, entitled "The Court of Poitiers." Despite his own equivocal position on the issue, Owen, *Eleanor of Aquitaine*, p. 155, characterizes Kelly's account of the courts of love as "one of the more extravagantly imaginative chapters of her biography."

10. In an otherwise balanced and serious account of Eleanor's urban policies, Edith Ennen calls her "Königin der Troubadoure," and says that when she took up residence on the continent after John's birth (which she dates 1167), "Eleonore hat das kulturelle Verdienst, zur Verbindung der höfischen südfranzösischen Poesie mit dem keltischen Sagenstoff beigetragen zu haben" ("Zur Städtepolitik der Eleonore," 42, 48). Even Martindale, in her admirable "Eleanor of Aquitaine," pp. 37–39, does not completely reject Eleanor's participation in debates like those described by Andreas Capellanus; she cautions that "vernacular writing cannot simply be discounted because historians may not be trained to read or interpret it." Régine Pernoud devotes a lengthy chapter to Eleanor as "La reine des troubadours," in *Aliénor d'Aquitaine*, pp. 160–76. See also Rosenberg, *Eleanor of Aquitaine;* Trouncer, *Eleanor: The Two Marriages*, esp. p. 157; and Seward, *Eleanor of Aquitaine*, pp. 111–13; Markale, *La vie, la légende, l'influence d'Aliénor*, esp. pp. 129–75 (Eleanor as "Reine des troubadours").

11. Gillingham, *Richard I*, pp. 44–46; Weir, *Eleanor of Aquitaine*, pp. 181–82, concluding "that the Courts of Love were nothing more than a literary fiction." For others who have taken the same position, see nn6–8 above.

12. In "Peinture murale," 95–96, Marc Thibout discusses the painting (discovered in 1964), reviews the bibliography, and seconds the cautious appraisal of its subject matter given by Suzanne Trocmé in an article published in *Bulletin de la Société des Amis du Vieux-Chinon* (1966), which I have not been able to consult. In analyzing the visual evidence relating to Eleanor I have relied on a paper, "The Image of Eleanor," written by my student Patricia Young in May 1982. I am grateful to her for permitting me to cite it.

13. The picture Owen reproduces in color appears in black and white in Seward, *Eleanor of Aquitaine*, p. 199; Owen adopts Seward's identification of the figures and dating of the painting. Weir reproduces the entire fragment, in *Eleanor of Aquitaine*, pp. 236–37. She calls the painting "controversial" and identifies the crowned figures as "probably represent[ing]" Richard I and Eleanor, whereas she thinks the young person beside the second crowned figure Jeanne of England ("or, less probably, Queen Berengaria") and the two young men in the rear Eleanor's grandsons Otto of Brunswick and Duke Arthur of Brittany. In contrast, Aurell, "Richard Coeur de Lion," 64, interprets the figures as "Henri II [the first crowned figure to the right, who is not shown] emmenant en captivité sa femme Aliénor d'Aquitaine, pour la punir d'avoir fomenté une révolte contre lui. La reine prend ici congé de Richard Coeur de lion: il lui tend un faucon, son animal favori." Beside offering his own analysis, Jean Flori calls attention to two other re-

cent interpretations: (*Richard Coeur de Lion,* pp. 48, 493 nn. 43–44). He rejects that of U. Nilgen, who thinks the picture shows Henry II with his four sons after their reconciliation in 1174. He generally agrees with the reading of Kenaan-Kedar, "Aliénor d'Aquitaine conduite en captivité," 317–30. He points out, however, that Jeanne, whom Kenaan-Kedar, like Weir, sees as the person next to the second crowned figure, was "alors" only nine years old. He does not believe that the figure both he and Kenaan-Kedar view as Richard is holding a falcon out to "Eleanor," but that "she" is giving it to him, since, he explains, the falcon was "son emblème, signe de pouvoir seigneurial, en symbole de sa confiance en lui pour assurer la continuité d'une action politique qu'elle ne peut désormais plus assumer." The ambiguities of the French leave it unclear whether Flori sees the falcon as Eleanor's or Richard's symbol. Flori thinks that Eleanor's open hand supports his reading, but he wisely adds that his interpretation, "bien entendu, demeure hypothétique comme toutes celles qui ont été jusqu'ici proposées."

14. Owen, *Eleanor of Aquitaine,* p. 33 pl. 2. The capital is now in the collection of the Metropolitan Museum of Art, the Cloisters. It is impossible to date precisely this capital and the seven other Langon capitals acquired by the Metropolitan Museum in the 1920s. The church, located 47 km. SE of Bordeaux, was consecrated during the rule of the seventh abbot of the priory's mother house, La Grande-Sauve, and hence between 1155 and 1183. According to departmental files at the Cloisters, no direct connection can be established between Eleanor and Henry, on the one hand, and the priory of Langon, on the other, although in 1155 the royal couple visited La Grande-Sauve (Sauve Majeure; 28 km. ESE of Bordeaux). Marie-Madeleine Gauthier surveys the history of the Langon capitals and examines each one individually, in "Les chapiteaux de Notre-Dame du Bourg," pp. 18–47, esp. 20 n7 (the date of the consecration of Langon), 21–24 (the capital with two crowned heads, identified simply as "Deux têtes couronnées"). Jacques Gardelles demonstrates the ubiquity of capitals depicting human heads in the region, in "La sculpture monumentale en Bordelais," 36, where he describes the Cloisters capital as "deux têtes couronnées se détachant d'une corbeille." I am grateful to Nancy Wu for her help with the capital.

15. Kelly, *Eleanor and the Four Kings,* frontispiece; of the capital she comments (p. xi) that it "is believed to be one of a number made to celebrate the progress which Eleanor and Henry made after their marriage in 1152 to efface from her domain the memory of Louis's overlordship" and asserts that it "shows the queen in the flower of her age and warrants all the chroniclers have recorded of her." Weir (*Eleanor of Aquitaine,* p. 236) states more cautiously that the "capital [is] said to represent Henry and Eleanor," although she goes on to declare that it is "one of several pairs of heads thought to have been carved to commemorate their nuptial progress through Aquitaine in 1152." Kelly also published a photograph of two

jamb figures of the central portal of Chartres and suggested that they might
have been viewed as Eleanor and Louis VII (*Eleanor and the Four Kings*, pl.
facing p. 21; see also p. xi); she proceeded to propose analyses of the characters of the putative "queen" ("welcoming, gallant, admirably sagacious,
mistress of herself") and "king" ("gaunt, solemn, self-accusing, bend[ing]
his gaze inward upon the appalling confusions of his own soul"). Following Kelly, Meade (*Eleanor of Aquitaine*, second pl. between pp. 200 and 201)
published images of another royal pair on the western portal of Chartres,
saying that they "represent[ed] a king and queen of Judah and [were] believed to be likenesses of Eleanor and Louis." All four statues are nimbed.
Again, I acknowledge my indebtness to Patricia Young.

16. Note, for example, Dumontier, with Bernage, *L'empire des Plantagenêts*,
who use Eleanor (termed "Aliénor, reine d'Occident") as the focal point
of a lavishly illustrated popular history of the age. Noting "the paucity of
information from contemporaries" regarding Eleanor, Owen remarks
that, in her recent biography of Eleanor, Alison Weir "has taken advantage
of this 'soft centre' to her study by comprehensively covering the activities of husbands and sons, and painting in the domestic as well as the political background of the period" (*The Times Literary Supplement*, October
15, 1999:36).

17. Broadhurst confirms the conclusion I proposed in 1976 (in "Eleanor of
Aquitaine: Parent, Queen, and Duchess," pp. 18–19), in her "Henry II of
England and Eleanor of Aquitaine," 53–84. In "La littérature anglo-
normande au temps d'Aliénor,"113–18, Mary Dominica Legge, apparently
reluctant to abandon the notion of Eleanor as patron yet unsure of precisely what she accomplished, concludes, "L'influence d'Aliénor sur la littérature anglo-normande n'est pas prédominante, mais il est difficile de
dire qu'elle n'existe pas." Flori presents Eleanor as a woman "fantasque
mais cultivée, amie des lettres, protectrice des poètes," and believes that she
took the initiative in assembling "de nombrex écrivains" at the English
court. He concludes, "Par elle et par son entourage, le jeune Richard
[Coeur de Lion] a probablement baigné dans une atmosphère
chevaleresque." See Flori, *Richard Coeur de Lion*, pp. 23–24, esp. 492 n44,
where he cites the works of Lejeune, as well, surprisingly, as Benton's revi-
sionary study of literary activity at the court of Champagne.

18. In "Eleanor, Abbot Suger, and Saint-Denis," in *Eleanor of Aquitaine*, ed. Kibler, pp. 81–114, Eleanor S. Greenhill proposed that Eleanor was a patroness of Suger's abbey church of Saint-Denis and a devotee and
propagator of the pseudo-Turpin, although neither of these hypotheses has
any documentary basis. Elizabeth M. Jeffreys endorses Greenhill's conclusions in "The Comnenian Background," 462–64 (linking Eleanor with the
construction of Saint-Denis and the Turpin, which she believes "emerged
from St Denis in the early 1140s"). So too does Caviness, in "Suger's
Glass," p. 267. Although she does not cite Greenhill's work, Lindy Grant
lists Eleanor with Louis VII as a patron of Suger's Saint-Denis: see Grant,

Abbot Suger, p. 250. Greenhill's ideas regarding Eleanor and the Turpin are influenced by those of Mandach, *Naissance et développement de la chanson de geste,* vol. 1:130–31, 385–87; see Greenhill, "Eleanor, Abbot Suger, and Saint-Denis," pp. 101–02, esp. n165. Mandach and Greenhill present idiosyncratic and imaginative interpretations of the relationship of (in Mandach's case) Henry II and (in Greenhill's) Eleanor to the chronicler Geoffroi de Breuil, prior from 1178 of Vigeois in the Limousin, who sent a copy of the Turpin to Vigeois's mother house, Saint-Martial of Limoges; on Geoffroi see Arbellot, "Étude sur Geoffroy de Vigeois," 135–61. Owen did not deal with Greenhill's hypotheses, doubtless because he does not seem to have consulted the essays collected in *Eleanor of Aquitaine,* ed. Kibler, which does not figure in his bibliography. I discuss (and reject) the Dyonisian provenance of the Turpin, in "Saint-Denis and the Turpin Legend," in *The* Codex Calixtinus, ed. Williams and Stones, pp. 51–88.

19. See esp. Meade, *Eleanor.* In 1963, Richardson and Sayles declared, "It may be that she was cursed by fate in being born a woman" (*Governance,* p. 326).

20. Mareille's *La Vie ardente d'Eléonore* is the first item in the "Bibliographie sommaire" that Jean Markale presents in his *La vie, la légende, l'influence d'Aliénor.* In his chapter, "La légende" (pp. 177–215), Markale concentrates on contemporary rumors about Eleanor. He lists Chambers, "Legends," in his bibliography, but was clearly more impressed by other works he cites, such as those by Mareille, Kelly, Pernoud, and Lejeune. In the description she gave on the Internet of her recent biography of Eleanor, Weir called Eleanor "sensual" and presented her as "submitt[ing] to a union with the handsome but sexually withholding Louis VII," and then "transcend[ing] the mores of society"; Weir characterized Henri II as "aggressively virile" and "hot-tempered." In her book, in which she professes her dedication to avoiding "the romantic mode of some earlier biographers," Weir describes William IX of Aquitaine as "[i]ntelligent and outrageously sensual" and Henry II as "a restless and impatient soul with a vigorous sexual appetite" (Weir, *Eleanor of Aquitaine,* pp. xviii, and captions on 236 bis). None of these books, however, sinks to the depths plumbed by Hillary Auteur (a pseudonym for Ted Gottfried), in his pornographic spoof, *The Scarlet Raptures.*

21. Walker, *Eleanor of Aquitaine,* pp. 161–62.

22. Plaidy, *The Plantagenet Prelude,* pp. 73–74; Strickland, *Lives of the Queens* 1:169 (describing Eleanor leading a dress parade of female warriors after taking the cross at Vézelay, and remarking "Such fellow-soldiers as queen Eleanora and her Amazons would have been quite sufficient to disconcert the plans and impede the projects of Hannibal himself"). On Eleanor and the Amazon myth, see Chambers, "Legends," 459–60, and Owen, *Eleanor of Aquitaine,* pp. 148–52. On Strickland and Eleanor, see Weir, *Eleanor of Aquitaine,* p. 354.

23. Green, *Lives of the Princesses* 1:218.

24. Stubbs, introduction to Walter of Coventry, *Memoriale* 2:xxviii. Weir (*Eleanor of Aquitaine,* p. 354) quotes a more sympathetic assessment by Stubbs, but unfortunately does not give its source.

25. Trouncer, *Eleanor: The Two Marriages* p. 157 (Eleanor's Gothic blood) and p. 223 (on her death).

26. See Lewis, "Birth and Childhood" chapter 7 in this volume, for Eleanor's sixth son. I have discussed with Professor Lewis the possibility that this son may have been a twin of one of the known children and may have died at birth before being named.

27. For Eleanor's ascendance, see Anselme, *Histoire généalogique* 2:519–22.

28. See Martindale, "'Cavalaria et Orgueill," pp. 87–116; repr. in Martindale, *Status, Authority,* no. X; *Les chansons de Guillaume IX,* ed. Jeanroy, pp. iii–iv; and Bezzola, *Les origines,* 2^2:262–71, and pp. 259–61 for relationships among William's forebears that may have affected his attitude to women. For William's wives, see Anselme, *Histoire généalogique* 2:519–20. Pavillon comments on William's wife Philippa, who became a nun of the order of Fontevraud, in *Vie dv Bien-hevrevx Robert d'Arbrissel,* p. 566; see also p. 564 for her appearance, under the date November 28 ("4 Cal. Decemb."), in a martyrology of Fontevraud's priory of Fontaines-les-Nones (near Meaux), as "Philippa Monacha Pictauen. comitissa," and p. 581, under the same date, in the third martyrology of Fontevraud, as "Philippa Pictauensis comitissa"; see also the copy of the martyrology of Fontaines edited in *Obituaires de la province de Sens* (Sens 4:193) (under the date 1117–18). William IX himself figures in the martyrologies of Fontaines and Fontevraud under the dates, respectively, of February 10 and 11 (4 and 3 "Idus Februarii"): see Pavillon, *Vie dv Bien-hevrevx Robert d'Arbrissel,* pp. 563, 577 ("Guillelmus Dux Aquitaniæ"), *Obituaires de la province de Sens* 4:189; see Anselme, *Histoire généalogique* 2:591, for William IX's death on February 10, 1126/27.

29. " . . .uns dels majors cortes del mon, e dels majors trichadors de domp-nas"; " . . .anet lonc temps per lo mon per enganar las domnas" (*Chansons,* ed. Jeanroy, p. 30).

30. *Chansons,* ed. Jeanroy, pp. 7–8.

31. On his poetry, see Bezzola, *Origines* 2^2:306; Belperron, *La "joie d'amour";* Lazar, *Amour courtois,* p. 69; Davis, "Guillaume IX d'Aquitaine," pp. 94–95.

32. Bezzola, *Origines* 2^2:293; and see *Chansons,* Jeanroy, ed., p. x.

33. Richard, *Histoire des comtes de Poitou* 1:478, 2:18, 45, 51. For his clash with Saint Bernard, see *S. Bernardi Vita Secunda,* in Migne, PL 185:503–06. William appears under the date March 28 in the martyrology of Fontaines-les-Nones: Pavillon, *Vie dv Bien-hevrevx Robert d'Arbrissel,* p. 563, where Pavillon cites the authorities that give the date April 9, accepted by Anselme, *Histoire généalogique* 2:521; see also *Obituaires de la province de Sens* 4:190.

34. Richard, *Histoire des comtes de Poitou* 2:18, 45.

35. I discuss the events following the death of William that culminated in the marriage of Eleanor and Louis and her coronation as queen, first at Bor-

deaux, and then, on August 8, a week after the death of Louis VII, at Poitiers, in *"Franks, Burgundians, and Aquitanians,"* pp. 34–38, 49–50.

36. Chaplais, "Le traité de Paris," 121–37, Martindale, "Eleanor of Aquitaine," pp. 24–26.

37. Geoffroi de Breuil, in RHF 12:436. On the expedition, see Grant, *Abbot Suger,* pp. 139–41; an unpublished paper on Geoffrey of Lèves, bishop of Chartres, which Dr. Grant was kind enough to permit me to read, emphasizes the important role Geoffrey played in preparing for the marriage.

38. Brown, *"Franks, Burgundians, and Aquitanians,"* pp. 48–53, 89–97.

39. "Ludouicus puer Pictauis coronatus est; et sic regnum Francorum et Aquitaniae ducatum quem nullus patrum suorum habuit nactus est" (Ordericus Vitalis, *Historia Æcclesiastica* 6:490); and see Brown, *"Franks, Burgundians and Aquitanians,"* pp. 38 n149, and 49.

40. Labande, "Pour une image véridique," pp. 178–79; Martindale, "Succession and Politics," pp. 39–40; see also Martindale, "Eleanor of Aquitaine," pp. 25–26.

41. "Erat inter secretarios regis miles eunuchus quem illa semper oderat et consueuerat deridere, fidelis et familiarissimus regi, sicut et patri eius antea fuerat, Terricus scilicet Gualerancius": John of Salisbury, *Historia Pontificalis,* p. 53. See also Labande, "Pour une image véridique," p. 185 n45.

42. Anselme, *Histoire généalogique* 2:520–21, 684–85; Martindale, "Eleanor of Aquitaine," pp. 26–27, and "Succession," pp. 35–37. Fredric L. Cheyette discusses the claim in "Women, Poets and Politics" p. 145, and see also p. 154, for Louis's attack on Toulouse. On Philippa of Toulouse, see n28 above.

43. On the relations between Bernard and Eleanor, and the peace achieved in 1144, see Grant, *Abbot Suger,* pp. 26, 37, 148–52. For the marriage of Alice Petronilla and Raoul of Vermandois, see Anselme, *Histoire généalogique* 1:533–34, and 2:528.

44. William of Newburgh, *Historia Rerum Anglicarum* 1:92. On the expedition, see Berry, "The Second Crusade," pp. 463–512.

45. John of Salisbury, *Historia Pontificalis,* ed. Chibnall, pp. 52–53, and 60–62, esp. 61. Duby relies on John in treating the divorce, in *Dames* 1:20–24.

46. Recounting the royal couple's stay in Antioch, John of Salisbury wrote (*Historia Pontificalis,* p. 53): "Cum uero rex eam inde properaret auellere, ipsa parentele mentionem faciens dixit illicitum esse ut diutius commanerent, quia inter eos cognatio in quarto gradu uertebatur et quinto. Vnde rex plurimum turbatus est; et licet reginam affectu fere immoderato diligeret, tamen acquieuisset eam dimittere si consiliarii sui et Francorum proceres permisissent. Erat inter secretarios regis miles eunuchus quem illa semper oderat et consueuerat deridere, fidelis et familiarissimus regi, sicut et patri eius antea fuerat, Terricus scilicet Gualerancius. Is ei persuasit audentius ne ipsam Antiochie morari diutius pateretur, tum quia cognato poterat nomine culpa tegi, tum quia regno Francorum perpetuum opprobrium imminebat si inter cetera infortunia rex diceretur spoliatus coniuge uel relictus." See Duby, *Medieval Marriage,* p. 58.

47. "Discordiam regis et regine, quae Antiochie concepta fuerat, auditis querelis utriusque seorsum omnino sedauit, prohibens ne de cetero consanguinitatis inter eos mentio haberetur; et confirmans matrimonium tam uerbo quam scripto, sub anathematis interminatione inhibuit ne quis illud impetens audiretur et ne quacunque solueretur occasione" (John of Salisbury, *Historia Pontificalis*, p. 61). Duby does not mention the papal pronouncement in recounting the divorce in *Medieval Marriage*, p. 59, or in *Dames* 1:20–24.

48. "Regi uisa est placuisse plurimum constitutio, eo quod reginam uehementer amabat et fere puerili modo" (John of Salisbury, *Historia Pontificalis*, p. 61).

49. Duby, *Dames* 1:23–24, views the steps the pope took as a remarriage of Eleanor and Louis ("Le pape Eugène III alla même jusqu'à remarier les conjoints, respectant scrupuleusement les formes").

50. Labande, "Pour une image véridique," 189–91; John of Salisbury, *Historia Pontificalis*, pp. 61–62.

51. Grant, *Abbot Suger*, pp. 283–86, analyzes the complex maneuvering that preceded Duke Henry's homage to Louis VII in September, 1151, and for background, pp. 148–49, 153–54, 171–72. See also Grant, "Suger and the Anglo-Norman World," pp. 63–64; and Aubert, *Suger*, p. 88; Suger, *Oeuvres complètes*, pp. 265, 384.

52. Torigni, *Chronique* 1:255.

53. On the divorce, see the chapters in this volume by Constance B. Bouchard and James A. Brundage.

54. William of Newburgh assesses Eleanor's motivations in selecting Henry as her future husband, in *Historia Rerum Anglicarum*, p. 93. Of the marriage, Torigni says that Henry married Eleanor "sive repentino sive praemeditato consilio" (*Chronique* 1:260). See also Martindale, "Eleanor of Aquitaine," pp. 39–40. John Gillingham invokes twelfth-century ideas about sexuality and procreation in considering why Louis VII agreed to divorce Eleanor, and provides useful insights into her relationship with Henry of Anjou, in "Love, Marriage and Politics," pp. 243–55.

55. Michael W. Cothren and I treat the following events in detail in "Twelfth-Century Crusading Window," 28–30 and figures 1–12. Martindale discusses Louis's reactions, in "Eleanor of Aquitaine," pp. 30–32.

56. Berger, "La formule 'Rex Francorum,'" 305–13.

57. William of Newburgh, *Historia Rerum Anglicarum*, p. 93; Labande, "Pour une image véridique," 197–98; Duby, *Dames* 1:25–26.

58. Labande, "Pour une image véridique," 191–93; Grant, *Abbot Suger*, pp. 283–86; Torigni, *Chronique* 1:256.

59. Brooke and Brooke, "Henry II, Duke of Normandy and Aquitaine," 88.

60. Richardson, "Letters and Charters," 193, and his introduction to *The Memoranda Roll for the Michaelmas Term of the First year of the Reign of King John*, pp. lxviii, lxxi, lxxiii.

61. Labande, "Pour une image véridique," 199; Richard, *Histoire des comtes de Poitou* 2:115.

62. Poole, *From Domesday Book to Magna Carta, 1087–1216,* vol. 3 of *The Oxford History of England,* p. 161; and Labande, "Pour une image véridique," 198.

63. Giraldus Cambrensis, *De Principis Instructione Liber* 8:301, 309; see Warren, *King John,* p. 2. I discuss Giraldus and his reliability in "Ritual Brotherhood," 366–70.

64. Anselme, *Histoire généalogique* 6:19–20 (dating Matilda's birth early in 1102, and Geoffrey's August 24, 1113). See also Chibnall, *The Empress Matilda,* esp. pp. 55–59.

65. Poole, *Domesday Book to Magna Carta,* pp. 128–29.

66. Poole, *Domesday Book to Magna Carta,* p. 326 n6; François-Souchal, "Les émaux."

67. Poole, *Domesday Book to Magna Carta,* pp. 165–66.

68. Labande, "Pour une image véridique," 199.

69. Brown and Cothren, "Twelfth-Century Crusading Window," 28–29.

70. Horrent, "Chroniques espagnoles et chansons de geste,"288, 292. I discuss the vase below. On the incident, see Martin, "L'escarboucle de Saint-Denis."

71. BnF, lat. 5480, p. 486 ("Anno ab Incarnatione domini. M.C.L.II. Regnante Lodouico Rege francorum Gisleberto pictauorum Episcopo et henrico pictauorum et andegauorum Imperium gubernante"); on this act, issued at Fontevraud in the abbey's favor, see below, at and following n144.

72. Torigni, *Chronique* 1:328, 356, 369; Green, *Lives of the Princesses* 1:216. The speed with which Eleanor produced children suggests that she did not nurse them, although in the twelfth century it was thought proper for noble women to do so. See *Le Chevalier au Cygne et Godefroid de Bouillon* 1:124–26; Renart, *Galeran de Bretagne,* lines 428–591 (esp. 559–91), 1030–34, 1106–23, and for background, pp. iii–v. See also Berger, *Blanche de Castille,* p. 21.

73. John's epitaph at Fontevraud records, "dumque erat annorum. [*sic*] ab illustrissimo patre suo Rege Henrico nobis & Ecclesiæ nostræ pio amore est oblatus, & à nobis per 5. annorum spatium nutritus," and Jeanne's states, less expansively, "quibus cum nutrita fuerat" (Pavillon, *La vie dv Bien-hevrevx Robert d'Arbrissel,* no. 90 at p. 585, and no. 96 at p. 588). See Bezzola, *Origines* 2²:287. Dana Sample discusses Jeanne's life before her marriage to Raymond of Toulouse in 1196, in "Joanna, Queen of Sicily."

74. Brown, "Eleanor of Aquitaine: Parent, Queen, and Duchess," pp. 17, 24. See Turner's valuable article, "Eleanor of Aquitaine and Her Children," esp. 324, 327, 331, and Huneycutt, "Public Lives, Private Ties." Andrew Lewis offers a useful assessment of my views, and those of Turner and Huneycutt, in his chapter in this volume. I welcome his correction of my endorsement of Jean Richard's conclusion (*Histoire* 2:150) that John was placed in his brother Henry's household after leaving Fontevraud. Nicholas Vincent presents John as "very much a mother's boy, brought up as the favourite of Eleanor of Aquitaine," in "Isabella of Angoulême," p. 204. Labande, "Filles,"

p. 107, cites Amy Kelly as his source for stating that Eleanor (born in 1161) was raised at Fontevraud with Jeanne (born in 1165).

75. See Lewis in this volume.

76. On Matilda, see Lewis in this volume; the obituary of Fontaines-les-Nones, in *Obituaires de la Province de Sens* 4:190 (under the date March 24); and Anselme, *Histoire généalogique* 2:721–22, 6:18.

77. Matilda was the widow of Henry I's only legitimate son William Aydelin. Her epitaph at Fontevraud gives the date of her death as May 22 ("11. Cal. Iunij") 1155, and says that she served (unwillingly) as Fontevraud's second abbess for five years ("transacto post electionem suam quinque annorum curriculo"): Pavillon, *La vie dv Bien-hevrevx Robert d'Arbrissel*, no. 95 at pp. 587–88; and, for Henry II's epitaph, no. 89 at p. 583; her deathdate is also recorded in the obituary of Fontaines-les-Nones, in *Obituaires de la Province de Sens* 4:191. On her, see Anselme, *Histoire généalogique* 6:17–18 (giving the year of her death as 1154); Crozet, "Fontevrault," p. 431 (dating her abbatiate 1150–64); Grant, *Abbot Suger*, p. 284 (saying she was made abbess in 1149); and Gaussin, "Politique monastique," 94 (dating her abbatiate 1149–55). Boase discusses Henry II's ties to Fontevraud, in "Fontevrault and the Plantagenets," 4–6. Note too that Henry's mother, Matilda, is described in the obituary of Fontaines-les-Nones (under the date September 9) as "benefactrix totius ecclesie nostre": (*Obituaires de la Province de Sens* 4:192). For Eleanor's visit to Fontevraud in 1152, see BnF, lat. 5480, p. 486, a charter issued by Eleanor at Fontevraud in Abbess Matilda's presence, which is discussed below, at and following n144.

78. Richardson, "Letters and Charters," 196 (noting that all writs issued in Eleanor's name are dated before Michaelmas 1163); see Labande, "Pour une image véridique," 204.

79. Labande, "Pour une image véridique," 202–204. For Eleanor's activities and authority, see Richardson's introduction to *The Memoranda Roll (1199–1200)*, pp. lxviii–xx, lxviii–ix.

80. François-Souchal, "Les émaux," 131, 137. Richardson, introduction to *The Memoranda Roll (1199–1200)*, p. lxix, discusses the authority Empress Matilda enjoyed in the absence of Henry and Eleanor.

81. Marguerite, daughter of Louis VII and Constance of Castile, was married in 1160 to Henry's son and namesake; she brought as her dowry the same borderlands in Normandy that Geoffrey of Anjou had relinqushed to Louis VII ten years before. On Henry's division of his lands, see Poole, *Domesday Book to Magna Carta*, pp. 328–31, and Richard, *Histoire des comtes de Poitou* 2:150; on young Henry's coronation, Labande, "Pour une image véridique," 205; and *Materials for Becket* 3:103.

82. On the investiture and its significance, see Barrière, "Le Limousin et Limoges au temps de l'émail champlevé," pp. 27–28. See also below, at, and following n135, for the cult of Saint Valérie and the importance of her ring.

83. *Gesta Regis Henrici Secundi* 1:30 n8.

84. Gillingham, *Richard I*, pp. 46–47; Poole, *Domesday Book to Magna Carta*, pp. 330–32; Richard, *Histoire des comtes de Poitou* 2: 164–65 Hardegen, *Imperi-*

alpolitik König Heinrichs II, p. 26; *Gesta Regis Henrici Secundi* 1:36; Vic and Vaissete, *Histoire générale de Languedoc* 6:53. On this occasion, Raymond witnessed a charter in which Henry confirmed certain rights for Fontevraud (*Recueil des actes de Henri II* 7[2]: no. CCCCLVII at pp. 5–6 [Delisle no. 300]).

85. *Gesta Regis Henrici Secundi* 1:42. Eleanor had many reasons for intriguing against her husband besides jealousy; see Martindale, "Eleanor of Aquitaine," pp. 43–44.

86. For Henry's reaction, see Labande, "Pour une image véridique," 212–13. Acknowledging the counsel of John Gillingham, Jane Martindale suggests that because she was a woman, Eleanor was less harshly treated than a male rebel would have been ("Eleanor of Aquitaine," p. 34). Giraldus Cambrensis reports that Henry considered divorcing Eleanor and sending her to Fontevraud as a nun: *De Principis Instructione Liber,* pp. 232, 306; Bienvenu, "Aliénor et Fontevraud," 21 n44, cites Amy Kelly as the source of the story.

87. Poole, *Domesday Book to Magna Carta,* p. 341.

88. *Gesta Regis Henrici Secundi* 1:305; Richardson, "Letters and Charters," 198 n6.

89. *Gesta Regis Henrici Secundi* 1:313, 333–34.

90. ". . .pro certo sciret, quod ipsa regina mater sua cum exercitu magno devastare vacaret terram suam": *Gesta Regis Henrici Secundi* 1:337–38.

91. Richardson, "Letters and Charters," 198–99.

92. Vic and Vaissete, *Histoire générale de Languedoc* 6:131, 133; Poole, *Domesday Book to Magna Carta,* pp. 344–46; Richard, *Histoire des comtes de Poitou* 2:243–45; and Giraldus Cambrensis, *De Principis Instructione Liber,* p. 246.

93. Baldwin discusses Philip Augustus's accession in *Philip Augustus,* pp. 3–24. Evergates offers interesting comments in "Aristocratic Women in Champagne," p. 77.

94. On these relationships see Anselme, *Histoire généalogique* 1:76–78, 2:840–42. On Marie's marriage to Henri, see Benton, "The Court of Champagne," 553–54 (pp. 3–4 in the reprint ed.).

95. For Henry's struggle against his sons and Philip Augustus, see Giraldus Cambrensis, *De Principis Instructione Liber,* p. 295; and *Gesta Regis Henrici Secundi* 2:50; Roger of Howden, *Chronica* 2:362–63, 366.

96. "In loco obscuro tantaeque majestati longe indebito" (Giraldus Cambrensis, *De Principis Instructione Liber,* p. 306); see *Gesta Regis Henrici Secundi* 1:7 ("contra dignitatem regni sui"). Henry's epitaph at Fontevraud reflects the same attitude. Attributing to Henry himself the decision to be buried at the abbey, the epitaph emphasizes the modesty of the house and interprets Henry's choice of burial there as a sign of his special dedication to Fontevraud (Pavillon, *La vie dv Bien-hevrevx Robert d'Arbrissel,* no. 89 at p. 583 ["sic in fine ipse maxime dilexit nos, ita scilicet vt nobis sinceræ veritatem dilectionis quam circa nos habebat, exhiberet, se nobis contulit, & concessit; & relictis propriis Ecclesiis per diversa terræ suæ spatia constitutis, licet maioris dignitatis sint & autoritatis, in Ecclesia nostrá inter pauperes Christi virgines & ancillas, sicut disposuerat, corpus ipsius traditur

sepulture"]). On the circumstances of Henry's burial, see Charles T. Wood, chapter 19 in this volume. François-Souchal discusses Henry's relations with Grandmont, in "Les émaux": 43, 135–42, 150; see also Gaussin, "Politique monastique," p. 90; Becquet, "La vie religieuse en Limrusin," p. 32, and, in the same volume, Boehm, "*Opus lemovicense.* La diffusion des émaux limousins," p. 44; and also Hutchison, *The Hermit Monks of Grandmont,* esp. pp. 53, 57–58, 60.

97. Wood, "Les gisants de Fontevraud et la politique dynastique des Plantagenêts," and Boase, "Fontevrault," 5–7, are especially useful; see also Gaussin, "Politique monastique," 90, 94. In the will he drew in 1182, Henry left two thousand silver marks to Fontevraud and its daughter-houses (*Collection of All the Wills,* ed. Nichols, p. 8). Henry left similar sums to the Cistercians and the Carthusians. He bequeathed just a thousand marks to the Cluniacs, but left three thousand marks to Grandmont and its dependencies. Nichols printed the will from Madox, *Formulare Anglicanum,* no. DCCLXVII at pp. 421–23.

98. *L'histoire de Guillaume le Maréchal* 1: lines 9503–10. It is not clear to me why Richardson ("Letters and Charters," 200) questions the report that Richard released his mother as one of his first acts. For Eleanor's activities in the years after the death of Henry II, Martindale, "Eleanor of Aquitaine: The Last Years," is fundamentally important. Ralph V. Turner gives a brief summary of her life in the years between the deaths of Henry and Richard, in "Eleanor of Aquitaine in the Reign of her Son Richard Lionheart" (paper presented at the Charles Homer Haskins Society Conference, Cornell University, November 1999).

99. "ut a propria persona sua argumentum eliceret captiones molestas esse hominibus, et jocundissimum animae refocillationem ab ipsis emergere" (*Gesta Ricardi Ducis Normanniae,* in *Gesta Regis Henrici Secundi* 2:74–75). Roger of Howden, *Chronica* 3:4–5, gives a slightly different account.

100. Richardson, "Letters and Charters," pp. 200, 211; *Gesta Ricardi,* in *Gesta Regis Henrici Secundi* 2:99.

101. For her release, see Roger of Howden, *Chronica* 3:303.

102. Gillingham, *Richard I,* pp. 125–26; Richardson, "The Marriage and Coronation of Isabelle of Angoulême," 311–13.

103. " . . .puella prudentiore quam pulcra": Richard of Devizes, *Chronicon,* p. 25. See his description of Eleanor as "femina incomparabilis, pulcra et pudica, potens et modesta, humilis et diserta." Martindale discusses this passage in "Eleanor of Aquitaine," p. 50. Gillingham (*Richard I,* p. 143, esp. n10) remarks that Richard of Devises "was presumably aiming at alliteration rather than accuracy" and notes that other chroniclers praised her beauty.

104. I discuss the two kings' encounter with Joachim of Fiore in Messina in "La notion de la légitimité et la prophétie," pp. 88–90.

105. Because of Lent, which ended on Easter day, April 14, Berengaria and Richard were not married until May 12, 1191, when they were wedded

and crowned in Limassol, on Cyprus: Gillingham, *Richard the Lionheart,* p. 166. See also Richardson, "Letters and Charters," 201.

106. Richardson, "Letters and Charters," 201–202; Gillingham, *Richard the Lionheart,* p. 179 and, for what follows, pp. 226, 229, and 233–36; Martindale, "Eleanor of Aquitaine," p. 49.

107. "ipsi saisirent in manu regis omnes terras et castella sua" (*Gesta Ricardi,* in *Gesta Regis Henrici Secundi* 2:236). See also Labande, "Pour une image véridique," 220 n233. For her authority, see Richardson, "Letters and Charters," 201–202.

108. Richardson, "Letters and Charters," 202; Labande, "Pour une image véridique," 223; Poole, *Domesday Book to Magna Carta,* pp. 364–66.

109. Roger of Howden, *Chronica* 3:202, 227, 229–32, 234; Gillingham, *Richard I,* pp. 247–48. Philip Augustus had recently received John's homage, further complicating Richard's relations with his brother. Labande discusses the situation Richard faced on his release, in "Pour une image véridique," 223; see also Poole, *Domesday Book to Magna Carta,* p. 366, and Warren, *Henry II,* pp. 44–45. In 1195, encouraging Richard to invade France, Henry VI sent him "coronam magnam auream, et valde pretiosam, in mutuae dilectionis signum" (Roger of Howden, *Chronica* 3:300–302).

110. Roger of Howden, *Chronica* 3:248; Labande, "Pour une image véridique," 224; Richardson, "Letters and Charters," 203; Richardson and Sayles, *Governance,* p. 153; Gillingham, *Richard I,* pp. 272–73.

111. Richardson, "Letters and Charters," 209–11, esp. 210; Vincent, "Isabella of Angoulême," pp. 190–92.

112. Roger of Howden, *Chronica* 3:251–52; *L'histoire de Guillaume le Maréchal* 1: lines 10341–48, does not mention Eleanor in discussing the peace. See Richardson, "Letters and Charters," 204.

113. Gillingham, *Richard the Lionheart,* pp. 276–77.

114. Bienvenu discusses the rhythm of her donations in "Aliénor et Fontevraud," 20–25. Her obituary records that she "Dedit itaque nobis in perpetuum C. lib. redditus in Marant recipiendas ad tunicas nostras singulis annis comparandas, et alias C. lib. redditus in Olerone ad eius, liberorumque suorum anniversaria celebranda, et L. lib. redditus in vinea de Marsilly super villam de Iaunay in territorio Pictau. sita. Cæterum Abbatiam illam quæ patebat eam introire volentibus sumptu proprio, muris circumclausit optimis, & necessariis crucem auream pretiosis lapidibus ornatam quæ in processionibus solemniter antefertur, et cuppam auream, & alia vasa aurea plurima & argentea, & ornamenta serica nostræ donavit Ecclesiæ": Pavillon, *La vie dv Bien-hevrevx Robert d'Arbrissel,* no. 97 at p. 589; quoted with some differences in spelling in Bienvenu, "Aliénor et Fontevraud," 26 n98; see also Crozet, "Fontevrault," 431.

115. Labande, "Pour une image véridique," 224; Vic and Vaissete, *Histoire générale de Languedoc* 6:173–74.

116. Poole, *Domesday Book to Magna Carta,* pp. 376–77; Richard, *Histoire des comtes de Poitou* 2:299, 313–14. Friedrich Hardegen presents a probing assessment

of Henry II's imperial ambitions in *Imperialpolitik*. Holt discusses the problems that Otto's recognition as count of Poitou would later cause for John, in "Aliénor," 97–98.

117. Alix died in or about 1197, according to Berman and Shadis, "A Taste of the Feast." Eleanor made a gift of 20 l. poit. to Alice's daughter Alice in 1199 (Marchegay, "Chartes de Fontevraud," 340–41.

118. Evergates presents a useful discussion of Marie's life in "Aristocratic Women in Champagne," pp. 76–80; he states that she was buried at Meaux, but does not mention her becoming a nun at Fontaines-les-Nones. She is described in a martyrology of Fontaines-les-Nones under the date March 11 ("5. Idus Mart.") as "Dom. Maria Reuerend. Monacha nobilissima campaniæ comitissa Franc. Regis filia" (Pavillon, *La vie dv Bien-hevrevx Robert d'Arbrissel*, p. 563 [noting that the martyrology was at Fontevraud when he consulted it]); and *Obituaires de la Province de Sens* 4:190 (giving the date March 8 or 11, 1198, and a fuller entry); and also Bienvenu, "Aliénor et Fontevraud," 18, esp. n18, and 24 n75. Anselme, *Histoire généalogique* 2:841, says nothing of her burial or final years, but dates her death March 11, 1198.

119. See Ralph of Coggeshall, *Chronicon Anglicanum,* p. 96. On the circumstances of Richard's death, see Gillingham, "The Unromantic Death of Richard I," 18–41, esp. 26–28 on Ralph of Coggeshall's reliability, repr. in Gillingham, *Richard Coeur de Lion,* no. 6; and also Gillingham, *Richard I,* pp. 324–26. Baldwin discusses the conflict between Philip Augustus and Richard that preceded Richard's death, in *Philip Augustus,* pp. 87–94. See also Perrier, "De nouvelles précisions sur la mort de Richard Coeur de Lion," 159–69, esp. 169, quoting a charter of Eleanor in which she says, "Sciatis autem nos interfuisse morti jamdicti filii nostri regis"; "quia dilectus noster (L), abbas de Torpiniaco, affuit nobiscum infirmitati et funeri carissimi filii nostri regis, et causa ejusdem exequias prae omnibus aliis religiosis laborauit." Richard appears in the third martyrology of Fontevraud as "charissimus amicus noster," under the date April 7 ("7 Idus Aprilis") (Pavillon, *Vie du Bien-hevrevx Robert d'Arbrissel,* p. 578), and as "dominus et amicus familiarissimus" in the obituary of Fontaines-les-Nones (*Obituaires de la Province de Sens* 4:190). His epitaph at Fontevraud gives the date of his burial, and says that he elected interment at the house because of the enormity of his sins, and asked to be interred at his father's feet "vt si non viuens, saltem moriens satis faciam" (Pavillon, *Vie du Bien-hevrevx Robert d'Arbrissel,* no. 89 at pp. 584–85 [mentioning Richard's donation to the abbey of wood of the True Cross and hairs of the Virgin]).

120. Richardson, "Letters and Charters," 206.

121. Roger of Howden, *Chronica* 4:88; Warren, *King John,* p. 50.

122. Labande, "Pour une image véridique," 221.

123. Chaplais, "Traité," pp. 121–37; Martindale, "Eleanor of Aquitaine: The Last Years," pp. 154–55. Richardson ("Letters and Charters," 205–206) believes that she probably did do homage to Philip Augustus for both Poitou and Aquitaine.

124. "karissimo filio nostro . . .sicut recto heredi nostro": *Rotuli Chartarum* 1¹:30, and for John's charter, p. 31. Neither act is dated, but Eleanor's follows an act of August 18, and John's of August 25. On the transaction, see Martindale, "Eleanor of Aquitaine: The Last Years," pp. 156–60; Holt, "Aliénor," 95–100; and Richardson, "Letters and Charters," 205–206.

125. On Jeanne and her son, see Anselme, *Histoire généalogique* 2:689, 691. For Jeanne's final days, see her epitaph at Fontevraud, in Pavillon, *Vie dv Bien-hevrevx Robert d'Arbrissel,* no. 96 at p. 588 (where the date July 11 ["5. Idus Iulij"] is given, and p. 580 for the correct date of her death, September 4 ["Prid. non. Septemb."], in the third martyrology of Fontevraud). Note (see n119 above) that the same abbot ("de Torpeniaco") who was with Eleanor at Richard's deathbed was present when Jeanne died. See also Bienvenu, "Aliénor et Fontevraud," 24–25, and Labande, "Filles," 109–11. On Raymond's tomb at Fontevraud, see Wood, "Les gisants de Fontevraud et la politique dynastique des Plantagenêts"; and his epitaph at Fontevraud, in Pavillon, *Vie dv Bien-hevrevx Robert d'Arbrissel,* no. 94 at p. 587. The effigies that adorned the tombs of Jeanne and Raymond were removed in the early seventeenth century when the abbess, Jeanne-Baptiste de Bourbon, decided to enlarge the choir of the church; she had statues honoring Jeanne and Raymond installed as part of the collective monument uniting the four surviving gisants that she commissioned. On the monument, see n172 below.

126. On the peace of Le Goulet of May 1200, see Baldwin, *Philip Augustus,* pp. 96–97, 269. At Fontevraud, Eleanor of Castile was remembered as "optimæ Ecclesiæ nostræ benefactrix" (Pavillon, *Vie dv Bien-hevrevx Robert d'Arbrissel,* p. 581 [the third martyrology of Fontevraud] under the date 3 [Cal.] November [October 30]).

127. Labande, "Filles," 107–108, for the ten children, including seven daughters (four of whom would become queens), of Eleanor and Alfonso VIII of Castile; see also Labande, "Pour une image véridique," 229–30, and Anselme, *Histoire généalogique* 1:81–82.

128. Baldwin, *Philip Augustus,* pp. 97–100, and Wood, "Les gisants de Fontevraud et la politique dynastique des Plantagenêts."

129. Martindale, "Eleanor of Aquitaine: The Last Years," pp. 151–52; Labande, "Pour une image véridique," 231; Poole, *Domesday Book to Magna Carta,* pp. 380–81; Richardson and Sayles, *Governance,* pp. 323–25.

130. Baldwin, *Philip Augustus,* pp. 98, 191–93; Labande, "Pour une image véridique," 232; Poole, *Domesday Book to Magna Carta,* pp. 381–82.

131. Baldwin, *Philip Augustus,* p. 194; Labande, "Pour une image véridique," 232–33.

132. Baldwin, *Philip Augustus,* p. 193.

133. "Ad vltimum tanto nobis effecta est vinculo sincerissimæ dilectionis quæ Religiones alias quasi respuens, velamen nostri ordinis suscipere, & in nostrâ præelegit Ecclesia sepeliri" (Pavillon, *Vie dv Bien-hevrevx Robert d'Arbrissel,* no. 97 at p. 589 [Eleanor's epitaph at Fontevraud, on which see n1

above]); quoted with some differences, in Bienvenu, "Aliénor et
Fontevraud," 26 n98. In the third martyrology of Fontevraud, Eleanor is
listed under the date March 30 ("3. Cal. April.") as "Regina Angliæ claris-
sima [*sic*, probably for *charissima*] mater nostra" (Pavillon, *Vie dv Bien-
hevrevx Robert d'Arbrissel*, p. 578, and see pp. 578–79, for Henry II as
"piissimus Pater noster" in the entry for the death of his son Henry, but as
"illustris Rex Angliæ" under the date of his own death, given as July 7
["Non. Iul."]; see no. 89 at p. 583, where he is designated the house's "pius
[piissimus] pater" and "pater noster charissimus" in his epitaph and, in
Richard I's, "benignissimus pater noster"). The only other woman commemorated as "charissima mater nostra" in Fontevraud's third martyrology
is Marie of Champagne, sister of Henri and Thibaud of Champagne, and
wife of Duke Eudes of Burgundy, who became a nun at Fontevraud after
her husband's death in 1162 and was buried there, having refused election
as abbess (Pavillon, *Vie dv Bien-hevrevx Robert d'Arbrissel*, pp. 579, 580, and
also no. 101 at pp. 591–92 [her epitaph]); Anselme, *Histoire généalogique*
2:840. Note as well, "excellentissima mater nostra," in the epitaph at
Fontevraud of Queen Eleanor of Provence, widow of Henry III of England, who died as a nun of the order in 1291 (Pavillon, *Vie dv Bien-hevrevx
Robert d'Arbrissel*, no. 99, at p. 590).

134. On the reliquaries, one of which is in the British Museum, the other in
Saint Petersburg, see Gauthier, *Émaux*, pp. 93–96; and *L'oeuvre de Limoges*,
no. 20 at pp. 116–18 (Élisabeth Taburet-Delahaye on the Saint-Petersburg
chasse, and the ring of Valérie); and see entry no. 86 at p. 278 (Taburet-
Delahaye on a reliquary of Saint Valérie dated ca. 1225–35, in the Louvre).

135. "Accipe dignitatis anulum, & per hunc in te Catholicæ fidei cognosce
signaculum, quia hodie institueris Dux, & Princeps Aquitaniæ, vt felix in
opere, locuples in fide, glorieris cum Domino dominantium, cui est honor
& gloria" (Godefroy and Godefroy, *Le ceremonial francois* 1:605–9, esp.
605–606 ["Forme de couronnement des anciens Ducs d'Aquitaine dans
la Ville Episcopale de Limoges. Colligée par vn nommé Helie, Prechantre
de la Cathedrale de ladite Ville, environ 1218. Ex veteri cod. Ecclesiæ
Lemovicensis"]). My suggestion that the details of the ceremony remained more or less fixed between Richard's investiture and the date of
the extant *ordo* may not be justified: see Jackson, "Manuscripts, Texts, and
Enigmas." For the *ordo* and its date, see Godefroy and Godefroy, *Ceremonial francois* 1:605, 608–09; and Schramm, *Der König von Frankreich*
1:128–29. On Richard's investiture and Valérie's ring, see also above, n82
and the accompanying text.

136. Note, in the prayer of bestowal, the phrase "dignitatis anulum," and in the
account of the ceremony written by Helias, precentor of the church, the
equation between "anulo Beatæ Valeriæ" and "Ducatus dignitate": see
Godefroy and Godefroy, *Ceremonial francois* 1:606, 609 (where Helias refers
to the crown as "garlanda redimitus aurea" and "circulus aureus," and
equates it with "Ducatus honore"); the account is also found in

RHF12:451–53. According to Geoffroy de Vigeois, in June 1172 Richard received the ducal lance and banner from the archbishop of Bordeaux and the bishop of Poitiers at the abbey of Saint-Hilaire of Poitiers, and sometime later was invested with the ring of Valérie in Limoges: RHF 12:442–43; see Flori, *Richard Coeur de Lion*, p. 40. Quoting Geoffroy's history, the author of a chronicle of Saint-Martin of Limoges (who reproduced the inaugural ceremonial) declared that the citizens of Limoges disputed Geoffroy's account, "quia in Ecclesia B. Stephani fit omnino novus Dux Aquitaniæ, et ibi est cappa qua induitur, et corona, et aliæ consuetudines scriptæ." He went on to comment, "De juribus et consuetudinibus Ducum parum sciunt Lemovicenses; quia Henricus Rex, ut dicitur, detulit in Angliam omnia scripta." See RHF 12:442.

137. Gauthier, "La légende de sainte Valérie."

138. Beech's chapter 17 in this volume cites and summarizes the longer studies dedicated to the vase.

139. "HOC VAS SPONSA DEDIT ANOR REGI LVDOVICO MITADOLVS AVO MIHI REX SANCTISQUE SVGERVS" (*Le trésor de Saint-Denis*, ed. Montesquiou-Fezensac and Gaborit-Chopin, no. 75 of the inventory of 1634, and esp. 3:63–64 and pl. 47). In Suger's rendition of the inscription in *De Administratione*, in Suger, *Œuvres*, ed. Gasparri, 1:152, Eleanor's name is given as "Aanor." Suger records that "in primo itinere Aquitanie regina noviter desponsata domino regi Ludovico dedisset."

140. See Panofsky's trans. in his ed. of Suger's *De Administratione*, p. 79, "as a tribute of his great love."

141. Pinches and Pinches in *Royal Heraldry* reproduce and discuss the obverse and reverse of a seal they say Eleanor of Aquitaine used "after the death of Henry II," pp. 19–20, and see p. 30, where they present no seal in discussing Eleanor of Provence. The seal they attribute to Eleanor of Aquitaine is in fact the second seal of Eleanor of Provence, the first queen of England to bear the title "Domina Hibernie," which appears as part of the legend on the reverse of the seal ("ALIANORA. DEI. GRACIA. DOMINA. HIBERNIE. ET. DVCISSA. AQVITANNIE"; the legend on the obverse is "ALIANORA. DEI. GRACIA. REGINA. ANGLIE"). Seward reproduces on the title page of each chapter the obverse of the first seal of Eleanor of Provence, implicitly attributing it to Eleanor of Aquitaine; it has the legend "ALIANORA. DEI. GRACIA. REGINA. ANGLIE. ET. DOMINA. HYBERNIE." Francis Sandford, Lancaster Herald, published images of both seals of Eleanor of Provence in his *Genealogical History*, pl. 57, the second and third seals. For the seals of Eleanor of Provence, see also Birch, *Catalogue of Seals in the British Museum* 1: nos. 791, 794 at pp. 98–99 (referring to the reproductions in Sandford's *History*, dating the first seal 1255–56 and the second 1262, giving the legends, and describing the object in Eleanor's left hand as a "sceptre ensigned with orb and dove"; see no. 791 at p. 99 for the legend on the reverse of the first seal, "ALIANORA : DVCISSA : NORMANNIE : ET : AQVITANIE : COMITISSA : ANDEGAVIE"). I am grateful to Hervé Pinoteau and Alan Stahl for their help with these seals.

142. For Eleanor's seals, see Eygun, *Sigillographie,* nos. 3–5 at pp. 159–60, and
   pl. I, no. 4. In working on the seals I have profited from the counsel of
   Brigitte Bedos-Rezak, George Beech, and Alan Stahl; I owe special
   thanks, again, to Hervé Pinoteau. On Roger de Gaignières, see Brown,
   The Oxford Collection. Roman, *Manuel de sigillographie française,* p. 101
   (see also p. 319), misleadingly presents the three drawings as depictions
   of a single seal, on which Eleanor is "coiffée d'une aumusse pointue, et
   de lourdes draperies chargent ses avant-bras; elle tient un rameau et un
   faucon."

143. Bedos Rezak, "Women, Seals," 64, and 78 n10. Although no image of the
   seal is preserved, Bedos Rezak believes that it "retained the nonroyal character of [the seals used by Eleanor's] predecessors."

144. "Sciant Vniuersi Sancte matris Ecclesie filij tam presentes quam futuri
   quod Ego Alienordis gratia dei Pictavorvm comitissa postquam a
   domino meo Lodouico uidelicet serenissimo rege francorum causa parentele disjuncta fui et domino meo henrico nobilissimo Andegauorum
   consuli matrimonio copulata. diuina illustratione tacta sanctarum uir-
   ginum fontis ebraudi congregationem uisitare concupiui et quod
   mente habui, opitulante gratia dei opere compleui. Veni enim deo
   ducente apud fontem ebraudum et capitulum supradictarum virginum
   ingressa sum. ibique corde conpuncta. laudaui concessi et confirmaui
   quicquid pater meus et antecessores mei deo et Ecclesie fontisebraudi
   dederant et precipue illam elemosinam quingentarum solidorum pictauensis monete. sicut dominus meus Ludouicus francorum rex tunc
   temporis maritus meus et Ego quondam dederamus secundum quod
   sua et mea scripta prolocuntur et ostendunt. omni prorsus occasione
   remota et absque ulla contradictione deinceps imperpetuum habendam
   humiliter concessi": BnF, lat. 5480, p. 486; see Eygun, *Sigillographie,* no.
   3, at p. 159. The names of nine witnesses precede the announcement
   that the act was concluded in the presence of Abbess Matilda in the
   common chapter of the nuns. For the dating clause, see n71 above.
   Martindale mentions the act in "Eleanor of Aquitaine," 32 n32. On the
   act, which Delisle copied from the original in 1870 and considered
   "très curieuse," see *Recueil des actes de Henri II* 4:127–28, and 7[1]:31–32,
   no. XXIV★ (Delisle, no. 22★).

145. For the text, see n71 above.

146. I am grateful to Charles T. Wood for pointing out to me the possible importance of the birds that appear on Eleanor's seals, and to Richard C.
   Famiglietti for advice on their significance.

147. Eleanor's dress is similar to the garb in which Saint Valérie is depicted in
   the two reliquaries of Saint Petersburg and London, which are illustrated
   in Taburet-Delahaye, in *L'oeuvre de Limoges,* no. 20 at pp. 116–17.

148. BnF, lat. 5480, p. 486, with the fragmentary legend "+ ALIENOR. DVCISSE.
   AQVITAN. . . . . CA. . . . . . ."). The images drawn for Gaignières were
   all drafted in pencil and ink on pieces of fine paper which were cut out

and pasted at the end of copies of the documents to which they were appended.

149. See below, for the consistency between the dimensions of the fragmentary seals of 1199, and the Gaignières drawings of the obverse and reverse of the seal appended to an act of 1200. Although Eygun, *Sigillographie,* no. 3 at p. 159, acknowledges that the source of the seal is a drawing, he accepts the drawing's dimensions as representing the seal's (which he gives as 46 mm. x 73 mm.).

150. Bedos Rezak comments on the prevalence of fleurs-de-lis on women's seals in the twelfth century and the first half of the thirteenth century in "Women, Seals," pp. 75–76, and also p. 64, fig. 2 (its appearance on the seal of Isabelle of Hainaut, wife of Philip Augustus, ca. 1180), and p. 70, fig. 10 (1258, nonnoble woman); and (as Brigitte Bedos-Rezak), in "Medieval Women," in Rosenthal, ed., *Medieval Women and the Sources of Medieval History,* p. 7, and at pp. 34–35, figs. 6 (1266), 7 (1210), and 10 (ca. 1154). See also n161 below.

151. For a detailed discussion of the dove as symbol of the Holy Spirit, see Didron, *Christian Iconography* 1:435–36, 441–451, 459–63, 493–94. Eucharistic doves were doubtless made in the Limousin in the twelfth century; for a thirteenth-century example, see Boehm, "Colombe eucharistique," in *L'oeuvre de Limoges,* no. 106 at pp. 318–19. I am grateful to Barbara Boehm for her advice and help.

Brigitte Bedos Rezak identifies as hawks the birds often found on women's seals after the middle of the thirteenth century. She sees them as a secular symbol, evoking the notion of hunting and the chase. She believes that the presence of the hawk "conveys an ambivalent perception of women," who, like hawks, were considered beautiful and also predatory. The use of this symbol, she thinks, reflects contemporary literature's "pessimistic assessment of the female as a threat to male psychological balance." See Bedos Rezak, "Women, Seals," pp. 75–77, and also her "Medieval Women," p. 7 (the hawk's "specific semiotic content relating to women: their beauty, their amorous conversation, and their cruelty"). Bedos Rezak does not discuss the English evidence. Of the three images she reproduces in her two articles, one (although early in date) clearly supports the interpretation she offers. This seal, appended to an act of 1186, shows a woman on horseback, with a bird on her outstretched left hand, evidently setting out for the hunt: Bedos Rezak, "Women, Seals," fig. 6 at p. 69 (Adele, countess of Soissons). Two other seals show women in poses similar to those in which Eleanor of Aquitaine is depicted on her seal. One is attached to an act of 1265 (Alix de Nemours), and one to an act of 1294 (Isabelle de Rosny). In both cases Bedos Rezak identifies the bird poised on the left hand as a hawk, although they seem to me to resemble doves: "Women, Seals," fig. 8 at p. 70 (1294); and Bedos Rezak, "Medieval Women," fig. 2 at p. 33 (1265). See also n142 above, for Roman's identification of Eleanor's bird as "un faucon."

152. On the seal of Edward the Confessor and the orb, see Bautier, "Échanges d'influences,"199–202; Bedos-Rezak,"The King Enthroned." For imperial background, and later scepters topped with doves, see *Age of Chivalry,* no. 14 at p. 203, and nos. 383–84 at pp. 368–69; Gaborit-Chopin, *Regalia,* pp. 75–78.

153. Birch, *Catalogue of Seals in the British Museum* 1:98, nos. 787–90 (seals of Matilda or Maud, and Adeliza, the matrix of whose seal was adapted from Matilda's).

154. These seals are illustrated in Sandford, *Genealogical History,* book 1, pp. A–B, and see also p. 54, for the seal of Henry II (and the quite different one of the young Henry, evidently influenced by French conventions); the seals of Richard and John are found on pp. 55–56. Henry II was the last of his line to employ an orb with cross and dove. On their seals (Sandford, *Genealogical History,* book 1, p. A), William I and William II hold a sword in the right hand and an orb surmounted with cross in the left.

155. "In Nomine patris et filij et spiritus sancti Ego Alienordis Aquitanorum et Normannorum ducissa simulque Andegauorum comitissa pro sancte et Indiuidue Trinitatis reuerentia et dilectione et pro animarum patris mei et matris mee salute et dilectissimi ducis Hainrici conjugis mei prosperitate ipsiusque et mei filij Gvillelmi incolumitatis subuectione et honore consilio et precibus venerabilium virorum pictauorum et Andegauorum supplicibus petitionibus [*sic*] domni Roberti Vindocinensis abbatis et monachorum eius adquiescens liberaliter in Elemosinam Vindocinensi Ecclesie dono et inperpetuum dimitto": BnF, lat. 5419, p. 80.

156. BnF, lat. 5419, p. 80; Eygun, *Sigillographie,* 160, no. 5 (who suggests, implausibly in my view, that this seal may simply be the counterseal Eleanor used in 1200, "mal dessiné et mal lu," for which see BnF, lat. 5480, p. 265, and below). The legend of the seal drawn for Gaignières ("+ s. ALIS [*SIC*]. . . . . NORMANORVM. DVCISSA. &. ANDEGAVIS [*SIC*]. COMITISSA") differs distinctively from that of the counterseal of 1200, which I give below.

157. Eygun, *Sigillographie,* pp. 159–60, no. 4, and pl. I, no. 4 (Angers, Archives départementales du Maine-et-Loire, Chartrier de Fontevraud, Angleterre, 2, no. 19); according to Eygun, the act is undated. The legends on the obverse (."... LIENO..... E. G....") and reverse ("."... VITANOR... NDEGA.....") are consistent with those of the Gaignières drawings of the seal and counterseal Eleanor used in 1200. The Service des sceaux of the AN now houses Eygun's collection of impressions, the Collection de Poitou, and has a mold of the seal Eygun describes and reproduces (see fig. 1.1).

158. AN, J 628, no. 5 (see Eygun, *Sigillographie,* p. 160); the act is dated 1199 and confirms the donation of a fief to Eleanor's "Karissimo Amico & Consanguineo" "Andree de Caluigniaco & heredibus suis"; for the seal and counterseal, see Douët d'Arcq, *Collection de sceaux* 3:263, no. 10006 (describing the object she holds as "un globe crucifère surmonté d'un oiseau," and identifying the place of issuance [*vallis Rodolii*] as "le Vaudreuil"). The pre-

cise location of Sainte-Sévère is unclear; note Sainte-Sévère near Cognac in the Charente, and Sainte-Sévère-sur-Indre near La Châtre in the Indre. The only letters visible on this fragment are what appear to be "ENO," in the same position as the corresponding letters on the seal described in the preceding note. I am grateful to Marie-Claude Delmas of the Archives nationales for her help with the two extant impressions of Eleanor's seal.

159. Eygun, *Sigillographie,* pp. 159–60, nos. 4–4a ("+ ALIENOR'. DEI. GRACIA. REGINE. ANGLORVM. DVCISSE. NORMAN."; "+ ALIENOR. DVCISSE. AQVI-TANORVM. ET. COMITISSE. ANDEGAVORVM"); and see the drawing made for Gaignières, in lat. 5480, p. 265 (fig. 1.1), following a copy of an act of 1200, which mentions Eleanor's late son Richard ("Karissimus filius noster Rex Ricardus cujus anima In pace quiescat eterna"). Because of the seal used by King John's wife Isabelle, Eygun hypothesized that the head of the figure on the reverse would have worn a band, which would have been replaced by a crown on the obverse (Eygun, *Sigillographie,* pp. 218–19, nos. 419a, 420a). The drawing made for Gaignières, however, clearly shows a crowned figure on both sides of the seal.

160. Doüet d'Arcq, *Collection de sceaux* 1:286–87, nos. 151–53 (Constance of Castile, Adele of Champagne, Isabelle of Hainaut). For the seal of Isabelle of Hainaut, see Bedos Rezak, "Women, Seals," pp. 63–64, and fig. 2. Bedos Rezak points out ("Women, Seals," p. 63) that the seal the dowager queen Bertrada of Montfort used in 1115 after the death of her husband Philip I declared her queen by grace of God, but suggests that Bertrada acquired the seal after Philip's death in 1108.

161. For the seal, see Posse, *Siegel* 1:pl. 19, no. 4; Sandford, *Genealogical History,* book 1, p. B; Chibnall, *Empress Matilda,* pls. 4–5; and Birch, "A Fasciculus of the Charters of Mathildis," 380–82, commenting on the absence of an orb, which she might have been expected to hold; see Bedos-Rezak, "Medieval Women," pp. 21–22 n74; and Birch, *Catalogue of Seals in the British Museum* 1:10, no. 54. The seal is smaller than those used by the kings of England. See Posse, *Siegel* 1:pl. 24, no. 1 (seal of Constance, wife of Henry VI, 1197); pl. 26, no. 1 (seal of Maria, wife of Otto IV, 1260); in each seal the woman's right hand holds a fleur-de-lis, and her left hand is pressed to her chest. See below, for the coins Matilda issued for England as "imperatrix" and "comitissa."

162. The seal is reproduced in Bedos Rezak, "Women, Seals," p. 70 no. 7; on it, see "Women, Seals," pp. 73–75 ("SIGILLVM CONSTANCIE DUCISSE NARBONE MARCHESIE"; "SIGILLVM CONSTANCIE COMITISSE THOLOSE"). See Douët d'Arcq, *Collection de sceaux* 1:381, no. 741, and see also 1:381–82, nos. 742–45 (the seals of Constance's son Raymond VI and grandson Raymond VII, depicted enthroned, with sword replacing Constance's orb; the legend on Raymond VII's seal identifies him as count of Toulouse "by grace of God"); Douët d'Arcq identifies the radiant orb that appears opposite a "croissant" on all the seals as an "étoile." For the orb with cross that Constance holds, see Bedos-Rezak, "Medieval Women," p. 21 n74; and Douët d'Arcq, *Collection des sceaux*

3:516–7, no. 11802 (Alix, queen of Cyprus, depicted with orb with cross in her right hand on her seal of 1234); Bedos-Rezak, "The King Enthroned," p. 63; Bautier, "Échanges d'influences," 199–202.

163. On Constance's seal, see Bedos Rezak, "Women, Seals," pp. 73–75; Bedos-Rezak, "Medieval Women," p. 22 n74. Anselme twice noted (*Histoire généalogique* 1:75, 2:687) that Constance "porta toujours la qualité [*le titre* in 2:687] de reine à cause de son premier mari." Anselme believed that Eustace was actually crowned, but no such ceremony seems to have been held. Nicholas Vincent notes that after the death of her first husband, John of England, in 1216, and until her own death in 1246, Isabelle of Angoulême retained the title of queen "by grace of God" and continued to use her queenly seal, despite her marriage in 1220 to Hugues of Lusignan ("Isabella of Angoulême," p. 206).

164. Bedos Rezak, "Women, Seals," 71–72; Bedos-Rezak, "Medieval Women," pp. 6–7; Pastoreau, *Traité d'heraldique*, p. 47.

165. Poey d'Avant, *Monnaies féodales de France* 2:1–4, 22–23, 28; see also the brief remarks of Dumas, "La monnaie dans les domaines Plantagenêt," 55. I am deeply indebted to Alan Stahl for his counsel on Eleanor's coinage.

166. On the so-called *DVCISIT/DVCISIA* coins, which seem to have been minted while Eleanor was duchess of Aquitaine, see Poey d'Avant, *Monnaies féodales de France*, pp. 78–79, who expresses reservations about this attribution ("Le type des monnaies attribuées à Eléonore me paraît une imitation du monogramme odonique combiné avec un autre ressemblant à celui de Cahors. Il ne faut pas songer à y voir des figures de blason"). He confesses that in assigning coins to her he "cède moins à ma conviction qu'à une opinion reçue." In 1990, in his valuable article, "Coinage in the Name of Medieval Women," Alan Stahl assigned the "ducissa" coinage to Eleanor, dating it after 1189 (see pp. 324, 328, 337 n14). In a recent conversation, he told me that he now believes that if these coins were created during Eleanor's reign, they were probably made soon after her father's death in 1137. Dr. Stahl termed the money "enigmatic," and cautioned that Eleanor's coinage awaits full investigation.

167. Poey d'Avant, *Monnaies féodales de France* 2:66–82 and pl. LIX.

168. See the valuable appendix listing coinage bearing women's names issued between 500 and 1500, in Stahl, "Coinage," pp. 328–33. For Matilda's coinage see Chibnall, *Empress Matilda*, pp. 121–23, and pls. 6a-b; for Clémence of Burgundy, see Nicholas, "Countesses as Rulers in Flanders," 117, 120. Cheyette discusses the court of Ermengard of Narbonne in "Women, Poets," esp. pp. 149–56. Vincent, "Isabella of Angoulême," p. 206, points out that after 1224 the name of Isabelle of Angoulême, John of England's widow, appears on coins of Angoulême (with the names of the king of France and her second husband, Hugues of Lusignan).

169. On the window, see Grodecki et al., *Le vitrail romain*, pp. 70–73. See also *L'oeuvre de Limoges*, p. 110. Weir uses the image of Eleanor on the cover of her biography of the queen.

170. On the date of Eleanor's effigy see Kathleen Nolan and Charles T. Wood in this volume. Following Alain Erlande-Brandenburg, Nolan argues that Eleanor commissioned not only Henry II's and Richard's effigies but also her own tomb, and, consequently, that she was responsible for its iconography. In view of the marked differences between the two male gisants, on the one hand, and her effigy, on the other, this seems to me questionable. Eleanor could, of course, have left instructions concerning the form of her effigy, and these orders could have been executed after her death by an artist working quite differently from the sculptor or sculptors responsible for Henry's and Richard's monuments. See Erlande-Brandenburg, "Le 'cimetière des rois' à Fontevraud," esp. 492, and his "La sculpture funéraire," pp. 564–68.

171. Duby's reflections on Eleanor's tomb (*Dames* 1:13–14) are moving and incisive. In *Women and the Book,* ed. Taylor and Smith, the editors present useful essays considering depictions of women and books, although none of the essays deals with Eleanor's tomb or with female gisants in general. The effigy of Richard I's queen Berengaria at the Cistercian house of l'É-pau shows her holding a squarish object, which Gillingham, *Richard I,* figs. 8–9, interprets as a book, but which could conceivably be a reliquary. See Trindale, *Berengaria,* p. 195.

172. Wood in this volume; and Louis Courajod, "Sépultures," 540–41; Gillingham, *Richard I,* pp. 266–67 esp. n73, 325. See also Enguehard, "Les travaux." Hallett describes his visit in 1902, and Napoleon III's abortive plan to give the tombs to Queen Victoria, in "Last Resting-Place"; on this project, see also Courajod, "Sépultures," 558. The monument is illustrated in Sandford, *Genealogical History,* plate between pp. 64 and 65 (reproduced in Erlande-Brandenburg, "'Cimetière des rois,'" 487, and in his "Sculpture funéraire," p. 572, fig. 2). On p. 65, Sandford reported the assistance of "F. Pavillion a Monk of Fout-Euraud" and of the abbess Jeanne-Baptiste de Bourbon, an illegitimate daughter of Henri IV of France, who before her death (on July 16, 1670) sent him the drawing of the monument (which he reported was placed against the north wall of the choir), which had been "delineated by her own Scenographer." On Jeanne-Baptiste de Bourbon, see Anselme, *Histoire généalogique* 1:150–51; the "Pavillion" who aided Sandford may be the "B. Pavillon" who was responsible for the richly documented *Vie dv Bien-hevrevx Robert d'Arbrissel,* published in 1667. At some point the four gisants were displayed side by side (Eleanor and Richard to the left, Henry and Isabelle to the right) in a small chapel of the abbey: see the photograph, unfortunately undated (attributed to Roger-Viollet), in Dumontier, with Bernage, *L'empire des Plantagenêt,* p. 130. The collective monument was also drawn for Roger de Gaignières in 1699. See Adhémar et al., "Les tombeaux." Bernard de Montfaucon published depictions of the individual monuments, in *Les monumens de la monarchie françoise* 2:113–14.

173. Stothard, *Effigies,* figs. 4–9, 13–14, esp., for Eleanor, figs. 6–7. An introduction to the book, including an account of Stothard's life, is prefixed to the

copy in the New York Public Library; written by Stothard's brother-in-law Alfred John Kempe, it was printed in 1832, doubtless in London. See p. 19 of Kempe's work, for Stothard's visit to Fontevraud in 1816.

174. On these monuments see Erlande-Brandenburg, *Le roi est mort*, pp. 135–37, no. 7, and figs. 43–46 (Childebert); 138–40, nos. 14–15, and figs. 47–49 (Chilperic and Fredegonde); 160–62, nos. 84, 86, and figs. 37–38 (Louis VII), 39 (Adelaide of Maurienne and Savoy). For the tombs of Count Henri of Champagne (1127–81), husband of Marie, daughter of Eleanor of Aquitaine and Louis VII, and his son and successor Thibaud (d. 1201), see Bur, "Les comtes de Champagne et la 'Normanitas'"; Bur, "L'image de la parenté"; and Dectot, "Ou périr ou régner?"; for the tomb of Henri, see *L'oeuvre de Limoges*, p. 445.

175. Katharine Hepburn's characterization of Eleanor, a phrase she used in conversation with me in February 1982.

176. Richard of Devizes commented of her (*Chronicon*, p. 60), "Et quis esset tam ferus aut ferreus quem in sua uota femina illa non flecteret."

CHAPTER 2

QUEEN ELEANOR AND AQUITAINE, 1137–1189

Marie Hivergneaux

> *The charter evidence reveals that the role played by Eleanor in her duchy during her two royal marriages is quite different from its traditional depiction.*

The aim of this study is to examine carefully the political role, the means of action, and the power that Eleanor of Aquitaine, queen of France and England, exercised in her hereditary duchy, Aquitaine. Annals and chronicles alone have previously been scrutinized; the charters that are an obligatory aspect of any such study of seigneurial power have been too much ignored until now. Fifty of Eleanor's charters survive from the fifty-two years considered here, those of her marriages to Louis VII of France (1137–52) and then to Henry II of England (1152–89).[1] Her surviving acts are undeniably fewer, more scattered, and less complete than those of her male counterparts. But by considering where Eleanor issued her acts, in whose favor, under what title, and with what witnesses, it is nonetheless possible to extract some information about her part in the duchy's government, the times when she was active there, and the methods she used. Her place within family and lineage as revealed by these charters, and the authority accorded her seal (that is, her capacity to authenticate her acts by herself, even when she was not merely confirming someone else's act), witness the reality and extent of her power. Finally, when the witnesses to her acts are recorded, we can reconstitute the personnel of her retinue to illuminate the extent of her prestige and influence, and better understand the ways in which she integrated herself in the power relations among lords and exploited them to her own ends.

Eleanor's 1152 divorce from Louis VII and her marriage to Henry of Anjou shortly thereafter brought about a shift in her political and familial alignments. The divorce and remarriage constitute a significant and convenient caesura to organize this study and to observe the modifications she introduced in her potential fields of action.

Eleanor's Capetian Marriage: An Apprenticeship in Legitimate Power

The twenty-odd acts in which Eleanor participated during her fifteen-year marriage to Louis VII are not evenly distributed over those years, perhaps due to changes in her official role in government. In fact, the surviving charters that refer to her are clustered, with one exception, in the six years preceding the Second Crusade. Louis mentioned her in an act of August 1137, but her first surviving charter dates only from 1139.[2] Thereafter, as her influence perhaps increased with age, she appears regularly with him in her own acts and in his. Her charter production appears to have reached an apogee during the preparation for the crusade, when she issued seven surviving charters within two years. If the crusade marks a logical pause in this production, it likewise denotes a true rupture that opens the troubled period preceding Eleanor's divorce from Louis, years that saw her virtually vanish from the acts of his government. Only one surviving charter has come down to us from these years, dated to the end of 1151 or the beginning of 1152, when she had effectively ceased to be part of the Capetian sphere.[3] But the charters concerning the queen are restricted not only in time. They are directed as well to a limited space: seventeen of the twenty acts discussed here deal not with Louis VII's domains, but with Aquitaine.[4]

Aquitaine: Joint Government, Restricted Power

Heiress of the duchy of Aquitaine, Eleanor married the Capetian heir at Bordeaux on July 25, 1137; less than one week later, he became King Louis VII. Despite this royal marriage, Eleanor's official participation in the French kingdom's affairs was—as far as extant charters indicate—restricted to no more than three references to her approval in Louis VII's acts.[5] Most probably these signs of her approval, all three of which concern estates in Paris or the Ile-de-France, are no more than a relic of Capetian queens' past association with royal decisions, that is of their role as *consors regni* (partner in royal power). The advance of Capetian royal power was already quite evident: its redefinition particularly manifested itself in the reappearance of a public administration centered on the king's court (*curia regis*), by the concentration of royal power upon the king's person, and by its corollary, the queen's exclusion from the kingdom's government.[6] This strengthening of the apparatus of government around the king, clearly accelerated under Louis VI (r. 1108–37), tended to strengthen the distinction between the public and private spheres of power, and ended by reducing the queen's official authority. Eleanor stands as one of the earliest victims of this process; despite her royal title, her political horizons thus remained essentially Aquitainian, extending only to the territory that was hers by right.

Aquitaine thus remained the only political sphere in which Eleanor might intervene officially, albeit irregularly. Despite the title "queen of the Franks [*Francorum regina*]" that her charters proclaim, she acted chiefly in her capacity as duchess, and with that title. But even this did not allow her an exclusive power of decision; Aquitaine was not exclusively reserved to her as an official sphere in which she could exercise power. Though Aquitaine was her own inheritance, Eleanor rarely appears alone in her surviving charters. Throughout her years as Louis VII's wife, she issued only four of these charters by herself, and all four confirm others issued by Louis. It is impossible to determine in all cases which spouse's act was issued first, but most frequently it was surely Louis; in any case, the form of his charters is always more finished. The remaining twelve charters from this period that mention Eleanor were issued by Louis with her consent. There is wide variation in the formulas that signify her approval: "with her agreement [*assentiente,* or *cum assensu*],"[7] "with her agreement and at her request [*assensu et peticione,* or *assensu et rogatu*],"[8] or "by her will and with her agreement [*voluntate et assensu*]."[9] Neither the queen-duchess's request or approval as expressed in these documents, however, nor their joint issue by both spouses is artificial or formal, and certainly neither one indicates the profound inequality between the couple that is often suggested. On at least one occasion, Eleanor employed the corresponding reverse formula in her charter confirming her husband's donation of liberties to the abbey of Notre-Dame at Saintes, which she granted "with the assent of Louis, king of the Franks and duke of the Aquitainians [*assensu Ludovici regis Francorum et ducis Aquitanorum*]."[10]

The administration of the duchy of Aquitaine thus appears to have been joint, with Louis VII's actions defining the limit of his wife's emancipation within a conjugal *societas* that embraced their patrimonies' common and intermingled interests.[11] If marriage had given Eleanor unrivalled prestige and guaranteed her ducal title, it allowed Louis to extend his power over a quasi-independent duchy, with the long-term prospect of its integration into the royal domain. The marriage likewise intertwined their rights, partly transferring Eleanor's economic and juridical rights to Louis and imposing upon him the necessity of her consent to any alienation from her personal inheritance.

These sixteen charters show that Eleanor governed Aquitaine at Louis VII's side, not alone, and they reveal her relatively limited sphere of action.

Their analysis is somewhat skewed by the nature of the sources: all sixteen charters witness her acting on behalf of ecclesiastical beneficiaries. In the spirit of her era's clerics, the humility of the religious sphere was better suited to a woman than was the exercise of power: a woman was more credible than a man when she made a religious donation. Real piety certainly motivated some of these gifts: when Louis VII confirmed donations of land previously made to the abbey of Saint-Vincent-de Nieuil "*assensu et peticione regine Alienordis,*" or provided a tomb for the duchess's mother, he was acting from filial piety as well as a desire to support the abbey's monks.[12] But these charters had multiple objectives, and their various levels of operation must also be kept in mind. A religious house was first and foremost a significant intercessor with the unseen, but as often as not it was also an influential "lord" administering numerous estates and sheltering many aristocrats within its walls. A donation of property to a monastery, or its confirmation, was thus an economic transaction and a religious practice seeking spiritual benefits, as well as the confirmation of social and political associations.[13]

From this perspective, Louis's and Eleanor's charters show them maintaining networks of fidelity in Poitou, the Aunis, and the Saintonge, areas that traditionally gave allegiance to the count-dukes of Aquitaine. They issued charters, for example, to the influential Templars of La Rochelle, masters of a large part of that city,[14] to the great landholder that was the Abbaye-aux-Dames at Saintes,[15] to the abbey of la Trinité-de-Vendôme with its possessions in Poitou, Saintonge, and Aunis and especially the isle of Oléron,[16] and to the greatest of Poitevin ecclesiastical barons, the abbey of Saint-Maixent, whose feudal networks extended over more than fifty parishes and which, as vassal to the count of Poitou, owed fifty foot serjeants for forty days.[17] To improve their control over a precarious frontier region, the couple likewise strengthened associations with the prestigious abbey of Fontevraud, an aristocratic women's convent on the borders of Poitou and Anjou, which attracted a large number of seigneurial widows and daughters of that region, from throughout the west, and even from much of the north of the kingdom. In 1146, Louis and Eleanor granted Fontevraud an annual rent of 500s. in Poitevin money, drawn from the issues of the Lenten fairs held at Poitiers and from that town's mint.[18]

The not inconsiderable economic character of these donations is equally evident. Eleanor and Louis VII manipulated lands as well as mills, rents, and financial privileges, such as those granted the abbey of Saintes on the exchange of moneys throughout that diocese.[19] At times, this economic character is not immediately apparent; financial questions were often avoided in acts concerning religious houses. Thus, during preparations for the Second Crusade, the couple granted or confirmed numerous privileges to religious houses without alluding to cash money or troops to be sent on the expedition. It would be astonishing if men of the Church had not contributed to the struggle against the infidel, but Louis VII's later orders from the Holy Land to Abbot Suger of Saint-Denis prove that the Templars and the Hospitallers had respectively lent him at least 2000 and 1000 marks of silver, which he at that time ordered Suger to repay.[20] Men and women of the Church were thus precious resources, sometimes financial but especially political, for the governance of an unstable and distant duchy.

The couple's visits to Aquitaine were, in fact, always relatively brief and made at wide intervals, so much so that they had to rely upon a few trustworthy lords whose support would allow them to watch over the duchy's affairs from a distance. As the great majority of the couple's Aquitainian charters issued from the royal chancery, however, they became increasingly normalized and, as a rule, recorded as witnesses only the great officers of the crown, whose attested presence was quite often a mere formality. Of the sixteen acts that mention Eleanor of Aquitaine, only a few afford a glimpse of those who assisted the royal couple in Aquitaine. The seneschal of Poitou, Guillaume de Mauzé, in office throughout the years of the marriage (1136–54), or Geoffrey, lord of Rancon, were among those who helped maintain ducal authority and who often traveled to the king and queen in the Ile-de-France.[21] This explains why nearly two-thirds of the surviving acts concerning Eleanor of Aquitaine were issued outside the duchy's boundaries; if all twenty-nine royal charters for Aquitaine from these years are taken into account, the percentage is only a third (ten acts), possibly explained by the particular circumstances of certain acts in which the duchess did not participate.

As the charters show, the administration of Aquitaine was, in fact, only partly a joint affair. The queen-duchess is named in, or confirmed in, only seventeen of the twenty-nine acts Louis VII issued for Aquitaine during their marriage. Of the dozen acts that do not correspond to the norm— that is, those in which Eleanor did not officially share—eight concern the settlement of litigation or the holding of a legal action, or convey threats to recalcitrant barons.[22] Louis VII settled cases not dealt with by the seneschal that were brought before the king's court or that maintained his control over judgments already rendered. Justice therefore seems to have arisen exclusively from Louis VII's competence. A major attribute of sovereignty and power was thus denied Eleanor, but the charters do not reveal whether this came about through the king's will, as the result of juridical incapacity born of woman's inability to lead the army, or some personal choice.

These acts attest as well to Louis VII's desire to renew the rights of the dukes of Aquitaine. Several carry the offensive to the fringes of Aquitainian territory, where ducal power remained most fragile: the viscount of

Brosse, the lords of the Limousin or the count of Angoulême were thus called to order in pleas brought before the king-duke by the abbeys of Saint-Benoît-du-Sault or Solignac, or by the bishop of Angoulême.[23] But in working to consolidate the duchy of Aquitaine, Louis VII was simultaneously seeking to heighten the image or the power of the Capetian royal office. Here perhaps lies a key to the queen-duchess's participation in the governance of Aquitaine, at least in some of its procedures: Louis could not entirely ignore Eleanor, duchess of Aquitaine in her own right.

Eleanor, A Legitimizing Authority for Louis VII

Louis VII had real need of his wife's legitimizing dignity to govern Aquitaine. Her legitimate title as duchess was carefully sustained, and even further developed to make the Capetian king the new titular lord of Aquitaine, a principality the king meant one day to integrate into the royal domain. Their first charters witness Louis's desire to attach himself firmly to the lineage of Eleanor's male ancestors. This was done all the more naturally because, at a lord's death, his successor had to confirm grants and associations his predecessor had personally established. Confirming the acts of Eleanor's father, Duke William X, and the earlier count-dukes thus allowed Louis to inscribe himself politically as their successor in everyone's eyes. Among the first abbeys to receive confirmations of their foundation charters, and the donations attached to them, were Notre-Dame de la Grâce-Dieu, founded by William X in the parish of Benon in the Aunis,[24] and Notre-Dame at Saintes, founded by Count Geoffrey Martel of Anjou and his wife Agnes, widow of the Poitevin count William V the Great.[25] When Louis and Eleanor honored Saint-Vincent de Nieuil as other counts of Poitou had done, they evoked her forebears' memory even more directly: her mother was buried there.[26]

Inscribing himself as the count-dukes' successor and upholding Eleanor's legitimate title as duchess was a sure means to legitimize Louis VII's joint authority. He insisted on several occasions upon the transfer of sovereignty brought about by their marriage. Thus in August 1137, in recognition of the marriage celebrated by the good offices of the archbishop of Bordeaux, the king-duke gave the archbishop, his suffragans, and all churches of his province the free canonical election of their prelates. He was able to do so because the province of Bordeaux "has come to us by the death of William, count of Poitou and duke of the Aquitainians, by way of marriage with his daughter Eleanor [*defuncto Aquitanorum duce et comite Pictavis Guillelmo, per filiam ipsius Alienoram nobis sorte matrimonii cedit*]."[27] But the transfer went even further: the emphasis on Eleanor's filiation as well as the conjugal tie made her ancestors those of Louis VII as well. In defining her primarily through her male ancestry, the advantages of Eleanor's status were transferred to Louis and upon the family group she had now entered. This was a procedure routinely utilized in a society in which kinship, power, and property were intimately linked, especially when female issue inherited power and prestige.[28] Thus, in the couple's charter in favor of La Grâce-Dieu, the twice-stated links of kinship define Eleanor's social status and affirm the transfer of property and legitimacy from her father to her husband: "Eleanor, then queen, wife of the said King Louis and daughter of the said Count William, praised and confirmed this gift of her father [*Laudavit etiam et confirmavit hanc eleemosynam patris sui Alienor, tunc regina, supradicti Ludovici regis uxor et praedicti Guillelmi comitis filia*]." Eleanor is here defined by her marriage since she is called both queen and King Louis's wife, a link that counterbalanced and augmented with its prestige the filial relationship recalled by the statement of her parentage and the references to her father's gift. The same charter specifies that Louis "took Eleanor to wife and obtained all the land [*Alienoram duxit in uxorem et totam terram obtinuit*]."[29] He thus set himself at the center of the argument, ready to receive all the benefits due him as Aquitaine's new master. In 1146–47 he based another confirmation to La Grâce-Dieu on the formula "by the gift of William, duke of the Aquitainians, father of the queen our consort [*ex dono Guillermi, ducis Aquitanorum, patris regine, lateralis nostre*],"[30] recalling, after ten years of marriage—and at a time when he urgently needed funds for his crusade—the legitimate basis upon which his authority rested. In relying on Eleanor's legitimacy, Louis VII could thus call the counts of Poitou as well as the kings of France his predecessors.

At the same time, Eleanor's position as heiress, and the legitimation of Louis VII's power that depended from it, afforded her certain prerogatives. Crucial examples are her royal title and, especially, her possession of a seal and the capacity to seal and authenticate documents—a symbolic evocation of the extent of its owner's power.[31] By proclaiming its owner's name and rank, the seal in effect embodied his/her official status; but from a legal point of view it also implied the rights of disposition of property. Eleanor's seal as queen of France is lost; nothing has been recovered of its iconography or the title it accorded Eleanor, but even at first glance its existence is exceptional: she was the first queen of France to possess a seal in her husband's lifetime, before widowhood, and to use it for business other than her private affairs. This privilege was certainly grounded in the fact that she was the first queen of France to possess her own territory (and that a vast one). This seal, used only when Aquitainian affairs were at issue, still preserved a certain seigneurial quality: just as her queenly title did not correspond to any true official power, it appears that her seal was not so much that of a queen of France as it was that of the duchess of Aquitaine. It was no less innovative nor prestigious for that, given the limited diffusion of the custom of sealing within the duchy itself.[32] But that limited diffusion may explain why, in the sixteen royal acts for Aquitaine in which Eleanor was involved, only three contain a sealing clause, and she verifiably attested only two of these, as late as 1146–47.[33] It is quite possible that she did not possess a seal before that time, but this could equally indicate that her involvement in the government of Aquitaine and in its affairs had become stronger than at the outset of her marriage. She appears to have used this seal at least twice, once when she confirmed one of Louis's acts and again to signify her full approval of one of their joint acts, both times in favor of the abbey of La Trinité-de-Vendôme.[34] The queen-duchess did not surreptitiously affix her seal to the latter act; remains of both seals survive on strings of yellow silk, and the charter's concluding phrase clearly refers to both: "I, Eleanor, queen, praised this [act] and have affixed my seal beside the seal of the lord king [*Ego Alienordis regina laudavi hoc et sigillum meum, cum sigillo domini regis, apposui*]." Possibly added by, or at the demand of, the beneficiary, this formula may also signify the queen-duchess's very active participation in the agreement.

While Eleanor is seen here sealing on the same basis as her royal spouse, it would be hard to insist that she effectively exercised the same power. The reality of the couple's sealing practice allows a greater appreciation of the extent of the queen-duchess's official power and the degree of her authority. The latter is witnessed by possession, and especially use, of a seal invested with real prestige and an authenticating power that was, to all seeming, identical to that of Louis VII as lord. But the public aspect of Eleanor's action was plainly limited. Louis VII took almost complete charge of sealing even the acts he and his wife issued together; likewise, it was he who issued most of the acts dealing with the governance of Aquitaine, even if they were issued with his wife's consent. If sealing an act reflects the status and the juridical capacities of a woman within her family and within the lineage, Eleanor during her first marriage stood on the periphery of government, in the margin of the official system of donation and decision, but never totally excluded because she legitimized it. The charters cast light on her public role in Aquitaine during this marriage, and it was far from being negligible though it was more restrained than is often asserted.

Eleanor's divorce from Louis VII, pronounced by a council at Beaugency on March 21, 1152, seems then to have opened to her, at the age of thirty, the way to greater autonomy in the governance of her duchy. She became the sole lord of Aquitaine—at least until her marriage with young Henry Plantagenet on May 18, 1152. She regained as well her place as vassal of the king of France. Thus Louis VII, watchful for his daughters' heritage, continued to style himself duke of the Aquitainians in virtue of his rights of guardianship and in response to the newlyweds' audacity: they had not obtained for their marriage the royal assent that Louis VII sought to impose on all his great vassals.

The Plantagenet Period: Discontinuous and Incomplete Power

During the thirty-seven years of her second marriage, Eleanor's diplomatic production for Aquitaine shows more maturity and autonomy but less continuity. The twenty-eight charters assembled for this study circumscribe two principal periods of activity. From 1152 to 1156, she issued ten charters, of which her husband confirmed only the last three. She is again found issuing documents for Aquitaine only between 1168–69 and her revolt in 1173; her assurance of the duchy's governance in these years is witnessed by fifteen acts, issued in her own name and that of her young son Richard, the future duke.

In contrast, between 1157 and 1168, besides her frequent childbearing, she primarily served as Henry II's second in England. After 1173, she disappears entirely from diplomatic sources. She resurfaces only twice, and then in very definite circumstances that reveal her deprived of all real power in Aquitaine. Throughout her second marriage, and despite a considerably inflated title (duchess of Normandy, countess of Anjou, and, from December 1154, queen of England), her inheritance thus played a significant role in her political life.

Freedom from Capetian Tutelage (1152–54)

The first three acts Eleanor issued in May 1152, alone and without marital confirmation shortly after her divorce and her quiet second wedding, reveal one major preoccupation: to affirm her authority over Aquitaine and to break with the Capetian past. That Louis VII continued to maintain his double title as king of the Franks and duke of the Aquitainians shows readily the difficulties in affording royal power a well-defined content and in expressing its authority over Aquitaine, still considered an autonomous political entity that could not be integrated into the Capetian domains.

To resume her inheritance into her own hands, Eleanor relied in particular upon three prestigious religious houses: the abbeys of Fontevraud, Saint-Jean de Montierneuf at Poitiers, and Saint-Maixent.[35] She began by reaffirming her legitimate rights to assume sovereignty over Aquitaine by herself, using the procedure employed by Louis VII during their marriage: she insisted on her lineage. When on May 26, 1152, she confirmed Montierneuf's privileges—as any new lord would do—she honored a house that her "great-grandfather, grandfather, and father [*attavus, avus, et pater*]" had enriched before her. By recalling this filiation, she invested herself with the same powers these forebears had exercised. In the act for Saint-Maixent issued next day, she turned her back on the Capetian horizon, openly referring to her divorce and explicitly stating that she had been "separated from the king by the Church's judgment [*a rege vero judicio ecclesie divisa*]." Then, insisting again upon that rupture, she attributed to herself the entire impulse behind the gift of the forest of La Sèvre, which she had made with Louis VII "almost without wishing to [*quasi nolens*]" in 1146; she took the forest back into her own hand and then granted it anew—now "with good grace [*ex bono voluntate*]." The contrast was facile but had the merit of showing her resolve to detach herself from an authority Louis VII meant to preserve in the name of his daughters' rights.

Until 1154, that is until Louis VII abandoned his title and his pretensions to the duchy of Aquitaine by an accord with Henry Plantagenet,[36] Eleanor was clearly the only authority officially recognized by so important a person as Archbishop Geoffrey du Lauroux of Bordeaux, who ended an act of October 24, 1153, with the formula "after Eleanor obtained the duchy of Aquitaine [*Alienordi autem ducatum Aquitanie obtinente*]," with no reference to Louis VII nor for that matter to Henry Plantagenet, who in any case did not assume the ducal title until the summer of 1153.[37] Further proof of her vassals' acceptance of Eleanor's authority was the authentication of at least two of her first three acts by her new seal, a small pointed oval (73 x 46 mm) bearing her titles as duchess of the Aquitainians and countess of the Poitevins, and so invested with the same official power as those of her father or her former husband.[38]

But this seal, like the title she used in her charter for the abbey of Fontevraud—"By the grace of God, countess of the Poitevins [*Gratia Dei Picavorum comitissa*]"[39]—betrays the fact that the power base of the count-dukes of Aquitaine remained essentially Poitevin, a situation apparently unchanged by fifteen years of Capetian control. Within Eleanor's entourage, continuity seems to have prevailed at first. Her retinue still consisted of traditional allies of comital power, in their front rank her near relatives, her uncle Viscount Hugh II of Châtellerault and his brother, Raoul de Faye. She quickly cemented their precious fidelity and support, for example in 1153–54 giving Hugh II the fief of Beaumont, the domain of Bonneuil-Matours, and hunting rights in the forest of Moulière northeast of Poitiers.[40] The charters also record the presence of other Poitevin lords such as Briand Chabot, Ebles de Mauléon (seneschal of Poitou in 1154), and members of the de Mauzé and de Melle families, loyal to the court of the count-dukes since the tenth century. It was, however, the officials, minor lords by birth, who stood beside Eleanor most faithfully. Among others, the charters note the continued presence of Hervey le Panetier from 1140 (he was rewarded with the *prévôté* at Poitiers in 1156–57), John de Forges, *prévôt* of Mervent and then of Oléron, and most especially Saldebreuil, in 1152 named constable of Poitou, an office he held for twenty years. As well, after Eleanor moved in 1153 to Angers—a convenient base from which to supervise her domains as well as those of her husband, who had left to battle Louis VII—the charters record the presence not only of these Poitevin lords and officials but, as well, of major Angevin officials such as Joscelin the seneschal of Anjou, Hugh the seneschal of La Flèche, and such lords as Briand de Martigné, later constable of Anjou.[41]

Given the few acts that survive for this period and their primary concern with religious houses, it is difficult to characterize the duchess's government. It is nonetheless evident that she now exercised an autonomy that had not been hers in previous years. She seems to have enjoyed true freedom regarding her inheritance, for she was able to administer it without any sign of her new husband's consent nor his confirmation. But this early freedom was progressively eroded, together with any uncertainty as to the definition of the foundations of her power. Her new seal, which guaranteed the exemptions from the rights of procuration she granted the abbey of La Trinité-de-Vendôme, now bore her titles as "duchess of the Aquitainians and the Normans and countess of the Angevins."[42] In amplifying her titulary and enhancing her prestige, however, this seal clearly referred to territories not hers by inheritance, and thus highlighted her status as the wife of Henry Plantagenet, whose titles would quickly outstrip her own.

Henry Plantagenet Takes Aquitaine in Hand (1154–57)

Once Henry II was assured of the English royal title, he could attempt what Louis VII had never managed to do: bring Aquitaine under his control and integrate it into the strong monarchy he meant to build. Henry's centralizing concept of power enclosed Eleanor's new autonomy in Aquitaine, and she gradually withdrew into the background of the duchy's official business and the records of its governance.

From an early moment in Henry's reign, Eleanor was in fact increasingly distanced from Aquitaine in a direct, physical sense as she was summoned to accompany Henry or journey elsewhere within the Plantagenet domains. On Easter of 1154, she traveled to Normandy, and at the end of that year she went to England to be crowned there with Henry. Thereafter she alternated visits on both sides of the Channel and began to appear, albeit obscurely, in certain charters.[43] After Henry had sworn fidelity to

Louis VII for Aquitaine and his other continental possessions on February 9, 1156, she returned to Aquitaine for the Christmas court held at Bordeaux in 1156, when the new king-duke solemnly received the Aquitainian barons' homages, previously reserved to the duchess alone. These events, far from lacking meaning for the duchy's political life, in effect marked the end of Eleanor's autonomy. The acts she issued thereafter were confirmed, indeed preceded, by similar acts of Henry II. For his part, Henry had already begun to act as the guarantor of acts previously issued by his wife; increasingly, he became the recognized legitimate holder of ducal power and authority.

Although Henry II thus swiftly assumed a dominant place in Aquitaine's governance, Eleanor was not wholly deprived of the chance to extend her official competence, if only in regards to ecclesiastical beneficiaries. In classic fashion, she confirmed the privileges of the abbey of La Sauve-Majeure in Bordeaux and a donation to Notre-Dame de Luçon,[44] but the use of her seal to guarantee an accord between third parties (the canons of Saint-Hilaire and their treasurer)[45] shows clearly that her seal still exemplified official power. She also acted to maintain order by ordering her *prévôts* to respect the immunities of the churches of Sablonceaux and Fontaine-le-Comte.[46]

Eleanor's share in Aquitaine's governance was visibly reduced from 1157. She no longer enjoyed the independence of the early years of her second marriage or, at least, no such liberty is reflected in the charters; it was evidently no longer of an official nature. True, she was preoccupied by at least eight pregnancies between 1153 and 1166, and her public role as regent for Henry II was concurrently expanding in England—well outside the geographical limits of this study, at the other end of the Angevin "empire" Henry II was struggling to unify and govern by himself. But her role in Aquitaine had so diminished that she vanishes from extant charters between 1157 and 1167; not a single act mentions her, either alone or jointly with Henry II.

The Return to Aquitaine and the Roots of Revolt (1168–73)

The spite or jealousy of a deceived woman was never expressed in charters and would be impossible to prove in any case. Certainly it did not underlie Eleanor's reappearance at the head of the Aquitainian administration late in 1167 or early in 1168. Rather, her reappearance underlines Henry II's inability to control all his domains through his own administration.[47] He put aside his centralizing policies, his hopes of creating a single homogeneous domain, and the effort to govern his lands personally and redistributed his powers within his family so those lands might be as firmly controlled as possible. This recourse to the idea of patrimony, which so often benefited women, returned Eleanor to her personal inheritance, a duchy wracked by frequent revolts but a region she knew well. To calm and contain the Aquitainians, Henry gave them back *their* duchess.

The six years the queen-duchess now spent administering Aquitaine saw the most elaborate production of charters in either of her marriages. She witnessed at least two extant acts and issued fifteen surviving charters whose full validity required no confirmation. During these years Henry II himself issued no acts for Aquitaine, and only two of his wife's acts refer to him as king. In the first, Eleanor took the abbey of Les Châteliers, in the isle of Ré, under her protection and exempted it from rents.[48] The second requires more attention, for she issued it in a less independent manner and in very exceptional circumstances. In this donation of an estate and its appurtenant rights to the chapter of Saint-Hilaire, she associated with herself Henry, "my lord the king [*dominum meum regem*]" and her son Richard. But when the act records its authentication with Eleanor's seal, the text expressly states that the donation was made "with the will and at the demand of my lord the king and my son Richard [*ex voluntate et mandato domini mei regis et Ricardi filii mei*]."[49] The grant initiated an anniversary mass to commemorate Earl Patrick of Salisbury, who while in the queen's service had been assassinated on March 27, 1168, by members of the Lusignan family, powerful Poitevin barons with strong leanings toward independence from comital authority. The late earl had been a personal friend of Henry II, and as military governor in Poitou had been responsible for Eleanor's safety. His murder touched Henry closely enough that he broke his silence on Aquitainian affairs to show his solidarity with his wife and to demonstrate that, even if ducal power was invested in several individuals, it united in the face of powerful rebels.

The couple's son Richard, enthroned as duke in 1170 while still a minor, took up his responsibilities only in 1174, when he issued, alone, two acts in favor of the town of Bayonne. This is why Eleanor, judicious governor in her own name during these years, associated him with herself ("I and Richard my son [*Ego et Ricardus filius meus*]") in two-thirds of the acts she issued in this period. It was not that she exercised power any the less in her own name in keeping with her rights, nor solely as the representative of husband or son. Thus her acts constrained her subjects by calling upon all the king's faithful followers *and hers* to respect her acts and the double authority that reigned over Aquitaine ("to the archbishops, bishops, abbots, counts . . . and all the king's faithful followers *and hers* throughout Aquitaine [*archiepiscopis, episcopis, abbatibus, comitibus . . . et omnibus fidelibus regis et suis totius Aquitanie*].")

The diverse contents of Eleanor's acts might tend to corroborate the idea that her power was now much fuller, less transitory, and geographically more widespread than it had been earlier. But if these acts show her manipulating rents and commodities that were economically significant, they also show that her authority extended only over a fairly limited region—the Poitevin heart of the count-dukes' possessions. Religious houses, moreover, remained her primary beneficiaries as she continued in her ancestors' and her husband's tradition to manifest the official power she represented by granting or renewing her protection over those houses, as for example her grants to the abbeys of La Merci-Dieu, Candeil, Les Châteliers or Dalon.[50] She suppressed new or excessive rents on the salt manufactured by men of the priory of Saint-Aignan in the Saintonge.[51] She restored vineyards to the priory of Saint-Pierre d'Oléron, a dependency of the abbey of Maillezais, to which she also confirmed rights over the sale of wheat at Maillé in lower Poitou.[52] Religious houses did not, however, monopolize her attention: laypeople figured in her acts in increasing numbers. She granted—or more than likely, sold—franchises on the sale and purchase of merchandise, and on tolls, to Geoffrey Berland, a rich merchant of Poitiers who at the end of the century obtained the very profitable concession of the marketplaces in that town.[53] She also exempted from all tax and rent Pierre de Ruffec, a townsman of La Rochelle, in exchange for a rent of 100s. to be paid to the abbey of Fontevraud.[54] Another sign of the recognition of her authority and official power was her confirmation and guarantee by her seal of acts between third parties, as when John de Longueville abandoned his claims to various revenues and gave all dependencies of the office of *bailli* at Angles and of the salt marsh of "Rosseria" to the priory of Fontaines.[55]

There is reason to believe that Eleanor was seeking during this period to confirm herself definitively as the head of the duchy, and even to distance herself increasingly from Henry II's policies. Already in 1168 and 1171, she held her own Christmas courts in Aquitaine, in her own domains, with her son but not her husband. The year 1172 appears to mark a more definite move in this direction. No charters survive from that event, but other sources confirm that late in June, she personally received King Alphonso II of Aragon (1162–96) and King Sancho VI of Navarre (1154–94).[56] Their discussions particularly bore on the ever-fragile diplomatic relations between the northern Iberian realms and the south of France, especially the county of Toulouse. In the same year, Eleanor was present and affixed her seal as witness to a grant to the priory at Montazais (a dependency of Fontevraud) by Mirable, widow of Robert de Sillé, a baron from Maine who had died in prison after rebelling against Henry II in 1168.[57] On this occasion she possibly conveyed a pardon from the king, but she might also have wished to keep her distance from his politics. Throughout this period, moreover, she consistently associated herself with

the influential and strategically located abbey at Fontevraud, which Henry
II had endowed more richly than Eleanor had previously done. She cor-
roborated the grant of a rent to Fontevraud by Henry II's steward Man-
asser Biset and his wife,[58] and especially after 1170, made several important
grants to the mother house at Fontevraud and its dependent priories. In
1170, she confirmed an estate to the priory at Soussis, and gave the nuns
there the right to take wood from the forest of Argenson for their fires and
for the priory's buildings.[59] In 1172, she augmented rights of usage to the
priory at Saint-Bibien.[60] At Fontevraud, she even attended the religious
profession of the wife of one Roger de la Coue.[61] Eleanor was possibly
pursuing and strengthening Henry's policies, but she could also have
wished to take up the abbey on her own and, via its influence, to attract to
herself the support of local barons who were ready to turn against the king
as count of Anjou.[62]

Finally, again in 1172—perhaps only by coincidence—Eleanor modified the form of address in three acts: instead of the words "to the king's
faithful followers and hers [*fidelibus regis et suis*]," there appears only "her
faithful followers [*fidelibus suis*]."[63] This seemingly affirmed for the future
the duchess's sovereign authority without reference to that of her husband.
The signs are admittedly ambiguous and this interpretation perhaps tentative. Together, however, these signs offer reason to suppose—especially in
light of the rebellion of 1173—that if the duchess's authority was recognized and her proprietary rights respected, her ability to conduct government was restricted. Hence Eleanor, determined to assert and free herself
to act in her own name as the head of the duchy, sought to govern more
freely, not only as young Richard's representative and most especially not
as her husband's.

The duchess of Aquitaine certainly did not control all elements of
power, nor the means available to express them. The duchy did not possess
a true chancery, no official organ like the English royal chancery that could
give regular, normative form to the ducal will.[64] Eleanor did not, however,
turn to Henry II's chancery for the preparation of her acts; rather, she drew
from the region's monasteries a few clerks whom she attached to her personal service—among them the notaries Jordan and, especially, Peter.[65]
Through their services she controlled her charter production, but in these
circumstances the written expressions of her power retained an air of dis-
organization—rather diminishing her credibility, especially in comparison
to documents routinely issued by the well-organized royal chancery in
England. That Eleanor herself had no such office explains why much business in Aquitaine was still moved by charters drawn up by beneficiaries
rather than donors. For Eleanor's charters in particular, it means that the
witness lists to her acts are not formalized as was the case with chancery

products; they can be relied upon to provide an overview of the duchess's retinue.

Though Eleanor had expanded her retinue somewhat, its makeup varied little. She still gathered about her primarily the barons of Poitou, most prominently her uncle Raoul de Faye, at this time seneschal of Aquitaine. In that capacity Raoul appears in at least ten of his niece's charters. Those who had the hereditary custody of ducal castles appear less regularly, such as Porteclie de Mauzé (three times) and William Maingot, lord of Surgères and a future seneschal of Poitou (1174–80) four times. Among the influential castellans who appear rarely, the most noteworthy were Count Audebert of La Marche, Count John of Vendôme, and the viscount of Thouars. Tradition names as a member of Eleanor's council the Norman Simon de Tournebu, guardian of the castle, who was made constable of the town in 1164; but if he was really among her advisors, he witnessed only one of her charters. Nonetheless Tournebu testifies to the appearance of some non-Poitevins in the queen's entourage; they were few, but one at least did have a certain influence on the direction of ducal policies. This was an Englishman, John de Belles-mains, bishop of Poitiers (1162–82), a close associate of Henry II until Thomas Becket's murder in December 1170, and still influential enough to serve as a notable intermediary between king and duchess; he witnessed at least five of her acts. But it is excessive to speak of an Anglo-Norman administration in Poitou.[66] Belles-mains was bishop of the town that was the center of Aquitainian political power, and as Eleanor made her principal residence there it was natural that the two found themselves together quite regularly. Nonetheless it is clear that though Henry II rarely appeared on the spot to deal personally with Aquitainian affairs, he kept himself well informed on such matters to the extent that Eleanor did not exercise complete freedom over the direction of her policies. Nor, evidently, did she control two major avenues of power, money and military action. In 1171, for example, it was Henry II who, at the request of the abbot of Saint-Martial in Limoges, checked the revolt of Count Audebert of La Marche. Financial records are lacking for the duchy before Eleanor's son Richard began to act as duke,[67] but her financial situation must have been quite restricted: unquestionably, the bulk of the ducal revenues went into Henry II's coffers.

Eleanor thus administered the duchy's daily affairs and must have participated in the development of certain political orientations and diplomatic strategies (primarily matrimonial). She was not without influence on ducal politics, but she remained subject to directions that, in the last analysis, were those of Henry II. Her situation in Aquitaine was essentially the same as that of her sons in the other Plantagenet domains. If she did not expressly instigate the revolt of 1173–74, her claims blended perfectly into it: each member of the family was demanding the true redistribution of power Henry II had promised in 1169. The revolt was noteworthy for the number of malcontents who opposed a royal authority they judged too firm and absolute, but their divergent interests ensured that the coalition remained fragile. And if Eleanor was the legitimate heir to Aquitaine, she had one serious handicap: her sex. As both a familial and feudal struggle, revolt thus ended for her not in the greater autonomy her sons achieved, but in the complete loss of her political role. She was consigned to the oblivion of a strict if honorable confinement, primarily in England, and for the next eleven years scribes and chroniclers observed an impenetrable silence about her.

Epilogue: Power Plays

When she at last reappeared on the Continent in 1185–86, Eleanor was restored to all the honors due her and reinvested with the ducal crown of Aquitaine. At Alençon, she appeared as principal donor in at least two acts in favor of the abbey at Fontevraud: she gave them an annual rent of 100*l.*, half to be drawn from the revenues of the *prévôté* at La Rochelle and half from those at Poitiers, and she founded a Fontevrist priory of Sainte-Catherine in La Rochelle.[68] But she made these grants "with the assent and will of my lord Henry, king of England, and of my sons Richard, Geoffrey and John [assensu et voluntate domini mei Henrici, regis Anglie, et Ricardi, Galfridi et Johannis, filiorum meum]." Henry quickly confirmed the charter.[69] Clearly these acts do not carry the same weight as Eleanor's earlier charters; they required authorization and confirmation from all male members of the Plantagenet family. This set piece exploited Eleanor and the power she could still pretend to exercise over Aquitaine. In reality, it was designed to bring Richard to heel, to compel him to end his revolt and to recognize his brother John's rights in Aquitaine; thus all Eleanor's living sons were called to assent to the grant. Once father and son had reconciled, silence again enveloped Eleanor, who never again acted officially,[70] either in Aquitaine or elsewhere, until true liberation came with Henry II's death on July 6, 1189.

★★★★★

In light of the charters, Eleanor's role and power in Aquitaine differ from historians' traditional descriptions. During her first marriage, her carefully affirmed and maintained legitimacy served as a basic tool for Louis VII's power and authority, but her official activity was limited. During the early years of her second marriage and especially in 1168–73, she enjoyed a recognized authority over her inheritance and exercised a more substantial if still partial power. Thanks to the patrimonial concept restored to deal with the challenges of the Plantagenet domains, she drew closer to, but never reached, the center of the decision-making process. This led her into the revolt of 1173–74 and forced her retreat into silence and the long years of political inactivity. Even if her status as a married woman did not restrict her official role in her inherited duchy, it imposed upon her certain constraints that varied according to the political atmosphere: Louis VII and Henry II associated her with power in different ways and assigned her different functions. Only in widowhood could she express herself fully through a greatly intensified charter production and attain at last the heart of power.

Notes

I wish to thank Martin Aurell for his careful and productive readings of this essay. The translation is the work of John C. Parsons, to whom I am very grateful.

1. Nearly 100 charters survive from the fifteen years of her widowhood (1189–1204).
2. At Bordeaux in August 1137. See Luchaire, *Louis VII*, no. 1 at p. 97; *Gallia Christiana*, 2: preuve 280.
3. Issued at Saint-Hilaire-sur l'Autize between October 1151 and February 2, 1152 [hereafter: October 1151 and February 2, 1152] in favor of the abbey of l'Absie (Luchaire, *Louis VII*, no. 268 at p. 386).
4. In sixteen of these seventeen acts, Eleanor participates in the governance of Aquitaine at Louis VII's side; the seventeenth only mentions her, but it requires careful attention because it makes explicit the Capetian conception of the role assigned her in Aquitaine as a royal spouse.
5. Luchaire, *Louis VII*, nos. 18, 119, 177.
6. See especially Facinger, "Medieval Queenship"; for an overview, see Bournazel, *Le gouvernement capétien*.
7. In charters issued at Poitiers, 1146 (*Revue des Sociétés Savantes* 5th ser. 3 [1872]:52 [copy by Paul Marchegay introduced by E. Hucher]); at Étampes, 1146 (Paris BnF, Collection Fonteneau, Fonds latin 18376–18404, vol. 15, fol. 779); and at Paris, April 28, 1147 X June 8, 1147 ("Cartulaire de l'abbaye de Sainte-Croix": 25–26 (no. 18).
8. In charters issued at Saint-Jean d'Angély and at Poitiers, 1141 (Pierre-Théodore Grasilier, *Cartulaires inédits de la Saintonge*, respectively nos. 49, 28; at Niort, 1141 (*Gallia Christiana*, 2: preuves 385–86); and at Saint-Hilaire-sur-l'Autize October 1151 X February 2, 1152 (Luchaire, *Louis VII*, p. 386 [no. 268]).
9. In charters issued at Orléans between April 24, 1143 X October 24, 1143 (Audiat, "Saint-Eutrope et son prieuré": 21–22) at Paris, August, 1146 X

April 19, 1147 (Giry, "Les Establissements de Rouen," 70–71; and at Étampes, August 1, 1146 X April 19, 1147 [Luchaire, *Louis VII*], p. 378 no. 176).

10. Grasilier, *Cartulaires inédits*, no. 29 at p. 36.

11. The idea and expression are those of Barthélemy, "Note sur le *maritagium*," p. 14.

12. *Gallia christiana*, 2: preuves 385–86.

13. On this point see Bloch, *La société féodale*, esp. p. 134. See also Gold, *The Lady and the Virgin*, p. 120.

14. Charter issued at Lorris, 1139; de Richemond, "Chartes," 25–26.

15. Charters issued at (Orléans?) December 28, 1140 (Grasilier, *Cartulaires inédits*, no. 48 at p. 51); at Saint-Jean d'Angély, 1141 (Grasilier, *Cartulaires inédits*, no. 49 at p. 52; at Poitiers, 1141 (Grasilier, no. 38 at pp. 35–36; and at Paris, 1141 (Grasilier, no. 39 at p. 36).

16. Charters issued in 1146 (Giry, "Les Establissements de Rouen," 2:72–73 (preuve no. 6), and at Paris, 1 August, 1146 X 19 April, 1147 (Giry, 2: preuve no. 5 at 70–71).

17. Charter issued at Étampes, 1146 (Paris, BnF, coll. Fonteneau, vol. 15 fol. 779). For the abbey's holdings and obligations, see the well-documented introduction to Richard's "Chartes de Saint-Maixent."

18. On Fontevraud, consult Dalarun's excellent *L'impossible sainteté* and, of the studies by Bienvenu, see especially "Aliénor et Fontevraud." For the 1146 grant see *Revue des Sociétés Savantes* 5th ser. 3 [1872]:52 n8.

19. Charters issued at (Orléans?), Dec. 28, 1140 (Grasilier, *Cartulaires inédits*, no. 48 at p. 51), and at Saint-Jean d'Angély, 1141 (Grasilier, no. 39 at p. 52).

20. Luchaire, *Louis VII*, letters nos. 236, 240.

21. This is particularly evident in the acts issued at (Orléans?) Dec. 28, 1140, in favor of Notre-Dame at Saintes (Grasilier, *Cartulaires inédits*, nos. 47–48 at pp. 50–51), and at Étampes in 1146 in favor of Saint-Maixent (Luchaire, *Louis VII*, p. 378 [no. 176]).

22. Luchaire, *Louis VII*, nos. 12–13, 74, 127, 129, 163, 269–70.

23. Luchaire, *Louis VII*, nos. 12–13, 74.

24. *Layettes*, ed. Teulet, 6:47 (no. 64). The royal couple's confirmation in this case appears at the bottom of an act of the papal legate Geoffroy de Lèves.

25. Grasilier, *Cartulaires inédits*, no. 28 at pp. 35–36.

26. *Gallia Christiana* 2: preuves 385–86.

27. *Gallia Christiana* 2: preuves 280–81.

28. Bedos Rezak, for example, argues this point from the women's seals she studied ("Women, Seals" and "Medieval Women"). See also Guerreau-Jalabert, "Note critique."

29. *Layettes*, ed. Teulet, 1:47 (no. 64).

30. Charter issued at Paris [August 1, 1146 X April 19, 1147] (Luchaire, *Louis VII*, no. 171 at p. 376).

31. See Bedos-Rezak ("Women, Seals" and "Medieval Women") and Chassel, "L'usage du sceau."

32. Cf. Chassel, "L'usage du sceau," and Eygun, *Sigillographie*.

33. Charters issued at Lorris, 1139 (Paris, BnF, Fonteneau, vol. 25, fols. 287–88; only the formula of the queen's approbation appears, not her attestation); at Paris, August 1, 1146 X April 19, 1147 (Giry, "Les Établissements de Rouen," 2: *preuve* 5 at pp. 70–71); and without location, 1146 (Giry, "Les Établissements de Rouen," 2: preuve 6 at pp. 72–73).

34. Giry, "Les Établissements de Rouen," 2 *preuve* 5 at pp. 70–71, and *preuve* 6 at pp. 72–73.

35. Respectively, charters issued at Fontevraud after May 18, 1152 ("Chartes," ed. Eugène Frédéric Ferdinand Hucher 53–54); at Poitiers, May 26, 1152 (Audoin, "Poitiers,"35–36 [acte 20]); and at Poitiers, May 27, 1152 ("Chartes de Saint-Maixent" 352–53 [acte 335]).

36. Peace was concluded in August 1154, to which date Louis VII had used the ducal title in at least 58 acts since his divorce from Eleanor in May 1152 (see the catalogue in Luchaire, *Louis VII*).

37. Richard, *Histoire des comtes de Poitou*, 2:116.

38. The seal was affixed to her acts for Fontevraud ("Chartes," ed. Hucher, and Saint-Maixent ("Chartes de Saint-Maixent"). For the unfortunately partial extant image of this seal, see Eygun, *Sigillographie*, pl. 3 at pp. 160–61.

39. See the act cited above, n35.

40. A grant known indirectly from the accounts and inquests held by Count Alphonse of Poitou (1253–69), and attested by several witnesses in the mid-thirteenth century (Bardonnet, *Archives historiques du Poitou*).

41. Abbé Charles Métais, "Cartulaire saintongeais," *acte* 62 at 103–04.

42. Métais, "Cartulaire saintongeais," *acte* 62 at 103–04.

43. E.g., the confirmation (Caen [1155–57]) of an act of Bishop Philip of Bayeux for the Norman abbey of Luzerne (*Gallia Christiana*, 11: *preuve* 16 at col. 82).

44. Respectively, acts issued at (Bordeaux?) Dec. 21,1156 (indicated in *Gallia Christiana*, 11: col. 869), and at Chizé, 1156–57 (Poitiers, BM, MS Fonteneau 14, fols. 251–52).

45. At Ruffec, December 1156 X March 1157 (Redet, "Saint-Hilaire de Poitiers,": *acte* 111 at 160.

46. Charter issued at Poitiers, 1156–57 (Pon, "Fontaine-le-Comte," 25–26 [acte 17]).

47. Bautier, "Empire Plantagenêt ou espace Plantagenêt?" The idea and even the existence of a Plantagenet "empire," dear to Jacques Boussard in his worthy and amply documented *Le gouvernement d'Henri II*, have been greatly tempered and nuanced; to speak of Plantagenet domains is surely more appropriate.

48. Charter issued at Poitiers [1169 X 1172] (Paris, BnF, Clairambault 1188, fol. 5r, a copy by Gaignières). I owe this reference to the kindness of Nicholas Vincent.

49. Issued at Poitiers, March 27 [1168 X 1172] (Redet, "Saint-Hilaire," *acte* 153 at 180–81).

50. Acts issued respectively at Poitiers [1169 X 1172] ("Cartulaire de l'abbaye de la Merci-Dieu") acte 87 at 78–79; at Chinon [1172] (Rossignol, "Une charte d'Aliénor"); Poitiers [1169 X 1172] (Paris, BnF, Clairambault 1188, fol. 5r); and at Périgueux [1169 X 1173] (Paris, BnF, Baluze 375 fols. 17v–18r, another reference generously communicated by Nicholas Vincent).

51. At Chinon ca. 1170 (Métais, "Cartulaire saintongeais," acte 70 at pp. 114–16). The priory of Saint-Aignan was a dependency of the abbey of La-Trinité-de-Vendôme.

52. Charters issued respectively at Poitiers, ca. 1170 (Paris, BnF, Fonteneau, vol. 25, fol. 71), and at Poitiers, [late 1170 X early 1171] (Lacurie, Histoire de l'abbaye de Maillezais, preuve 51 at pp. 271–72).

53. Issued at Chinon [1169 X 1174] (Audoin, "La commune," acte 22 at 39–40).

54. Issued at Chinon, 1172 (Marchegay, "Chartes de Fontevraud,"135–36).

55. Issued at Poitiers [1169 X 1173] Marchegay, Cartulaire du Bas-Poitou, p. 109.

56. Richard, Histoire des comtes 2:161; Labande, "Pour une image véridique," 206.

57. At Chinon, 1172 (Paris, BnF, coll. Fonteneau, vol. 15, fol. 48).

58. Issued at Fontevraud [1168 X 1169] (Recueil des actes de Henri II 1:404; the rent of 20s. was intended for the purchase of herrings during Lent).

59. Issued at Saint-Jean d'Angély [1169 X 1173] (Marchegay, "Chartes de Fontevraud," 329).

60. Issued at an unknown location [1169 X 1172] (Paris, BnF, lat. 5480, vol. 2, p. 22, a vidimus of 1220 copied by Gaignières).

61. Lost original charter known from the seventeenth-century copy of the Grand cartulaire de Fontevraud, Angers, Archives départementales du Maine-et-Loire, 101 H 225 bis, pp. 90–91.

62. Hypotheses advanced by Bienvenu, "Aliénor et Fontevraud," 15–27.

63. Issued at Poitiers [1169 X 1173] (Marchegay, Cartulaire du Bas-Poitou, p. 109). See also (Marchegay, "Chartes de Fontevraud,"135–36.

64. Richardson, "The Letters and Charters."

65. Jordan, clerk and notary, appears three times in Eleanor's acts and Peter, notary and chaplain, eight times.

66. An idea explored and discussed by Boissonnade, "Administrateurs laïques."

67. Richard, Histoire des comtes, p. 169; after the revolt of 1173–74, Henry II offered Richard half the duchy's revenues and the possession of four castles.

68. Marchegay, "Chartes de Fontevraud," 330–31; the latter foundation is known only from the inventory of the Fontevraud cartulary prepared by Père Lardier, preserved in the Archives départementales du Maine-et-Loire (see Grand cartulaire de Fontevraud, Angers, Archives départementales du Maine-et-Loire, 101 H 225 bis, pp. 90–91).

69. Recueil des Actes de Henri II, 2: acte 465C at p. 270.

70. One indication of Eleanor's restricted liberty is that her personal expenses were consigned to the Pipe Rolls—e.g., £20 in 1181–82 (Martindale, "Eleanor of Aquitaine," p. 35 n36).

CHAPTER 3

ELEANOR OF AQUITAINE
IN THE GOVERNMENTS OF HER SONS
RICHARD AND JOHN

Ralph V. Turner

An examination of Eleanor of Aquitaine's career during Richard Lionheart's and John's reigns challenges the picture of her as "an essentially frivolous woman," showing her fighting to preserve intact the Plantagenet possessions.

The marriage of Eleanor of Aquitaine and Henry II produced two sons, Richard I the Lionheart, and John Lackland, who survived to succeed, between 1189 and 1216, to the English throne, the duchy of Normandy, the Angevin domains in the Loire valley, and Eleanor's patrimony in Aquitaine. Though her reputation derives largely from earlier events in her life, especially her unhappy marriages to two kings, she exercised her greatest political power as a widow. Eleanor manifested her strongest maternal feelings in Richard and John's adult years, as she struggled to help them secure their inheritances and preserve their possessions. She did not follow many noble widows' example and live quietly on her dower lands, though the purpose of dower was to "liberate the new lord's house from the presence of his mother, so that he would have by him only his wife."[1] As one of her biographers, Régine Pernoud, has written, Eleanor had accumulated during her 1174–89 imprisonment treasures of energy that she would spend without counting the cost during her sons' reigns, the most burdensome, active, and eventful years of her life.[2] An examination of Eleanor's career in those years, taking into account some fifty surviving *acta,* adds depth to one-dimensional accounts of her by misogynist medieval writers, and by modern authors absorbed in courtly literature. By 1189, romance and coquetry had no relevance for the aged Eleanor of Aquitaine; the evidence of her last years challenges the widespread view that she was "an essentially frivolous woman" whose life was a series of scandals.[3]

This "incomparable woman" dedicated her energies to seeing her sons firmly in control of their territories.[4] Scholars have assumed that her primary concern was her own duchy of Aquitaine, but she seems never to have doubted that her ancestral lands belonged within the larger Angevin "empire" that Henry II had assembled, and she fought to hold together for Richard and John the far-flung Plantagenet possessions.[5] In the first half of Richard's reign, Eleanor's efforts to protect his position while he was absent on crusade, and then in prison, were phenomenal for a woman of her age. While she held no official position in England's government comparable to that of Philip II's mother in France, the respect due her as queen-mother gave her a prominent part in English politics during the turbulent years of 1190 to 1194, when the regency was threatened by her younger son Count John of Mortain and by Philip II. She was a prominent force in England, enforcing royal directives, prohibiting papal legates' movements, attesting royal charters, and attending the *magna curia regis.* She acted in a governing capacity in Anjou after Richard departed from Chinon in June 1190; for example, she sat with the seneschal of Anjou at Saumur to settle a dispute between the town's mayor and the abbess of Fontevraud.[6] Upon Richard's death in April 1199, she flew into action after five years of repose to promote her last surviving son's succession to the Plantagenet heritage. Indeed, Eleanor was busiest in the months after Richard's death, circulating about Anjou and Aquitaine to prevent partition of the Angevin "empire" between John and her grandson, Arthur of Brittany.[7]

Eleanor's royal sons each had strong feelings for her. During their reigns, she took precedence over their wives, enjoying a queen-regnant's perquisites.[8] As duchess of Aquitaine she was rich and powerful in her own right, and though the division of the duchy's resources between Eleanor and Richard is unclear, she evidently felt able to make grants from the revenues of Poitou's *prévôtés.* Richard provided her with an income independent of annual exchequer grants by confirming the dower lands granted her by Henry II and adding lands that Henry I and Stephen gave their wives; as duke of Normandy, he granted her added income from farms of Norman *prévôtés.* As Henry II's wife, Eleanor had received queen's gold, a gold mark for every hundred silver marks paid to the king as feudal relief or as offerings for favors; she continued to collect this payment even after

Richard married Berengaria of Navarre, and John Isabelle of Angoulême. While Richard settled on Berengaria all Gascony below the river Garonne, his mother's dower lands in England, Normandy and Poitou would pass to Berengaria only after Eleanor died.[9] Three members of Eleanor's household received annual grants from the English exchequer: Adam of Wilton, her chapel clerk; Adam her cook; and Osbert, known simply as "the queen's man." Her cook's duties must have extended beyond the kitchen, for in April 1194, Richard granted Adam land in Cumberland "for his service which he performed for our dear mother and our dear nephew Otto, son of the duke of Saxony." In 1200, about a year after his accession, John too rewarded the labors of his mother's servants.[10]

Following Henry II's death, Richard ordered Eleanor's release and empowered her to hold England until he arrived to take it for himself; though she was not officially regent, some writs issued by the chief justiciar were authorized "by the queen's precept."[11] She traversed the kingdom and dispatched royal representatives to the counties to release captives imprisoned for offenses against forest law, or those held by the king's will and not by the law of the realm, while those imprisoned by due process were to be freed if they found sureties for their appearance at trial. Also her agents went about taking free men's oaths of fidelity to their new king.[12] Richard met Eleanor at Winchester soon after he landed at Portsmouth on August 13, and she joined his retinue as he made his way to Westminster for his coronation. In preparation for the queen-mother's participation in the coronation festivities, over £100 was spent on clothing, furs, horse-harness and other items for her and her entourage.[13]

Eleanor continued to share in governing as she accompanied her son about England in the autumn of 1189. She issued very few charters concerning English matters, however. An exception is a charter for Maurice of Berkeley confirming his right to the Berkeley barony, issued by Eleanor on the same day that Richard issued other charters confirming properties. Maurice doubtless sought a royal charter because his barony was newly created for his father by Henry II, and he proffered a 1000-mark offering.[14] In November, Eleanor took a hand in the archbishop of Canterbury's longstanding quarrel with the monks of Christchurch Cathedral. When a papal legate landed in England to settle the controversy, Eleanor prevented his proceeding beyond Canterbury. Several days later, she was present with Richard and a number of prelates for a discussion of the long-simmering dispute between the archbishop and the monastic chapter at his metropolitan cathedral.[15]

In the spring of 1190, Richard provided funds for Eleanor to attend a great council at Nonancourt in Normandy, where he laid out plans for governing his lands during his expedition to the Holy Land.[16] Richard generously gave his younger brother control of almost half of England but also gave John scope for causing great trouble. Two checks that Richard expected to restrict his brother's power were Eleanor's influence and John's oath to remain out of England during his brother's absence, but neither worked as expected. First, Eleanor was away from England for several months in 1190 and 1191, accompanying Richard as far as Chinon in Anjou, then criss-crossing Aquitaine to conduct Richard's bride to Sicily for their marriage. After the queen-mother returned to England in 1191, however, she exerted enough maternal pressure on John to prevent his joining Philip II following the French king's premature return from the crusade in the summer of 1191. John's promise at Nonancourt not to return to England for three years was soon undone, apparently through Eleanor's request that Richard free John from that oath.[17] With Eleanor far away on her journey to Spain and Sicily, John soon surfaced "in active mischief."[18]

Eleanor's weightiest cares, dynastic continuity and the unity of the Plantagenet holdings, animated her desire to see Richard married and the father of a son. In 1169, he was betrothed to Alice, daughter of the French king Louis VII and half-sister of Philip II; but Richard balked at marrying her, possibly because of rumors that his own father had seduced her.[19] Despite Eleanor's anxieties, Richard showed little concern for the succession, confident he would survive the dangers of an expedition to the Levant and live long enough to sire heirs.[20] At Messina in Sicily, before sailing for the Holy Land, he named as his heir Arthur of Brittany, son of his late brother, Geoffrey. Eleanor was wary of Richard's potential heirs: his only living brother, John, his nephew Arthur, and his illegitimate half-brother Geoffrey, a cleric in minor orders. Despite doubts about her youngest son's character, Eleanor apparently viewed him as the logical successor should Richard die childless; possibly her wish that Richard should release John from his oath to remain outside England reflects concern for his prospects as heir. Eleanor can hardly have sympathized with Geoffrey, her late husband's bastard, and she opposed Richard's honoring Henry II's wishes by naming him archbishop of York.[21] But the religious vows Geoffrey had to take before his consecration did weaken his claim to the succession, and, like John, he was barred from England for three years.

Despite Eleanor's fears for the succession, historians err in depicting Richard as "bullied into marriage by his formidable mother." John Gillingham rejects, as attempts to discredit Richard's capability as a ruler, suggestions that Eleanor handled the marriage negotiations. Richard's Pyrenean marriage must be seen as part of his plan for stabilizing Gascony by allying with Berengaria's father, Sancho VI (d. 1194) and her brother, Sancho VII. For Gillingham, the match was "an ingenious diplomatic device . . . to cut his way through a thicket of political problems." Navarre and other

Christian kingdoms in northern Spain played important roles in the politics and diplomacy of southwestern France, and Richard's alliance with Navarre protected his southern flank from aggression by the count of Toulouse and antagonistic Aquitanian nobles.[22] But it was Eleanor, aged sixty-seven, who brought Berengaria to Sicily, where Richard wintered in 1190–91. No doubt, she reassured Sancho VI about the honesty of her son's intention to set aside his French fiancée in favor of Berengaria. Sancho would have sought assurances that Richard had extricated himself from that betrothal, a difficult task since Richard would not win Philip II's assent to break off the betrothal until March 1191. By late January 1191, Eleanor and Berengaria had crossed the Alps and continued southward until Richard met them on March 30 at Reggio.[23] Richard married Berengaria during a May 1191, detour to Cyprus en route to Jerusalem.

Dissatisfied with her last-born son and her grandson as heirs, Eleanor hoped that Richard and Berengaria would have a son; but the marriage remained childless, and uncertainty hovered over the Plantagenet succession. Richard's patronage of his brother John, count of Mortain, in his strongly governed kingdom and his wealthiest French province, established him in so powerful a position that some of Richard's subjects suspected that the king did not expect to return to England. They feared that if he did, "[h]is brother, already no less powerful than he and eager to rule, would defeat him and drive him out of the kingdom."[24] Richard's grants to John seemed an implicit declaration of his intent should he die overseas; an explicit statement would have encouraged John's bad behavior much sooner, as Henry II's unhappy experience with young King Henry showed. In fact, John saw his advantage, for his open moves against the English regency only began after Richard's recognition of Arthur of Brittany as his heir late in 1190.

Arthur was unacceptable to Eleanor as heir. His very name was "a badge of Breton independence and hostility toward the Plantagenets."[25] After her husband Geoffrey died in 1186, Constance and the Breton aristocracy harbored powerful hostility toward their suzerain, the duke of Normandy; and it aroused Eleanor's desire to block little Arthur from becoming head of the Plantagenet house.[26] Constance's fury against the Angevins blinded her to the advantages that an upbringing at his uncle's court might give her son, an opportunity to strengthen ties with Richard that could win him formal nomination as the childless king's heir. In 1196, when Richard demanded custody of the boy, Arthur was instead hidden away and then dispatched to Philip II's court. With Arthur a pawn of the French monarch, neither Eleanor nor Richard could bear to contemplate his succession.

After Arthur's flight to Paris, the aged queen's eyes possibly fixed on another grandson as a potential heir: Otto of Brunswick, son of Henry II's

and Eleanor's daughter Matilda and her husband Henry the Lion.
Richard's nomination of Otto as count of Poitou in the spring of 1196 is
difficult to explain, for it seems to contradict his earlier tenacity in seeking
to hold on to his southern inheritance. Eleanor's influence may have inspired Richard's grant; if she had become reconciled to the fact that he
would not father an heir, she may have sought to have someone solidly established in her patrimony to prevent any succession struggle there upon
her death.[27] Or possibly Otto's new position marked a step in grooming
him as head of the Plantagenet house. After Emperor Henry VI's death in
1197, however, the grander possibility arose of Otto's accession to the imperial throne, and he returned to Germany to pursue his candidacy. With
Otto's withdrawal and Arthur of Brittany in Philip II's household, Richard
tacitly acknowledged his brother John as his heir.[28] Yet Arthur would continue to worry his grandmother, since he provided "a trump card" for his
Capetian protector to play in Philip's great political game against John after
Richard died in 1199.[29]

Once Eleanor and the archbishop of Rouen reached Normandy, she
seems to have passed the winter of 1191–92 at one of her dower manors,
Bonneville-sur-Touques.[30] Soon, however, she had to deal with the collapse of Richard's scheme for governing England, which was breaking
down due to English resentment against his Norman-born viceroy,
William Longchamp. His position as chancellor—keeper of the king's
seal—witnessed Richard's confidence in him and seemed to confirm his
supremacy, and he was concentrating in his own hands all authority over
the central administration. Pope Clement III's nomination of Longchamp
as papal legate in England added to his power, giving him jurisdiction over
English ecclesiastical offices. Despite Longchamp's administrative gifts and
Richard's confidence in him, William as a low-born foreigner lacked the
English baronage's respect; his financial extortions, imperious manner, and
ignorance of English customs soon roused the barons' incipient xenopho-
bia, inspiring mockery of his physical appearance and innuendo about his
private life. In governing the kingdom, the chancellor faced difficulties as
well in curbing the ambitions of Count John, who required delicate handling because he was not only an overmighty magnate, but a likely successor to the English throne.[31]

John seized the opportunity created by Longchamp's unpopularity to
enhance his position by heading baronial opposition to the chancellor's au-
thoritarian rule. The two met in July 1191 but failed to find a compromise;
at a second meeting later in the summer, John secured Longchamp's
promise to support his succession should Richard not return from the crusade. For a time before sailing from Sicily, Richard refused to listen to
complaints from England about his agent's high-handed conduct. Though

some authorities have credited his mother's arrival at Messina as confirm-ing accusations against Longchamp and causing him to take action, Eleanor had been absent from England too long to have been aware of the trouble; by the time she met Richard at Messina late in March 1191, he had already sent home letters responding to the alarming reports of his viceroy's conduct.

Royal agents were sent to England as counterweights to Longchamp's authority. Most important was Walter of Coutances, archbishop of Rouen and a longtime royal servant, who accompanied Eleanor on her return to Angevin territory from Sicily. They departed only three days after Eleanor arrived at Richard's court in Messina, not waiting to see Richard set sail for the East on April 10. Walter arrived in England by April 1191, in time to try to mediate the quarrel between the chancellor and John. He carried with him Richard's letters, whose contents undermined Longchamp's au-thority by forcing him to share authority with Walter, as one who knew the king's will. The other counterweight was Geoffrey Plantagenet, the king's half-brother, whom Richard had nominated as archbishop of York. Once installed in England as archbishop, Geoffrey could be expected to re-strain Longchamp's legatine domination of the English Church. On her re-turn journey to Angevin territory, Eleanor stopped in Rome to lobby the pope for Geoffrey's swift consecration as archbishop; she spent heavily to purchase support at the *Curia,* changing 800 marks with Roman money-changers.[32] When Geoffrey landed at Dover in September 1191 on his way to take possession of his see, Longchamp overplayed his hand by arresting him. After two great councils stripped Longchamp of his authority as chief justiciar, he fled to Normandy by the end of October. The council declared John supreme governor of England and gave him custody of all royal cas-tles; but Walter of Coutances headed the administration, taking on the chief justiciar's duties without the title.

The queen-mother was a central figure in Walter of Coutances's coun-sels from September 1191 until the end of 1193. Her backing gave credi-bility to his administration. In January 1192, she had to deal with Philip II's demands for the release of his sister Alice, betrothed to Richard since child-hood, but whom he had steadfastly refused to marry.[33] In Normandy, Eleanor learned of John's flirtation with Philip and sailed for England on February 11, 1192 to alert Walter of Coutances and to intercept her son be-fore he crossed the Channel to join Philip's court. At a series of councils, "through her own tears and the prayers of the nobles," John was persuaded to promise not to go to Philip for the time being.[34] While in England, Eleanor found time to join the Londoners' appeal for easy terms for a citi-zen saddled with an amercement of over £500 arising from a counterfeit-ing case.[35] She also sought, unsuccessfully, to reconcile at a London council two quarrelling northern prelates—Archbishop Geoffrey of York and Bishop Hugh du Puiset of Durham.[36]

When the exiled Longchamp excommunicated former English government colleagues and placed his diocese of Ely under an interdict, Walter of Coutances excommunicated him in retaliation and seized his episcopal estates.[37] In Cambridgeshire in 1192, Eleanor saw the misery that Longchamp's ecclesiastical sanctions were causing the inhabitants, when "a people weeping and pitiful" lamented that their relatives were denied burial in consecrated ground. She was a prime factor in forcing Coutances and Longchamp to patch up a quarrel that was causing such woe to innocent people, persuading them to withdraw their excommunications and Walter to restore the Ely estates. A contemporary chronicler asks, "And who could be so savage or cruel that this woman could not bend him to her wishes?"[38] A modern authority notes that in this episode, Eleanor's determination in dealing with two powerful prelates was "entirely typical of Angevin methods of government: it might have been employed by Henry or Richard."[39]

When news arrived early in 1193 of Richard's imprisonment in Germany, Eleanor assumed a position of direct authority in England.[40] In March, she dealt with the return of Longchamp, seeking to resume his papal legateship, but discussion with Walter of Coutances and the barons convinced her to give up any hope of reconciliation between the two quarrelling prelates; Longchamp left England, never to return. John had menaced the kingdom's peace since Philip II's return from the crusade, and as soon as he learned of his brother's imprisonment, he rushed to the French court to do homage to Philip for the Plantagenet continental domains. When John returned to England, declaring Richard dead and demanding recognition as king, Eleanor rallied the government to the captive king. The result was John's revolt in 1193–94, still underway when Richard reached England in March 1194.[41] The possibility loomed of a French invasion to aid John, and Eleanor took action to defend England from a hostile fleet, ordering the coasts facing Flanders strongly fortified. According to one chronicler, these commands were issued "by the mandate of Queen Eleanor, who ruled England at that time."[42]

Eleanor's role in an 1193 Canterbury election illustrates her influence in Richard's absence. The see of Canterbury fell vacant twice while the king was beyond the sea. Eleanor was absent from England during the first election in autumn 1191, when Walter of Coutances as justiciar unsuccessfully sought election for the candidate named in Richard's letters from Palestine. Eleanor was active as her son's agent in the second Canterbury election, made necessary by the new archbishop's sudden death only a month after his consecration. Only early in 1193, while Richard was a prisoner in Germany, did his will become known, when he nominated his trusted adviser in the Holy Land, Bishop Hubert Walter of Salisbury. The king sent three letters in March authorizing the monks of Christchurch Cathedral to hold an election and supporting Hubert's candidacy. The first letter, to the monks, commanded them to hold their election with the advice of Queen Eleanor and William of Sainte-Mère-Eglise, a trusted royal clerk; the second, to Eleanor, recounted Hubert's work at the Roman *Curia* and the German emperor's court in seeking his release and asked her to work for his election; the third urged government officials to support Hubert. The Canterbury monks elected the king's candidate in May 1193, the occasion marred only by the perennial spat between the prelates of the province and the Christchurch monks over the right of election.[43] Unaware that the election had taken place in keeping with his wishes, Richard wrote from Germany again in early June to urge his mother to settle the matter by going to Canterbury herself.[44]

Richard's captivity must have raised Eleanor's memories of her own confinement, and letters written for her by Peter of Blois witness her "passionate, wrathful frenzy to secure his release." Letters seeking papal support for Richard's release expressed her almost religious devotion for her captive son; he was described as "the soldier of Christ, the anointed of the Lord, the pilgrim of the cross."[45] When Emperor Henry VI pressured Richard to surrender England to him as an imperial fief subject to an annual tribute of £5,000, Eleanor advised her son to accede to the demand to speed his release.[46] An immediate issue was the raising of the staggering ransom the emperor demanded for Richard's release. In a letter to Eleanor and the regency council in April 1193, Richard urged them to begin raising quickly an initial 70,000 marks to expedite his release in exchange for hostages. Eleanor and Walter of Coutances approved a levy of one-quarter of the value of all movable goods, 20s. on each knight's fee, and all churches' gold and silver with the exception of the austere Cistercian and Gilbertine houses, which could contribute their wool crop.[47] In early June, the queen-mother attended a council at Saint Albans at which trustees were named to hold the money raised for the ransom; they would deposit the treasure at St. Paul's Cathedral in chests sealed with Eleanor's and the archbishop of Rouen's seals. Despite the demand for altar plate, she gave the monks of Saint Albans a charter redeeming a gold chalice they had given.[48]

The emperor released Richard in February 1194, when he summoned his mother and Walter of Coutances to bring the ransom to Germany. Eleanor reached Cologne in time for the feast of the Epiphany on January 6, and by January 17 had arrived at Speyer, where her son was held. She attended an assembly of bishops and magnates at Mainz on February 2, to consider final terms for the release; two days later, Richard was finally freed. He landed in England on March 13; as his wife Berengaria remained on the continent, it was Eleanor who accompanied him on a progress about the realm. In late March and early April, she attended a great council held at Nottingham to reorder the realm, and on April 17 at Winchester Cathedral a solemn crown-wearing, symbolically reasserting Richard's sacral status as king. She perambulated with him until he reached Portsmouth on April 24, where he waited more than two weeks for a favorable wind to take him to Normandy.[49]

Once Richard's position in England was restored, Eleanor could return to France knowing that the realm was secure despite his continued absence fighting Philip II from mid-1194 until his death in 1199. Evidently, some time after she and Richard returned to France, she reconciled him with John at Lisieux.[50] She settled not at Poitiers but at Fontevraud Abbey, within the diocese of Poitiers though on the frontier of Anjou and Poitou. Henry II's Angevin forebears and Eleanor's ancestors had been generous to the abbey, as had Henry himself, but she had not proven particularly bounteous before 1185, when she founded a Fontevraudist priory at La Rochelle.[51] Once settled at the dual convent and monastery, she made it her chief residence for the rest of her life, and her benefactions increased. Her residence at a religious house did not mean that she had withdrawn from the secular world; rather, she chose the Loire valley house as "a convenient base of operations, situated in a strategic position" for assisting her sons in their struggle against their nemesis, Philip II.[52]

Little evidence of Eleanor's activitives survives from Richard's last five years, while he was resisting his Capetian rival.[53] Perhaps she joined Richard's Christmas court in Poitiers in 1195, but no extant charters witness her presence; his remaining Christmases, observed in Normandy amidst warfare, were unlikely to have been festive. Occasional documents witness Eleanor's continued intervention in matters of state. An 1196 charter announces the settlement in her presence at Fontevraud of a dispute between the abbey of Bourgueil and her men of Jaulnay in Poitou.[54] The next year, she joined Walter of Coutances in asking the king to remit a debt Hugh Bardolf, a longtime royal servant, owed for justice in a suit against the earl of Chester; Richard canceled half of it.[55] In 1198, the Christchurch monks sought her intervention in their still-simmering dispute with the archbishop of Canterbury.[56]

When Richard was fatally wounded at the siege of Chalus, near Limoges, in early April 1199, Eleanor rushed to his sickbed. After he died on April 6, she accompanied the body to Fontevraud for burial there on Palm Sunday. Richard's death without an heir of his body left uncertainty over the succession to the Angevin territories: English and Norman magnates opted for his brother John, but the nobles of Anjou, Maine, and

Touraine proclaimed as their lord his nephew, Arthur of Brittany. The uncertainty enabled Philip II to revive his family's policy of pitting one Plantagenet against another, and he supported young Arthur's claims.[57] Though in her mid-seventies, Eleanor roused herself to win John's recognition as heir to Henry II's entire legacy. Because of her deep distrust of her Breton daughter-in-law Constance, who had handed over her son to Philip II, Eleanor had no wish to see the Angevin "empire" partitioned between her son and grandson. Indeed, the succession struggle following Richard's death can be seen as a conflict between the two mothers, each fighting for her own son's rights.[58]

While John worked to secure Normandy and England, Eleanor asserted control over lands to the South. Anjou and Maine were threatened by an invading force led by Arthur and Constance, and when they had occupied Le Mans, Philip II went there to take the boy's homage; then the Breton prince moved on to Tours. As John hurried to Rouen to be invested as duke of Normandy on April 25, Eleanor, in company with one of Richard's mercenary captains led an army that ravaged Anjou, while faithful Poitevin nobles marched northward to Tours to confront Arthur's army.[59] Unlike his brother, John was not in possession of Aquitaine when he succeeded to the English throne, and the possibility of troublesome action by Philip II necessitated Eleanor's assertion of authority over her duchy. While John sailed to England for his coronation on May 25, she hastened to Aquitaine by the end of April to take her subjects' homage. As one of her charters states, "God having left us still in the world, we have been obliged, in order to provide for the needs of our people and the welfare of our lands, to visit Gascony."[60] Also to secure her duchy, she sought out Philip in mid-July to do homage to him, denying him an excuse for interference in her domains on Arthur's behalf. From April through July 1199, Eleanor traversed her duchy from Loudun near the Angevin border to Bordeaux, issuing charters confirming properties and privileges to win support for John.

The duchess made grants to Poitevin nobles to purchase their support for her youngest son—for example, returning to William de Mauzé his land of Marans that Richard had confiscated.[61] She sought to rally to John members of Poitevin families with a tradition of ducal service, notably two families of middling nobility, the Mauléons and the Maingots of Surgères, who had loyally served the Plantagenets as *prévôts* and seneschals.[62] The Mauléons, with holdings along the Atlantic coast of Poitou, at Aunis on the Ile de Ré and the Ile d'Oléron, were hereditary comital custodians of the Poitevin lordship of Talmond, one of Richard's favorite hunting grounds. Ralph de Mauléon sought to profit from the disputed succession in 1199 by offering himself to whichever candidate promised more. When he claimed lordship over Talmond and La Rochelle by right of inheritance, Eleanor was willing to grant him Talmond but refused to surrender complete control over the profitable port of La Rochelle, offering him instead £500 annually from the profits of its *prévôt* plus the castle of Benon.[63] The Maingots, hereditary custodians of the comital castle of Surgères, were another family with a history of service to the counts of Poitou; Eleanor cemented William III Maingot's loyalty by recognizing him as lord of Surgères.[64] Eleanor also sought to win the support of Andrew de Chauvigny, one of Richard's faithful Poitevin knights, with a grant of Saint-Sever-sur-l'Adour; but she failed here, for Chauvigny rallied to Arthur's cause.[65] Probably it was from Eleanor, about this time, that Hugh l'Archéveque, lord of Parthenay, recovered his castle of Secondigny that Richard had taken from him.[66] Some time before the end of 1199, Hugh IX of Lusignan gained possession of the county of La Marche, which his family had long sought. According to a Limousin chronicler, he gained it by abducting the aged Eleanor and extorting the county from her; equally likely, however, is her grant of the county as a reward for Hugh's support for John.[67]

On a spring and summer circuit of her domains in 1199, Eleanor sought as well to shore up the loyalty of townspeople and ecclesiastics. The people of Bordeaux petitioned her to abolish "certain evil impositions, unheard of and unjust," that Richard had imposed; she obliged. In July, John confirmed to the citizens of Bordeaux "all liberties and customs" that she had conceded and confirmed by charter. Other towns in Aquitaine, such as La Rochelle, Niort, and Poitiers, also benefited from Eleanor's charters granting them communes in return for acceptance of a military obligation by their militias.[68] Eleanor granted charters to religious houses confirming lands and privileges: to Montierneuf at Poitiers, Saint-Eutrope at Saintes, Fontaine-le-Comte, Notre-Dame de Charon, the archbishop of Bordeaux, Saint-Croix at Bordeaux, La Sauve-Majeure near Bordeaux, and Grandmont in Limousin.[69] In the attempt to win her subjects to John's side, she issued more charters in the months after Richard's death than at any other time in her widowhood; roughly forty of her fifty *acta* from 1189–1204 date from 1199 and after. Yet because she granted away ducal resources to purchase support for John, ducal power declined dangerously in Poitou and Gascony.

By the end of July 1199, Eleanor had left Aquitaine for Normandy, and at Rouen she exchanged charters with John. She ceded Poitou (and all Aquitaine is implied) to her son and took his homage; in turn, the county's bishops and lay nobility pledged John their homage, fealty, and service. He then issued a charter returning the province to her for her lifetime or for as long as she wished, to rule as *domina*. John's charter established for mother and son the sort of joint rights over property commonly shared by husband and wife; neither could alienate possessions without the other's consent. John would appoint the seneschals who headed the administration in Poitou and Gascony, but Eleanor's authority was genuine.[70] The arrangement was "a diplomatic masterstroke," preserving the English king's title as duke of Aquitaine and guaranteeing his authority in southwestern France, yet allowing no excuse for the Capetian king's intervention over the succession on the duchess' death.[71]

In early autumn 1199, John came to terms with Arthur's leading supporter among the nobility of Anjou and Maine, William des Roches, who had come to believe that Philip II was manipulating the boy to his own advantage. Des Roches managed to remove Arthur from Philip's custody and in October at Le Mans, a formal treaty of reconciliation ended—for a time—the contention between John and his nephew. This forced Philip to come to terms with John early in 1200 with the treaty of Le Goulet, which appeared to solidify the English king's position with a permanent peace. By its terms, Philip recognized John's right to Anjou and ratified Brittany's status as his fief; but John failed to gain custody of Arthur, and the boy returned to Paris. To seal the treaty, a Capetian-Plantagenet marriage was arranged: Philip's son and heir, Louis, would marry John's niece, Blanche of Castile, daughter of his sister Eleanor and King Alfonso VIII.[72] Once again, the aged queen-mother set off for Spain to fetch a royal bride, passing through the familiar territory of her youth on her last lengthy journey. In Roger of Howden's words, "Aged and wearied by the labors of her long journey, Queen Eleanor withdrew to the abbey of Fontevraud and remained there." She may have stayed at Poitiers occasionally, however, for she witnessed a charter there in February 1202.[73]

But in August 1200, John created another opportunity for Philip II and Arthur of Brittany. Having set aside his marriage to Isabella of Gloucester, he married another Isabelle, daughter and heir of Count William Taillefer of Angoulême, without regard for her prior betrothal to Hugh IX, lord of Lusignan and recently installed as count of La Marche, the head of an important clan in lower Poitou. On the surface, this marriage appeared an astute diplomatic move; the Angoumois was a strategic region, on the route between Poitiers and Bordeaux, and would have kept out of Lusignan's direct control castles that could threaten the Plantagenets' passage from Poitou to Gascony. Yet when John tore young Isabelle from her fiancé's household, he committed "an unprovoked act of dishonor" that was bound to affront the Lusignan family.[74] John may have viewed preventing Hugh's marriage as a plus, but his theft of his vassal's betrothed not only angered and humiliated the Lusignans, it outraged other powerful nobles on Poitou's southern fringe. John made no effort to compensate the Lusignans; instead, his contemptuous treatment spurred Hugh's clan to revolt.

By autumn 1201, Hugh had taken his complaint against John to the court
of Philip II, suzerain over Poitou. Philip's court on April 28, 1202, condemned John for failure to appear in Paris to answer Hugh's charges.[75] This
led to another round of the long Capetian-Plantagenet conflict, with
Philip taking advantage of the crisis to revive Arthur of Brittany's claim to
a share of the Plantagenet heritage. The young duke rejected his vassalage
to John for Brittany, and Philip recognized him as his vassal for Anjou,
Poitou, and Brittany. The revived conflict would end in Arthur's death and
Philip II's annexation of Normandy.

Eleanor sought to shore up John's position in Poitou by winning over
Aimery, viscount of Thouars, the most important Poitevin noble, with a
dozen castles dominating the north and west of the county. The viscount's
loyalty was problematic; he had supported John in the spring of 1199 but
had turned toward Arthur and Constance that autumn, once John revoked
Aimery's custody of Chinon castle in order to reward William des Roches
for removing Arthur of Brittany from Philip II's clutches. Also about this
time, Aimery's brother, Guy of Thouars, had become the third husband of
Arthur's mother, Constance of Brittany.[76] In February or March 1201, the
queen-mother, though ill, summoned Aimery to Fontevraud and entreated
him to remain faithful to John. In a letter to her son describing the visit,
she reported that Aimery had renewed his fealty and that she would act as
pledge for the viscount's good behavior. Aimery also wrote to John, giving
his account of the meeting and assuring the king of his loyalty.[77] Sir Maurice Powicke commented, "But for the prompt action of Eleanor, therefore, the house of Thouars might have become a most dangerous ally of
the house of Lusignan."[78] In 1202, however, Aimery joined William des
Roches, John's seneschal in Anjou, in deserting the English king and align-
ing with Arthur's forces.

Once more in Philip II's care, the fifteen-year-old Arthur afforded the
Capetian king a weapon against John. In the summer of 1202 Philip put
the boy at the head of an invasion force headed for Poitou.[79] At age seventy-eight, Eleanor left Fontevraud for Poitiers to keep her homeland
from falling into his hands. When she stopped at Mirabeau Castle north of
Poitiers near the end of July, she found herself under attack by Arthur's
forces and the Lusignans. For once in his largely listless defense of his continental domains, John's feelings for his mother moved him to energetic,
unaccustomed speed. With a mobile force of mercenaries, he made a
forced march of eighty miles from Le Mans in less than two days to surprise the besiegers and free Eleanor. In the most decisive military action of
his career, John caught the enemy force by surprise and captured a number of important rebels, including Arthur, the Lusignan brothers, and Andrew de Chauvingny.[80]

John's good fortune did not last, however, for as usual he over-reached himself. The deaths of a number of his captives from harsh conditions of imprisonment, and his probable murder of young Arthur led to defections by major magnates of Anjou and Poitou, and the loss of the Loire valley by the spring of 1203. By the end of that year, his defense of Normandy had failed, and he fled to England.[81] Early March 1204 saw the fall of the great fortress of Château-Gaillard, built by Richard I to dominate the Seine valley; and less than a month thereafter, on April first, Eleanor of Aquitaine died at the age of eighty. An Angevin chronicler described the king's reaction: "By her death the king, most violently saddened, feared greatly for himself and was disquieted more than enough to withdraw from Normandy."[82] His chronology is wrong, but the writer doubtlessly captured the depth of John's feeling for his mother. Obviously, Eleanor's death had a direct impact on Poitou, and nobles such as Aimery of Thouars, who had remained loyal to the Plantagenets out of respect for their duchess, now rushed to do homage to Philip of France.[83]

Historians' unfavorable estimates of Eleanor's political impact generally dwell on her early life and her marriages to Louis VII and Henry II. For example, Elizabeth A.R. Brown has written, "Her passionate pride and jealous dedication to upholding her rights and status led her to undertake and execute vendettas aimed simply at avenging indignities she had suffered." Brown acknowledges the importance of Eleanor's two royal sons to her and her role in their reigns, but concludes: "Self-sufficient, self-concerned activist that she was, she tended to view them as instruments of her will, or obstacles blocking its exercise, rather than as individuals to be nurtured and cherished." Brown continues in a psychohistorical mode, placing on Eleanor responsibility for John's "paranoia and unprincipled opportunism."[84] Such a judgment seems to go beyond the limited evidence of the charters and chronicles surviving for the last fifteen years of Eleanor's long life. Certainly she showed genuine devotion to the integrity of the block of lands that Henry II had amassed; as Bishop Stubbs wrote, despite her failed marriage, she was "naturally averse to the dismemberment of his empire."[85] In her sixties and seventies, at an age when most great ladies would have retired from activity, Eleanor of Aquitaine threw herself energetically into the cause of protecting and preserving intact the Angevin "empire" for her last sons, Richard and John.

Notes

1. Duby, "Women and Power."
2. Pernoud, *Aliénor d'Aquitaine,* p. 257.

3. Martindale, "Eleanor of Aquitaine," pp. 23–24, 35–50. See also Jane Martindale, "Eleanor of Aquitaine: The Last Years." For Eleanor's acta, see Baldet, "Recherches sur la reine Aliénor."

4. Richard of Devizes, *Chronicon,* p. 25.

5. E.g., Martindale, "Eleanor of Aquitaine," pp. 32–33: the "needs of the territories which she had inherited south of the Loire were always uppermost in her thoughts."

6. For her activities in England, 1190–94, West, *Justiciarship,* p. 65; Landon, *Itinerary of Richard I,* pp. 2, 13, 16, 18, 26. On her role in Anjou, CDF, ed. Round, no 1091 at pp. 387–88.

7. Richardson, "Letters and Charters," 207.

8. Richardson and Sayles, *Governance,* p. 153.

9. For grants from Poitevin *prévôtés,* e.g., that to Fontevraud from the *prévoté* of Oléron, Marchegay, "Chartes de Fontevraud." On her dower and Richard's Norman grants, Richard of Devizes, *Chronicon,* p. 14; Howden, *Chronica,* 3:2; Powicke, *The Loss of Normandy,* p. 234; Gillingham, "Richard I and Berengaria of Navarre." For queen's gold, Richardson, "Letters and Charters," 209–11.

10. Pipe Roll 6 Richard I; Pipe Roll 7 Richard 1, pp. 119, 173; Pipe Roll 8 Richard I, pp. 101, 275; Pipe Roll 9 Richard I, p. 120; Pipe Roll 1 John, p. 21; Pipe Roll 4 John, pp. 131, 172; Pipe Roll 6 John, pp. 113, 145. For Adam the Cook, Pipe Roll 5 Richard I, p. 75; Pipe Roll 7 Richard I, p. 27; Pipe Roll 8 Richard I, p. 21; Pipe Roll 1 John, p. 210, 212; Pipe Roll 4 John, p. 254; Pipe Roll 6 John, pp. 141, 142; *Cartae Antiquae Rolls 1–10,* p. 96 (no. 195). For Osbert, Pipe Roll 5 Richard I, p. 154; Pipe Roll 7 Richard I, p. 251; Pipe Roll 7 Richard I, p. 251; Pipe Roll 4 John, pp. 12, 271; Pipe Roll 5 John, pp. 5, 224; Pipe Roll 6 John, pp. 17, 102; *Rotuli Chartarum,* pp. 71 (grant to Nicholas fitz Richard "for the service which he made to Lady Eleanor our mother and to King Henry our brother"), 71b (to Adam, Eleanor's cook).

11. Pipe Roll 1 Richard I, pp. 163, 180.

12. *Gesta Regis Henrici Secundi,* 2:74–75; Ralph of Diss, *Opera Historica,* 2:67.

13. Pipe Roll 1 Richard I, pp. 223–24.

14. Landon, *Itinerary of Richard I,* p. 13; Sanders, *English Baronies,* p. 13 and n6.

15. *Gesta Regis Henrici Secundi,* 2:97; Landon, *Itinerary of Richard I,* pp. 16, 18.

16. Pipe 2 Richard I, pp. 2, 131.

17. Howden, *Chronica,* 3:32, 217, does not credit Eleanor with securing John's release from the oath; Landon, *Itinerary of Richard I,* p. 198.

18. Stubbs, *Historical Introductions to the Rolls Series,* p. 224.

19. Gillingham, "Richard I and Berengaria of Navarre," pp. 129–30.

20. A March 1191 treaty with Philip of France made provisions for anticipated sons (Landon, *Itinerary of Richard I,* p. 230).

21. Landon, *Itinerary of Richard I,* p. 3.

22. First quotation, Gillingham, "Legends of Richard the Lion Heart," p. 189; second quotation, Gillingham, "Richard I and Berengaria of Navarre," pp.

120. For historiography, see Gillingham, "Richard I and Berengaria of Navarre," pp. 121–22, 130–32.

23. Landon, *Itinerary of Richard I*, pp. 45, 193–94.

24. Richard of Devizes, *Chronicon*, p. 6.

25. Meade, *Eleanor of Aquitaine*, p. 332.

26. Carter, "Arthur I," pp. 200–203; Labande, "Pour une image véridique,"225–26.

27. Richard, *Histoire des comtes de Poitou*, 2:300.

28. Hillion, "La Bretagne et la rivalité capétiens-plantagenêts,"118–19; Landon, *Itinerary of Richard I*, app. E, pp. 207–208; Richard, *Histoire des comtes de Poitou* 2:300–02; Labande, "Pour une image véridique," 225–26; Holt, "Aliénor," 97–99.

29. Duby, *France in the Middle Ages*, p. 218.

30. Richardson, "Letters and Charters," p. 201.

31. West, *Justiciarship*, p. 73.

32. Howden, *Chronica*, 3:100; Pipe Roll 3 Richard I, p. 29.

33. Richard of Devizes, *Chronicon*, p. 58; Owen, *Eleanor of Aquitaine*, pp. 84–85.

34. Richard of Devizes, *Chronicon*, pp. 60–64; *Gesta Regis Henrici Secundi*, 2:236–37.

35. Pipe Roll 4 Richard I, p. 303.

36. *Gesta Regis Henrici Secundi*, 2:237–38; Appleby, *England without Richard*, p. 102.

37. Richard of Devizes, *Chronicon*, pp. 53–54.

38. Richard of Devizes, *Chronicon*, pp. 59–60.

39. Richard of Devizes, *Chronicon*, pp. 59–60; Martindale, "Eleanor," p. 49.

40. Elizabeth A.R. Brown, "Eleanor of Aquitaine: Parent, Queen, and Duchess," p. 21; Richardson, "Letters and Charters," 201–202.

41. Landon, *Itinerary of Richard I*, App. E., p. 205.

42. Gervase of Canterbury, *Opera Historica*, 1:515; see also Landon, *Itinerary of Richard I*, pp. 204–205. The queen-mother assured the prior and monks at Canterbury that fortifications erected there at her prayer would not diminish their liberties.

43. Cheney, *Hubert Walter*, pp. 45–46; Turner, "Richard Lionheart,":7–8.

44. Landon, *Itinerary of Richard I*, p. 76.

45. First quotation, Brown, "Eleanor of Aquitaine: Parent, Queen, and Duchess," p. 21; second quotation, Rymer, *Foedera*, 1:58. Lees, "Letters of Eleanor to Pope Clement III," dismisses these letters as examples of "rhetorical exercise masquerading in the guise of an historical letter." Most authorities, however, accept them as genuine.

46. Howden, *Chronica*, 3:202–03.

47. Howden, *Chronica*, 3:208–10; Landon, *Itinerary of Richard I*, p. 75.

48. Landon, *Itinerary of Richard I*, p. 76; Howden, *Chronica*, 3:208–11; Devizes, *Chronicon*, ed. Appleby, pp. 42–43.

49. Landon, *Itinerary of Richard I*, pp. 86–93.

50. Howden, *Chronica*, 3:134, 252.

51. Bienvenu, "Aliénor et Fontevraud"19, 21; Martindale, "Eleanor of Aquitaine," p. 20. For Eleanor's benefactions, see Marchegay, "Chartes de Fontevraud," 204, 330–31, and a number of grants from 1199 and later in Marchegay, 124–35, 338–39, 340–41, 390; also a rent from her *prévoté* of the Ile d'Oleron for the souls of Henry II, young Henry, "potens vir rex Ricardus," and other sons and daughters (Marchegay, "Chartes de Fontevraud," 337–38).

52. Bienvenu, "Aliénor et Fontevraud," 23–24.

53. Richardson, "Letters and Charters," 205.

54. CDF, p. 338 (no. 1092).

55. Pipe Roll 9 Richard I, p. 98.

56. *Chronicles and Memorials of the Reign of Richard I*, 2:437–48 (Epistolae Cantuarienses).

57. Powicke, *Loss of Normandy*, p. 133.

58. Carter, "Arthur I," p. 200.

59. Howden, *Chronica*, 4:88; Baldwin, *Philip Augustus*, pp. 94–95.

60. Owen, *Eleanor of Aquitaine*, p. 95, citing Kelly, *Eleanor and the Four Kings*, p. 353.

61. Marchegay, "Chartes de Fontevraud,"224–35; in return, William granted the nuns of Fontevraud £100 for clothing.

62. Favreau, "Les débuts de la ville de La Rochelle," 9.

63. Boussard, *Le gouvernement d'Henri II*, pp. 117, 125; Painter, "Castellans of the Plain of Poitou," p. 34; Richard, *Histoire des comtes de Poitou*, 2:335–36; CDF, pp. 389–90 (no. 1099), with John's confirmation, *Rotuli Chartarum*, p. 24b.

64. *Rotuli Chartarum*, p. 25.

65. CDF, p. 473 (nos. 1306–07); Devailly, *Le Berry*, pp. 438–41.

66. *Rotuli Litterarum Patentium*, p. 11, shows it in Hugh's possession in 1202.

67. Citations in Painter, "The Lords of Lusignan," p. 66. The chronology is confused. Labande, "Pour une image véridique," 227 n268, dates the incident to the end of 1199, when in his account Eleanor was en route to Castile; but that journey was in connection with Blanche of Castile's betrothal and so did not take place until after the 1200 treaty of Le Goulet. For the latter explanation see Warren, *King John*, p. 68.

68. "Recueil de documents concernant la commune de la ville de Poitiers,"49–52, nos. 26, 27; John's confirmation is *Rotuli Chartarum*, pp. 4b, 5b; Labande, "Pour une image véridique," pp. 228–29.

69. "Recueil des documents relatifs à l'abbaye de Montierneuf de Poitiers," 182–86, no. 112; CDF, p. 473 (no. 1304); "Cartulaire de l'abbaye de la Grace Notre-Dame ou de Charon," 22–23; Pon, "Fontaine-le-Comte,"39–40; *Gallia Christiana* 2: instrumenta 3899–90; Rymer, *Foedera* 5.i:80; CDF, pp. 450–51 (no. 1248); *Cartulaire de l'église collégiale Saint-Seurin*, p. 349 (no. 351); Audiat, "Saint-Eutrope et son prieuré," (no. 7), and Eleanor's grant to Grandmont of salt-works at Bordeaux and free passage of their ships on the Garonne, *Rotuli Chartarum*, pp. 62–62b.

70. Holt, "Aliénor."
71. *Rotuli Chartarum*, pp. 30–31; CDF, pp. 389–90 (no. 1099); Ralph de Mauléon did liege homage to Eleanor when she granted him Talmond. See Holt, "Aliénor," 96–97; Richardson, "Letters and Charters," 205–07.
72. Powicke, *Loss of Normandy*, pp. 134–35.
73. Howden, *Chronica*, 4:107, 114–15; Pon, "Fontaine-le-Comte," no. 27.
74. William Chester Jordan, "Isabelle d'Angoulême," 824.
75. Ralph of Diss, *Opera Historica*, 2:174; Baldwin, *Philip Augustus*, p. 98.
76. Roger of Howden, *Chronica*, 4:97.
77. Eleanor's letter is Rymer, *Foedera* 1:81–82; *Rotuli Chartarum*, pp. 102b–103; Aimery's letter is *Rotuli Chartarum*, p. 102b.
78. Powicke, *Loss of Normandy*, p. 143.
79. Powicke, *Loss of Normandy*, p. 138.
80. Ralph of Coggeshall, *Chronicon Anglicanum*, pp. 137–38; Labande, "Pour une image véridique," 232.
81. Baldwin, *Philip Augustus*, pp. 191–96.
82. *Recueil d'annales angevines et vendômoises*, p. 21. Andrew Lewis's revision of Eleanor's birthdate as 1124 instead of 1122, accepted by Alfred Richard and others, makes her age at death eighty, not eighty-two (Lewis, chapter 7 in this volume).
83. Gillingham, *Richard Coeur de Lion*, p. 70.
84. Brown, "Eleanor of Aquitaine: Parent, Queen, and Duchess," pp. 23–24, a view that she restates in this volume (chapter 1).
85. Stubbs, *Historical Introductions*, p. 453.

CHAPTER 4

WIFE, WIDOW, AND MOTHER:
SOME COMPARISONS BETWEEN
ELEANOR OF AQUITAINE AND NOBLEWOMEN
OF THE ANGLO-NORMAN AND ANGEVIN WORLD

RáGena C. DeAragon

Comparing Eleanor of Aquitaine with countesses of the Anglo-Norman and Angevin world affords insight into the queen as a female aristocrat and as an individual.

One of the most famous women in medieval European history, Eleanor of Aquitaine has been the subject of many biographies, celebrated in literature, drama, and film. She was undoubtedly an extraordinary woman, but in what ways? How are we to interpret her actions? We may have a general understanding of the contexts for the men of her day but, as Jane Martindale remarks, "it is considerably more difficult to formulate any standards by which the political and social activity of a twelfth-century queen can be assessed—even one who played such a prominent position on the European stage as Eleanor had done all her life since her father's death."[1]

Until recently, relatively little was known of the lives of medieval noblewomen, and therefore most interpretations of Eleanor's life have been founded primarily in relation to men of her class, other medieval queens, medieval literature, or authorial presuppositions about gender. I propose, instead, to examine Eleanor as daughter, heiress, wife, mother, grandmother, and widow (roles that were not strictly political or regal), in comparison

with countesses who lived in the Anglo-Norman and Angevin realms between ca. 1070 and 1230. In attempting such a comparison, I recognize that
interpretation is the name of the historian's game and that no absolute standards exist by which any historical figure can be assessed. I also recognize
that the current state of research on individual medieval women—even
those of high rank—means that mine must be a very preliminary under-
taking. We do not yet fully understand the complexities and nuances of the
world Eleanor inhabited, but periodically testing our assumptions against
insights gleaned from prosopographical research can be helpful. It is not my
purpose here to recount Eleanor's life but rather to provide contexts for
evaluating her life and actions. My results reinforce views about the unique-
ness of some aspects of Eleanor's life and actions while also clarifying those
ways in which she was similar to her noble female contemporaries. This
analysis also urges some caution about using available evidence for determining the emotions and motivations of the people of high-medieval western Europe.

When Duke William X of Aquitaine died in April 1137, his thirteen-
year-old daughter Eleanor had been his presumptive heir for some seven
years.[2] Recently betrothed to the son of Louis VI of France, she was still
living in her father's household. Her own daughters would be betrothed
and given into their fiancés' custody at much younger ages: Marie at eight,
Alice at three; Matilda was betrothed at nine, sent to Saxony at eleven and
married at twelve; Eleanor was sent to Castile at eight and probably wed
not long thereafter; and Joanna went to her fiancé in Sicily at eleven. Two
of Louis VII of France's daughters joined the Angevin royal nursery when
even younger: Margaret, betrothed in her cradle to Eleanor's son Henry,
was married to him when she was two, and Alice arrived aged nine as
Richard's betrothed. In the twelfth century, many an aristocratic girl of
thirteen was already married, or betrothed and living in the household of
her in-laws-to-be.[3] Thus Eleanor's continued residence in Duke William's
domains, rather than at the Capetian court, is cause for remark, especially
with her father leaving on pilgrimage to Compostela. Louis VI surely had
felt some need to have so worthy a prize as the heiress to Aquitaine and
Poitou safely in his own household. Perhaps the widowed William X had
been reluctant to part with his daughter, or perhaps the terms of the betrothal had not been fully sorted out at the duke's death.[4] Perhaps William
had been considering remarriage, which might have seen the birth of a son
to supplant Eleanor as the duke's heir. Whatever the reason, it is surprising
that she was unmarried and still living in Aquitaine at the time of her father's death.

Eleanor's biographers consistently comment on the emotional component of her two marriages. Historians justifiably consider whether twelfth-

century familial relations ever attained the warm, loving solidarity so movingly described in the literary biography of Earl William Marshal of Pembroke. That work's touching deathbed scene, when the dying Earl William asks for a last kiss from his wife Isabel, calling her his "dear love," is said to have brought tears to the eyes of most of those present and, no doubt, to many a reader. Modern romantic sentiment would certainly be satisfied if a marriage between two people of such disparate fortunes and ages evolved into a loving relationship. (William married Isabel in his late thirties or early forties, when she was no more than twenty and probably about eighteen.)[5] While other strongly idealized elements of the *Histoire* of William Marshal should caution against too romantic an interpretation when it is used as historical proof, other evidence substantiates the conclusion that a sense of strong partnership, genuine esteem, and respect developed between Earl William and his wife.[6] If chroniclers can be trusted in these matters, other comital couples whose marriages seem to have been successful on emotional as well as familial and practical bases include Earl Robert III ("Blanchmains") of Leicester (d. 1190) and Petronilla de Grandmesnil (d. 1212), and perhaps Isabel de Vermandois (d. ca. 1147) and Earl William de Warrenne II of Surrey (d. 1138). The earl of Leicester often referred to Petronilla as "his dearest wife," an uncommon epitaph for a husband to use in charters. Countess Petronilla not only attested many of Robert's charters; she was also reputedly one of his most important advisors. The couple jointly led an invading force of Flemish soldiers into East Anglia in 1173, in support of the rebellion of the young King Henry, and were captured and sent abroad into captivity together.[7] If the English chronicler Henry of Huntingdon was referring to Earl William de Warrenne II when he mentioned an unnamed but high-ranking lover of Isabel de Vermandois during her marriage to Count Robert of Meulan (d. 1118), then their marriage, immediately after Count Robert's death, was probably a love match.[8] But these couples whose happiness was publicly known and remarked upon represent a tiny proportion of the total number of noble couples. Is it wise to assume that members of the aristocracy, Eleanor included, expected such emotional satisfaction within their marriages and would be unhappy if they did not achieve it? Experience should teach us how difficult it is to judge our contemporaries' happiness from their actions, let alone those who lived over eight centuries ago.[9]

Another relationship that carries heavy emotional baggage in the modern world is that between individuals and their mothers-in-law. Given aristocratic males' relatively early ages at first marriage, and the very young ages at first marriage for aristocratic females, many a mother lived to see at least her eldest son married, but evidence is scant for the nature of relations between mothers- and daughters-in-law of this period. Both

Eleanor's husbands had widowed mothers alive at the time they married her. Louis VII's mother, Adelaide of Maurienne (d. 1154), outlived the span of his marriage to Eleanor, of whom Adelaide was reputedly not fond. Since Adelaide retired from court to her dower lands within a year of Eleanor's arrival in Paris, and later took a second husband, she apparently played little role in the royal couple's lives.[10] Henry II's mother was quite different. Claimant to the English throne in her own right, Matilda "Empress" (1103?–67) maintained some authority and regal presence in Normandy during her son's reign. The nature of her formal power there is not entirely clear, but for the most part she freed Henry to attend to the governance of other areas of his domains.[11] Surely it is no coincidence that Henry II sent Eleanor to preside in Poitiers in 1168, the year after Matilda died. As Eleanor had by then finished with childbearing, she may have been filling much the same role in Poitou as Matilda had filled in Normandy.[12] A widow might retire to her dower lands, as Adelaide of Maurienne had done, or to a religious community, graciously or grudgingly turning over the management of the royal household to her successor. Adelaide's departure may have been grudging, for she had been the most powerful Capetian queen until that time.[13] Others have noted that, like her daughter-in-law, Matilda "Empress" had married as a second husband a count of Anjou much younger than herself, and that for both women this was a demotion in status. While Matilda initially might have had reason to resent her son's marriage without her consultation, and to fear the reprisals that the marriage might prompt from Louis VII, she could have had, or evolved, some sympathy for Eleanor, especially after the birth of her first grandchild, William, in 1153. The two women seem, however, to have met only rarely. We really have no basis on which to decide how they got along, other than hunches based on our reading of their personalities. Among the nobility, I know only of Petronilla (d. 1212) and Loretta de Braose (d. ca. 1266), successive countesses of Leicester, whose examples provide limited insight into this common relationship. The elder dowager countess, Petronilla, challenged Loretta's right to certain dower lands in 1205. She claimed that these estates were part of her rightful inheritance as heir to the Grandmesnil honor, which complicated an already difficult succession to the Leicester honor and cannot have endeared Petronilla to her beleaguered daughter-in-law. The courts eventually awarded a lucrative manor to Petronilla in partial recompense.[14]

Given Eleanor's limited contact with her first mother-in-law, Queen Adelaide cannot bear responsibility for the problems between Eleanor and Louis. Though the motives on both sides are generally understood, it is not clear who initiated their divorce; there were more political motivations for the divorce on Louis's part, but it has been suggested that Eleanor was the real instigator.[15] Yet only one earlier countess in twelfth-century western Christendom is known to have initiated a divorce: Countess Beatrice of Guines (d. 1146). Heir to a cross-Channel estate, Beatrice in 1137 had married Aubrey de Vere III (d. 1194), heir to a sizeable English barony. Young Vere was to safeguard Beatrice's hold in Guines against a rival male claimant. Almost immediately following his installation as count of Guines in 1138, however, he returned to England, abandoning his wife and ignoring several summons to return to Guines. Admittedly, there was much to keep him busy in England: the civil war between Stephen and Henry II's mother Matilda had intensified, Aubrey's father had been murdered, and he himself had been made earl of Oxford by Matilda "Empress." When the Guines party finally sought an annulment ca. 1145, it may have come as a relief to both spouses.[16]

If some of Eleanor's contemporaries did believe that she had initiated her well-publicized divorce, her actions may have inspired other noblewomen to follow in her footsteps. Constance (d. 1201), heir to the duchy of Brittany and the English earldom and honor of Richmond, and widow of Eleanor's son Geoffrey (d. 1186), married (1187) as her second husband Henry II's nominee, Earl Ranulf III ("de Blundeville") of Chester (d. 1232). Constance's relationship with Ranulf was turbulent, undermining the king's likely intention that the earl would maintain a strong Angevin presence in Brittany. The independent Constance, staunch supporter of her son Arthur's claims to the Angevin patrimony, suffered a fate similar to that of her former mother-in-law: in 1196 Ranulf captured her en route to finalizing negotiations with Richard I and confined her in at Beuvron for at least a year. Soon after her release, she seems to have sought an annulment of the Chester marriage, and chose a third husband for herself: the Angevin nobleman Guy de Thouars (d. ca. 1213).[17] Matilda de Mandeville (d. 1236), countess of Essex in her own right and by marriage countess of Hereford, instituted annulment proceedings in 1232 to free herself from her second husband, the Wiltshire lord Roger de Dauntsey (d. 1238). She received her annulment by April 1233, though a papal review board overturned the decision three years later.[18] Castles and lands that comprised Matilda's inheritance and dower, and from which she had made grants "in free widowhood" during those three years, were ordered restored to Dauntsey in July 1236, a few months before Matilda died.[19]

Some historians have been surprised by, or critical of, Eleanor of Aquitaine because only two months elapsed between her divorce and remarriage. They have suggested only personal or emotional reasons for that swiftness or for the divorced queen's choice of Henry of Anjou as a second husband. As Jane Martindale has pointed out, however, political reasons compelled Eleanor's rapid acquisition of a second husband, as did concerns for her personal safety.[20] A significant number of Anglo-Norman and Angevin countesses who remarried did so within a year or two of being widowed. The briefest interval of widowhood among these women may, indeed, have lasted no more than a few days. Henry of Huntingdon reports that Earl William de Warrenne of Surrey married Isabel de Vermandois, countess of Meulan and Leicester, in 1118 while her first husband Earl Robert was on his deathbed, but it is more likely (if less titillating) that they married almost at once after Robert's death.[21] The heiress Lucy, later countess of Chester (d. ca. 1138), married Earl Ranulph ("le Meschin") of Chester (d. ca. 1129) within a month of the death of her first husband Ivo Taillebois (d. ca. 1094); she married again within a year of Ranulph's death.[22] During the civil wars of Stephen's reign, perhaps because of the turbulent times, some widowed countesses remarried quite soon, generally within six months to a year. To some degree, the wealthier and younger the widow, the shorter the interval between her marriages.[23] The chronology of these countesses' second and third marriages suggests that Eleanor's contemporaries may have been less dismayed by the brief interval between her marriages than by the speed with which she became pregnant after her second wedding.

Eleanor's eleven childbirths were spaced over twenty years and continued into her forties. This was by no means a record, though her children's survival to adulthood is remarkable: she and Henry II may have lost only two children. Countess Isabel of Pembroke (d. 1220), wife of Earl William Marshal (d. 1219), and her daughter and namesake Countess Isabel of Gloucester (d. 1239/40), both equalled Eleanor's record, even producing five children of each sex. But all three women were surpassed by Isabel de Vermandois, who had thirteen children by two husbands. For the forty-seven countesses of the Anglo-Norman and Angevin periods known to have given birth at least once, the average number of recorded children per mother is 3.9.[24] Despite the long delay before her first successful pregnancy with Louis VII, then, Queen Eleanor was more fecund than the average ranking noblewomen of that period, and she may have produced exceptionally healthy children.[25]

Much has been made of Eleanor's "neglect" of her offspring during their childhoods, especially her abandonment of her two daughters by Louis VII after their divorce. Yet I am struck by evidence for the extent of her contact with the children of her second marriage.[26] Those children sometimes travelled with her, even crossing the Channel as infants in her entourage. Soon after her daughter Matilda's birth in the summer of 1156, Eleanor crossed to the continent with three of her older children (all under the age of three), and returned to England the next year while pregnant with Richard.[27] Given the dangers of twelfth-century travel, and the obvious bother of travelling with small children under any conditions, one would expect that the children would have been entrusted to caretakers, as her elder daughter by Louis VII must have been while her parents were on crusade. Eleanor's 1160 visit to Normandy with five-year-old Henry and Matilda, aged four, had a compelling practical purpose: young Henry's marriage to his betrothed, Louis VII's daughter Margaret, in order to secure her dowry, the Vexin.[28] Perhaps the most potentially dangerous of any of Eleanor's winter crossings with her children took place in January 1163, when she and Henry II returned to England with the French Margaret and their own daughters, Matilda, six, and one-year-old Eleanor. But other journeys were undertaken with the royal children in the hazardous late fall or winter months, as well as during more felicitous times of the year.[29] It also appears that some or all of her children were often with their parents during Christmas festivities until 1166, when Eleanor gave birth to John while young Henry celebrated with his father at Poitiers.[30] It is probably wrong to picture the queen standing on the deck of a ship holding an infant in her arms while a toddler clutches her skirt. But such frequent travel in her children's company argues against the view of Eleanor as a neglectful mother who was uninterested in her children until they became politically useful to her as adults. For no other noblewoman do we have similar evidence of such close contact with her children, but nonetheless we do not assume an absence of motherly concern. Contact is not equivalent to affectionate concern, of course, but here the evidence is insufficient. It is unlikely, for example, that messages between mothers and children would have been preserved.[31] As with many working mothers today, she could well have chafed at the necessity of being separated from her children even as she relished the challenges that kept her from them. For the medieval aristocratic mother, was there any equivalent to the modern "quality time" with children? The queen's critics levelled many charges against her, but being a bad mother was not among them. Had Eleanor been particularly neglectful by the standards of her day, her many detractors would have pointed out such a fault.

Among the "faults" thus ascribed to her was her visible nonconformity to the standards expected of, and imposed upon, the wives of powerful men. Even while married, Eleanor may have tried to act with the freedom generally accorded only to widows. In Linda Mitchell's words, "Independent noble widows were ubiquitous in thirteenth-century England. They controlled large amounts of land, they frequently preferred to remain single, and they were fully capable of handling their families and their tenants with an iron fist."[32] But Eleanor's independence occasionally had unpleasant repercussions: Louis VII removed her from Antioch by force, and Henry II confined her in England for sixteen years. She is not the only

wife known to have suffered captivity at her husband's orders: I have noted
above Constance of Brittany's imprisonment by Earl Ranulf of Chester,
and Countess Agnes of Oxford (d. ca. 1214) and Countess Isabel of
Gloucester and Mortain (d. 1217) were also confined for various periods.
The first earl of Oxford, Aubrey de Vere (d. 1194), had tried to divorce his
young third wife, Agnes of Essex, and shut her up in one of his castles after
she appealed her case to the pope on May 9, 1166. The bishop of London
learned of her predicament and ordered the earl, under threat of God's justified wrath, to restore her to liberty, permit her to seek counsel, and to
treat her as his wife at table and bed while the pope had the case under
consideration.[33] Countess Isabel's captivity was less strict than Agnes's but
lasted much longer. Her first husband, Eleanor's youngest son John, divorced her in 1200 on grounds of consanguinity; when they had married
in 1189, John had been count of Mortain, but by the time of their divorce
in 1200 he wore the crown of England and may already have chosen Isabel's replacement. John kept his ex-wife shut away and her inheritance in
his own hands, though he later awarded part of it to Isabel's nephew, her
eldest sister's son; occasionally, he sent her gifts of wine and cloth.[34] Only
when the king decided to shop her marriage for 20,000 marks, which Earl
Geoffrey de Mandeville III of Essex (d. 1215) agreed to pay in 1214, did
John release Isabel and the remainder of her inheritance.[35]

The beginning of Queen Eleanor's fifteen-year widowhood coincided
with her release from captivity in 1189. The chances are very good that
had she been a vassal rather than the mother of two kings, she would have
taken a third husband despite her age, or paid the fine for royal permission
to remain single. During her son Richard I's reign (1189–99), 66 percent
of widowed countesses in England remarried, and of the remainder, many
paid the crown to control their own marital rights.[36] The choice might not
be a matter of personal preference, as Countess Hawise of Aumâle and
Essex (d. 1213/14) discovered. Left childless at the death of her first husband Earl William de Mandeville I of Essex in 1189, Hawise is said to have
resisted pressure to marry Richard I's nominee for her second spouse:
William de Forz, a Poitevin who was to command Richard's fleet on the
imminent crusade. In retaliation, Richard ordered that her chattels be
seized and sold. Hawise capitulated and married William after less than a
year's widowhood. In one respect the marriage was a success, for despite
William's absence on crusade and his death in 1195, the couple produced
a son and heir to Aumâle. Hawise's second term as a widow may have been
even shorter than her first, for Richard I's need for funds had not diminished. A minor lord from Artois, Baldwin de Béthune, became her third
husband before July 1196; at his death in 1212, Hawise paid King John
handsomely for the right to remain single.[37]

Scholars have long noted that the succession to the English crown did not follow the same rules of inheritance that the royal courts applied to the landholding class. Considerations other than strict adherence to primogeniture could and did prevail when it came to who would wear the crown—the sex of the claimant, for example, as in the case of Henry II's mother, Matilda. But by the end of the twelfth century, the aristocracy of England had accepted the custom of primogeniture, which could prevail despite relatives' wishes and permit a female, or a minor of either sex, to inherit to the exclusion of an adult male. Beatrice de Say (d. ca. 1197) discovered the strength of this custom after the death of her nephew, Earl William de Mandeville of Essex (d. 1189). William's nine-year marriage to Countess Hawise of Aumâle was childless, and in 1189 his heir was his paternal aunt Beatrice, then in her eighties. She wished to turn over the Mandeville honor to her younger son, Geoffrey de Say (d. 1214), rather than to the daughters of her deceased elder son William (d. ca. 1177). Richard I was then preparing for his crusade and, desperate for funds, allowed an exception to the rule of primogeniture for an appropriately large sum of money. But when Geoffrey de Say fell behind on his payments, Geoffrey fitz Peter (d. 1213), husband of Beatrice's eldest granddaughter, was well-positioned within the royal administration and successfully advanced his wife's claims to the earldom. Fitz Peter arranged to have his counteroffer accepted and eventually became earl of Essex in his wife's right.[38] Queen Eleanor's support for her youngest son John as Richard I's heir, to the exclusion (and eventual death) of her grandson Arthur of Brittany, is reminiscent of, if more successful than, Beatrice de Say's attempt to advance her younger son at the expense of her granddaughters.

Mothers and grandmothers probably played a larger role in family marriage negotiations than has been recognized, suggesting or even selecting spouses for their children and grandchildren. Scholarly focus on feudal lords' legal rights over the marriages of minor heirs and heiresses, and the assumption that fathers negotiated their children's marriages, has distracted attention from the examples we have of female involvement in the process. Certainly Eleanor had a hand in the selection and safe delivery not only of Berengaria of Navarre as a bride for her son Richard I, but also of her granddaughter Blanche of Castile as a wife for the future Louis VIII of France.[39] Countess Emma of Guines (d. ca. 1140)—rather than her husband, Count Manasses (d. 1137)—was reportedly responsible for selecting Aubrey de Vere III as a husband for her granddaughter Beatrice, heir to Guines.[40] Yet even if widowed, a mother's involvement in such matters is generally hidden from view, though we know that the dowager Countess Margaret of Winchester arranged her daughter Hawise's marriage to Earl Hugh de Vere of Oxford in 1222/23 (and paid the crown 400 marks for the license).[41]

Aristocratic women of all levels patronized religious houses, both as wives and as widows. Some were founders or cofounders of houses, and not just houses for women. The full story of women's contributions to monasticism is yet to be written, but some conclusions can be drawn.[42] Thanks to monastic scribes and sixteenth- and seventeenth-century antiquarians, we possess sufficient records to ascertain where many countesses made their benefactions. (By reason of this evidence, we are, in fact, likely to know more about this than almost anything else about medieval aristocratic women.) Most dowager countesses did not have the independent resources to found a religious house of any size on their own, though hospitals and canonries might not be beyond their pocketbooks. Among the few who did so in their widowhoods were Countess Ela of Salisbury, who founded Lacock Abbey and later became its abbess; Countess Lucy of Chester, founder of Stixwould priory for Cistercian nuns; and Countess Judith of Northumbria, who established the Benedictine nunnery at Elstow. Queen Eleanor, as the wealthiest heiress in Western Europe, had the funds to found even an expensive Benedictine monastery but chose to establish a cell of Fontevraud at La Rochelle ca. 1180.[43]

While the dowager queen spent many of her later years at Fontevraud Abbey, old age need not automatically have led to religious retirement for royal or aristocratic women. Only ten percent of the dowager countesses I have studied for the period 1066–1230 are known to have joined a religious community, adopted a formal religious life, or retired informally to a monastery.[44] Again, we are hampered by a dearth of evidence for most, but even if we amplify that percentage to account for the records' silence, we must conclude that a majority of widowed countesses did not choose a formal religious life or setting for retirement. Such a choice may have been predicated on personal and familial factors. Countess Ela of Salisbury, for example, seems to have hoped that her entry into the community at Lacock would allow her to surrender her inherited title and estates to her son.[45] Queen Eleanor apparently chose Fontevraud for several reasons. She and her family had a close association with the monastery, and she had been its patron for many decades. Its location on the frontiers between Poitou and Anjou symbolized the link between her lineage and that of King Henry; perhaps it appealed to her as an order subject to the rule of an abbess.

Many aristocrats of both sexes devoted considerable time to planning their funeral and burial arrangements, though their wishes could be, and occasionally were, overturned by surviving kin. As Christopher Daniell has noted, "The monasteries were the preferred choice [for burial], not because the person might have been a generous benefactor, but because it was the family's traditional resting place."[46] But for a woman, which family? Natal? Marital? And which husband: first, last, most beloved, most eminent? There seems to have been some freedom of choice in terms of burial site for widows, perhaps slightly less for noblewomen who were married at the time of death. Of the nineteen countesses whose final dispositions are known, there is a fairly even distribution between those who were buried with their husbands, those entombed in religious houses they founded or patronized, and those who were laid to rest in a patrilineal mauseoleum.

At least six Anglo-Norman and Angevin countesses were buried beside their comital spouses. This set includes two of the three wives of Aubrey de Vere III, first earl of Oxford: Eufemia (d. 1153/54) and Agnes of Essex (d. ca. 1214), who were interred beside him in his family's foundation at Colne in Essex.[47] In or about 1153, Vere's second wife Countess Eufemia issued one of the few existing charters recording the wishes of any twelfth-century woman for the disposition of her remains. Most likely on her deathbed, she granted 100 shillings' worth of land from her *maritagium* to Colne Priory and stipulated that her body be buried there.[48] The dowager Countess Adeliza of Eu (d. ca. 1198) must have requested burial with her first husband, Count John, at Foucarmont, for she had given permission for him to take the cowl there before his death.[49] Her second husband, Alured de St. Martin, had founded a Cistercian abbey at Robertsbridge in Sussex, which Adeliza had also patronized, and if she had predeceased Alured he would most likely have had her interred in his foundation.[50] Stipulating that one's heart be buried in a different place than one's body could provide a compromise when one wished to resolve competing loyalties. The dowager Countess Christine of Essex (d. 1232) chose that option. Her body was laid next to that of her first husband, Earl William de Mandeville II of Essex (d. 1226/27), in the Gilbertine house at Shouldham founded by his father Earl Geoffrey fitz Peter (d. 1213); but her heart was apparently taken to Binham Priory, to which she and her parents Robert fitz Walter and Gunnor de Valoines had contributed.[51]

Another six dowager countesses apparently favored for their final resting places houses associated with their parents. These six included heiresses, such as Countess Denise of Devon (d. 1221), daughter of the prince of Déols, and Countess Isabel of Surrey (d. 1203), daughter of Earl William de Warenne, who inherited their patrimonies in their own right; or Countess Philippa of Warwick (d. 1265), an heiress of the Basset family. As heiresses, these women may have been encouraged to maintain a permanent association with their patrilineage in this manner. While another heiress, Countess Alice de Gant of Northampton (d. ca. 1185), requested burial at the Gilbertine house at Sempringham that she had supported, she was probably interred at the Augustinian house at Bridlington established by her paternal grandfather Walter de Gant.[52]

Five dowager countesses were buried in religious houses they themselves had founded or patronized. In the case of Countess Ela of Salisbury
(d. 1261), her eventual status as a cloistered nun and abbess of Lacock
Abbey assured her right to be laid to rest there.[53] Countess Rohese of
Essex (d. ca. 1167) retired to the Gilbertine priory at Chicksands she had
cofounded with her second husband, Payn de Beauchamp (d. ca. 1156), but
seems to have lived there as a pensioner rather than as a vowed member of
the community. She was eventually interred there in a place of honor beneath the chapter house floor.[54] Rohese apparently attempted to have her
eldest son, Earl Geoffrey de Mandeville III of Essex (d. 1166), buried at
Chicksands rather than at Walden Abbey, which his father Earl Geoffrey I
(d. 1144) had founded. When apprised of the planned destination of her
son's funeral cortège, Rohese approved a plan to ambush it and bring his
body to Chicksands. Her plan failed when the cortège was alerted to the
threat and took a different route.[55] The site of burial clearly had several lay-
ers of meaning for members of the aristocracy.

It is unclear exactly what role, if any, Queen Eleanor played in Henry
II's burial at Fontevraud, but she was certainly involved in Richard I's burial there and stipulated that she be interred with her son and husband.
Eleanor almost certainly commissioned the effigies that marked the royal
burials in the nave of the church at Fontevrault and endowed there the
commemoration of the anniversary of her death.[56] Thus the queen was
able to fulfill all three options I delineate above: Fontevrault had been patronized by her ancestors as well as Henry's; the royal couple had added
their own benefactions; and it was the final resting place of her husband
and favorite son. At the same time, this act allowed her to maintain at least
a semblance of family solidarity.

One aspect of Eleanor's life story that has generally invited comment is
her longevity. At the lowest estimate, she was eighty years old at her death
in 1204. By modern standards that is not exceptional for an upper-class female, but it has seemed extraordinary for people of premodern times.[57]
One obstacle to ascertaining whether Eleanor's lifespan was unusually long
for her time is our lack of information on birth and death dates for almost
everyone of the twelfth and thirteenth centuries. The births and deaths of
aristocratic daughters, moreover, were less likely to be noted in surviving
records than those of sons. As I have stated elsewhere, however, in those
few cases for which we have sufficient evidence to deduce life spans, a significant number of countesses lived beyond their seventieth birthday.[58]
These include Countess Bertrade of Chester (d. 1227), Countess Cecily of
Hereford (d. 1204/07), Countess Ela of Salisbury and abbess of Lacock (d.
1260), Countess Eleanor of Salisbury (d. 1232/33), Countess Isabel of Oxford (d. 1245), and Countess Lucy of Chester (d. ca. 1138). One of the

longest-lived of the queen's contemporaries was Countess Loretta of Leicester, who died in 1266 when she was at least eighty-six years old (she spent sixty-six of those as a childless widow, and at least forty-five as a recluse associated with Hackington, near Canterbury).[59] And over six percent of the landholding widows whose approximate ages are recorded in the 1185 *Rotuli de Dominabus et Pueris et Puellis* (a total of eighty-two women) are listed as seventy or older.[60] Queen Eleanor was probably not, therefore, exceptionally long-lived for a woman of her class and time, but she did remain extremely active until the very end of her life. While no other elderly noblewoman of the period seems to have undertaken long, arduous journeys, or endured a siege in their late seventies as Eleanor did, several appear to have been active, capable, and valued members of their society far into old age. The king consulted Countess Loretta concerning "the rights and liberties of the earldom and honor of Leicester" just a year before her death.[61] Beatrice de Say, née Mandeville, inherited the estate of the earls of Essex in 1189, when in her eighties and, as noted above, was considered competent to arrange its transfer to her surviving younger son, Geoffrey de Say.[62] Countess Isabel of Oxford actively collaborated in her final years with the bishop of Carlisle to build a larger priory for the Dominicans just south of the town of Oxford.[63]

On the basis of these comparisons, we can identify ways in which Eleanor of Aquitaine's career was like and unlike those of other noble women of her time. She was betrothed fairly late for an heiress of her status and wealth, and though she experienced a late first pregnancy she was ultimately a more prolific childbearer than many other noblewomen. The frequency and number of her pregnancies does not seem to have jeopardized her health and certainly did not cut short her life. Divorce freed her from a difficult spouse but cost her personal contact with her daughters by Louis VII, though again we have no way of knowing how this affected any of them. Only one comital divorcée had children by her divorced spouse: Countess Juliana of Norfolk (d. 1199/1200) may have maintained or reestablished a relationship with her son and heir Roger Bigod, for in several of his grants to religious houses he mentioned her by name, and he paid her outstanding debts after her death.[64] For the children of Eleanor's second marriage, there is ample and unique evidence of fairly regular contact in the children's youth with all but the youngest, but the evidence provides too little information to judge emotional connections between mother and child. In common with aristocratic widows who remarried, Eleanor took a second husband very soon after her divorce. She was not the first or only noble wife kept in captivity by a husband's command, though hers was the longest confinement before 1230. Like many wealthy women, she founded and supported religious houses but, as most noble widows did not retire to a religious community, her retreat to Fontevraud Abbey was a matter of personal and political choice. The queen was unusually active for all but the last few years of her life. Like other mothers, grandmothers, and particularly widows, she played a vigorous role in family matchmaking and burial arrangements.

Desmond Seward has said that Eleanor of Aquitaine "will always remain a fascinating enigma."[65] Perhaps she has seemed puzzling in part because we have too little knowledge of her world. We may have turned to romance to fill the gaps in our understanding because we have lacked sufficient contexts for understanding her. Though as queen she was set apart from other noblewomen in rank, wealth, and influence, Eleanor shared some aspects of her life with her aristocratic sisters. Many of the differences I have identified, however, stem perhaps more from Eleanor's personality and choices than from her regal status. As with so many perennially intriguing figures in history, our fascination with Eleanor may be sparked by her individual response to the circumstances of her life. It has been difficult to judge the full individuality of those responses when knowledge of her female contemporaries was lacking. Research on her regal and comital sisters will help us to understand this famous and fascinating woman.

Notes

My thanks to John Carmi Parsons and Bonnie Wheeler for the opportunity to expand my horizons; to R.M. Volbrecht, R. Mortimer, and H. Braun for their support; to Sir J.C. Holt for setting my research sights on aristocratic widows; and in memory of colleagues and friends Victoria Chandler and Tom Keefe. I am indebted to the ACLS, the College Colloquium of the Association for Religion and the Intellectual Life, and Gonzaga University for funding my research.

1. Jane Martindale, "Eleanor of Aquitaine," pp. 44–45.
2. See Lewis, chapter 7 in this volume.
3. Below the level of royalty, few cases of such practices are known in detail. Because of an appealed suit, we know that Agnes, daughter of the royal constable Henry of Essex, was handed over to the custody of her betrothed, Geoffrey de Vere II, when she was three years old. As Geoffrey's household was not equipped to deal with such a small child, Agnes remained for three years in the custody of his brother, the earl of Oxford (*Letters and Charters of Gilbert Foliot* p. 215 n162).
4. Brown states that the duke did not arrange Eleanor's betrothal to young Louis, but put her and his lands in Louis VI's guardianship before he left for Compostela ("Eleanor as Parent, Queen, and Duchess," pp. 12–13). I find it difficult to believe that, given Eleanor's age, her father would not have arranged her betrothal at the same time, unless he gambled that as her

guardian, Louis VI would secure her betrothal to his son and heir as soon as word of the duke's death reached him.

5. Mullally, "Portrayal of Women," 358–59. But Duby, *William Marshal,* pp. 15 and 124–25, says William was almost fifty, Isabel at most seventeen. Painter, *William Marshal,* p. 76, says that Isabel was "some" nineteen years old and William over twenty years her senior. Crouch, *William Marshal,* pp. 61–62, says Isabel was no older than twenty, and William about forty-two years old.

6. Mullally, "Portrayal of Women," pp. 358–60.

7. *Jordan Fantosme's Chronicle,* pp. 72–79. The chronicler portrays Countess Petronilla as a major influence on her husband during the rebellion against Henry II; when she urges him to action, the earl is reported to have responded, "I needs must take your advice, for greatly have I loved you" (pp. 72–73). For an example of Earl Robert's use of the superlative in a charter, see Dugdale, *Monasticon* 6.2: no. 3 at p. 1079.

8. Henry of Huntingdon, *Historia Anglorum,* ed. Greenway, p. 598 n39. One other couple reputed to have been well-matched emotionally as well as socially were Earl William de Mandeville II of Essex and Countess Hawise of Aumâle. Ralph de Diceto suggested that the happiness of their marriage was foreshadowed because their wedding took place on the feast of St. Felix (January 14) (*Opera Historica,* ed. Stubbs, 2:3). That alone would hardly constitute acceptable evidence of a loving relationship, though it is interesting that in several of the bequests Hawise made long after William's death, when she had twice remarried, he is described as her husband ("domini mei") in *pro anima* clauses with no mention of her subsequent spouses. In one charter, Hawise specifies that she is in free widowhood after the death of her (third) husband Baldwin de Béthune, but only Earl William is mentioned in the *pro anima* clause, again as "domini mei" (Dugdale, *Monasticon* 5: no. 3 at p. 334).

9. Alexander, "Medieval Biography," 357–58.

10. On Queen Adelaide's career, see Owen, *Eleanor of Aquitaine,* p. 17, and Nolan, "The Queen's Body," pp. 249–67. See also Facinger, "Medieval Queenship," 1–47.

11. Chibnall, *Empress Matilda,* pp. 159–162.

12. My thanks to John Carmi Parsons for suggesting this point.

13. Labarge, *A Small Sound of the Trumpet,* p. 47; Facinger, "Medieval Queenship," 3–48.

14. Powicke, "Loretta, Countess of Leicester," p. 255.

15. Owen, *Eleanor of Aquitaine,* p. 30–31.

16. There is some doubt that the marriage was consummated; the bride was young and sickly. See Lambert of Ardres, *Historia Comitum Ghisnensium,* chap. 60 at p. 591. See also Duby, *Medieval Marriage,* p. 101 n35.

17. Johns, "Wives and Widows of the Earls of Chester," 127–28.

18. Cokayne, *Complete Peerage* 5:134 and 6:458–59.

19. *CPR 1232–1247,* p. 154; *Annales Monastici,* ed. Luard, 3:144.

20. Martindale, "Eleanor of Aquitaine," pp. 42–43.

21. Henry of Huntingdon, *Historia Anglorum,* ed. Greenway, p. 307.

22. Ingulph of Crowland, *Chronicle of the Abbey of Crowland,* trans. Riley, pp. 258–60; Cokayne, *Complete Peerage* 3:166, and 7: appendix J, pp. 743–44.

23. DeAragon, "Dowager Countesses," 95. Countess Rohese of Essex, for example, remarried within six months of the death of her first husband, Earl Geoffrey de Mandeville II of Essex, in 1144; he had died excommunicate while in rebellion against King Stephen, and her sons were minors.

24. DeAragon, "Dowager Countesses," 91.

25. Moore, "The Anglo-Norman Family," 153–96.

26. Turner, "Eleanor of Aquitaine and Her Children," 321–35.

27. Owen, *Eleanor of Aquitaine,* pp. 45–46.

28. Owen, *Eleanor of Aquitaine,* p. 48.

29. Owen, *Eleanor of Aquitaine,* pp. 50, 55.

30. Owen, *Eleanor of Aquitaine,* p. 55.

31. Powicke, "Loretta, Countess of Leicester," p. 255.

32. Mitchell, "The Lady is a Lord," 72.

33. *Letters and Charters of Gilbert Foliot,* p. 215 n162. Agnes eventually prevailed, however, and her marriage was declared valid by Pope Alexander III.

34. Warren, *King John,* p. 139.

35. Cokayne, *Complete Peerage* 5:691; *Annales Monastici,* ed. Luard, 3:45; Warren, *King John,* p. 202. Her second marriage was short-lived; within two years, the earl died in a tournament accident.

36. DeAragon, "Dowager Countesses," 97.

37. Stenton, *The English Woman in History,* p. 36. Warren, *King John,* p. 189, states categorically that the widowed Countess Hawise was King John's mistress, though she was at least the same age as the king and probably a bit older, and not widowed in John's reign until she was at least forty-six years old.

38. Turner, "The Mandeville Inheritance," 147–72.

39. Owen, *Eleanor of Aquitaine,* pp. 82–85, 96–97.

40. Lambert of Ardres, *Historia Comitum Ghisnensium,* p. 583.

41. Cokayne, *Complete Peerage* 10:215 n"f."

42. For some useful studies, see Thompson, *Women Religious;* Elkins, *Holy Women of Twelfth-Century England;* Cownie, *Religious Patronage in Anglo-Norman England;* and Penelope D. Johnson, *Equal in Monastic Profession.*

43. Marchegay, "Chartes de Fontevraud," 133.

44. DeAragon, "Dowager Countesses," 93–94.

45. *Women of the English Nobility,* p. 201 n32.

46. Daniell, *Death and Burial in Medieval England.*

47. *The Itinerary of John Leland,* appendix 1, p. 146.

48. *Cartularium Prioratus de Colne,* no. 56 at pp. 29–30; Dugdale, *Monasticon,* 6:101.

49. Cokayne, *Complete Peerage* 6:157; *The Cartulary of Blythe Priory,* 1:xix.

50. Dugdale, *Monasticon* 5:66.

51. Cokayne, *Complete Peerage* 5:132.
52. Cokayne, *Complete Peerage* 6:645–46.
53. Cokayne, *Complete Peerage* 11:382.
54. *Itinerary of John Leland* 5:150.
55. Round, "Who Was Alice of Essex?" 250.
56. Nolan, chapter 18 in this volume; Martindale, "Eleanor of Aquitaine," p. 17.
57. Labarge, *A Small Sound of the Trumpet,* p. 51; see also Brown, chapter 1 in this volume, and Lewis, chapter 7 in this volume.
58. DeAragon, "Dowager Countesses," p. 92.
59. Powicke, "Loretta, Countess of Leicester," pp. 247–72. All but Countess Cecily were mothers, and of those, all but Countess Eleanor appear to have interacted with their children, even in old age. Countess Bertrade and Countess Isabel played significant roles in their sons' lives, serving as guardians before the boys came of age and apparently continuing to advise their sons as earls in the early years of their majorities.
60. *Rotuli de Dominabus et Pueris et Puellis.* The ages returned, especially for widows aged over forty, are not particularly accurate, but the estimations can still be useful.
61. Powicke, "Loretta, Countess of Leicester," p. 267.
62. Turner, "Mandeville Inheritance," 148.
63. Jarrett, *The English Dominicans,* p. 82.
64. London, British Library, MS Cott. Vesp. E14, fols. 44–44v; Oxford, Bodleian Library MS Tanner 425, fol. 44v; *The Great Roll of the Pipe for the Second Year of King John,* p. 39.
65. Seward, *Eleanor of Aquitaine,* p. 256.

CHAPTER 5

ALIANORA REGINA ANGLORUM: ELEANOR OF AQUITAINE AND HER ANGLO-NORMAN PREDECESSORS AS QUEENS OF ENGLAND

Lois L. Huneycutt

This study of Anglo-Norman queens of England (1066–1152) explores when and how Eleanor's career deviates from patterns of the previous century and argues that, as England's queen, Eleanor was unable to build upon precedents set by the most successful of her Anglo-Norman predecessors.

The outlines of Eleanor of Aquitaine's career as queen of England and France are well known to the scholarly community. The story of her life as it is so often presented to us is replete, in all the wrong proportions, with dramatic elements of wealth, beauty, power, motherhood, sexual misadventure, and marriages gone awry. The extremes that describe Eleanor— her wealth, her relationships with her royal husbands and sons, her reputation as a poet and patroness, her longevity—make it easy to dismiss her as an exception to the silence, passivity, and anonymity that we "know" were the lot of most medieval women (and, for that matter, most medieval men). But how well do we "know" Eleanor? Personally, perhaps as well as we ever can; there are shadows in any reasonable portrait of her that we can draw from the sources. We "know" her lineage—but what we really know are names and a few legends surrounding her troubadour ancestors. We know nothing of her early education or to what extent she was exposed to

the courtly culture of southern France before she wed King Louis VII and
went to live in Paris. The number of literary works that can actually be
linked to her patronage is surprisingly limited. Her patrimony brought un-
precedented wealth and territory to the Capetian and Angevin monarchies,
but, again, there is much to be learned about her relationships to these rich
southern domains throughout her long life. Finally, we know much about
Eleanor's marriages, her children, and family troubles—but nothing of her
personal views on marriage, childbirth, childrearing, or her relationships
with most of her grown children.[1] Surviving narratives, letters, and charters
reveal something of her patronage patterns, especially toward the religious
order of Fontevraud, but even these documents have not been systematically examined.

We are often left, then, with legends and myths; if the Eleanor who poisoned fair Rosamond has long been discarded, other tales persist. Modern
scholarly ideas about Eleanor are often tainted with the Eleanors of novels, film, and popular biography.[2] And while we can work our way through
these Eleanors, it is sometimes equally difficult to uncover the "real"
Eleanor within the works of medieval chroniclers, some of whom are as
opinionated as the mythmakers of the recent past. But these chroniclers
are, I suggest, valuable when we look at what the authors communicate
about their implicit assumptions. When they praise or condemn Eleanor,
they often tell us less about what "really happened" than about what they
expect a twelfth-century queen should and would do. Their expectations
were often grounded in knowledge of what previous queens had done, either for good or ill.

Within this framework of medieval perceptions and expectations, I
propose to begin a new dialogue about Eleanor of Aquitaine, one that
sees her career within the contexts of twelfth-century queenship and
seeks to identify points of comparison with, and departure from, what
might be called the "norms" of Anglo-Norman and Capetian queenship.
Only in recent years could a study such as the one I am proposing be
carried out. Even a decade ago no such contexts existed. Since about
1990, a number of important works have appeared that, taken together,
allow us to compare queens' lives and careers across times and space in a
meaningful way, even given the dearth of biographical data that is too
often the case with even the most visible of these women. In these
monographs, scholars interested in "queenship" have usually taken one of
two approaches, or a combination of both. They either look at an individual woman in terms of conformity to or deviation from a biologically
dictated life cycle, exploring questions of birth and lineage, betrothal and
marriage, childbearing and childrearing, and so on through widowhood,
death, and burial. Others look at queenship in terms of a model that does

not ignore lineage and marriage but focuses also on what is sometimes called an "office" of queenship.[3]

I use the term "office" cautiously but deliberately. Nothing like a modern office with job description, salary, regular means of appointment, or specific duties existed within any royal administration during the central medieval period, and certainly not for the king's wife. Her position was fluid, her power always dependent upon her relationships to husband and offspring. And yet, there were ceremonial acts, public obligations, expectations to be met, and regular sources of income from lands and monies that were among the prerogatives of queenship. Recent studies tracing these issues have shown some continuity and evolution over time, and it is with this continuity of responsibilities, expectations, and prerogatives in mind that I use the term "office." Such institutional studies typically explore the amount and type of a queen's resources, the degree to which she could control them independently, and the extent to which an individual woman participated in "public affairs." Of course, in the twelfth century, "public affairs" might include anything from presiding over a meeting of the *curia regis* to sitting in judgment over accused criminals, or making decisions and issuing charters in the king's name. As queens distributed lands, money, and offices to court favorites and to religious or educational institutions, patronage studies have also been important and fruitful: following a trail of queenly donations can reveal patterns of religious devotion or suggest reassessments of queens' sponsorship of literary and artistic activities. Many recent works on queenship also take advantage of anthropological insights by demonstrating the importance of ritual in creating and manipulating public perceptions of the queen.

John Carmi Parsons has recently offered a third way to assess the importance of a medieval queen within the society over which she reigned. In his monograph on Eleanor of Castile (d. 1290), first consort to Edward I of England, Parsons admits the impossibility of a truly satisfying biographical study since many details of Eleanor of Castile's life, particularly of her early life, are unknown to modern historians. Seeking the origins of medieval and early-modern commentators' markedly contradictory assessments of his subject, Parsons reconstructs "the formation of popular perceptions" of Eleanor of Castile, "examining theme and context within the intricate relationships between queen and realm. The sources must ultimately be turned to the reconstruction of thirteenth-century English society's experience of Eleanor, both as woman and as queen."[4] This study of norms and expectations of the society in which a queen lives suggests new insights into the nature of queenship itself, and has fruitfully identified expected sources of tension and harmony as a queen interacted with her realm. From this recent work on the women who ruled before and after

Eleanor of Aquitaine emerges an exciting new field that combines traditional political and constitutional history with insights from multiple disciplines and approaches, a field of inquiry that seems to point the way to
a new understanding of Eleanor of Aquitaine within the contexts of contemporary English queenship.

This chapter offers another step toward putting Eleanor back into the
spotlight, not by offering new details of her career but by seeking to qualify
the perception that Eleanor stands "alone of all her sex" as an active, sometimes controversial, queen-consort in twelfth-century England. This prosopographical approach looks at Eleanor's marriage alliances, relations with her
spouse and children, control of wealth, patronage, and public activities, all in
comparison with those of the four Anglo-Norman queens who preceded
her. The women under scrutiny here are Matilda I, or Matilda of Flanders
(d. 1083), wife and queen of William the Conqueror; Matilda II, also called
Edith-Matilda or Matilda of Scotland, the first queen of Henry I, who married him shortly after his accession in 1100 and died in 1118; Adeliza of
Louvain (d. 1151), Henry's second wife and the only one of the Anglo-Norman queens to outlive her spouse; and King Stephen's wife Matilda III, or
Matilda of Boulogne (d. 1152). Examining the activities and historical reputations of these women opens perspectives on the normal course of high-
medieval queenship and identifies points of departure from those norms that
have contributed to Eleanor's modern reputation.

In her classic article on Capetian queenship, Marion Facinger argued
that Louis VI's queen, Adelaide of Maurienne, who reigned from 1115
until her husband's death in 1137, stood at "the apogee of Capetian queenship."[5] It is becoming increasingly clear that the same era also represents an
apogee for English medieval queenship. Margaret Howell points out that
Matilda of Flanders and Matilda of Scotland each had her own household
and domestic officers, control of her own lands, and that each controlled
her own lands and headed a regency government in her husband's absence.[6] The Anglo-Norman era was no golden age even for the most aristocratic of women, but the Anglo-Norman queens did have some
advantages not shared by their immediate predecessors or successors. To
some extent, they stand out as "good queens" simply because they stand
between the controversial later Anglo-Saxon queens and the controversial
thirteenth- and fourteenth-century Eleanors and Isabellas. There are also
personal, perhaps chance, reasons for their success. The Anglo-Norman age
saw four queen-consorts in a row who enjoyed contemporary chroniclers'
near-universal approbation and seem to have had harmonious (dare I write
"happy"?) relations with their spouses. Save for Adeliza, each produced at
least one son, fulfilling their primary duty to secure dynastic succession.
Even beyond personalities, structural factors also allowed the Anglo-

Norman queens their privileged positions. The first two Matildas were trusted queens of kings who ruled on both sides of the English Channel, and as the king's wife and deputy, they each exercised what amounts to vice-regal authority in their respective realms—Matilda I usually presiding in Normandy, and Matilda II in England in her husband's name during several of his continental sojourns. Adeliza of Louvain married Henry I after his administration had matured to the point that it no longer needed the oversight of a family member during the king's absences. Yet like the other Anglo-Norman queens, Adeliza enjoyed substantial control over generous dower property or patrimonies, and like them she seems to have administered that property more independently than would be the case in the thirteenth century or later. Civil war forced Matilda III to take a more active role during her years as England's queen. She assumed leadership of Stephen's government during his captivity and planned several military campaigns during their troubled reign.[7]

The "life-cycle" approach is most easily adapted to a comparative framework, so I will begin there and move to a discussion of the institutional aspects of Anglo-Norman England. There were several times in a queen's life when she was most likely to be of interest to chroniclers, or when she most likely left a record in the narrative sources. First among these is the her marriage and coronation. The negotiations leading to a queen's marriage, and the attendant ceremonies, allowed chroniclers to comment upon a particular woman's suitability, to describe what she brought to the marriage, or to speculate on the reasons for a particular alliance. Sometimes their narratives also pass on colorful and unlikely legends, the kind of "telling anecdote" that serious historians once scorned but that medieval chroniclers deliberately used to crystalize the character or other personal qualities of their subjects. One such anecdote was used to predict the future greatness of Duke William of Normandy. Matilda of Flanders was a daughter of the Flemish Count Baldwin V and his wife, Adela, daughter of the French king Robert the Pious. When told that her father wished her to marry William the Bastard of Normandy, young Matilda is said to have raged that his base birth made him unworthy of her. To avenge this insult, William rode to her father's castle and beat Matilda soundly. The attack made her more enthusiastic about the alliance; she declared that if William were courageous enough to attack her in her father's castle, he obviously had the necessary audacity to accomplish deeds worthy of her bloodline.[8]

Henry I's marriage to Matilda of Scotland also occasioned controversy. This Matilda was the elder daughter of King Malcolm III of Scotland and his queen, Margaret, a descendant of the line of Alfred the Great. A marriage between Matilda and the newly crowned Henry carried the possibility of an heir who would unite the bloodlines of conquerors and conquered. The marriage would also secure the Scottish border, freeing Henry's attention for expansion into Wales and the extension of his continental holdings. But Matilda had been educated in English monasteries, and on more than one occasion had been seen in public wearing a nun's habit. Rumors that she had taken religious vows, or that her parents had meant her for the Church, were circulating when Henry I offered to marry her, and Archbishop Anselm of Canterbury refused to perform the wedding until her status was clarified. Eadmer of Canterbury, Anselm's secretary and constant companion, wrote in the 1130s to defend Anselm against charges that he had wrongly allowed the royal wedding. Eadmer's account shows us a determined Matilda, aware of her bloodline, wanting desperately to become England's queen and aggressively countering any possible objections to the marriage. She sent messengers to Anselm as soon as he returned to England from his continental exile, explained her circumstances, and agreed to testify on her own behalf before an ecclesiastical council. Eadmer tells us that when she was declared free to marry, she received the verdict with a "happy expression."[9] Other writers speculated on the reasons for the marriage. William of Malmesbury reports that Matilda brought little or nothing to the marriage in the way of material goods and spoke instead of a long-standing affection between Henry and Matilda. Several chroniclers agreed that this marriage was indeed a love match. As Matilda was the sister of the king of Scotland, it does seem unlikely that she brought no land or treasure to her marriage, though she may have brought too little to satisfy contemporary expectations.[10]

Three years after Matilda's death in 1118, Henry married a daughter of Godfrey, count of Lower Louvain and duke of Brabant (1106–1128, died 1139) and his first wife, Ide, daughter of Count Henry III of Namur. The marriage seems to have been arranged quickly, prompted by the drowning in 1120 of Henry's only legitimate son, William. The chroniclers are silent on Adeliza's desires or reaction, commenting only that she had the requisite beauty, morals, and character to become England's queen. In addition to giving Henry an opportunity to father more children, the marriage strengthened England's existing diplomatic alliances within the German empire. Henry's decision to have the wedding performed by a diocesan bishop, Roger of Salisbury, led to a dispute with the archbishop of Canterbury, resulting in the articulation of the archbishop's right to serve as royal chaplain anywhere in England.[11] Matilda III, a niece of Matilda II and of the Scottish kings of the early twelfth century, was married to Stephen when his prospect of mounting the throne was remote. We know nothing of her reaction to the marriage. She was countess of Boulogne in her own right, and her wealth and lands greatly brightened Stephen of Blois's economic future. She also brought the prestige of kinship to Europe's most illustrious crusading family: her paternal uncles, Godfrey of Bouillon and Baldwin I, reigned in Jerusalem in the early twelfth century. Matilda's English bloodline became important when Stephen acceded to the throne upon Henry I's death, for through her mother, a sister of Matilda II, her children also carried the blood of the old West Saxon ruling house.

The Anglo-Norman queens were all chosen for their bloodlines and for the political alliances they represented, and the chroniclers hint that "the Matildas" especially were conscious of their worth in that regard. It is also clear from the narratives, however, that medieval commentators (much like modern popular journalists) preferred to believe that a degree of love, or at least mutual affection, obtained for these royal matches. Here Eleanor of Aquitaine appears as a spectacular failure, for her initially harmonious relations with Louis VII and Henry II deteriorated rather swiftly. Modern writers tend to see Eleanor as a woman who took control of her own fate, differentiating herself from the passivity and acceptance believed to be characteristic of other medieval women. With the possible exception of Adeliza, none of the Anglo-Norman queens can be characterized as women who passively accepted fates determined by others. Each seems to have been at least content with her lot, with Matilda II actively seeking to enter marriage. Perhaps the biggest surprise in the marriage alliances of the Anglo-Norman queens is the lack of tangible wealth the women brought to their marriages. Wealth in the form of land was a factor only in the alliance of Matilda of Boulogne and Stephen—and their marriage was not initially a royal alliance. Eleanor of Aquitaine was twice chosen as a royal bride, and in both instances, her landed wealth seems to have been the deciding factor in the alliance. Such wealth is one area in which Eleanor truly stands out from her twelfth-century predecessors, and the extent of her holdings was clearly a noteworthy point for contemporary chroniclers. Her desire to maintain control over her inheritance was clearly an issue in the later twelfth century, but as we shall see, the Anglo-Norman queens did retain control over their smaller dower properties. To whatever extent they violated Angevin legal expectations, Eleanor's demands do not appear out of line with her predecessors' experiences.

Any medieval queen's position often rested on her perceived influence at court rather than on formal institutional powers. The Anglo-Norman queens realized that it was to their advantage at least to appear to have special access to their husbands. Their sexual proximity to the king was one tool with which to forge perceptions of such access, which could allow them to intercede with the king and influence his decisions. Courtiers flattered or bribed the queen to do so, churchmen wrote didactic treatises and letters attempting to direct her intercession, and the Anglo-Norman queens ably persuaded their publics that they indeed had a powerful influence over the king's actions.[12] Matilda II and Matilda III were particularly adept at manipulating the language of persuasion and intercession to their advantage; the wording of Matilda II's documents makes it clear that she considered the intercessor's role an important one, and Matilda III's appeals to Henry of Winchester during Stephen's captivity cannot be other than a carefully staged act of intercession.[13] This is an area in which Eleanor of Aquitaine deviated from perceptible norms: when the sour relations between the queen and her kings became known in court and throughout the realm, her access to the many rewards of successful intercession must also have been lost.

Another time when a queen became visibly interesting to the realm was during pregnancies and births, particularly the birth of a first son and heir. Medieval monarchs, indeed noble families in general, faced many problems regarding their families' futures. Given the medieval rate of infant mortality a couple needed to produce several sons to ensure male succession; but if many sons survived to adulthood, providing for them all could dilute family wealth, force a division of its holdings, or expand the number of potential successors to the father's position. Faced with the choice of too many heirs versus no heir at all, medieval royal families seem to have preferred the first option. Matilda I, for example, gave birth to four sons and up to five daughters. She seems to have been closest to her eldest son, Robert Curthose, who was groomed to succeed his father as duke of Normandy. The names of Matilda and Robert appear frequently together in charters and other Norman acta. At one point when Robert and his father were at war with each other, William found that Matilda had sending Robert messages and probably gifts. The chronicler Orderic Vitalis has Matilda responding with a speech that ought to erase many doubts about medieval family affection. William expresses his outrage that his wife, whom he asserts he loves as his own soul and has trusted with his wealth and his authority, would provide aid and succor to his enemies. Matilda responds with incredulity, wondering why anyone would doubt a mother's affection for a firstborn child. She swears that if Robert were dead and her lifeblood were needed to raise him up, she would gladly let it pour forth for him.[14] Chroniclers seem to assume that a queen should produce many children in order to secure the succession; it is when there are few or no children what the writers believe an explanation is in order. Matilda II produced only a son and a daughter, a fact that medieval chroniclers felt they had to explain. William of Malmesbury says that she was "satisfied with a child of either sex" and retired to a separate life secluded from Henry's busy court, while others suggest that Henry was disgusted by her habit of kissing the open sores of lepers and refused to put his lips to hers.[15] Extant descriptions of Matilda II and her young children are limited to one chronicle, describing Matilda's visits to Merton Priory and her habit of bringing William so he could play on the grounds.[16] Her daughter left England at the age of eight to join her betrothed, the German emperor Henry V. A letter survives from the emperor to Matilda II thanking her for her assistance in some matter of mutual concern. While that concern is unspecified, the letter was possibly written during negotiations leading to the betrothal, showing that Matilda II participated in arranging her daughter's future.[17] Adeliza was assumed to be barren after several years went by and no children were born to the royal couple. Her childless state led to a succession crisis, but somewhat surprisingly, there were no calls for an annulment or other end to her marriage. Her failure to bear a child distressed her, and she sought spiritual advice from the Bishop Hildebert of LeMans, whose comforting letters to her survive.[18] Matilda III gave birth to at least five children of whom two, Baldwin and Matilda, died in infancy before Stephen acceded to the throne. After she became queen, Matilda III commemorated these children in gifts to the Augustinian priory at Holy Trinity Aldgate in London, suggesting a degree of remembrance and grief for very small children rarely noted in medieval sources.[19] Matilda III also personally arranged her son Eustace's marriage to a French princess. There are few hints about the early experiences of the Anglo-Norman queens' children, but adult relations were expected to be amiable; indeed Orderic excuses Matilda I's partiality for the feckless Curthose as something that was to be expected. The limited evidence available also suggests that the royal mothers were routinely involved in decisions about their children's future and in training their children for those futures.

Examination of the normal course of family relationships within the Anglo-Norman royal family provides insights that helps us understand Eleanor of Aquitaine's much-romanticized family life in new ways. Among issues that have troubled commentators is Eleanor's seeming abandonment of her daughters with Louis VII. This early separation was, clearly, less a problem for medieval commentators than modern critics. Medieval mothers and daughters were routinely parted early. Matilda II, for example, cannot have been much more than seven when she was sent from Scotland to England for her education. Her own daughter left England at the age of eight to be educated in Germany in anticipation of her marriage to the future emperor. Another set of relationships that is just beginning to be explored is that of a married queen to members of her natal family. Historians have generally assumed that married daughters ceased to be of interest to their families of origin, but this certainly was not the case with royal brides. Marriage to a foreign king did not mean that a woman was cut off from her natal family or that she ceased to identify herself with her ancestors. The

Conqueror and Matilda I commemorated her family in the names of at least four of their children: Henry, Constance, Matilda, and Adela. Robert, the name chosen for their eldest son, was William's father's name but may have also ultimately recalled Matilda's royal grandfather, King Robert II of France. Matilda II commissioned a biography of her mother, Margaret of Scotland, which she used to help shape her own role as queen.[20] Matilda II and Adeliza actively promoted their siblings' interests and those of even more distant relatives. One account specifically notes that Matilda II's brother, David of Scotland, secured his bride, the widowed countess of Huntington, through Matilda's intercession.[21] Matilda may also have promoted her sister Mary's marriage to Count Eustace of Boulogne. In widowhood, Adeliza granted English lands to a brother and a cousin, in the latter case specifying that the gift was in honor of the cousin's marriage. Her brother attested several of her charters and established a memorial in her name after her death.[22] Before Stephen acceded to the English throne, when the county of Boulogne was the highest honor their children could expect, Matilda III commissioned a life of her saintly paternal grandmother, Ide of Boulogne. She and Stephen also named one of their sons Baldwin, probably in honor of her uncle, the ruling king of Jerusalem.[23] Eleanor of Aquitaine was unusual in having few natal relatives, though that is how a girl becomes an heiress, after all. Her perceived close relations with her uncle, Raymond of Antioch, provoked scandal during the Second Crusade, but one need not join in medieval gossip to understand the appeal of a suddenly re-discovered older, powerful male relative to a woman perhaps already anxious to free herself from an unhappy marriage.

Another area where Eleanor differed from her Anglo-Norman predecessors was her longevity. Of the four Anglo-Norman queens, only Adeliza outlived her husband, with whom she had no children. She made a rather quick second marriage and did her best to live a quiet life during the English civil war. Henry's II's mother, Empress Matilda, lived until 1167, but she never really reigned over England and spent most of her son's reign on the Continent. The last true "queen-mother" in England had been Emma of Normandy (d. 1052), whose family politics were nothing if not controversial.[24] Though it would seem hard to rival the drama of Emma, her multiple marriages, and multiple sons, Eleanor succeeded in doing so. As many have pointed out, it was as queen-mother that Eleanor proved most influential and energetic as she actively supported Richard and, to some extent, John.

The medieval queen-consort's power and influence always depended on her relations with others. The primary relationship was of course with her husband, but natal relatives and children were also important. Institutional issues also factor in, to help or damage a woman's chances of success in her role. A queen's access to resources and control over property could be crucial. Several scholars have attempted to reconstruct the holdings of England's medieval queens, and have succeeded to some degree, but there are many obstacles to the reconstructive process. Royal charters are the logical place to begin such a survey, but vital facts about the nature of land transactions are often concealed beneath charters' formulaic phrasing. For instance, charters that record a queen's granting away or exercising control over certain properties rarely reveal whether she is giving land of her own or acting in a vice-regal capacity. What may look like a donation from the queen turns out to be merely a royal confirmation of someone else's gift. Another problem with relying on charters to reconstruct holdings is that charters normally record alienations of land, and while it is helpful to know what a queen granted away, such grants rarely specify anything about properties or privileges the queen retained. It is also dangerous to assume that a charter represents a decision made by the queen herself. A charter issued in the queen's name could have been drawn up, sealed, and witnessed by royal officers without her personal involvement. Nevertheless, when combined with other record and narrative sources, charters do suggest possibilities and patterns in the extent of a queen's holdings and the degree of control she exercised over them.[25]

Some have speculated that there was, in late Anglo-Saxon England, a group of lands that traditionally formed part of the queen's holdings. The phrase "queen's demesne" is sometimes used, usually in reference to estates in Rutland and surrounding counties that were associated with at least queens Aethelthyrth and Emma in the late tenth and early eleventh centuries. Later, Matilda II and some of the Angevin queens appear in the records administering these lands. No one has claimed that every queen held the lands; that would be impossible if a widowed queen lived into succeeding reigns and retained as dower those lands assigned her as queen-consort. Marc Meyer has argued that, although most later Anglo-Saxon queens held properties of nearly equivalent values, there was little or no true continuity in queenly landholding patterns before 1066.[26] In Edward the Confessor's reign, for instance, the Godwin family held enormous amounts of land, and the holdings of his queen, Edith, reflect her status as a member of that clan as much or more as they do her status as Edward's queen. Edith lived into the Conqueror's reign, retaining most of her holdings, so William I assigned new lands to his queen, Matilda I. After Matilda died in 1083, William I granted most of her English property to the baron Robert Fitz Hamon. By the time Henry I became king in 1100 and married Matilda II, the lands held by the Confessor's widow were again part of the royal demesne, and it was largely from these estates that Matilda II's dower was assigned. Meyer's conclusions have been challenged as premature by Pauline Stafford, who has pointed to the need for a larger history of royal lands in the later Anglo-Saxon era before the queen's landholding patterns or lack thereof can be discerned.[27] There may not have been a group of traditional queenly holdings in the Anglo-Saxon era, but it seems the Normans thought that there were, and Henry I went out of the way to associate these lands with his own Anglo-Saxon queen. Matilda II was assigned lands in and around the city of London, including custody of a wharf district on the Thames then known as "Ethelred's hithe" but called "Queenhithe" ever after. When Matilda died, many of her properties were assigned to her successor, Adeliza, who also got a number of lands not previously associated with the queen-consort. Adeliza's widowhood and her wish to retain control of her lands challenged Matilda III, whose charters often claimed authority over the lands that her aunt, Matilda II, had held. The widowed Adeliza issued charters claiming control over the same properties, once even specifying that Henry had given her these lands "as his queen and as his wife," as if to claim dower rights as well as rights of queenly office. Both queens, for instance, claimed custody of Barking and Waltham abbeys, which had formed part of Matilda II's demesne.[28] In later years, Eleanor of Aquitaine drew royal servants from among Waltham's canons, as did Isabella of Angoulême and Eleanor of Castile in the thirteenth century.[29] Custody of Barking Abbey, and the Queenhithe revenues, also often made up part of the thirteenth-century prerogatives and rights of a queen-consort. It appears that the Anglo-Norman queens were indeed beginning to see themselves as holding something like an "office," including regular sources of income and customary prerogatives, and later evidence suggests that Eleanor of Aquitaine became keenly aware of her rights and privileges over the course of her tenure as England's queen, especially during widowhood. It is also clear that the thirteenth-century queens did not independently control their lands.[30] It may well be that Eleanor's reign will prove to be a turning point that saw the queen's lands and income brought more closely under the jurisdiction of the king's officers. If so, the process of removing lands from the queen's personal jurisdiction may hinge as much on personal factors, such Henry II's lack of trust in his wife, as on impersonal trends, including the rise of administrative kingship.[31]

It was probably during Eleanor's reign that the systematic collection of queen's gold began, but there are hints that this custom originated in Henry I's reign. Hugh the Chanter, York's champion in the Canterbury/York disputes, included in his chronicle an account of one action by Bishop Ranulf Flambard of Durham that describes a bribe to be offered to Queen Matilda II to use her influence in York's favor. Writing about 1130, Hugh reports that Flambard offered the king a thousand marks of silver, and the queen one hundred, for a favorable verdict in the dispute over whether

York's archbishop should profess obedience to Canterbury. According to this highly partisan narrative, Henry refused to listen to the northern bishop, "knowing full well which side could make the better offer."[32] Flambard, William II's chief financial officer, undoubtedly knew his way around the court better than most, but offers such as his may not have been unusual, and it may be no coincidence that he offered the queen ten percent of the amount offered to the king. According to the *Dialogus de scaccario,* written during Henry II's reign, Queen's Gold was a surtax on monies proferred to the king: "those who voluntarily engage to pay coined money to the King, must know that they are likewise bound to the Queen, although that was not stated." Queen's Gold was also due on amercements of the Jews and the ransom of moneyers. The *Dialogus* explains that whoever offered a sum of one or two hundred marks to the king owed the queen "one mark of gold for one hundred marks of silver, two for two hundred, and so on." The money was collected by a queen's clerk, who attended the twice-yearly accounting at the Exchequer. Even if monies owed to the king were remitted, "it will be for the queen to decide about her share, and without her consent, nothing can be remitted or respited." The *Dialogus*'s author acknowledged confusion over whether Queen's Gold was due on sums less than a hundred marks, indicating that the question was in litigation and not yet resolved.[33] This confusion may indicate that Henry II's officials were trying to resurrect an earlier practice that had lapsed under Stephen, or that they were in the process of creating a new practice. Recent work on thirteenth-century queens has shown that Queen's Gold formed a significant source of revenue, but extant sources do not permit us to know when sustained and systematic collection of Queen's Gold began, or how long it continued.[34] An 1167 gift to King Henry II included "one hundred marks of gold to the king and one to the queen," which H.G. Richardson saw as evidence that gold was being collected for Eleanor of Aquitaine before her 1173 disgrace. It is not clear at what point Queen's Gold was allowed only to the current queen-consort. Eleanor seems to have possessed rights to Queen's Gold as part of her dower revenues, which she retained until her death despite the presence of Richard's and John's queens. Indeed, the earliest direct evidence of the collection of Queen's Gold comes from Richard's reign, in a chronicle recording a settlement reached on Queen's Gold owed Eleanor by the monks of Bury St. Edmund's. But even at that date, the chronicler referred to the tax as a "custom of the kingdom." About the same time, the canons of Waltham Holy Cross, who had been providing a clerk to collect the money, received Eleanor's assurance that their service was voluntary and constituted no precedent. Only after Eleanor died in 1204 did John's queen, Isabelle of Angoulême, receive her mother-in-law's dower rights, presumably including Queen's Gold.

Another point of comparison is the composition of the queen's household and the makeup of her staff. Who were the queen's officers? Where and how were they recruited? How much overlap was there between the king's household and the queen's? In deference to Heather Tanner's work on Matilda of Boulogne and Laura Gathagan's on Matilda of Flanders, I will limit my comments here to the queens of Henry I, Matilda II and Adeliza. Each drew chaplains, chancellors, and other officials from the lands over which they exercised jurisdiction. In some cases, officers attested charters solely for the queen or attested the king's charters only in conjunction with the queen. It appears that each of these women was familiar enough with her properties to choose servants from them, and that both understood the patronage potential of their positions. For ambitious clerics, service in the queen's household carried the potential for advancement. Two of Matilda's chancellors were promoted to bishoprics, as were two of Adeliza's. In both cases, members of the queens' natal families remained close to the queens and were part of their households. Matilda II was especially associated with her younger brother David, later David I of Scotland. David was raised in the English court, and attested several of the queen's charters and some of the king's, where David's name usually appears on Henry's charters in conjunction with his sister's. Matilda is said to have interceded on David's behalf in securing him a rich bride and the honor of Huntingdon.

The rise of administrative kingship has been adduced as a factor in the diminishing power of the thirteenth-century queen. The position of Matilda I and II as virtual regents for their husbands allowed them more room to maneuver within the public sphere than most queen-consorts enjoyed. Both issued charters that only the king or someone acting in his name could have granted, and both appear sitting in judgement in lawsuits. Both, in short, exercised all the prerogatives of sovereignty. Matilda III was forced by the circumstances of the war between Stephen and the empress to take on sovereign duties, and was a major catalyst in securing Stephen's release after he had been captured by the empress's forces. Adeliza took little part in governing the realm, never served as a regent, and does not appear as part of the king's curia. C. Warren Hollister assumed Henry I preferred to keep Adeliza by his side in hopes of conceiving a son and heir, and this does seem to have been the case, particularly until about 1130.[35] Personal inclination probably also contributed to Adeliza's absence from the public sphere, but so did the diminishing need, as Henry's government developed, for day-to-day administrative involvement by members of the royal family. Adeliza was a French-speaking noblewoman from Lotharingia who could not have had the same interest in England as Matilda II and Matilda III, who had been raised mostly in England and were descendants of Anglo-Saxon kings. Analysis of Eleanor of Aquitaine's role must take structural and personal factors into account as we examine the queen's marginalization over the course of the thirteenth century. Somewhat surprisingly, very little has been done to reconstruct the administrative structure Eleanor employed.

The last area deserving further study that I wish to mention is that of patronage—of religious houses and movements, the arts and literature. All of the Anglo-Norman queens displayed their piety through founding or giving grants to ecclesiastical houses. All are known to have maintained an international correspondence with continental churchmen. Each queen used gifts to religious houses and orders as a way of furthering her own interests or those of her family. Matilda II and Adeliza were also literary patrons. Besides the life of her mother noted above, Matilda II commissioned the Anglo-Norman version of the life of St Brendan and may also have been the patron of William of Malmesbury's *Deeds of the Kings of England*. I argue elsewhere that Matilda II consciously fostered a taste for Anglo-Saxon metalwork and embroidery as part of her self-concept as an Anglo-Saxon princess.[36] The chronicler Henry of Huntingdon quoted a Latin poem written to celebrate Adeliza's beauty, but she is perhaps best remembered as a patron of French literature. She sponsored Philippe de Thaon's *Bestaire,* and the Anglo-Norman version of the *Voyage of St Brendan* was re-dedicated to her; Geoffrey Gaimar implies that she commissioned a lost verse biography of Henry I from the poet David.[37] This verse biography may represent Adeliza's attempt to write the history of her husband's reign in much the same way that queens Emma and Edith used texts to shape an historical picture of themselves and their husbands. The flurry of donations Eleanor of Aquitaine made in Henry's memory may be part of her attempt to commemorate her husband. The language of these charters will likely repay careful scrutiny by historians sensitive to the possibility that Eleanor used these gifts to shape an historical portrait of her late husband.

As a woman of incomparable wealth and almost incredible longevity, Eleanor of Aquitaine was "alone of all her sex" among the twelfth-century queens of England. Yet, in her role and in the scope of her activities as queen of England, she is eclipsed by her predecessors. Twelfth-century commentators expected a queen to exercise public power wisely, to participate in shaping the cultural life of the realm, and to safeguard the interests of her children. They also expected that the king and queen would trust each another and that the queen would act for the well being of her husband and the realm. Eleanor's seeming refusal, or inability, to act within the expectations of a wife and consort thus placed her in a unique position. Further investigation of the complex interplay between the personal factors of her shifting relations with her husband and children, combined with the timing of certain changes in the administrative structure of the queen's household during Henry II's reign, might well reveal the impetus behind some institutional developments within the royal administration. Eleanor's personal difficulties with Henry may have forced changes that would prove detrimental to the status of the queen far beyond her own reign. It is within the context of medieval expectations of queenship, as well as within the framework of the rise of administrative kingship, that Eleanor of Aquitaine should be scrutinized and judged.

Notes

1. See Turner, "Eleanor of Aquitaine and her Children" and my reservations about his conclusions in Huneycutt, "Public Lives, Private Ties."
2. Kelly, *Eleanor and the Four Kings.*
3. The list of biographical and institutional publications has become too long for inclusion here. The starting place ought to be the works of Pauline Stafford and John Carmi Parsons cited in this volume.
4. Parsons, *Eleanor of Castile,* p. 6.
5. Facinger, "A Study of Medieval Queenship," 29.
6. Howell, *Eleanor of Provence,* p. 260.
7. Heather Tanner addresses the career of Matilda of Boulogne, too long ne-glected by historians, in chapter 6 in this volume; thus I focus on the queens of William I and Henry I. The military actions are described in *Gesta Stephani,* pp. 81–85.
8. These rumors, which appear with varying details in a number of late and unreliable chronicles, have been ignored completely by William's modern biographers. See Douglas, *William the Conqueror* and Bates, *William the Conqueror.* Strickland, *Lives of the Queens* 1:27, considered Matilda's beating merely a form of "Teutonic courtship." The fullest medieval account oc-curs in a Tours chronicle excerpted in RHF 11:348. For the impediments to the marriage and the explanations that have been offered, see Douglas, *William the Conqueror,* appendix C.
9. Eadmer, *Historia novorum,* pp. 121–26.
10. I argue elsewhere that Matilda may have received northern lands and her mother's personal treasure; see Huneycutt, "Another Esther," chap. 3.
11. Eadmer, *Historia novorum,* pp. 290–293.
12. Farmer has treated clerical and monastic encouragement of the interces-sory role of aristocratic wives in "Persuasive Voices." The ramifications of queenly intercession are discussed by Huneycutt, "Intercession," Parsons, "Queen's Intercession," and McCartney, "Ceremonies and Privileges of Office."
13. Malmesbury, *Historia Novella,* pp. 57, 66.
14. Orderic Vitalis. *Historia Ecclesiastica* 3:102–103.

15. Aelred of Rievaulx, "Genealogia regum anglorum"; William of Malmesbury, *De gestis regum anglorum* 2:494.

16. Colker, "Latin Texts concerning Gilbert, Founder of Merton Priory," 250.

17. The letter is printed in the "Codex Udalrici," entry 142, p. 259.

18. Hildebert of Lavardin, "Epistolae," in *Opera omnia.*

19. *The Cartulary of Holy Trinity Aldgate,* nos. 973, 977 at pp. 192–93.

20. Huneycutt, "The Idea of the Perfect Princess."

21. "Vita et passio Waldevi comitis," in *Chroniques anglo-normandes* 2:126–27.

22. See Wertheimer, "Adeliza of Louvain" in which she discusses *Reading Abbey Cartularies,* 31, 33.

23. Nip, "Godelieve of Gistel and Ida of Boulogne," in *Sanctity and Motherhood,* pp. 212–13.

24. Stafford, *Queen Emma and Queen Edith.*

25. In some cases, of course, the details are spelled out. One of the most striking of these is in the charter of Queen Adeliza, widow of Henry I, giving a manor to Reading Abbey on the first anniversary of Henry's death. The charter grants "my manor of Easton which my lord the most noble King Henry gave to me as his queen and wife [Eastonam manerium meum quod dedit mihi Dominus meus nobilissimus rex Henricus ut regine ut sponse sue]" (*Reading Abbey Cartularies* 31:301).

26. Meyer, "The 'Queen's Demesne.'"

27. Discussed in Stafford, *Queen Emma and Queen Edith,* pp. 126–30.

28. See Huneycutt, "Another Esther," chap. 3.

29. For Geoffrey, Matilda's chaplain and dean of Waltham, see Tanner, chapter 6 in this volume. Between Richard's 1189 coronation and Christmas 1992, the abbot of Waltham was responsible for finding a clerk to collect the Queen's Gold. Eleanor conceded that the abbot had done so "by her request and by grace and not by duty or custom pertaining to the abbey." See *Waltham Abbey,* ed. Ransford, entry 36, pp. 26–27.

30. See Howell, *Eleanor of Provence,* and Parsons, *Eleanor of Castile.*

31. A comprehensive discussion of queenly revenues in the thirteenth century and beyond is Johnstone, "The Queen's Household," 5:231–289; see, however, the important correctives in Margaret Howell, "The Resources of Eleanor of Provence as Queen Consort," and Parsons, *Eleanor of Castile,* pp. 75–86; also Richardson, "Letters and Charters," 209–11.

32. Hugh the Chanter, *The History of the Church of York,* pp. 46–47.

33. *Dialogus de Scaccario,* pp. 121–22.

34. There were attempts to collect Queen's Gold in the reign of Charles II, when William Prynne compiled a legal brief for Catherine of Braganza, asserting her rights to this ancient form of revenue, collection of which had apparently lapsed. See Prynne, *Aurum reginae.* A paleographical study of the first surviving Pipe Roll from John's reign suggests that a clerk had carefully checked through and noted whether Queen's Gold was due, and if so, in what amount. There are even cases where the clerk was unsure if a fine was due and so indicated by marking "dub' de auro." See Pipe 7 John,

p. xxxvi. Part of the problem is that in the twelfth century, Queen's Gold was only extraordinarily recorded as income separate from that of the king.

35. See, for instance, Hollister, "Administrative Kingship," p. 230 n23. This is also the argument put forth by Wertheimer in "Adeliza of Louvain."

36. Huneycutt, "Proclaiming her Dignity Abroad."

37. Wertheimer, "Adeliza of Louvain," pp. 108–109.

CHAPTER 6

QUEENSHIP: OFFICE, CUSTOM, OR AD HOC?
THE CASE OF QUEEN MATILDA III
OF ENGLAND (1135–1152)

Heather J. Tanner

This chapter examines the career of Eleanor of Aquitaine's predecessor, King Stephen's wife Matilda of Boulogne, whose obligations and activities were shaped by custom established by previous queens and the ad hoc needs of king and realm. Eleanor of Aquitaine followed some of the precedents Matilda had set, but her lack of lands in England and the extension of royal bureaucracy circumscribed her power.

A rekindled scholarly interest in political history, broadened by feminist historians' newer currents, has directed fresh attention to the exercise of public power and authority by women in general and queens in particular, especially those of the Middle Ages. Though individual queens have attracted many historians' interest today, few have investigated Matilda III of England (d. 1152), wife of King Stephen (r. 1135–54). The evidence for Matilda's active political career considered in this chapter raises questions about twelfth-century women's relationships to power.[1] Did she wield power in virtue of her office, through her relationships to her husband or male relatives who did govern, or a combination of the two? Did she act publicly by custom, as an officeholder, or on an ad hoc basis? In the twelfth-century context, did the rise of bureaucratic kingship, and a gradual separation of the royal household from sites of governance, really effect a decline in queenly power, as has been suggested? Matilda, like her Anglo-Norman predecessors, shared in the governance of the realm—a power derived from anointment and marriage and shaped by custom and political exigency. While Eleanor of Aquitaine followed some of the precedents set by Matilda III, the scope of her power was curtailed both conceptually, as reflected in the coronation ordo, and practically by her lack of English lands and the extension of royal bureaucracy.

As no contemporary text specifically addresses queens' duties or rights in England, the outlines of queenship are most clearly observed in the English coronation ordo.[2] The so-called "Edgar" ordo of 973 was amended under William the Conqueror, particularly the section on the queen's coronation. Like the king, she was anointed with oil (oleo), formally invested with a ring for holiness, innocence, and purity, and with a crown for glory and honor. She did not formally receive a sword, virge, scepter, or royal pallium.[3] The revised ordo made three statements about queenly power: it derived from God ("constituit reginam in populo"); the queen shared royal power ("regalis imperii . . . esse participem"); and the English people would be governed by the king's power and the queen's virtue and foresight ("reginae virtutis providentia gubernanda").[4] Transformed by unction like the king, the queen was set apart from other layfolk: she was not merely noble, but royal. The coronation thus indicated that she did exercise royal power, albeit hers was not as extensive as the king's. Her power was clearly gendered: Anglo-Norman queens governed not by "imperium" (the power of command, closely tied to military command), but by "providentia" and "virtus." This gendering of royal power was doubly nuanced. First, "virtus" carried a variety of meanings, several of which cluster around concepts of goodness, worth, merit, and virtue. These qualities were not strictly gendered in the twelfth century; any Christian could strive for and achieve them. But "virtus" also signified male-gendered qualities of manliness, strength, and courage, translated into political theory as "charisma, divine favor and actual power."[5] The king's "virtus" allowed him to defend the realm and so was central to definitions of good kingship. The coronation ordo likely referenced both sets of meanings; the queen shared in governance through her Christian virtue as well as through divinely bestowed grace and power.

Second, while queens' silent investiture with the scepter denied them a separate right of judgment, their seals certainly represented them holding these symbols of rule and royal clemency that they informally received during their coronations.[6] Matilda III's seal, like her aunt's, depicts her with a fleur-de-lis scepter in her right hand a bird to her left.[7] Official sigillographic representation with their scepters, however they received them, publicly manifested both the "potestas reginae" and a blurring of the gendered division of power, for royal justice as portrayed in the ordo was not solely a king's domain. Queens were expected to intercede—to temper the kings' laws with mercy. As John Parsons argues, "the scepter's persistent floriation in art and on the queens' seals strongly recalls the flowering rods of Aaron and Jesse, Biblical images commonly seen as figures of the Virgin Mary."[8] Such symbolism implied a queen's mediatory role and was intensified by her place to the king's left, near the virge of justice and equity he held in that hand. Queenly intercession was seen as a feminine act—Christ as law, Mary as mercy; woman as peacemaker; wives as forces of moral persuasion in the home.[9] But twelfth-century queens also issued judicial decisions,[10] and their roles as royal counselors and judges were seen as masculine activities. Thus Matilda's coronation signaled her entry into an office in which she was expected to rule with the king. This sharing of power and governance was confirmed, usually at the major feasts of Easter, Whitsun, and Christmas, by the custom of crown-wearings by king and queen, which reiterated regal power and authority through lavish patronage and entertainment.[11] Stephen continued the custom, especially in the first years of his reign when his treasury was full; his Christmas court after his release from captivity in 1141 included a ceremonial recrowning of himself and Matilda by the archbishop of Canterbury.[12]

The coronation ordo, including the queen's reception of a scepter, its implications regularly restated by crown-wearings, clearly implies that queenship was an office and that the queen had a role in the realm's governance. While she attained this office by marriage, her powers were not merely delegated, to be exercised in the king's absence or illness. A queen wielded both direct and indirect power, and its origins lay at the nexus of conjugal tie and queenly office. This blending of public and private, office and family, can also be seen in the inheritance of kingship (or countship). A king's power—his office and lands—was inherited from a family member and legitimized by coronation. Lands and offices, including those of a monarch, could be transmitted through male or female lines.[13] Henry I designated his daughter, the empress Matilda, as heir to his throne and his domains in England and Normandy, just as his contemporary, Baldwin II of Jerusalem (r. 1118–31), chose his daughter Melisende to inherit and rule as queen-regnant.[14] Thus inherited, power fostered a desire to keep familial properties intact to be handed on to heirs—sons by preference, daughters if need be. As any noble (and especially royal) couple's first duty was to produce heirs, queens remained at their husbands' sides until the succession was ensured. As Matilda I and Matilda III had children before their coronations, their role in governance was little affected by childbearing; Matilda II's and Eleanor's children arrived in the first years of their marriage, freeing them to participate in governance. Adeliza of Louvain, Henry I's second queen, was an active patron and curialis but had no role in governance: childlessness limited her prominence to the court alone.[15]

A queen's ability to fulfill her office was also rooted in wealth and, to a lesser degree, her ability to depend on family support. In this her power was like that of any political actor of the time. Anglo-Norman queens had several possible sources of revenue: inherited property (land or moveable wealth), lands assigned from the royal demesne, gifts, and Queen's Gold (a surtax on certain revenues at the Exchequer). From her father, Count Eustace III of Boulogne, Matilda inherited the French counties of Boulogne and Lens, including the valuable port of Wissant, and the English honor of Boulogne, tenth largest secular holding after the royal demesne.[16] These French lands were not extensive, but the city of Boulogne lay on the Roman road from Amiens and Paris, and the easy Channel-crossing from Wissant made it most convenient for the Anglo-Flemish wool trade. Shipping tolls were thus a handsome source of income, and the port itself was useful in transporting Flemish mercenaries to Stephen's army in England.[17] As appears from the patterns of her patronage analyzed below, Matilda's inherited lands were the main source of her income, and Stephen relied on her during his reign to manage the county and honor of Boulogne. This de facto control of her patrimony during her marriage was anomalous: an English heiress's lands were usually controlled by her husband, and she confirmed only permanent gifts from her patrimony.[18]

Matilda's substantial inheritance, like her successor Eleanor's, lessened the need for Stephen to assign her lands from the royal demesne. By custom, queens were assigned lands and revenues to maintain household and office, but there was little continuity in the estates that later became known as the queen's dower.[19] The property a queen might inherit from her family, a queen-dowager's possible survival, and political exigencies all influenced the amount of land a queen might hold. This last was an important consideration, for the succession to the English throne was contested throughout the Anglo-Norman period, and kings had to weigh their queens' needs against the need to attract and maintain the loyalty of English nobles. Thus while Matilda I held extensive lands in England, the survival to 1075 of Edward the Confessor's widow Edith, as well as William I's representation of his kingship as a legitimate inheritance from Edward, meant that Matilda did not hold the same lands Edith had held.[20] In Matilda III's case, many estates held by earlier queens lay in parts of England outside Stephen's control, and Queen Adeliza was allowed to retain her dower to ensure her loyalty to Stephen.[21] Matilda did receive three sources of revenue with enduring ties to English queens—the royal abbeys of Barking and Waltham and the London wharf estate called Queenhithe. As few records from Waltham and Barking survive for this period, it is difficult to judge Matilda's involvement with them.[22] Rosalind Ransford argues that Adeliza of Louvain was Waltham's advocate or titular head until she retired to Afflighem in 1150; Matilda III would then have received the advocacy, and we know she freed the abbey from gelds and scots, a strictly royal prerogative.[23] She also patronized Holy Trinity Aldgate, a Waltham dependency founded by Matilda II, and controlled at least a portion of Queenhithe: by charter, Stephen granted Queenhithe to St. Martin le Grand in London to hold as freely as Matilda had held it.[24]

No charters or letters granting gifts to Matilda survive, and the lack of Pipe Rolls from Stephen's reign precludes any estimate of her revenue from Queen's Gold. The origins of this surtax on certain Exchequer revenues for the queen's use are unknown, nor is it clear how systematic its collection was. Our earliest evidence for the custom comes from Henry II's reign, but while the *Dialogus de Scaccario* and Jocelin of Brakelond's chronicle prove the custom was established before that reign, it is unclear whether (or if) this was under Henry I or Stephen.[25] The tax was due on voluntary offerings to the king in coin, on the moneyers' "redemptio" and on amercements of the Jews.[26] The rate of taxation was 10 percent of the debt for offerings of one hundred marks or more, and perhaps on offerings as low as ten marks.[27] Even if the king pardoned the debt owed him, he could not excuse his wife's share; summons for Queen's Gold were made separately from those for the king's debt, and the queen had a clerk at the Exchequer to account for and receive the revenue. Records from later reigns indicate that Queen's Gold never became a major source of revenue and it probably was not in Matilda III's day.[28] However irregular the income from Queen's Gold, its mechanisms of collection and pardon support arguments for the existence of a queenly office and for queens' exercise of regal authority.

Wealth was an important tool of rulership, and Anglo-Norman queens customarily enjoyed resources sufficient to allow them an effective share in governance. Like other monarchs, moreover, Stephen and Matilda could call upon additional means to govern: traditional mobilization of kin-based action groups for military actions, peace negotiations, and such matters of mutual interest; or the administrative structures evolved under Henry I— Exchequer, coram rege, itinerant justices, sheriffs, hundred courts, household, and the familia regis or military household. The king and queen's tenants in the honor and county of Boulogne provided consistent support; when Matilda undertook the siege of Dover in 1138, she called on "friends, kinsmen and dependents of Boulogne" to blockade the port.[29] Her paternal relatives were few, but Pharamus of Boulogne, grandson of Eustace II's bastard son Geoffrey, served her as castellan at Dover and commanded the royal army in 1141.[30] Stephen's nephews and bastards filled ecclesiastical posts and helped to cement alliances,[31] and his brother, Bishop Henry of Winchester, was prominent at court. The couple also created or fostered loyalty through their children's marriages and betrothals: their eldest surviving son Eustace married Constance of France, their daughter Matilda was betrothed to Waleran of Meulan (a key ally in England and Normandy), and their son William married Isabella, heiress of William de Warenne III, earl of Surrey.

An Anglo-Norman queen was, then, expected to share in governance by virtue of her office; in that capacity she could call upon the royal administration, revenues from her lands, and the charisma and royal power conferred by coronation. As they worked to fulfil such expectations, queens' functions or duties were shaped by predecessors' actions as well as by political exigency. Matilda III could draw upon the precedents of Matilda I (1066–83) and Matilda II (1100–18), who participated at the royal curia, witnessed royal writs, and took part in the *coram regis;* they governed in the kings' absences,[32] extended patronage to churchmen and artists, judged suits, and interceded with their husbands to obtain mercy or benefits for others.[33] Matilda II had issued acta exercising specifically regal powers and served in the Exchequer and on occasion as a diplomat.[34]

Matilda III's models probably also included *The Life of St Margaret.* As Lois Huneycutt argues, this *vita* of Margaret of Scotland—Matilda II's mother and the grandmother of Matilda III—was written "as a didactic tool for Matilda [II], to instill in her an ideal of queenly behavior, and to provide a pattern which she could follow in her daily activities." In the *Life's* picture of queenship, "All things which were fitting were carried out by order of the prudent queen; by her counsel the laws of the realm were put in order, divine religion was augmented by her industry, [and] the people rejoiced in the prosperity of affairs." Margaret was depicted as "busy among 'the tumult of lawsuits and the many-sided cares of the kingdom'" and involved in church reform as well as acts of personal piety.[35] Matilda III too participated in government business, witnessed royal acts, judged cases, issued writs, interceded for others, and patronized reform monasteries. To such customary activities there was an added ad hoc element: civil war during much of Stephen's reign required Matilda to participate actively in diplomacy and to take an occasional stint as military commander.

Matilda was involved in political affairs almost from the start of Stephen's reign. She did not accompany him to England in December 1135, nor did she attend his coronation, for she had just borne her son William.[36] She was in England for his Easter court in 1136 and was crowned on March 22 in Westminster Abbey. Her actions between Easter and the next Christmas court, which she also attended, are unknown.[37] As she witnessed no charters issued while Stephen was besieging several rebellious lords, she probably remained in or near London awaiting the birth of her fifth child, late in 1136. Matilda went to Normandy with Stephen in March 1137, probably for the entire five-month campaign.[38] Stephen established his authority in Normandy and won the support of Louis VI of France; his son Eustace did homage for the duchy.

The first two years of Stephen's reign were the busiest period of Matilda's curial activity. Of her fifty-eight attestations to Stephen's charters, fifteen fall within this two-year period.[39] These totals are slightly skewed because, at his 1136 Easter and Christmas courts, the king issued a flurry of confirmation charters, of which Matilda witnessed six. Excluding these, she attested ten charters in 1136 and three in 1137, above her average of three attestations per year for the rest of the reign. Issuing confirmation charters was a traditional gesture at a new king's accession; such acts, and the splendor of the courts at which they were issued, disseminated and declared Stephen's and Matilda's authority.[40] Her position and authority were affirmed when Stephen granted her custody of Barking Abbey, long associated with English queens.[41]

After this period of curial activity, Matilda turned her attention and talents to alliance formation. Early in 1139, she worked with the papal legate Alberic of Ostia to restore peace between Stephen and her maternal uncle, King David of Scotland. Alberic saw that Matilda hoped to bring about peace and, through her, appealed to Stephen, who at first rebuffed them both. But she persisted, and in the end her shrewdness and eloquence triumphed.[42] After inducing Stephen to make peace, Matilda represented him at the peace conference. A truce was agreed upon at Durham in April 1139, and was confirmed by the queen and King David's son Henry. Clerics praised wives who persuaded their husbands to perform good acts, and as a negotiator and diplomat in 1139, Matilda carried this topos into the official domain.[43] Privately, she convinced Stephen of the utility of a truce; publicly, she negotiated the peace on his behalf.

Matilda's diplomatic efforts also included, in February 1140, her son Eustace's betrothal and marriage to Constance of France.[44] In part a response to the Empress's arrival in England and the onset of civil war, the marriage strengthened the Anglo-French alliance of 1137. Chroniclers do not reveal who proposed the marriage, but the king's choice of his wife to carry out the negotiations reflects his confidence in her eloquence and shrewdness as well their partnership: he could have chosen one of his brothers, Bishop Henry of Winchester or the French curialis, Count Theobald of Blois. Matilda may thus have fostered a custom of queenly involvement in the marriages of royal children.[45] On her return from France in May 1140, Bishop Henry arranged for her and Robert of Gloucester to negotiate at Bath for peace between Stephen and the Empress, but nothing came of the meeting. In the same year, Matilda uncovered Earl Ranulph of Chester's plot to ambush Henry of Scotland on his return home; she induced Stephen to escort Henry to Scotland and so protected the Scottish alliance.[46] She also acted on Stephen's behalf to restore peace with Count Thierry of Flanders, uncle of the Empress's husband, Count Geoffrey of Anjou. No chronicle details the peace process, but grants to Thierry's foundation at Clairmarais by Stephen, Matilda, and William of Ypres perhaps sealed the agreement.[47]

In addition to active diplomacy, Matilda commanded Stephen's military forces. Facing three major rebellions in 1138, Stephen chose her to besiege Dover, while he was similarly occupied at Hereford. The choice was unusual as women rarely directed sieges, but it reflects their partnership. As noted earlier, Matilda's appeal to relatives, friends, and tenants in Boulogne was crucial to a successful blockade of the port, and Dover's surrender in December 1138, assured a vital conduit for mercenary soldiers.[48] Upon Stephen's capture at Lincoln on February 2, 1141, the queen took control of Stephen's army and government and retired from London into Kent with William of Ypres. With the royal forces in disarray, she turned to diplomacy and negotiation. From her base in Kent, she called on Stephen's men across England to demand his release, "made supplication to all, importuned with prayers, promises, and fair words for the deliverance of her husband."[49] At a legatine council called by Bishop Henry of Winchester on April 7 to settle Stephen's deposition, Matilda sent her clerk, Christian, to read a letter requesting Stephen's release.[50] Matilda's letter derailed Henry's carefully choreographed transfer of power; Archbishop Theobald and the bishops refused to recognize the Empress without Stephen's express permission, and the London delegation left giving only vague promises of tepid support. Although Stephen released the bishops from their oath, the Londoners remained obdurate and it was only with the defection of Geoffrey de Mandeville, castellan of London, that the Empress was able to enter the City around June 20. Within four days, the Queen ousted the Empress from London. Matilda skillfully used military pressure and the Empress's lack of diplomacy to regain the city.[51] Though Empress Matilda rallied her forces in Oxford, her situation continued to deteriorate. Queen Matilda used her eloquence to win back the allegiance of Bishop Henry and Geoffrey de Mandeville, and the countersiege of Winchester yielded the ultimate negotiating counter with the capture of Robert of Gloucester, the Empress's half-brother and military commander.[52] Robert, by the queen's order, was imprisoned at Rochester, and negotiations were conducted by Queen Matilda, the Empress, and the countess of Gloucester. In early November, Stephen and Robert were freed.[53]

The year 1141 was thus a turning point in the reign. Queen Matilda had functioned throughout with supreme royal authority, commanding Stephen's army and his followers' loyalty. Despite her efforts, however, Stephen's dominion after 1141 was limited in the Midlands and the North, and nonexistent in the West; and lost in Normandy by 1144. His intinerant court still transacted government business, but he relied upon Matilda to oversee governmental affairs in London and to administer the honor of Boulogne. Fifty-six percent of Matilda's charters and her attestations of Stephen's charters that specify a location are dated in London or within a forty-mile radius of the city; none of her charters written in England was prepared more than eighty miles from London.[54] Matilda's presence in areas where Stephen had reasonable control strengthens the argument that she functioned in his stead or headed the royal administration while he was occupied with military affairs.[55] Her presence in or near London was doubly advantageous. First, it is likely, if unprovable, that she oversaw the collection of revenue at the Westminster Exchequer. Second, she apparently inspired strong loyalty in her English tenants, in the Londoners, and in the Boulonnais. The need for men and money made it vital that London trade flourished and that the ports of Wissant and Dover remained open.

One of the most significant areas of Matilda's royal and curial activity was the exercise of justice and the maintenance of peace. In 1137, she assisted in a case between the castellan of London and Holy Trinity Priory that was pled at the *coram regis*.[56] Matilda acted swiftly to circumvent rebellion by incarcerating some citizens of Rochester whose lord opposed Stephen.[57] She and her predecessors also maintained their own court (*curia regine*) where they heard pleas touching Waltham.[58] The queen's authority extended to all royal lands, not just those assigned for her use. Four of her judgments and writs concerning the royal demesne have survived. Only one of these, concerning the soke of Cripplegate, has previously been regarded as evidence of Matilda's wielding royal power (in the guise of a regent). In this charter, Matilda ordered John the sheriff that the canons of St. Martin le Grand should hold the soke of Cripplegate freely.[59] This act's regal nature is indicated by the fact that Cripplegate was not under Matilda's jurisdiction as countess and by the diplomatic phrase that R.C. van Caenegem has characterized as viceregal: *rex precepit per breve suum*."[60] The charter has been dated to 1141 on the grounds that she acted as regent (or regally) only in that year; but there is no internal affirmation of the date, and since John the sheriff is not found elsewhere in the sources before 1155–56, the act probably originated after 1141. In the second charter (1143/47), Matilda announces an end to a lawsuit over a half hide in Mashbury, land apparently in the Mandeville family until Stephen stripped Geoffrey de Mandeville of his properties in 1143.[61] The case was heard in the curia regis, "in audientia regis Stephani et mea," and the lack of a charter from Stephen (though clearly present at the proceedings) supports the idea that the queen's regal authority allowed her to act. Matilda also issued a charter (1143/47) resolving a land dispute between St. Martin le Grand and Baldwin of Wissant. The land at Good Easter had, prior to 1088, been part of the honour of Boulogne, and Baldwin was constable of Boulogne, but Matilda's authority in this matter was royal not comital.[62] The case was presented by St. Martin's dean, not by a comital official, in the *curia regis,* "apud regem et apud me," and once again, Stephen did not issue a confirming writ. Finally, Matilda ordered the sheriff of Essex to ensure that St. Martin's held the marsh of Maldon in peace. The marsh, a holding of Geoffrey de Mandeville, had reverted to the king in 1143, thus, Matilda's writ (1147/52) reflects her regal authority to command a royal official to see that justice was done on royal demesne land.[63]

Matilda conducted her administration of royal and comital affairs with the aid of her own household and occasional support from Stephen's curiales and household officers. Of the four acta noted above, only that of the Mashbury suit preserves its witness list; five of the six attestors are among Stephen's most frequent attestors.[64] Further analysis of the witnesses to her charters reveals solid correlation between Stephen and Matilda's most regular attestors, especially Richard de Lucy and William Martel, a steward. The prevalence of royal *curialis* among the king's and queen's attestors supports the shared nature of their governance. Stephen's campaigning and Matilda's base in London meant, however, that there was a minimal sharing of household officials.[65] Though the queen relied upon her own *familia* to carry out her duties, she routinely commanded royal officials, such as sheriffs and justices, to execute her orders.[66] Despite the decrease in the number of royal officials after 1141, Henry I's institutional innovations persisted throughout Stephen's reign.[67] Therefore, Matilda's active political role suggests that the growth of bureaucratic kingship did not diminish queenly power before 1154.

Custom as well as the close working relationship between Matilda and Stephen led churchmen to ask her to intercede with him. As noted earlier, she assisted the legate Alberic in promoting peace between Stephen and King David. Bernard of Clairvaux wrote her twice, the first time to remind her of a promise to give a tithe to the abbot of La Chapelle (Boulogne).[68] In a six-year dispute over Henry Murdac's confirmation as archbishop of York, Bernard appealed to Matilda to champion Henry's cause, writing that his petition "concern[s] your own salvation and the glory of *your* kingdom."[69] The two also worked together to establish the peace between Stephen and Count Thierry of Flanders.[70] In 1148, Eugenius III called on Matilda's wisdom and piety, asking that she and Stephen accept a profession of loyalty rather than an oath of fealty from Bishop Robert of Lincoln, whom the Empress appointed during Stephen's captivity.[71] Bernard's and Eugenius's letters demonstrate Matilda's intercessory function as well as the shared rule of the royal couple. Matilda also intervened to restore smooth relations between Stephen and Archbishop Theobald after Stephen had exiled him for disobediently attending the Council of Reims (March 1148).[72] Theobald resided at St. Bertin Abbey near Boulogne while the queen and William of Ypres aided negotiations for Theobald's return and the lifting of the papal interdict.

Matilda's patronage rarely intersected with the needs of state that she helped govern with such energy and skill. Her grant and confirmation of Stephen's gift to Clairmarais, Thierry of Flanders's Cistercian foundation, were made to foster an alliance. She and the king encouraged Aubrey de Vere II's second marriage by adding the manor of Ickleton to the dowry of his bride, Eusemia; the gift may have helped secure Aubrey's loyalty.[73] Her promotion of her chaplain Ralph as prior of St. Martin's fortified that priory's close links to the royal chancery.[74]

Matilda's political patronage was undeniably limited as was her literary or artistic sponsorship.[75] There can be no question, however, of her support of the reforming monastic orders: Austin canons, Cistercians, Knights Templar, Savignacs, and Arrouasians.[76] Her gifts to these orders may reflect the royal role of protector of the faith and the custom established by her grandmother and aunt. She and Stephen founded several houses—Longvilliers (Savignac, 1135), Cressing-Witham (Templars, 1137, Witham added, 1147–48), Cowley (Templars, 1138–39), Coggeshall (Savignac, 1140), Lillechurch (St. Sulpice, 1148), and Faversham (Cluniac, 1148). Matilda also patronized the secular colleges of St Martin and Holy Trinity in London, and founded the hospital of St. Katherine by the Tower.[77]

The specific orders Matilda patronized were determined by her own family ties and Stephen's. Savigny attracted Stephen's and Matilda's patronage through his position as count of Mortain in Normandy; founded by the hermit-preacher Vitalis of Mortain, this reforming order spread rapidly with the support of Henry I, Stephen, and their courtiers. Stephen and Matilda founded several Savignac houses; their gifts to the order came chiefly from Stephen's lands.[78] Matilda issued Coggeshall's foundation charter and exempted it from tolls and customs on her English and Boulonnais lands. The Arrouasians, of which her father's chaplain was a founder, received grants from her holdings at Merck in the Boulonnais.[79]

The Boulonnais and Blesois comital families' distinguished record as crusaders inspired Matilda's and Stephen's interest in the Templars, the order she patronized most extensively. Her father had confirmed the earliest known grant to the Templars in England, and both Stephen and

Matilda had ties to the order's earliest founders: Hugh de Payens was from Champagne, a region controlled by the Blois family, and Godfrey of St. Omer was a vassal of the counts of Boulogne. Osto of Boulogne, Grand Master of the Temple in England ca. 1147–57, was Stephen's curialis and witnessed two of Matilda's charters as well as the 1152 settlement between Stephen and Henry of Anjou.[80] From her English holdings she founded and endowed houses at Cressing and Cowley; Stephen and Eustace added gifts and confirmations.[81]

Matilda's patronage of Holy Trinity Aldgate and St. Martin le Grand in London stemmed from familial and royal associations. Matilda II had founded Augustinian Holy Trinity, and Matilda III was associated with the house before 1135. Her son Baldwin and daughter Matilda were buried there.[82] The queenly association was continued with Eleanor; her son Henry was baptized there.[83] Matilda gave the canons custody of St. Katherine's by the Tower, and the land and church at Braughing.[84] The Braughing grant may have been motivated by the election as Holy Trinity's prior of Ralph, Matilda's confessor at least since Stephen's coronation and probably before. St. Martin's had provided several clerks to Stephen's household; Matilda's brother-in-law Henry of Winchester was dean from 1139 to 1171 and since Henry I's time, St. Martin's prebends had served as benefices for royal household clerks. Six such clerks are known, among them Matilda's and Stephen's chaplains, Richard of Boulogne and his son Robert.[85]

From 1148, Matilda devoted much of her time to a new house intended as the family's burial place. Faversham was colonized from Cluniac Bermondsey, an initially surprising choice given Matilda's and Stephen's interest in the reforming orders. The Cluniac combination of splendor and reform was eminently suitable for a royal mausoleum, and their choice mirrored Henry I's foundation of Reading.[86] Faversham had "an unusually long choir of considerable splendor and archaic design, with the royal tombs at its focal point."[87] Whereas previous Anglo-Norman royal family members were buried separately in their chosen monastic house, the magnificence of this family mausoleum suggests a conscious promotion of their dynasty and Eustace's succession. Fontevraud served this same function under the direction of Eleanor of Aquitaine. As with her other patronage, there were strong familial connections with Cluny that strengthened the dynastic aims of this foundation.[88] Faversham's first prior was formerly the prior of Bermondsey, a house where Matilda may have been educated and that had received her mother's patronage and served as the countess' gravesite.[89] Matilda's father and grandmother, Countess Ida, had founded Cluniac houses at Le Wast and Rumilly, where they retired and were buried; Stephen's mother, Countess Adela, retired to Cluniac

Marcigny late in life, his brother Bishop Henry was a Cluniac monk, and Henry I had founded the Cluniac house at Reading where he was buried.[90] The splendor, family ties, and prestige of Cluny made Faversham a potent symbol of dynastic aspirations.

While Matilda's monastic patronage reveals a queenly concern for fostering reform, it is harder to assess her personal piety. She once used her royal authority to order the monks of St. Augustine's at Canterbury to disregard an archiepiscopal interdict and celebrate mass for her while she stayed there, but contemporary chroniclers do not describe her as deeply devout or saintly.[91] Her lack of a saintly reputation is in contrast to the eminent piety of her aunt Matilda II, who washed and kissed the feet of lepers, and the holiness of Matilda III's grandmothers, Bl. Ida of Boulogne and St. Margaret of Scotland.[92] But her patronage does indicate interest in female spirituality. Her daughter Mary was a nun at St. Sulpice, Rennes, founded by Ralph de la Futaie, one of many hermit monastic founders in Brittany and Maine; Ralph modeled his foundation on Fontevraud, a double order particularly associated with women.[93] The Arrouasians and Savignacs had strong associations with women, and Stephen and Matilda founded (1135) a Savignac nunnery at Longvilliers in the Boulonnais.[94] Matilda gave ten marks to Godstow nunnery and attended the dedication with Stephen, and gave an acre in Faversham to the nun Helmid for life, with reversion to St. Augustine's.[95] Her interest in female monasticism and spirituality accords with her desire to elevate standards of ecclesiastical life in her lands; her interest in reform might also be seen in the fact that none of her chaplains was promoted to the episcopacy.[96]

In her last years, Matilda took a less prominent role in the governance of England. Stephen's military activities began to decrease significantly with the death (October 1147) of Robert of Gloucester, commander of the Empress's army, and the Empress's departure for Normandy early in 1148. With the uneasy peace, Matilda became primarily an advisor. She continued to witness and issue charters with the same frequency as earlier in the reign.[97] Matilda was present at Robert de Chesney's election to the see of Lincoln (December 13, 1148). She oversaw work at Faversham and worked with Archbishop Theobald to resolve tensions at Stratford nunnery; in 1148, Matilda and Stephen founded a new Sulpician house at Lillechurch and settled Mary there.[98] Matilda's diminished public presence from 1147 also reflects the need to groom Eustace, now of age, to succeed as king. Thus her activities attracted little attention as chroniclers focused on Eustace's military activity and on Stephen's decision to leave him in charge of London in 1149. Eustace's responsibilities were emphasized in a new coinage issued at York ca. 1145, that displays two figures, Stephen and probably Eustace.[99] From 1150, Stephen tried to assure his son's succession, sending the archbishop of York for papal sanction for Eustace's coronation. That mission failed. He tried again in April 1152, calling a church council in London that Matilda attended; but, led by Archbishop Theobald, the bishops refused to crown Eustace.[100] This was Matilda's last public appearance; she died on May 3, and was buried at Faversham.

Matilda's office, initiated and broadly defined by the coronation ordo, gave her royal power and authority to share in governance. Her obligations and activities were shaped by custom established by previous queens and the ad hoc needs of king and realm; she thus surpassed customary queenly roles as curialis, patron, and intercessor. Matilda III's thorough integration into the governance of the realm was not repeated in Eleanor's years as queen of England. Eleanor's coronation followed a new model that emphasized the queen as progenitor of royal heirs and subordinate to the king rather than as sharer of royal power.[101] Though Eleanor acted as regent in England between 1156 and 1158 and in Poitou on several occasions from 1165 on, her writs suggest delegated rather than shared royal authority.[102] In England, her power was limited by the lack of lands assigned to her use and by the elaboration of financial and judicial administration. Whereas Matilda III's inheritance allowed her to play an integral role in politics by securing the Londoners' loyalty and a steady supply of mercenaries, Eleanor's inheritance provided her with more extensive power in Poitou and Aquitaine than in England. Until 1163, Eleanor withdrew funds from the Exchequer by her own writ, but unlike her Anglo-Norman predecessors, she was not a member of its council nor did she issue judgments from the royal court.[103] Eleanor's counsel and diplomatic activities, in contrast to Matilda's, are rarely mentioned. She did, however, encourage the 1159 Toulouse campaign and supported Henry in the Becket affair and the coronation of young Henry.[104] Eleanor was not a prominent curialis; she rarely witnessed Henry's charters or interceded to secure the king's mercy.[105] She did follow in Matilda's footsteps in her promotion of her sons, cultivation of dynastic goals through the Fontevraudian tombs, and patronage that reflected her family's traditions. For Matilda, to be queen encompassed a variety of functions—curialis, diplomat, judge, intercessor, and "regent." Through a combination of factors, Eleanor's role as queen was much more restricted.

Chart 6.1 Chronological Range of Matilda's Charters and Attestations

Year	Regesta II Charter No. or Reference*	Attestation Avg. (incl. avg. from Chart 6.2)	Charter Issuance Avg.
1136	204, 284, 341, (½) 506, 678, 944, 945, 946, 947, 948, 949, **CPC t. 250, f. 268r–v**	11.5	1.4
1137	(½) 288, 312, (½) 506, 598, **843**	4.0	1.4
1138	(½) 288, (½) **850**	1.5	.8
1139	(½) 477, (½) 478, (½) 479, 667, (½) **850**, (⅓) **207**	4.3	1.5
1140	(½) 477, (½) 478, (½) 479, 921, (⅓) **207**	4.3	1.0
1141	276, (⅓) **207, 24, 530**	2.6	3.0
1142	**26, 195**	1.8	2.8
1143		2.0	1.1
1144		2.0	1.5
1145	(⅓) **541**, (⅓) **553**, (⅓) **539**	2.0	2.5
1146	471, (½) 694, 736, (⅓) **541**, (⅓) **553**, (⅓) **539**	4.5	2.5
1147	(⅓) 402, (½) 511, (½) 694, (½) 760, (½) 846, (⅓) **541**, (⅓) **553**, (⅓) **539**, (½) **512**, (½) **513**, (½) **845**, (½) Cox #2	4.3	4.7
1148	(⅓) 402, (½) 511, (½) 760, (½) 846, (½) **512**, (½) **513**, (½) **845**, (½) Cox #2	4.2	2.5
1149	(⅓) 402, 633(?)	3.0	1.4
1150	(⅓) 185	2.0	1.5
1151	(⅓) 185, **157**(?)	2.0	2.5
1152	(⅓) 185	2.0	1.5
Total		58.0	33.0

Notes: **bold** = Charters issued by Matilda; normal = Matilda's attestations of Stephen's charters; (?) = tentative date

*ERO is the Essex County Record Office; CPC is Collection Picardie, BNF (Paris); Cox, "Two Unpublished Charters"; Vincent, "Six New Charters." See n. 39 for discussion of the calculation of the averages.

Chart 6.2 Chronological Range of Matilda's Charters and Attestations of Stephen's Charters: Attestations with More Than Three Year Dating Range

Year Range	Regesta III Charter No. or Reference (averages added to Chart 6.1)
1136–39	718
1136–40	643
1136–45	162
1136–46	662, Davis **167**
1136–47	**243**
1139–45	757
1139–46	483, 508, **509**
1139–47	446, **556**
1139–49	**76**
1139–52	35, 36, 538, 743, 830
1140–46	507
1140–52	34
1141–52	Vincent, no. 11
1142–47	200, **196**
1143–47	**198, 550, 557**
1143–48	Vincent, no. 6
1143–52	**149**
1146–52	Davis 166, ERO D/Du 102/28
Dec. 1147–May 1152	184, 501, 957
1147–52	**503, 548**
Dec. 1148–May 1152	**221, 224**
1148–52	**301**
1136–52	249, 376, 505, 829, 956, 960, **239b, 239d, 917**

Notes: **bold** = Charters issued by Matilda; normal = Matilda's attestations of Stephen's charters; see Chart 6.1 for the abbreviated references.

Chart 6.3 Comparison of Frequency of Attestation of Royal Charters

Rank	Attestor	Number of Attestations for Stephen	Number of Attestations for Matilda
1:4	William Martel	186	6
2:7	Robert de Ver	145	2
3:1	Richard de Lucy	144	11
4:7	Richard de Camville	70	2
5:0	Roger le Poer	61	0
5:6	Henry bp Winchester	61	3
5:3	William de Ipres	61	7
6:0	Aubrey de Ver	57	0
6:0	Queen Matilda	57	n/a
7:8	Nigel bp Ely	48	1
8:6	Henry of Essex	43	3
9:0	Alex. bp Lincoln	40	0
10:0	Roger bp Salisbury	39	0
10:0	Hugh Bigod	39	0
11:7	Simon de Senlis	37	2
12:8	Adam be Beaunay	36	1
12:2	Warner de Lusor	36	8
12:4	Eustace ct Boulogne	36	5 (or 6)
13:0	William de Albino	34	0
14:0	Fulcolne de Oilli	32	0
15:8	Waleran de Meulan	31	1
16:0	Roger de Fecamp	29	0
16:0	Robert de Clare	29	0
16:0	Roger de Fraxinet	29	0
17:0	Adelulf bp Carlisle	27	0
18:0	Turgis of Albrinc	25	0
18:4	Theobald Abp Cant.	25	5
19:8	William de Chesney	22	1
20:7	Robert bp Hereford	21	2
20:0	Baldwin de Clare	21	0
21:0	Robert de Gant	20	0
22:0	William Abp Cant.	17	0
22:0	Wm III de Warenne	17	0
23:6	Hilary bp Chicester	15	3
23:0	Bernard bp St David	15	0
24:0	Philip d'Harcourt	12	0
0:5	Ralph, Q' chancellor	0	5

Notes: Ranking column: The first number signifies rank among Stephen's attestors; the second number signifies rank among Matilda's attestors. For example, William Martel is the most frequent attestor of Stephen's charters, and the fourth most frequent attestor of Matilda's.

bp = bishop; ct = count; Abp = archbishop; Q' = Queen's

Notes

1. Excluding bibliographies and articles, recent work includes: Stafford, *Queens, Concubines and Dowagers*; *Women and Power in the Middle Ages,* ed. Erler and Kowaleski; *Women and Sovereignty,* ed. Fradenburg; *Medieval Queenship,* ed. Parsons; *Queens, Regents and Potentates,* ed.Vann. Of modern historians of Stephen's reign, R.H.C. Davis discusses Matilda's actions in most detail (*King Stephen,* 3rd edn., p. 48–67).

2. The lack of treatises and specula also applies to kings in this period. For medieval conceptions of kingship, see *The Cambridge History of Medieval Political Thought, c. 350–c. 1450;* Galbraith, "Good Kings and Bad Kings"; and Tanner, "Trial by Chronicle."

3. Schramm, *History of the English Coronation,* pp. 28–31; Schramm, *Three Coronation Orders,* pp. 53–61 (king), 61–64 (queen).The *Te deum* was sung for Matilda I in 1068, but it is unknown whether the other Anglo-Norman queens' coronation ceremonies included the *Te deum* (Cowdrey, "The Anglo-Norman *Laudes regiae*").

4. Schramm, *Three Coronation Orders,* pp. 62–63. The ordo used for later queens stressed their dynastic maternity and subordination to the king (Parsons, "Ritual and Symbol").

5. Lewis, *An Elementary Latin Dictionary,* p. 924; Peters, *The Shadow King,* p. 22.

6. No impressions or descriptions of Matilda I's seal exist, for her scepter and crown see *Les abbayes Caennaises,* ed. Musset, no. 16. Matilda II's seal shows her standing with an orb in one hand, and in the other a scepter with a fleur-de-lis finial, a bird above the center petal (*Letters,* ed. Crawford, p. 24). Adeliza's seal was modeled on Matilda II's (*Reading Abbey Cartularies,* nos. 370, 535).

7. *Sir Christopher Hatton's Book of Seals,* no. 424). Her four extant original charters lack seals (RRAN, 3: nos. 506, 550 ; 3: nos. 149, 243, 503, 539), while three (RRAN, 3: nos. 24, 76, 843), not preserved as originals, refer to her seal.

8. Parsons, "Ritual and Symbol," p. 65.

9. Huneycutt, "Intercession"; Parsons, "The Queen's Intercession"; and Farmer, "Persuasive Voices."

10. RRAN, 3: nos. 506, 550.

11. Schramm, *English Coronation,* pp. 31–32, 43; Richardson, "Coronation in Medieval England." Henry of Huntingdon notes Stephen's splendid 1136 Easter court, but for 1140 says "all that made the court splendid . . . had disappeared. The treasury . . . was now empty" (Henry of Huntingdon, *Historia Anglorum,* ed. Arnold, p. 267). Biddle, "Seasonal Festivals,"argues that the location and frequency of crown wearings was less fixed or regular than often implied; as the custom in fact declined under Henry I, Stephen's practice does not prove anarchy or loss of prestige.

12. Gervase of Canterbury, *Opera historica* 1:123.

13. Hudson, *Land, Law and Lordship,* pp. 108–22; Martindale, "Succession and Politics."

14. Chibnall, *Empress Matilda*, pp. 51–53; Huneycutt, "Images of Queenship" 64; and Huneycutt, "Female Succession."

15. For Matilda I's family, Douglas, *William the Conqueror*, pp. 393–95, and Barlow, *William Rufus*, pp. 441–45; for Matilda II's, Chibnall, *Empress Matilda*, pp. 8–9; for Matilda III, see n36 below.

16. The honor of Boulogne included lands in eleven counties, concentrated in Essex; revenue in 1086 was £770 (Hollister, "Magnates and 'Curiales,'" p. 99).

17. *Actes des comtes de Flandres*, nos. 30 clause 2, and 41 clause 2.

18. Holt, "Feudal Society and the Family"; Milsom, "Inheritance by Women"; and Green, "Aristocratic Women."

19. Meyer, "The Queen's 'Demesne'" "Huneycutt, *Another Esther*, chap. 2; and Parsons, *Eleanor of Castile*, pp. 75–76.

20. Apart from letting the Empress stay at Arundel in September 1139, Adeliza was loyal to Stephen. She held Stanton Harcourt (Oxon.), Aston (Herts), Northolt (Sussex), Betchworth (Surrey), Heytesbury (Wilts.), advocacy of Romsey and Waltham Abbeys (RRAN 3: nos. 140, 220, 629, 679, 697, 723, 793, 918, 921), and the honor and castle of Arundel (R.H.C. Davis, *King Stephen*, 2nd. edn., p. 137). Malmesbury, *Historia Novella*, p. 3, states that at the Council of London (1126), Henry I gave Adeliza the earldom of Shrewsbury. By September 1139, the widowed Adeliza had married Henry I's butler, William d'Aubigny; Stephen granted William the earldom of Lincoln in 1139, but ca. Christmas 1141 transferred that earldom to William de Roumare and made d'Aubigny earl of Sussex (Davis, *King Stephen*, pp. 137–38). In 1150, Adeliza retired to the convent of Afflighem; lands assigned her as queen were probably then transferred to Matilda III. For Adeliza's activities during Stephen's reign, see Wertheimer, "Adeliza of Louvain," 109–15.

21. The Confessor's widow Edith and Matilda II, for example, held extensive lands in Rutland and, in Devon (Lifton and revenues in Exeter); Matilda I also held many estates in Devon, but none were available for Stephen to grant Matilda III (Meyer, "Queen's 'Demesne'," 105–13; Huneycutt, *Another Esther*, chap. 2). Stephen successfully defended Exeter in 1136, but it was lost to him by 1142 (*Gesta Stephani*, p. 44).

22. Matilda II and Adeliza held the advocacy of Waltham and Barking (RRAN, 2: xxxiv–xxv, nos. 525, 802, 1199; *VCH Essex*, 2: pp. 86, 120, 125, 177). For Matilda III and Waltham, RRAN, 3: nos. 31, 915; none of her extant charters concerns Barking. Wilton and Romsey also had longstanding ties to English queens. Stephen apparently allowed Adeliza to retain Romsey (RRAN, 3: nos. 722–24). Matilda III's great-aunt Christina joined Romsey in 1085; Matilda II (and probably her sister Mary, Matilda III's mother) were educated there (*Anglo-Saxon Chronicle*, E text, a. 1085; Eadmer, *Historia*, pp. 121–26).

23. *Waltham Abbey*, ed. Ransford, p. 12, note to no. 19. Three of Adeliza's charters for Waltham survive (*Waltham Abbey*, ed. Ransford, nos. 16–18); her continuing advocacy is implied by the Empress's notification that she had

granted Waltham to Adeliza (RRAN 3: no. 918). Matilda III's grant to Waltham is RRAN 3: no. 917.

24. Lands in London's wharf area, called "Ethelred's hythe" until the mid-twelfth century, became known as "Queenhithe" as they were routinely granted to queens of England. Matilda II had public toilets installed here and Eleanor of Aquitaine received revenues from Queenhithe (*VCH Essex* 6:59; Brooke and Keir, *London 800–1216*, pp. 315–18; Wolffe, *The Royal Demesne*, pp. 230–35). But William of Ypres apparently held the farm of Queenhithe, while Matilda gave £10 from Queenhithe to fund the hospital of St Katherine by the Tower (RRAN 3: nos. 501–04).

25. *Dialogus de Scaccario*, pp. 122–23; *Jocelini de Brakelonda Cronica*, p. 46; Patricia M. Barnes, "The Anstey Case," p. 22.

26. *Dialogus de Scaccario*, pp. 122–23. Voluntary offerings were sums or gifts for a liberty, manor, farm, wardship, justice in a suit or "anything else which may seem to [the offerer] to augment his convenience or dignity" (*Dialogus de Scaccario*, pp. 119–21). They appear to include reliefs (inheritance fines). Moneyers paid *redemptio* to inherit the right to strike coins and to receive a new die when coinage changed. Stephen made four official coin issues: ca.1136, ca.1145, ca.1150, and ca. 1154 issued respectively by a minimum of 162, 50, 47 and 80 coiners. Matilda would have received 1 percent of the *redemptiones* by approximately 259 moneyers (Blackburn, "Coinage and Currency," pp. 156–57, 194). The Jews paid £2000 into the Exchequer in 1130 and an aid was taken in 1159, but no known aids were levied on the Jews in Stephen's reign (Green, "Financing Stephen's War," 105 n107). Green notes that Thomas of Monmouth's life of St. William of Norwich has the Jews say to Stephen, "We are . . . your tribute-payers every year, and frequently your friends of necessity, since [we are] always faithful to you and your kingdom [and] not un-useful."

27. Eleanor of Aquitaine asserted her right to Queen's Gold on fines of 10 marks (*Dialogus de Scaccario*, p. 123).

28. Johnstone, "The Queen's Household," 5:231–39. Pipe and Hundred Rolls list Queen's Gold sporadically from John's reign; the highest revenue appears in the thirteenth century under Eleanor of Castile: £2875 in 1286–89, and £1564 in 1289–90 (Yoshitake, "The Exchequer in the Reign of Stephen"; Parsons, *Eleanor of Castile*, pp. 81, 83–84).

29. Tanner, *Between Scylla and Charybdis*, pp. 194–96; Orderic Vitalis, *Historia Æcclesiastica*, 6:521.

30. Matilda's bastard half-brothers died or vanished from record before she wed Stephen in 1125; her paternal uncles Duke Godfrey of Lower Lorraine, Defender of the Holy Sepulchre (d. 1100), and King Baldwin I of Jerusalem (d. 1118), were childless. But her maternal Scottish kin were of diplomatic value to her (as discussed herein).

31. Stephen's bastard son Gervase was abbot of Westminster; a natural daughter wed Hervey le Breton, who held Devizes castle for Stephen (1140–41) and was made earl of Wiltshire in 1141. Stephen nominated his nephew

Henry de Sully as bishop of Salisbury and archbishop of York in 1140 and imposed another, William fitz Herbert, as archbishop of York, 1143–47 and 1153–54. A third nephew, Hugh du Puiset, was treasurer of York 1143–53 and bishop of Durham 1153–95.

32. West, *Justiciarship,* p. 25, thinks Matilda was regent after Roger of Salisbury fell in 1139 and during Stephen's 1141 captivity; in contrast, Cronne, *Reign of Stephen,* p. 188, thinks Roger was Stephen's only regent and that Matilda behaved as expected of any noble lady. I reject such terminology for Anglo-Norman queens, arguing they routinely shared royal power and governance. See also Hollister, "Administrative Kingship"; Bates, "Origins of the Justiciarship."

33. The best summary of Matilda [I] of Flanders's career is van Houts, "Matilda of Flanders,"; my thanks to Dr van Houts for sending me a copy of her work. For a case Matilda I judged in 1075, Paris BnF, coll. Moreau, t. 31, fol. 81r-v. On Matilda II of Scotland, see Huneycutt, "Images of Queenship" and *Another Esther.*

34. Huneycutt, "Images of Queenship," 65. Matilda II granted augmentations to fairs, ordered a confiscated ship to be returned to its rightful owner, and provided safe conducts; no noble or ecclesiastic could have exercised these powers.

35. Huneycutt, "Perfect Princess," 81, 89–91.

36. Matilda's children were Baldwin (b. ca. 1126, d. before December 1135), Eustace (b. 1130/31, d. August 10, 1153), Matilda (b. ca. 1134, d. late 1138/early 1139), William (b. before December 26, 1135, d. October, 1159), and Mary (b. 1136, d. 1182) (*Burke's Guide,* p. 194). I modify Burke's account in two respects. First, it seems unlikely that Baldwin was the eldest son: the counts of Boulogne had named their heirs "Eustace" since the early eleventh century. Burke's birth order probably rests on the assumption that Eustace became count of Boulogne (Christmas 1146) at 15 or 16. (The name "Baldwin" honored Matilda's uncle Baldwin I of Jerusalem [r. 1100–18]). Second, the Anglo-Norman dynastic name "William" suggests the third son was born after Henry I died and Stephen decided to claim the throne.

37. She perhaps reached England by January 4, 1136, the date of Henry I's funeral (RRAN 3: no. 678, dated 1136–37, probably January 4, 1136; and see no 944. for her coronation). For her presence at the Christmas court, see Gervase of Canterbury, *Opera Historica,* 1:96.

38. RRAN 3: nos. 945–49.

39. See Chart 6.1 and 6.2. In 1139–40 and 1146–8, Matilda averaged 4.3 attestations per year; the average was 3.0 for the other years of the reign. There are two charts; Chart 6.1 records charters with date ranges of under three years; Chart 6.2 records those with ranges over three years. To calculate the average attestations or issuance, equal portions have been assigned to each year of the date range. For example, charter No. 506 has a date range of 1136–37, and thus there is (½) 506 in the 1136 and (½) 506 in the 1137 column. The abbreviations are as follows: Davis = R.H.C. Davis,

King Stephen, 3rd ed.; ERO=Essex County Record Office; CPC=Bibliothèque national (Paris), Collection Picardie; D.C. Cox=D.C. Cox, "Two Unpublished Charters of King Stephen for Wenlock Priory"; Vincent=Nicholas Vincent, "Six new charters of King Stephen: The royal forest during the anarchy." My thanks to Dr. Vincent for allowing me to consult the charter transcripts prior to publication.

40. Richardson, "Coronation in Medieval England," p. 128.

41. RRAN 3: nos. 31, 915. The Barking grant can be dated between 1136 and March, 1137.

42. John of Hexham, *Continuation* 2:300; the quote is from Richard Prior of Hexham 3:176.

43. John of Hexham, *Continuation* 2:300; Richard of Hexham, *Chronicle* 3:176, 178; Farmer, "Persuasive Voices," pp. 517–43.

44. William of Newburgh, *Historia Rerum Anglicarum* 1:44; continuator of Florence of Worcester, in Florence of Worcester, *Chronicon ex Chronicis,* 2:125.

45. Minimal information exists on the betrothals of Matilda III's children other than Eustace. Matilda I was perhaps involved in her daughters' betrothals to Harold of Wessex, Alfonso of León, and Stephen of Blois (Douglas, *William the Conqueror,* pp. 393–95). Emperor Henry V sought Matilda II's support for his marriage to her daughter, but negotiations were conducted by his envoys and Henry I (Chibnall, *Empress Matilda,* pp. 15–16). John Carmi Parsons notes later queens' roles in their daughters' marriages in "Mothers, Daughters, Marriage, Power."

46. William of Malmesbury, *Historia Novella,* p. 44; John of Hexham, *Continuation* 2:306. Ranulph claimed some of the land given to Henry and King David by the Durham treaty.

47. *Les Annales de Saint-Pierre de Gand,* p. 166; Johan Buzelin, *Annales Gallo-Flandria* (Douai, 1624), p. 232. For the grants, see RRAN 3: nos. 194–95, 200 (Matilda's charter was issued in Boulogne).

48. Orderic Vitalis, *Historia Æcclesiastica* 6:521; Torigni, *Chronica,* ed. Howlett, 4:135.

49. John of Hexham, *Continuation* 2:310; *Gesta Stephani,* p. 127; Gervase of Canterbury, *Opera Historica* 1:19.

50. William of Malmesbury, *Historia Novella,* pp. 54–57.

51. *Gesta Stephani,* pp. 122–23. She harshly and abusively rejected the queen's and Bishop Henry's request to recognize Eustace's inheritance of the honor of Boulogne, and rejected the Londoners' petition to reduce their taxes. See Green, "Financing Stephen's War," 106–07 and *Reading Abbey Cartularies,* nos. 463–4 for the Londoners support of Stephen.

52. William of Malmesbury, *Historia Novella,* p. 58; William of Newburgh, *Chronicle* 1:45. Stephen apparently went to Lincoln leaving the two women under Mandeville's protection; Geoffrey allowed Matilda to retreat into Kent but kept Constance in the Tower. The incident might explain Stephen's seizure of Geoffrey's lands and titles at Michaelmas 1143.

53. William of Malmesbury, *Historia Novella,* p. 61; *Gesta Stephani,* p. 133; Florence of Worcester, *Chronicon* 1:134; Gervase of Canterbury, *Opera Historica* 2:74.

54. The geographical range of Matilda's charters (in bold) and attestations are as follows: London, total of twenty-seven (**24, 207, 224, 243, 512, 513, 541, 845,** 185, 402, 446, 471, 477, 479, 483, 501, 508, 511, 542, 633, 694, 760, 829, 830, 846, ERO D/Du 102/28, Vincent, no. 11), Westminster, total of nine (**239b,** 506, 743, **843, 845,** 944, 947–99), Bermondsey (**550,** 505, 957), Windsor (**539,** 35, 36, Cox no. 2), Rochester (**157**?, 198), Colchester (**239d**), Canterbury (**301**?, 162, 276), Castle Hedington (**503**), Reading (**850,** 678), St Albans, (662), Oxford, (**221**?, 478, 643, 667), Barking (34), Winchester (204, 341), Stamford (249), Eye (288), Marlborough (312), Cheshunt (538), Waverley (921), Guildford (960), Osinforth, (Davis, 167), Coggeshall (Davis, 166), Saffron Waldon (Vincent, no. 6), Lens (**26**), Boulogne (**196**), Lyon-la-Foret (598), no location, total of seventeen (**76, 149, 195, 509, 530, 548, 553, 556–57, 917, 184, 200, 284, 718, 757, 956,** CPIC t. 250 f. 268r-v). For Stephen this percentage is approximately 25 percent.

55. Probably for expediency's sake Stephen relied on Roger, Henry I's regent, until Roger's arrest in June 1139 for disturbing the peace of the court (White, "Continuity in Government," pp. 118–19). Roger attested thirty-nine of Stephen's charters and issued two charters of a regal nature (RRAN 3: nos. 313, 397). Of six writs addressed to Roger, five concern his see; the sixth, touching Barking Abbey, is addressed to him as regent (RRAN 3: nos. 31, 351–52, 525, 784, 786).

56. RRAN 3: no. 506.

57. "The Miracles of St. Ithamar," 435. Although it is not certain that the Queen Matilda in question is Stephen's wife, it seems most likely. Matilda III issued two charters from Rochester and incarcerated Robert of Gloucester there in 1141, RRAN 3: nos. 157, 198.

58. RRAN 3: no. 915.

59. RRAN 3: no. 530.

60. The statement of shared royal authority is echoed in other viceregal or regental charters, e.g., those of Bishop Roger of Salisbury (RRAN, 3: nos. 313, 397) and van Caenegem, *Royal Writs,* pp. 134, 159, 163–64. Both Roger and Matilda use the phrase, *precipio ex parte regis et mea* in "viceregal" charters (RRAN 3: nos. 313, 530); emphasis mine.

61. RRAN 3: no. 550.

62. RRAN 3: no. 557; Westminster Abbey archives, Muniment book 5, fol. 18r. For a discussion of the conflict see R.H.C. Davis, "The College of St Martin-Le-Grand," 16; West, *Justiciarship,* p. 25 uses this case and the previous to argue for Matilda's position as regent.

63. RRAN 3: nos. 548, 276; Davis, "The College of St Martin Le-Grand," 16–17.

64. The witnesses are Henry, bishop of Winchester; William of Ypres; Richard de Lucy; William Martel; Robert de Ver; and Robert de Salcheville. Writs,

from Henry I's reign, had few witnesses and they were primarily household officials (Caenegem, *Royal Writs,* pp. 148–49). See Chart 6.3.

65. None of Stephen's chancellors, masters of the scriptorium, butlers,
chamberlains, or marshals attested any of Matilda's charters; RRAN 3:
ix–xxi. Matilda developed her own set of officials, drawn from her comital holdings, who attest only her charters and none of Stephen's, with
the exception of her chamberlain Hubert, who attested four of
Stephen's charters. Three of Matilda's chancellors are known to us:
Ralph (ca. 1137–ca. 1141), Thomas (1142), and "A." (1147–52); we
know of five clerks and two chamberlains (RRAN 3: x, xiii, xix; William
of Malmesbury, *Historia Novella,* p. 58).

66. RRAN 3: nos. 149, 157, 509, 512, 530, 548, 550, 843, and 845 (9 of her
33 charters). Eleanor also routinely called upon royal officials (Richardson,
"Letters and Charters," 196, 201, 204).

67. Some historians argued that Stephen consciously decentralized government through his reliance on the earls and that this process was furthered
by the civil war. For a summary see Stringer, *Reign of King Stephen,* pp.
50–59. White, "Continuity in Government," p. 142, argues for a continuity of governmental institutions and practices between the reigns of Henry
I and Henry II. During Stephen's reign, royal administration was less effective but not dismantled.

68. Bernard of Clairvaux, *Letters,* p. 448. *Vita Sancti Bernardi,* RHF 14:373,
where Bernard is said to have helped Matilda in childbirth; he refers to her
son's recent birth in Migne, PL 182: col. 522. Bernard was in Flanders in
1131 and 1138; to my knowledge, Matilda was not in Boulogne in 1138,
so the letter likely refers to Eustace's birth.

69. Bernard of Clairvaux, *Letters,* pp. 267–68, emphasis mine.

70. Bernard witnessed Matilda's 1142 grant to Clairmarais (RRAN 3: no. 195).

71. Migne, PL 180: col. 1249.

72. Saltman, *Theobald,* pp. 25–30; Gervase of Canterbury, *Opera Historica,*
1:135. Eugenius ordered an interdict to be placed on England in July;
Theobald had returned to England by October and shortly thereafter settled his differences with Stephen.

73. On Aubrey, see Davis, *King Stephen,* pp. 140–41. See also *Cartularium Prioratus de Colne,* no. 56; RRAN 3: no. 242.

74. RRAN 3: xi, xiii–xv.

75. Other than Geoffrey of Monmouth's dedication of one copy of his history
to Stephen, there is no evidence of royal patronage of literature or art in
this reign (Legge, *Anglo-Norman Literature,* pp. 27–33; Bezzola, *Origines*
2:436–70). She may have commissioned the *vita* for her grandmother Ida
while she was countess (Nip, "Godelieve," pp. 212–13). The absence of this
type of patronage in Matilda of Boulogne's case most probably reflects the
financial demands of paying for mercenaries throughout most of Stephen's
reign, not the queen's disinterest or a deficiency of education.

76. Matilda also confirmed her grandmother Ida of Boulogne's gift to Bec, and
an agreement between Canterbury cathedral and Matilda of Saint-Saëns

(RRAN 3: nos. 76, 149). St. John's, Colchester, was also a recipient of her and her father's patronage; she granted the house Tey manor and exchanged East Donyland for Lillechurch (*Cartularium monasterii S. Johannis Baptiste de Colecestria,* p. 47; RRAN 3: nos. 221, 224, 239b, 239d). For gifts to the Cistercian houses of Clairmarais and Mortemer see Bouvet, "Le récit de la fondation de Mortemer"; RRAN 3: nos. 195, 196, 198.

77. On monasticism in England in Stephen's reign, Knowles and Hadcock, *Religious Houses;* Holdsworth, "The Church"; Guilloreau, "Les fondations anglaise."

78. Longvilliers was jointly founded by Stephen and Matilda, Auvry, *Histoire de la Congrégation de Savigny,* 2:247–48. Stephen founded Eagle (Templars), Ivychurch (Augustinian canons), and two Savignac houses, Furness (1125–27) and Buckfast (1136) (*The Lancashire Pipe Rolls,* p. 301, and CDF, ed. Round, no. 800). For Coggeshall, RRAN 3: no. 207.

79. RRAN 3: nos. 24–26 (including Stephen's grant).

80. *The Cartulary of the Knights of St John,* no. 212; *Records of the Templars in England,* ed. Lees, pp. xlviii-ix; RRAN, 3: no. 195, 272, 843.

81. RRAN 3: nos. 843–47, 850–53, 865. She also gave Cottered (Herts.) to the Templars (*Records of the Templars in England,* ed. Lees, pp. 43, 71).

82. Holy Trinity Aldgate "became the core of the 'queen's soke'" (Brooke and Keir, *London 800–1216,* p. 318). For family affiliations of the house, Parsons, "Burials and Posthumous Commemorations of English Queens," p. 330.

83. Saltman, *Theobald,* p. 345.

84. RRAN, 3:xi-xiii, nos. 503, 512–13. The Braughing charter was issued between August 1147 and April 1148.

85. Richard attested three of Matilda's charters and two of Stephen's (RRAN 3: nos. 177, 196, 198–99, 243; for references to him and to Robert, see nos. 536, 539–40, 553–54). Her gifts to St. Martin's can be dated ca. 1145–47, about the time Richard of Boulogne died.

86. *Reading Abbey Cartularies,* p. 15.

87. Elizabeth M. Hallam, "Royal Burial and the Cult of Kingship,"369–70; Philip, *Excavations at Faversham,* 7–17, 36; Tefler, "Faversham Reconsidered," 215–220. Faversham was 370 ft. in length. The choir's eastern end was extended by 6 bays to house the royal tombs and a monument decorated with Burgundian scalloped moldings and red, purple, and gold paint; tiles in this area were decorated with four rampant lions in a medallion. The western arm of the nave had cylindrical piers with spiral moldings, internal basket capitals, and chevron moldings (Philip, *Excavations at Faversham,* pp. 10, 15, 41).

88. Parsons, "Burials and Posthumous Commemorations of English Queens," pp. 320–21; Hallam, "Royal Burial and the Cult of Kingship," p. 339–80.

89. Gervase of Canterbury, *Opera Historica,* 1:138–39; *Annales Monasterii de Bermundseia,* 3:432; for the foundation, RRAN 3: nos. 300–02, and for Clarembald, RRAN 3: nos. 505, 550, 957.

90. *Reading Abbey Cartularies,* p. 15.

91. Gervase of Canterbury, *Opera Historica* 1:139; Saltman, *Theobald,* p. 71.

92. Huneycutt, "Perfect Princess," pp. 81–98; "De B. Ida vidua, Comitissa Boloniae in Gallo Belgica," AASS (April 13), pp. 139–50; Huyghebaert, "La Mère de Godefroid de Bouillon"; de Gaiffier, "Sainte Ide."

93. Burton, *Monastic and Religious Orders,* p. 95; de Bascher, "Robert d'Arbrissel"; on Fontevraud as especially a women's order, see Gold, *The Lady and the Virgin,* pp. 103–05.

94. Auvry, *Histoire de la congregation de Savigny* 2:247–48 (the foundation charter is lost; it is unclear whether Matilda or Stephen was the true founder). Stephen founded Savignac houses at Furness (1125–27) and Buckfast (1136) (*The Lancashire Pipe Rolls,* p. 301; CDF, ed. Round, no. 800).

95. RRAN 3: nos. 157, 336; Thompson, *Women Religious,* pp. 167–69, 203.

96. Holdsworth, "The Church," pp. 212–15. No lack of opportunity prevented the promotion of her chaplains; thirteen dioceses in England had two or three bishops in Stephen's reign. His failure to secure miters for nephews (above, n31) perhaps influenced Matilda's decision.

97. See Charts 6.1 and 6.2.

98. Her attestations decrease from an average of 4.3 in 1147 to 2.0 in 1150–52 (Charts 6.1 and 6.2). On Lillechurch, see Saltman, *Theobald,* p. 107 and charter no. 155. Mary went to Romsey Abbey ca. 1154 but was taken from there to marry Matthew of Flanders in 1160.

99. Torigni, *Chronica,* ed. Howlett, 4:160–63, 169–70; Gervase of Canterbury, *Opera Historica* 1:147, 149–51; Henry of Huntingdon, *Historia,* pp. 287, 293; *Gesta Stephani,* pp. 218–19, 222–24, 226, 230, 238. For the coinage, see Blackburn, "Coinage and Currency," p. 183; the second figure has been identified as Matilda and the issue dated 1141, but Blackburn argues that the "numismatic evidence points to an even later date . . . no earlier than c.1145 . . ." If this is right, the figure was probably Eustace.

100. Saltman, *Theobald,* pp. 37–38.

101. Gervase of Canterbury, *Opera Historica,* p. 160; Parsons, "Ritual and Symbol," p. 62.

102. *Reading Abbey Cartularies,* nos. 466–67; Dugdale, *Monasticon* 3:42, 88; *Early Charters of the Cathedral Church of St Paul, London,* no. 48; *Chronicon monasterii de Abingdon* 2:225; John of Salisbury, *Letters* 1: nos. 32, 115, and 2: no. 136; Eyton, *Henry II,* pp. 40–43, 86, 93, 112, 129, 137–38, 144.

103. Eyton, *Henry II,* pp. 40, 43, 51, 58; Richardson, "Letters and Charters," p. 195.

104. Brown, "Eleanor of Aquitaine: Parent, Queen, and Duchess," p. 16; Torigni, *Chronica,* ed. Howlett, 4:201–02; Eyton, *Henry II,* p. 86.

105. Eleanor witnessed two of Henry's English charters, both for Holy Trinity Priory, Eyton, *Henry II,* p. 6, and one of his French charters, *Recueil des Actes de Henri II* 1:541.

CHAPTER 7

THE BIRTH AND CHILDHOOD OF KING JOHN:
SOME REVISIONS

Andrew W. Lewis

> *This reexamination of the record of John's early years, and of his place in the family group, tends to confirm the view already advanced by some scholars that Eleanor spent considerably less time with him than she had spent with his older brothers.*

The birth and childhood of King John have received attention not only in biographies of the king himself but perhaps especially in scholarship on Eleanor of Aquitaine, and that for two reasons.[1] First, for several decades now, historians have seen the birth of Eleanor's youngest child as representing a change in her life cycle—as the end of the years of almost constant childbearing in her marriage to Henry II and prelude to the brief period in which she was Henry's deputy in Poitou, then to the longer one in which she was his captive in England.[2] Second, in recent studies John's childhood has been the subject of a scholarly debate centered on what models of familial practice may properly be used as a framework within which to assess Eleanor's impact on the development of John's personality. At issue has been whether, as one scholar has suggested, Eleanor's almost total absence from John's life during his early years would have contributed significantly to the formation of the "paranoia and unprincipled opportunism" that characterized John the adult; or whether, as another has argued, Eleanor's style of parenting was typical of her class. This view posits a family system in which mothers bore children but did not nurture them or directly participate in their upbringing; servants, tutors, or other surrogates performed those functions. From this latter perspective, John would have been no more psychologically deprived in respect to his parents than were most other sons in royal or great noble families of the time. His isolation from Eleanor would thus not be exceptional and would not account for the peculiar formation of his personality.[3]

Close inspection of the scholarship on John's childhood reveals, however, a discrepancy in quality between the imaginative and insightful lines of analysis that scholars have advanced, and the state of the factual base on which parts of that analysis have been founded. Crudely put, we as a group have too trustingly accepted the word of our predecessors in respect to certain of the biographical data, most of which have appeared to be so basic that we have assumed that they had long since been established. As a consequence, the accepted record is flawed in numerous regards. Most of these are small points. Indeed, some of them may appear initially to be mere details of little more than antiquarian interest. In practice, however, the data are sufficiently scant that even seemingly inconsequential errors are sometimes susceptible of distorting our view of genuinely significant issues. In the interest, therefore, of better securing our base for ongoing investigation, the present article will seek to establish more exactly certain of the data concerning John's earliest years.

The supposed facts are as follows. John is said to have been born at Oxford, his parents' fifth son, the youngest child of a mother who herself had been born in 1122. The year of his birth (1166 or 1167) is disputed. So is the day (24 or 27 December). Early, perhaps when Eleanor took up residence in Poitou in January 1168, he was placed at Fontevraud Abbey, where he remained for five years. He is thought subsequently to have entered the household of his eldest brother, Henry, the young King, where he would have received the customary training of a boy of his class.[4] Almost all of these statements are either inaccurate, as yet inadequately documented, or subject to qualification.

To review these points in the order of reference above, there is no credible authority for saying that John was born at Oxford. The claim rests entirely on a late source: a prose addition, itself of unknown date, to the verse chronicle written by Robert of Gloucester during the reign of Edward I (1272–1307).[5] The reference to Oxford in this addition is, moreover, one of several interpolations in a longer passage composed of notes that the glossator derived from the chronicle of Robert of Torigny.[6] The insertion may represent an authentic tradition; it may equally well be no more than an echo of a similar record, found only three sentences earlier in Robert of Gloucester's text, regarding the birth of John's older brother Richard.[7]

The most nearly corroboratory evidence that can be affirmed from contemporary sources is that Eleanor does appear to have been in England at the time of John's birth.[8]

As for his place in the family group, John was his parents' youngest child, but not their fifth son: he was the fifth whose name is recorded. Ralph of Diceto who, as dean of Saint Paul's at London, was in a position to know, wrote that Henry II and Eleanor had *six* sons, two who died in childhood and four who survived.[9] One of the former would have been the eldest son William (1153–56); the other a son whom other contemporary writers did not mention and whose existence modern historians have overlooked. The rapid succession of births between those of William (1153) and Geoffrey (1158) leaves no time for the unrecorded births of any other children during those years. This previously unnoticed son must, therefore, have been born either between the births of Geoffrey (September 1158) and Eleanor (ca. September 1161), or between those of Eleanor and Joan (October 1165).[10]

For Eleanor of Aquitaine's age, most recent scholars have relied on Alfred Richard, the great modern specialist on the counts of Poitou. But details of this sort were not among Richard's strengths as a scholar. Moreover, he vacillated in his statements on the subject, and his argument is circular. Thus, when speaking of Eleanor's birth, he wrote that it was only from knowing that she was eighty-two years old when she died, in 1204, that one could place her birth in 1122. Yet when speaking of her death, he gave her age as "*about* eighty-two years," while citing no source to that effect.[11] Even if such a source were adduced, moreover, one might question how reliable it would be, that is, whether writers that late—most of whom would have been much younger than she—would have known exactly how old Eleanor was. One may place greater confidence in the genealogical text composed at Limoges in the later-thirteenth-century records a presumably earlier tradition that she was thirteen years old at the time of her father's death, in April 1137.[12] Not only would more people at that time, before the passing of generations, have been likely to have known her age but, because by canon law a woman had to be at least twelve years old in order to marry, the information would have had a practical relevance. By contrast, Eleanor's exact age at the time of her death had none.

The next issue, the date of John's birth, requires detailed examination because of a contradiction in the sources: Robert of Torigny placed the birth in 1167, Ralph of Diceto in 1166.[13] William Stubbs considered Torigny the better authority, but Stubbs was using a very old edition of Robert's chronicle.[14] In it, the record of John's birth, Robert's last notation for the year 1167, figured, with no indication of break, immediately after a note on the appearance of two meteors on Christmas Eve of that year.

Since Robert began the year at Christmas, it seemed from the position of these notes that he placed John's birth precisely on December 24, 1167. Stubbs adopted that date, and most recent British and American scholars have followed him on the subject.[15]

That interpretation would have been valid had Robert been more systematic in his manner of composition, that is, had he written in unified sequence for each year. In fact, he did not. Writing contemporaneously, as he learned of events, he appears to have made notes on separate sheets or tablets that his clerks, after some interval, transcribed into the working copy of the chronicle, sometimes with disregard for chronology.[16] In some cases, events are recorded under the year during which Robert heard of them rather than when they actually occurred: for example, the election of Maurice of Sully as bishop of Paris in 1160, which the chronicle attributes to 1161.[17] For others, scribal carelessness may be the explanation, as when Robert's scribe entered under the year 1168 the record of the departure of Henry II's daughter Matilda for her marriage to the duke of Saxony; other sources establish that Matilda left for Saxony in September 1167.[18] One finds such inattention even in respect to extremely important events. For example, the note that Becket was canonized "in the following year" was inserted on an erasure in the entry for 1171, which was one year early, since in fact the canonization of Becket did not occur until 1173.[19]

Stubbs did not know, but the critical editions published since he wrote reveal, that the record of John's birth was an insertion into the original transcription of Robert's entry for 1167. Paleographically distinct, the note was entered, after completion of the body of the entry, in the space left blank for the rubric of the year 1168.[20] Given what is now known about Robert's method of redaction, one may prudently infer no more than that the insertion was made at that spot because that was where there remained space in which to write it. Its position does not signify that Robert intended this note to be a sequel to the record of the meteors, that is, that he attributed the birth to December 24. Indeed, given the numerous errors by Robert or his clerks in respect to chronology, one may question whether the chronicle can be trusted even as to the year.

Ralph of Diceto, by contrast, did not write until perhaps fifteen to twenty years after John's birth. He did, however, use older notes or records; he was well informed and was generally careful in his work.[21] Moreover, his attribution of John's birth to 1166 is reinforced by his later remark that John was "vix bene septenni[s]," barely seven years old, in February 1173 when Henry II betrothed him to the daughter of the count of Maurienne.[22]

The only other contemporary who mentions the birth was a canon at Laon who wrote in the second decade of the thirteenth century. This writer does not record the year but states that John was so named because he was born around the time of the feast of St. John, that is, December 27.[23] This source is late, and the writer was inaccurate on some matters, but his statement that John was born in December and Diceto's that John had just recently turned seven in early 1173 appear mutually corroborative as to the month.[24]

One strand in French scholarship has viewed December 27, 1166, as John's birthdate. This opinion stems, however, from Alfred Richard's misinterpretation of the canon of Laon. Richard read the text as saying that John was born *on* the feast of St. John rather than *around* that time; he then attempted to reconcile this date with the evidence of Robert of Torigny on the basis that, since Robert had calculated the beginning of the year from Christmas, December 27, 1167, by his system pertained to the year 1166 by modern reckoning.[25] There are problems with this explanation. First, the canon of Laon did not give a precise birthdate. Second, since Ralph of Diceto also began the year at Christmas but placed John's birth in 1166, the manner of reckoning the year cannot account for the discrepancy in dates.[26] A slight variant, however, could do so. For if John were born in England around the middle of December, Ralph, at London, could have learned of the birth prior to Christmas. By contrast, Robert, at Mont-Saint-Michel, would not have learned of it until some time afterward, that is, in 1167 as reckoned by the Christmas style.

A more solid means of addressing the issue of the year of John's birth may lie in the indirect evidence furnished by the itineraries of Henry II and Eleanor of Aquitaine. As best they can be reconstructed, these itineraries show that Eleanor was in England in late 1166.[27] In respect to late 1167, the record is obscure, and there are problems with the sources.

From the Pipe Roll it appears that Eleanor was in England for at least part of the fall in 1167, prior to crossing to Normandy at a date no later than December 1167.[28] Whether she attended the "great court" that Henry II held at Argentan at Christmas that year is not recorded (although she and the king commonly did keep Christmas together).[29] By the spring of 1168, she was in Poitou where Henry, facing a rebellion by several great lords of the region, placed her in charge of his administration. The first event recorded of her time there was the slaying in her presence of the earl of Salisbury, on about April 7, 1168.[30] When Eleanor would have reached Poitou can only be inferred from the vague record of Henry II's itinerary. Henry was in the north when he learned of the revolt in Poitou. He rushed southward, seized the rebel castle of Lusignan, ravaged the region, placed fighting men and provisions in his own castles, then left the queen behind in care of the earl of Salisbury while he himself returned northward to meet with Louis VII near Mantes on April 7.[31] A charter issued probably on his journey northward shows him to have been at Angers on

March 24.[32] Since Henry is said to have left Eleanor behind (*relicta*), it follows that she was already in Poitou by that date.[33]

If one believes the biography of William Marshal, Henry II and Eleanor were in England when reports of the revolt in Poitou reached them. The king at once summoned his forces and hastened to the continent, bringing Eleanor with him. There they followed a circular route through Normandy, then traveled through Maine and Anjou to Poitou.[34] If this version is accurate—at least in general outline, whether or not in all particulars—it would indicate that Henry and Eleanor crossed over to England after Christmas 1167 and that word of the revolt reached them there in January or February 1168. It would also imply that the entry in the Pipe Roll relative to Eleanor's crossing to Normandy referred to an earlier crossing by the queen and her entourage rather than to her embarkation with Henry preparatory to their march to Poitou. If so, the conjecture that she may have attended Henry's Christmas court at Argentan is strengthened.[35]

From this reasoning it follows that if John was born in England and in the month of December, Eleanor's itinerary for 1166 is compatible with the assignment of the birth to that year. By contrast, it is not clear where she was during December 1167. She appears to have been in England until December at the earliest. That element, however, need not be crucial, because it is only on the flimsiest evidence that one can argue a priori for placing John's birth in England. By contrast, the evidence that implies that Eleanor traveled that month to spend Christmas at Argentan raises very serious doubts whether that could have been the year of the birth, since it seems unlikely that she would have undertaken such an arduous trip within two weeks of the birth. From this analysis, 1166 would seem to be the more probable date.

Two other fragments of evidence point to the same conclusion. As has been seen, in 1167 Henry II and Eleanor may have kept Christmas together at Argentan. In 1166, by contrast—and atypically—they were apart at Christmas. More strikingly, Eleanor was in England and Henry at Poitiers, where he had his eldest son join him for the occasion.[36] For Henry, on the only Christmas in his reign that he spent at Poitiers, to have summoned his heir—doubtless to show the Poitevins their future lord or overlord—yet to have failed to summon and display his queen, the Poitevin heiress, seems anomalous. If, however, Eleanor was pregnant and approaching term at that moment, the omission is convincingly explained.

If one investigates to see where Henry II and Eleanor were nine months before the supposed birthdate, the sources accord perfectly for 1166 but for 1167 are, again, problematical. In 1166, Henry II and Eleanor were both in Normandy during March.[37] For 1167 their itineraries are less well known. Henry was at Rouen at some time in February, at Grandmont during Lent (probably March), and on campaign in Auvergne after Easter (April 9).[38] Eleanor's whereabouts during the same period are not clearly known. Some evidence seems to indicate that she was in England. But nothing places her on the Continent in March.[39]

In sum, converging lines of evidence point to 1166 as the probable year of John's birth and to England as the place. From the chronicles alone, there would seem to be no sure way to establish a preference between Robert of Torigny's testimony and that of Ralph of Diceto. From the itineraries of Henry II and Eleanor, however, probabilities emerge. If John was born in December, in 1166 Henry and Eleanor were together during the month in which John would have been conceived, and Eleanor was in England during the month he would have been born. In 1167, they probably were not together in March, and she may or may not have been in England in December.

The evidence reviewed thus far, though pertinent to factual exactitude regarding John, contributes perhaps more substantively to our understanding of Eleanor. For one theme in scholarship on the queen has been the rapid succession of the births of her children by Henry II during the 1150s: William in 1153, followed by Henry in 1155—Henry II and Eleanor had been apart for much of the interim—then Matilda in 1156, Richard in 1157, and Geoffrey in 1158. Then the pace seemed to slow, with the births of Eleanor in 1161, Joan in 1165, and John in 1166, or, as it appeared to some, 1167.[40] One scholar has suggested that stillbirths may have intervened between some of the later births.[41] Others have assumed that the approach of menopause lowered Eleanor's fertility in the 1160s.[42]

Revisions proposed in this chapter require some modification of our image of Eleanor during her later childbearing years. First, if 1124 is accepted as the year of her birth, she was two years younger than most scholars have assumed. Second, establishment of the year of John's birth places the end of her childbearing one year earlier than many had believed. Thus, if the revisions proposed for these dates are accepted, Eleanor would have had her last child not when she was forty-five but at the age of forty-two. In addition, the discovery of a previously unnoticed son increases by one the number of offspring known to have been born to her between 1159 and 1164. Accordingly, the idea that Eleanor's fertility decreased as she neared menopause appears tenuous. That the births of Joan and John occurred only fourteen months apart casts doubt on that thesis in any case; the suspicion of merely a single miscarriage or stillbirth during those years would undermine it completely.

There remain for review the issues of John's years at Fontevraud and his placement in his brother Henry's household. The latter of these may be disposed of quickly: it is a modern myth founded on a misreading of the *Gesta regis Henrici II*. The text says merely that in August 1170 Henry II, gravely ill, in anticipation of death entrusted John to the young King, "that he might advance him and maintain him."[43] Nothing positively indicates that John entered his brother's household then or later, and the body of evidence strongly suggests that he did not.[44]

The matter of John's time at Fontevraud is more complicated. Recent scholars have based their discussion of the subject entirely on a note by Alfred Richard, itself based on the entry for John in a series of obituary notices on eminent patrons of Fontevraud, preserved in the cartulary of the abbey.[45] The obituary notice records the death of King John, who "was given to us and to our church as an oblate by his most illustrious father King Henry and for a period of five years was cared for by us."[46] Seeing in this placement an element that markedly differentiated John's childhood from those of his brothers, historians have sought to draw all possible meaning from Alfred Richard's terse report. In so doing, they have gone beyond the explicit terms either of his note or of the obituary notice itself—assigning the placement to an approximate date (1168 or 1169), attributing the initiative to Eleanor (thus by implication linking it to her withdrawal to Poitou), or conjecturing that the placement indicates an early plan, later discarded, to prepare John for an ecclesiastical career.[47]

This notice, of late composition, is probably based in part on reminiscences or oral traditions within the abbey, but nothing in it arouses suspicion as to accuracy. One might question whether in fact the author knew which of John's parents had placed him at Fontevraud, but there seems no reason to doubt that it was Henry. Within the family system, a decision of that sort would almost certainly have fallen within the father's jurisdiction.[48] The description of John as an oblate, however, is problematical unless the term is understood to denote any boy, other than a temporary guest, who had been lodged at the abbey. In fact, the peculiar character of Fontevraud renders it highly unlikely that John was placed there to be trained for an ecclesiastical career; for Fontevraud was a "double abbey," ruled by an abbess, in which the women outranked and were served by the men. As such, it would have been a questionable environment in which to rear a king's son intended for high office in the church's exclusively male hierarchy.[49]

On balance, the evidence seems more to suggest that John's placement at Fontevraud represents a provision of child care for him. Moreover, his sister Joan, who was only one year older than he, was also there, probably at the same time and for the same reason.[50] The years involved may be identified by indirect means. One may presume that John was there when very young, that is, before he had reached the age at which he would be placed under the direction of men for training in the masculine skills of his class. For both children, the *terminus ante quem* is set by their crossing from Normandy to England with their father on July 8, 1174, during the later phases of the Great Revolt.[51] Since John was in England, at least at certain times, in 1176, 1177, 1178 or 1179, and 1182, the five years he spent at Fontevraud could only have preceded July 1174.[52] Similarly, Joan was in England in May 1176, when ambassadors from William II of Sicily came to seek her hand in marriage for their king.[53] From the *terminus ante quem* one may seek a *terminus a quo*. No date can be set for Joan; the obituary notice composed for her at Fontevraud says that she had been "cared for" or "reared" by the nuns but gives no indication of how long she was with them. For John, greater precision is possible: the reference to five years in the obituary notice for him implies that his placement dates from 1169 or early 1170. John would therefore have been at the abbey from the age of around three until he was seven or seven and a half; Joan, from an undetermined age until she was eight or eight and a half. Nothing suggests that the older sibling next in age, Eleanor, ever lived at Fontevraud. Indeed, she appears to have been in Aquitaine with her mother precisely in 1169, when envoys from Alfonso VIII of Castile sought her as bride for him, and she was sent to Castile the next year.[54] The elder children appear not to have lived at Fontevraud, either.[55] A pattern thus emerges. Only the two youngest of the children were placed at Fontevraud. Their time there corresponds to years when their mother was almost always absent in Poitou and Aquitaine. This synchronism, and the contrast between the arrangements made for these children and as much as is known about the early childhood of their elder siblings, suggests that Eleanor's absence should be considered a major element in the decision to place them in an abbey.

One must ask why, of all the abbeys in the Angevin empire, Fontevraud should have been the one chosen. Two elements conspicuously favor Fontevraud: its location and the gender of the religious. First, given Eleanor's designation as royal deputy or regent in Aquitaine, an English abbey would have been inaccessible to her. But within the parents' Continental lands, the central location of Fontevraud would make it accessible to both Henry and Eleanor, he from Normandy or Anjou, she from Poitou, for such parental functions as they chose to fulfill. Second, for the care of young children, an abbey of nuns would have been preferred over a community of monks, and that for at least two reasons: first, Joan was female, and second, at their stages of life both children would have needed female attendants. Among convents of nuns, Fontevraud was the one with the closest ties to both sides of John's family. Its ties to Eleanor's ancestors are well known, but those to Henry II's family were even closer, since his aunt Matilda of Anjou had been a nun, then abbess there.[56] Moreover, at

precisely the time Joan and John were placed at Fontevraud, King Henry's
first cousin, Matilda of Flanders, was a nun there. Whether her presence in
the abbey was a significant factor in determining the selection of
Fontevraud for the children is impossible to assess. Daughter to a sister of
Henry II's father, Geoffrey Plantagenet, she was the only older female col-
lateral relative of high birth within the closer ranks of the extended family whom they would have known—all the others, except for Count
Geoffrey's illegitimate children, were geographically distant. What nurturing Matilda of Flanders might have offered the children one cannot know.
A younger child herself, she had taken her vows as a nun at the age of fourteen and probably had had little if any contact with children, during the
twelve or more years since then.[57] She would at least have contributed to
the oversight of the children's upbringing as a representative of the family
and as a model for them of whatever social skills were expected from
young members of great princely families.[58]

From these revisions a slightly altered image of John's childhood emerges,
perhaps especially in relation to his mother. John was barely one year old
when Henry II put Eleanor in charge of his government in Poitou. Perhaps at that time, the king thought the assignment temporary, that Eleanor
would bring some calm to the region, freeing him to deal with pressing
matters in the north. Whatever the initial plan, it was not until a year, perhaps a year and several months, later that John was placed at Fontevraud.
This lag is comprehensible if one views it in relation to the prolongation
of Eleanor's stay in Poitou. In the meanwhile, John, and perhaps Joan,
would have been left at royal residences, probably in England. As time
passed, this arrangement apparently proved unsatisfactory—hence the
move to Fontevraud, with the possibility for immediate oversight by
Matilda of Flanders or others, and for intermittent contact with Eleanor.
Modern historians have assumed that, since Eleanor stayed principally in
Poitou during those years, such contact was slight if it occurred at all. In
fact, little is known about Eleanor's itinerary during this period. She may
very well have made visits to Fontevraud of which there is no record.[59]
Nothing, however, suggests that John resided with her for any period of
time. The conclusion appears inescapable, therefore, that throughout his
early childhood John saw less of his mother than had his brothers.

After the Great Revolt of 1173–74, John does not appear to have been
placed in his eldest brother's household. Thus the possibility for fraternal
attachment, which has been hypothesized on that basis, did not exist. Instead, John is found sometimes in his father's company, sometimes in that
of others. By this time, however, he was of an age to be placed in the

household of someone other than his parents. During these years, he may have seen no less of his father than had his brothers at the same stage in their lives; certainly, however, he saw less of Eleanor than they had.[60]

In two other significant regards as well, John's upbringing was different from that of his brothers. First, because of his position as youngest child and the seven-year difference in ages between himself and Geoffrey, he had no brother close to him in age with whom he could be reared and therefore bond. Second, as the youngest, and also because of the early age at which his sisters were sent off for marriage, John had totally different relationships with them than did his brothers. He did not know his oldest sisters at all; they had both left before he could have had lasting memories of them. Joan he knew; she would have been his companion during much of his childhood—but she was sent off to be married when he was nine. With an absent mother either sent away or allowed to retire as a consequence of menopause, absent sisters, and no grandmother, John's family, as he would have experienced it, was notably lacking in female presence.

With respect to John and his brothers, one is perhaps dealing in all these regards more with differences in degree than with differences in kind. John's case was unique, however, in that in each regard he would have experienced greater deprivation than did his siblings. By that measure, it would be misleading to see the outlines of John's upbringing as conforming to a norm for boys of his class, though it may have been less unusual for younger sons in large families. That said, another adjustment to our view should be considered. By any reasonable standard, those traits that Henry II and Eleanor brought to the rearing of their sons had unfortunate results. One is dealing with a bad lot. It is hardly surprising that John, whose experiences would appear to have been even worse than those of his brothers, should have turned out even worse than did they.

Notes

1. Among biographies of John, see in particular Norgate, *John Lackland,* pp. 1–8; Warren, *King John,* pp. 17, 26–30; Turner, *King John,* pp. 20–25.
2. Labande, "Pour une image véridique," 203–08; Brown, "Eleanor of Aquitaine: Parent, Queen, and Duchess," p. 17; Duby, *Dames du XIIᵉ siècle,* pp. 32–33. Because of the historiographical importance of Professor Brown's 1976 article, I cite the original version throughout. See also, however, the revised and expanded version published as chapter 1 in this volume.
3. For the first of these views, Brown, "Eleanor of Aquitaine: Parent, Queen, and Duchess," pp. 17, 24. For the second, Turner, "Eleanor of Aquitaine and Her Children," 325–26, 329, and Turner, *King John,* pp. 20–24, 35–38. For a thesis of much greater involvement by Eleanor in her children's lives, see

Honeycutt, "Public Lives, Private Ties" in *Medieval Mothering,* ed. Parsons and Wheeler, pp. 297–98, 306–08. One effect of Huneycutt's analysis is to delineate differences between John's rearing and that of his brothers.

4. Warren, *King John,* pp. 17, 26; Turner, "Eleanor and Her Children," 327, and Turner, *King John,* pp. 20, 23–24; Richard, *Histoire des comtes de Poitou* 2:155, 375.

5. Robert of Gloucester, *Chronicle* 2:484.

6. Torigni, *Chronica,* ed. Howlett, 4:195, 207, 221, 233, 252.

7. The detail on Richard's birth is also an addition; it is not found in Torigni, *Chronica,* ed. Howlett, 4:195. It does appear, however, that Richard was born at Oxford: Ralph of Diss [de Diceto], *Opera historica* 1:302.

8. Eyton, *Henry II,* pp. 103–04, 108; see also below, nn27–36.

9. Ralph of Diss, *Opera Historica,* 2:16–17, and 2:269–70.

10. For the births, except Matilda's, see Torigni, *Chronica,* ed. Howlett, 4:176, 183, 195, 197, 211, 226; Eyton, *Henry II,* pp. 54–55. For Matilda, see Ralph of Diss, *Opera Historica,* 1:302; Eyton, p. 18. The length of the interval between the births of William and Henry is explained by Henry II's absence in England from January 1153 until April 1154, while Eleanor remained on the Continent (Torigni, *Chronica,* ed. Howlett, 4:171–79; Gervase of Canterbury, *Opera Historica,* 1:151–58). After Henry, other children (Matilda, Richard, and Geoffrey) were born at the rate of one per year from 1156 through 1158. Professor Brown and I have discussed the possibility that the younger son who died was the twin of one of the previously known children and that he died soon after birth. Upon reflection, I believe that Diceto's statement that this son died "in childhood, *pueritia,*" should be taken to mean that he survived early infancy. For that reason, both here and below (text following n42), I view him as the fruit of a separate pregnancy. Since William died at the age of slightly less than three years, it appears that Diceto was using the word *pueritia* in the sense (derived from Augustine) of denoting the time before a boy learns to speak, rather than the probably more common definition (derived from Isidore) of the age between seven and fourteen years; see Sears, *The Ages of Man,* esp. pp. 56, 125.

11. Richard, *Histoire des comtes de Poitou* 1:488 and n1, 2:437 (emphasis added).

12. "Fragmentum genealogicum ducum Normanniae et Angliae regum," in RHF 18:241. The source is Paris, BnF latin 5452, an early fourteenth-century manuscript from Saint-Martin of Limoges containing copies of earlier materials from Saint-Martial of Limoges. I cite the relevant sentence from fol. 70v: "M.C.XXXVI, quinto idus aprilis quod tunc fuit in parasceue obiit Willelmus palatinus comes pictauensis, ultimus dux acquitanie relinquens Iudovico francorum regi . . . [In 1136, on the fifth ides of April, which in that year was Good Friday, William, count palatine of Poitou and the last duke of Aquitaine, died at Saint James in Galicia, leaving his only daughter, named Eleanor, aged thirteen years, whom he had begotten of the sister of the viscount of Châtellerault, and the principal-

ity of Aquitaine, to Louis, king of the French]." Initial reaction to this source may be skepticism as to its reliability because of the number of errors it contains. Fuller investigation, however, reveals that the text is essentially a pastiche of excerpts from the chronicle of Geoffroi de Vigeois and that most of the errors are from Geoffroi's record of events from outside the Limousin; see Geoffroi de Vigeois, Chronica 1.43, 44, 48, 53, 55, 56, 72, 2.6, pp. 302, 304, 308–10, 327, 332. By contrast, although the sentence pertinent here was adapted from Geoffroi (p. 304), the death date of William X and Eleanor's age are interpolations drawn from a different source. The note on William is accurate: He died on Good Friday, April 9, 1137. The citation of the year as 1136 may be a copyist's error, or it may reflect the style of reckoning the year from Easter that was introduced at Limoges in the thirteenth century; see Guibert, "Les formules de date." Moreover, since Geoffroi had not mentioned William's children other than Eleanor, a later writer who relied on his chronicles could well have assumed that she had been an only child. The provenience of the manuscript and the author's dependence on Geoffroi, point to Limoges as the place of composition. The mention of Edward I in the piece implies a date of composition after 1272. A somewhat later date may be preferred, for the text calls the two Constances, wife and daughter of Geoffrey, son of Henry II, "Berta" and "Brita" respectively. "Berta" may be a scribal corruption of "Brita" and translated as "the Breton woman," used disrespectfully in place of the given name because of anti-Breton sentiment prompted by resentment of Arthur of Brittany, by marriage viscount of Limoges, who, beginning in 1277, quarreled bitterly with the abbot and monks of Saint-Martial; see *Chroniques de Saint-Martial de Limoges*, pp. 135–136, 140, 180, 197–198; see also ibid., pp. 172–73, 175–76. The amount of detail on William X may suggest that for these interpolations the author drew on written material that is now lost. In subsequent studies I shall examine other texts from this manuscript. Among recent scholars, Labande cites this source in a footnote but, in the corresponding text, leans toward the date advanced by Richard, "Pour une image véridique," 176–77. Later (233), when Labande says that "she died at the age of eighty-two years, at Poitiers, according to a single chronicler," he cites as source the "Chronicae Sancti Albini Andegavensis." This source does say that Eleanor died at Poitiers, but says nothing about her age (*Chroniques des églises d'Anjou*, ed. Marchegay and Mabille, p. 53). Duby, *Dames du XIIe siècle*, p. 14, is the only scholar I have seen who has accepted 1124 as the year of Eleanor's birth.

13. Torigni, *Chronica*, ed. Howlett, 4:233; Ralph of Diss, *Opera Historica* 1:325.

14. William Stubbs, introduction to Walter of Coventry, *Memoriale* 2:xvii n3 (hereafter: Walter of Coventry, *Memoriale*). Stubbs used a 1726 reprint of the text of this chronicle that Johann Pistorius had published in 1513 (Walter of Coventry, *Memoriale* 2:xvii n3; see also Howlett's preface to Torigni, *Chronica*, ed. Howlett, 4:lxvi-lxvii).

15. Walter of Coventry, *Memoriale* 2:xvii n. 3. Earlier, Norgate had hesitated between 1166 and 1167 (Norgate, *England Under the Angevin Kings* 2:130 n7; by 1902, she had adopted 1167 (Norgate, *John Lackland* p. 1). For 1167, see also Poole, *From Domesday Book to Magna Carta*, p. 330; Warren, *Henry II*, p. 78; Turner, "Eleanor and Her Children," 325, and Turner, *King John*, p. 20. But for December 24, 1166, see Warren, *King John*, p. 17.

16. Torigni, *Chronica*, ed. Howlett, 4:lix-lxi.

17. Torigni, *Chronica*, ed. Howlett, 4:211.

18. Torigni, *Chronica*, ed. Howlett, 4:234; Eyton, *Henry II*, p. 109; *The Great Roll of the Pipe for the Thirteenth Year of the Reign of King Henry the Second, A.D. 1166–1167*, Pipe 11, pp. 2, 18, 19, 37, 194.

19. Torigni, *Chronica*, ed. Howlett, 4:250.

20. Torigni, *Chronica*, ed. Howlett, 4:233 n7. The earlier edition by Delisle had also signalled the note as an addition (Torigni, *Chronique* 1:369 n6).

21. Stubbs, preface to Ralph of Diss, *Opera Historica* 2:xv-xvi.

22. Ralph of Diss, *Opera Historica* 1:353.

23. "Ex chronico anonymi canonici, ut videtur, Laudunensis," in RHF 13:679.

24. Among inaccuracies, note the canon's statement, RHF 13:679, that "they nicknamed him John 'Lackland' because he was born after his father had divided his lands among his sons," although that did not happen until 1169.

25. Richard, *Histoire des comtes de Poitou* 2:140–41; Labande, "Pour une image véridique," 203.

26. Thus his entries for 1170, 1171, 1172, 1187, 1192 and 1195 all begin with events which occurred on or immediately after December 25 (Ralph of Diss, *Opera Historica* 1:337, 342, 350; 2:47, 103–04, 124).

27. Eyton, *Henry II*, pp. 103–04, 108.

28. Eyton, *Henry II*, p. 112.

29. That Torigni, *Chronica*, ed. Howlett, 4:234, specifies that Henry "held a *magna curia* in his new hall" at Argentan may imply that the occasion was unusually grand. Note the lack of such comment in Torigny's notes on where Henry kept Christmas in 1166, 1168, and 1169 (Torigni, *Chronica*, ed. Howlett, 4:229, 240, 244).

30. Torigni, *Chronica*, ed. Howlett, 4:235–36.

31. Torigni, *Chronica*, ed. Howlett, 4:235–36; John of Salisbury, *Letters*, 2:562–67 (ep. 272).

32. *Recueil des actes de Henri II* 1: no. 267 at pp. 414–15.

33. Torigni, *Chronica*, ed. Howlett, 4:236: " . . . relicta ibi regina cum comite Patricio Salesberiensi [having left the queen there with Earl Patrick of Salisbury] . . ."

34. *L'Histoire de Guillaume le Maréchal* 1:58–60 (lines 1565–1618).

35. The *chanson* of William Marshal was based on William's own recollections as transmitted to the poet by William's son and confidants, and its general credibility is high. In the present context, I view it with some reserve on particular details. Since William accompanied the royal forces

from England to Normandy and then Poitou, I see no reason to doubt his report that Henry had been in England when he issued the summons. As for Eleanor's whereabouts at that moment, one may wonder how precise the poet's information was. I would not exclude the possibility that Henry had left her on the Continent when he went to England, then had her join him as he passed through Normandy on the way to Poitou. None of the other movements hypothesized here for the royal couple would have been out of the ordinary. Henry not uncommonly kept Christmas on one side of the Channel, then crossed to the other between January and early March; see Eyton, *Henry II,* pp. 15–16, 58, 77–78, 132–35. In some years Eleanor, or she and some of their children, spent Christmas with Henry on the Continent and then crossed to England (Eyton, *Henry II,* pp. 20, 24, 49).

36. Eyton, *Henry II,* pp. 103–104, 112.
37. Eyton, *Henry II,* pp. 92–93, 98; Torigni, *Chronica,* ed. Howlett, 4:226, 228; Ralph of Diss, *Opera Historica* 1:318.
38. Eyton, *Henry II,* pp. 104–106; Torigni, *Chronica,* ed. Howlett, 4:229–30.
39. v pp. 108–09. Torigni, *Chronica,* ed. Howlett, 4:233, states that Eleanor crossed to England with her daughter Matilda in 1167; if accurate, this would place her on the continent before that time. Eyton, however, puts her crossing in 1166. The lack of any mention in the Pipe Roll of a crossing by Eleanor between late 1166, when she appears in England, and late 1167, when she traveled to the continent, supports Eyton on this point.
40. For the dates of birth see above, n10.
41. Warren, *Henry II,* p. 78.
42. Labande, "Pour une image véridique," 202–03; Brown, "Eleanor of Aquitaine: Parent, Queen, and Duchess," p. 16; Duby, *Dames du XIIe siècle,* p. 32.
43. *Gesta regis Henrici secundi* 1:7. I cite the translation in Norgate, *John Lackland,* p. 3.
44. The few extant references to John between 1173 and 1182 show him not under the Young King's care but under that of his father or others the king appointed (Norgate, *John Lackland,* pp. 7–8).
45. Richard, *Histoire des comtes de Poitou* 2:375.
46. Paris, BnF, lat. 5480, p. 5: "Migr[avit] Johannes Rex Anglorum et Dux Aquitanorum et Comes Andegavorum, ab illustrissimo patre suo Rege Henrico nobis & Ecclesie nostre oblatus est et a nobis per 5 annorum spacium nutritus, cumque autem Regni Anglie suscepit gubernacula dilectione non modica nos dilexit, et Ecclesiasm nostram suis beneficiis ampliavit [Died: John, king of the English and duke of the Aquitanians and count of the Angevins. He was given to us and to our church as an oblate by his most illustrious father King Henry and for a period of five years was cared for by us, and when he assumed the government of the kingdom of England he felt great affection for us, and he increased our church by his benefactions.]" BnF, lat. 5480 is a seventeenth-century manuscript. The

obituary notices in it were drawn from the "Grand nécrologe" of Fontevraud, a codex of unknown date which is no longer extant; *Répertoire,* ed. Lemaître, pp, 1204, nos. 2901, 2903.

47. Poole, *Domesday Book to Magna Carta,* p. 425 and n1; Warren, *King John,* p. 26; Turner, *King John,* p. 23, and "Eleanor and her children," p. 325. The error on John's age has been repeated most recently by Lewis, "Philip the Cleric," 125 n64.

48. Henry II clearly intended to be in charge of the successional arrangements for his sons; the only times he shared that role were when one or more of them successfully challenged his decisions, and then he shared it with one or more of them, not with Eleanor (Warren, *Henry II,* pp. 108–11, 117–18, 596–99). But for societal background, in which royal mothers had sometimes attempted to play a role in arranging successions but had been excluded by the fathers, see Lewis, "Successions ottoniennes et robertiniennes," pp. 51–53.

49. On the regime at Fontevraud, see Smith, "Robert of Arbrissel's relations with Women," pp. 180–84. In respect to John being styled an oblate at an age when, presumably, he would have been judged too young to take orders of any sort, note for comparison that Louis VII's nephew, Philip of Dreux, had been accorded clerical status when no older than four or five (Lewis, "Philip the Cleric," 123–26).

50. BnF, lat. 5480, p. 4: "Ipsa . . . nobiscum cum quibus nutrita fuerat parvo tempore manens apud Rothomagum pergens [she . . . after staying for a short time with us, by whom she had been reared, went onward to Rouen] . . ."

51. Ralph of Diss, *Opera Historica* 1:382; Turner, "Eleanor and Her Children," 327—drawing in part on Norgate, *John Lackland,* p. 7—interpreted Gervase of Canterbury's statement that at the time of the outbreak of the revolt of 1173–74 only John "remained with his father" to mean that John left Fontevraud at that time. Since, however, the first half of the sentence containing that report records that the other sons had just fled from their father, Gervase may mean merely that only John remained in territories still controlled by Henry II (Gervase of Canterbury, *Opera Historica* 1:243). Since in May and June 1174 Henry II was in the border region between Anjou and Poitou, he may well have retrieved the children at that time; see Ralph of Diss, *Opera Historica,* 1:379–80.

52. Norgate, *John Lackland,* pp. 7–8. Note that John was in Normandy at other times during some of the same years.

53. *Gesta regis Henrici Secundi* 1:115–16, 120; Ralph of Diss, *Opera Historica,* 1:408, 414.

54. Green, *Lives of the Princesses* 1:264–67.

55. Henry and Matilda certainly did not; see references in Turner, "Eleanor and Her Children," 324, 326–27. Nor, apparently, did Richard, since the obituary composed for him at Fontevraud does not mention such a placement (BnF, lat. 5480, p. 1).

56. *Gallia Christiana* 2:1318–19. For references to this Matilda in charters of Henry II for Fontevraud, see *Recueil des actes de Henri II* 1:37, 50, 76, nos. 30, 44, 69. For benefactions to Fontevraud by Henry's grandfather Fulk V and by his father, Geoffrey Plantagenet, BNF lat. 5480, pp. 89–90, 131, 321–26. For Eleanor's family ties to Fontevraud, Brown, see "Eleanor of Aquitaine: Parent, Queen, and Duchess," pp. 11–12; BnF, lat. 5480, pp. 363, 365.

57. *Gallia Christiana* 2:1320. This Matilda was the daughter of Thierry of Alsace, count of Flanders, and Sibyl, sister of Geoffrey Plantagenet. Matilda was at Fontevraud by 1157, when her father confirmed donations he had made to the house at the time she became a nun there (BnF, lat. 5480, p. 315). She became abbess in 1187 and died in 1191. For other relatives— children of Sibyl countess of Flanders, or of Eleanor's sister, Petronella countess of Vermandois—see Erich Brandenburg, *Die Nachkommen Karls des Grossen*, pp. 12–13, 14–15, 44–45.

58. This point may raise the question of whether a prime reason for the choice of Fontevraud for the children's placement was the aristocratic background of its nuns. That hypothesis would be problematical. During the late twelfth century, a certain number of the nuns there came from the high nobility; but the origins of the great majority of the religious, and even some of the abbesses, are unknown.

59. Thus she could have stopped at Fontevraud in connection with her stay at Caen in June 1170; she may also have seen John at, or en route to or from, Henry II's Christmas court at Chinon in 1172, which she attended (Labande, "Pour une image véridique," p. 205; Eyton, *Henry II*, pp. 137–38, 170).

60. A related difference between John's experience and those of his oldest brothers is that, for such time as they spent with their mother, she provided a relatively stable, predictable environment. Certainly she traveled, but she also spent long periods in a given region, sometimes with her children either with her or nearby (Eyton, *Henry II*, pp. 69–70, 78–79, 85–86, 93, 108, 112). For John, by contrast, active contact with a parent would have been with Henry II, who was incessantly on the move.

CHAPTER 8

A TASTE OF THE FEAST:
RECONSIDERING ELEANOR OF AQUITAINE'S
FEMALE DESCENDANTS

Miriam Shadis and Constance Hoffman Berman

> *Historians of the Middle Ages have traditionally reproduced genealogies by following male lineages across generations, often missing interesting relationships among powerful women. As the first taste of a potentially rich feast, we reconstruct here the lives of Eleanor's granddaughters on the female side (that is, the daughters of her daughters).*

Jacqueline Murray's lovely video introduction to a study of medieval women describes the subject of this volume as "the remarkable Eleanor of Aquitaine, wife of two kings and mother of two kings, and a powerful ruler in her own right."[1] But Eleanor was also the mother of two queens and grandmother of many more. Through her daughters and their female descendants, Eleanor had lasting influence—cultural and political as well as genetic—over a wider Europe than the empire built by her second husband, Henry II of England, and lost by their youngest son, King John.

Eleanor of Aquitaine has been seen as the last powerful French queen— or rather, as a postscript to a series of earlier, more powerful women. Indeed, Eleanor's perceived ability to rule, or the lack thereof, first in France and then in England, has signified the demise of women's power after the 1180s. This interpretation is seen particularly in the early and much-cited study of medieval queenship by Marion Facinger (Meade).[2] That study, along with David Herlihy's "Land, Family, and Women in Continental Europe, 701–1200," was

an important component in the evidence cited by Joan Kelly (-Gadol)'s famously contested article, "Did Women have a Renaissance?"[3] Recent work
on various regions of medieval Europe by historians of secular and religious
life, however, has shown that not only does much of women's history remain
to be written, but the entire periodization of women's position vis-à-vis that
of men needs to be revised.[4] This has consequences for what we can know,
or thought we could know, about Eleanor and her descendents.

Much confusion about women's roles in the Middle Ages has arisen
from misplaced assumptions about how published document collections
for the Middle Ages reflect the larger set of all surviving sources, many of
which remain hidden in archives. Comparing evidence on women found
in the published documents for the early Middle Ages (which now include
nearly all surviving sources for the period up to ca. 1000) with that found
in published documents for the period after the turn of the millennium,
historians have concluded that women's power and authority declined in
the later period. But this approach assumes that the published documents
mirror without distortion the larger set of documents that remain in the
archives, an assumption that is proving to be increasingly invalid. The early
Middle Ages are much better published than the later Middle Ages because
publication of sources has often been supervised by national and local
commissions who first brought into print their oldest and most precious
documents. But more recent archival forays are showing that what has
been published from the later Middle Ages are precisely those sources in
which women are less likely to be found. For instance, even published collections of later medieval documents such as monastic cartularies or collections of monastic archival materials—from which a relatively unbiased
sample of women's activities might be anticipated—do not wholly reflect
the state of the archives: records for male religious houses have been much
more frequently published than those for religious women. This editorial
bias has had consequences for the writing of medieval secular women's history as well as the history of women's religious life, for recent archival research suggests that women in positions of power and authority in the later
Middle Ages were more likely to favor women's religious communities,
whether with their gifts, their requests for prayers, or their entrance into
such communities at the end of life.[5]

Final verdicts on women's status in the period 1000–1500 CE must
await additional archival work to redress the imbalance between an ill-
published later Middle Ages and an almost exhaustively published early
Middle Ages. But what archival investigation has been carried out is bringing to light much more evidence of powerful women in the generations
following Eleanor's.[6] New methodologies are allowing us to note more
clearly elements that earlier historians seem to have overlooked, even in

published materials. David Herlihy pioneered the use of charter evidence in writing medieval women's history, but we can point to more recent and innovative work by Elizabeth Makowski, Marilyn Oliva, Caroline Bruzelius, Bruce Venarde, and Jeffrey Hamburger.[7] Given the enormous range of documentation that is only now beginning to be used to give significant attention to women of all kinds, we are convinced that the evaluation of women's position in the later Middle Ages vis-à-vis their position in the early Middle Ages will continue to shift in the coming years.

Methodologies for the study of history are also changing, with special significance for the study of women. Greater sophistication and subtler use of "interdisciplinary" materials—art, narrative, archeology, literature, and other elements that make up medieval studies—have shown the absolute necessity of exploiting those sources to understand medieval women in all their dimensions. Furthermore, new theoretical constructs include a sustained and sophisticated interest in motherhood as a framework of analysis; studies of ritual in regard to women, especially concerning rites of birth, death, and the preservation of memory; and an understanding of gender and its social construction in all periods, whether in tension with or in replacement of "sex." Miriam Shadis's work, for example, emphasizes some of these theoretical frameworks in discerning women's roles through the chronicles of the high Middle Ages, demonstrating another important element in the problems of periodization: for the period after ca. 1100, narrative sources become more widely available, but they are found more frequently for some areas than others. Such narratives are now being reread from a variety of perspectives, including the sometimes seemingly contradictory feminist and postmodern. For example, Gabrielle Spiegel's positioning of narratives and other texts within their "social logic" has provided a crucial tool for thinking about the place of women in the past; other theoretical positions include ever-expanding conceptions of the practices of power, particularly in conjunction with the privileges of authority, or Judith Bennett's call to understand the continuities in medieval women's lives as well as the obvious changes that constitute a history for women.[8] The place of continuity is important in our view, for life did not change ca. 1000 or even ca. 1200 as much as some have thought. We expect that more continuity will become apparent as fresh materials of every nature are published and analyzed. Although evidentiary bases do sometimes change, we are finding that women continued in the later Middle Ages to be as important as women in the earlier Middle Ages in terms of control of property and hence of substantial economic resources, particularly as patrons of the church. In terms of geographical continuity, one of the things our work demonstrates is that both the historiography on women and the available evidentiary base vary from country to country (in a modern sense of Europe), much more than medievalists sometimes assume.[9]

In many senses, a primary reason for writing about Eleanor of Aquitaine's female descendants is to show how many of those women enjoyed substantial importance as players on the political scene and, in their control of economic resources, as patrons of the religious life. Interesting continuities and intersections in both political power and religious patronage (for which we often have the better documentation) can be observed among Eleanor's granddaughters and even her great-granddaughters. In the larger sphere, this shows the importance of thirteenth-century religious women whose archives are revealing many fresh documents, and the secular, often royal women who were donors, patrons, and eventually entrants into such religious communities. Thus, despite contentions that followed Joan Kelly's schema, the thirteenth century did not see a marked decline in female power in either the secular or monastic spheres.[10] In fact, patronage documents of the thirteenth century reveal that foundations of women's religious communities of all kinds increased. In part this reflected a noticeable presence of women in positions of leadership at the level of the highest political authority.[11]

The power of thirteenth-century women in many regions of Europe, particularly at the very top of society, may stem from an ethos often associated with northern France (but part of the very breath of life south of the Pyrenees) that included crusading as a necessary adventure for knights. Such an ethos has been identified by Jonathan Riley-Smith as associated with particular crusading families in northern France, but other geographical areas have not been explored as thoroughly in this regard as far as we are aware.[12] The linguistic frontiers of the period that were beginning to form what eventually become political boundaries appear to have had little effect on crusading ideals, at least at the highest level of society. At the royal level at which Eleanor's daughters, granddaughters, and great-granddaughters operated, the ideals of the Crusade and the conquest of Muslim-held lands were pivotal—and in no case more so than in that of Eleanor's daughter Leonor (4), who is a central figure in our story.[13] She is less known than women in France and England primarily because of modern biases that have made the history of the Iberian peninsula less central to the story that medievalists usually tell.[14] The thirteenth-century power of women like Blanche of Castile (4.3), her cousins and sisters, and their daughters was perhaps an unanticipated side-effect of an extremely violent, male-dominated age in which the ideology was one of increased attention to individual male lineages. The reality, of course, was that male heirs might die before they could inherit their family's domains, or succeed as minors, or go on Crusade, leaving women to rule in their absence. Whether or not such factors are associated with a strict theory of primogeniture, as Duby has been seen as arguing, or with more fluid familial schemes for the preservation of property, remarkable numbers of heiresses appeared in the thirteenth century. The appearance of such heiresses was primarily a consequence of deaths in combat of male heirs from certain families who, by insisting on the religious or social benefits of crusading, exposed themselves not only to the perils of warfare but to many new diseases.

That the genealogies of so many families show repeated failure of male heirs in the thirteenth century, however, informs us that women did not cease to obtain positions of power and authority at western European society's highest level after Eleanor of Aquitaine's death in 1204. Several of her daughters, granddaughters, and great-granddaughters became important rulers. New methodologies suggest, indeed, that the very increase in misogynous attacks on women, mostly by monastic authors, which might at first be seen as evidence of a decrease in women's prestige, can be read instead as proof of an increase in numbers of powerful communities of religious women and the increased access of secular women to real political power. While not all issues can be resolved by studying Eleanor of Aquitaine's female descendants and following the female line rather than the male, such an excursion does nonetheless turn inside out some of our assumptions about certain relationships. Studying the female also reminds us of cognatic family relationships, which are as equally close as, but more fluid than, agnatic ties, and which are often forgotten in standard presentations that trace only male lines.[15]

The marriages of Eleanor of Aquitaine's five daughters created or strengthened ties between their respective fathers and important allies, but were not negotiated for the dynastic concerns of either Louis VII or Henry II. In this respect, we can consider the women's incorporation into their marital dynasties, but also that such marriages afforded the women new arenas for individual action. After her divorce from Louis VII and marriage to Henry of Anjou in 1152, Eleanor was isolated from the two daughters she had borne Louis, Marie (1) in 1145 and Alix (2) in 1150—though John F. Benton's claims that she never saw them again are probably overstated.[16] Shortly after Louis VII's second wife, Constance of Castile, died in childbirth in 1160, he took as his third queen, Adele of Champagne, with whom he produced the future Philip Augustus in 1165. This marriage marked a drastic shift in Capetian diplomacy, allying Louis with the house of Champagne/Blois against the growing power of the Angevin house, which had acquired Eleanor's vast Aquitanian domains through her second marriage. For the house of Blois/Champagne, this change in alliance patterns coincided with a shift in territorial interest toward the burgeoning wealth of Champagne's towns, in the eastern portion of their domains. After mid-century, these eastern areas became the crucial holdings for a family that had previously concentrated its attentions to the west of Paris, on the territories of Blois, Chartres, and Tours, from which the family had created the inheritance of its eldest sons. At Thibaut IV of Blois's death in 1152, however, the situation reversed. Thibaut's eldest son, Henry I of Champagne (r. 1152–81), received the eastern domains, while those west of Paris went to the younger sons, Thibaut V of Blois (r. 1152–91) and Stephen of Sancerre (r. 1152–90). This shift was also reflected in the eastward-moving ecclesiastical career of the fourth son, William, bishop of Chartres 1165–68, archbishop of Sens 1168–75, and finally archbishop of Rheims 1175–1202.[17]

The diplomatic concerns created for the Capetians by the sudden eruption of Angevin power, and the sisters' potential kinship to the royal line of England as well as that of France, were bound to raise the profile of Louis VII's daughters by Eleanor of Aquitaine, for while Marie (1) and Alix (2) remained his sole direct heirs, it was important to arrange to marry them to his allies. Thus, when Louis married Adele of Champagne, he also arranged for his daughters by Eleanor to marry Adele's brothers.[18] A charter recording a gift to Marie's teacher, Abbess Alice of Mareuil, reveals that Marie was sent after her betrothal for the rest of her childhood to the abbey of Avenay, near Épernay in Champagne; Alix may have been there as well, though possibly she remained in Paris with Queen Adele.[19] In 1164–65, Marie married Henry I, future count of Champagne,[20] and about a decade later, probably in 1174, Alix married Thibaut V of Blois, who held the more important of the family's lands west of Paris.[21] Usually known as Marie of Champagne, the elder sister has received considerable attention from recent historians, who have debated her patronage of letters and of "courtly love." Much of what may be known of the younger sister, Alix, remains to be extracted from the charters, but the outlines of Marie's life as reconstructed from such documents were set out by Theodore Evergates in detail in 1999. Widowed in 1181, Marie died in 1198, and Alix, a widow from 1191, died probably in 1197.[22]

Eleanor of Aquitaine's second marriage to Henry II of England (r. 1154–89) produced, in addition to six sons, three daughters: Matilda (3, 1156–89), Eleanor, or, as she came to be called, Leonor (4, 1161–1214), and Joanna (5, 1165–99).[23] Henry's need to settle his new dynasty among the established ruling lineages of Europe took his daughters far from their parents' court, but only Leonor really successfully established herself elsewhere, even as ties to her parents' court and natal family remained central. Matilda and Joanna have received little sustained interest from historians, largely because they have been overshadowed historiographically by their politically more interesting brothers Richard and John, who achieved what Matilda and Joanna could not: kingship. What interest these sisters have garnered involves their relations to their father and brothers, as exemplified by one historian's comment: "Kings, also, had to make provisions for their daughters . . . [usually giving them] in marriage, together with a cash dowry, to a neighbouring prince. Thereafter the costs of supporting them were borne by their husband's family. This is what happened to Matilda . . . and to Joan."[24] Closer examination of the course of the sisters' lives, however, challenges assumptions embedded within this statement and suggests directions for further research.

Matilda (3) remained close to and indeed dependent on her parents well after her marriage. Her early life is obscure, but she seems to have spent a fair amount of time in her mother's company, traveling with Eleanor in September 1160, in 1165, and in 1167.[25] Probably by the end of 1167, in her twelfth year, she had left England "cum infinita pecunia et apparatu maximo," to marry Henry "the Lion" of Brunswick, duke of Bavaria and Saxony (1129–95).[26] Matilda's new husband, however, found himself in grave conflict with Emperor Frederick I, and Henry II was prevailed upon to intercede on his son-in-law's behalf, if only to assure his daughter's interests. The English chronicler Roger of Howden explains that "for love of her father the king of England," Frederick I allowed Matilda to retain her dower when the emperor seized Henry the Lion's domains; even if the duchess followed her husband into exile (which she did), "the emperor granted her that he would appoint his custodians for the safe-keeping of her dower."[27] In 1182, Matilda and Henry the Lion, with their children and followers, thus became dependents at Henry II's court; Matilda remained in her parents' domains for the rest of her life and was often in her mother's company.[28] Henry II died in July 1189, and only weeks afterward, Matilda followed him in death.

The year 1189 was also significant in the life of Joanna (5), Eleanor of Aquitaine's youngest daughter by Henry II. Born at Angers in 1165, in 1189 Joanna was married to King William II of Sicily, and for some time her life was characterized by Sicily's Mediterranean context. Further examination of Joanna's life at the wealthy, even decadent court of William "the Good" might illuminate the ways in which western brides have been seen as becoming exotic through their experiences in the south and east. Such interrogation-problematizing the supposed glamour and sophistication of a luxurious, multicultural, orientalized court in comparison with a putatively dour and religious northern French one-would be particularly important for unraveling and understanding the historiography of Eleanor of Aquitaine's eastern "exploits." Joanna's marriage, regardless, remained unsuccessful by medieval standards, as it was without issue, and when

William died in 1189, his aunt Constance succeeded him as ruler of Sicily.[29] Constance's cousin and counter-claimant Count Tancred of Lecce captured Joanna and held her hostage until 1191. Rescued by her brother Richard, Joanna's life became organized by his political and military aims and continued to be characterized by misadventure. In 1191 she was briefly reunited with her mother, when Eleanor delivered Berengaria of Navarre to Sicily to be Richard's bride. Joanna and Berengaria spent the next two years together, suffering shipwreck and other indignities off the coast of Cyprus but essentially providing Richard a "court away from court" as he slowly proceeded to the Holy Land. The women left Palestine in 1193 and went to Rome, where they stayed for about six months, and then traveled to Pisa, Marseilles, and finally Poitiers. On the last leg of the trip they were accompanied by Count Raymond VI of Toulouse, whom Joanna married in 1196. The union proved disastrous; Raymond was unreliable, irresponsible, and unpleasant.[30] After bearing a son in 1197, Joanna was left to face a rebellion alone and fled to Eleanor's court at Rouen. Pregnant and ill, Joanna insisted upon being admitted to the abbey of Fontevraud and, despite her irregular situation, her wish was granted. Joanna died there in childbirth during the delivery of a son who lived just long enough to be baptized; she was buried "inter velatas" at Fontevraud.[31]

It was the second of Eleanor of Aquitaine's Angevin daughters, her namesake Leonor (4), who most exemplified the qualities of command that Eleanor of Aquitaine seemed to have passed on to all of her daughters and their daughters in turn. Leonor was born in 1161; Robert of Torigny (d. 1186), chronicler-abbot of Mont-Saint-Michel in Normandy, stood as one of her godparents and took a special interest in the princess: he recorded her birth at Domfront and followed her life as best he could.[32] Her marriage to Alfonso VIII of Castile may have helped secure the new Pyrenean frontier that Henry II's marriage to Eleanor of Aquitaine had created for the Plantagenet ruler's domains.[33] The dates given in English chronicles for Leonor's marriage to Alfonso vary; negotiations probably started ca. 1169 and were concluded sometime in 1170, when Leonor was eight or nine and Alfonso fifteen or sixteen.[34] Although the Castilians claimed Gascony as Leonor's dowry, there is no conclusive proof that Henry II willingly risked dismembering his wife's inheritance in this manner, and Alfonso's attempts to control the region and subsequent ephemeral claims derived from this precedent ultimately proved burdensome to Leonor's heirs.

The marriage was advantageous to both families, but it is probably important to remember that Henry II's daughter was in some sense marrying up. For Henry II, the marriage affirmed the status of his own line, legitimizing his position and that of his wife as royal, not merely comital, and may have helped stabilize the frontier of Aquitaine with an ally to the south.[35] For Alfonso, alliance with the Plantagenets held out the promise of assuring himself a legitimate heir and brought him an important ally to whom he turned for support in his disputes with Sancho VI of Navarre.[36] After forty-four years of marriage, during which they produced at least ten children, both Alfonso VIII and Queen Leonor died in October 1214.[37]

Unlike her sisters, Matilda (3) and Joanna (5), Leonor (4) probably ex-cited less comment from contemporaries because she in some respects led the most conventional life.[38] Many of her activities as queen of Castile re-main obscure because she so often acted alongside her husband, King Al-fonso. She also must have exercised considerable political power in his absences, but for Leonor we must argue much more by analogy than from documentation for such activities. We do know that Alfonso VIII expected to rely on her: his will in 1204 stated very clearly that Leonor was to rule along with their son Fernando in the event of the king's death. A fascinat-ing reference to a list of debts which "she has in her possession" suggests the extent to which this queen may have been involved in royal adminis-tration.[39] In 1214 Leonor held the regency not for Fernando who was by then dead, but for her son Enrique after the death of her husband in early October. As she herself died on October 30 that same year, we may spec-ulate that she succumbed to the same unexpected illness that killed her husband and may not have been well throughout her brief regency. Leonor's only significant act of which we are aware from this period is her commissioning of the regency of king and kingdom to her eldest daugh-ter, Berenguela (4.1), the former queen of León.[40] The unique brevity of Leonor's regency means that documentation of her powers and activities normally associated with periods of widowhood is lacking.[41] It is through her patronage of the church during her lifetime that we are more likely to see her actions, as is discussed below with regard to las Huelgas.

By the 1180s, the court of Alfonso VIII and Queen Leonor (4) was reach-ing maturity as a peninsular and continental power. There would be some low moments, as in the dismal defeat by the Almohads at the battle of Alarcos in 1195, but in general Alfonso's and Leonor's children were born into a newly influential and powerful family. In late twelfth-century Castile, the Christian Conquest exemplified the church's growing power and led as well to changes in political organization. As the frontier moved southward, the process of re-populating deserted areas began, posing new challenges for government.[42] The constant threat of warfare and political intrigue characterized the polit-ical contexts of Eleanor of Aquitaine's Iberian progeny. The deaths of those of Leonor's sons who lived beyond a few months, and the major events of her daughters' adult lives, were all defined by these contexts. In such circum-stances, the presence of violence and disorder provided another role for women apart from reproduction and ruling: that of peacemaker. The role of women in securing peace, whether through marriage, motherhood, or negotiation, was real and well-documented. As the daughter of Eleanor of Aquitaine and Henry II of England, Leonor had been brought up to expect that she was destined to serve them through her marriage; it would seal an alliance or bring her family prestige. Leonor's marriage to Alfonso was Henry II's metaphorical marriage to higher status. The experience of being a tool of such ambition must have been significant as Leonor prepared her daughters to be married women. She would expect no less of her children.

Four of Leonor's (4) daughters made important royal marriages, to kings or future kings of León, France, Portugal, and Aragón. The marriage that shows Leonor's greatest influence (and thus, the important political role of the queen) was her daughter Berenguela's (4.1) consanguineous marriage to Alfonso IX of León.[43] The *Cronica Latina* tells us that no peace was possible between Castile and León "unless the king of Castile united his daughter the lady Berenguela to the king of León, in *de facto* marriage, because it could not be allowed by law as these kings were related in the second degree."[44] Archbishop Rodrigo Jiménez de Rada of Toledo also attributed the marriage to a desire for peace, explaining that because of consanguinity Alfonso VIII rejected the marriage for his daughter, but Queen Leonor persuaded him otherwise.[45] By December 17, 1197, at age seventeen,[46] Berenguela married her father's cousin Alfonso IX and became queen of León.

Though it is likely that the kings had requested a papal dispensation for the marriage, it does not appear that one was actually issued by Pope Celestine III, who seemed inclined to let things take their course and neither condemn nor approve the action.[47] But the problem of so prominent a consanguineous marriage was not ignored, and at least two chroniclers went to some length to attribute responsibility for the situation to Queen Leonor (4). They implied that for her, the ends justified the means; peace was worth any price. There is evidence to suggest that at the very least Queen Leonor had some part in the decision. De Rada says that Leonor was prudent and wise and, understanding the dangers of continued warfare, recommended that matters could be resolved by such a marriage.[48] The *Primera Crónica General* suggests that as Leonor was a very wise and understanding woman, the great men of both realms went to her to plead for the ending of the war:

> She understood the dangers of these things and the deaths that resulted from this hatred, and that this could be resolved by this marriage . . . [T]hey went to her and talked with her in secret, . . . and they set out their reasons, because they held her in such esteem, saying that between the kings so many

good things could come of this marriage and so many evil things could be ended, that it was more a mercy than a sin . . . The queen, as she was very understanding as we have said, when she heard such good reasons from the *omnes buenos* declared that this pleased her heart, and that she desired that this marriage be contracted.[49]

Leonor's putative role in these negotiations indicates the Castilians's high anxiety about the illicit nature of the consanguinous marriage, coupled with the imperative that it nonetheless succeed.

As for the Leonese, as Gonzalez points out, consanguineous relations were almost traditional. The same problems that caused competition (i.e., blood relations) could only be resolved by marriage, which was, of course, prohibited by the Church because of those very blood relations. Thus, Leonor was not only credited with promoting peace but was also made responsible for what could be seen as a difficult, possibly unpopular moral decision. Furthermore, as queen, Leonor was understood to have great influence with her husband. The great men of the realm, who exploited her position of influence in this way, thus recognized a queen's important and appropriate political role.[50]

Berenguela of Castile (4.1) remained Alfonso IX's wife until 1203 or 1204, when Innocent III finally effected their separation; the marriage had lasted long enough, however, for the couple to produce five children.[51] Following her divorce, Berenguela returned to her parents' court in Castile, and in 1214 her dying mother, Queen Leonor (4), named her regent for Berenguela's young brother Enrique I. After Enrique's troubled minority and premature death in 1217, Berenguela briefly inherited the crown of Castile and soon abdicated in favor of her son Fernando III. She helped to rule and eventually to unite Castile and León in 1230.[52]

In 1201, Queen Leonor's (4) daughter Urraca (4.2), best known to historians as the sister not chosen by Eleanor of Aquitaine to marry Louis of France, instead married Alfonso, heir to the Portuguese throne. This couple produced at least four children before her death in 1220, including the sons who reigned as Sancho II and Alfonso III, a daughter, Alionor (4.2.1), who married King Waldemar of Denmark, and a son known as Fernando de Serpa. Though Urraca's career remains to be fully explored, it is evident that she was consistently named in her husband's charters, and so appears representative of the high status of Portuguese queens in the first two centuries of that realm's existence. Urraca may have contributed to her husband's dynastic prestige in influencing the choice of the Cistercian abbey of Alcobaça as a royal burial site, carrying to Portugal the traditions of royal burial she would have known from Las Huelgas, which was ultimately traceable to the transformation Eleanor of Aquitaine had effected at Fontevraud.[53]

Queen Leonor's (4) youngest daughter to become a queen was also named Leonor (4.4). She was born in 1200/01 and in February 1221 married the young king of Aragón, Jaume I, then about thirteen. This marriage produced one child, Alfonso (1228–60), who died estranged from his father and without issue. Divorced from Jaume in 1229, Leonor returned to Castile, from where she apparently continued to influence her son, but eventually retired to (and perhaps became a nun at) the family retreat of Las Huelgas near Burgos, where she died in 1244.[54]

Leonor of England's (4) youngest surviving daughter, Constanza (4.5), never married and became a nun at the family foundation of Las Huelgas. She was evidently never abbess there but held a position of power at the abbey, directing its operations as if she were abbess. Constanza's presence in the foundation's earliest years sealed the family connection to the house, which in turn helped confirm the position of Cistercian women in Iberia and in the broader European world.[55] The possibility of the Fontevraud model, especially in terms of its use as a family necropolis, emphasizes Eleanor of Aquitaine's strongest legacy in the intertwining of biological family, women's piety and the practice of power, and an institution that has lasted to this day. That possibility was reflected as well in the accomplishments of Leonor's other daughter, Blanche of Castile's (4.3) foundations at Royaumont for Cistercian monks, and at Maubuisson and Le Lys for Cistercian women, discussed below.

One arena in which Eleanor's daughters and other female descendants wielded a great deal of influence was, of course, monastic patronage. While clearly a close association would eventually develop between Eleanor of Aquitaine (along with Henry II) and the community of nuns at Fontevraud, little indicates that either the counts of Anjou or those of Poitiers and Aquitaine were founders of that abbey.[56] A propensity for the support of religious women was an important characteristic shared by many of Eleanor of Aquitaine's female descendants. Excellent documentation of their endeavors survives and indicates how such women in positions of power behaved and thought. A growing tie to the Cistercians for many of those descendants began with the foundation of the female abbey Las Huelgas in Burgos by Alfonso VIII of Castile and Queen Leonor (4).[57] This institution may have served as a summer home for the court, and from its inception was conceived as a royal necropolis. Its endowment, unusual in that the abbess of Las Huelgas exercised very independent powers, signifies the most important donation Leonor and Alfonso made to the church. Leonor may have brought to her marriage a desire to patronize female religious houses that culminated in the foundation of Las Huelgas, which seems to have been endowed at her specific request.[58]

Las Huelgas was the most spectacular single foundation by any of Eleanor of Aquitaine's daughters and, through its eventual function as a royal necropolis, linked Leonor (4) to Fontevraud, the house her mother would eventually treat as a royal mausoleum.[59] It is significant in this context that while Eleanor of Aquitaine's monastic patronage in England was not extravagant, her patronage on the Continent, especially in Aquitaine, increasingly assumed a dynastic coloration.

Las Huelgas offers a point of contact as well with Leonor's daughter Queen Blanche (4.3) of France, who like her parents favored the Cistercian order and whose foundations shared the preference for supporting the prayers of religious women associated with familial support of the nuns of Fontevraud. Indeed, Cistercian nuns are central to much of the religious patronage of the granddaughters and great-granddaughters of Eleanor.

As regent of France, Blanche (4.3) negotiated the treaty ending the Albigensian Crusade in 1229. Its favorable terms for the Cistercians are usually attributed to the fact that Blanche's collaborator in the negotiations was the Cistercian Abbot Élie Guarin of Grandselve but, with her parents' example before her, she probably needed little persuasion to support the Cistercians.[60] She was certainly responsible for converting Louis VIII's testamentary bequest for the foundation for his soul of a house of Victorines into the house of Cistercian monks at Royaumont that served at least temporarily as a royal necropolis.[61] Blanche also made bequests and supported those of others to houses of Cistercian women in the Paris region in the second quarter of the thirteenth century, and she herself founded two, at Maubuisson and Le Lys. Her original dower lands in the Artois region were exchanged and perhaps supplemented by Louis IX between 1237 and 1240, when Blanche received 1500li. of Paris annually from the crown's general revenues, as well as the towns of Meulan, Pontoise, Étampes, Dourdan, Corbeil, Melun, Crespy-en-Valois, la Ferté-Milon, and Pierrefonds.[62] From those sources she founded and built an abbey of Cistercian nuns at Maubuisson in 1236, near the royal residence at Pontoise.[63] Probably beginning in 1244, she contributed to the establishment of a second abbey of Cistercian women at Le Lys near Melun.[64] To found the latter she sent her friend and cousin Alix of Mâcon (1.1.1), Eleanor of Aquitaine's descendant through Marie of Champagne (1), to be the first abbess.[65] Several royal infants were buried at Royaumont, and while Blanche's body was buried at Maubuisson her heart was interred at Le Lys in 1253.[66]

Blanche's (4.3) cousin Countess Isabelle of Chartres (2.2) is likewise noted for her patronage of religious houses.[67] Isabelle made gifts to a number of Cistercian houses for men, such as the 1221 confirmation of earlier gifts by her brother Count Louis of Blois to the Cistercian monks of Notre-Dame-la-Trappe and to Vaucelles and Barbeaux.[68] She also gave and confirmed gifts to the Cistercian nuns of Saint-Antoine-des-Champs in Paris and those of les Clairets, founded by her cousin Countess Matilda of Perche (3.1).[69] Isabelle was, moreover, the founder of two, if not three, houses of Cistercian nuns. The earliest was the priory of Moncey near Tours, which was probably dependent on Savigny in the thirteenth century; evidence is limited but suggests Moncey's association with Isabelle and her first husband, Sulpice of Amboise.[70] Isabelle founded the house of Cistercian nuns at Lieu-Notre-Dame de Romorantin in 1221, using land in the castellany of Romorantin that Isabelle had inherited.[71] Her third foundation was at Eau-lez-Chartres, which Isabelle founded with her second husband, John de Montmirail, in 1226, possibly on land from his family.[72] Concentrating her resources increasingly on Lieu-Notre-Dame, Isabelle eventually diverted to it revenues that had earlier been given to Cistercian men's houses.[73] She confirmed all her gifts to the nuns at Lieu-Notre-Dame in her will of 1249, a charter the nuns of Lieu copied onto the opening page of their cartulary. In her last testament Isabelle endowed a chapel at Lieu-lez-Romorantin, "for her own soul and for that of her dear cousin Blanche of Castile."[74] While Blanche was of course Isabelle of Chartres's cousin and almost exact contemporary, we have as yet found no indication of how she and Blanche had shaped the intimacy implied by the commemorative chapel Isabelle founded for the two of them.

Isabelle of Chartres (2.2) confirmed gifts to the Cistercian nuns at les Clairets, founded by her cousin Countess Matilda of Perche (3.1), daughter and namesake of Matilda, duchess of Saxony (3). In 1189 Matilda's uncle Richard the Lionheart had married her to Geoffrey III, son of Count Rotrou of Perche.[75] In 1204, as the widowed countess of Perche, Matilda began the process of founding the house at les Clairets near Nogent-le-Rotrou, west of Chartres. A bull of Innocent III, dated January 1204, took under papal protection the prioress, sisters, and monastery of les Clairets, who "ought to follow the practice of the brothers of Cîteaux," and confirmed the gifts of their founder, Countess Matilda of Perche; Innocent exempted the nuns from tithes in the typical formula found in many earlier Cistercian privileges.[76] The bull tells us that Matilda had made the foundation because her late husband had not fulfilled his Crusading vow and wished instead to found a religious house, and that he charged her with the choices of site, of religious men or women, and their order. Matilda died before May 1213 when her son, Count Thomas of Perche, confirmed her gifts "to the nuns of les Clairets, of the Cistercian order."[77] Further research may reveal more on this Matilda, sometimes called Matilda of Brunswick, countess of Perche, an emperor's sister and granddaughter of Eleanor of Aquitaine.[78] Religious patronage was a common activity of noble women of the time. Its importance to us today is that it is through the documentation of their patronage that we can often piece together accounts of their lives, as we do, for instance and apparently for the first time, here with regard to Alix of Blois (2). Whether Eleanor's granddaughters were extraordinary in their bequests is difficult to tell. Certainly Eleanor herself had no role model for this activity in her own mother, but it is possible that she learned something from the example of her mother-in-law, the empress Matilda.[79]

The above material suggests that familial background may have encouraged aristocratic women's religious patronage in certain directions. The same women who are seen exercising such support of abbeys of religious women to which they might decide to retire to die were also leaders in the exercise of political and economic power. Too often they cannot be seen in this activity or documented as acting independently of their male consorts, however, for such power is best documented when men were away or had died. Thus, though it is likely that the most expert politician among Eleanor's daughters was Leonor (4), because she died in the same year as her husband Alfonso and because Alfonso's military activity was relatively local and confined to Iberia, we have little documentation of Leonor's independent activity. Even in the literary arena, moreover, economic and political power are more likely to be documented by poets, musicians, and ecclesiastics when such power has been exercised to their benefit; for both these reasons, we must be constantly aware that documentation is uneven. A glance at some of Eleanor's female descendents for whom we can document the exercise of that power suggests what was in fact probably a larger exercise of such power by all of them. It also shows the various ways in which political power for women could be documented—when they served as regents, acquired power in their own right by inheritance, or exercised it through their influence over ruling husbands or sons.

The literary texts praising Eleanor of Aquitaine's daughter Marie of Champagne (1), for example, were perhaps a consequence of the political power she wielded during a series of regencies in Champagne, after her conventual upbringing and a number of years at the side of an older husband. Her first regency came between June 1179 and February 1181, while Count Henry was in the East; his death soon after his return from the Holy Land brought about Marie's second regency, from March 1181 to May 1187, for her young son Henry II of Champagne (r. 1181–97). In fact, Marie was regent for all but about three years of her son's reign, for he went to the East in 1190, there married Queen Isabelle of Jerusalem, became king himself, and never returned to Champagne. Marie's third regency thus lasted from her son's departure for the East in May 1190 until his death there in 1197, and continued for her underage son Thibaut until her own death in March 1198, at the age of about fifty-three. Evergates thus counts fifteen years of regency in the last twenty years of Marie of Champagne's life.[80] It is likely that Marie's sister, Countess Alix of Blois (2), served as regent in Blois after Thibaut V left for the East and following his death there in 1191. At that time, Alix's eldest surviving son Louis was aged no more than fourteen, and she presumably would have continued as regent for some years.[81]

Surely the best-known female regent among Eleanor of Aquitaine's immediate descendants was her granddaughter Blanche of Castile (4.3). Blanche and her sisters together also document for us the patterns of power that we cannot document, but can argue existed, for Queen Leonor of Castile (4). Probably the most famous of Leonor's children, Blanche is often identified with her grandmother Eleanor, not only because Blanche returned at marriage to France and came to know at least some relatives from her grandmother's first marriage, but also because of the journey the two women took in 1200, in preparation for Blanche's marriage, to the future Louis VIII of France. The journey of Eleanor and Blanche will always tantalize historians, but speculation about Eleanor's possible tutelage of Blanche remains just that. Born to Leonor and Alfonso VIII in 1188, Blanche was sent to France as a result of the Treaty of Le Goulet between England and France, which proposed a marriage between Philip Augustus's son Louis and one of English King John's nieces. Eleanor of Aquitaine went to Castile to choose one of her granddaughters for this purpose and, after deciding on Blanche, escorted her across the Pyrenees. Eleanor accompanied Blanche no further than Bordeaux, nor did she attend the twelve-year-old girl's marriage to fourteen-year-old Louis, which had to take place in English territory because France was under interdict as a consequence of the dispute over Philip Augustus's repudiation of Ingeborg of Denmark. All this occurred after Richard I's death, so it was Blanche's uncle John who, upon becoming king of England, contributed the sums and castles settled on Louis and Blanche by the marriage treaty.[82]

The next twenty-three years of Blanche's (4.3) life are obscure; she and Louis apparently produced few extant records, so we can say little of her position as the king of France's adolescent daughter-in-law growing up at his court. It was several years before the marriage was consummated; Blanche's first child arrived only in 1205, her eldest son Philip in 1209, and the future Louis IX in 1214. It must be assumed that in those first years at the royal court the young couple studied, played, and were instructed together in the arts of rulership. They would have become intimate with younger relatives, like Jeanne (1.2.1) and Marguerite (1.2.2), the future countesses of Flanders who were there under Philip Augustus's wardship from at least 1208 until 1212 (in 1208 they were eleven and eight). The adolescents and children may have gleaned religious instruction in part from the illuminated *bibles moralisées* that were being produced at this time, one of the most sumptuous of which has been directly associated with Blanche herself.[83] Through tales of her childhood visits to Las Huelgas, Blanche may also have instilled among the younger children an interest in the Cistercians, particularly the patronage of Cistercian women. It was probably in Paris with Blanche that Jeanne and Marguerite learned to call unhesitatingly upon the Cistercian General Chapter, whether for creating new houses of monks or nuns, or (as we know in the case of these two successive countesses of Flanders) to ask for the services of Cistercian lay-brothers.[84] Certainly all of them learned to ask for Cistercian prayers for their souls, their parents', and the safe births of their relatives' male heirs; for instance, Blanche of Castile in 1222 petitioned the General Chapter of Cîteaux for the Order's prayers for her soul and her parents' souls.[85]

Once her eldest son was born and the Capetian succession secure, Blanche (4.3) began to play more active roles. Most likely it was she who induced her father-in-law to confirm in 1214, in celebration of young Louis's birth, the Parisian properties of the recently established abbey for Cistercian nuns at Saint-Antoine-des-Champs.[86] Blanche also evidently interceded successfully with Philip Augustus for financial assistance to her husband in connection with the ill-fated invasion of England in 1217.[87] With Philip Augustus's death in 1223, Louis VIII and Blanche were crowned king and queen. Louis VIII's three-year reign is little studied, but it is apparent that he was only beginning to extricate himself from his father's policies and advisors when he died in 1226, on a campaign against the Albigensian heretics in the Midi.[88] In keeping with her husband's testament, Blanche assumed the regency for their son Louis IX. She ruled the realm for at least the next decade, so effectively that Robert Fawtier thought she might be regarded as one of the kings of France.[89] Blanche's policies, however, are only beginning to emerge as distinct from those of her father-in-law, husband, or son. Extant documents for Blanche and her husband during Philip Augustus's reign are few, but Louis IX's reign coincides with an enormous increase in documentation produced by the bureaucracy that had begun to be created in Philip Augustus's time. Much remains to be published among public and private documents for mid thirteenth-century France.[90]

A certain amount of confusion thus continues to surround the early reign of Louis IX and Blanche's (4.3) regencies for him. Blanche served as regent from 1226 to an undeterminable date in the mid-to-late 1230s, perhaps as late as 1242, and again from 1248 to her death in 1252 during his first crusade. Louis seems to have been content to allow Blanche to dictate the directions of his religious patronage even after he married Marguerite of Provence in 1234. Only after he took a crusading vow during a serious illness in 1244 was there a major shift in his patronage and piety. It is not so much that Louis ended the support of the Cistercians his mother favored to give more attention to the mendicants, the beguines, and the foundation of hospitals, as that his crusade became the all-encompassing goal of his charitable activities to which royal funds were increasingly devoted.[91] Blanche's support for the Cistercians and their responsiveness to her agenda is evident in Louis IX's many confirmations and in the continued support and negotiation with them by her younger sons Alphonse of Poitiers and Charles of Anjou.[92]

Blanche's (4.3) success as queen and regent of France and especially as a royal mother and patron are highlighted by the French contexts of her life, but her Iberian connections remained strong. Particularly interesting is the fostering of her nephew Alfonso of Portugal, second son of her sister Urraca (4.2). Perhaps drawing on the example of her father-in-law, who married Countess Jeanne of Flanders (1.2.1) to a Portuguese prince, Blanche seemingly destined Alfonso of Portugal for life as a French lord. He married the heiress Matilda of Boulogne, but seized the chance to claim the Portuguese throne in 1248, when his brother Sancho II's incompetence in the face of episcopal and papal opposition brought about the Portuguese king's deposition. As Alfonso III of Portugal, Blanche's nephew repudiated the childless Matilda, though he retained the title count of Boulogne for some time thereafter.[93]

Eleanor of Aquitaine's daughters and granddaughters are for the most part well-known examples of women who served as regents for sons when fathers departed on crusade or died while sons were too young to be able to rule in their own names. Such situations arose not infrequently in the Middle Ages, and any aristocratic wife and mother had to be prepared to step in to fill such a temporary vacuum. A complete lack of male political presence was by no means unknown among the medieval nobility, however, and in such cases a noblewoman would enter into a position of power in her own right. Examples of such female inheritance of sovereign authority can also be found among Eleanor of Aquitaine's descendants. While there are some examples of heiresses who from a young age inherited power in their own right, in other cases, for instance that of the daughters of Alix of France [countess of Blois (2)], such women were adults and had already married several times before they inherited lands and titles.

A series of deaths among Countess Alix of Blois's (2) children left only daughters in the direct line. Possibly not until after Alix's death, her elder surviving son Count Louis left for the crusade to die at the siege of Adrianople in 1205. His young son succeeded as Thibaut VI, and though married twice, he left no heirs at his death in 1218, by which time Alix's only surviving descendants were her daughters Marguerite (2.1) and Isabelle (2.2), Thibaut VI's paternal aunts. Philip Augustus then agreed (evidently in return for a hefty payment) to allow the sisters to inherit Blois and Chartres, but he separated the counties. These granddaughters of Eleanor of Aquitaine divided the family holdings, with Marguerite, probably born in the late 1170s, inheriting Blois.[94] Her first marriage placed her at the center of the circle of late twelfth-century northern French "courtly love." According to Reto Bezzola, Marguerite in her first marriage (ca. 1189) became the third wife of the first *trouvère,* Huon d'Oisi; this explains her appearance in his poems. Her second marriage, probably in 1192, was to Count Otto of Burgundy, a son of Emperor Frederick I; her third, probably ca. 1200, was to Gautier II, lord of Avesnes in Hainaut, who in 1218 became count of Blois in her right. Although Marguerite's date of death is sometimes given as 1230, she evidently survived Gautier and appears alone in a charter of 1230, granting rights to hold a market or fair to the abbey of the Madeleine in Châteaudun, and another of 1235. She probably retired soon thereafter to Fontevraud and was probably dead in 1241, the year of the death of her only child, Marie of Avesnes, whose children with John of Châtillon continued the line of the counts of Blois.[95]

Marguerite's younger sister, Isabelle (2.2), was born about 1180 and inherited Chartres when in her late thirties and in her second marriage. She had a daughter, Mathilde (2.2.1), by her first husband, Sulpice, lord of Amboise. Isabelle's second husband, John de Montmirail, lord of Oisy, was styled count of Chartres in charters, with Isabelle as countess, until his death without issue ca. 1240.[96] After John's death, Isabelle exercised comital power in her own right for nearly another decade, during which time knight service was provided by Richard de Beaumont, husband of her daughter, Mathilde of Amboise. Isabelle died in the winter of 1247–48; Mathilde succeeded her as countess of Chartres, and like her received as well the castellanies of Romorantin and Millançay-en-Sologne.[97] When Mathilde died childless in 1256, her cousin a younger John of Châtillon reunited Chartres with Blois.[98]

As described by the chronicler Gislebert of Mons, Marie of Champagne's (1) daughter Marie (1.2) married the future Baldwin IX of Flanders at Valenciennes in 1186, when she was about twelve and he about fourteen. They became count and countess of Flanders in 1194 but had no living children until the turn of the century, when two daughters were born to them, Jeanne (1.2.1) in 1199/1200 and Marguerite (1.2.2) in 1202/03. Baldwin went on Crusade in 1202 and was elected emperor of Constantinople after the 1204 capture of that city by the Crusaders. Marie ruled Flanders in his absence and then, leaving their infant daughters, set off to join Baldwin in the East. She died in 1204 before their reunion, he died in 1205; their daughters, Jeanne and Marguerite, grew up as Philip Augustus's wards or hostages in Paris. Philip arranged Jeanne's marriage to Ferdinand of Portugal in 1212, when the couple assumed control of Flanders. Unwilling to be the French king's puppet, however, Ferdinand conspired against Philip and was captured at the battle of Bouvines in 1214; imprisoned at the Louvre in Paris, he was released only in 1226. Jeanne ruled alone as countess during his captivity and again after his death in 1233, until her second marriage to Thomas of Savoy in 1237; she died in 1244. Jeanne's only child, Marie of Portugal, died young, and her sister, Marguerite, succeeded her as countess of Flanders (1244–78). In fifty-two of the sixty-six years between 1212 and 1278, then, these great-granddaughters of Eleanor of Aquitaine ruled the economically important Flanders region without the assistance of counts-consort.[99]

Marie of Champagne's (1) sons succeeded in turn as counts of Champagne, but there was a battle about which grandchild should inherit because Count Henry II appears to have left the county to his younger brother at a time when he had no heirs. Then, going to the East, he married Queen Isabelle of Jerusalem with whom he produced two daughters, Alice (1.3.1) and Philippa (1.3.2). Alice married King Hugh I of Cyprus, ruled there as regent, and died in 1246; Philippa married into the powerful Champenois family of the counts of Brienne. These sisters claimed to have inherited the county of Champagne itself. However, the Champenois branch of the family, descended from Marie of Champagne's younger son Thibaut III, had Count Henry II's marriage to Queen Isabelle of Jerusalem invalidated and their two daughters bastardized, but were not able to quell Alice and Philippa's considerable political importance.[100]

What we have documented here about Eleanor of Aquitaine's female descendants is a tantalizing taste of a larger feast of family relationships from the thirteenth century and of the possibilities of tracing descendants through the female line. That these relationships were important to the women themselves is not only evidenced through the actions such as those of Isabelle of Chartres (2.2) in regard to Blanche of Castille (4.3), but also, perhaps more concretely, through the naming practices followed by Eleanor of Aquitaine's descendents. The use of the name Eleanor or its variants is most clear among her Iberian progeny, through whom the use of the name returned to England. Although Alfonso VIII and Leonor of England's (4) daughter of the same name, Leonor (4.4), was not her parents' first child nor first daughter, her birth marks a point of departure for the royal families of medieval Christian Iberia, for it introduced the name Leonor into the familial canon. This was not only a logical choice as appropriate names became exhausted (her older sisters were named for a range of paternal female ancestors), but a direct tribute to her grand-mother, Eleanor of Aquitaine, who had visited the Castilian court shortly before Leonor's birth.[101] This Leonor had no daughters, but the name became a first choice for several generations of her family. Berenguela (4.1) of Castile (as queen of León), for example, named her first child Leonor (4.1.1). While that child died in infancy, the name was continued by Berenguela's son Fernando III, whose daughter Eleanor of Castile married Edward I of England.[102] Berenguela's younger son, Alfonso de Molina, named a natural daughter Leonor, and we have seen that the name was also used by Urraca of Portugal (4.2). Eleanor was the name of the sister of Arthur of Brittany and became a frequent name among King John's offspring—his daughter Eleanor who married Simon de Montfort, for example, and her daughter of the same name.[103] In con-trast, the daughters of Eleanor of Aquitaine and Louis VII seem to have excised their mother's name from naming patterns; it appears nowhere among their descendants nor, for that matter, among the offspring of Matilda (3) or Joanna (5), Eleanor of Aquitaine's daughters by Henry II, whose futures lay with France. That Eleanor does not appear in subse-quent times in France can be seen as a significant absence. It is inverted evidence suggesting the power Eleanor had in France and the ire that the Capetians felt at the loss of her important inheritance. The very omission of the name Eleanor from the French naming canon may be the most lasting tribute to her importance.

It is a relatively simple matter to lay out the patterns and outlines of these women's lives, historiographic and archival "traditions" notwith-standing. More complex is the problem of interrogating a genealogy which in the extreme may seem preternaturally imbued with feminine power. Clearly, many powerful and important European men and women of the High Middle Ages did not trace their ancestry back to Eleanor of Aquitaine (and yet perhaps shared identity with her in more significant ways as patrons and politicians.) At the same time, given the medieval emphasis on family, consanguinity, marriage, and procreation as political tools—and, increasingly from the eleventh century on, the romance of genealogy—we should not be surprised to find the heirs of one of the richest individuals of the twelfth century taking up their stations throughout Europe.

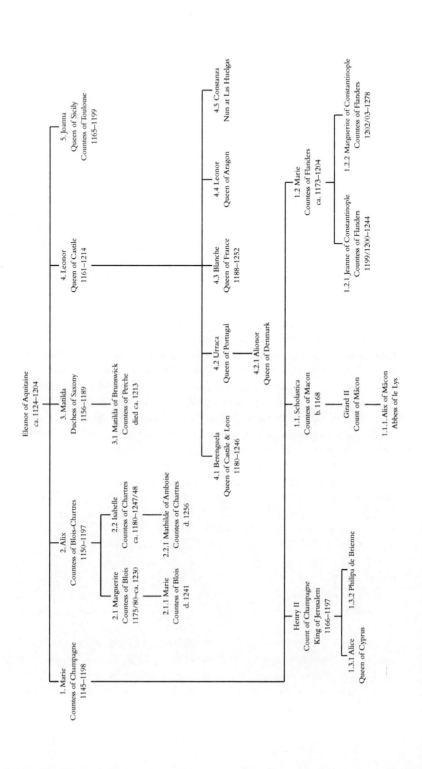

Notes

We would like to thank Caroline Bruzelius, who first introduced us, and the editors of this volume for their patience. In addition, Constance Berman would like to thank Jean Aikin, Michelle Armstrong-Partida, Yun Xiang Gao, Andrea Gayoso, Janice Faris, Erin Jordan, Margaret Lande, and Katherine Tachau. We dedicate this work to our grandmothers, mothers, and mothers-in-law, as well as to our children.

1. Murray, *Women in the Middle Ages.*
2. Facinger, "Medieval Queenship." Facinger searched published French royal charters to the beginning of the thirteenth century; the downward curve she identified for the twelfth century (the period of Eleanor of Aquitaine's queenship) was then extrapolated to the rest of the Middle Ages by Renaissance historians. Facinger Meade also published *Eleanor of Aquitaine.* See also Shadis, "Blanche of Castile."
3. Herlihy, "Land, Family, and Women in Continental Europe"; given its terminal date and the declining trends Herlihy identified in the twelfth century, his study too was read to imply a twelfth-century decline that continued after 1200. See Kelly-Gadol, "Did Women Have a Renaissance?"; cf. Herlihy, "'Did Women Have a Renaissance?'" For the later Middle Ages, see Harris, "A New Look," which attributes to a prevailing paternal preference for marrying off daughters rather than consigning them to convents a decline in noblewomen's foundations of convents and in their legacies to established houses.
4. This has been a trend in our own work. Berman argues that the case for Cistercian nuns means describing a different development for the Cistercian Order (Berman, *Cistercian Evolution,* and "Abbeys for Cistercian Nuns." Cf. Shadis, "Piety, Politics, and Power").
5. Du Faur, "L'abbaye de Voisins," 180, comments that a house of nuns "peut encore présenter quelque intérêt." Cf. *Cartulaire de Voisins,* ed. Doinel. A nineteenth-century study of the countesses of Blois traces only the wives of men who ruled the county; those who inherited in their own right, such as Isabelle of Chartres (2.2) and Marguerite of Blois (2.1), discussed below, are given only two sentences in Dupré, "Les comtesses de Chartres," 227. Duby, *Rural Economy,* p. 151, cites the account book and charters for the Cistercian abbey of Maubuisson as if for a house of monks, not nuns.
6. See *Aristocratic Women,* ed. Evergates.
7. In general, see Herlihy, "Land, Family, and Women in Continental Europe." Many of Herlihy's relevant articles were collected in a posthumous volume, *Women, Family, and Society.* See also Makowski, *Canon Law and Cloistered Women;* Oliva, *The Convent and the Community;* Hamburger, *Nuns as Artists;* Venarde, *Women's Monasticism;* Bruzelius, "Seeing is Believing." Important insights on widows have been contributed by a recent study of early modern notaries' families in Nantes; see Hardwick, *The Practice of Patriarchy,* esp. pp. 129–41.

8. Spiegel, "Social Logic," 59–86; Bennett, "Confronting Continuity," 73–94; "Introduction" to *Women and Power,* ed. Erler and Kowaleski, pp. 1–19.

9. See for example the arguments by Rucquoi, *Histoire médiévale de la Péninsule ibérique.*

10. Such miscalculation is also seen with regard to monastic women when Jean Leclercq underestimated women's importance in the later Middle Ages because he counted only houses of women in the mendicant Orders (Leclercq, "Monachesimo femminile," pp. 61–99).

11. See for example, Erin Jordan, "'For the Safety of my Soul.'"

12. Riley-Smith, *The First Crusaders.*

13. From this point, discussion in this chapter can be most readily followed by reference to the genealogical table at the end of this chapter. Each of Eleanor of Aquitaine's female descendents discussed here has been assigned a number that shows her descent from Eleanor's daughters, who are numbered 1 through 5. Each generation is then indicated in a similar sequence. For example, Marie of Champagne, Eleanor's oldest daughter, is numbered 1; her daughters are numbered 1.1 and 1.2, granddaughters 1.1.1, et cetera. To avoid disrupting the narrative, each woman is numbered in a paragraph only when her name is first mentioned.

14. It is too simplistic to attribute the neglect of the study of women in the later Middle Ages to assertions by such scholars as Georges Duby, who appears to argue (for example, in the articles translated by Postan as *The Chivalrous Society,* that women's importance declined in the later Middle Ages. Duby provided stimulating ideas for our teaching and research but had little real control over the discourse of North American scholarship; cf. the articles in *Aristocratic Women,* ed. Evergates. Much early work on medieval women relied on published records (one had to start somewhere).

15. Our approach is obviously modeled on that of Labande, "Filles," 101–12.

16. Benton, "The Court of Champagne," 551–91; McCash, "Marie de Champagne and Eleanor of Aquitaine," 193–209.

17. Evergates, *Feudal Society,* pp. 2–4; see also the family tree and chronological table in *Feudal Society,* ed. and trans. Evergates, pp. xxv–xviii.

18. For marriage as a tool, see Baldwin, *Philip Augustus,* pp. 269–72. Unfortunately, the study of earlier women in this area by Livingstone, "Aristocratic Women in the Chartrain," pp. 44–73, does not cover the last quarter of the twelfth century.

19. For the Avenay charter, dated 1158, see Evergates, *Feudal Society,* no. 45 at p. 64; Evergates dates Marie's betrothal to 1153.

20. The couple produced at least four children: Henry (born July 29, 1166), Scholastica (1.1, born ca. 1168), Marie (1.2, born ca. 1173), and Thibaut (born May 13, 1179). See Labande, "Filles," 102, and Bouchard, *Sword, Miter, and Cloister,* pp. 278–79.

21. Evergates, "Aristocratic Women," pp. 76–79, and see our note 22.

22. For Marie (1), see preceding notes. Alix (2) is often said to have died ca. 1183, but see *Cartulaire des Vaux-de-Cernay,* nos. 79 (1187: Count Thibaut

with Countess Adelicia [Alix], sons Thibaut, Louis, and Philip, and daughters Marguerite [2.1] and Isabelle [2.2]; 106 (1196: Adelicia [Alix] countess of Blois acts for the soul of her husband Thibaut); 107 (1196: Louis acts at the request of his mother, Countess Adelicia of Blois); *Cartulaire de Tiron,* nos. 329 (1183: Thibaut V and his wife Countess Adelicia, daughter of Louis VII, and their sons and daughters Thibaut, Louis, Marguerite and Isabelle); 319 (1185: moved by prayers of his wife Alix with their sons Thibaut and Louis and daughters Marguerite and Isabelle); 337 (1192: Louis with his mother Countess Adelicia of Blois, his brothers Thibaut and Philip and sisters Marguerite, Isabelle and Alix); 340 (1195: Alix after the death of her husband in March 1191 retired with four children to Tiron); 341 (1202: confirmation by Louis). For Alix's children, see also *Cartulaire de Châteaudun,* nos. 36 (1190) with 37 (1190: the son Louis confirms a gift by Bernard Deacon, suggesting Louis is of age); 43 (1200: Count Louis of Blois and Clermont attests to a gift to the Cistercians at l'Aumône by Geoffrey of Brulon); the notes for no. 80 (1202) mention a charter of Count Louis of Blois and Clermont, with confirmation by his wife Katherine, son Thibaut, and daughter Jeanne, and his brother Philip and sisters Marguerite and Isabelle; 90 (1230: Countess Marguerite of Blois confirmed a fair to this house); 100 (1235: Countess Isabelle of Chartres, 20s. rent on the tolls of Chartres). One charter in the Cartulary of Grand-Beaulieu is dated 1215 for Alix, Countess of Blois. It is very likely this is a scribal error, transposing Roman numerals MCCXV (1215) for MCXCV (1195). Alix disappears from the charters after 1197 and her son Louis takes over in that year. Internal references to Louis's clerk (Louis died ca. 1202–03) and witness lists corresponding to 1193–97 make 1215 increasingly unlikely, but point to Alix's activity into 1197 (*Cartulaire de la Léproserie de Grand-Beaulie,* nos. 195 at p. 77 [1215/1195]; 168–69 at pp. 66–67 [1197]). Many thanks to Michelle Armstrong-Partida for assistance in locating these charters. See also Brown, chapter one in this volume, n.117 for Eleanor's gift to Alix's daughter Alix in 1199.

23. Of Eleanor and Henry II's sons and their children, William died at an early age (1153–56); Henry (1155–83) married Marguerite of France but left no surviving issue; Richard (1157–99) succeeded Henry II in 1189 and had no issue by his wife Berengaria of Navarre; Geoffrey (1158–86) wed Constance of Brittany and had two surviving children—Arthur (1187–1203), who died in suspicious circumstances, and Eleanor (1184–1241), who lived for decades in close custody in England; John (1166–1216) became king of England in 1199. By his second wife, Isabelle of Angoulême, John had three legitimate daughters, Joan (1210–36), Isabelle (1215–41), and Eleanor (1216–75) who married first William Marshal the younger and then Simon de Montfort. John had at least one illegitimate daughter, also Joan (d. 1238), who married the Welsh Prince Llewellyn. On Geoffrey's daughter Eleanor see a note in Howell, *Eleanor of Provence,* p. 23.

24. Gillingham, *Richard Coeur de Lion,* p. 34. Leonor (4), on the other hand, has played a persistent, if peripheral role in the historiography of thirteenth-century Castilian rulership. The most recent survey of her life is Vann, "Medieval Castilian Queenship," In her forthcoming *Berenguela of Castile,* Miriam Shadis expands upon and diverges from Vann's argument.

25. Torigny, *Chronique* 4:207, 225, 233.

26. Torigny, *Chronique* 4:234 and n3.

27. Howden, *Chronica* 2:269. Matilda's (3) son Henry was probably born before these events, but she may have borne the future Emperor Otto IV soon after her arrival in Normandy. Her son William was born at Winchester a few years later. Howden, *Chronica* 2:269, states that Matilda arrived at her parents' court with her husband and "filiis et filabus suis," and while in Normandy gave birth to a son in 1181. Matthew Paris, however, states that Henry and Otto arrived with their parents in Normandy in 1182, and mentions no daughter; he states that William was born at Winchester in 1183 (Matthew Paris, *Chronica Majora* 2:318–19).

28. The illuminated dedication leaf of a psalter commissioned by Matilda (3) and her husband Henry the Lion, around 1188, clearly identifies the couple, Henry's parents, and his imperial maternal grandparents. Matilda is depicted along with her father and her grandmother, the empress Matilda and an "unidentified laywoman." Van Houts, *Memory and Gender,* pp. 97–98, says "There is no sign of Matilda's mother, Queen Eleanor, unless one assumes that the laywoman, without crown or royal insignia and tucked away in the corner without an identifying label is Eleanor." Van Houts suggests that Matilda instructed the artist to omit or disguise Eleanor because Matilda was dependent upon her father, who at the time of this portrayal had imprisoned Eleanor. This is also suggested by Owen, *Eleanor of Aquitaine,* p. 58. Possibly Matilda made the decision to include the "insignificant" laywoman for Eleanor, and including her mother in this way (when Eleanor was not in Henry's good graces) was a form of protest. The chronicles cited throughout this essay suggests that Matilda and Eleanor spent considerable time together when Matilda was in exile and even when Eleanor was "locked up."

29. Torigny, *Chronique* 4:303, tells of Joanna's (5) son Bohemond's baptism and investment as duke of Apulia, but this is unconfirmed elsewhere. For a prime example of the assumption of the East's exoticizing influence on a western woman, see the chapter "Antioch the Glorious" in Kelly, *Eleanor and the Four Kings,* pp. 52–63.

30. At the time, the match must have seemed a good idea to the Plantagenets and especially to Eleanor of Aquitaine, for it seemed likely to bring Toulouse under their influence.

31. Howden, *Chronica* 4:96. Joanna's (5) surviving son became Raymond VII of Toulouse, who upon defeat in the Albigensian Crusade would negotiate the treaty of Paris in 1229 with his first cousin, Blanche of Castile (4.3), regent of France. Under its terms, Raymond's daughter Jeanne, his heir at

the time, was to marry Louis IX's younger brother, Alphonse of Poitiers; they were respectively great-granddaughter (through Joanna), and great-grandson, through Leonor (4) and Blanche of Castile, of Eleanor and Henry II. Jeanne and Alphonse died without heirs in 1270–71 in the course of Louis IX's second Crusade, and under the terms of the 1229 treaty, Toulouse reverted to the French king. See a discussion of this marriage in Wakefield, *Heresy, Crusade and Inquisition,* pp. 165–66, which contains all relevant literature and a genealogical table.

32. Torigny, *Chronique* 4:295, 303, calls her "carissimam dominam meam et filiam in baptismate," notes her son Sancho's birth ca. Easter 1181, and refers to her daughter Berenguela (4.1), though not by name: "Circa Pascha, Alienor, filia regis Anglorum, uxor Anfulsi regis de Castella, peperit filium, et vocatus est Sanchius; peperit etiam ante filiam unam" (Torigny 4:211). In regard to Leonor's (4) date of birth, see Matthew Paris, *Chronica Majora* 1:315, gives 1162, but Torigny seems more reliable here given his special relationship to Leonor.

33. Vann, "Medieval Castilian Queenship," pp. 128–29.

34. Most scholars accept this date (Gonzalez, *Alfonso VIII* 1:188–90; Flórez, *Reinas Católicas,* p. 504); Warren, *Henry II,* p. 13, says 1176 but probably follows Howden, the only chronicler to give this date, which Stubbs calls a "sad blunder" by Howden. It is interesting that Leonor's (4) marriage receives less attention from this chronicler than her sister Joanna's (5) (Howden, *Chronica* 2:105 and n1). Torigny, *Chronique* 4:247, has the marriage in 1170.

35. Warren, *Henry II,* p. 223.

36. Sancho VI had taken advantage of Alfonso VIII's long nority to reclaim territory in the border region between Castile and Navarre. In their disputes, Alfonso and Sancho turned for resolution to Henry II, who decided in Alfonso's favor (Gonzalez, *Alfonso VIII* 1:185, 787–89, 793; O'Callaghan, *Medieval Spain,* pp. 235–39). Analysis of Leonor's (4) lands held in dower suggests that this marriage was an essential element of Alfonso's strategy in dealing with Navarre (Vann, "Medieval Castilian Queenship," pp. 129–30; Shadis, *Berenguela of Castile* (forthcoming).

37. Gonzalez, *Alfonso VIII* 1:194–212, documents three sons and seven daughters born between 1180 and 1204; two other sons and a daughter may be attested in less trustworthy sources. Of Leonor's (4) three (or five) sons, only one survived to reign briefly as Enrique I of Castile (b. 1204, r. 1214–17); he died at thirteen from an accidental blow to the head. Leonor's surviving daughters are discussed below in text.

38. Vann, in "Medieval Castilian Queenship," argues that Leonor (4) may have served as a model for Alfonso X's ideal queen articulated in his *Siete Partidas.* This argument is problematic, since Alfonso X's mother Beatrix of Swabia and perhaps his grandmother Berenguela (4.1), both of whom he knew, would also fit his archetype, whereas his great-grandmother Leonor died well before his birth. In any case, Vann nicely point out Leonor's

model qualities. Historians close to her time were less sure of Leonor's reticent perfection, assigning her responsibility for more pragmatic political decisions: see Shadis, *Berenguela of Castile* (forthcoming).

39. Gonzalez, *Alfonso VIII* 3: no. 769 at p. 344 (dated December 8, 1204) "Item, pateat cunctis quod ego teneor persoluere creditionibus meis, nominatim illis quorum nomina scripta sunt in quaterno meo, cuius exemplar tenet domina regina . . ."

40. In charters from early in Enrique I's reign, the executors of Alfonso VIII's final will reiterate the validity of Berenguela's (4.1) regency; see, for example, Gonzalez, *Alfonso VIII* 3: no. 963 at p. 664, which states "hoc fecimus cum consilio domine Berengarie, regine Legionis et Gallecie, cui mater sua regina domina Allionoris dimisit regnum et filium et omnia regni iura, sicut dominus rex bone memorie dimiserit ipsi Allionori regine." See also documents no. 970 and 976.

41. The lack of documentation for Leonor's (4) activities is due as much to poor survival of Castilian royal documents as any gendered activity or lack thereof on her part.

42. Alfonso IX of León called the first definite meeting of a representative *cortes* in 1188 (comparable to the Provisions of Oxford in 1258 in England, and Edward I's calling of parliament in the later thirteenth century). Another impetus to this development was the increased study and application throughout Christendom of Roman law (as opposed to, or more appropriately, layered on top of, customary law), which provided theoretical framework for the practice of government (O'Callaghan, *Cortes of Castile-León*, p. 15). On how these developments affected women see Dillard, *Daughters of the Reconquest*.

43. In 1157 Alfonso VII had divided his kingdom between his sons; Ferdinand, the younger, received León and Sancho, Castile. Sancho died in 1158, leaving a child (Alfonso VIII) vulnerable to noble ambition and a Leonese uncle eager to bring Castile under his own authority. Competition between Castile and León continued into the next generation between Alfonso VIII and Fernando's son, Alfonso IX, king of León since 1187. See general history for the kingdom(s) of León-Castilla in this period, including those studies by Gonzalez cited in the bibliography at the end of this book. For the most recent analysis of Alfonso VII, see Reilly, *Alfonso VII*.

44. *Cronica Latina*, ed. Brea, chap. 15 at p. 50.

45. Rodrigo Jiménez de Rada, *De rebus hispanie* 7:31 at p. 253.

46. The first contemporary reference to Berenguela (4.1) is dated May 1, 1181, a charter drawn up in Burgos to record Alfonso and Leonor's (4) gift of land to Berenguela's nurse Estefanía and her husband, presumably for their services (Gonzalez, *Alfonso VIII* 2: 367). By that date Berenguela's brother Sancho was named in Alfonso's acts, but a gift to the bishop and church of Palencia on July 1, 1181 shows that Berenguela's status had changed: "I the abovenamed King Alfonso, together with my wife Queen Leonor and with my daughter the Infanta Berenguela, give, grant, and con-

firm . . ." (Gonzalez, *Alfonso VIII* 2:373). Most of Alfonso VIII's acts do not specify an heir, but he occasionally took advantage of chancery practice to reaffirm his association with his heir, son or daughter. When Sancho, Fernando, or Enrique were alive and heirs apparent, they appeared in the above form; when there was no son, Berenguela so appeared as heir presumptive. Though born before Sancho, for example, Berenguela only began to appear as heir after his death and until Fernando's birth in November 1189. Emphasizing Berenguela's presence and consent was clearly a way of reiterating her status, and perhaps was even more important for a daughter than for a son.

47. There appears to be no text of Celestine's condemnation or approval; Gonzalez, *Alfonso IX* 1:100, suggests Celestine was influenced by Spanish prelates who desired peace and supported the marriage. Howden says a dispensation was granted, probably assuming that one must have been granted simply because the marriage did take place. Howden also comments that the marriage took place "pro bono pacis" (Howden, *Chronica* 3:90).

48. Rodrigo Jiménez de Rada, *De rebus hispanie*, 7:31 at p. 253. See also Florez, *Reinas Católicas* 1:464. The *Crónica Latina* does not mention Leonor's (4) role.

49. Alfonso X, *Primera Crónica General*, chap. 1004 at pp. 682–83. The *Primera Crónica General* also suggests that the "omnes buenos" foresaw that the marriage would ultimately be dissolved, whether by the pope or some political force, but that the birth of heirs in the meantime would more than offset this possibility. Perhaps the *Primera Crónica's* authors were reading later events into earlier history; at the time he married Berenguela (4.1), Alfonso IX's children by his first (also consanguineous) marriage to Teresa of Portugal had been declared legitimate, so any children by Berenguela were potentially removed from inheriting the throne of León.

50. Gonzalez, *Alfonso IX* 1:95. Interestingly, Eleanor of Aquitaine is noticed in the historiography of this moment. Discussing this marriage, Linehan, *History and Historians,* pp. 257–58, writes: "According to the Archbishop Rodrigo fifty years after the event, Alfonso VIII opposed his daughter's marriage to the king of León because it was unlawful. However, Alfonso's English wife . . . Queen Eleanor [4] could see the advantages for Castile of this particular *pro pace* marriage . . . The daughter of Henry II of England, Eleanor had presumably inherited this calculating ability from her mother rather than her father . . . [S]he put the common good, peace and quiet, and the welfare of the *patria* above a little bit of incest."

51. The firstborn, Leonor (4.1.1), died a child; her birth was followed by those of Constanza, Fernando, Alfonso, and Berenguela. Citing Lucas of Túy, Gonzalez, *Reinado y diplomas de Fernando III* 1:62 nn4–5, says Leonor died on November 12, 1202, and postulates her birth in the second half of 1198, the earliest possible date. Fernando was born in 1201, Constanza probably in 1199, Alfonso in 1202, and Berenguela in 1204.

52. Shadis, "Political Motherhood," pp. 335–58.

53. Gonzalez, *Alfonso* VIII 1:203–04. Typical would be this confirmation from 1217: "Ego Alfonsus IIus dei gratia Port. Rex una cum uxore mea Regina domna Urraca et filiis nostris Infantibus domno Sancio et domno Alfonso et donna Alionor istam cartam suprascriptam . . ." Earlier generations of this relatively young monarchy also recognized the queen in royal charters, as well as royal sisters and aunts who inhabited the court (*Portugaliae Monumenta Historica* 1:396–97). The question of Alcobaça is open, as Urraca's (4.2) husband effected her burial there and Urraca's patronage patterns are unknown. Alcobaça became an important royal mausoleum; its choice represents a major shift in the policy of choosing Cistercian women as caretakers of the dead, and John Parsons theorizes that Urraca brought Castilian burial customs to Portugal ("Mothers, Daughters, Marriage, Power," p. 75) On royal tombs at Alcobaça see Boaventura, *Abbadia de Alcobaça,* Notice no. 5 at pp. 17–20.

54. Leonor's (4.4) was another case in which consanguinity was the excuse, not the reason, for divorce. The *Cronica Latina,* chap. 54 at p. 99, says Leonor and Jaume were divorced by a papal legate "propter incestum notorium," and Jaume says as much in his autobiography: *Llibre dels fet,* chap. 140 at 2:137. A more likely reason was personal incompatibility. For Alfonso's relations with his father see Bisson, *Crown of Aragon,* pp. 62, 67–68. Leonor's interesting case remains to be fully explored; on her possible foundation of Santa María de Duero, a female Praemonstratensian abbey near Almazán, see Gonzalez, *Reinado y diplomas de Fernando III,* pp. 86, 249–54. See also Shadis, *Berenguela of Castile,* forthcoming.

55. For Constanza (4.5) and the distinctive positions of royal women (professed and lay) within the abbey's hierarchy, see Shadis, "Piety, Politics, and Power," p. 208. See also Gayoso, "'Lady' of Las Huelgas."

56. See *Grand cartulaire de Fontevraud,* vol. 1. There is one passing reference to a meeting between the abbess and Louis VII, in no. 378 (1146), but this is not a conveyance to the nuns; there are no references to Eleanor and no charters from Henry for the nuns.

57. Leonor's (4) patronage extended as well to the royal foundation of the Hospital del Rey in Burgos, which in her lifetime was often called the "Hospital de la reina." See Vann, "Medieval Castilian Queenship," p. 135, and Shadis, *Berenguela of Castile,* forthcoming.

58. *Documentación del Monasterio de las Huelgas* 1: no. 12. Alfonso X noted that his great-grandfather built the monastery "por los muchos ruegos et por el grand afficamiento de la muy noble reyna donna Leonor, su mugier" (Alfonso X, *Primera Crónica General,* chap. 1006 at p. 685). Regarding this endowment's influence on Leonor's (4) daughters and granddaughters' patronage see Shadis, "Piety, Politics, and Power," pp. 202–27.

59. Kelly, *Eleanor and the Four Kings,* p. 159, thought Leonor (4) might have been brought up at Fontevraud, but Andrew Lewis notes in this volume that no extant source supports that theory. Shadis, "Piety, Politics and

Power," pp. 203–04, argues that Fontevraud served as an important model for Leonor's foundation and patronage of a house of Cistercian women at Las Huelgas. In both cases, the use as a family mausoleum was secondary and only came some time after the foundation, for it is clear to those of us who are monastic historians that in such patronage the primary concern is the support of prayers by the nuns, not family burials. Leonor continued to have ties with Fontevraud Las Huelgas; see the act of June 30, 1190, in which Leonor and her husband conceded an annual rent to Fontevraud for prayers for the soul of her father Henry II, who had been buried at Fontevraud in 1189 (Gonzalez, *Alfonso VIII* 3: no. 551; Shadis, "Piety, Politics, and Power," 202–27).

60. Wakefield, *Heresy, Crusade and Inquisition,* pp. 126–27.

61. Clause 22 of Louis VIII's will, in RHF 17: 304, says, "Praeterea volumus ut omnes lapides nostri pretiosi qui sunt in coronis nostris vel extra coronas, vendantur, et de pretio eorum construatur nova abbatia de ordine Sancti-Victoris in honore beatae Mariae Virginis, et omne aurum quod est in coronis vel annulis, vel aliis jocalibus, similiter vendatur ad opus praedictae abbatiae." See also Dimier, *Saint Louis et Cîteaux,* pp. 121–23.

62. Berger, *Blanche de Castille* pp. 314–5; the lands and revenues settled on Blanche (4.3) as dower in 1240 would constitute the resources from which she would endow her communities of nuns at Maubuisson and Le Lys.

63. There is much unpublished Maubuisson material in Pontoise, archives départmentales du Val d'Oise, sér. 72H 1–236, but see Kinder, "Blanche of Castile and the Cistercians"; Dutilleux and Depoin, *L'abbaye de Maubuisson;* l'Épinois, "La fondation de Maubuisson"; Bonis, *Maubuisson;* Dutilleux and Depoin, "Inventaire de Maubuisson," pp. 1–6.

64. Dimier and Delabrouille, *Notre-Dame-du-Lys;* L'Huillier, "Inventaire de Notre-Dame du Lys; Prieur, *L'abbaye royale du Lys;* Paris, BnF, lat. 13892, "Cartulaire du Lys," fol. 104.

65. For Alix of Mâcon's (1.1.1) descent from Eleanor of Aquitaine, see the genealogical table for this chapter. See also Dimier, *Saint Louis et Cîteaux,* and LeGoff, *Saint Louis,* p. 167 n2.

66. Royaumont was nearly complete by 1239 when Blanche (4.3) began work at Maubuisson, to which she planned to retire and where she was buried. Blanche provided all sums for the building of church, cloister, conventual buildings, and cloister enclosure for Maubuisson, which she referred to as Notre-Dame-la-Royale. Although her church has been destroyed, other buildings survive and there have been careful excavations of the site. Building records are in Pontoise, archives départmentales du Val d'Oise, sér. 58 H, 1–58, esp. no. 4, Registre de Maubuisson, parchment codex entitled "Achatz et heritages." It appears that Le Lys had a slower gestation than Maubuisson and its endowment was more dependent on continued land consolidation after Blanche's death. Nonetheless, of the 300 li. annual rent to which Louis IX limited his mother's alienations in alms during a period of stringent cuts in royal expenditures prior to his first crusade, Blanche

granted 100 li. in rents (one-third the total) to Le Lys. Each abbey was to house 120 nuns. On the size of this house see Berman, "How much?"

67. She also paid for some of the windows at Chartres cathedral (*Cartulaire de Notre-Dame de Chartres,* no. 294 [1249]).

68. *Cartulaire de la Trappe,* p. 1 (1221). In *Cartulaire de Tiron,* no. 57, Isabelle countess of Chartres and Lady of Amboise (2.2) grants 100s. rent (June 1221); see also *Cartulaire de l'abbaye royale du Lieu,* nos. 45–47.

69. Paris, Archives nationales, S*4386, Cartulaire de Saint-Antoine, fols. 1r–1v (1236), has two grants by John and Isabelle (2.2); *L'abbaye royale de Notre-Dame-des-Clairets,* no. 63 (1279), confirms a gift by the late Isabelle.

70. See Bondéelle-Souchier, "Les moniales cisterciennes et leurs livres manuscrits," pp. 193–336, for a gazetteer for all Cistercian houses of nuns in France (Moncey at p. 306), and Cottineau, *Repertoire topo-bibliographique;* Berman, "Abbeys for Cistercian Nuns," pp. 83–113.

71. *Cartulaire de l'abbaye royale du Lieu,* nos. 29 (1245), 38 (1245), 25 (1239).

72. *Cartulaire de l'abbaye de Notre-Dame de l'Eau,* nos. 4 (1225), 5 (1225), 9 (1226), 10 (1227), 13 (1228), 16 (1229); Isabelle (2.2) ceased to give it her attention within a short time after her husband's death.

73. E.g., *Cartulaire de l'abbaye royale du Lieu,* nos. 45–47.

74. *Cartulaire de l'abbaye royale du Lieu,* no. 1 (1247).

75. Howden, *Chronica,* 3: 3.

76. "Quod Gaufridus quondam comes Perticensis, maritus noster, in suorum compunctus recordatione peccatorum et metuendi diem judicii cordis oculis anteponens, pro redemptione suae animae et nostrae, nec non antecessorum nostrorum pariter et haeredum, dedit et concessit ... moriens nos vocavit et ad perficiendum quod proposuerat sub fide nostri matrimonii nos adjurans, insuper nos, fide corporaliter praestita, obligavit ad hoc effectui mancipandum, nostrae reliquens optioni, quatenus de quo placeret ordine monachos, vel sanctimoniales religiosas eligeremus, eisque locum aedificandae abbatiae competentem et idoneum, et redditus cum suorum hominum consilio providerimus." *(des Clairets,* no. 4 [1204]).

77. "Monialibus de Claretis, Cisterciensis ordinis," *(L'abbaye royale de Notre-Dame-des-Clairets,* no. 5 [1213]); by 1214, a charter records a gift to the nuns by Geoffrey of Saint-Quentin when his sister Agatha entered the house (*L'abbaye royale de Notre-Dame-des-Clairetts,* no. 6 [1214]). Count Thomas of Perche made gifts in 1215 and 1217 (*L'abbaye royale de Notre-Dame-des-Clairets,* nos. 7 [1215], and 10 [1217]).

78. Thomas and Matilda (3.1) perhaps had a daughter Helisende, wife of one of the lords of Triennel; see La Cour-Notre-Dame cartulary, Auxerre, A.D. Yonne, H787. Helisende did not, however, inherit the county of Perche. In 1218 Count Thomas's successor was his paternal uncle William, then bishop of Châlons, who confirmed earlier gifts by Count Thomas and Countess Matilda. He granted the nuns three arpents of land adjoining those that his predecessors had given so that they would celebrate an anniversary for his soul (*L'abbaye royale de Notre-Dame-des-Clairets,* nos. 13

[1218], 14 [1218]). At William's death the county reverted permanently to the crown.

79. See Chibnall, *Empress Matilda,* esp. pp. 177–94.

80. On the regencies, Evergates, "Aristocratic Women," pp. 76–79; on the power of women, see the illuminating remarks by Cheyette, "Women, Poets and Politics," pp. 138–77. Marie died a nun at Fontaines-les-Nones (Brown, chapter 1 of this volume, n.118).

81. For Alix's (2) children see above, note 22. Louis, elder of the two sons who survived Thibaut V, could have been no more than fourteen when he became count in 1191. Certain of Alix's other descendants are discussed below.

82. Berger, *Blanche de Castille,* pp. 3–10.

83. Discussed in Tachau, "God's Compass," 7–33.

84. Schneider, *Vom Klosterhaushalt,* pp. 28–55, discusses lending of lay-brothers, including the countesses of Flanders's requests for them.

85. See petitions for parents and fertility in *Statuta capitulorum generalium,* e.g., no. 12 (1236), a request by Louis IX and his mother Blanche (4.3) for prayers for the late Louis VIII, Blanche's mother, and other siblings.

86. Bonnardot, *L'Abbaye royale de Saint-Antoine-des-Champs.*

87. Sivéry, *Blanche de Castille;* Berger, *Blanche de Castille,* pp. 1–10.

88. Only two monographs have appeared since Petit-Dutaillis, *Louis VIII:* Choffel, *Louis VIII,* and Sivéry, *Louis VIII.*

89. Fawtier, *Les capétiens,* trans. as *The Capetian Kings of France,* says at p. 28 of the English version: "To all intents and purposes she may be counted among the Kings of France."

90. On bureaucratization, see Baldwin, *Philip Augustus,* esp. pp. 137–75.

91. Jordan, *Louis IX.*

92. Alphonse of Poitiers gave to the nuns of la Cour Notre-Dame (Berman, "The Labors of Hercules," 45–63). In return for promises to build abbeys in southern Italy, Charles of Anjou inveigled a tithe from the Cistercians for his Italian campaign (Bruzelius, "ad modum franciae," 402–20); Louis IX gave a gift for his sister Isabelle (*Cartulaire de l'abbaye royale du Lieu,* no. 81 [1242]).

93. As king, Alfonso III married Beatrix, a natural daughter of Alfonso X of Castile. Their first two children were named Branca and Diniz (Blanche and Denis), obvious tributes to Alfonso's French past. Alfonso also asserted his Iberian lineage, however, calling himself "son of Alfonso II King of Portugal and Queen Urraca [4.2]," and "son of Alfonso of Portugal and the grandson of Alfonso of Castile." In this, Alfonso imitated his brother Sancho, perhaps claiming the same lineage to bolster his claims to the same throne. It is interesting to note in this context that the deposed Sancho III took refuge with his Castilian relatives. See *Portugaliae Monumenta Historica,* 1:606, 610, 651; Livermore, *A History of Portugal,* p. 132.

94. For Countess Alix's (2) children see above, note 22. Baldwin, *Philip Augustus,* pp. 277, 342, reports Gautier of Avesnes, Marguerite's (2.1) husband in 1218, paying relief for his succession to Blois through his wife.

95. See note 22 and *Statuta capitulorum generalium* 2:1228, no. 8 and indices. We cannot verify that Marguerite (2.1) entered Fontevraud; for her activity as a patroness and subject of poetry, see Bezzola, *Origines* 3.2: 436–49. Marie's 1241 will confirms exchanges of property her husband Hugh made with Isabelle countess of Chartres (1.2) ("karissima matertera mea, Ysabellis comitissa Carnotensis"), and gave up any claims they had with Isabelle's daughter Mathilde (2.2.1) ("karissima consanguinea mea Matilda") [*Layettes*, ed. Teulet, 2: no. 2002). Marguerite's grandson John de Châtillon in 1256 reunited the two counties of Blois and Chartres (Chédeville, *Chartres et ses campagnes*, pp. 42–43); *L'abbaye royale de Notre-Dame-des-Clairets*, no. 63 (1279), confirms Marie's gift of 100s. annual rent over the fulling mills of Chartres made by John de Châtillon, count of Blois and Chartres (reconfirmed in no. 169 [1282] by John's daughter and heir Jeanne, countess of Chartres, and her husband Pierre d'Alençon, son of Louis IX). Isabelle is not named in les Clairets's extant necrology (*L'abbaye royale de Notre-Dame-des-Clairets*, p. 238), though Countess Marguerite of Blois appears there. In 1228, Marguerite is mentioned in the Statutes of the Cistercian General Chapter when an anniversary mass was granted for her and for Blanche of Navarre—the Statute suggests that she was still alive at that point, but possibly near death? See *Statuta capitulorum generalium*, vol. 2, p. 66, 1228, no. 7 and 8.

96. *Cartulaire de l'abbaye de Notre-Dame de l'Eau*, nos. 4 (1225), 5 (1225), 9 (1226), 10 (1227), 13 (1228), 16 (1229), 24 (1235), 27 (1239), are all contracts with John and Isabelle (2.2); nos. 29 (1240) and 31 (1242) are for Isabelle as a widow; the late Isabelle is mentioned in no. 87 (1279).

97. *Cartulaire de l'abbaye royale du Lieu* contains many charters for Isabelle (2.2) and Mathilde (2.2.1), but few for their menfolk; no. 25 (1239) has Isabelle with her daughter Mathilde and Mathilde's husband Richard of Beaumont; nos. 121 and 129 are by Isabelle alone in February 1247; no. 1, in May 1247, is Isabelle's will.

98. *Cartulaire de l'abbaye de Notre-Dame de l'Eau*, no. 50 (1256) after Mathilde's (2.21) death; *Cartulaire de l'abbaye royale du Lieu*, no. 2, may be Mathilde's will (misdated 1245 for 1255).

99. Nicholas, "Countesses as Rulers in Flanders," pp. 127–35. Jordan, "For the Safety of My Soul," emphasizes religious patronage; for the countesses' involvement with the Beguines, see also Galloway, "Discreet and Devout Maidens," pp. 92–115.

100. On Alice of Cyprus (1.3.1) see Edbury, *The Kingdom of Cyprus;* there is some discussion of this case in Baldwin, *Philip Augustus*, pp. 197–98, and in LeGoff, *Saint Louis*, p. 111. See also Schabel, "Frankish Pyrgos," pp. 349–60. All evidence is collected in an unpublished University of Iowa M.A. paper by Janice Faris, "Alice, Queen of Cyprus," spring 1993. Marie of Champagne's (1) younger son, Thibaut III of Champagne, was born in 1179 and lived to rule only four years (1197–1201), the first year under Marie's regency. In 1199 he wed Blanche of Navarre, by whom he had a

daughter, Marie, and a posthumous son Thibaut IV (1201–53), for whom
Blanche of Navarre was regent (1201–22). Blanche was able to uphold the
legitimacy of her son's claims to Champagne in part by giving up her infant daughter, Marie, to be brought up at Philip's court, and by promising
that she herself would not remarry without the king's permission (Evergates, "Aristocratic Women," p. 81). It appears likely that Philip Augustus
found it expedient to allow widows to remain unmarried, rather than risk
the consolidation of rival counties such as occurred with the marriage of
Matilda of Auxerre to Guy of Forez ca. 1226; on this see Baldwin, *Philip
Augustus,* p. 278. The child Marie would have been brought up at the
Capetian royal court in the company of Blanche of Castile and the future
Louis VIII, and for at least four years, from 1208 or so until 1212, with
those other wards or hostages of Philip Augustus, Jeanne (1.2.1) and Mar-
guerite (1.2.2), the future countesses of Flanders.

101. It was a nice coincidence that it was also her mother's name. We may safely
assume, however, that the child was not named for her mother; amongst
their sons Leonor (4) and Alfonso never used the name Alfonso, but rather
Sancho (Alfonso's father), Fernando (the first king of Castile, Alfonso's paternal ancestor, and his uncle, Fernando II of León), and Enrique (Leonor's
father, Henry II Plantagenet). These practices fit trends suggested by
Bouchard, "Migration of Women's Names," 1–19.

102. Alfonso X, *Primera Crónica General,* chap. 1048 at p. 735, is explicit on this
point, describing Fernando III's daughter by Jeanne of Ponthieu as "una fija
quel dixieron donna Leonor, del nonbre de su visauuela donna Leonor
muger del noble rey don Alfonso . . ." The same source (chap. 1036 at p.
720) notes that Fernando had had with his first wife a daughter Leonor,
who died as a child. One may quibble over the dates of birth of Leonor
(4.4), daughter of Leonor of England (4), and Leonor (4.1.1), daughter of
Berenguela of Castile (4.1). Dates of birth are approximate: both Leonors
were born at around the same time. Each was named for her maternal
grandmother, initiating a trend linking Iberian royal women with Eleanor
of Aquitaine. For Eleanor of Castile, see Parsons, *Eleanor of Castile.* Queen
Leonor's daughter Mafalda (4.6), or Matilda, was perhaps named for her
paternal great-grandmother, Henry II's mother, the empress Matilda, an
unusual but not unique use of the name among Iberian royalty.

103. See the genealogy in Maddicott, *Simon de Montfort,* pp. xxiv-xxv.

CHAPTER 9

THE CANON LAW OF DIVORCE
IN THE MID-TWELFTH CENTURY:
LOUIS VII C. ELEANOR OF AQUITAINE

James A. Brundage

> *Louis VII and Eleanor of Aquitaine terminated their marriage through an action*
> *brought under the rules of the canon law. This chapter outlines the substantive and*
> *procedural law relevant to that action.*

When the troubled marriage of King Louis VII (r. 1137–80) to Eleanor of Aquitaine (ca. 1124–1204) finally reached the stage at which the parties wished to terminate their union, they turned to the church's judicial system to determine whether and under what terms they could do so. That they did so as a matter of course was the result of a complicated and lengthy process. Jurisdiction over marital disputes had for centuries been a contentious issue in medieval France, but by 1152 the result was clear. The church had won almost complete control over marriage litigation, and the parties to such disputes had no option but to submit to ecclesiastical judgment on the matter.[1]

The reigning authorities on current church law concerning marriage and other matters in 1152 were contained in a recently completed book by a Bolognese canonist named Gratian.[2] Gratian entitled his work the *Concordia discordantium canonum*, or *A Harmony of Clashing Canons*, but common usage among lawyers and non-lawyers alike soon replaced that colorful if cumbersome title with the more manageable *Decretum*, or *Decree*, by which the book has ever since been universally known.[3] Anders

Winroth has recently identified an early and relatively short recension of the work, which survives in four manuscripts and probably dates from ca. 1140.[4] The expanded, or vulgate, recension that was taught in medieval law schools, almost twice as long as the earlier one, was being used as a textbook at Bologna by about 1150, and at Paris not long after that.[5]

The canon law of marriage and divorce as it appeared in Gratian's book recognized eight grounds on which a marriage could be annulled and the parties could be allowed to remarry. They were consanguinity (blood relationship), affinity (relationship by marriage), sexual incapacity to consummate the marriage, *ligamen* (an existing valid marriage to someone else or a binding commitment to enter the religious life), marriage below the minimum age permitted by canon law, lack of free consent by the parties to a marriage, error of person, and (with qualifications) disparity of religion or adultery.[6]

The grounds for divorce in the case that Louis VII brought against his marriage to Eleanor of Aquitaine were consanguinity. Prevailing canonical doctrine on this matter in 1152 taught that persons related within seven degrees of blood kinship could not lawfully marry one another. If they attempted to do so, their marriage was null and void.[7] Church law also required the couple to separate under pain of excommunication and infamy;[8] if they remained together, they would be committing incest.[9] This seven-degree rule prevailed over another, that forbade marriages between two people who shared an ancestor within four or five generations of themselves.[10] As matters stood in 1152, however, two general church councils, as well as regional councils in France, had within living memory reiterated the seven-degree rule.[11]

The seven-degree rule had the effect of prohibiting unions within an extraordinarily wide range of potential marriage partners. In effect any couple who shared one great-great-great-great-great grandparent could not marry each other. One calculation shows that, even under a set of minimal assumptions, a prospective bride or groom could easily have almost 3,000 relatives within the forbidden degrees of blood relationship.[12] It is scarcely surprising that church authorities ultimately decided to reduce from seven degrees to four the genealogical range within which marriage was forbidden, reasoning that the seven-degree rule "often led to difficulties," a considerable understatement.[13] That change took place, however, only at the Fourth Lateran Council in 1215, some sixty-three years after Louis and Eleanor divorced.[14]

The circumstances of the couple's marriage are well known. Eleanor's father, Duke William X of Aquitaine (r. 1127–37), fell ill while on pilgrimage to Santiago de Compostella and died there on April 9, 1137. On his deathbed, William named King Louis VI of France (r. 1108–37) as

guardian for Eleanor, his daughter and heiress. Louis hurriedly arranged for
her to marry his son, Louis VII. He did so in the nick of time: the marriage was celebrated, publicly and with appropriate pomp, at Bordeaux on
July 25, 1137, and Louis VI was dead within the week.[15] Disturbing rumors that the new king's marriage violated church law soon began to cir-
culate among the French kingdom's power elite. John of Salisbury reports
that Bishop Bartholomew of Laon knew that the couple were related to
each other and took the trouble to check the degree of consanguinity between them.[16] St. Bernard of Clairvaux (1090–1153) complained in an
1143 letter to Bishop Stephen of Palestrina about Louis VII's cheek in lec-
turing others about improper marriages while he remained coupled with
a woman to whom he was related in the third canonical degree.[17] Though
Bernard apparently calculated the relationship incorrectly, his complaint
was justified: the royal couple was indeed more closely related to each
other than canon law allowed. Eleanor's great-grandfather, William VIII of
Aquitaine (r. 1050–88) had married Audiarde, daughter of Duke Robert I
of Burgundy (d. 1076), a brother of Louis VII's great-grandfather, King
Henry I (r. 1031–60). King Robert II (r. 996–1031), father of Henry I and
Robert of Burgundy, was thus a common ancestor of Eleanor and Louis
VII. They were accordingly related in the fourth degree on his side of the
family tree and in the fifth degree on her side.[18]

We do not know when or under what circumstances Louis and Eleanor
became aware of this problem. John of Salisbury reports that Eleanor raised
the issue in 1148, while she and Louis were at Antioch during the Second
Crusade. According to John's report, the issue arose amid what sounds very
much like a family quarrel, during which Louis demanded that Eleanor accompany him to Jerusalem, while she wished to stay at Antioch with her
uncle Raymond, to whom she was attached, perhaps more closely than was
altogether proper. In the course of the dispute, John tells us,

> [W]hen the King made haste to tear her away, she mentioned their kinship,
> saying it was not lawful for them to remain together as man and wife, since
> they were related in the fourth and fifth degrees. At this the king was deeply
> moved; and although he loved the queen almost beyond reason he consented
> to divorce her if his counsellors and the French nobility would allow it.[19]

John's story thus makes it clear that by March 1148, Eleanor knew her
marriage was consanguineous. John strongly implies, moreover, that up to
this point Louis had been unaware of it and that when he learned of it, his
first reaction was to consider divorce.

Relations between Louis and Eleanor remained strained, John reports,
until the autumn of 1149, when the couple passed through papal territory

on their return from the Holy Land to France. At Tusculum on October 9 they met Pope Eugene III (r. 1145–53), whose reaction upon learning of the couple's estrangement was to attempt to reconcile them and head off a divorce. According to John of Salisbury:

> He reconciled the king and queen after hearing severally the accounts each gave of the estrangement begun at Antioch, and forbade any future mention of their consanguinity: confirming their marriage, both orally and in writing,[20] he commanded under pain of anathema that no word should be spoken against it and that it should not be dissolved under any pretext whatever. This ruling plainly delighted the king, for he loved the queen passionately, in an almost childish way. The pope made them sleep in the same bed, which he had had decked with priceless hangings of his own; and daily during their brief visit he strove by friendly converse to restore love between them.[21]

John of Salisbury is a credible witness and we must, I think, give his account great weight. He described his evidential criteria in the prologue to the *Historia pontificalis* in these terms: "In what I am going to relate I shall, by the help of God, write nothing but what I myself have seen and heard and know to be true, or have on good authority from the testimony or writings of reliable men."[22] We have ample reason to think him as good as his word. He could not have witnessed the exchange he reports between Louis and Eleanor at Antioch, but this was presumably one of the episodes he related on "the testimony or writings of reliable men." John knew and was on friendly terms with many influential participants in the crusade, including the papal legate Cardinal Guido and the counts of Flanders and Champagne, any of whom could well have been privy to goings-on in the royal household.[23]

One might have hoped for some corroboration of John's report in the work of Odo of Deuil (d. 1165) an eyewitness to the events of the Second Crusade. As Louis VII's chaplain, Odo was in an excellent position to know about events in the royal household. His account of the crusade, however, is essentially a paean to Louis VII's merits, and it is perhaps not surprising that he says nothing of the quarrel at Antioch.[24] There is also reason to believe that he may have revised his text (presumably after the queen's marriage to Henry of Anjou), in the process excising nearly all references to her.[25]

John of Salisbury almost certainly had reliable, first-hand information of the royal couple's encounter with Eugene III, for John spent the years 1148–52 at the papal curia and was probably in the papal entourage at Tusculum.[26] One might wonder why Eugene III admonished Louis and Eleanor to remain in wedlock when, as we have seen, their marriage clearly violated then-current rules against consanguineous marriages. The answer must surely be that he adopted this position in virtue of his power to dispense from the prescriptions of man-made law when individual circumstances made this appropriate.[27] Contemporary canonistic teaching held that the church's consanguinity rules fell into this category, as they were part of neither natural nor divine law.[28] Eugene III, we can be sure, was well abreast of juristic opinion—too much so, in the view of his former novice master.[29]

The pope's attempt to reconcile the estranged royal couple worked for a few years. Then, in the spring of 1152, according to the anonymous *Historia gloriosi regis Ludovici VII,* certain relatives and associates of the king informed him that he and his wife were related within the forbidden degrees of consanguinity.[30] In view of John of Salisbury's account, it seems highly unlikely that the king was greatly surprised at this, but the *Historia's* author tried to put the best face on Louis's actions. "Hearing this," he tells us, "the king no longer wished to have her as his wife against Catholic law." It seems inherently unlikely, however, that Louis was greatly troubled by qualms of conscience. He had, after all, received a papal dispensation from the impediment of consanguinity. Indeed, he had also received a papal command not to proceed with the divorce action he had contemplated in 1149, and had evidently complied. Now, at the beginning of 1152, Louis finally determined to divorce Eleanor. Evidence for the reasons for Louis' change of mind is not entirely reliable. We have hearsay anecdotes from chroniclers who were not present, and modern historians' abundant, sometimes fanciful, inferences from those statements. About the most we can say with reasonable certainty is that dynastic considerations—specifically Eleanor's failure to bear a son—probably played a role.[31] Suger of St.-Denis's death in January 1151 was another likely factor that sped the divorce to its conclusion.[32] Suger had been a restraining influence on both parties; his death made it easier for Louis and Eleanor to move toward the solution both apparently now desired.

Louis took the initiative and, once he had decided to proceed with the divorce, followed the appropriate protocol to institute proceedings. He consulted his diocesan ordinary, the bishop of Paris, and probably through him approached Archbishop Hugh of Sens, metropolitan of the ecclesiastical province within which Paris was situated. The archbishop, in turn, convened a synod consisting of himself and the archbishops of Reims, Rouen, and Bordeaux, at least some of their suffragan bishops, and an indeterminate number of barons and other great men.[33] The choice of the archbishops was probably dictated by jurisdictional (and, no doubt, political) considerations. The principal residences and landed properties of the parties were concentrated within those four ecclesiastical provinces, and on that basis, the archbishops could legitimately claim jurisdiction over the case.

A venerable rule of canon law dating back to the sixth century held that the place of residence of the defendant should determine the venue of the court in contentious matters,[34] but the trial in this case took place on more-or-less neutral ground, at the castle of Beaugency in the county of Blois, on the north bank of the Loire roughly midway between Blois and Orléans. We can reasonably assume that the parties (or their legal advisers) and the four archbishops negotiated this arrangement.

The synod of Beaugency convened on March 18, 1152. No formal trial record now exists, or probably ever did exist. What we know of events at Beaugency comes entirely from narrative sources, which give a sketchy outline of what took place. According to one account, the bishop of Langres proposed that the assembly inquire into allegations of Eleanor's adultery; the archbishop of Bordeaux, her subject, rejected that proposal and suggested instead that the synod consider whether she and Louis had married within the forbidden degrees of consanguinity.[35] Procedurally, this greatly simplified the trial. Consanguinity could be proved by the sworn testimony of two or three credible witnesses, and the synod adopted this course.[36] There is no evidence that other issues were seriously discussed, and the testimony on consanguinity was not contested.[37] The archbishop of Sens immediately declared the marriage annulled, adding that since the parties had married in good faith, their two daughters were legitimate. Having completed their business, the members of the synod forthwith dispersed. King Louis and Eleanor, now his former wife, parted ways at once.[38]

That brings us to what most lawyers would regard as the nub of this or any divorce action: the property settlement. Division of the matrimonial estate is nearly always the most difficult and hotly contested issue in divorce, especially when both parties want to dissolve the marriage. How far the property issues had been settled in advance of the synod at Beaugency is not clear from the narrative sources, which are all we have to go on, since no written agreement on these matters—if there ever was one—seems to have survived.

The property division in this case apparently followed, at least in broad outline, the prevailing customary law of northern France, although it must be added that the details of that law in the mid-twelfth century are uncertain, because few *coutumes,* or written statements of customary private law, survive from before the thirteenth century.[39] Thirteenth-century *coutumes,* which may well reflect twelfth-century practice, distinguish three types of matrimonial property: the family lands (*propres, héritages*) that each party brought into the marriage, lands acquired during the marriage (*acquêts, conquêts*), and movable property (*meubles*). At the termination of a marriage, each party retained the family lands with which he or she had entered the marriage. Acquests and movables were treated as community property and partitioned equally between the parties.[40]

We have no information as to how Louis and Eleanor divided their acquests or movable property. Each retained the family lands they had brought into the marriage. True, Louis made a brief attempt to secure control of some of Eleanor's lands, but soon abandoned the idea.[41] He could well have calculated that the risks were too great to justify the huge investment of resources that the venture demanded. Even had he succeeded in the short run, retaining control of Eleanor's patrimony would almost certainly have required more money, time, and manpower than he could readily afford.[42]

These, then, are the legal contexts of the divorce between Louis VII and Eleanor of Aquitaine. They could not, of course, have foreseen the long-term consequences of their divorce or Eleanor's subsequent marriage to Henry of Anjou. They acted well within their legal rights. We can only wonder whether they would have thought it wise to pursue those rights as they did, had they any inkling of what the future would bring.

Notes

1. Daudet, *Les origines carolingiennes;* Esmein, *Le mariage en droit canonique* 1:25–31; Helmholz, *Marriage Litigation,* p. 5.
2. For what little evidence about Gratian himself exists, see Noonan, "Gratian Slept Here," 145–72.
3. Stephan Kuttner explored the methodological implications of the musical metaphor in Gratian's original title for his little book in "Harmony from Dissonance."
4. Winroth, "The Two Recensions of Gratian's Decretum," 22–31. Winroth's conclusions have been confirmed by Weigand, "Zur künftigen Edition des Dekrets Gratians," 32–51, and Larrainzar, "El decreto de Graciano del Códice Fd 9, 421–89.
5. Kuttner, "Les débuts de l'école canoniste française," 193–204.
6. Brundage, *Law, Sex and Christian Society,* pp. 242–45; Gaudemet, *Le mariage en occident,* pp. 195–221.
7. Gratian, C. 35 q. 2 & 3 c. 1, c. 17, c. 19. Gratian's text is cited throughout from the standard edition of the vulgate version in vol. 1 of the *Corpus iuris canonici,* ed. Friedberg. For the canonistic citation system employed here see Brundage, *Medieval Canon Law,* pp. 190–94.
8. Not even kings could trifle with these threats. See Vodola, *Excommunication.* Landau, *Die Entstehung des kanonischen Infamiebegriffs,* and Migliorino, *Fama e infamia.*
9. Gratian C. 35 q. 2 & 3 c. 9.
10. Gratian C. 35 q. 2 & 3 c. 19 and 20, as well as Gratian's comments in d.p.c. 19. For a detailed account of the development of these rules see Freisen,

Geschichte des canonischen Eherechts, pp. 371–405; at pp. 406–39, Freisen also explains the methods for computing the degrees of blood relationship.

11. The First Lateran Council (1123) c. 9, and the Second Lateran Council (1139) c. 17, in *Decrees of the Ecumenical Councils,* ed. Alberigo, 1:191, 201. See also the Council of Clermont (1130) c. 12 and the Council of Reims (1131) c. 16, in *Sacrorum conciliorum,* ed. Mansi, 21:439–40, 461.

12. Flandrin, *Families in Former Times,* p. 24.

13. Modern writers have often criticized the medieval church's consanguinity rules, none more harshly than Maitland, *The History of English Law,* 2:389: "Behind these intricate rules there is no deep policy, there is no strong religious feeling; they are the idle ingenuities of men who are amusing themselves by inventing a game of skill . . . to be played with neatly drawn tables of affinity and doggerel hexameters . . . When we weigh the merits of the medieval church and have remembered all her good deeds, we have to put into the other scale as a weighty counterpoise the incalculable harm done by a marriage law which was a maze of flighty fancies and misapplied logic."

14. Fourth Lateran council (1215) c. 50, in *Constitutiones Concilii Quarti Lateranensis,* pp. 90–91. This canon was later incorporated into the official papal law book, the *Decretales Gregorii IX,* and thus forms part of the *Corpus iuris canonici,* where it appears as X. 4.14.8.

15. Suger, *Vie de Louis VI le Gros,* ed. Waquet, pp. 280–83, trans. Cusimano and Moorhead as *The Deeds of Louis the Fat,* pp. 156–57. The text of William X's testament bequeathing Aquitaine and Poitou to Eleanor appears in the *Chronicon comitum Pictaviae,* in RHF 12:409–10, s.a. 1137.

16. John of Salisbury, *Historia pontificalis,* c. 23, p. 53.

17. Bernard of Clairvaux, Epist. 224 in Bernard, *Sancti Bernardi Opera* 8:93 [91–93].

18. Duby, *Medieval Marriage,* p. 55 n91.

19. John of Salisbury, *Historia Pontificalis,* c. 23 (trans. Chibnall, p. 53).

20. No such document is known to survive.

21. John of Salisbury, *Historia pontificalis* c. 29 (trans. Chibnall, p. 61).

22. John of Salisbury, *Historia pontificalis,* prologue (trans. Chibnall, p. 4).

23. Constable, "Second Crusade," 274.

24. Constable, "Second Crusade," 217.

25. Odo of Deuil, *De Profectione Ludovici VII,* p. xxiii n67.

26. Chibnall, introduction to John of Salisbury, *Historia pontificalis,* pp. xvii, xxi–xxiii.

27. Gratian C. 1 q. 7 c. 11–17; all of these canons appeared as well in collections assembled by Gratian's predecessors, e.g., Burchard of Worms, *Decretum* 1.197, and Ivo of Chartres, *Decretum* 2.78 and 5.312 (c. 11); Ivo's prologue (c. 15–16); and especially Alger of Liège, *De misericordia et iustitia* (c. 16–17).

28. This was certainly Gratian's opinion; see C. 35 q. 1 d.p.c. 1. The Fourth Lateran Council (1215) c. 50 expressly stated the same view when enun-

ciating the change from the seven-degree rule to the four-degree rule (X 4.14.8).

29. Bernard of Clairvaux, *De consideratione,* 1.13 in *Sancti Bernardi Opera* 3:408–09. Bernard took a decidedly dim view of lawyers, their works, and their pomp; see Brundage, "St. Bernard and the Jurists," pp. 25–33.

30. *Historia gloriosi regis Ludovici VII* in RHF 12:127.

31. Louis and Eleanor had two daughters, the younger born after the reconciliation at Tusculum (Howden, *Chronica* 1:214). Louis was to marry twice more before his third wife at last bore him a son.

32. William of St.-Denis, *Vita Sugerii,* in RHF 12:111.

33. At this period, synods were still the usual forums for resolving disputes involving ecclesiastical law (Brundage, *Medieval Canon Law,* pp. 41–42, 120–21; Cheney, *English Synodalia,* pp. 1–33; Gescher, "Synodales," 358–446; Hinschius, *Das Kirchenrecht* 5.1:278–81). Church courts presided over by trained lawyers only begin to appear at the end of the twelfth century, as a corps of professional canon lawyers was taking shape (Brundage, "The Rise of Professional Canonists," 26–63).

34. Gratian C. 11 q. 1 c. 15, 16.

35. Thus Markale, *La vie, la légende, l'influence d'Aliénor.* I have been unable to verify Markale's source for this report.

36. Gratian C. 35 q. 6 c. 2–4.

37. *Historia gloriosi regis Ludovici VII* in RHF 12:127; Torigny, *Chronica* 4:174 (s.a. 1152); Gervase of Canterbury, *Chronica,* in his *Opera Historica* 1:149 (s.a. 1152); William of Newburgh, *Historia* 1:92; William of Tyre, *Chronicon,* 2:770; Matthew Paris, *Chronica Majora* 2:186 (s.a. 1150).

38. *Historia gloriosi regis Ludovici VII* in RHF, 12:127; Gervase of Canterbury, *Chronica* 1:149 (s.a. 1152).

39. Gilissen, *La coutume,* pp. 80–85.

40. Donahue, "What Causes Fundamental Legal Ideas?" 66–67, 70–72, and Donahue, "English and French Marriage Cases," pp. 339–66.

41. Gervase of Canterbury, *Gesta regum,* in his *Opera Historica* 2:75; *Chronicon Dolensis coenobii,* in RHF 12:456 (s.a. 1152); *Chronicon Turonensi,* in RHF 12:474 (s.a. 1152).

42. Fawtier, *The Capetian Kings of France,* p. 24.

CHAPTER 10

ELEANOR'S DIVORCE FROM LOUIS VII: THE USES OF CONSANGUINITY

Constance Brittain Bouchard

> *The divorce of Eleanor and Louis VII was the culmination of one hundred and fifty years during which the Capetians had tried to balance the personal and political choice of marriage partners with the church's definition of incest.*

One of the most famous divorces in history took place in 1152, when King Louis VII ended his marriage to Eleanor, duchess of Aquitaine, his wife for the previous fifteen years. The official reason for the divorce was consanguinity: they were connected by blood within fewer than the permitted "seven degrees," being related within four degrees on his side and five on hers. That is, he could count four generations back to their common ancestor, while she counted five. In modern terms, they were third cousins once removed.[1] The blood relationship between them was more an excuse for a divorce than the real reason, however, as the relationship had been well known for years and had even been excused by the pope.[2] In this chapter, I shall discuss this paradigmatic divorce, concentrating especially on the union between Louis and Eleanor as a locus of blood-ties binding together much of the upper nobility of the medieval west. A study of their blood relationship is revelatory of the ways that consanguinity was understood and used in the twelfth century.

Such a famous divorce has, not surprisingly, long been interpreted as much more than the rather sorry end of a union between two individuals. It has instead, as indeed it was during the twelfth century, been taken as emblematic of the changing rules and experiences of marriage during the period. Thus at the end of the twentieth century, a period of increased awareness of feminist issues, the story was often retold as an example of female independence. Several scholars have recently suggested that the divorce was Eleanor's idea, that she, a spirited southern woman who never became used to the dourness of northern France, used consanguinity as a convenient excuse to leave a loveless and unsatisfying marriage.[3]

While the consideration of women as active agents rather than merely powerless victims is of course to be encouraged, it is difficult in this case to accept Eleanor as one who fashioned her marital situation to meet her own needs. She may well have chosen Henry II as her second husband out of all the would-be dukes of Aquitaine presenting themselves in 1152, but she had been powerless to leave Louis until he decided that the lack of a male heir made a divorce imperative. Women who produced heirs when they were supposed to, as Eleanor did when married to Henry II—a marriage that must have become even less satisfying than her marriage to Louis, given Henry's decision to keep her locked up for years—were not given the option of leaving.

Another interpretation of this divorce has been that it is indicative of how thoroughly the church "controlled" aristocratic marriages, forcing even the most powerful nobles to bow to the church's model of marriage as forbidden between relatives.[4] The imposition of a broad definition of consanguinity on Europe's nobility has even been taken as a rather cynical effort to keep noble families from consolidating their power through cousin marriages—indeed, as an effort to force them to dissipate their wealth through exogamous unions so that they could not mount an effective challenge to ecclesiastical authority.[5]

But this view does not accord with the evidence. Even aside from the facts that "the" church did not exist as a monolithic entity, and that most bishops and powerful abbots, the sons and brothers of important noblemen, were in consequence more disposed to their families' interests than otherwise, seven forbidden degrees would have serious overkill if the incest laws' purpose had merely been to disperse family patrimonies. To keep property in the family, the closest possible kin-marriages would have been necessary, even brother-sister unions, a level of incest forbidden in all societies. Medieval nobles attempted nothing like so close a degree of relationship in arranging their marriages.

The situation was much more complicated than can be explained by a simplistic view of the church forcing a broad definition of incest on unwilling secular nobles. Blood ties were one of many factors members of the nobility had to consider when creating their unions, but they were also one of the tools these nobles could use to get out of unproductive marriages in an age when, at least officially, divorce was not possible at all. In addition, it is striking that, even though it was widely recognized almost from the outset of their marriage that Eleanor and Louis were related, the first reaction of the hierarchical church was *not* to make them divorce but rather to keep them together.

Here it must be understood that this divorce, a case of a prominent couple breaking up on the grounds of consanguinity with the divorce the husband's idea, not the bishops, was not typical of the entire Middle Ages, only of the twelfth century. After the "seven forbidden" degrees had been established as the norm in the early Middle Ages, in the later ninth and tenth centuries the greatest noble families, including Eleanor's and Louis's ancestors, had tried to avoid such marriages in the first place.[6] In the eleventh century, in contrast, they began to marry cousins, not first cousins or even generally second cousins, but often third cousins—the same degree of relationship as that between Louis and Eleanor. Bishops routinely preached against these cousin marriages, and several such unions, including some involving the Capetians, were dissolved against the wishes of the principals, as discussed below. Eleanor and Louis were thus far from the first couple in that lineage to be criticized for a cousin marriage. In yet another change in the twelfth century, the church hierarchy stopped trying to break up such consanguineous unions as their first response and instead stressed the indissolubility of marriage, while the spouses themselves made much more of the degree of their relationship—that is, if they wished for other reasons to end their marriages.

The outlines of the 1152 divorce are fairly clear.[7] Louis and Eleanor had been married for fifteen years but had had only one child, a daughter, when the queen accompanied her husband on the Second Crusade. Her behavior on the expedition was considered scandalous, and when they stopped in Rome on the way home the pope felt it necessary to try to reconcile the couple. Discussion of their blood relationship was already widespread, however, and when their second child proved to be another daughter, Louis determined to go ahead with a divorce. A council of bishops assembled at Beaugency officially separated him and Eleanor on the grounds of consanguinity. Almost immediately thereafter, she married Henry of Anjou, soon to become king of England as Henry II, to whom she was related just as closely as she was to Louis; Louis shortly afterwards married Constance of Castile, to whom he was related even more closely than he was to Eleanor.

To understand the ramifications of this divorce, it is first necessary to discuss exactly how Eleanor and Louis were related (see Fig. 10.1). The evidence in the primary sources is quite clear, but there has been a surprising amount of confusion in the scholarly literature about their relationship.

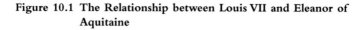

Figure 10.1 The Relationship between Louis VII and Eleanor of Aquitaine

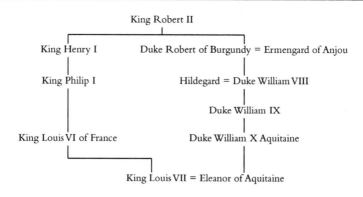

Most commonly it is assumed that Hugh Capet's wife, Adelaide, was from Aquitaine,[8] and that this connection made consanguineous the marriage between Eleanor and Louis. The chief difficulty with this view is that there is nothing in the sources to support it.[9] The reasoning, going back to Ferdinand Lot,[10] is circular: we know that Eleanor and Louis were blood relatives, we do not know the origins of Hugh Capet's wife, and therefore she must provide the link to Aquitaine. As shown below, however, there was a well-documented marriage two generations later between the Capetian lineage and the family of the dukes of Aquitaine, a marriage that, had Hugh Capet's wife come from Aquitaine, should not have been possible even under the most lenient interpretation of consanguinity at the time. There is thus no reason to postulate a connection between Louis VII and Eleanor via Hugh Capet's wife. Such a marriage by Hugh Capet would not, moreover, have produced the blood relationship "within four or five degrees" of which John of Salisbury said the bishop of Laon accused Eleanor and Louis.[11] Had Hugh married a woman from Aquitaine, the common ancestor for Eleanor and Louis would have been Hugh's putative father-in-law, and thus Louis would have been related to his wife within six degrees, not four. Thus it is necessary to look elsewhere for the basis of their connection.

The actual relationship between Eleanor and Louis can be established via the second alliance of Duke Robert of Burgundy (1031–1075), the first Capetian duke of Burgundy.[12] Sometime around 1050, Robert repudiated his wife, Helias of Semur, to enter into a union with Ermengard, daughter of the count of Anjou.[13] With Ermengard, Robert had a daughter, Hildegarde, who married Duke William VIII of Aquitaine.[14] Thus, Hildegarde was the grandmother of Duke William X of Aquitaine, and Eleanor's great-grandmother. Both Eleanor and Louis were therefore descendants of King Robert II (Duke Robert's father). In Louis VII's case, there were four generations from him back to this common ancestor (through Louis VI, Philip I, and Henry I to Robert II), whereas in Eleanor's case there were five generations (William X, William IX, Hildegarde, and Duke Robert to Robert II).

As already suggested, the marriage—and subsequent divorce—of Eleanor and Louis was far from the first time that issues of consanguinity had been raised that affected members of their families. Originally, in the tenth century, the great nobles themselves had avoided consanguineous marriages. Hugh Capet at the end of that century wrote to the Byzantine emperor to ask (unsuccessfully) for a bride for his son Robert II, complaining that "There is no one equal to him whom we can give him in marriage, because of our kinship with neighboring kings."[15] Robert II's son, Henry I, went even further afield and married a Russian princess, allying the Capetians with virtually the last princely family available to whom they were not already related, and this at the first moment in which that family's conversion to Christianity made such a marriage thinkable.[16] Such was the appeal of Russian alliances to western princes seeking wives of the upper nobility to whom they were not already related, that in the years following Henry I's marriage, a number of western princes took Russian wives, including the emperor Henry IV, whose second wife was a Russian princess.[17] But as indicated by the need of these kings to look for wives so far away, by the beginning of the eleventh century the most powerful nobles were often left with no choice: the only women of sufficiently exalted background to make appropriate spouses were related to them within the forbidden degrees. Thus in the eleventh century, consanguineous unions among the most powerful noble lineages began to appear. The initial reaction of the church hierarchy was to end such unions as quickly as possible.

Robert II himself became embroiled in controversy over a consanguineous marriage after his father failed to obtain the desired Byzantine bride for him. Hugh Capet married Robert instead to Rozalla-Susanna, the widowed daughter of the last king of Italy.[18] She was of noble birth and not related to him, but there was a significant drawback to this union: she was much older than Robert, perhaps twice his age. According to the chronicler Richer, Robert soon divorced her because she was too old, but was left without any suitably noble women to marry who were not also his cousins. Immediately upon Hugh Capet's death in 996 (and disregarding his wishes), Robert married his cousin Bertha.[19] A daughter of the king of Burgundy, she was far closer to Robert's age than Rozalla-Susanna.

Figure 10.2 The Relationship between Robert II and Bertha

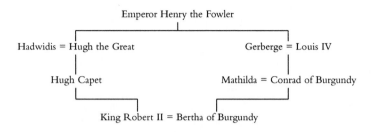

But Robert and Bertha were related within three degrees, much too closely for anyone to overlook their relationship (see Fig. 10.2).[20] Over the next few years, popes Gregory V and Sylvester II and ecclesiastical councils pronounced anathema against Robert for this "incestuous" union. Even before he became pope, indeed, Sylvester II had tried unsuccessfully to persuade Bertha out of a marriage to Robert.[21] Robert initially refused to leave Bertha, apparently returning to her even after they had been divorced and he had remarried,[22] which certainly suggests that dissolving their union for consanguinity had not been *his* idea. Repeated preachings against him by bishops and threats of anathema had their effect, however, and he eventually left her for good. Robert finally married Constance of Arles, the mother of his children (including Duke Robert of Burgundy).[23]

Thus, the first blatantly consanguineous union involving Louis VII's ancestors ended disastrously. But the difficulties that had made Hugh Capet seek a Byzantine bride for his son, and then an aging Italian princess, continued. One of the striking aspects of the union a generation later between Duke Robert of Burgundy and Ermengard of Anjou, the marriage that eventually led to the dissolution of Louis VII's marriage to Eleanor of Aquitaine, was that it was itself a consanguineous alliance (see Fig. 10.3). John of Fécamp complained to the pope that Duke Robert had left his "legitimate" wife for a "consanguineous" union with Ermengard.[24] They were related through the counts of Anjou: Duke Robert's mother, Queen Constance of Arles, was a niece of Count Geoffrey Greymantle of Anjou, and Ermengard was a daughter of Geoffrey Greymantle's son, Count Fulk Nerra. Robert and Ermengard therefore were related within three degrees (i.e., they were second cousins).[25]

But the union between Duke Robert and Ermengard of Anjou, the union that produced the eventual link between the Capetians and the dukes of Aquitaine, did not end in divorce as did Eleanor's and Louis's mar-

Figure 10.3 The Relationship between Robert of Burgundy and Ermengard of Anjou

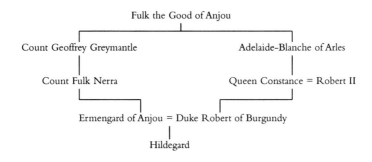

riage a century later—or, for that matter, as had the marriage between King Robert II and Bertha of Burgundy fifty years earlier. Instead, Robert and Ermengard seem to have stayed together for the rest of their lives, for when Duke Robert died in 1075, he was commemorated along with Ermengard at the newly-founded monastery of Molesme.[26] The details are very obscure, but their commemoration together at the monastery suggests that, presumably after Robert's repudiated first wife died, he had simply married Ermengard. A well-placed woman like Ermengard, of a more powerful family than Robert's first wife had been, was a tempting enough prize for Robert to risk ecclesiastical censure, especially at a time when the French bishops were more concerned with proving to a suddenly activist papacy that they had not used simony to obtain their offices, and when the popes were too preoccupied by a growing struggle with the emperors to spare much concern for a duke's adultery with his cousin. Thus, the marriage between Robert and Ermengard, a marriage everyone apparently knew was consanguineous, indicates that a noble couple of the eleventh century just might be able to defy the incest regulations.

Louis and Eleanor, of course, did not "get away" with marrying their cousins, at least not in the long run, but there were several other eleventh-century marriages involving the Capetians in which cousins married each other. It should again be noted that this was a new phenomenon in the eleventh century. Here it is also significant that Robert II, at the beginning of the eleventh century, was the last Capetian who had to give up an alliance with a cousin against his will. His difficulties with staying in such a marriage against ecclesiastical opposition were doubtless an influential example when his son, Henry I, decided to marry a Russian princess. But the Capetians after Robert II, including Duke Robert of Burgundy, were more successful in ignoring the censure put on those who committed what the church considered incest.

Here it is also worth noting that despite ecclesiastical opposition, Philip I, grandson of King Robert II and king of France at the end of the eleventh century, was successful as his grandfather had not been in managing to stay with the woman he loved. Like Duke Robert a generation earlier, Philip left his wife for a woman connected to the counts of Anjou—in his case, Bertrada de Montfort, the current countess. She was not herself Philip's cousin; her first husband, Count Fulk Réchin, was. Accused of both adultery and incest, Philip had to face efforts by bishops and even the pope to make him leave her; that he was under sentence of excommunication from Pope Urban II at the time the First Crusade was organized may have given him a convenient excuse not to go. On several occasions Philip promised to leave Bertrada, but never did so. The popes, who desperately needed the king of France's support during their struggles with the Empire, eventually turned a blind eye, and Philip remained with Bertrada for the rest of his life.[27]

When young Louis VII married the duchess of Aquitaine in 1137, there was thus a well-established century-long tradition of Capetians entering into incestuous unions without having those marriages dissolved. In 1137, no one would have raised consanguinity as an impediment to the royal heir's marriage to such a wealthy and well-placed young woman as Eleanor. Therefore their divorce fifteen years later cannot have been due merely to the discovery that they were related. As scholars have long argued, it was Eleanor's failure to produce a male heir that most concerned Louis VII; consanguinity provided an excuse for a rupture that Louis wanted anyway.

The extent to which consanguinity could be employed as a convenient excuse for divorce was noted at the time by Bernard of Clairvaux, who complained that on the grounds of consanguinity, Louis VII was forcing the breakup of marriages that he found politically troublesome. To Bernard, this went against Christ's teaching that no one "put asunder" what God had "joined together" (Matt. 19:6). Bernard himself, however, was conflicted as to whether it was appropriate for a couple to remain in a consanguineous union. In the same letter in which he warned Louis against too-ready dissolution of consanguineous unions, he also remarked on Louis's "effrontery" in trying to lay down the law on incest to others, when he himself was living with a woman to whom he was related within three degrees.[28] Bernard exaggerated the nearness of Louis' relationship to Eleanor, but he still saw very clearly the extent to which consanguinity could be used as an excuse to break up a union—either by the couple themselves or by outsiders to whom the marriage had become an irritation.

Figure 10.4 The Relationship between Louis VII and Constance of Castile

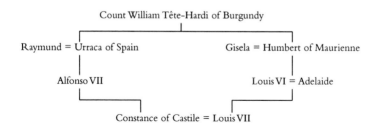

Against the pope's wishes, Louis managed to persuade a council of French bishops to grant him a divorce from Eleanor on the grounds of consanguinity, but his professed concern that he was sinning in staying married to his cousin could not have been as sincere as he led the bishops to believe, for he promptly married a woman even more closely related to him. Constance of Castile, his second wife, was also his second cousin due to the marriage at the end of the eleventh century of the son of the count of Burgundy into the Castilian royal house at the same time his sister married the count of Maurienne, by whom she had Adelaide, Louis VII's mother (see Fig. 10.4).[29] For her part, the newly-divorced Eleanor soon married a man as closely related to her as Louis VII had been (see Fig. 10.5).[30] Their second marriages, therefore, additionally indicate the extent to which consanguinity (at least a relationship within four or five degrees) had, by the twelfth century, become a convenient mechanism for powerful nobles to obtain a divorce they wanted anyway. On the other hand, they were quite prepared to ignore such a degree of relationship if that suited their needs instead. And Louis VII was not the only king who divorced a wife in the 1150s. Frederick Barbarossa, emperor and king of Germany, divorced his first wife to marry Beatrix of Burgundy, a very well-placed heiress who, thanks to the deaths of her father and uncles, had become a much more desirable marriage partner than his current wife. As Louis had done a few years earlier, Frederick claimed consanguinity as an excuse to get out of a marriage that had become politically untenable.[31]

The difficulties of such "divorce on demand" were fully recognized by the organized church by the second half of the twelfth century. In 1190, Pope Clement III declared that if witnesses who knew a couple were related failed to speak up at the time of their marriage, their testimony would not be accepted later.[32] Earlier generations of intermarriage meant that by

**Figure 10.5 The Relationship between Eleanor of Aquitaine and
Henry II**

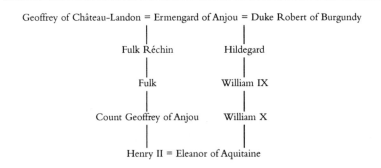

Geoffrey of Château-Landon = Ermengard of Anjou = Duke Robert of Burgundy

Fulk Réchin   Hildegard

Fulk   William IX

Count Geoffrey of Anjou   William X

Henry II = Eleanor of Aquitaine

the end of the twelfth century, there were very few unions among the aristocracy that involved no relatives within seven degrees, and rather than
allow the most visible and most powerful sectors of society to continue dissolving inconvenient marriages so readily, the church hierarchy changed the
definition of consanguinity. At the Fourth Lateran Council of 1215, the
number of forbidden degrees was reduced from seven to four, and a flood
of marriages followed that would earlier have been considered incestuous.[33]

Louis and Eleanor's divorce, then, marked a key transition in both the
aristocracy's and the church's attitudes toward consanguinity. In the tenth
century, marriages within "seven degrees" had been forbidden by developing canon law and were generally avoided (at any rate within five or six
degrees) by the most powerful nobles. In the eleventh century, however,
the powerful began to marry third and fourth cousins, and although the
church's initial reaction was highly negative, eventually those who wanted
to remain in such unions were able to do so. In the twelfth century, in contrast, it was the greatest nobles who attempted to exploit the canon law on
consanguinity in order to leave unprofitable marriages, whereas it was the
spokesmen of the church who tried to make them stay together. By the
beginning of the thirteenth century, after generations of couples had
twisted the ecclesiastical law on incest to suit their own purposes, a practice of which Louis and Eleanor were only the clearest example, the
church hierarchy chose indissolubility over consanguinity as a principal
concern. Louis had manipulated the church's own laws in 1152 to gain a
divorce over the pope's objections, but after Lateran IV only the closest
marriages, those between first and second cousins, were routinely subjected to ecclesiastical penalty—and the nobles themselves had almost
never attempted such unions.

Notes

1. For medieval methods of calculating degrees of consanguinity see Bouchard, "Consanguinity," 269–71.
2. John of Salisbury, *Historia Pontificalis,* chap. 29 at p. 61. See also Duby, *The Knight, the Lady, and the Priest,* pp. 192–95.
3. Owen, *Eleanor of Aquitaine,* p. 25; Duby, *Women of the Twelfth Century* 3, 1:8.
4. Duby, *Medieval Marriage,* pp. 62–63. Duby's analysis here is nuanced by the extent to which he sees church leaders as committed to preserving the indissolubility of marriages, even if they were consanguineous.
5. The view of Goody, *The Development of the Family and Marriage,* pp. 39–47, 123–25. See also Brundage, *Law, Sex and Christian Society,* pp. 606–607.
6. Bouchard, "Consanguinity," 271–73. Le Jan, *Famille et pouvoir,* p. 322, has argued, in contrast, that in the tenth century many great noble families contracted consanguineous marriages. Almost all the examples she cites, however, are from the ninth century, before families began worrying about consanguinity, or else are of family trees in which gaps in the evidence have had to be filled by conjecture. Jackman, *The Konradiner,* p. 139 n230, argues that the great noble families who appear to have avoided marriages with those related less closely than six degrees might in fact have been more closely related to their spouses if all cognate lines were considered. The difficulty with this argument is that neither they nor modern scholars were aware of any such closer ties; although some unrecognized blood relationships surely existed, if unrecognized these cannot have influenced the choice of spouse.
7. The events and principal sources are summarized in Duby, *Medieval Marriage,* pp. 54–62.
8. See, for example, Lewis, *Royal Succession,* p. 12 and n28. This position has been argued most recently by Settipani, *La préhistoire des Capétiens,* pp. 415–19.
9. The sole direct evidence generally cited is a charter, known only from copies of a *vidimus* from the late fourteenth century, in which a woman from Aquitaine, named Adela, is listed with a husband named "Eblo." The editor of this charter "corrected" "Eblo" to "Hugo," assuming her husband must have been Hugh Capet: see *Recueil des actes de Lothaire,* ed. Halphen and Lot, pp. 108–10, no. 48. Without better evidence, however, it is difficult to accept this identification. See also Bouchard, "Patterns of Women's Names," 17 n28.
10. Lot, *Derniers Carolingiens,* pp. 358–61.
11. John of Salisbury, *Historia Pontificalis,* ch. 23, p. 53.
12. For Duke Robert, see also Bouchard, *Sword, Miter and Cloister,* pp. 256–58.
13. "Genealogiae comitum Andegavensium," p. 247. The approximate date is known from a letter of John of Fécamp to Pope Leo IX, complaining that Duke Robert had left his legitimate wife for a union with another woman (Migne, PL 143:799–800). See also Duby, *The Knight, the Lady and the Priest,* p. 90.

14. *La chronique de Saint-Maixent,* ed. Verdon, p. 138; "Genealogiae comitum Andegavensium," p. 247. Jean Richard suggests that the two youngest of Duke Robert's sons, neither of whom inherited any authority in Burgundy, might also have been born to his union with Ermengard (*Les ducs de Bourgogne,* p. 14).

15. Gerbert, *Die Briefsammlung Gerbertss,* Letter 111, pp. 139–40.

16. Thietmar of Merseburg, *Chronicon* 4.38, MGH SS 3:785; Bouchard, "Consanguinity," p. 277. See also Facinger, "Medieval Queenship," 1–48; and Dhondt, "Sept femmes," 35–70.

17. Vernadsky, *Kievan Russia,* pp. 74–83, 340–43.

18. The best overview of Robert II's three marriages and two divorces remains that by Pfister, *Robert le Pieux,* pp. 41–69.

19. Richer, *Historia,* ed. Latouche, 4.87 and 4.108 at 2:286, 330.

20. In modern terms, Robert and Bertha were second cousins. Their grandmothers, Hadwidis and Gerberge, were sisters, daughters of Henry the Fowler, king of the Germans. Hadwidis married Hugh the Great, King Robert's grandfather ("Tabula Ottonorum," MGH SS 3:215). Her sister Gerberge married Louis IV and was the mother of Mathilda, queen of Burgundy (Siegfried of Gorze, letter to Poppo of Stablo, in *Geschichte der deutschen Kaiserzeit,* 2:714–18; Alberic de Trois-Fontaines, *Chronica,* MGH SS 23:782 s.a. 1024). Mathilda's daughter Bertha married first the count of Blois and then King Robert II (Hugh of Fleury, "Modernum regum Francorum acta," MGH SS 9:387).

21. Richer, *Historia,* ed. Latouche, 4.108 at 2:330; Council of Rome 998, in *Sacrorum Consiliorum,* ed. Mansi, 19:223–30; Helgaud of Fleury, *Epitoma,* chap. 17 at p. 92.

22. Adalbero of Laon, "Rythmus satyricus," 24, p. 795. See also Lot, "La chanson de Landri," 1–17.

23. Glaber, *Five Books of Histories,* 3.7 at p. 106 and n"b" (see also p. xci); Helgaud of Fleury. *Epitoma,* chap. 10 at p. 74; "Chronica de gestis consulum Andegavorum," p. 43; "Genealogiae comitum Andegavensium," p. 248.

24. Migne, PL 143:799–800.

25. See the family trees in Bachrach, *Fulk Nerra,* pp. 262, 265. Bachrach discusses only Ermengard's two earlier marriages, not her union with the duke of Burgundy.

26. Petit, *Histoire des ducs de Bourgogne,* 5:386.

27. For Philip's attempts to stay with Bertrada, see Duby, *The Knight, the Lady, and the Priest,* pp. 3–18, and Fliche, *Philippe I.*

28. Bernard of Clairvaux, *Sancti Bernardi Opera* 8, Letter 224, p. 93.

29. For Raymond of Burgundy's marriage to Urraca of Castile, and his sister Gisela's marriage to Humbert of Maurienne, see Bouchard, *Sword, Miter and Cloister,* pp. 273–75. Raymond and Urraca were the parents of Constance of Castile's father, Alphonso VII of Castile (Giselbert of Mons, *Chronicon Hanoniense,* MGH SS 21:515).

30. They shared a great-great-grandmother, Ermengard of Anjou, who married first Geoffrey of Château-Landon, by whom she was ancestor of the later counts of Anjou, and then Duke Robert of Burgundy, as noted above. See also Bachrach, *Fulk Nerra,* pp. 201–02.

31. For Beatrix of Burgundy, see Bouchard, *Sword, Miter, and Cloister,* p. 277.

32. X 4.18.2, ed. Friedberg, *Corpus iuris canonici* 2: col. 318.

33. Lateran IV, canon 50, ed. Hefele, *Histoire des conciles* 5.2:1372–73; Baldwin, *Masters, Princes, and Merchants,* 1:332–37; Duby, *Knight, Lady, and Priest,* p. 209. See also Bouchard, *"Strong of Body, Brave and Noble,"* pp. 94–97.

CHAPTER 11

THE RECIPROCAL LOYALTY
OF ELEANOR OF AQUITAINE
AND WILLIAM MARSHAL

Evelyn Mullally

*The Anglo-Norman verse biography of William Marshal (ca. 1226) affords brief but
favorable glimpses of Eleanor of Aquitaine unobtainable from any other source. In
1168, she lavishly rewards his part in rescuing her from a Poitevin ambush; after her
son Richard I's accession, William supports her in the government of England during
Richard's absence.*

One source that gives an unequivocally positive image of Eleanor of
Aquitaine is the Anglo-Norman verse biography of William Marshal,
composed ca. 1226 and edited a century ago as the *Histoire de Guillaume le
Maréchal.*[1] Tantalizingly brief as are the *Histoire*'s episodes concerning
Eleanor, they are our only source for certain events in her life that, though
mentioned in every biography of her, have never been studied in their full
context. William Marshal had an extraordinary life, from his relatively obscure birth ca. 1147 as the younger son of a minor knight to his final eminence as regent of England from 1216 to his death in 1219. One of the most
fascinating and enjoyable narratives of Eleanor's day, the *Histoire* recounts an
amazing number of adventures and reversals of fortune, culminating in
William's detailed and uplifting death scene. As well as being a primary
source for the history of the Plantagenets, the text is a mine of information
on aspects of social history, such as tournaments and family relationships,

though unfortunately for our purposes, its insights are entirely from a masculine point of view (as is, of course, the case with virtually all narrative sources of the time).

Dominica Legge long ago noted with regret that the *Histoire* was better known to historians than to students of literature. It is to be hoped that the forthcoming edition will increase its readership,[2] though historical narratives in verse even now run the risk of falling unluckily between two stools. Political historians tend to treat anything written in rhyme as "poetry" and, as such, not quite worthy of serious consideration as documents. Literary historians tend to treat such writings as creative works of art and search them for subtle artistic purpose. It is important to remember that at this period, anything written for secular consumption will be written in the vernacular and in the simple rhyming couplet, the medium most suited to oral delivery. Though very well written, William's biography is down-to-earth and factual, and largely devoid of literary allusion. In a later age, it would certainly have been written in prose.

If the format is banal, however, the content and purpose of the text are original, indeed unique. Unlike chroniclers who recorded the events of a reign or a region, the *Histoire*'s author concentrates on one individual's life, the earliest known biography of a man who was neither king nor saint. William was certainly a remarkable individual, and the author has no hesitation in telling us at the outset of his narrative that he will relate the life of the best knight of the age (ll. 15–17). William's faithful and self-effacing squire, John of Earley, was the source of most of the work's personal details and perhaps its actual author.[3] The epilogue indicates that the work was composed to preserve William's memory for his children. The prologue alludes to a larger audience, though as the *Histoire* survives in only a single manuscript it seems not to have reached a wide public. It is nonetheless a most valuable witness to the mentality of Eleanor's contemporaries.

William's life is the life of a man in a man's world. Remarkable woman though she was, Eleanor is only briefly mentioned in a text of over 19,000 lines. The *Histoire*'s great themes are William's courage, worthiness, and above all loyalty in the service of successive lords. The key rhyme is *Mareschals/leals;* the author misses no chance to emphasize his hero's integrity, remarkable in an age when conflicts of feudal loyalty were common and when so many lords he knew acted with violence and greed.

William's father was an example of the ruthless, ambitious man of the period. John Marshal let nothing stand in his way: when he could not defeat Earl Patrick of Salisbury, he decided to join him. To that end he unceremoniously discarded a wife with whom he had been perfectly happy and married Patrick's sister. A son of this second marriage, William counts for nothing in his father's struggle for power. Desperate to keep his castle of Newbury, John gives his little son as a hostage to King Stephen to guarantee a pledge he does not intend to keep. Only Stephen's unusual tenderheartedness spares the boy's life. When William reaches his early teens, his father sends him to a Norman kinsman who supports him, eventually knights him, and equips him, albeit meagerly. William returns to England after participating in continental tournaments, but there is no further mention of his father. William instead seeks out his maternal uncle Patrick, for whom, as events were to show, he has warm filial feelings.

Through Patrick of Salisbury, William's first, critical encounter with Eleanor takes place in the spring of 1168, when he would have been about twenty-one. The barons in Eleanor's territory of Poitou rebel against King Henry II. The author severely criticizes the Poitevins who, he claims, were ever disloyal to their lords even when he was writing, nearly fifty years after these events (ll. 1577–80). On this occasion King Henry hears that the Poitevins have laid waste all the region except his castles. He rides to the rescue, accompanied by Eleanor and certain barons, including Earl Patrick, who brings with him his nephew:

> Will[ame], li pruz Mareschals,
> Li pruz, li senés, li leals,
> Qe si[s] uncles pout tant amer
> Ovec lui repassa la mer. (ll. 1597–1600)

[William, the brave Marshal, the brave, the wise, the loyal man, whom his uncle loved so much, crossed back over the sea with him.]

In Poitou, Henry asks Patrick to escort the queen, an office he gladly accepts. Unfortunately, he lacks a safe-conduct and is not riding fully armed. The Poitevins spy their passage and ambush them. Realizing the danger, Patrick gets Eleanor safely inside a castle but refuses to flee. Unarmed on his palfrey, he fights back, shouting for his war-horse, which arrives while his men are still in the rear, struggling into their armor. As he mounts his *destrier*, Patrick is fatally speared in the back. The unnamed killer is denounced as a traitor (l. 1648). Whoever he is, the author has already attributed responsibility for Patrick's death to Geoffrey de Lusignan, the most prominent of the rebellious Poitevins, for he has named him as leader of the ambush:

> Gefreis de Lesingnan sanz dote
> Esteit sires de cele rote,
> Qui unques a nul seignorage
> Ne volt porter fei ne homage,

N'unkes ne vot estre soz jou,
Toz jors i out del peil del lou. (ll. 1623–28)

[Geoffrey of Lusignan without doubt was the leader of this band, Geoffrey
who would never give faith or homage to any lordship and who never
agreed to be under any yoke: there was always a hair of the wolf there.]

Geoffrey is implicitly responsible for Patrick's death, though the biographer records his denial:

" . . .bien sai que li Mareschals
Ne fu unques malveis ne fals.
Si ne m'ainme il pas, por veir,
Quer tel chose cuide saveir
Certes, que je unques ne fis,
Quer unches sun uncle n'ocis." (ll. 6453–58)

[I know well that the Marshal was never evil or false. And I know indeed
that he has no love for me because he thinks he knows something I never
did, for I never killed his uncle.]

Geoffrey then recommends Henry to take William's advice (ll. 6517- 24).
Other chroniclers attribute the murder to Geoffrey's brother Guy,[4] but it
is unlikely that William thought Guy was guilty. He later spent two years
on crusade and in 1187 left the Holy Land on excellent terms with Guy,
by then king of Jerusalem (ll. 7289–95).[5]

When William sees the blow that has killed his uncle, he nearly goes
mad with grief because he cannot reach the killer to avenge Patrick's
death. Unarmed save for his hauberk, William lays about him like a fam-
ished lion (ll.1660–67). His horse is killed under him, but he fights off the
Poitevins on foot with his back to a hedge until one of them stabs him
from behind the hedge. Bleeding profusely, he is taken prisoner, his captors
little inclined to help him. If they knew his identity, they would kill him;
they believe the more he suffers, the more readily he will pay a ransom.
Returning to base, they lodge one night in a house where a lady smuggles
bandages to him. Nevertheless, his sufferings as a wounded prisoner are
acute. Geoffrey's wars with the king would be too long to relate, says the
author (ll. 1860–63). Instead he records Eleanor's generosity to William:

Mais la reïne ostaja,
Quant ele pout, le Mareschal
Qui trop par out ennui & mal
En la felenesse prison;

Ce fu laidesce & mesprison.
Quant de prison fut delivrez
& a la reïne livrez
Li Mareschals, molt lu[i] fu bel,
C'unkes nus, des le tens Abel,
Tant vos di sanz plus & sanz mains,
N'eschapa de si cruels mains.
A vis lu[i] fu qu'ore ert en l'or,
Quer la reïne Alïenor
Li fist atorner son afaire
Come a tel bachiler dut feire.
Chivals & armes & den[i]ers
& beles robes voluntiers
Li fist doner, cui qu'il en peise,
Quer molt fu vaillante & cortoise. (ll. 1864–82)

[But the queen gave hostages when she could for the Marshal, who had suffered torment and pain in the cruel prison. [His imprisonment] was insulting and wrongful. When the Marshal was freed from prison and handed over to the queen, he was very happy, for no one, since the time of Abel (let me tell you without more ado) escaped from such cruel hands. It seemed to him then that he was very well off, for Queen Eleanor equipped him with what was fitting for such a man. No matter who might object, she gave him horses and arms and money and plenty of fine robes, for she was very worthy and courteous.]

William's heroism is motivated by his feelings for his uncle rather than by loyalty to Eleanor, but she takes responsibility for his sufferings in her defense. The lavishness of her gift is an expression of personal power, independent of her husband. She plays a more active part here than former queens, who had been confined to the roles of mother, charitable or cultural patroness, and intercessor.[6] No quality is more insistently recommended to the medieval prince than liberality. It is not enough to say that in any work produced for a patron, praise of liberality will have a self-interested motive. Lavish, even apparently reckless generosity from ruler to subject is a demonstration of power. The text that most strongly seized the imagination of the twelfth century was Geoffrey of Monmouth's *Historia Regum Britanniæ,* and the episode selected for endless elaboration in fiction was the plenary court at Caerleon-on-Usk where King Arthur confirms his supremacy by justifying his reputation as a generous giver.[7] Rash boons and neglected heroes complicate romance plots, but the assumption remains that a "worthy and courteous" ruler must reward lavishly. In anthropological terms, Eleanor's generous gifts to William might be seen as having an element of the potlatch.

On a personal level, however, it is not clear from the text that they actually met. Eleanor arranged for William to be freed and for compensation to be given him ("fist atorner . . . fist doner"), but no personal interview is mentioned, though it is most likely that one took place. It is also highly probable (though again, there is no evidence from the text) that her recognition of William's courage and loyalty was at least indirectly responsible for the big break in his career. After coming to Eleanor's notice, he distinguishes himself as a knight so that kings, queens, dukes, and counts talk of him (ll. 1901–04). In 1170, when Henry decides with Eleanor's consent to crown their eldest son Henry, then aged fifteen, he sets William, about twenty-three, to guard and teach the young king (ll. 1943–45). In due course William knights the youth (ll. 2097- 2101), and despite dramatic reversals of fortune in the next years, his rise to greatness starts there.

Over twenty years pass before another meeting with Eleanor is recorded, and the last sixteen of those years she passes as her husband's prisoner. In 1189, Henry rewards William's faithful service by promising him a rich bride, the damsel of Strigoil—Isabel, daughter of Richard de Clare (better known as Strongbow) and granddaughter of Diarmaid Mac Murchada, king of Leinster. Heir to lands in England, Wales, and Ireland, she is indeed a great prize. But Henry dies at Chinon before he can fulfil his promise, and William has to contend with the new king, Richard. William has reason to be apprehensive of his fortunes under the new regime: not long before, he had killed the rebellious Richard's horse under him. Fortunately, Richard has the sense to value William's proven worth and loyalty. He confirms the grant of the heir of Strigoil and entrusts William with messages to England on his behalf. As soon as Henry is buried, William sets off in haste but is injured in an accident at Dieppe. Nevertheless he continues his journey and carries out Richard's commands. In the text, Richard does not mention Eleanor, so it is conceivably on his own initiative that William goes to Winchester to tell her of Henry's death and free her from confinement. It seems that someone else preceded him with the news; William finds her at liberty and, unsurprisingly, happier than she had been. The biographer recounts William's second meeting with Eleanor with tantalizing brevity:

Li Mar[eschal] en Engleterre
Fist bien ce qu'il i out a querre,
De ce k'aparteneit al conte,
Si comme l'estorie le conte;
E la reïne Alïenor
Qui out le nom d'ali e d'or
Trova delivree a Wincestre

Plus a ese k'el ne sout estre.
Quant out fini toz les messages,
Comme cointes e comme sages,
Si porchaça la damisele
D'Estregoil qui fu bone e bele. (ll. 9503–14)

[The Marshal did everything in England that he had sought to do concerning the Count (King Richard), as the source relates; and he found Queen Eleanor, whose name was composed of ali and or, at liberty in Winchester, happier than she was accustomed to be. When he had delivered all the messages in a wise and prudent fashion, he went to find the damsel of Strigoil who was good and beautiful.]

The parenthetic reference to the meaning of Eleanor's name is striking. She is almost the only woman named in the text, the only one whose name is analyzed. The comment on her name is quite out of character for this writer. As women play a minor role in the society he describes and are always subordinate to men, they are usually identified only by their relationship to a father, husband, or brother and referred to simply by a title. If there is no trace of antifeminism in the narrative, neither is there any literary idealization of women, nor any special status accorded to women, even those of high rank. William's wife, with whom he had a happy marriage and ten children, is never referred to by name. Before her marriage, she is the "damisele" or "pucele d'Estregoil"; after it, she is simply "la contesse."[8]

Eleanor's remarkable case is therefore a tribute to her extraordinary personality. William's biographer was not the only writer to single out her name and transmit or invent an etymology for it. According to the chronicler Geoffroi de Vigeois, Eleanor was "another Anor," after her mother Anor—her name was made up of Alia and Anor.[9] In *L'histoire de Guillaume le Maréchal,* the word "ali" causes particular difficulty. Paul Meyer suggested that it might be a form of "aloi," alloy, and that the author may have been implying that her good qualities, the gold, were not without alloy, adding that if so, the author would not have been wrong.[10] This is surely mistaken. There were plenty of hostile comments about Eleanor in her time, but Marshal's biographer presents only a favorable side; "ali" must have a positive meaning. For D.D.R. Owen, it connotes a coin minted from gold, which is in keeping with the context.[11] Another possibility would be that "ali" is a form of "alli," or alliance. As duchess of Aquitaine, Eleanor had provided the Angevins a golden alliance; Henry II had profited from it in the past as Richard was about to now.

At Richard's accession, Eleanor regains power. There are glimpses in the text of her intervention in the strife between her sons. In 1190, along with the Chancellor William of Longchamp, she warns Richard on crusade that

his brother John is allying with the king of France and that he risks losing
his kingdom if he does not return (ll. 9808–20). Richard is captured on his
return in 1192 and unlike John, Eleanor is distraught: " . . . dolente en fu
sa mere, / mes n'en pesa pas a son frere (ll. 9821–22) [His mother was
grieved, but his brother was not sorry]."

Meanwhile, in 1191, Longchamp is deposed and replaced by Archbishop Walter of Rouen. As Chief Justiciar, Walter rules wisely in Richard's
absence with the counsel of the barons, William Marshal, and the queen:

> Molt se garda de fere mal.
> Par le conseil del Mar[eschal]
> E par les barons ensement
> Ouvra [il] bien & sagement,
> E par conseil de la reïne
> Qui la esteit en cel termine. (ll. 9871–82)

[He took great care to do no wrong. He acted well and wisely, by the advice of the Marshal and of the barons, and also by the advice of the queen,
who was there at that time].

The threat to Richard becomes acute early in 1193 when John, who has already captured Nottingham, fortifies Windsor. Walter and the barons besiege
Windsor and send for William, who arrives accompanied by the Welsh
barons who owe him allegiance since his marriage to Strongbow's daughter.
Richard's supporters, including Eleanor, meet him with joyful ceremony:

> Molt li firent joiose encontre,
> Quer en grant joie fu meüe
> Trestote l'ost por sa venue.
> E Alïenor la reïne
> Mere le rei, [qui] enterine
> Li fu, unques ne volt son mal,
> Fist molt grant joie al Mar[eschal]. (ll. 9908–14)

[They welcomed him very joyfully, for the whole army went out in great
joy to meet him; and Queen Eleanor, the king's mother, who was entirely
loyal to him and never wished him harm, welcomed the Marshal warmly].

The young man Eleanor had liberated and rewarded over twenty years earlier is now a powerful figure who can reciprocate her loyalty with welcome counsel and support.

In 1202, when John has succeeded his brother, Eleanor is again in danger in Poitou when she is besieged at Mirebeau (about 15 miles north of

Poitiers). Once more the Poitevins are on the attack, again including Geoffrey de Lusignan but now led by her grandson, Arthur of Brittany. John hastens to rescue her and defend his interests against his nephew (ll. 12059–12116). After this, Eleanor vanishes from the tale. Her death in 1204 is not mentioned, for the author is taken up with William's part in John's turbulent career. Yet, writing over twenty years later, he creates the impression of a great queen who practised the aristocratic virtue of liberality, gave wise and prudent counsel, and valued and reciprocated the loyalty of a man like William Marshal.

Notes

1. *L'histoire de Guillaume le Maréchal*, pp. 255, 268, 304. A new edition by A.J. Holden is in preparation for the Anglo-Norman Text Society, with translation by Stewart Gregory and historical notes by David Crouch.
2. Legge, *Anglo-Norman Literature*, p. 308. The principal historical studies of William's life are: Painter, *William Marshal*; Duby, *Guillaume le Maréchal*, trans. as *William Marshal*; Crouch, *William Marshal*.
3. Evelyn Mullally, "Did John of Earley write the *Histoire de Guillaume le Maréchal?*"
4. See *L'histoire de Guillaume le Maréchal* 3:25–26.
5. Like Eleanor herself, the Lusignans quickly became the stuff of legend. See *Le Roman de Mélusine*, which includes a detailed family tree.
6. On the queen's role as intercessor in the early twelfth century, see Huneycutt, "Intercession." I am grateful to my colleague Judith Green for this reference.
7. Geoffrey of Monmouth, trans. Thorpe, pp. 225–30.
8. Mullally, "The Portrayal of Women." The Anglo-Norman verse chronicle which records the marriage of Isabel's mother names no aristocratic women; the only female named in it is a violently vengeful camp follower called Alice (Mullally, "La colonisation de l'Irlande.")
9. Geoffroi de Vigeois, *Chronicle*, RHF 12:434–35, cited by Kelly, *Eleanor and the Four Kings*, p. 6.
10. *L'histoire de Guillaume le Maréchal* 3:121.
11. Owen, *Eleanor of Aquitaine*, p. 110. In a different context, another scholar notes that at the beginning of her reign as queen of the English, Eleanor had established some financial independence for herself by instituting payments known as the Queen's Gold, but it is unlikely that any reference is being made to this in 1189 (Meade, *Eleanor of Aquitaine*, p. 180). Queen's Gold is discussed in this volume by Huneycutt, chapter 5, and Tanner, chapter 6.

CHAPTER 12

SCANDALIZING DESIRE:
ELEANOR OF AQUITAINE
AND THE CHRONICLERS

Peggy McCracken

In accounts of Eleanor's adulterous passion for a Muslim sultan, post-twelfth-century chronicles reveal anxieties about gender, sexuality, and sovereignty that continually surfaced in medieval definitions of queenship.

Most historical accounts characterize Eleanor of Aquitaine as a strong-willed woman who knew what she wanted, and many stories about her—both medieval and modern—portray her desire as a dangerous threat to the powerful men in her life. She is represented this way in some of the earliest accounts of her life as queen of France, most prominently in chronicles that record her voyage to the East with Louis VII. In 1148, Eleanor accompanied the king to Antioch, and her affection for her uncle, Raymond of Antioch, was regarded with suspicion by some in her entourage; several chroniclers recorded rumors of an adulterous passion between the queen and her uncle. Over the course of the Middle Ages, chroniclers transformed Eleanor's close relationship with her uncle into a scandalous, adulterous passion for a Muslim sultan. While the fictitious elaborations of Eleanor's story do not offer historically reliable information about the queen herself, their representation of her scandalous desire for adultery might say something about the institution of queenship in the medieval West in the twelfth and thirteenth centuries. The ways in which the story of Eleanor's adultery is recounted, revised, and elaborated may speak some of the anxieties about gender, sexuality, and sovereignty that continually surfaced in medieval definitions of queenship. In particular, these narratives articulate the imperative of legitimate childbirth within the royal family, the complex and contested question of the queen's sovereign authority, and above all, an uneasy recognition of the queen's access to influence and power as the king's sexual partner.

Eleanor in Antioch

The story of Eleanor's scandalous desire begins in Antioch. John of Salisbury offers one of the earliest accounts of the queen's suspicious affection for her uncle Raymond. Writing about fifteen years after the events, he reported that:

> . . . the most Christian king of the Franks reached Antioch, after the destruction of his armies in the east, and was nobly entertained there by Prince Raymond, brother of the late William, count of Poitiers. He was as it happened the queen's uncle, and owed the king loyalty, affection and respect for many reasons. But whilst they remained there . . . the attentions paid by the prince to the queen, and his constant, indeed almost continuous conversation with her, aroused the king's suspicions. These were greatly strengthened when the queen wished to remain behind, although the king was preparing to leave, and the prince made every effort to keep her, if the king would give his consent. And when the king made haste to tear her away, she mentioned their kinship, saying it was not lawful for them to remain together as man and wife, since they were related in the fourth and fifth degrees.[1]

This incident was also recorded by William of Tyre, who wrote between 1170 and 1184, some twenty to thirty years after the events. William describes the love affair as a form of revenge Raymond took against the king of France, who had refused to help him enlarge his territory. Whereas John of Salisbury simply states that Eleanor did not wish to return to France and preferred to stay in Antioch with her uncle, William claims that she was a willing participant in adulterous intentions, if not adulterous acts:

> Raymond had conceived the idea that by [Louis's] aid he might be able to enlarge the principality of Antioch . . . When Raymond found that he could not induce the king to join him, his attitude changed. Frustrated in his ambitious designs, he began to hate the king's ways; he openly plotted against him and took means to do him injury. He resolved also to deprive him of his wife, either by force or by secret intrigue. The queen readily assented to this design, for she was a foolish woman. Her conduct before and after this time showed

her to be, as we have said, far from circumspect. Contrary to her royal dignity, she disregarded her marriage vows and was unfaithful to her husband.[2]

In other chroniclers' accounts, the topos of secrecy characterizes the incident as a scandal, something that should not be spoken about. Gervase of Canterbury, writing in 1188, about the same time as William of Tyre, records that after the royal couple returned from Jerusalem there was "discord" between them concerning things that happened on the crusade and that are probably best passed over in silence.[3] Richard of Devizes's ostensibly flattering portrait of Eleanor, written in the early thirteenth century, praises her as "an incomparable woman, beautiful yet virtuous, powerful yet gentle, humble yet keen-witted."[4] A marginal note in the manuscript of the chronicle, however, contains the words: "Many know what I would that none of us knew. This same queen, during the time of her first husband, was at Jerusalem [sic, for Antioch]. Let no one say any more about it. I too know it well. Keep silent." The marginal note both announces the secret and hides the truth. Ruth Harvey has noted that "[t]he annotation is arranged in the form of an inverted triangle and surrounded by a thick wavy line whose flourishes exert an irresistible attraction on the reader's eye."[5] The marginal annotation in Devizes's chronicle gives the truth the status of a scandalous secret.

The twelfth-century chroniclers offer roughly contemporaneous, though not eyewitness accounts of the events at Antioch. All suggest that something scandalous happened; all attempt to explain the visit to Antioch and the subsequent royal divorce with reference to what Eleanor *wanted,* identifying her desire as scandalous. Even in William of Tyre's account, where Raymond initiates the liaison, blame ultimately shifts to Eleanor: "The Queen readily assented . . . for she was a foolish woman." What actually happened at Antioch between Eleanor and her uncle can never be known with certainty. Whether or not there were grounds for doubting her fidelity, it is indisputable that she was suspected of adultery by some in the royal entourage, and Louis also appears to have had misgivings about her behavior: a letter from Suger advises him to hide his anger against the queen until after their return to France.[6] Eleanor was never formally charged with adultery, and the rumored liaison with her uncle did not end the royal marriage. She and Louis were apparently reconciled by the pope when they stopped in Italy on the way back to France, and in 1150 the queen gave birth to a second daughter. But despite this ostensible reconciliation, three years after the events at Antioch, Eleanor and Louis were divorced on the grounds of consanguinity.

Although the chroniclers cited above do not insist upon Eleanor's desire for her uncle as the direct cause of her divorce from Louis, their focus on events in Antioch emphasizes the particular implications of a queen's adultery for her husband and for his government. In the Middle Ages, adultery was a crime and a sin, but when a queen was accused of adultery, the charge's consequences went beyond personal guilt or injury. Suspected sexual transgression not only put into question the legitimacy of any heirs to the throne; it also demonstrated the king's lack of authority in his own household and, by extension, in his kingdom. The relationship between the king's authority and his wife's sexual fidelity is implicitly acknowledged in the chronicles that record the suspicions about Eleanor's relationship to her uncle, particularly in William of Tyre's account, where Raymond's desire to damage the king takes the form of a seduction of the queen, to which Eleanor "readily assented . . . for she was a foolish woman."

Yet moral judgments about the queen's character expressed in chroniclers' accounts of Eleanor's conduct do more than censure the woman who threatens to betray a sovereign husband. Narratives about the queen's "foolishness" with her uncle also speak about the political anxieties provoked by the representation of a queen's sexuality. The scandalous desire represented in chroniclers' accounts may cover a related anxiety—not about the queen's betrayal of her husband but about the power the queen enjoyed as the king's sexual intimate. An exploration of how the queen's desire is shown to be scandalous may reveal some of the anxious tensions that could be provided in French aristocratic society by the prospect of the influence over the king enjoyed by the woman who legitimately shared his bed.

The Queen and the Sultan

The story of Eleanor's adultery was told with more and more vehemence over the course of the Middle Ages. Indeed, in some texts Eleanor's unbridled sexual desire becomes a sort of all-purpose historical explanation for events that occurred during her two royal marriages. In an early-thirteenth-century chronicle, Helinand de Froidmont identifies her desire as the cause of a war between her former and current husbands. "The abandoned wife of Louis king of the French was carried off by Henry, count of Anjou and duke of the Normans, thereafter king of England. That brought about a war between them. It was on account of her lasciviousness that Louis gave up his wife, who behaved not like a queen but more like a [whore]."[7]

It is understandable that with the benefit of hindsight, chroniclers might exaggerate the crimes of the woman who took from France the vast lands Eleanor transferred to England by her marriage to Henry of Anjou. But in a particular—and peculiar—group of chronicles, her transgressions are extended to account indirectly for the failure of the Second Crusade. These texts attribute to Eleanor not the suspect affection for her uncle vaguely described by John of Salisbury and William of Tyre, but a determined desire for adultery with a Saracen prince who, in several versions, is identified as the Muslim leader Saladin.[8] The queen's desire is identified as a sexual transgression that threatens her husband's sovereignty.

The *Récits d'un Ménestrel de Reims* is a thirteenth-century text that seems to have had a great influence on subsequent accounts of Eleanor's stay at Antioch. It recounts Louis VII's marriage to Eleanor of Aquitaine, who was "a very evil woman. And she held Maine, Anjou, Poitou, Limoges and Touraine, and had a good three times as much land as the king had."[9] I quote here a rather long passage from the *Ménestrel de Reims* in order to offer an idea of the kinds of changes made to the story told by John of Salisbury and William of Tyre and to establish a reference point for subsequent textual treatments of the queen's adultery.

In the Ménestrel's account, the king and queen of France travel to Tyre (not Antioch), where they spend the winter. The queen's uncle is absent in this story, and her husband is presented as a weak and ineffectual leader in contrast to Saladin, whose courtesy and bravery are known to the queen:

> When Saladin perceived [the king's] softness and foolishness, he challenged him several times, but the king did not want to undertake a battle. And when Queen Eleanor saw the weakness that the king carried in himself and she heard about the goodness, prowess, wisdom and generosity of Saladin, she loved him greatly in her heart, and she sent one of her messengers to him with her greetings. Saladin understood that if he could win her, she would take him as her lord and renounce her religion. When Saladin understood this from the letter that the messenger had given him, he was very happy, for he knew well that she was the most noble lady in Christendom and the richest. He had a ship readied . . . and sent it to Tyre with the messenger, and they arrived there a little before midnight.
>
> The messenger went . . . into the chamber where the queen waited for him. When she saw him she asked, 'What news?' 'Lady,' he said,' Here is the ship all ready and waiting for you. Now hurry, so that we will not be seen.' . . . She chose two ladies and two trunks full of gold and silver that she intended to send to the boat. When one of the ladies understood her plan, she left the room as quietly as she could and went to the bed of the king, who was sleeping. She woke him and said, 'Sire, things are going badly; my lady wants to go to Ascalon with Saladin and a ship is waiting for her in the port. For God's sake, sire, hurry up.'
>
> When the king heard this he jumped up, dressed himself and armed his men and went to the port. And he found the queen who already had one foot on the ship. He took her by the hand and led her back to his chamber. And the king's men captured the ship and all those inside, for they were so surprised that they could not defend themselves.

The king asked the queen why she wanted to do this. 'In God's name,' said the queen, 'because of your worthlessness; for you are not worth a rotten apple. And I have heard so much good said of Saladin that I love him more than you. Know for a truth that you will never have any pleasure from possessing me.' Then the king left her and had her well guarded, and he was advised to return to France, for her was running out of money and he was gaining nothing there but shame.

The king took to sea with the queen and returned to France. There he took counsel from his barons about what he should do with the queen, and he told them how she had acted. 'By faith,' said the barons, 'the best advice we could give you is that you let her go, for she is a devil and if you keep her any longer we fear that she will kill you. And above all, you have no children with her.' The king followed this advice and he acted foolishly: it would have been better to have walled her up; then he could have kept her great lands all his life and avoided the bad things that happened afterwards, as you will hear recounted below.[10]

Although Eleanor is clearly guilty of adulterous desire in the Ménestrel's account, the king also comes off badly. Not only is Eleanor's betrayal directly related to Louis's "softness and foolishness," but he is blamed for the loss of her lands and should have prudently found a way to retain Eleanor's territory for the French crown. Louis's unwillingness to fight may recall the failure of the Second Crusade, and his weakness is emphasized in the identification of the queen's lover as Saladin, the Muslim leader who took Jerusalem from the Christians in 1187. Anxiety about French sovereignty may also explain this account's insistence on the lack of a royal heir: the Ménestrel eliminates two royal daughters in his *Récit* (one born after the couple's return to France), and the counsellors' claim that Louis has no children with the queen hints at contemporary anxieties about the absence of a son and heir in the royal family.

The Ménestrel's version of events is closely followed in the *Chronique normande* of Pierre Cochon, a notary of the archbishop of Reims. This fifteenth-century text repeats the Ménestrel's emphasis on Eleanor's wealth. The queen has "three times as much land as the king," and Saladin is delighted to have the queen because she is "the richest and most noble woman in all Christendom." Eleanor plans to escape with Saladin, and the king seizes her with one foot already on board the ship. Louis returns to France with the queen and asks his barons for advice. They counsel him "to let her go to the devil in Normandy where she had come from. That was bad advice because it would have been better if he had walled her up. And besides, he had no child from her."[11] This version abridges the Ménestrel's account, and the conclusion is a little different. Although the queen's extensive holdings are emphasized at the beginning of the account—"Les barons vouldrent que le roy fust mariés à la ducesse de Normandie nommée Lyennor, laquelle tenoit trois tanz de terre plus que le roy, tant en Almaigne que ailleurs"—the judgment that the king should have walled up the queen is linked to her lack of children rather than to the loss of her lands.[12]

Another text probably related to the Ménestrel's account is the fourteenth-century *Chronique abrégée* found in a fifteenth-century manuscript at the Bibliothèque Nationale in Paris. Its narrative begins with the council of Clermont in 1095 and ends in 1328. This chronicle includes the story of Eleanor's adulterous desire in a shorter version than that given by the Ménestrel, but, like the Ménestrel's version, it stresses the importance of the queen's property ("she held Normandy, Poitou, Anjou and Maine"), identifies Saladin as the queen's lover, and blames the king for losing the queen and her lands:

> When the queen was taken, the king asked what he should do with her. He was advised to send her back to the country of which she was the ruler. And he did so and sent her out of the country, which was a foolish thing to do. For it would have been better to wall her up because all the land would have remained in the king's hands. It did not happen like that, for Countess Eleanor returned to her country and had more land than the king of France . . . When [Louis] returned from the East and learned that his wife had remarried with King Henry of England he knew that he had acted foolishly by not walling up Countess Eleanor, but it was too late.[13]

A last example of the narrative scandalizing of the queen's desire may be offered from a *Chronique de Flandres,* thought to have been written at Saint-Omer in the first half of the fifteenth century. Of the chronicles I have cited, this is the least like the *Récits d'un Ménestrel de Reims,* though several narrative elements strongly suggest a relationship to the *Récits* or one of its analogues. It records the story of the Second Crusade and of Eleanor's adulterous passion for a sultan during a siege at Antioch.

> An extraordinary thing happened during this siege, for Eleanor, the queen of France, who had stayed at Tripoli, had become so involved with the Sultan Rehaudin [variants: Jehoudin; the Sultan of Babylon] that she meant to go away with him. The king was in Antioch, and as soon as he was told he mounted his horse and rode all night long, and when he arrived there he found that the queen had already left to get on the ship. And the king seized her immediately and brought her back with him. After that, the king took leave of the king of Jerusalem to return to his country . . . [He] went to Rome and asked the pope that by his authority a divorce be made between him and Eleanor, who was lady of Touraine, Anjou, Poitou, Agénois and Gascony.[14]

In this version, the queen's lover is not Saladin but is still a sultan. Unlike other accounts, this one acknowledges Eleanor and Louis's two daughters (in a passage following the one cited above), but the second daughter is born before the departure for the East rather than after the king and queens' return to France. As in some of the other versions, the adultery is the direct cause of the annulment of the royal marriage; the pope's reconciliation is absent. There is no explicit mention of the loss of the queen's great lands, but it is suggested by the enumeration of her domains.

These chronicles were written in different periods and in different regions and serve different ideological, political, and narrative purposes.[15] Yet they all recount Queen Eleanor's transgressive desire for a Muslim prince. Obviously the incident explains how France lost a queen and her lands and how England gained control of French territories. But the form of the explanation—the insistence on the queen's adulterous passion—merits further examination. In this context, the chronicles that recount Eleanor's scandalous desire to leave her king for a Muslim nobleman are more about queenship than about any particular queen. Indeed, Eleanor is not always the protagonist in this story. The fifteenth-century *Deuxième cycle de la croisade* recounts a queen's attempted flight with Saladin, but here it is the unnamed wife of Louis VII's son, Philip II Augustus. This queen meets Saladin in France, falls in love with him, and tries to seduce him. Saladin initially resists, claiming that he would betray both God and the king if he accepted her love, but when the queen threatens to take revenge for his refusal, he changes his mind: "'Do not take action, Madame,' he said, 'for we would both be in great peril, and I would rather grant your request than suffer shame or damage to my body.' And he embraced her then and kissed her with pleasure.'"[16] Saladin leaves France, the king and queen go on crusade, and on the pretext of converting Saladin, the queen goes to his castle, where she intends to stay permanently. One of the king's knights forces her to return to the king; Philip sends her back to her father the king of Aragon, "renouncing her company because of her outrageous life and the ill will she had shown in wishing to live among the Turcs."[17] This account at least places Saladin in a plausible chronology—Philip Augustus indeed met him in battle—but Philip was a widower when he went on crusade, and he never married a king of Aragon's daughter. That the story of an adulterous liaison with Saladin (or a sultan) was transferred from queen to queen suggests that its most important characters are a queen—not necessarily Eleanor of Aquitaine—and a sultan.

These accounts of a queen's attempted flight with a Muslim sultan may be seen as an anxious representation of a queen's sexuality as a threat to her husband's sovereignty. The link between the queen's desire and the king's authority becomes even clearer when the chronicle accounts about

Eleanor and Saladin are read alongside another medieval narrative form: romances about queens whose adulterous desire causes political disruption in their husbands' courts. In romances such as *Le roman des sept sages de Rome,* queens try to seduce one of their husbands' vassals and when they are rejected, they try to use their influence over the king to destroy the vassal. The story of the seductress queen elaborates the Potiphar's wife motif, and the story of the desire for power realized through sexual predation proliferates in its associations with queens in twelfth- and thirteenth-century narratives.

Seductress Queens

Le roman des sept sages de Rome may stand as a model for what I am calling romances about seductress queens.[18] There are several extant versions of the story, but the basic plot is unchanged in each account: an empress tries to seduce her stepson, he rejects her, and she accuses him of trying to seduce her. The emperor vows to execute the son who has betrayed him, but after a succession of proofs and counterproofs, the falsely accused son succeeds in convincing the emperor that his wife, not his son, is the sexual predator. The enlightened emperor then identifies his wife's insatiable sexual desire as the origin of her treachery: "O false woman and miserable creature, you didn't have enough to satisfy your carnality and luxuriousness in me and your lover, but in addition you want my son for your evil!"[19] In the king's view, the queen's sexual voracity demonstrates her evil nature, and in romances like *Le roman des sept sages de Rome,* queens are shown to be ruled by an indiscriminate concupiscence that disrupts the king's government of his court when the queen tries to destroy his relationship with his heir in order to avenge a rejection of her sexual advances.

The association of betrayal and sexuality in the portrait of a queen would not seem to need much explanation. In the context of medieval queenship, however, it may have historically specific importance. The queen's ability to influence her husband's government is a manifestation of political influence, even when her influence is only temporarily effective. Since the queen-consort does not govern directly, but owes her position to her marriage, the queen's power in these romance examples depends on her personal relationship with the king—since in these romances she has no children through whom she might claim the respect usually accorded to the mother of the king's heirs. In the thirteenth-century *Châtelaine de Vergi,* another romance about a woman who tries to seduce her husband's vassal, that personal influence is located entirely in a sexual relationship: a duchess succeeds in dictating her husband's conduct toward his vassal by using sexual blackmail.[20] *La châtelaine de Vergi* recounts the story of a duchess, not a queen, but the ducal court in this romance shares the structure of feudal royal courts. This noble wife's participation in political decisions in her husband's court and the counsel she offers him also characterize the position of the medieval queen-consort. As in romances about queens who use their influence to pursue vengeance for sexual rejection, the duchess's power and authority take the form of a sexual manipulation that threatens to corrupt the proper government of the feudal court.

The characterization of the queen's sexual relationship with the king as a source of power and influence is not an invention of medieval romance. John Carmi Parsons and Lois L. Huneycutt have noted how the medieval queen's ability to intercede effectively with the king is linked to her intimacy with her husband.[21] That the queen had a sexual relationship with the king gave her an access to the sovereign that was recognized as both influential and important. The chronicles that recount Eleanor's passion for Saladin, like romances about seductress queens, suggest that the queen's influence over her husband could also provoke anxiety about the relationship between proper government and privileged access to the king.

Changes in queenship in Europe during the twelfth and thirteenth centuries distanced the queen from the powerful position as an informal coregent that she had enjoyed in earlier centuries, and located her power primarily in her influence on her husband.[22] While historians of medieval queenship have shown that such influence was openly recognized, even codified in rituals, it could also provoke anxiety about the queen's sexual influence, and this anxiety surely contributed to the representation of queens whose transgressive sexual desire is shown to present a danger to their husbands.

That Eleanor of Aquitaine might become the focus for an expression of anxieties about queenship and sexuality is understandable for several reasons. First, of course, she was linked to sexual scandal by the accounts of her conduct at Antioch, and while her reported demonstrations of affection for her uncle were not necessarily the cause of the dissolution of her marriage, they were followed by a royal divorce and France's loss of her inheritance. A more important source of anxiety about Eleanor's sexual influence over the king may be seen in William of Tyre's assertion, repeated by William of Nangis, of Louis's "immoderate" affection for Eleanor.[23] The queen's sexual influence on the king is not disturbing as long as it is properly contained within the parameters suggested by ritual. But when—through the king's excessive desire and the queen's transgressive expression of desire—it escapes the functions scripted by royal rituals of intercession and succession, it may be seen to threaten the king's sovereignty, particularly if the queen is a wealthy sovereign in her own right.

In what I am defining broadly as a family of post-twelfth-century nar-ratives about Eleanor of Aquitaine's adulterous affair in the Holy Land, the queen's power is defined in terms of sexuality (her choice of sexual part-ner) and in terms of property (the ability to transfer her lands to the part-ner of her choice).[24] The identification of Eleanor's lands in these accounts is not quite accurate. Eleanor controlled a vast territory equal to about one-third of Louis's, but she did not hold Normandy, Anjou, or Touraine—these were in fact Henry's lands.[25] Chroniclers would surely have known the difference. The conflation of Eleanor's territory with Henry's possessions indicates the narrator's knowledge of the events that followed the royal divorce in France: the consolidation of Eleanor's and Henry's lands under the English crown. It may also explain the consistent assertion that King Louis should have "walled up" his wife to avoid los-ing her lands. If the chroniclers wrote with the knowledge of Henry II's imprisonment of Eleanor in 1173–89, they may have taken it as a retro-spective lesson for the French king.

Henry "walled up" his wife to prevent her further participation in their sons' rebellion, a legitimate concern since Eleanor was involved in succession politics throughout her life.[26] Linked to any representation of Eleanor's marriage to Louis VII, and featured by the chroniclers, is the lack of a royal heir. Whether or not Eleanor's conduct in the Holy Land indicates a desire to escape her marriage, Louis certainly had rea-sons to get rid of a wife who had not produced sons.[27] In the Ménestrel's account, at the same time that the narrator claims that the king should have walled up his wife (would she eventually produce sons?), the king's barons grasp at a solution to a potential succession crisis: "The best advice we could give you is that you let her go . . . above all, you have no children with her." The barons' advice may also suggest a less explicit reason for repudiating the queen immediately. The emphasis on the king's lack of children with the queen may sug-gest suspicions that Eleanor's relationship with Saladin had gone be-yond an exchange of letters. It may hint at illegitimacy, the disputed paternity of any child of the queen's.[28] It may also implicitly suggest—for both king and barons—the added anxiety of a union between a Christian woman and a Saracen prince.

This is surely the reason for Saladin's presence in the story, whether his partner is Eleanor of Aquitaine or the wife of Philip Augustus. Not only is Saladin renowned for his courtliness and prowess in the medieval legends that surround him, but he is a figure already associated with a scandalous union between a Christian woman and a Saracen prince. The thirteenth-century romance *La fille du comte de Pontieu* recounts that Saladin is the great-grandson of a French woman and the sultan of Aumarie.[29]

The suggestion of illegitimacy and miscegenation, the implicitly articulated relationship between sexuality and power, and the explicit acknowledgment of succession concerns make chroniclers' accounts of Eleanor of Aquitaine's adulterous desire for Saladin less a story about Eleanor herself than a story about queenship in which Eleanor has become exemplary. Eleanor is featured as a famous example of a woman who misuses her sexual power, an idea captured in Helinand de Froidmont's assertion that Eleanor's scandalous desire caused Louis to "abandon" her—"It was on account of her lasciviousness that Louis gave up his wife, who behaved not like a queen but more like a whore"—and then the king had to fight a war because of her wantonness.[30] Chroniclers' accounts of Eleanor's scandalous desire may be seen as part of a discourse about queenship in which anxieties about the queen's influence over her husband are expressed in the representation of the queen's adulterous desire as an exemplary transgression. This is nowhere more evident, perhaps, than in a sermon *exemplum* recorded by Etienne de Bourbon:

> I have heard that when a certain queen of France desired one master Gilbert de la Porée, she called him to her . . . Seeing that he had fair hands, she said, taking him by the hands, 'Oh, how fitting if these fingers should touch my sides!' Withdrawing his hand, he said, 'Lady, let this not be done, for if my fingers thus touched you, with what could I ever eat again?'[31]

The editor of this text refers to rumors about Eleanor of Aquitaine's "galanteries," and suggests that the unnamed queen of the exemplum may be she; and Gilbert de la Porée, bishop of Poitiers, was in fact Eleanor's contemporary. While the exemplum, like the *Récits d'un Ménestrel de Reims,* may indicate that by the thirteenth century Eleanor was associated with promiscuous behavior, it also suggests that an unnamed queen, any queen, offers an exemplary representation of the dangerous combination of sexual desire and power.

The insistence of Eleanor's adulterous desire and the particular ways in which her desire is shown to be scandalous suggest that Eleanor was not just a villain of history but an emblem of the dangers of the queen's sexual intimacy with the king. If changes in the institution of queenship over the course of the Middle Ages produced anxieties about women's access to power through the influence they might gain as the sexual partner of the king, those anxieties may be expressed in romance narratives that recount how a queen's transgressive sexual desire threatens her husband's government of his court, or in chronicle accounts of a queen who seeks to deny giving her body and lands to a Christian king and instead offers them to his Muslim enemy. The association of the queen's dangerous influence and transgressive sexual desire found in romance narratives like *Le roman des sept sagees du Rome* finds an echo in chronicle accounts of Eleanor of Aquitaine's actions in the East, where the queen's scandalous desire is recounted not only as a displaced representation of cultural anxiety about queenship but as an exemplary tale that represents the queen's power to corrupt government as a dangerous and scandalous sexual desire.

Notes

Linda Seidel, Ellen McClure, John Carmi Parsons, and especially Sharon Kinoshita offered perceptive questions and comments on earlier versions of this essay. I am very grateful for their help.

1. "Anno uero gratie millesimo centesimo quadragesimo nono uenerat Christianissimus rex Francorum, fractis in oriente uiribus, Antiochiam, ibique a principe Reimundo, fratre Guillermi bone memorie comitis Pictauensis, honorifice receptus est. Erat enim regine patruus, et regi fidem, amorem, et reuerentiam debebat ex multis causis. Sed dum ibi morarentur ad nauragi exercitus reliquias consolandas, fouendas et reparandas, familiaritas principis ad reginam et assidua fere sine intermissione colloquia regi suspicionem dederunt. Que quidem ex eo magis inualiuit quod regina ibi uoluit remanere, rege preparante recessuim; eamque princeps studuit retinere, si pace regis fieri potuisset. Cum uero rex eam inde properaret auellere, ipsa parentele mentionem faciens dixit illicitum esse ut diutius commanerent, quia inter eos congatio in quarto gradu uertebature et quinto." See John of Salisbury, *Historia Pontificalis,* pp. 52–53. On consanguinity in relation to the royal divorce, see Brundage, chapter 9 in this volume, and Bouchard, chapter 10 in this volume.

2. "Erat, ut praemisimus, sicut et prius et postmodum manifestis edocuit indiciis, mulier imprudens, et contra dignitatem regiam legem negligens maritalem, tori conjugalis fidem oblita." Translation from William of Tyre, *Deeds Done Beyond the Sea* 2:180, based on William of Tyre, "Historia rerum," 1:752.

3. Gervase of Canterbury, *Chronica,* in Gervase of Canterbury, *Opera historica,* 1:149, cited by Owen, *Eleanor of Aquitaine,* pp. 110–11.

4. Harvey, *The Troubadour Marcabru,* p. 133, citing Richard of Devizes, ed. Appleby, pp. 25–26.

5. Harvey, *The Troubadour Marcabru,* p. 133.

6. Suger, Epistola LVII in Migne, PL 186.1378: "De regina conjuge vestra audemus vobis laudare, si tamen placet, quatenus rancorem animi vestri, si est, operiatis, donec Deo volente ad proprium reversus regnum et super his et super aliis provideatis." Cited by Harvey, *The Troubadour Marcabru,* p. 235 n40.

7. Helinand de Froidmont, *Chronicon,* ed. Migne PL 212: cols. 1057–58; cited by Owen, *Eleanor of Aquitaine,* p. 111.

8. Needless to say, these versions offer an entirely fictitious account of Eleanor's relationship with Saladin, whom she never met and who would

have been about eleven years old when she was at Antioch. I will return to
the importance of the substitution of Saladin (or a sultan) for Raymond,
but the importance of the East (Antioch, Tyre) as a setting for Eleanor's
adultery deserves a fuller exploration than it receives here.

9. " . . . qui mout fu male famme. Et tenoit le Mainne et Anjo et Poiteu et
Limoge et Tourainne, et bien trois tans de terre que li rois ne tenoit . . .
Quant Solehadins aperçut sa molesce et sa nicetei, si li manda pluseurs fois
bataille; mais li rois ne s'en vout onques mellier. Et quant la roine Elienor
vit la deffaute que li rois avoit menée avec li, et elle oï parleir de la bontei
et de la prouesce et dou senst et de la largesce Solehadin, si l'en ama dure-
ment en son cuer, et li manda salut par un sien druguement; et bien seust
il, se il pouoit tant faire que il l'en peust meneir, elle le penroit à seigneur
et relanquiroit sa loi. Quant Solehadins l'entendi par la letre que li drugu-
menz li ot baillie, si en fu mout liez; car il savoit bien que ce estoit la plus
gentis dame de crestientei et la plus riche. Si fist armeir une galie et mou-
voir d'Escaloingne où il estoit, et aleir à Sur atout le druguement; et arriverent à Sur un pou devant la mie nuit.

Et le druguemenz monta amont par une fause posterne en la chambre la
roine qui l'atendoit. Quant elle le vit, si li dist: 'Queis nouveles?–Dame, dist
il, veez ci la galie toute preste qui vous atent. Or dou hasteir, que nous ne
soiens perceu.–Par foi, dist la roine, c'est bien fait.' Atant prist deus damoiseles et deus coffres bien garniz d'or et d'argent, et les en vouloit faire
porteir en la galie, quant une de ses damoiseles s'en perçut, et se parti de
la chamber au plus coiement qu'elle pot, et vint au lit dou roi qui dormoit,
et l'esveilla et li dist: 'Sire, malement est; ma dame s'en veut aleir en
Escaloigngne à Solehadin, et la galie est au port qui l'atent. Pour Dieu, sire,
hastiez-vous.'

Quant li rois l'oï si saut sus, et se vest et s'atourne, et fait sa mesnie armeir
et s'en va au port. Et trouva la roine qui estoit ja d'un pié en la galie; et la
prent par la main, et la ramainne arriere en sa chambre. Et la mesnie au roi
retindrent la galie et ceus qui estoient dedenz; car il furent si sourpris qu'il
n'orent pouoir d'eus deffendre.

Li rois demanda la roine pourquoi elle vouloit ce faire. 'En non Dieu, dist
la roine, pour vostre mauvestié; car vous ne valez pas une pomme pourrie.
Et j'ai tant de bien oï dire de Solehadin que je l'ain mieuz que vous; et
sachiez bien de voir que de moi tenir ne jorrez vous jà.' Atant la laissa li
rois et la fist très bien gardier, et ot conseil qu'il s'en revenroit en France;
car si denier li aloient faillant, et il n'aquestoit là se honte non.

Si romonta sour meir atout la roine et s'en revint in France; et prist conseil à touz ses barons que il feroit de la roine, et leur conta comment elle avoit
ouvrei. 'Par fois, dient le baron, li mieudres consaus que nous vous sachiens
donner, ce est que vous la laissiez aleir; car c'est uns diables, et se vous la
tenez longement nous doutons qu'elle ne vous face mourdrir. Et ensour-
quetout vous n'avez nul enfant de li' (*Récits d'un Ménestrel de Reims*, p. 4).

10. *Récits d'un Ménestrel de Reims*, pp. 4–7.

11. "Les barons vouldrent que le roy fust mariés à la duchesse de Normandie nommée Lyennor, laquelle tenoit trois tanz de terre plus que le roy, tant en Almaigne que ailleurs. Or avint que le roy out volenté d'aler outre mer conquerre la Terre-Sainte, et s'apresta et garny, et se mist sur mer, et mena sa fame avec lui: dont il fist que fol, si comme vous orrés après. Et arriverent à Sur, que plus ne tenoient Chretianz in cele contrée, et fu là tout l'hiver. Et Salhadin les pourforchet et ammonestet d'avoir la bataille. Et la royne Liennor, qui oy parler de la grant proesche et de la noblesche et largesse, ama Salhadin, et luy fist savoir qu'i la venist querre par certain message, et elle s'en iroit avec luy. Et quant Salhadin sut qu'elle l'amoit, il n'ut omcques si grant joie, considéré que c'estoit la plus rice de Chretienté et la plus noble. Si aplica une gallée ordenée pour le fait, et y envoia certain messager où plus se fioit. Quant elle sut que la gallée estoit au port venue, ele fist ses trussiaus de ses meilleurs joiaux et d'or et d'argent, et envoia par nuit par ses privés. Après ce, se mist à voie pour entrer en la galée; mais il n'est rien qui ne soit seu: le roy le sut, et la hasta et suy de si près que elle avoit .j. pié à entrer enz; et prist le roy gallée et tout et cheulz qui la venoient querre, et se retourna en France, lui et ses gens; et conta à ses barons tout l'affaire de point en point, et qu'i le conseillassent comme il an feroit. S'il lui conseillerent qu'i la lessat aller au deable en Normandie don't elle estoit venue: dont ce fu malvès conseil qu'il eust miex vallu qu'il l'eust enmurée. Et avec ce, il n'avoit de lui nul enfant" (Cochon, *Chronique normande,* pp. 2–3).

12. Cochon, *Chronique normande,* p. 2.

13. " . . . li rois Loys fu mariez a la ducesse elienor qui estoit moult riche dame. Car elle tenoit normendie et poitau aniou et le maine . . . quant le roy Loys ot espouse celle elienor qui estoit ducesse daniou une pieche apres il qui estoit moult preudons si dist que il vouloit aler outre mer. Il y ala et le royne elienor ala avecques lui ne li roi ne l'en pot detourner . . . Quand li roys Loys fut oultre mer il trouva le soudan Salphadin. Le royne elienor lama et sen vault aler avecques le soudant et cestoit le plus beaux sarrasins du monde. Le roine elyenor fu prinse prouvee ainsi quelle devoit entrer en le nef la ou ses choses estoient appareillies et on sot lestat par une de ses demoiselles qui dit comment le besogne aloit. Quant le royne fu prise li roys demande que il en feroit. Il lui fu loue que on le renvoiast en son pais dont elle estoit dame. Et il si fist et le bouta hors de la compagnie. Dont il ouvra moult nichement. Car il vaulsist meulx quelle eult este emmuree si fust demuree toute le terre en le main du roy. Il ne fu mie ainsi car la comtesse elienor revint en son pais et avoit plus de terre que navoit le roi de France . . . Quant il fu venus doultre mer et il sot comment sa femme sestoit remariee au roy henry dengleterre si sot bien que il avoir nichement ouvre de ce que il navoit emmuree la contesse elienor mais cest trop tart" (*Chronique abrégée,* Paris BnF, fr. 9222, fols. 16v–17r).

14. "Or durant ce siége avint une moult grant merveille; car la royne de France Aliénor, qui avoir séjourné à Triple, avoit tant fait devers le soudan

Rehaudin, qu'elle s'en devoit aler avoec luy. Tantost on le fist sçavoir au roy, qui estoit à siége devant Ascalogne. Li roys monta et s'en ala toute nuit; et, quant il vint là, il trouva que la royne estoit jà venue à la galée, pour y entrer ens; et tantost li roys la prit et la ramena avoec luy. Après ce, li roys prit congé du roy de Jhérusalem et s'en revint vers son pais et arriva à Brandis, et de là s'en revint à Romme et parla tant à l'Apostole que par son autorité (luy revenu à Estampes) fut la départie faite de luy et d'Aliénor, qui fut dame de Touraine, d'Anjou, de Poitou, d'Agénois et de Gascongne" (*Istoire et Chroniques de Flandres,* pp. 44–55). For the sultan of Babylon variant, see Paris, "La légende de Saladin," 437 [284–89, 354–65, 428–58, 486–98].

15. For yet another example, see the "Extrait d'un abrégé de l'histoire des rois de France," *RHF* 12:229.

16. " . . . 'Non férés, madame,' fet il, 'car en peril serions vous et moy, et mieulx aime ottroyer vostre requeste que avoir honte ne dommage de mon corps" (*Saladin,* ed. Crist, p. 97).

17. " . . . ançois le renvoya au roy d'Arragon son pere, renonçant a la compaignie d'ycelle par lex excusacions de sa vie oultrageuse et de la male voulenté qu'elle avoit eue de vouloir converser aveq les Turcz" (*Saladin,* ed. Crist, pp. 155–56).

18. I study these romances in more detail in *The Romance of Adultery,* pp. 144–70. For an edition of the two verse versions of *The Romance of the Seven Sages,* see Speer, *Le roman des sept sages de Rome.*

19. "O faulce femme et miserable creature, tu n'avoies pas souffisance pour accomplier ta charnalite et luxure de moy ne de ton rybaul, mais vouloyes encores mon filz pour pis faire!" (*L'ystoire des sept sages,* ed. Paris, p. 160).

20. *La châtelaine de Vergi,* vv. 566–72.

21. Parsons, "Queen's Intercession," and Huneycutt, "Intercession."

22. Facinger, "Medieval Queenship."

23. *Chronique latine de Guillaume de Nangis,* 1:44.

24. Martindale discusses the territorial basis of Eleanor's power in "Eleanor of Aquitaine," pp. 23–33.

25. Here I develop a suggestion from Sharon Kinoshita.

26. On Eleanor as a mother, see Brown, "Eleanor of Aquitaine: Parent, Queen, and Duchess," revised as chapter 1 in this volume. See also Turner, chapter 3 in this volume, and Lewis, chapter 7 in this volume.

27. Martindale, "Eleanor of Aquitaine," p. 41, notes that "for dynastic reasons King Louis needed the separation rather more than Eleanor."

28. It may be worth emphasizing that I am discussing a fictional account and its implication for the construction of medieval queenship. After her return to France, Queen Eleanor gave birth to another daughter, whose legitimacy was not questioned.

29. *La fille du comte de Pontieu, conte en prose.* See my discussion of this text in *The Romance of Adultery,* pp. 124–35. Even when Queen Eleanor's lover is

not Saladin, as in *La chronique de Flandres,* he is still a sultan, not a Western prince like her uncle Raymond of Antioch.

30. See above, n7.

31. *Anecdotes historiques,* p. 212. I am grateful to John Parsons for bringing this text to my attention.

CHAPTER 13

DAMNED IF SHE DIDN'T AND
DAMNED WHEN SHE DID:
BODIES, BABIES, AND BASTARDS IN
THE LIVES OF TWO QUEENS OF FRANCE

John Carmi Parsons

> *This chapter contrasts the mythologizing receptions of Eleanor of Aquitaine and Marie Antoinette, whose long years as childless queens of France reputedly elicited rumors of adultery, incest and sexual ridicule of their husbands.*

Throughout history, the queen who fails in her first obligation, to provide an heir to her husband's realm, has rarely failed to attract notice. Some childless royal marriages elicited legends of celibacy and sanctity, as with Emperor Henry II and his wife St. Cunegunde, or with King Edward the Confessor. But childless medieval queens were more likely to attract criticism. Margaret of Anjou's eight years of childless marriage to Henry VI of England led to charges that she was unfit to be queen; when she bore a son in 1453, rumor insisted that the father was not the feeble king, but his cousin (and Margaret's), the Beaufort duke of Somerset. In fourteenth-century Naples, Queen Sanchia of Aragon's Franciscan piety was blamed for her childlessness, and so far from sharing the Confessor's sanctity, his widow, Edith, was allegedly pursued to her deathbed by rumors of her adultery. Little wonder that Constance of Sicily, aged forty and after childless years as Emperor Henry VI's wife, reputedly bore her only son in a marketplace to ensure sufficient witnesses to attest that the child was hers.[1]

This chapter focuses on the contexts and implications of disparaging gossip about childless queens by interrogating the mythologizing receptions of the two most romanticized of all the queens of France: Eleanor of Aquitaine (ca. 1124–1204) and Marie Antoinette of Austria (1755–93). This may seem an odd pairing, but remarkably similar tales were told of these two women: that they openly scorned their husbands' sexual performance and that they committed adultery and incest. However suggestive the immediate similarities in these tales, it remains to be seen if any factors really linked these tales' genesis and the queen's initial failure to bear children or, if not, whether these externally similar tales indicate that common themes linked the two lives across six centuries. I therefore survey the reasons for either woman's childlessness, the criticism each endured, what is known of their reactions to their situations, and the tales of derision, adultery, and incest that circulated about both.

The sources for Marie Antoinette's case are naturally more plentiful and detailed than those for Eleanor of Aquitaine.[2] Her life has, however, been misunderstood ever since Stefan Zweig's 1932 biography of the queen carved in stone the belief that her husband, Louis XVI, had an inelastic foreskin (medically known as phimosis) that made intercourse impossibly painful for him.[3] Zweig's source was a 1774 report by a Spanish envoy to France, who collected valets' gossip on the condition of royal bedlinen and the state of Louis's manhood as he rose from bed in the morning. The envoy soon retracted his "diagnosis," but Zweig made it the decisive factor in the couple's plight.[4] A friend of Sigmund Freud, Zweig was convinced that sexual frustration caused the queen's relentless pursuit of costly amusement and either suppressed evidence that confuted this idea or misrepresented sources to support his thesis.[5] Louis XVI did not suffer from phimosis.[6] The truth about his conjugal performance appears in a letter from the queen's brother, Emperor Joseph II, to their brother Leopold of June 9, 1777, just after Joseph had visited Versailles. Zweig quoted from this letter[7] but suppressed its frank details of the couple's intimacies that Joseph had heard from the pair themselves. Louis was fully capable of normal relations, but initiated intimacy only out of duty and admitted frankly to Joseph that he had "no taste for it." As Joseph described matters, Louis in effect practiced an oddly inert form of *coitus interruptus:* in His Imperial Majesty's words, the Most Christian King needed only "to be . . . pushed, or beaten, to make him ejaculate . . . like donkeys."[8]

Recent historians have found further evidence to weaken Zweig's thesis. Maria Theresa's envoy at Versailles reported in 1777 that Joseph II had cleared Louis's head of "the extraordinary idea that he was endangering his health by fulfilling his conjugal duties." Some argue that as a child of Maria Theresa's puritanical court, the queen was a prude (which was probably true), or that her own libido was so listless that Louis's shortcomings would have bothered her little but for her family's wish that she bear a son. Others suggest that Louis's useless attentions so repulsed her that she avoided him. Certainly Joseph II regretted that his sister was not of a more amorous nature, called the pair "two complete fumblers," and ascribed their problems to mutual "laziness, clumsiness and apathy."[9] But whatever advice he gave Louis worked: in the third week of August 1777, Marie Antoinette at last became the true queen of France.[10] Her first child arrived in December 1778, after which she conceived at least five times in fairly regular succession through the autumn of 1785.[11]

No sources comparable to Joseph II's letter exist to cast light on Louis VII and Eleanor of Aquitaine's relations, but some reasons can be suggested for the couple's few pregnancies. Eleanor wed Louis VII at thirteen, in 1137, and had an unsuccessful pregnancy shortly thereafter; she bore her first child ca. 1145, eight years after marriage, and her second five years later.[12] Louis VII thus impregnated her three times in fifteen years; his second wife, Constance of Castile, had two children in six years (1154–60), and his third, Adela of Champagne, was likely pregnant twice in five or six years (1160–66). And, as Andrew Lewis shows in this volume, Eleanor and Henry II had nine children in thirteen years. John of Salisbury twice says that Louis VII loved Eleanor immoderately, but, contrasted to their procreative frustration while married, their successes with other spouses suggest that their conjugal life was indeed unsatisfactory in some way, perhaps even biological, that we cannot now identify.[13]

The consequences of the two queens' delayed childbearing were not limited to personal disappointment. Even apart from diplomatic scrutiny of Marie Antoinette's early failure to conceive, she and Louis XVI during those seven years endured open humiliations that, in the view of modern writers, had a marked effect on both. Eighteenth-century Parisian fishwives asserted the privilege of speaking as they pleased to the royal family and publicly told the queen to "open her legs and get on with it," berating her thus within the palace of Versailles in 1775 when they came to congratulate Louis's brother on the birth of a son. When the queen once playfully took to pelting Louis with bread at dinner, he genially asked his war minister how to meet the barrage; to a frigid silence, the minister said, "Sire, I should spike the gun!" His remark painfully showcased a prevalent belief that Louis XVI was impotent. Contemporary engravings graphically show a baffled queen vainly enticing a flaccid king, and rumor later ascribed her children's paternity to various courtiers with whom she allegedly had shared her favors. In the face of such talk the bulky, awkward, and shy Louis XVI became ever more aloof; unwilling or unable to curb his lively wife, he indulged her diversions.[14] We cannot know if Eleanor of

Aquitaine was as openly rebuked for her childlessness with Louis VII, but she surely had to contend with the literal or figurative presence of her mother-in-law, Adelaide of Maurienne, who had had seven sons with Louis VI.[15] The closest we are likely to come to Eleanor's real feelings is the account of her meeting with Bernard of Clairvaux in 1144, during which she is said to have expressed fears that God had closed her womb.[16] Given the publicity that surrounds royal procreation even today, it is by no means impossible that, apart from personal hopes for children, Eleanor as queen of France was, or was made to be, conscious enough of her childless state to seek a holy abbot's advice.

Both women were said to have gone even further in expressing their feelings. It is doubtful that Marie Antoinette habitually called Louis XVI "the poor man" in any sense, sexual or other. But she knew of the prints of their useless couplings and the pamphlets describing her adulterous or lesbian affairs: copies were left conspicuously lying about Versailles, and the king and queen even found them under their dinner napkins. Such awareness affords a stark honesty to her remark to a courtier in 1777: "I should neither be grieved nor very annoyed if the king were to develop a passing and temporary attachment, as he might thereby acquire more vitality and energy."[17] This authentic and widely-reported comment echoes Eleanor of Aquitaine's reputed remark that Louis VII's attentions left her unsure whether she had wed a king or a monk, and that marriage to the duke of Normandy (later Henry II of England) would be more to her taste. But this tale's reliability must be carefully weighed: the earliest version appears not in a French text contemporary with Eleanor's marriage to Louis, but in the *Historia Rerum Anglicarum* by the English writer William of Newburgh, written probably between 1196 and 1198—well after Henry II's death.[18] The tale could fit the scenario of a sexually incompatible couple, as may be implied by their procreative plight. But the tale jars with the report of Eleanor's plaint that God had closed her womb, which if true would mean that she and Louis were having relations often enough that her barren state was puzzling. The Newburgh tale's late date, its English source, and its unlikely attribution to Eleanor of an admitted attraction to Henry while still Louis VII's wife—we may as well insist that Marie Antoinette really did say "Let them eat cake"[19]— imply that Newburgh's tale was meant to suggest Eleanor's inclination to adultery. Newburgh's choice to report it may be seen, then, as part of that strain of anti-Angevin feeling Jane Martindale notes in English writings of the twelfth and early thirteenth centuries.[20]

Despite the lack of reliable foundation for Eleanor's remark evident to modern observers, neither queen's contemporaries would have found it difficult to credit these reports. The story of Eleanor's plaint to Bernard reflects the medieval tendency to blame a wife for a barren marriage, deepening a queen's dilemma by making her presumed bodily failure a shadow on the king's virility. Any man's strength was judged in part by the number of sons he fathered; for a king, identified with his realm's strength and fertility, failure to sire children was a particular fault. As Louis VII's virility was thus shadowed by the lack of a son with Eleanor, his subjects could deem him lacking in the fullness of his powers, and ultimately in moral or political authority.[21] To whatever extent Eleanor's contemporaries knew or believed Newburgh's tale, then, they could have understood it as a woman's calculated insult to a male royal body. Unlike Eleanor's alleged remark about Louis VII, Marie Antoinette's about Louis XVI is authentic, and contemporaries could have concluded that it affirmed his impotence, even more disastrously menacing his authority. Belief in any report that a queen had spoken of her husband in such manner would have had few positive consequences for herself or the king. The results are obvious in Marie Antoinette's case: a corollary of Louis XVI's presumed impotence was the belief that his queen must be unfaithful. As a young woman whose husband ignored her, she welcomed—even encouraged—male flattery, but with the much-debated exception of the Swedish Count Axel Fersen, no proof exists that she strayed. Joseph II sharply criticized much of her behavior but admitted in 1777 that she had not mislaid her virtue, though he felt that she remained chaste less through circumspection than inborn aversion. The testimony of this experienced observer, who knew the queen well must be given its due and argues that Marie Antoinette's love life was legendary in more than one sense of the word.[22]

As to continuing speculation about Eleanor of Aquitaine's adulteries, some weight could attach to Bishop Geoffrey of Langres's brief (and quickly dismissed) demand at the queen's 1152 divorce proceedings that her adultery be examined. Geoffrey had accompanied the royal party on crusade and must have observed the couple's behavior; but his motives in disparaging Eleanor do not bear scrutiny. Geoffrey was Bernard of Clairvaux's cousin, one of his first companions at Clairvaux and a former prior there. Clairvaux lay within Geoffrey's diocese; Bernard had attacked the morals of Geoffrey's Cluniac predecessor as bishop, got that election quashed in 1140, and promoted his cousin's election. Bernard was the royal divorce's strongest clerical supporter, and possibly his circle hoped to justify the divorce on such moral grounds as he had used to secure cassation of the election of Geoffrey's predecessor, to impugn Eleanor's honor and lessen her potential as a wife to some other lord. Geoffrey's allegation in 1152 may not, then, reflect real knowledge of Eleanor's behavior.[23] Later medieval and early modern English ballads had William Marshal fathering the queen's eldest son with Henry II and made one of her Angevin daughters the child of a

French friar, but no known contemporary rumor alleges that anyone other than Louis VII or Henry II fathered her children.[24] Thanks to the influence of Amy Kelly's highly-colored account, the myths of Eleanor's many lovers have latterly rested on Andreas Capellanus's now-rejected report of the "courts of love" at which she allegedly presided in Poitiers. These myths have no bearing on the realities of her life.[25]

The tale of Eleanor's incest with her uncle Raymond of Poitiers, prince of Antioch, is one of those familiar stories that assumed recognizable shape only well after the fact, and every later author who reports it seems to know more than any earlier writer has been able to tell us.[26] Whether medieval kings charged their wives with adultery for political or moral reasons, such cases usually ended for the wife in swift repudiation, imprisonment, or repatriation—none of which happened to Eleanor.[27] That she and Louis VII were on bad terms after their 1148 stay at Antioch cannot prove that she had committed adultery. The pope was later able to reconcile them, they had another child whose paternity Louis accepted, and they divorced only four years later, hardly suggesting that her actions at Antioch included adultery, let alone incest. At Antioch, Louis initially agreed to leave Eleanor not for her sexual misdeeds but because of their kinship, and it is unlikely that he had serious doubts about her relations with Raymond. John of Salisbury, the earliest writer to report the events in Antioch, refers to constant conversations between Raymond and Eleanor but, as Archbishop William of Tyre's later account implies, this may reflect no more than Raymond's cultivation of his niece so that she might induce Louis to grant Raymond's request for military aid. Her reunion with her uncle, a reminder of youth and home, perhaps highlighted existing problems in her marriage. As duchess of Aquitaine, moreover, Eleanor likely wished for personal and political reasons to help her uncle and other Poitevins in Antioch, and in such case she would have been angered by Louis's refusal to help Raymond. Or she may have balked at leaving Antioch to avoid further danger after the harrowing journey through Asia Minor, especially the defeat at Mount Cadmos for which Louis's retinue might already have been blaming her.[28] As James Brundage and Constance Bouchard note in this volume, the crucial aspect of the events at Antioch was that Eleanor there openly remarked her kinship to Louis. Bernard of Clairvaux had censured that kinship in 1143, but it is uncertain that it had bothered Eleanor or Louis before their quarrel at Antioch.[29] Louis may well have been furious that she disputed his military decision or troubled by her assertion of an uncanonical union. But the notion that his anger was kindled by her adultery appears only in the works of later medieval and modern writers.[30]

A greater threat to Eleanor's political future and personal reputation was the allegation that before her second marriage she had been intimate with

Henry II's father, Count Geoffrey of Anjou. As Margaret Pappano notes in this volume, that liaison would have made Eleanor's marriage to Henry void in canon law, their children bastards and, as the issue of incest, monstrous as well (one point on which Henry II might ultimately have agreed).[31] But Eleanor's reputed affair with Count Geoffrey is, again, first noted not in French sources but in later, if still contemporary, works by the British writers Gerald of Wales (Giraldus Cambrensis) and Walter Map. This implies that like William of Newburgh's tale of Eleanor's sexual derision of Louis VII, rumors of her liaison with Geoffrey of Anjou were part of English writers' anti-Angevin sentiments, as noted above, and that they circulated to cloud the legitimacy of her children with Henry and the Angevin court's moral authority.[32] Neither the allegations of Eleanor's misconduct at Antioch nor those of her affair with Geoffrey will bear close scrutiny, but in the minds of contemporaries and later readers, the two tales could well have reinforced each other to create the picture of an incestuously faithless wife.

Easily the most appalling aspect of Marie Antoinette's final ordeal is the charge of incest with her son, brought at her trial before the Revolutionary tribunal in October 1793. She was accused of teaching the boy to masturbate and, in prison after Louis XVI's death, of taking the boy to bed with herself and the late king's sister to attempt intercourse, so that he suffered a hernia. These ghastly charges arose after the child was taken from his mother's care in July 1793. His new guardians found him masturbating and saw in his groin a bandaged injury, which he had in fact sustained at play while still with his mother; Revolutionary prosecutors soon steered him into confirming the version of his mother's behavior they wished to force on an innocent reality. The charge's political aim has been clear to historians of the French Revolution. Fears of plots to restore the monarchy were widespread; charges that the queen resorted to incest to weaken her son and dominate him after her political schemes put him on the throne fitted neatly with an identity imposed on her in pamphlets of the 1780s—a new Agrippina, the mother who sought sexual dominance over her son, Nero.[33]

Reports that Eleanor of Aquitaine and Marie Antoinette committed incest are, then, no more credible than tales of their habitual adulteries. Tales of Eleanor of Aquitaine's adultery, incest, and sexual mockery during her union with Louis VII postdate her marriage to Henry II; they first appear in English writings, not in French sources, but are made to relate to her years as Louis VII's wife. Such chronological and geographical factors of origin suffice, or should suffice, to raise large doubts as to the tales' veracity. The only contemporary remark linked to her procreative problems with Louis is her alleged plea in 1144 to Bernard, which conveys not sexual contempt for Louis but fear that her own body was flawed. The calumnies against Marie Antoinette have, again with one exception—her comment on Louis XVI's apathy—proved as baseless as those against her twelfth-century predecessor. But in contrast to Eleanor's case, the tales about Marie Antoinette were contemporary with her marriage to Louis XVI, and ascribed her childlessness not to the female bodily failure Eleanor allegedly feared in 1144 but to the king's impotence. These tales about two women who lived six centuries apart are therefore alike only superficially. But however baseless, the invented reports of ridicule, adultery, and incest indelibly marked both queens' images, and elicit examination of the contexts in which the tales arose. The tales suggest only one point of contact: both women's bodies were subject not only to a husband's authority but to the dictates of monarchy and realm. It is irrelevant whether these tales tell us what the two women really did; what matters is the uses that were made of the tales and what attitudes they reveal toward these eminent wives.

This realization raises a fundamental question: whether childlessness really had all that much to do with the genesis of tales about these queens. In Eleanor of Aquitaine's case, it did not. The late, non-French origins of the first reports of her sexual misconduct show that her early childlessness with Louis was not the originating ground of these stories. Nor was the lack of a son, though there is little doubt that they were able to obtain a divorce because they had no heir to assure the royal lineage's survival and with it, the link between power and patrimony that in the medieval centuries remained vital to the identity and integrity of realm and people.[34] Six centuries later, Marie Antoinette's desiring body was observed in relation to a French monarchy vastly more evolved and geographically extended than that of the twelfth. As a result of its growth and mystique, the Bourbon monarchy was ironically less flexible than its twelfth-century ancestor. Despite Habsburg fears, divorce was never considered; Louis XVI and Marie Antoinette remained married, long childless and exposed to sexual innuendo. In so far as continuation of the royal lineage involved a single couple's fecundity, moreover, Marie Antoinette's childlessness mattered little. Male royal succession was now established as fundamental public law in France; if Louis XVI was slow to sire a Dauphin, he had two living brothers, one of whom had two sons, and princes of the blood were not lacking. The association of lineage and sovereign power could have persisted had the queen never borne a child. Whether or not it mattered that a particular royal couple produced children, however, they were all expected to do so. Royal pregnancies focused obsessive attention; their absence pejoratively exposed royal bodies, especially a queen's.[35] Childlessness itself does not, then, signify in these cases; rather, the central focus must be the way in which childlessness foregrounded queens' desiring bodies, and especially the stress the resulting tales placed on relationships between those bodies and the body politic.

The complexities of those relationships were grounded in the same questions of gender and power that defined and redefined queens' positions and methods. Constance Berman and Miriam Shadis deplore in this volume a schematization of women's power in the later Middle Ages that has inscribed a decline in women's capacities outside a domestic sphere.[36] As regards queens—and other women, who were told to regard queens as exemplars of proper behavior[37]—Berman and Shadis suggest correctives to accounts deriving from Marion Facinger's argument that as queen of France, Eleanor of Aquitaine suffered from a contraction in queenly power after a perceived high-water mark under Adelaide of Maurienne. True, the rise of royal bureaucracy and organized jurisprudence from the eleventh century was transforming formal government operations into a male preserve. At the same time, the *Policraticus* by Eleanor's contemporary John of Salisbury gave the body politic its classic medieval formulation as patterned on the human body. Morphological analogy exemplified an ideal cooperation among that body's members, but no function John detailed—administrative, military, conciliar, or ecclesiastical—nor any bodily member to which these functions corresponded, implied a female body. A king's male frame, especially, embodied his realm and betokened its strength and vigor; its impermeability figured the security of the realm's boundaries from intrusion or invasion.[38] To a body politic so imagined, women in general, queens in particular, were outsiders, their pervious bodies perilous openings that could threaten the realm. Subjected by royal ritual to the king's body as the site of supreme authority, the queen's body could not serve as the seat of power.[39]

These developments did not bar kings' wives from all access to power, but they did critically affect representations of a queen's position and the methods open to her. The rise of bureaucracy meant that, as reflected in the disappearance of queens' names from witness lists to twelfth-century English and French royal charters, the advisory role of a king's wife was no longer officially publicized. Adelaide of Maurienne was the last queen of France whose name appears as a witness to royal charters, as Eleanor of Aquitaine was the last queen of England whose name was so advertised. She was also the last queen of England to issue royal writs in her own name, and to serve regularly as regent.[40] Of course, charters and other records that witness such changes were written from a male perspective, and do not prove that queens' power was contracting. But the way they were *seen* to perform their roles changed significantly. It was no longer visibly, in the council chamber, that a queen fulfilled the duties the coronation *ordo* urged upon her as a counsellor, mediator, or intercessor with the king. Given her primary function as the mother of his children, the focus of her activities was now the bedchamber, in which at least one thirteenth-century queen chose to receive petitioners as a means to advertise her intimate relationship to the king as the real base of her power. As this intimate, wifely access to the king was not rightly subject to (male) official restraint, any formal limits on her voice implied by her advertised presence in the council chamber fell away. Whatever other parts of the regal anatomy she did or did not command, she was always assumed to have the king's ear. But any wife, queen or subject, who was seen to abuse an ecclesiastically sanctioned access to her husband menaced the right order of society.[41] Thus a queen's persuasive influence, inextricably tied to her sexual and domestic role as bedfellow, could seem to threaten the order idealized and represented by evolving male officialdom in ways not understood to exist when her place was affirmed in written acts that announced the king's decisions. The queen was left uneasily poised between the official and the domestic, a position that heightened fears about her ability to sway the king and her potential role in court intrigue.[42] Chroniclers witnessed these anxieties about queenly influence by focusing on the approved performance, or the perceived corruption, of a queen's domestic roles as wife or mother. If later medieval portrayals thus make it seem that queens' power had declined, they none the less witness, by criticizing behavior as inappropriate or by praising compliant and selfless deeds, consorts' continued eminence as exemplary figures to society, as potential participants in court intrigues, or as fomenters of conflict, especially in the familial contexts that remained central to dynastic politics. Significantly, Peggy McCracken sets within this same changing political terrain her study of the increasingly prominent image of the adulterous queen in Old French romance.[43]

Active in the twelfth and early thirteenth centuries, Eleanor of Aquitaine stands at the center of these shifts in medieval queens' power bases. One queenly reaction might be seen in her taunting of Thierry Galeran, a "male" official whose lack of male attributes perhaps left him more vulnerable to derision than other male advisors. And rather than slight Louis openly, as William of Newburgh's unreliable tale has it, it would have been safer to mock an advisor as a symbol of male authority (though substituting eunuch for king as the target for such mockery might tacitly suggest the same sexual derision she was later said to have expressed toward Louis). But if queens no longer shared openly in formal consultation, medieval royal government was always personal and, surely in Eleanor's day, directed from the royal household, whose domestic model gave that household's women effective if informal means to persuade royal business. As Facinger rightly noted in 1968, moreover, Eleanor's position as Louis VII's wife was unlike that of any earlier Capetian queen: she was the first to bring so great an in-heritance to her marriage. Her domains tacitly gave her activity, informal or otherwise, greater weight than the behavior of previous queens in France or England.[44] Certainly she was seen to seek a wider field of action than was open to her as the wife of kings, but her reputed effort to exploit her motherhood of future kings portrayed her as resorting to just the kind of domestic intrigue now seen as inimical to the official, male-dominated or-dering of government. Failure exposed her to contemporary rebuke as a disobedient wife who defied her husband's authority and an unnatural mother who turned her sons against their father.[45]

Marie Antoinette also stood in an uncertain relationship to monarchy in a changing society. Jean-Jacques Rousseau denounced political roles for women but, echoing the twelfth-century changes noted above, felt that ab-solute monarchy's personal rule favored women's political activity. The power of an absolute ruler like the king of France was unlimited by an as-sembly whose members were by implication male; his court remained a household writ large, and Rousseau saw few restraints on any of its women who sought political influence. But they could win their ends only in un-official venues and by means less rational than emotional and, in the last resort, sexual. This negative image of the "public woman" was apropos to the reign of Louis XVI's grandfather Louis XV (r. 1715–74), whose mis-tresses, Mmes. de Pompadour and du Barry, wielded political influence known to all Europe.[46] The informal, sexually grounded influence of those mistresses touches on an aspect of eighteenth-century French absolutism that crucially affected Louis XVI and his wife. The regal body was no longer mere metaphor for the realm; the ritual evolved at Versailles under Louis XIV manifested the royal presence as vital to the realm's government and life.[47] But Louis XV used his office to enable his indulgence of per-sonal desires, and like Louis XVI disliked the public parade of royal life; the latter's liking for ironwork, plastering, or clambering up on Versailles' roof to shoot stray cats hardly evoked the majesty that haloed Louis XIV's least gesture. Versailles' role as France's political and cultural center faded too, as it became only one among many eighteenth-century royal residences. In addition to Marie Antoinette's fantasy realm at the Petit Trianon, she de-fied custom to become the owner of an estate at Saint-Cloud, where she and Louis XVI luxuriated in simple informality.[48] Louis approved her lik-ing for simplicity over the ceremonial that had advertised Bourbon power, but the absence of royal bodies from public view weakened belief in the king's person as inviolable, favored conjecture on royal bodies, and fed the sexual rumors that plagued the couple.[49]

The results were disastrous for Marie Antoinette. She might have given herself to good works until the Almighty saw fit to open her womb, but as

Joseph II fulminated and historians have long observed, she paraded her-self in ways and venues inappropriate to her dignity. Rather than live in pious obscurity like earlier Bourbon queens she, like Louis XV, identified the privacy she craved not with anonymity but with personal indulgence. She frequented her minions' gambling dens and masked balls in Paris where—recognized despite disguises she fondly believed hid her iden-tity—she mingled with the demimonde (or worse).[50] Such ill-advised be-havior inevitably favored speculation on her sexual activity; like Margaret of Anjou, Henry VI of England's long-childless wife, Marie Antoinette was held to dominate a weak king while indulging her sexual desires else-where. She was thus aligned with the unseemly influence of Louis XV's mistresses, her hold over Louis XVI emotional, manipulative, and devi-ous—exactly the sort of improper female dominance Rousseau had de-cried.[51] Joseph II in 1777 had indeed likened his sister's relationship with the king to that of a high-handed royal mistress, not a compliant wife, and for the anonymous author of a 1789 London edition of the *Essais his-toriques sur la vie de Marie-Antoinette,* Mme. du Barry (Louis XV's most in-famous mistress, and in truth a former prostitute) "almost honored a dishonorable position,"while Marie Antoinette had "prostituted an estate that seemed invulnerable to degradation."[52]

Pervasive changes in eighteenth-century French political thought deep-ened the implications of such perceptions of Marie Antoinette's situation. As theories arose of a body politic independent of royal bodies or lineages, *la Nation* and *le peuple* were eclipsing lineage-based politics. The queen, whose maternal body was meant to continue the royal lineage, was thus in an especially vulnerable position. Marie Antoinette's delayed maternity and its impact on both spouses' images played directly to the Revolution's rhetorical needs: complexly interwoven tales of Louis XVI's impotence, his wife's derision, and her adultery subverted confidence in the Bourbon line's legitimate continuity and the need to preserve a link between lineage and sovereign authority. Loss of faith in monarchy's central mystique fur-thered the Revolution's aim of dissolving that link; but to achieve that goal, the queen's body must be morally demonized and mortally destroyed. Stefan Zweig correctly noted that the sexually explicit attacks on Marie Antoinette became really poisonous only after she bore children, especially her first son in 1781.[53] But the image of a wanton queen did not shift blame for childlessness from Louis XVI's allegedly impotent body to his wife's. By signifying a tottering regime's inability to meet its problems and fostering the belief that his wife's children were bastards, Louis XVI's im-potence was too irresistibly useful a tool for the Revolution to abandon.[54] In contrast to the queen once shown futilely titillating a limp Louis, for example, Marie Antoinette appears in one Revolutionary print enjoying a close encounter with a male insurgent. This image appropriated that of her adultery to inscribe the *Ancien Régime*'s impotence and to imply monarchy's revitalizing (re)union with a masculine *Nation*. But by making the queen partner to this revival, the print cast monarchy as feminine and thus hostile to *le peuple*'s interests, now to be assured by a masculine *République*. The print thus echoes the belief that a wife's adultery feminizes her husband: an immoral queen emasculated king and monarchy alike.[55]

This view of the queen appears in one of the most libellous works about her, Louise de Keralio's *Les crimes des reines de France* (1791), which lumped her with Brunéhaut, Frédégonde, and Catherine de Médicis as examples of evil queens. This work's allegorical frontispiece shows an aged king, slumped senseless on his throne; the scepter is taken from his hand by a voluptuous diademed female nude, whose one visible leg ends in a scaly fishtail. The usurping consort is thus shown as a mermaid or siren, an ancient sign of the prostitute once used against Mary, queen of Scots, during her liaison with Lord Bothwell.[56] By extending adultery's senses to include prostitution, the Keralio engraving implies wider aspects to the sexual dangers associated with queens as male rulers' desiring wives. Most significantly, prostitutes (and witches) were thought in the Middle Ages and later to be able to prevent conception. Given the unreliability of the tales of both queens' adulteries, a *prima facie* response is that if either woman took lovers in her childless years, it is odd that she conceived so tardily. But that neither queen profited from such second thoughts suggests that adultery rumors about childless queens could imply the use of contraceptive lore to conceal adultery.[57] (Marie Antoinette's rumored lesbianism also explained sexual licence without pregnancy.)

Transferring belief in marginal women's arcane contraceptive wisdom to eminent women by tales of adultery or prostitution could return the blame for a childless royal marriage from the king's male body to his wife's, but it would at the same time deepened her dilemma.[58] Any notion that a childless queen was adulterous or wanton had yet wider implications. As Charles Wood points out, medieval women in general were accorded more respect as mothers than as wives, and André Poulet affords this fact particular relevance by showing that a royal mother's presumed lack of self-interest as she acted in her children's (and the realm's) interest prepared the way for the French female regents of the Middle Ages.[59] A childless queen obviously could not profit from assumptions of ideal maternal disinterest; a belief that as an adulteress/prostitute she might use contraceptive techniques implied that she was driven by a self-interest that could work to the realm's detriment.[60] It would have been natural, then, for Eleanor of Aquitaine to assume a mediator's ideally neutral role between Louis VII and the count of Champagne, as Bernard supposedly urged her in 1144.

Like other childless queens, such as Richard II's wife, Anne of Bohemia, Eleanor might thus have appeared as a selfless, nurturing maternal figure.[61] In this respect, some significance attaches to Lois Huneycutt's remark in this volume that Eleanor's relationships with her kings did not allow her to adopt the intercessor's compliant role, and indeed, the queen's temperament may not have favored such activities. As Jane Martindale has noted, the one occasion on which Eleanor as queen (mother) of England is known to have acted as anything like a mediator presents her not as a supplicant but as an authority figure: she acted to relieve the sufferings of the people of the diocese of Ely, but not by humbly begging the bishop to set matters right—she peremptorily ordered him to do so. It is unlikely that her subjects would have seen her in the selfless, maternal guise that might have softened the image of a meddlesome wife and mother chroniclers inscribed after the 1173–74 revolt.[62] Ideas that Marie Antoinette was similarly ruled not by idealized maternal feelings but by a powerhungry self-interest clearly prepared the 1793 charges of incest with her younger son; just as vile was a pamphleteer's 1789 claim that she poisoned her elder son, who died in that year.[63] (Plausibly echoing this tale, the Keralio frontispiece prominently displays a dead infant in the foreground.[64]) A woman so lacking in maternal virtue that she could kill a long-awaited son to give her self-interest rein through perverted ascendancy over his brother, surely could not properly nurture *la Nation*. As pamphlets repeatedly claimed, Marie Antoinette had to destroy the Revolution to save the monarchy; as the prostitute-queen had dominated an impotent husband, she must control her son by any means available.[65]

Whether or not the pollution associated with queens' bodies was phrased in sexual terms, its relevance surpassed the sexual. Within their husbands' realms, queens were often seen as foreign intruders, and both Eleanor of Aquitaine and Marie Antoinette have been cast in this mold: Eleanor as a cultural colonizer from the permissive South, Marie Antoinette from France's hereditary enemy, Austria. The latter was seen to import alien customs, wrecking Versailles's networks of etiquette to enjoy the less protocol-ridden life of the Viennese court. The nobility's status-affirming ceremonial roles were menaced by her dislike of formality and her abolition, as queen, of many customary court usages. Her upstart minions ousted the nobility from privileged access to her; in the 1770s and 1780s, these piqued patricians invented the tales of her love affairs.[66] Her few cultural interests were significant: she brought the Austrian composer Gluck to Paris and promoted his works over those of the Parisian favorite, Piccini.[67] By wearing muslin or lawn dresses from the Austrian Netherlands, she appeared to be out to enrich Habsburg subjects and ruin the silk weavers of Lyon.[68] In short, she was colonizing France as an outpost of her own culture. Even sexual rumors about her stressed her alien body: eighteenth-century France knew lesbianism as "the German vice." The epithet "l'Autrichienne"("the Austrian woman") included a robust pun— "chienne" means "bitch"—that implied a bodily mutation echoed in Revolutionary prints that imposed her head on a harpy's body or made her part of a hybrid mammal: Louis as a horned goat, she as a wolf with Medusa-like serpentine locks adorned by Junoesque peacock plumes. Also likened to a monkey, tigress, panther, spider, and vampire, her body became alien to the human race itself as well as geopolitically foreign.[69] Related charges against her climaxed in 1793, when she was accused of plotting to dismember France itself and give to Austria the duchy of Lorraine, her father's original inheritance.[70]

Many authors offer a similar cultural critique of Eleanor of Aquitaine by arguing the history of northern Frankish disdain for Occitan morals.[71] But while Eleanor's status as an in-marryer at the Capetian and Angevin courts was complex, as Pappano shows in this volume, explicit contemporary associations between Eleanor's behavior and her Occitan origins are lacking.[72] Bernard of Clairvaux's much-quoted letter to the noble Sophia shows that his opinion of ornate aristocratic ladies' dress was similar to the eleventh-century chronicler Raoul Glaber's report of the strange clothes worn by the Provençal retinue of Constance of Arles (d. 1032), third wife of Robert II of France (r. 996–1031): such raiment bespoke a moral laxity that menaced the purity of Robert's court. *Pace* Eleanor's biographer Alison Weir, however, Bernard did not link such display to Eleanor, nor the South, when in his letter to Sophia he savaged contemporary fashion, referring to ladies mincing about in rich attire as "daughters of Belial."[73]

The author of the *Epitoma vitae Rotberti Regis,* an adulatory life of Constance of Arles's husband, further criticized her for the greed that was seen to underlie her management of royal wealth, especially the jewels and bodily ornaments over which she exercised special vigilance.[74] Such critiques can link Constance and Eleanor through queens' shared attentiveness to ornament and attire. Splendor was as much a tool of rulership as armed force or largesse, and since Carolingian times a queen's duty to assure courtly grandeur, linked to her responsibilities as royal housekeeper and manager of royal wealth, associated her with the maintenance of fitting splendor in royal attire. In Constance's day, the scope of a queen's activities was extended by her control and allocation of royal wealth, but by Eleanor's time, as noted above, male officials were assuming the control of such treasure. To regain lost ground, queens perhaps more ardently exploited traditional associations with splendor: as in the reclothing episode in Chrétien's *Erec and Enide,* royal wives' dress was expected to reflect regal wealth and power. Significantly, this episode is prepared when Erec, a king's son, insists that only Queen Guenevere can rightly give his bride, Enide, the rich robes that will properly adorn her at Arthur's court.[75] But the image of a queen as guardian of dignity and display was easily turned to criticism. If a clerical author wished to praise kingly largesse, he might depict queenly thrift as greed, or preoccupation with adornment as vanity, as Glaber implied for Constance of Arles. Insistence on attire suited to royal dignity could also appear as vanity, whether at the hands of a cleric praising pious sobriety as in Bernard's "daughters of Belial" letter, or one lauding a virtuous king's austerity: one of Louis IX's clerical eulogists used an exchange on this topic between Louis and his wife to stress Louis's rational response to what the writer implied was her vainglory.[76] Evidence for Eleanor of Aquitaine's raiment is admittedly slight: the first Pipe Roll of Henry II's reign notes in 1154–55 the huge sum of £100 for a robe (a full outfit, not one garment) for her, but consistent information is unavailable. Chroniclers do not remark her ostentation in dress, unlike that of the upstart Thomas Becket, whose rich dress as chancellor was noted in contrast to the plain garb Henry II favored. Such comparisons suggest that Eleanor's dress was sufficiently compatible with her rank as to merit no remark or that she, like other queens, was so eclipsed by her husband that her attire went unnoticed. But with her taste for power and informed political instincts, it is unlikely that she would have ignored so ready a means to advertise her status, especially given the wealth she could draw from her inheritance. There is food for thought in W.L. Warren's suggestion that Henry delegated not to the queen but to Becket the task of advertising regal splendor.[77]

In Constance of Arles's case, then, a focus on bodily adornment implied foreignness, greed, and moral laxity. Eleanor's childless years with Louis VII could have left her, too, an unsubdued alien, exposed to insinuations that adornment proved her desire to attract the opposite sex. If, as Henry II's wife, she tried to proclaim her status through her clothing, her efforts would not appear to have met with enough success to merit the chroniclers' attention. But even if critics did not exploit bodily adornment to conjure a queen's alien status, such factors could serve her ill: tales of Marie Antoinette's lavish spending on jewels convinced many that her invented role in the Diamond Necklace Affair—including a midnight tryst with a cardinal in the palace gardens—was genuine.[78]

If Marie Antoinette's initial childlessness and reputed misdeeds made her a vehicle to assail a feeble monarchy, we must ask why portrayals of Eleanor of Aquitaine turned her into an immoral consort who, like her successor in France six centuries later, could appear as an emasculating threat to Angevin power in England. Modern historians occupy a vantage point from which to appreciate the long-term results of Henry's judicial and administrative reforms. But from that same vantage point, it appears that as those reforms controversially furthered the growth of royal power, many in England saw a potential for tyranny; King John's abuse of the system Henry initiated would affirm the ruinous results if a devious king controlled the administration. Modern scholars who focus on changes in England, moreover, often ignore Henry's failure to maintain control in his and Eleanor's continental domains, or to stave off the Capetian threat, facilitated by his sons' jealousies, that dominated the last years of Henry's reign. Gerald of Wales reported Henry's last words—"Let the rest go as it will. I care no more for myself, nor for aught in this world," and "Shame, shame on a conquered king!"—to imply that Gerald did not see Henry's reign as an unqualified success.[79]

Such attitudes could have favored Eleanor's emergence in the chroniclers' pages as a means to criticize Angevin power. As Tolhurst notes, Gerald of Wales is among the earliest English chroniclers to give a markedly negative portrayal of Eleanor; such unflattering portrayals increase in her sons' reigns, when her profile was higher than in Henry II's time and as John's erratic behavior bedeviled English political life; Tolhurst sees the chroniclers' representations of Eleanor in these years as fostering a noticeable decline in her reputation.[80] Later English chroniclers did not overlook the tactic of commenting adversely on queens to criticize their husbands' rule. The thirteenth-century writer Matthew Paris (d. 1259), for example, often assailed Henry III (r. 1216–72) by censuring the Queen Eleanor of his own day, Henry's beautiful but (in many eyes) politically overactive Provençal wife (d. 1291).[81] Matthew's attitude toward the beauteous but intrusive Eleanor of Provence and toward Eleanor of Aquitaine, whom he described as lovely while noting that she might have incited her sons' revolt against Henry II,[82] links the two queens' transgressive desires through their beauty and foregrounds queenly desire's role in gendered constructions of sovereignty.

Thus a primary attribute of the tales about Eleanor of Aquitaine and Marie Antoinette is their use of the queens' bodies to "prove" disagreeable truths about royal governance.[83] Regardless of her beauty, Eleanor of Aquitaine's vast inheritance, divorce, and remarriage were bound to attract comment. Chroniclers made her transfer of Aquitaine to Henry a sign of her lust for him, though we must ask if he desired her beauty or her domains (and vice versa); Louis VII's ardor for Eleanor had reputedly exposed him to her sexual scorn. Her case thus suggests fresh nuances to the resonances of queenly desire. Eleanor's inheritance complicated the question, noted by Pappano, of a queen's sovereign desire: Aquitaine invested what were seen as Eleanor's whims with meanings lacking in other queens' desires. The defeat at Mount Cadmos, for example, was legendarily linked to

Geoffrey de Rançon's fealty to Eleanor as countess of Poitou and the favor she showed him as *her* vassal, not Louis VII's.[84] And since, as noted earlier, Eleanor's wish to help fellow Poitevins at Antioch may have had a central role in the events there in 1148, such conflicting loyalties between herself and Louis could have figured as importantly in the collapse of their marriage as did any personal problems between them. Given Elizabeth A.R. Brown's suggestion that Eleanor may have incited her sons against Henry II because he excluded her in 1173 from the count of Toulouse's homage, which she saw as her due as duchess of Aquitaine, such rivalries could have undermined her relationship with Henry as much as they may have troubled her first marriage. Or, to return to Lois Huneycutt's point, any ambitions Eleanor's domains nourished, and their contribution to her poor marital relationships, would have deepened her inability to profit from the intercessor's compliant role.[85] Marie Antoinette's alleged plan to give Lorraine to Austria is a helpful contrast: if her imagined crimes could acquire territorial associations even though she had no hereditary right in Lorraine as Eleanor had in Aquitaine, the duchess of Aquitaine's supposed desires were all the more readily associated with a lack of national fidelity linked to her foreignness.[86] Another example, noted in this volume, is Eleanor's creation of a royal mausoleum at Fontevraud, which Charles Wood sees as honoring her own lineage rather than the Angevin house. Here we see, again, the substance her inheritance could give to the actions that manifested her desires. In creating this mausoleum, moreover, Eleanor initiated a tradition of some significance to later queens. Few of these women enjoyed the inherited resources Eleanor could deploy, but they could use the burial practices she inaugurated to assert their lineages and kindred against their children's appropriation to patriarchal royal ends. Such dissent by queens from an ideally passive biogenetic role suggests just the kind of resistance to passivity Pappano associates with the complexities inherent in queens' sovereign desires.[87]

If a queen's childlessness could signify resistance through related images of unsubdued foreignness, adultery, or unnatural maternity—incestuous, infanticidal, or parricidal—her desiring, (non)reproducing body itself could appear as a site of resistance to male authority. A childless consort could not claim a place within a body politic imagined as male; failure stressed an alienness unsubjugated to the king's authority. If this unsubdued alien betrayed her marriage or mocked the king's sexual powers (or was thought to do so), she had ridiculed, even feminized, the male frame that embodied, protected, and invigorated the realm.[88] A queen's childlessness could, then, imply not only regal impotence or queenly infertility, with all the dangerous assumptions that might surround either situation. As in Queen Sanchia of Naples's case, it could also imply pious (or in other cases, profane) resistance to marital relations and, by extension, to male authority—perilous images for a couple who figured divine models of community to their subjects.[89] Medieval queens knew how much in their lives hinged on producing an heir. Childless queens menaced with divorce, like Philip Augustus's first wife Isabelle of Hainaut in 1184, fought to stay at their lords' sides to prove their fertility, asserting their desiring bodies in ways that implied resistance to royal wishes even as the women sought to re-inscribe themselves as submissive wives.[90] Such resistance could also be portrayed as an inversion of the natural sexual order. Marie Antoinette's maternity was depicted as infanticidal and incestuous to stress the threat of her return to an improper political dominance. The perils represented by the queen who openly named Louis XVI's marital torpor, and allegedly turned to infanticide and incest to assure an impure political dominance, are manifest in a Revolutionary print in which she delightedly straddles a male partner who lies prone beneath her.[91] As belief in Eleanor of Aquitaine's reputed remark on Louis VII's monkishness implied his sexual inferiority to her, her inheritance could have suggested that she might put herself "on top" politically. Madeline Caviness points to a plausible visual clue to Aquitaine's place in Eleanor's political thinking: the east window she donated in the cathedral at Poitiers, her chief residence as countess of Poitou. At the window's base, it is her body, not Henry II's, that occupies the more prestigious position in the composition, to the viewer's left of the cross the pair are donating—the site usually reserved to the male as legitimate powerholder. Eleanor's alleged ridicule of Louis VII would have furthered belief in her adultery; such tales made her the more active and hence masculinized sexual partner, again threatening the male ruler's feminization. Eleanor only improbably considered pitting herself against Louis VII: for one thing, she had no Capetian son to enlist as she evidently, and necessarily, inveigled her Angevin sons against Henry II. But with Elizabeth A.R. Brown's suggestion that the queen incited her sons' revolt after Henry excluded her from the count of Toulouse's homage, we again confront Aquitaine's role in her political thinking. Certainly she was fleeing there when Henry's men captured her in 1173.[92]

In Eleanor's case, with queenly desire openly expressed in ways easily construed as resistant or transgressive, with queenly whims afforded substance or even autonomy by her domains, we may well ask about her subjects' responses. In the literary text Pappano discusses, Arthur upsets the management of courtly desire by not rewarding Lanval with his other knights. But as in the life of William Marshal Evelyn Mullally discusses, Eleanor could bestow gifts independently of Henry.[93] Unfettered by the need to transform desire for herself into a likeness of desiring the king, Eleanor could attract desire to herself. In this sense, she played perilously at transgressing the limits of desire for the king as

distinct from desire for herself. Such desire is explicit in a much-quoted
t   w   e   l   f   t   h   -
century *minnesing:*

> Were all the world mine
> From the sea unto the Rhine,
> Its loss to me would be no harm
> If the queen of England
> Lay within my arms.[94]

A wishful admission that Eleanor's intimacy could equal "all the world . . .
from the sea unto the Rhine" aligns her lordship with the desires she attracted. More specifically, if less provocatively, queenly desire as expressed
in (imagined) adultery foregrounds a failure to transform desire for her
into desire for the king and the effects this had on her role in shaping relationships of domination and subordination for the realm at large. A king
who, like Arthur in Lanval, cannot foreclose desire for the queen by managing her desires as well as his subjects', cannot focus loyalty on himself nor
control resistant elements within his realm. Eleanor's case, like Marie Antoinette's, shows that this was a sovereign dilemma in life as well as literature. If Henry II could not limit the whims manifest in Eleanor's actions,
which referentially suggested such bodily yearnings as the tales about her
implied, he could not be expected to control his realm. Louis XVI's failure to impregnate Marie Antoinette and to control her transgressive behavior reflected a political impotence parallelled by the sexual incapacities
her derogatory remark appeared to confirm.

Clearly, royal wives and politics were a hazardous combination, and
such women could be drawn into such situations without being politically
active themselves: as vehicles for commentary, they served the interests of
royal adherents and critics alike. Consequently, while the tales discussed
here add nothing to what is known of either queen's life, they can suggest
much about the societies that invented and received them, and especially
about attitudes toward women who might wield power and the ways in
which they were seen to do so. Tales of Eleanor's adultery might have
served to mitigate the threat to Capetian interests that arose from the
Angevin and Aquitanian inheritances' union but, as the tales first appear in
English works, it seems that her body became a blank canvas on which
English writers inscribed anxieties as Henry II's reforms fueled the growth
of royal power. William of Newburgh tells us only superficially of Eleanor's
immoral longings. His tale will have had its genesis not in her sonless marriage to Louis VII, but in her fecundity with Henry II: ironically, her body
threatened England and France only when she and Henry II did produce

that clutch of sons, heirs to burgeoning royal power, whose legitimacy might be clouded by tales of her adultery. Marie Antoinette's initial failure to produce an heir entrenched belief in Louis XVI's impotence, and her children's presumed bastardy challenged the need to preserve an untainted royal line. Her remark on Louis XVI's apathy, and Eleanor's alleged complaint about Louis VII, contrasted supposedly disinterested or impotent kings to other men who might satisfy the queens, and compared an overly pious king to more profane men—or a failing monarchy to sturdier forms of government.

As Lynn Hunt's study of the calumnies against Marie Antoinette shows, times of change or crisis focus attention on the bodies of the eminent or powerful.[95] Marie Antoinette's experience was more obviously crisis-related than Eleanor's, but both women lived during cultural and political shifts that profoundly influenced portrayals of women and women's roles. Such scrutiny and criticism of the queens' bodies offers a key to the similar tales about them: despite the six centuries between them, and notwithstanding that hardly any of these tales rest on reliable evidence, the two queens are linked by the precarious relationship between women's sexual bodies and the body politic. The twelfth and eighteenth centuries reimagined that body to privilege the male frame and the female body was made intrusive and threatening, to be subjected and excluded.[96] The most visible of women, queens suffered especially: all wives were directed to the domestic sphere, but queens remained inescapably exposed, examined, and exploited.[97] But if tales about these queens implied their children's bastardy, the tales' ultimate aims were dissimilar in one significant respect. Those about Eleanor addressed one royal lineage's hold on power but did not dispute a fundamental link between power and lineage. In the eighteenth century, that link remained vital only to royal ideologies; it had to be ended if the Revolution were to succeed. The upheavals of the late eighteenth century ensured that the tales about Marie Antoinette more surely subverted Bourbon authority than those about Eleanor of Aquitaine had loosened the Angevin hold on power, but the tales' primary ground remains the complex relationship between the body politic and the body of a male powerholder's wife. True, in the last analysis such tales probably would not have arisen had either woman borne a son soon after she married: Eleanor and Louis VII might not have divorced, and Louis XVI's impotence would not have been imagined. But that later historians could damn these two women for the years when they didn't have children, and that contemporaries damned them when they did, again highlights the fragile position of a male powerholder's wife, which remains brittle even today (and not only in hereditary monarchies).

Stefan Zweig's flawed study of Marie Antoinette created new tales for old, but he was at least able to look beyond royalist hagiography and republican calumnies of the nineteenth and early twentieth centuries to steer a new course, and subtitled his work "The Portrait of an Ordinary Woman."[98] Observing the invention and reception of legends that such eminent women as Marie Antoinette or Eleanor of Aquitaine attracted, and setting their lives within the contexts of the societies that created and received such illusive accretions, are primary requisites to shaping fresh understandings of their motives, decisions, and actions. No one will sensibly call Eleanor of Aquitaine ordinary, but stripping away the legendary overlays to her life, and considering how and why they arose, are the first steps on a path whose exploration has been long delayed.

Notes

Bonnie Wheeler, Jo Goyne, Elizabeth A.R. Brown, Peggy McCracken, and Mark Ormrod read this chapter in preparation and offered helpful suggestions. Any oversights are my own responsibility.

1. On Cunegunde, AASS March 1:265–80; Glaber, *Five Books of Histories,* pp. 94–96; *Vitae Henrici et Cunegundis Imperatorum,* pp. 787–828; Klauser, *Der Heinrichs—und Kunegundenkult;* Elliott, *Spiritual Marriage,* index at p. 359 s.v. "Cunegund (empress)." On Edward the Confessor and Edith, Stafford, *Queens, Concubines and Dowagers,* p. 165, and *Queen Emma and Queen Edith,* pp. 72–73, 260–65. On Margaret of Anjou, Lee, "Reflections of Power," 183–217; Dunn, "Margaret of Anjou," 199–217; Chamberlayne, "Crowns and Virgins," pp. 47–68, and "Margaret of Anjou," pp. 107–43; and Maurer, "Margaret of Anjou." On Sanchia of Naples, see Musto, "Queen Sanchia," pp. 179–214. For Empress Constance, van Cleve, *Emperor Frederick II,* ch. 1, pp. 13–37; Kantorowicz, *Frederick the Second,* pp. 3–5, and Abulafia, *Frederick II,* pp. 89–90.

2. Standard monographs used here are Zweig, *Marie Antoinette;* Castelot, *Queen of France;* and Cronin, *Louis and Antoinette.* Lever, *Marie-Antoinette,* offers fresh record evidence but fails to address questions of gender and politics. Isabelle comtesse de Paris, *Moi, Marie-Antoinette,* imagines the queen's self-examination in her last hours. My thanks to Bonnie Wheeler for drawing my attention to Lever, and to Jeremy du Q. Adams for lending me his copy of the countess's work.

3. Zweig thought the marriage was unconsummated for seven years as Louis feared the circumcision needed to correct matters. The surgery was performed and the marriage consummated in 1777 after the queen's brother, Emperor Joseph II, visited Versailles to stiffen Louis's resolve (*Marie Antoinette,* ch. 2 [pp. 21–31], ch. 11 [pp. 125–35], and ch. 12 [pp. 136–43]). Belloc, *Marie Antoinette,* pp. 102–03, 136–37, 539–42, hinted at some such problem in terms that prove he knew of the Spanish envoy's 1774 letter. But

in 1909 Belloc clearly felt it impossible to print the details Zweig gave in 1932.

4. Cronin, *Louis and Antoinette,* p. 406. Louis XVI was medically examined several times after marriage. One verdict was that intercourse "depended on the young prince's volition; no physical obstacle would stand in the way when his mind was made up." Scrutiny in 1772 revealed something described as common in teenagers that required no surgery (probably a tight frenum). Examination in 1775 disclosed "a lack of self-confidence, fear and childish timidity [and] a cold, late-blooming temperament." Louis may have feared that relations weakened the male body (Lever, *Marie Antoinette,* pp. 40–41, 92, 108–09). There is no proof he ever had such an operation, which for an adult demands several days' bedrest. His diary shows he never stopped horseback riding in spring or summer 1777, a pastime impossible just after adult circumcision (Cronin, *Louis and Antoinette,* pp. 406–09; Lever, pp. 92–93). Neither the queen's letters to her mother, nor the latter's to her envoy, refer to surgery in 1777; nor does Louis's December 21, 1777, letter to Joseph II imply surgery (Baccque, *Body Politic,* p. 44: "I am sure of having done what is necessary . . . [S]ince your trip, things have gotten better and better until a perfect conclusion").

5. Zweig never cited two letters available to him in which Marie Antoinette told her mother, empress Maria Theresa, that she believed her marriage was consummated on the night of July 21–22, 1773, and that Louis XV was informed (texts in Cronin, *Louis and Antoinette,* Appendix B at pp. 409–11; Lever, *Marie Antoinette,* pp. 40–41). Admittedly, the 1773 letters state only her belief that the union was consummated but, regardless, Zweig suppressed them. As with his omission of the Spanish envoy's retraction of his 1774 letter (text above) and his suppression of crucial portions of Joseph II's letter (text below), Zweig's failure to give such evidence its due cannot be overlooked.

6. Cronin, *Louis and Antoinette,* pp. 406–09, suggests the Austrian envoy spread the phimosis story to blame the king for the pair's childlessness. Intriguing in this diplomatic context is a 1758 report from Louis XV's envoy to Russia that Grand Duke Peter, heir to that throne, had a physical impediment to intercourse that could be amended by the same procedure Louis XVI allegedly underwent. The envoy doubted if Peter had consummated his marriage to the future Catherine II who, after years of marriage, almost certainly needed outside help in 1754 to conceive the future Paul I. (The accepted account is that Peter's aunt, Empress Elizabeth, urged Catherine to take a lover and conceive an heir [McGrew, *Paul I,* pp. 22–26]). Similarities between the 1758 French report and the 1774 Spanish letter on Louis XVI are hard to ignore. Cf. a 1778 report to Versailles that the homosexual Gustavus III of Sweden pushed an aide into his wife's bed to gain an heir (Lever, *Marie Antoinette,* p. 118), and the brutal diplomatic speculation on whether Francis II of France could father a child (Fraser, *Mary, Queen of Scots,* pp. 65, 94–95).

7. Zweig, *Marie Antoinette,* p. 130.

8. Bernier, *Secrets of Marie Antoinette,* pp. 217–18. As early as May 2, 1777, Joseph had given Leopold a less detailed version of this explanation for Louis's lack of conjugal success (Bernier, *Secretss of Marie Antoinette,* p. 216).

9. Louis's disinterest in women was noted early on (Castelot, *Queen of France,* pp. 9, 27; Cronin, *Louis and Antoinette,* p. 407; Baccque, *Body Politic,* pp. 39–44, 48; Hunt, "Bodies of Marie Antoinette," p. 116. For theories on his apathy, see Cronin, *Louis and Antoinette,* pp. 49–50, 157; Lever, *Marie Antoinette,* pp. 108–09 (" . . . fumblers"); for other versions of Joseph's phrase, Baccque, *The Body Politic,* p. 44; Cronin, *Louis and Antoinette,* pp. 158, 408 ("laziness . . . apathy"). For the queen's youth at Maria Theresa's court, her prudery and low sex drive, Bernier, *Secretss of Marie Antoinette,* pp. 12, 78, and (for the 1777 quote) 216, and Bernier, *Words of Fire,* p. 56. The queen wanted children but was happy when Louis left off relations in her first pregnancy, and she resumed them only months after that birth (Lever, *Marie Antoinette,* pp. 114, 124, 127); she slept alone for months after a 1783 miscarriage, and was gloomy in her 1784–85 pregnancy (pp. 156, 161). She was so distressed at the early signs of her last pregnancy, later in 1785, that her doctors delayed confirming it (Lever, *Marie Antoinette,* p. 183).

10. A diplomatic report to Vienna says that the battle was won at ten A.M. on August 18, 1777. For this report and her letter to her mother of August 30, 1777, stating that victory was achieved more than a week before and that Louis had repeated the effort on August 29, see Lever, *Marie Antoinette,* p. 112 (dating the letter August 29; all other works give August 30 [full text with that date in Bernier, *Secrets of Marie Antoinette,* pp. 223–24]). The date August 18 is doubtful. On August 19, the queen told her mother: " . . . my own state . . . is unfortunately always the same . . . But I do not despair; there is a slight improvement, which is that the king is more eager than before . . ." (Bernier, *Secrets of Marie Antoinette,* pp. 222–23). Zweig, *Marie Antoinette* [1933], p. 136, significantly varies this sentence: "As regards my virgin state, it is unfortunately still the same . . ." In the original, Zweig inserted "jungfräulicher" parenthetically (*Marie Antoinette* [1932; 1961], p. 135); his English translators made it integral to the sentence. As the queen's letter of August 30 states the battle was won more than a week earlier, and as she reported no change on August 19, a likelier date is between August 20 and 22. Zweig [1933], p. 136, cites the Spanish envoy's letter giving August 25, but the queen's report must be preferred. She told her reader of her new situation late in 1777 (Campan, *Memoirs,* p. 127).

11. The children arrived in December 1778; October 1781; March 1785; and July 1786; she miscarried in 1780 and November 1783 (von Isenburg-Büdingen and von Loringhoven, *Stammtafeln,* 1.2, tafel 7). Bernier, *Secrets of Marie Antoinette,* pp. 275–76, gives Maria Theresa's letter of August 1, 1779, noting the queen's letter of "the sixteenth"(presumably July), and reading in part: " . . . all our fine hopes are gone; and I must admit that I really counted on them. Nothing is lost; you are both very young, in good health, and you love

one another, so it will easily be made up . . . Thank God you had no hemorrhage, inconvenience or weakness!" Bernier gives no letter from the queen of July 16, 1779, but the empress's words imply that the letter of that date had reported a miscarriage. This would appear to be the pregnancy ended by the queen's exertion in closing a carriage window (Campan, *Memoirs*, p. 141).

12. Martindale, "Eleanor of Aquitaine," pp. 17–50, is most helpful; Brown, chapter 1 in this volume, notes that most monographs on Eleanor are imaginative or romanticizing. Works used for this chapter include Kelly, *Eleanor and the Four Kings*; Meade, *Eleanor of Aquitaine*; Owen, *Eleanor of Aquitaine*; and Weir, *Eleanor of Aquitaine*.

13. Lewis, chapter 7 in this volume. For Constance's daughters, see Baldwin, *Philip Augustus*, pp. 19–20, and Kessler, *Richard I*, p. 31. On Adela of Champagne's daughter Agnes, see Baldwin, p. 536 n46, follows earlier accounts and dates Agnes's birth at 1166 or later, for which there is no reliable evidence; her birth may only have been portrayed as following that of the future Philip II in August 1165. LoPrete, "Adela of Blois," p. 317, sees Stephen of Blois's large family by Adela of Normandy as a sign of sexual compatibility between spouses. On Louis VII's affection for Eleanor, see John of Salisbury, *Historia Pontificalis*, pp. 53 ("licet [rex] reginam affectu fere immoderato diligeret"), 61 ("[rex] reginam uehementer amabat et fere puerili modo").

14. Baccque, *Body Politic*, pp. 29–75 and plates 1–4; Castelot, *Queen of France*, pp. 109, 120; Cronin, *Louis and Antoinette*, pp. 129–30, 163; Campan, *Memoirs*, pp. 89–90. See also Hunt, "Bodies of Marie Antoinette," pp. 108–30.

15. On Adelaide, see Nolan, "Queen's Body and Institutional Memory," pp. 249–67.

16. Brown, chapter one in this volume.

17. She called Louis "the poor man" in a 1775 letter to an Austrian count, who showed it to Maria Theresa who, with Joseph II, scolded the queen sharply enough to ensure she would not repeat herself. Whether or not the letter was widely known, a popular song had her calling Louis "a sorry lout"(Castelot, *Queen of France*, pp. 102–04; Bernier, *Secrets of Marie Antoinette*, pp. 171–72 [Maria Theresa to the queen, 30 July 1775). For the queen's 1777 remark, see Castelot, p. 124, and Lever, *Marie Antoinette*, p. 94 (noting a duke's offer to lend Louis his mistress). For the availability of prints and leaflets at Versailles and the queen's awareness of them, Lever, *Marie Antoinette*, p. 64; Zweig, *Marie Antoinette*, p. 152; Campan, *Memoirs*, p. 136.

18. William of Newburgh, *Historia rerum Anglicarum*, 1:128–29: " . . . illa [regina] maxime moribus regiis offensa et causante se monacho non regi nupsisse. Dicitur etiam quod in ipso regis Francorum conjugio ad ducis Normannici nuptias suis magis moribus congruas aspiravit . . ." On the date of the *Historia*, see Gransden, *Historical Writing*, p. 263.

19. This most familiar of Marie Antoinette's legends was perhaps inspired by Louis XVI's aunt Victoire (1733–99), who once heard the people lacked bread and said, "But if only they could resign themselves to eating

piecrust!" (Castelot, *Queen of France,* p. 26). Rousseau ascribed a like remark
to "a great Princess" who, given the date of his work, cannot have been
Marie Antoinette (Lever, *Marie Antoinette,* p. 224 n1 [at pp. 325–26]).

20. Martindale, "Eleanor of Aquitaine," pp. 40–42, notes at 41 n49 this "build-
up of anti-Angevin propaganda, completed as late as 1216." Cf. the
chronology of critical chronicle references to Eleanor noted by Tolhurst,
chapter 15 in this volume.

21. Brown, chapter 1 in this volume; Bullough, "Medieval Medical and Scientific Views," 485–501; Parsons, "Pregnant Queen," p. 44 (see also Ortner,
"Gender and Sexuality in Hierarchical Societies," p. 384).

22. Cronin, *Louis and Antoinette,* pp. 136–37, 158, and Bernier, *Secress of Marie
Antoinette,* p. 216 (Joseph II to Grand Duke Leopold, June 9, 1777: "Her
virtue is intact, even strict, but less through forethought than inborn dis-
position"). For her love of flattery, see Lever, *Marie Antoinette,* p. 91, and
Castelot, *Queen of France,* p. 127. On Fersen, see Loomis, *Fatal Friendship.*
There is no doubt of Fersen's place in her affections, but their letters, and
much of his journal, were destroyed by Fersen himself or made illegible by
his heirs after expurgated texts were printed in the nineteenth century.
Current consensus is that if they ever were lovers, it was for one night in
February 1792 (Zweig, *Marie Antoinette,* pp. 237–47; Castelot, *Queen of
France,* pp. 176–88 at 182; Cronin, *Louis and Antoinette,* pp. 343–44; Lever,
Marie Antoinette, p. 272).

23. The bishop mentioned neither incidents nor persons (Brundage, chapter 9
in this volume). On Bishop Geoffrey (de la Roche-Vanneau) of Langres's
relations with Bernard (who administered Geoffrey's diocese during the
crusade), see Colloque de Lyon-Cîteaux-Dijon, *Bernard de Clairvaux,* pp.
56, 96, 121, 357, 392, 532, 538. On Geoffrey and the crusade, see Odo of
Deuil, *De Profectione Ludovici VII,* p. 6 n4. On Bernard's approval of the divorce, see Meade, *Eleanor of Aquitaine,* p. 148; Owen, *Eleanor of Aquitaine,*
p. 31; Weir, *Eleanor of Aquitaine,* pp. 87–88. Weir, p. 77, says Eleanor was "the
subject of defamatory rumors" before the divorce but typically cites at p.
77 n6, as if contemporary and authoritative, the English chronicler
Matthew Paris (d. 1259).

24. Parsons, *Eleanor of Castile,* pp. 226–31. That there were no friars in Eleanor
of Aquitaine's lifetime disproves the allegation, but significance attaches to
the allegation that the "friar" was a foreigner.

25. On Andreas's unreliability on the "courts of love," and imaginings of
Eleanor's sex life based thereon, see Brown and Pappano in this volume.
The great proponent of Andreas's work as indicative of Eleanor's love life
is Kelly: see her "Eleanor of Aquitaine and Her Courts of Love," 3–19, and
Eleanor and the Four Kings, pp. 157–67; Meade, *Eleanor of Aquitaine,* pp.
251–54, sees the "courts" as attacks on male supremacy; but in addition to
Brown and Pappano, cf. Owen, *Eleanor of Aquitaine,* pp. 152–56, and Weir,
Eleanor of Aquitaine, pp. 181–82.

26. See the evolution of accounts of Eleanor's part in the Second Crusade and in particular of events at Antioch in McCracken in chapter 12 and Tolhurst in chapter 15 of this volume.

27. Adulterous royal wives were given short shrift in medieval Europe. In 1314, two of Philip IV of France's daughters-in-law were imprisoned when their affair with two Norman knights was revealed. The third daughter-in-law was imprisoned as she allegedly knew of the others' offense and had not reported it; presumably as she was heir to the county of Burgundy, her husband (later Philip V) was eventually allowed to reunite with her (McCracken, *Romance of Adultery*, pp. 171–75 and references at p. 171 n1). In a twelfth-century Hungarian case known to Louis VII and Eleanor, a Kievan-born queen of Hungary allegedly caught *in flagrante* was repatriated; her son was denied a claim to the Hungarian throne (Odo of Deuil, *De Profectione Ludovici VII,* pp. 34–39; Bak, "Queens as Scapegoats," p. 226. Llywelyn ap Iorwerth of Wales (d. 1240) repudiated his wife Joan (d. 1238, King John's bastard daughter) and hanged her lover (*Calendar of Ancient Correspondence Concerning Wales,* pp. 51–52). Count Philip I of Flanders (d. 1191) hanged his wife's alleged lover in a cesspit (Duby, *Le Chevalier, la Femme et le Prêtre,* p. 215—omitted from the English version). In some cases, political reasons likely prompted adultery charges. It was almost certainly for this reason that Lothar II of Germany accused his wife Teutburg of adultery when trying to repudiate her in the 850s and 860s, to wed his concubine Waldrade (Airlie, "Private Bodies and the Body Politic," 12).

28. Martindale, "Eleanor of Aquitaine," p. 40, suggests Eleanor wanted to help her uncle and other Poitevins at Antioch. John of Salisbury's account of the royal pair's visit to the papal court stresses papal prohibition of discussion of the couple's kinship, with no reference to adultery (Brundage, chapter 9 in this volume), implying that what came between them was not Eleanor's sexual conduct but her reference to the marriage's canonical status; cf. McCracken, chapter 12 in this volume. John of Salisbury's source for the events at Antioch was possibly Thierry Galeran, the eunuch Eleanor had mocked and the only individual John names among Louis's advisors as the king addressed Eleanor's actions at Antioch. John's quote from Ovid's *Heroides,* as discussed in this volume in chapter 16 by Pappano, "Marie de France, Aliénor d'Aquitaine," may or may not be a coded reference to incest between Eleanor and Raymond. It may be merely a clerical display of classical knowledge; Thierry could have used it when he gave John his version of events, or John could have added it as he wrote his account.

29. Brundage and Bouchard in this volume. Weir, *Eleanor of Aquitaine,* pp. 67–70, cites John of Salisbury's early version of the queen's reference to her blood kinship with Louis, but Weir takes as factual the suspect elaboration in late twelfth- and thirteenth-century reports of events at Antioch, failing to note that that this elaboration appears in English works, not French. At pp. 67–68, Weir takes as reliable later, oblique remarks by William of Tyre, Gervase of Canterbury, and Richard of Devizes, none of whom says that

Eleanor and Raymond were lovers, and concludes that Eleanor did commit incest since "all . . . reliable contemporary evidence" points to her wandering eye at this time; but at p. 91, Weir says no contemporary evidence supports later twelfth-century claims that Louis VII "repudiated [sic]" Eleanor for adultery. Kelly, *Eleanor and the Four Kings*, pp. 60–63, reaches no definite conclusion on the events at Antioch; Meade, *Eleanor of Aquitaine*, pp. 107–08, says only that Louis suspected the queen and Raymond were lovers; Owen, *Eleanor of Aquitaine*, pp. 24–25, cites only John of Salisbury on Louis's suspicions about the relationship (which Owen does not see as adulterous) and Eleanor's assertion of a consanguineous marriage.

30. McCracken, "Scandalizing Desire." While William of Tyre's account implies that Eleanor adulterated her marriage before and after the stay in Antioch, he no more explicitly names her liaison with Raymond than does John of Salisbury.

31. Pappano, "Marie de France, Aliénor d'Aquitaine"; for canon law on affinity caused by fornication, Brundage, *Law, Sex and Christian Society*, pp. 194–95, 356–57. Perhaps for this reason, Richard I later claimed Henry II had seduced Richard's betrothed, Alice of France: such an affair would have established affinity between Richard and Alice that would have made marriage impossible (*Chronica Monasterii de Melsa* 1:256: "[Ricardus] publicabat Henricum dudum patrem suum dum ipsam Alician in sua custodia retinerat, de ea unam filiam sed jam mortuam procreasse"). On the veracity of Richard's claim cf. Kessler, *Richard I*, pp. 29–45. On incest producing monstrous children, see Warnecke, *Anne Boleyn*, pp. 191–233. Warnecke rightly argues that such beliefs were common, but my citation does not endorse her contested application of them to Anne Boleyn's case.

32. Martindale, "Eleanor of Aquitaine," pp. 40–42 at 41 n49, notes that Giraldus and Walter Map give different accounts of Eleanor's affair with Geoffrey; Kelly, *Eleanor and the Four Kings*, p. 77, stresses the later date of Giraldus's work and that Map admits he is reporting mere gossip. See also Pappano in this volume.

33. Castelot, *Queen of France*, pp. 379–80; Hunt, "Bodies of Marie Antoinette," pp. 114–15. Pre-1789 pamphlets accused the queen of incest with Louis XV, Louis XVI's brother the count of Artois, and her father, Emperor Francis I (Hunt, "Bodies," p. 123). Zweig, *Marie Antoinette*, pp. 419–25, deals with the 1793 charge in Freudian terms: at a preliminary inquiry for the queen's trial, Louis XVI's sister said that the boy had for some time practiced "*plaisirs solitaires,*" for which she and the queen had punished him. Zweig ascribes to that punishment the boy's compliance with the prosecutors.

34. In this volume, see Brown, Brundage and Bouchard. On the association of royal lineage and the realm's integrity, Nelson, "Inauguration Rituals," p. 71.

35. Parsons, "Pregnant Queen," p. 52.

36. Shadis and Berman, chapter 8 in this volume.

37. Parsons, "Violence, the Queen's Body."

38. Gierke, *Political Theories*, pp. 22–24; Ullmann, *History of Political Thought*, pp. 123–24; Nelson, "Inauguration Rituals," p. 71; Black, *Political Thought*, pp. 14–17.

39. Parsons, "Violence, the Queen's Body"; San Juan, "The Queen's Body and Its Slipping Mask," p. 21; Parsons, "Pregnant Queen," p. 49, and "Ritual and Symbol," pp. 60–77.

40. In general, Facinger, "Medieval Queenship," and Parsons, *Eleanor of Castile*, p. 72. On Eleanor and Aquitaine during her marriages, in this volume see Hivergneaux, Brown, and Turner, who stress Eleanor's activity as queen-mother after 1189. But a queen-mother is not the same as a queen-consort, and Aquitaine alone made Eleanor a figure of European stature. In reference to that inheritance, Richardson and Sayles described her position after Henry II's death as anomalous among the medieval queens of England (Richardson and Sayles, *Governance of Medieval England*, pp. 153–54.

41. By "ecclesiastically-sanctioned access," I mean the wifely obligation to assure a husband's way of life (Farmer, "Persuasive Voices," 517–43). On receiving petitioners in the bedchamber, see Parsons, "Ritual and Symbol," pp. 67–68, and Ormrod, "In Bed with Joan of Kent," pp. 277–92.

42. Parsons, "Queen's Intercession," pp. 147–77, and *Eleanor of Castile;* Howell, *Eleanor of Provence.*

43. Parsons, *Eleanor of Castile*, pp. 69–75, and "Queen's Intercession," pp. 149–51; Howell, *Eleanor of Provence*, esp. chap. 11, pp. 255–86; McCracken, *Romance of Adultery*, pp. 4–15. For Eleanor's declining reputation among late twelfth-century chroniclers, in this volume see McCracken and Tolhurst.

44. Facinger, "Medieval Queenship." In this volume, Huneycutt and Tanner each discuss English queenly traditions in reigns before Henry II's. Stafford, *Queen Emma and Queen Edith,* discusses eleventh-century Anglo-Saxon queens. Chibnall, *Empress Matilda,* probes the career of Henry II's influential mother; Eleanor of Aquitaine's first mother-in-law, Queen Adelaide (see above, n13). With her domains and taste for power, Eleanor of Aquitaine perhaps hoped to equal such women, as Shadis and Berman in this volume suggest, many of Eleanor's female descendants emulated her.

45. Norman bishops condemned her at the time of the 1173–74 revolt: "Lamenting together, we all deplore that you, a most prudent woman, turn from your lord . . . Worse, you urge the progeny of the king and yourself to rise against their father, as in the prophet's words, 'I nourished and brought up sons who spurn me [Is. 1:2].' . . . [R]uin will fall on the king's sons and their heirs . . . Lest this matter go from bad to worse, return with your sons to the husband with whom you must live and whom you should serve, lest worse things be imputed to you or your sons . . . [W]arn your sons, for whom their father has endured such anguish, trials, and labors, to be subject and devoted to him . . ."(my translation from Petri Blesensis ep. 154, Migne PL 207: cols. 448–50).

46. On Louis XV's first eminent mistress, Mitford, *Madame de Pompadour.* No adequate study of Mme. du Barry exists, but see Laski, *Trial and Execution*

of Madame du Barry, and Haslip, *Madame du Barry.* See also Cronin, *Louis and Antoinette,* pp. 32–34, 40–43, 60–63; Castelot, *Queen of France,* pp. 25–26, 44–56; Mitford, *Madame de Pompadour,* pp. 108–09.

47. Foucault, *Power/Knowledge,* p. 55.

48. French queens had never owned private property (Cronin, *Louis and Antoinette,* pp. 55, 112–15, 427–28; Castelot, *Queen of France,* pp. 27, 181, 191; Lever, *Marie Antoinette,* p. 167; Chartier, *Cultural Origins of the French Revolution,* pp. 178–80). The Bourbon monarchy's concurrent loss of style and power is engagingly traced in de Gramont, *Epitaph for Kings.*

49. The 1997 film *Mrs. Brown* dramatizes political debate, extending to abolition of the monarchy, that was favored by rumors of Queen Victoria's intimacy with her servant John Brown, rumors fanned by her absence from public life after her husband's death. The most sensible account of this relationship is in Longford, *Queen Victoria,* pp. 323–45. Cf. the film *The Madness of King George* for similar debate while that king was absent from public life during a lengthy 1788 illness.

50. Campan, *Memoirs,* p. 114 (the queen thought she was unrecognized at balls, but others pretended not to notice her). Louis XV's wife, an inveterate gambler, confined such activities to her state apartments at Versailles (Mitford, *Madame de Pompadour,* pp. 30–32).

51. For Hunt, "Bodies of Marie Antoinette," pp. 109, 112, court politics' secretive nature fostered the queen's dissimulation, a particularly feminine vice for the eighteenth century. In 1793, she was charged with teaching Louis to promise one thing in public while secretly opposing the Revolution (Castelot, *Queen of France,* p. 369; Cronin, *Louis and Antoinette,* p. 389). Her disastrous efforts at diplomacy before 1789 were directed from Vienna to further Habsburg interests (Castelot, *Queen of France,* p. 368; Lever, *Marie Antoinette,* pp. 114–18, 155–56, 160–62).

52. Bernier, *Secrets of Marie Antoinette,* p. 127 (Joseph II to his brother Leopold, June 9, 1777: "[she] has the kind of power to be expected from a royal mistress, not the kind a wife should have"); Hunt, "Bodies of Marie Antoinette," pp. 108–30; Maza, *Private Lives and Public Affairs,* pp. 178–82, the quote at 182.

53. Zweig, *Marie Antoinette,* pp. 152–53.

54. The Revolution's image of Louis as a gluttonous, drunken and, significantly, castrated pig was, like his impotence, a useful political metaphor (Baccque, *Body Politic,* pp. 68–75).

55. Baccque, *Body Politic,* pp. 51–55. On female adultery's subversive and feminizing effects, see Brandes, "Like Wounded Stags," pp. 227–30.

56. Fraser, *Mary, Queen of Scots,* pp. 308–09 and pl. 28. There is a full-page print of the Keralio frontispiece in Maza, "The Diamond Necklace Affair," p. 83, though at p. 82 Maza says the siren-queen pierces the king's heart with a spear; she clearly seizes a scepter. Prosecutors in 1793 compared the queen to Brunéhaut, Frédégonde, and the Médecis (Hunt, "Bodies of Marie Antoinette," p. 109).

57. Nelson, "Why Witches Were Women," pp. 346–47; Leyser, *Medieval Women: A Social History,* pp. 104 (suggesting some effort to deny such information to "loose women"), 130–31.

58. Parsons, "Family, Sex, and Power," p. 5; Hunt, "Bodies of Marie Antoinette," pp. 108–30.

59. André Poulet, "Capetian Women," pp. 110–11; for England, cf. Parsons, *Eleanor of Castile,* p. 45.

60. Herman of Tournai, *De Restauratione Sancti Martini Tornacensis,* chap. 18 at p. 282, says Countess Clemence of Flanders, sister of Pope Calixtus II and aunt of Eleanor of Aquitaine's Capetian mother-in-law Adelaide of Maurienne, used "female arts" to prevent conception after bearing three children in three years. She feared civil war over the Flemish inheritance, but Hermann moralized that the early deaths of all her children were divine punishment for her actions.

61. *Vita Sancti Bernardi,* RHF 14:376; Parsons, "Pregnant Queen," p. 52.

62. This act of intervention—not true intercession—occurred in 1192, when Eleanor was effectively regent for the absent Richard I; Martindale, "Eleanor of Aquitaine," p. 49, notes that Richard of Devizes praises Eleanor's actions on this occasion in "far from conventional" terms, and that the remedy she provided "lay in her power of command," not in a mediator's role. Cf. nn80, 85 below.

63. Hunt, "Bodies of Marie Antoinette," p. 118, citing the 1789 edition of the *Essais historiques,* first published in 1781. The tubercular boy was known to be doomed long before he died, to his parents' inconsolable distress (Cronin, *Louis and Antoinette,* pp. 29–30, 279; Castelot, *Queen of France,* pp. 230–31; Lever, *Marie Antoinette,* pp. 156, 183, 187–88, 207–08). For the pamphlet, see Hunt, "Bodies of Marie Antoinette," pp. 118–26.

64. The body lies near a peacock, emblem of Juno, queen of the gods, who contested Jove's power over mortal lives. The juxtaposition of peacock and infant corpse recalls that in her Hellenic guise as Hera, the queen of the gods sought to kill the young Hercules, Zeus's son by a mortal.

65. Hunt, "Bodies of Marie Antoinette," pp. 113–14. On *la* (masculinized) *République's* nurturing abilities and the male assumption of maternal behavior, cf. Sheingorn, "The Maternal Behavior of God," pp. 77–100, and Hale, "Joseph as Mother," pp. 101–16.

66. For her flouting of protocol and abolition of ceremonial, see Cronin, *Louis and Antoinette,* pp. 197–98; Campan, *Memoirs,* pp. 69–74; Castelot, *Queen of France,* p. 47 for her ridicule of elderly courtiers, and p. 149 for her clique's role in alienating the nobility. Ladies who had served Louis XV's wife were offended by the new queen's disdain for the late queen's regard to etiquette (" . . . do not imagine that a Queen, born an Archduchess of Austria, can give so much interest and enthusiasm to them as a Polish Princess who became Queen of France [Castelot, *Queen of France,* pp. 20, 84].)" Accusing rivals of immoderate or deviant sexual behavior was a familiar political tool at Versailles from the 1750s. Nobles excluded from the queen's coterie in the 1770s and 1780s thus resorted

to established practice when they invented her love affairs (Bernier, *Words of Fire*, p. 57).

67. Castelot, *Queen of France*, pp. 66–69; Cronin, *Louis and Antoinette*, pp. 125–27; Campan, *Memoirs*, p. 107, is explicit on the queen's lack of cultural interest.

68. Cronin, *Louis and Antoinette*, p. 212; Castelot, *Queen of France*, pp. 174–75; Lever, *Marie Antoinette*, p. 153.

69. Castelot, *Queen of France*, p. 144; Hunt, "Bodies of Marie Antoinette," pp. 122–23; for the prints, see Schama, *Citizens*, pp. 66, 550. Almost predictably, she was said to use a dog for sexual pleasure (Bernier, *Words of Fire*, pp. 140–41).

70. After he wed Maria Theresa in 1736, Duke Francis of Lorraine was adopted as heir to the last Medici Grand Duke of Tuscany. Lorraine went to Stanislas Lezczynski, the Polish ex-king whose daughter was Louis XV's wife, and was united to France when Lezczinski died in 1766 (Acton, *Last Medicis*, pp. 300–01). For one early consequence of the queen's paternal descent, see Castelot, *Queen of France*, pp. 31, 39. At her 1793 trial, she gave her surname as "de Lorraine d'Autriche," which the prosecutors used to imply that she meant to give Lorraine to the Habsburgs (Castelot, *Queen of France*, pp. 367, 391).

71. For northern disapproval of Aquitanian customs, see Labande, "Pour une image véridique," 180.

72. Pappano, chapter 16 in this volume. Language may have played a role in Eleanor's distinctness in England. Richard of Devizes's account of her 1192 encounter with people in Cambridgeshire, reduced to misery by the bishop of Ely's interdict on his estates, states that "There was no need for an interpreter . . . they spoke through their tears" (quoted and translated in Martindale, "Eleanor of Aquitaine," p. 49), implying that otherwise an interpreter would have been needed. Cf. a 1275 incident in which Edward I's Castilian-born queen needed an interpreter to communicate with townspeople at St. Albans (Parsons, *Eleanor of Castile*, p. 64).

73. Bernard of Clairvaux, *Letters*, no. 116 at pp. 174–77. Weir, *Eleanor of Aquitaine*, pp. 35–36, wrongly implies that the letter refers to Eleanor. The parallel with Constance of Arles is, however, a telling one for, like Eleanor, Constance was censured for meddling in the royal succession: when her eldest son Hugh died in 1027, she supported as the new heir her third son, Robert, over the second, later Henry I, whom Robert II favored (Adair, "Constance of Arles").

74 Even when Robert knew such ornaments were stolen, he regarded the losses as alms to the thieves despite what were portrayed as Constance's strident objections. See Adair, "Constance of Arles."

75. Chrétien de Troyes, *Erec and Enide*, pp. 18–19, 21–22. On the peasant Griselda's reclothing at her wedding to a marquis, as related to the meanings of royal women's dress, see Parsons, "Violence, the Queen's Body."

76. Parsons, "'Loved Him, Hated Her,'" p. 287, and *Eleanor of Castile,* p. 53 and n164; Stafford, *Queen Emma and Queen Edith,* pp. 105, 115–17, and *Queens, Concubines and Dowagers,* pp. 106–107. Even a queen's idealized role as mediator could appear as feminine manipulation of male egos on an emotional basis linked to such bodily states as pregnancy (Leicester, "Of a fire in the dark," 164; Parsons, "Pregnant Queen," p. 45).

77. For the robe, see *English Historical Documents 1042–1189,* p. 407; it is undescribed, but the splendor its cost implies suggests it was made for the December 1154 coronation or Eleanor's churching after the birth of her second son in February 1155—dynastic occasions to which display was appropriate. On Becket, see Barlow, *Becket,* pp. 25, 38, 55, 75–76, and Warren, *Henry II,* pp. 78–80 and 207. For kings overshadowing wives, e.g., Parsons, *Eleanor of Castile,* p. 44 (on Edward I's dislike of royal trappings, Prestwich, *Edward I,* p. 108). That Henry II kept Eleanor in obscurity for most of their marriage, even before 1174, is agreed by Facinger, "A Study in Queenship," 1–47; Warren, *Henry II,* pp. 18–21; and Brown, "Eleanor of Aquitaine: Parent, Queen, and Duchess."

78. On this endlessly analyzed tragicomedy, see Maza, "Diamond Necklace Affair," pp. 63–89; Lever, *Marie Antoinette,* pp. 173–82; Cronin, *Louis and Antoinette,* pp. 236–58.

79. Giraldus Cambrensis, *De Principis Instructione Liber* 8:295–97; for Gerald's reliability, see Brown, "Ritual Brotherhood," 366–70. On Henry II's reforms in England, Warren, see *Henry II,* pp. 241–396; Sayles, *Medieval Foundations of England,* pp. 402–03. If Gerald invented Henry's words, that invention suggests something of contemporary views of Henry's reign.

80. Eleanor's failure to adopt the intercessor's submissive posture could also have contributed to perceptions that she did not meet ideals of queenly behavior (see n62 above and n85 below).

81. Tolhurst, "Whatever Happened to Eleanor?"; Howell, *Eleanor of Provence,* pp. 5, 36, 42; Parsons, "'Loved Him, Hated Her,'" pp. 279, 289–91. Chroniclers put words into John's mouth blaming his queen, Isabella of Angoulême (1187?–1246), for the loss of Normandy and Anjou (Jordan, "Isabelle d'Angoulême," 821–52; cf. now Vincent, "Isabella of Angoulême," pp. 165–219).

82. Matthew Paris, *Chronica Majora,* 2.

83. Parsons, "'Loved Him, Hated Her'," pp. 279–98.

84. Chambers, "Some Legends Concerning Eleanor of Aquitaine," 459–68, with comments in Owen, *Eleanor of Aquitaine,* p. 24.

85. Huneycutt, in this volume; Parsons, "Queen's Intercession," pp. 147–77, and "Pregnant Queen," pp. 39–61. As for other reigns in which queens were blamed for their husbands' harsh rule, a lack of submissive queenly behavior could construct a king's perceived severity (Parsons, *Eleanor of Castile,* pp. 152–55), and cf. above, nn62, 80. That Eleanor of Aquitaine did not routinely mediate gave Henry II fewer chances to show magnanimity than otherwise would have been the case.

86. Pappano, in this volume.

87. Nolan, Wood, Pappano in this volume; Parsons, "'Never was a body buried,'" pp. 326–30; and see the introduction to this volume.

88. McCracken, *Romance of Adultery,* esp. chap. 1, pp. 25–51. On subversive and feminizing effects of female sexual ridicule, see Abu-Lughod, "Romance of Resistance," pp. 320–21.

89. Parsons, "Violence, the Queen's Body"; on divine models of community, Parsons, "'Never was a body buried,'" pp. 334–35 n57.

90. Parsons, "Violence, the Queen's Body." Even a childless wife not menaced with divorce, such as Adelicia of Louvain, sought spiritual comfort from a renowned bishop (Huneycutt, "*Alianora Regina Anglorum*").

91. De Baccque, *Body Politic,* pl. 5; see also Davis, "Women on Top," pp. 147–90.

92. Bullough, "Medieval Medical and Scientific Views," p. 496, notes beliefs that the soul could experience somatic sexual change: "if a man let a woman move towards any degree of equality, she would be liable to somatic change and apt to challenge him for control." Brandes, "Like Wounded Stags," pp. 227–30, notes beliefs that female adultery's feminizing effects on husbands can also be somatic. On the Poitiers window, see Caviness, "Anchoress, Abbess, and Queen," pp. 128–29; for the prestige accorded the viewer's left, see Fraser, *Mary, Queen of Scots,* pp. 238–39, 241 (Lord Darnley became titular king when he wed Mary, but as queen by right she signed documents at the left.) Stafford, "Emma: The Powers of the Queen," pp. 3–4 and pl. 1, discusses the Winchester *Liber vitae's* full-page portrayal of King Cnut and Queen Aelfgifu-Emma, stressing the illumination's ambiguities while noting that the artist aligns Emma with the Virgin Mary as a sign of the queen's exalted power on earth. Stafford does not remark Emma's position to the viewer's left of the cross she and Cnut present, but notes Emma's visual prominence in the composition and suggests that her identification as "Aelfgifu Regina" stresses the English identity she acquired with her first marriage to Ethelred II. Emma's position to the viewer's left may reflect the importance of her Norman and English identities to Cnut's reign. A twelfth-century German illuminator perhaps relegated Eleanor of Aquitaine to visual unimportance, see van Houts, *Memory and Gender,* pp. 96–97, and comment by Shadis and Berman, "A Taste of the Feast,"n28 in this volume.

93. Mullally, "Reciprocal Loyalty." Eleanor's ability to distribute gifts and attract loyalty (or desire) herself, rather than to the king, may suggest why Arthur in Lanval distributes gifts himself rather than delegate to Guenevere (Pappano, "Marie de France, Aliénor d'Aquitaine," at n62). Cf. Henry II's possible assignment to Becket, not Eleanor, of the advertisement of royal splendor (above at n77), and implications for the preservation of hierarchy identified in queens' ritual gift distribution (Enright, *Lady with a Mead Cup,* pp. 1–37; Nelson, "Women at the Court of Charlemagne," p. 54.

94. "Wær du werlt alliu mîn,/ von dem mere unz an den Rîn,/ des wolt ich mich darben/ daz diu künegin von Engellant/ læge an mînem arme"(*Des Minnesangs Frühling*, p. 1 [my free translation]). It cannot be doubted that this queen was Eleanor, as implied by Kelly, *Eleanor and the Four Kings*, p. 101.

95. Hunt, "Bodies of Marie Antoinette," p. 109. McCracken, *Romance of Adultery*, p. 30, notes that fictional medieval queens' bodies became the focus of such rumors as might well have fed suspicions of adultery.

96. For early modern tightening of patriarchal authority and royal marriage, Freccero, "Marguerite de Navarre," pp. 132–49. Kelly (Gadol) article "Did Women Have a Renaissance?" is contested (Shadis and Berman, in this volume,"n2). But Kelly's point that social change does not necessarily have positive results for everyone—especially women—is apposite here.

97. Harding, "Medieval Women's Unwritten Discourse on Motherhood," 201–202, argues that women tried to "keep the maternal body out of verbal circulation," restricting talk of pregnancy to women so they might "exert a measure of control over their own bodies." A queen could not enjoy such female intimacy: her pregnancies were matters of state.

98. I prefer this rendering of Zweig's 1932 German subtitle, *Bildnis eines Mittleres Karaktere,* to the 1933 English translation's *The Portrait of an Average Woman.*

CHAPTER 14

TEMPERING SCANDAL:
ELEANOR OF AQUITAINE AND
BENOÎT DE SAINTE-MAURE'S *ROMAN DE TROIE*

Tamara F. O'Callaghan

> *Since Eleanor of Aquitaine is likely to read his work, Benoit's creation of Briseida and portrayal of Helen of Troy are attempts to praise Eleanor and avoid her wrath.*

Eleanor of Aquitaine has long been regarded by medievalists as a great patron of the literary arts at the Angevin court.[1] One text frequently associated with her is Benoît de Sainte-Maure's *Roman de Troie*, the *roman d'antiquité* that widely popularized the story of Troy in the Middle Ages.[2] But the passage commonly cited as evidence of Eleanor's patronage does not appear in the poem's prologue or epilogue, as might be expected of a dedication, but rather well into the poem's narrative. Having concluded his story of the inconstant Briseida—a woman who relinquishes Troilus, her Trojan lover, for Diomedes, her Greek captor—Benoît starts a lengthy diatribe against all faithless women who change their loves so quickly and so easily:

> Femme n'iert ja trop esgaree:
> Por ço qu'ele truist ou choisir,
> Poi durent puis li suen sospir.
> A femme dure dueus petit:
> A l'un ueil plore, a l'autre rit.
> Mout muënt tost li lor corage.
> Assez est fole la plus sage:

Quant qu'ele a en set anz amé
A ele en treis jorz oblïé
Onc nule ne sot duel aveir.
Mout lor pert bien de lor saveir:
Ja n'avront tant nul jor mesfait
Chose ne rien que tant seit lait,
Ço lor est vis, qui que les veie,
Que l'om ja blasmer les en deie.
Ja jor ne cuideront mesfaire:
Des folies est ço la maire.
Qui s'i atent ne qui s'i creit
Sei meïsme vent e deceit. [ll. 13438–56]

[A woman will never be very upset:
As long as she finds where to look anew,
Her sighs will not last much longer.
Sorrow lasts briefly in a woman:
She cries with one eye, but laughs with the other.
Their hearts change very quickly.
The wisest is foolish enough:
All she has loved for seven years,
She will forget in three days.
Not one has ever felt sorrow.
They think very highly of their wisdom
It seems to them that they
Never do anything so wrong or vile,
No matter who sees them do it,
For which they should be blamed at all.
They never believe their misdeeds:
This is the greatest of their follies.
He who relies on or believes them,
Deceives and sells himself].[3]

Benoît suddenly interrupts this condemnation with a careful supplication to an unnamed lady whom he fears may criticize his harsh words:

De cest, veir, criem g'estre blasmez
De cele que tant a bontez
Que hautece a, pris e valor,
Honesté e sen e honor,
Bien e mesure e saintée,
E noble largece e beauté;
En cui mesfait de dames maint
Sont par le bien de li esteint;
En cui tote scïence abonde,

A la cui n'est nule seconde
Que el mont seit de nule lei.
Riche dame de riche rei,
Senz mal, senz ire, senz tristece,
Poissiez aveir toz jorz leece! [ll.13457–70]

[In truth, I fear to be blamed for this,
By that one who has so many good qualities
Who has nobility, esteem and merit,
Virtue and judgement and honor,
Goodness and temperance and purity,
And noble generosity and beauty;
In whom the misdeeds of many women
Are cancelled by her goodness;
In whom all knowledge abounds,
To whom there is no equal
Who may be in the world in any law.
The powerful lady of a powerful king,
Without evil, without anger, without sorrow,
May you have joy forever!]

Many critics have interpreted this passage as a dedication to Eleanor and even as evidence of her patronage of Benoît as a court poet.[4] Recent scholarship has, however, made a strong case against such claims.[5] As Karen Broadhurst convincingly argues, the passage does not state that Benoît deliberately wrote his *Roman* for Eleanor or at her request.[6] In fact, the unnamed "riche dame de riche rei" cannot be definitively identified as the queen, though other possible choices are pretty much limited to one of her daughters, Queen Eleanor of Castile or Queen Joan of Sicily, or Louis VII's daughter Marguerite, wife of Eleanor's eldest son Henry the Younger. Certainly, Eleanor of Aquitaine seems the most likely candidate, especially since the term "riche rei" was associated with Henry II.[7] If we accept her identity as the lady—and I think we must—then the passage makes it very clear that, despite the lack of textual evidence to suggest that Eleanor commissioned the work or was the intended audience, Benoît considered her to be a likely reader of his poem. We are now left with a puzzling question: why would Benoît interrupt his castigation of fickle women, such as Briseida, to address Eleanor in such manner? Certainly, his words are those of flattery, for he praises the lady for all her "bontez" in great detail as well as for her "bien," which has the power to expunge the misdeeds of every other woman. Yet, placed as they are in the midst of a vehement, antifeminist diatribe, his words also seem obsequious, as though he is somehow trying to cajole Eleanor for fear of her reaction to his story at this point.

Thus we need to consider seriously just *how* Eleanor might have read the *Roman* in order to understand the passage and its full significance.

Benoît wrote the *Roman de Troie* sometime between 1165 and 1170,[8] drawing largely on two brief pseudohistorical accounts of the Troy story, Dares Phrygius' *De excidio Troiae historia* and Dictys Cretensis's *Ephemeridos belli troiani* (respectively ca. sixth and fourth centuries CE, although they claim to antedate Homer as firsthand accounts of the Trojan war). At over 30,000 lines, the poem expands substantially upon Dares's and Dictys's accounts, and intertwines the story of the Trojan war with the love relationships of Jason and Medea, Paris and Helen, Diomedes and Briseida, and Achilles and Polyxena. Although we know that Benoît used Ovid to "flesh out" his version of the story, many of the descriptions and details are entirely of his own creation. Nowhere is this more apparent than with the character of Briseida, a literary figure who will be the source of Giovanni Boccaccio's Criseyda, Geoffrey Chaucer's Criseyde, Robert Henryson's Cresseid, and William Shakespeare's Cressida. Although her initial appearance is clearly based on Dares's Briseis, the slave-concubine of Achilles taken from him by Agamemnon and eventually restored,[9] the love-triangle of Troilus, Briseida, and Diomedes is wholly original to Benoît. Briseida, beloved of the Trojan warrior-prince Troilus, is traded to the Greeks and, after two long years in the Greek camp, ultimately succumbs to the unrelenting advances of Diomedes. As Douglas Kelly points out, such literary invention is highly unusual since medieval writers tended to recreate—that is, draw on antecedent material and present it in a new version that conforms to his, her, or a patron's conception of the source—rather than to invent entirely new material.[10] With Briseida's story, Benoît will illustrate the dire consequences of a love relationship that develops under the shadow of a past, more legitimate love on the part of the woman.

But why? Does not Benoît have that same story in the love relationship of Paris and Helen? After all, the theft of Helen by Paris is the infamous catalyst for the Trojan war. What could be a more dire consequence than that? Without question, Benoît must have intended the story of Briseida and Diomedes to parallel the love affair of Paris and Helen, for the two stories mirror one another in terms of plot structure more than any of the others in the poem: Helen and Briseida are both taken forcibly from their people and their husband/lover; they both succumb to a new love with disastrous results; Paris and Helen's love brings about the downfall of Troy; Briseida and Diomedes' love brings about the social condemnation of Briseida by both her own people and the Greeks. Nevertheless, there seems to be more at work here, for Benoît's accusation of female faithlessness, a charge which he showers so vehemently on Briseida, could just as easily apply to Helen— in some ways, even more so since Briseida takes a full two years to change lovers, while Helen takes only a few days. And yet, he remains surprisingly silent. He condemns Helen neither for her extra-marital relationship with Paris nor for her mistreatment of her lawful husband, Menelaus. There is, in fact, only the briefest of references to the Greek king's pain and anguish upon discovering that his wife has been taken (ll. 4787–89). Benoît rarely mentions Menelaus but, when he does, he emphasizes only the Greek king's sociopolitical motivations for declaring war on Troy, stating that Menelaus undertakes the battle in retaliation for the "hontage" or "shame," shown to his wife (l. 4943) and for the "damage" or "injury," brought upon his kingdom (l. 4944).[11] Never once does Benoît suggest that Menelaus is personally shamed or that he pursues Helen because he loves her. With this silence, Benoît permits the love affair between Paris and Helen to develop almost untainted by the scandal of adultery.[12]

The love narrative of Paris and Helen is a story that a twelfth century audience would have readily considered the direct cause of the Trojan war. Although Paris and Helen's is the most catastrophic of all the love narratives in the *Roman de Troie*, Benoît portrays their love relationship as the most positive. This apparent idealization of an adulterous affair that has such tragic consequences for so many has been the subject of considerable critical debate.[13] Many critics, in particular Rosemarie Jones, have observed that Benoît presents the relationship as ideal, but none have adequately explained why he does so.[14] As Lee Patterson argues in his analysis of the *Roman de Troie*,

> [Paris and Helen's] love may be an effect of the Trojan desire for revenge for the abduction of Hesione and may be in itself illicit. But Benoît nonetheless represents it in terms that invoke a different, brighter world, in which *Amors* is not a device of statecraft and where gifts of Venus entail only happy consequences. Adulterous love is the efficient cause of the Trojan war, but the straightforward link between personal immorality and historical disaster established by the narrative is then undone by Benoît's empathy for the lovers yearning for a realm in which private but by no means solely carnal desire can be fully legitimized.[15]

Indeed, the lovers' bliss is seemingly untouched by the catastrophic events they set in motion. Benoît conveys no sense of immorality or wrongdoing on Paris and Helen's part.

This sympathetic portrayal of erotic love is even more remarkable since Helen is just as guilty of faithlessness as is Briseida. Benoît never criticizes Helen or her behavior in any way. Although he suggests that Helen is attracted to Paris when she first sees him and that she "Ne se fist mie trop laidir" [did not act too outraged] (l. 4505) by her abduction and even gives

a "semblant del consentir" [appearance of consent] (l. 4506), Benoît gives
no concrete evidence of her guilt in the affair beyond mere speculation
and innuendo.[16] This flattering portrayal of Helen is quite different from
the view presented twenty years later by another Angevin court writer,
Joseph of Exeter, in his version of the Troy story. Upon her abduction,
Joseph's Helen literally assaults Paris in an effort to satisfy her carnal desire:

> . . . non iam oscula reddit,
> non reddenda negat Helene, sed pectore toto
> incumbens gremium solvit, premit ore, latentem
> furatur Venerem, iamque exspirante Dione
> conscia secretos testatur purpura rores.
> proh sceles! an tantis potuisti, pessima, votis
> indulsisse moras exspectabatque voluptas
> emptorem? o teneri miranda potentia sexus!
> precipitem in lucrum suspenit femina luxum
> nec nisi conducto dignatur gaudia risu.

> [Now Helen's kiss is real,
> And she grants many more. With all her heart
> She opens up her loins; with eager mouth she steals
> His dormant love, and as their passion pants its gasp
> A guilty redness witnesses her secret dews.
> For shame, foul whore! Could you allow delays for such
> Desires? Was pleasure put on hold to wait upon
> A purchaser? What power of the tender sex,
> That woman should withhold her headstrong love for gain,
> Nor deign to laugh or show delight except for hire!][17]

Benoît's Helen is no such virago, filled with lustful aggression; she is cautious and concerned with issues of marriage and fidelity (ll. 4741–48). Paris
responds to her with the *courtoisie* of the ideal suitor in the twelfth century,
for he says,

> Or ai mon cuer si en vos mis,
> E si m'a vostre amor espris,
> Que del tot sui enclins a vos.
> Leiaus amis, leiaus espos
> Vos serai mais tote ma vie:
> D'iço seiez seüre e fie.
> Tote rien vos obeïra
> E tote rien vos servira [ll. 4741–48].

> [Now I have placed my heart so in you,

And your love has so burned me,
That I am completely enclined toward you.
Loyal beloved, loyal spouse
You will henceforth be all my life:
Of this fact you may be certain and confident.
All will obey you
And all will serve you.]

The references to "mon cuer" and "vostre amor" make clear the mutuality of their love. Paris also stresses his fidelity with the repetition of "leiaus" and the vow of marriage, yet the vow should be problematic. Helen is, after all, another man's wife; however, not even that, it seems, can stand in the way of true love. The consummation of the lovers' relationship is the complete antithesis of that described by Joseph of Exeter:

Mout l'a Paris reconfortee
E merveilles l'a honoree.
Mout la fist la nuit gent servir. [ll. 4769–71]

[Greatly did Paris comfort her
And marvellously did he honor her.
Greatly did he serve her well that night.]

Understated and decorous, the description simply implies the physical, particularly with the play on "reconfort" and "honor." The two behave as true lovers in a courtly romance.

This idealization of the relationship continues with Paris and Helen's arrival at Troy. As they enter the city, Paris takes Helen's horse by the reins and leads her at his side "De li honorer [to honor her] (ll. 4815–16)." Helen is no captive or fallen woman, for this simple gesture venerates her as Paris's equal, both in his eyes and the eyes of the Trojans who watch their arrival. The Trojan tribute continues as Priam comes to greet them both and to take the reins of Helen's horse from his son for the rest of the journey (l. 4846). This courteous display not only demonstrates the honor shown to Helen by the Trojan king, but also indicates an acceptance of Helen on the part of the Trojans. Priam emphasizes their approval of her by informing the silent woman that in Troy she will be a "dame del païs [lady of the homeland] (l. 4852)." It is a significant episode, for it is almost a complete inversion of Briseida's departure for the Greek camp. Like Paris, Troilus takes hold of the reins of Briseida's horse (l. 13425); the purpose of his gesture is neither to honor or control her, however, but rather to guide and comfort her, albeit temporarily, as he leads her away from her people, to an unknown fate. And just as Paris hands over the reins of Helen's horse to

Priam, so Troilus hands those of Briseida's horse to Diomedes, but he conducts her without celebration to the Greek camp (l. 13529). It is consequently impossible to read the two love episodes in the *Roman de Troie*
without noticing how one parallels the other. Like a mirror, each heroine
is both the reflection *and* the inversion of her counterpart.

As Barbara Nolan states, with the figure of Helen, "Benoît gives a first
glimpse into the image of the changeable, unfaithful woman he will develop more fully in the character of Briseida."[18] This observation could not
be more true: despite the similarities in the two women's behavior, Benoît
provides a "glimpse" and nothing more. Does Benoît create the story of
Briseida and Diomedes simply to parallel Paris and Helen's relationship in
the same way he mirrors Jason and Medea's story with that of Achilles and
Polyxena? Perhaps, but this answer does not justify Benoît's significant silence with respect to Helen's conduct, especially when he is so verbose
concerning Briseida's actions. It is to the historical context within which
Benoît wrote the *Roman de Troie* that we must turn in the hope of finding
a better solution to this problem.

Like the other *romans d'antiquité*, the *Roman de Troie* was written for a
court audience.[19] That the Angevin court should be so preoccupied with
stories of the great classical civilizations is hardly surprising since the
twelfth century witnessed a surge of interest in myths that purported to
prove that the Normans and the English possessed a classical heritage and
were descended from the nobility of Troy, in particular.[20] A century after
the Norman invasion, a sense of nationalism had begun to develop between the two peoples "through the common law which [the royal gov-
ernment] applied throughout the kingdom, through the 'self-government
at the king's command' which administered the law, and through the resentment which the king's overseas wars and taxes aroused."[21] Benoît
wrote his poem not simply to entertain, but to present the story of Troy as
a myth of descent:

> A cultural myth is, in the simplest sense, a remembered story that endures be-
> cause it does not lose its hold over a people's imagination. The longevity of
> an origin myth offers the most telling measure of its vitality and resonance,
> its continuing capacity to absorb and interpret experience. As it survives or-
> ganically within a culture and inspires its imaginative works, this myth testi-
> fies to the belief that the past can shape the present and, by extension, the
> future. The belief that there is a vital connection running through the stages
> of a people's history underlies any myth of cultural identity.[22]

That the *Roman de Troie* was perceived as such a myth is evidenced by the
fact that a thirteenth-century manuscript of the Bible in verse translation

includes the entire poem in the Book of Exodus.[23] Although such a textual combination may seem strange to us, medieval scholars were simply using the histories of the only earlier peoples they knew in order to determine the origins of their own people.[24] In such a way, biblical history and literary fiction are conflated to create one unified myth of origins, and the Trojan court becomes part of the Norman and English identity, something to be revered and even emulated.

As a linear narrative, such myths emphasize the importance of unbroken lineage for a culture.[25] Accordingly, much of the *Roman de Troie* focuses on the concern for *lignage,* specifically how *fine amor* destroys its very essential perpetuation for a people. With the story of Jason and Medea, which begins the poem, Benoît emphasizes Medea's betrayal of her father and her people rather than her brutal punishment of Jason and his new wife. He ends the story with Jason and Medea's return to Greece, claiming that he does not find anything else about them in his source:

> Jo ne le truis pas en cest livre,
> Ne Daires plus n'en voust escrire,
> Ne Beneeiz pas ne l'alonge,
> Ne pas n'i acreistra mençonge. [ll. 2063–66]

> [I find no more in this book;
> Dares did not wish to write more,
> And Benoît does not lengthen it,
> Nor will he add lies to it.]

Benoît has been using Ovid thus far to augment Dares's version of the episode. The *Metamorphoses* and, to a lesser extent, the *Heroides* provide the missing ending, yet Benoît evidently makes a conscious choice not to include it. Although he comments that he must now finish the tale of Jason and Medea in order to proceed to the main focus of his work, the Trojan war (ll. 2043–44), he has already devoted over 1,300 lines to their story; a few more at this point do not seem very significant. He also presents Medea as Aeetes's only child (ll. 1215), another intentional change to his sources, and, in doing so, effectively downplays the cruelty traditionally associated with her. These deliberate alterations and omissions allow Benoît to shift the focus of the story's "moral" in a new direction. Whereas Jason is clearly guilty of betrayal, Medea is not, in Benoît's view, completely blameless, for

> Grant folie fist Medea:
> Trop ot le vassal aamé,
> Por lui laissa son parenté,
> Son pere e sa mere e sa gent. [ll. 2030–33]

[Great was Medea's recklessness;
She loved the vassal too much,
For him she abandoned her family,
Her father, her mother, and her people.]

She loved too much and, as a result, forsook her family and her people. Her overwhelming passion for Jason effectively destroys a dynasty, for Colchis is left without an heir. Thus Benoît illustrates the effect that love can have not only on the individual who experiences love but also on a people.

The decided emphasis on Medea's destruction of the Colchian lineage, rather than on her brutality, is a unique interpretation of the Jason and Medea story and one that will prove to be essential for uniting the *Roman de Troie* as a whole. The theme is interwoven throughout the poem, linking major and minor episodes. Priam states explicitly on two occasions that his decision to send an embassy to Greece for the return of Hesione is for the purpose of avenging the Greek's outrage to his "lignage" [ll. 3213–14, 3687–88]. Paris uses the same argument to convince his men to steal Helen when he first sees her (ll. 4384–86). In the love story of Achilles and Polyxena, Priam also worries that, by allowing Achilles to marry Polyxena, he is undermining the Trojan lineage (ll. 17940–42), while Hecuba uses the promise of Polyxena as a means of obtaining revenge on the Greek hero for his part in the destruction of her lineage on the battlefield (ll. 21897–99). Even Briseida and Diomedes's story illustrates this theme for, as a direct result of their mutual love, they are ultimately left without a homeland of their own.

Needless to say, the question of lineage was also a significant one for Henry II. Later chroniclers refer to his line's alleged descent from Satan as though it were a well-established rumor, for even Henry's son, Richard I, is recorded as making reference to it.[26] But, more importantly, the twelfth century was a period of great upheaval and uncertainty with respect to the English throne, a situation that was only resolved with Henry's succession. After Henry I's death in 1135, Britain was left in a precarious political situation. The king's legitimate heir, William, had drowned in the "White Ship" disaster of 1120. Although Henry had wanted his daughter, Matilda, to inherit the throne, the barons instead chose his nephew, Stephen of Blois. As we all know, however, Matilda did not accept this decision and waged a war that lasted until 1148, when Stephen was finally defeated. Still, the barons refused to accept her as queen, and eventually Stephen returned to the throne. None the less, Matilda did win in having her son, Henry of Anjou, declared Stephen's heir with the Treaty of Winchester of 1153.[27] Thus Henry succeeded Stephen in 1154 after a long period of war and political uncertainty. He also came to the throne with Eleanor, whom he had married in 1152, and it is to Eleanor of Aquitaine that we must return our attention for a fuller understanding of Benoît's *Roman de Troie*.

Eleanor's importance to the question at hand cannot be overemphasized, for her life is in many ways a mirror image of Helen's story. In marrying Eleanor, Henry had not only wedded the daughter and heiress of Duke William X of Aquitaine, but the "cast-off" wife of Louis VII, king of France. Her unhappy marriage to Louis was dissolved by a council of French clergy a mere eight weeks before she wed Henry, whom she had only met once before.[28] Historians have debated whether or not her marriage to Henry was a love match. Robert de Torigny, a contemporary Norman chronicler, makes a point of noting that he is unsure if Henry wed Eleanor "sive repentino sive praemeditato consilio [suddenly or by premeditated deliberation]."[29] Writing after 1160, Gervase of Canterbury specifically describes Henry's desire for Eleanor as one based on lust for her possessions as well as for herself:

> Dux vero generositate feminae et maxime dignitatum quae eam contingebant cupiditate illectus, amoris et morae omnis impatiens, paucis secum assumptis sociis viam longiorem discurrit in brevi; infra tempus modicum conjugio illius jam olim concupito potitus est.

> [But the duke, enticed by the woman's high birth and especially by lust for the holdings she possessed, unable to endure love and any delay, took a few companions with him and made the longer journey in short order; within a brief time he attained his long-desired union.][30]

Gerald of Wales even suggests that Henry and Eleanor engaged in "adulterino concubito [adulterous sexual intercourse]" before they married.[31] Thus, like Helen, Eleanor remarried under the shadow of a past legitimate union as well as to her former husband's greatest political enemy. Even the names of the two women, Aliénor and Heleine, suggest a connection, albeit unintentionally, for in French they sound very like one another.

Consequently, Benoît is faced with telling a story that parallels contemporary events a little too closely. Rather than castigate Helen for her behavior and possibly offend the queen, he creates another woman, Briseida, whose story, although similar, is a less obvious match for Eleanor and her position in the Angevin court. Briseida is not a queen, but an aristocratic woman; she is not taken at will to the enemy camp, but rather sent; she does not relinquish her past love quickly, but waits almost two years to do so. Benoît even takes the added precaution of interrupting his lengthy

diatribe against unfaithful women, such as Briseida, with a careful supplication to Eleanor. Thus, by adding the wholly original story of Troilus, Briseida, and Diomedes, Benoît is able to criticize a woman for behavior such
as Helen's—and, by extension, Eleanor's—without fear of reprisal. Even
more importantly, the addition allows him to idealize the story of Paris and
Helen, thereby creating a romantic analogy to Henry and Eleanor's relationship. With the succession of Henry and Eleanor, Britain has a new
"Paris" and a new "Helen," who will rule over a new "Troy."[32]

Such an analogy helps to explain Benoît's unexpected silence regarding
Menelaus and his relationship with Helen, since the Angevin court would
hardly appreciate any significant attention being drawn to the queen's previous marriage. There are, in fact, other textual parallels between the Trojan and Angevin courts. Following Dares, Benoît says that Hecuba had
eight children, five sons and three daughters (ll. 2930–55); Eleanor and
Henry had eight children, five sons (the oldest of whom died in childhood) and three daughters.[33] In addition, Benoît pays considerable attention to Trojan culture in terms of its richness and refinement, the best
example perhaps being the portrayal of Helen and Paris's *Chambre de
Beautés*. The emphasis on the artistic splendor of the Trojan court echoes
that of the Angevin. More significant perhaps is the description of the rebuilding of Troy after its first destruction:

> Mout la troverent deguastee,
> Mais cent tanz mieuz l'ont restoree;
> Mout la refirent bele et gente. [ll. 3001–03]

> [But they restored it one hundred times better;
> They rebuilt a very beautiful and pleasant city.]

He includes many details regarding the reconstruction, including the
specifics of the parapets, city walls, roads, and Ilion, the principal fortress.
In particular, Priam has built a luxurious hall made of marble and ebony
with walls encrusted with precious stones and decorated with magnificent
sculptures (ll. 3099–3110). So large is this room that there is enough space
for "ses granz maisniees" [his great household] (ll. 3113–14). The depiction
of the rebuilding of Troy echoes Henry's considerable efforts during his
entire reign to strengthen and repair the castles throughout his domains.[34]
The chronicler Robert of Torigny describes on many occasions the king's
architectural enterprises, particularly his fortification of the queen's palace
at Poitiers and of the fortress-palace at Rouen, which included the building of a great hall, a site that, in 1162, would serve as the assembly room
for his vassals from Normandy.[35]

As a myth of descent, the *Roman de Troie* presents both the purported origins of the Angevin court, made more obvious by the parallels between Helen and Eleanor, and a pattern to shape the future of the Angevin dynasty through the theme of lineage and its preservation. Thus Benoît's story of Troy does not conclude with the end of the Trojan war and the subversion of social order but with the reconciliation of lineage so that familial lines are seen to continue, thereby restabilizing society. Certainly, the stories that conclude the poem can be generalized as tales of vengeance, for Benoît tells of Nauplus's revenge for his son's death, of Agamemnon's murder and Orestes's retaliation, of Pyrrhus's revenge for the death of his grandfather, of Pyrrhus's death at Orestes's hands, and of Ulysses's death at the hands of his own son, Telegonus. I would, however, disagree with Lee Patterson that the poem's ending, particularly the story of Ulysses, completes the general disaster of the Greek homecoming.[36] The last two stories focus as much on the reestablishment of hereditary lines as on themes of vengeance, leaving the reader with a more positive view of the conclusion of the Trojan war. In relating the story of Pyrrhus, Benoît describes how the Greek follower marries Hector's widow, Andromache, who already has a son, Laodamas, by the Trojan prince. With Pyrrhus she has another son, Achillides, and the two half-brothers, Trojan and Greek, grow up together to become close friends even after Pyrrhus's death (ll. 29777–810). More significant perhaps is the story in which Ulysses is killed by his illegitimate son, Telegonus, whom he fathered by Circe. As Benoît retells the episode, the emphasis is as much on the uniting of Telegonus with his half-brother, Telemachus, as it is on Ulysses's death. The story and, more importantly, the poem do not conclude with the Greek hero's death but with a description of Telemachus's reign over his father's kingdom with the help of his half-brother, "Ensemble o lui un an e plus" [together with him for over a year] (l. 30270).[37] When Telegonus eventually returns to Circe's island, he rules there and enjoys a similar peace. The erotic passion involved in the conception of an alternate lineage—Telegonus—results initially in death and potential chaos, but ultimately the conflict is resolved by a harmonizing of familial lines.

Thus the *Roman de Troie*, which begins with a tale of deceit and betrayal leading to the end of a dynastic line, finishes with reestablished peace and familial descent by a new generation. It is a similar promise that Henry offers Britain, for the twenty years preceding his reign were ones of devastating war. Upon succeeding Stephen, and already married to Eleanor, Henry II brought the potential of political stability and a new lineage. However, history cannot be shaped in the same way as a literary work. While Henry's reign may be characterized as one that established order and organization in diverse dominions, his relationship with Eleanor proved to be anything but ideal. Although little is known of the early years of their marriage, by 1174 Eleanor was imprisoned for sixteen years for her part in her sons' rebellion against their father.[38] Nor did Henry fare much better with his children. In addition to young Henry's attempted uprising, Richard and John joined forces with Philip II, king of France, against their father at the end of his reign. Their act of betrayal dealt what is traditionally regarded as Henry II's death blow, for the king died three weeks after his defeat in France against Richard and Philip. Ironically, Henry's life ends in an almost peculiar inversion of the Ulysses story. Richard and John's treasonous actions in all likelihood hastened their father's death, and the two brothers, in contrast to Telemachus and Telegonus, do not afterwards live in accord: Richard is perhaps best remembered as an absentee ruler, and John, who governed in his absence, continually plotted against his brother.[39] Ironically, it is Henry II's very *lignage*—so important to him, so crucial to the *Roman de Troie*—that ultimately undermined his kingship.

It is in an earlier historical context, however, that Eleanor would have read the *Roman de Troie*. When first written, Benoît's poem must have been, for her, more than a myth of descent for a nation. Not only could she see herself and Henry in Benoît's presentation of Helen and Paris, but Troy's exotic, oriental setting might well have reminded her of the marvellous Byzantine court of Manuel Comnenus which, as Louis's wife, she visited during the Crusades in 1147. And, in the anachronistic presentation of Troy as a model of *courtoisie,* she would have recognized the prefiguration of her own twelfth-century culture, a *civilisation courtoise*.[40] Thus, in the invention of Briseida, Benoît creates a foil for both Helen and Eleanor, for her literary depiction does not merely echo and contrast Helen's; it also illuminates the brilliance of the Trojan—and, by extension, the Angevin—queen. Benoît underscores this point with the passage eulogizing the "Riche dame del riche rei," making it unquestionably explicit that no reader, not even Eleanor herself, should view Briseida as the reflection of either queen. Eleanor of Aquitaine, in all likelihood, did not commission the *Roman de Troie,* and we cannot say definitively that she was the intended reader—but we can argue that she was the expected reader, one who would have easily recognized herself and her royal sovereignty in Benoît's presentation of Helen and the Trojan war.

Notes

This article was prepared while the author was a postdoctoral fellow through the Social Sciences and Humanities Research Council of Canada.

1. This has been most strongly argued by Kelly in *Eleanor and the Four Kings;* Labande in "Pour une image véridique"; and Lejeune, "Rôle littéraire d'Aliénor."

2. All references are to Benoît, *Le Roman de Troie.*

3. Unless otherwise noted, all translations are my own.

4. In particular: Haskins, "Henry II as a Patron of Literature," p. 75; Schirmer and Broich, *Studien,* pp. 19, 78, and 199; Bezzola, *Origines* 3:271–91; Flutre and Mora, "Benoît," p. 139b; Dronke, "Peter of Blois," 186; Baumgartner, "Repères," p. 25; B. Nolan, *Chaucer and the Tradition of the* Roman Antique, p. 41.

5. Broadhurst, "Henry II and Eleanor of Aquitaine." This detailed study of the passages of texts associated with Henry and Eleanor contends that the royal couple's role as literary patrons has been grossly exaggerated.

6. Broadhurst, "Henry II and Eleanor of Aquitaine," 73.

7. Broadhurst, "Henry II and Eleanor of Aquitaine," 73–74; see especially Cowper, "Date and Dedication of the Roman de Troie," 380; Walter Map, *De nugis curialium,* p. 450, cited in Broadhurst "Henry II and Eleanor of Aquitaine," n5.

8. The dating of the *Roman de Troie* is discussed by Constans in the introduction of his edition of the poem (6:182); though Constans dates it between 1155 and 1160, recent critics, such as Baumgartner, "Repères," pp. 11–13, give a date between 1165 and 1170. Cf. n33 below.

9. In classical tradition, it is not Achilles's desire to marry Polyxena that causes him to refuse to fight in the Trojan war but the loss of Briseis. Benoît evidently did not realize that Dares's Briseis is the same woman as Dictys's Hippodamia, daughter of Brises, for elsewhere in the *Roman de Troie,* beginning at l. 26747 he retells the story of Agamemnon's taking of Hippodamia.

10. D. Kelly, "The Invention of Briseida's Story," 222–23.

11. Agamemnon also appeals to issues of "shame" and "injury" when he encourages Menelaus to declare war on Troy (ll. 4973–78).

12. The scandal of adultery associated with Eleanor during her marriage to Louis is discussed in this volume by McCracken in chapter 12, and Parsons in chapter 13.

13. R.M. Lumiansky, "Structural Unity in Benoît's *Roman de Troie,*" 415, believes that Benoît dramatizes the courtship of Helen in order to increase the love interest; Jones, *Theme of Love in the Romans d'Antiquité,* pp. 47–50, argues that Benoît deliberately idealizes the couple because their love is mutual; B. Nolan, *Chaucer and the Tradition of the* Roman Antique, p. 109, interprets Paris and Helen's relationship as one of private, "foolish" love.

14. Jones, *Theme of Love in the Romans d'Antiquité,* p. 47: "These changes [to the story of Paris and Helen] would tend to suggest that Benoît has deliberately placed this couple in a favourable light."

15. Patterson, *Chaucer and the Subject of History,* p. 118.

16. Here Benoît adheres strictly to his source, for Dares describes Helen as "non invitam" [not unwilling] X.23, implying her possible collusion rather than asserting it [*Daretis Phrygii*]; rarely does Benoît fail to expand upon his source material, particularly with respect to the love narratives.

17. Joseph of Exeter, *Trojan War I-III* 3:329–38; the translation is from A.G. Rigg and Carin Ruff's forthcoming complete translation of the work, with critical commentary.

18. B. Nolan, *Chaucer and the Tradition of the* Roman Antique, p. 108.

19. Legge, *Anglo-Norman Literature*, p. 75.

20. Eley, "Myth of Trojan Descent," 28–29; Reynolds, "Medieval *Origines Gentium*"; Joly, *Benoît*, p. 112; Birns, "The Trojan Myth: Postmodern Reverberations."

21. Reynolds, "Medieval *Origines Gentium*," 385.

22. Howe, *Migration and Mythmaking*, pp. 2–4.

23. Jean Bonnard, *Les Traductions de la Bible en vers français au moyen âge.* Eley, "Myth of Trojan Descent," 30 n15, notes that the *Roman de Troie* is also found with Wace's chronicles and parts of the *Histoire ancienne jusqu'à César.*

24. Reynolds, "Medieval *Origines Gentium*," 378.

25. The issue of genealogy in historical narratives is more fully discussed in Spiegel's "Genealogy."

26. Giraldus Cambrensis, *De Principis Instructione Liber,* 8:301, 309; Brown also notes this belief ("Eleanor of Aquitaine: Parent, Queen, and Duchess," p. 15).

27. Warren, *Henry II*, pp. 12–53.

28. Warren, *Henry II*, p. 42.

29. Torigni, *Chronica*, ed. Howlett, 4:165.

30. Gervase of Canterbury, *Opera Historica*, 1:149.

31. Giraldus Cambrensis, *De Principis Instructione Liber*, 8:300.

32. In chapter 16 in this volume, Margaret Pappano well argues the idea that a literary text could have this degree of historical referentiality, particularly in terms of its connection to Eleanor.

33. One of Hecuba's "daughters" is actually a daughter-in-law, Andromache. Eleanor's children with Henry II were William (1153–56); Henry (1155–83); Matilda (1156–89); Richard I (1157–99); Geoffrey (1158–86); Eleanor (1162–1214); Joan (1165–1199); and John (1166–1216). Ferrante, *Glory of Her Sex,* p. 116, also suggests that this parallel between the number and composition of the two women's offspring would have allowed Eleanor to identify herself with Helen. Andrew Lewis's chapter 7 in this volume establishes that Eleanor and Henry in fact had nine children, of whom one son (name unknown) died in infancy. That son lived briefly enough to merit only a passing reference to him by a single chronicler, and his birth date is unknown. But as the chronology of the eight other births is well established, this boy presumably lived out his brief life between the births of Geoffrey (1158) and Eleanor (1162), or between 1162 and Joan's birth (1165). In any event, this son's existence means that if Benoît did

write the *Roman de Troie* at a time when Eleanor and Henry II had had eight children, he must have done so *before* John's birth in 1166. Cf. above, n8.

34. Warren, *Henry II,* pp. 234–36.
35. Torigni, *Chronica,* ed. Howlett, 4:106, 209–10; Richard, *L'Histoire des Comtes de Poitou* 2:141.
36. Patterson, *Chaucer and the Subject of History,* pp. 121–22 n91.
37. As we have seen with the story of Jason and Medea, Benoît does not hesitate to adapt his source material when he wants to end a narrative at a particular episode, even if it is not the traditional conclusion; had he so wanted, he could have done the same here.
38. Consequently, it is not surprising that Joseph of Exeter, writing some time in the 1180s, had no apparent reservations about portraying his Helen as a wanton aggressor.
39. Warren, *Henry II,* pp. 594–630.
40. Baumgartner, "La Très Belle Ville," p. 52. For more discussion of anachronism in twelfth-century French literature see A. Petit, "L'Anachronisme."

CHAPTER 15

WHAT EVER HAPPENED TO ELEANOR? REFLECTIONS OF ELEANOR OF AQUITAINE IN WACE'S *ROMAN DE BRUT* AND LAWMAN'S *BRUT*

Fiona Tolhurst

> *The drastic shift in the portrayal of Queen Guenevere as Lawman transforms Wace's version of the Arthurian legend is most likely the result of the decline in Eleanor of Aquitaine's reputation in annals and chronicle histories at the turn of the thirteenth century.*

Anglo-Norman treatments of the Arthurian legend during the twelfth and thirteenth centuries offer strikingly varied presentations of Guenevere. Having defined how Geoffrey of Monmouth's presentation of Arthur's queen in the *Historia Regum Britanniæ* reflects his interest in the life of Empress Matilda, I then wondered whether Guenevere's portrayals in the works of Geoffrey's translators—Wace's *Roman de Brut* and Lawman's *Brut*—might likewise reflect an interest in the life of a female historical figure. Using feminist and New Historicist methodologies, I have identified both broad patterns of connection among female characters in each translation and specific patterns of connection between Guenevere in these two texts and Eleanor of Aquitaine. The drastic shift in the portrayal of Queen Guenevere as the Arthurian legend gets transformed from Wace's *Roman de Brut* into Lawman's *Brut* is certainly consistent with the two poets' respective treatments of female characters. However, given Wace's connections with Eleanor of Aquitaine and Henry II as well as Lawman's composition of his Brut during a period of increasingly misogynist rhetoric, Eleanor emerges as the most likely female historical figure to whom these two writers respond. Consequently, the decline in Eleanor of Aquitaine's reputation in annals and chronicle histories at the turn of the thirteenth century offers the most plausible explanation of the decline in the reputation of Guenevere as Eleanor's fictional counterpart.

Eleanor's reputation among her contemporaries is difficult to assess because both twelfth- and thirteenth-century chroniclers and nineteenth- and twentieth-century biographers tend to blur history and legend. Both groups consequently vacillate between vehement but often formulaic praise, and vilification based on less-than-solid evidence. Just as the legend of Eleanor's role as literary patron has been grossly exaggerated when one scholar cites another's hypothesis as fact, but other distortions of her role in history have resulted from the disparate portrayals the queen's many biographers have created.[1] If some inaccuracies have resulted from the mixing of legend and history, other more recent ones have arisen from the assumption that Eleanor can be shown to have played a role in matters of state only if her name appears on charters and other documents.[2] Karen Broadhurst's useful corrective to the blending of legend and history that debunks the myth of Eleanor's patronage of courtly literature has led me to search for evidence of the supposed connection between Eleanor and Guenevere long assumed by literary critics and biographers alike.[3] This investigation of the twelfth- and early thirteenth-century annals and chronicle histories mentioning Eleanor suggests that the decline in Guenevere's reputation as we move from Wace to Lawman might well be connected to the concurrent decay of Eleanor's reputation among historical chroniclers, a connection that helps to position Wace's *Roman de Brut* and Lawman's *Brut* more precisely among histories and *historiæ*.[4]

Eleanor in Annals and Chronicle Histories

While Margaret Pappano suggests in this volume that Eleanor of Aquitaine might have been perceived to threaten an agnate system of inheritance,[5] medieval chroniclers responded ambivalently to the many aristocratic women in France who controlled land. Given their ambivalence, however, chroniclers' increasingly negative response to Eleanor of Aquitaine argues instead that, perhaps because her power was greater than that of other noblewomen, chroniclers saw her as a political threat to her two royal husbands. Elizabeth A.R. Brown's chapter in this volume notes several facts regarding Eleanor's lineage, official roles, influence over her sons, and competencies that could have encouraged mysogynist chroniclers to portray her negatively. In addition, as Pappano states, a French stereotype of Occ-

itans as having a "warlike, passionate nature and interest in love,"[6] or a more
general assumption that all women are overly emotional, might have col-
ored Eleanor's portrayal. Late twelfth- and early thirteenth-century chronicle histories depict her as a woman driven by her passions, but it is difficult
to attribute such a portrait of a powerful female figure to a single stereotype or image of women given the political complexities of the twelfth
century. Because agnate and cognate systems of inheritance co-existed into
the twelfth century, there was considerable confusion over the definition
of a queen's appropriate role. It is not surprising, therefore, that twelfth-
century romances and *historiæ* respond in various ways to the issue, especially when discussing the political impact of adultery, as we see in Wace's
and Lawman's portrayals of Guenevere.

Annals become the most common form of historical writing in the thirteenth century;[7] these are usually anonymous, containing little if any editorial commentary. Consequently, these sources say little about Eleanor. When
they do discuss her, however, they tend to make negative comments. These
remarks suggest that information of varying accuracy about Eleanor of
Aquitaine circulated as travelers visited various abbeys where the annals were
written. Antonia Gransden notes that monastic authors of annals treat King
John with more caution during his lifetime than after his death—partly because these historians lacked critical distance on recent events or, in some
cases, feared "alienating valuable friends."[8] Although this pattern might apply
to Eleanor as well, her relatively sparse coverage in the annals makes that determination unlikely. Despite this sampling problem, however, a pattern
emerges in the monastic annals in regard to their presentation of Queen
Eleanor. Thirteenth- century annals note most of the major events in
Eleanor's life—her divorce and remarriage in 1152, her coronation with
Henry II in 1155, her children's births, release from prison in 1189, her
freeing many of Henry's political prisoners when Richard acceded to the
throne, her conducting Berengaria to Richard, and her death in 1204—and
the few editorial comments made about Eleanor in relation to these events
are negative.[9] Furthermore, the more detailed annals, such as those of Dunstable and Worcester, include more of these negative evaluations.[10] The
Worcester annals, for example, note that Eleanor's marriage to Henry followed closely upon her divorce from Louis VII, while the more detailed
Chronicon of Thomae Wykes depicts her divorce as bitter and her marriage to
Henry as the result of lust.[11] Similarly, while some annals note the rebellions
of Henry II's sons without mentioning Eleanor's possible role in them, the
Dunstable annals say that Richard and Geoffrey rebelled "consilio matris" [in
consultation with, or according to the plan of, their mother].[12] Many annals
likewise note the Second Crusade without comment, but the more expansive accounts, like those of Waverley, criticize the entire crusading-pilgrim

group of which he notes that Eleanor was a member; it explains that through "rapina pauperim et ecclesiarum spoliante [pillage of the poor and plunder of the churches]," the pilgrims in 1147–49 brought on themselves famine, pestilence, and defeat at the hands of the pagans.[13] Thus the annals portray Eleanor neutrally if their coverage is minimal and negatively if it is reasonably detailed. Following a similar pattern are the chronicle histories, which portray Eleanor neutrally and, in some cases, positively when they say little about her.[14] In addition to this variation in the degree of detail that correlates with the amount of criticism Eleanor receives, there is another pattern at work in the annals that also applies to the chronicle histories. Despite their limited space for critique, annals written in the last years of the twelfth century and the early ones of the thirteenth describe Eleanor's role in the Second Crusade, her marriage to Henry II, her possible encouragement of her sons' rebellions, and her personality more negatively than do earlier annals. Chronicle histories likewise reflect this decline in the queen's reputation, but they do so more powerfully. Because they provide fuller accounts than annals, chronicle histories contain extensive editorial comments and therefore offer stronger evidence of this decline in Eleanor's reputation. Examining the chronicle histories enables us to trace how historians portrayed her personality and some of Eleanor's roles—in the Second Crusade, her marriage to Henry II, and her sons' rebellion—more negatively after the turn of the thirteenth century.

Because Eleanor's conduct on the Second Crusade with Louis is the aspect of her life that chroniclers most discuss and that they evaluate in the most disparate ways, it best illustrates the downturn in Eleanor's reputation. The only account written before the Second Crusade and the failure of Eleanor's marriage to Louis VII praises her for providing a good role model for other nobles and for the great resources her wealth brought to the effort in the Holy Land.[15] Odo of Deuil, "the 'official' historian of the Second Crusade, has virtually nothing to say about Eleanor," as Berry remarks.[16] Writing early in Henry II's reign, the English chronicler Henry of Huntingdon blames French arrogance and the crimes of the pilgrim group for the Second Crusade's failure.[17] Although Robert of Torigni wrote later in Henry's reign, he also blames the pilgrims as a group, not Eleanor specifically.[18] John of Salisbury, who was at pope Eugenius's papal curia from 1148 to 1152, provides an insider's view of tensions in the royal marriage during the Crusade but puts less emphasis on Louis's knowledge of his queen's adultery than on his fear of the shame that she might abandon him or be taken from him.[19]

Archbishop William of Tyre, who finished his *Historia rerum in partibus transmarinis gestarum* in 1184, relied on secondhand information for his account of the Second Crusade.[20] Nevertheless, William attacks Eleanor for unchaste behavior more explicitly than did John of Salisbury, however, presenting her adultery as a political attack on Louis VII.[21] As Margaret Pappano notes in this volume, William labels Eleanor "mulier imprudens [an imprudent woman]," who committed adultery "contra dignitatem regiam negligens legem maritalem, thori conjugalis fidem oblita [contrary to (her) queenly dignity, disrespecting (her) marriage contract (and) the vow of fealty to (her) marriage bed]."[22] Because she commits this sin with a man who manifestly desires to humiliate Louis, William of Tyre's account suggests the political threat Eleanor embodies, and he underscores this point by explaining that the king "clam egressus est [secretly left]" Antioch after discovering Eleanor's betrayal.[23]

Covering events through 1198, the English chronicler William of Newburgh broadened and strengthened the monastic authors' attack on Eleanor's conduct, paving the way for other historians to condemn her.[24] He broadened the attack by blaming the pilgrims' lavish lifestyle and the ease with which they could fornicate, which angered God against them, on the presence of women on the Second Crusade.[25] In addition, he strengthened the attack by accusing Eleanor of undermining the crusade in several ways: insisting on travelling with Louis, encouraging an inappropriate lifestyle by bringing her chambermaids, willfully disputing with Louis to facilitate her future divorce, and using her power to obtain a divorce motivated by lust for Henry.[26] Roger of Howden (d. 1201) more subtly condemns Eleanor by suggesting Eleanor's loss of wifely honor. He blames the crusade's failure on the troops who committed "omni genere scelerum [every type of wickedness]"—including adultery and fornication—and on French "superbia [arrogance]," but he suggests Eleanor's supposed criminality when he says Louis divorced her because many noblemen "jurantibus . . .illam demeruisse uxorem suam esse [took oaths that she was no longer fit to be his wife]."[27] Gerald of Wales mounts a still more vehement attack, as we might expect given his resentment of the fact that Henry II never appointed him to the principal Welsh bishopric. Gerald explains that because of Eleanor's sinful acts in Palestine, her divorce and remarriage, and Henry's sins, the royal couple was cursed in their sons; by underscoring his comment with the medieval equivalent of "enough said [satis est notum]," he implies that they deserved this fate.[28] Later French and English chroniclers blame the presence of Eleanor and other women for the Second Crusade's failure, as does the thirteenth-century English chronicler Matthew Paris when he notes Louis's passionate desire to take Eleanor on crusade.[29]

Just as there is a marked shift in the chronicler's portrayal of Eleanor's role on the Second Crusade as the twelfth century ends, there is a conspicuous change in the portrayal of her marriage. Henry of Huntingdon, writing at the beginning of Henry's reign, presents Eleanor's divorce and remarriage neutrally, noting only that marrying Eleanor greatly increased Henry's power.[30] Robert of Torigni (whose *Chronique* ends in 1186) states that he was unsure whether Henry married Eleanor "sive repentino sive praemeditato consilio [either hastily or with premeditated deliberation]."[31] Gervase of Canterbury, who might have continued his work into the thirteenth century, claims Henry married out of lust for Eleanor and her possessions. Developing a "doubtful account" at the turn of the thirteenth century,[32] Gervase also emphasizes Eleanor's personal role in arranging her own marriage, creating a tale of a messenger whose role shades into that of pander, as Margaret Pappano notes in this volume.[33] Walter Map's *De Nugis Curialium* (1181–92) suggests the possibility of Eleanor's inappropriate premarital relations when he describes how Eleanor "iniecit oculos incestos [cast unchaste/lewd eyes]" on Henry and married him through an "iniustum machinata diuorcium [unjustly gotten separation (she) arranged]."[34] Pappano also suggests that William of Newburgh (writing ca. 1196–98) uses syntax to imply Eleanor's disregard for her daughters and to connect her unworthiness as a mother to "her shifting national allegiance and compulsive desire."[35] Ralph of Coggeshall, whose *Chronicon Anglicarum* covers events from 1066 to 1223, treats Eleanor's divorce and remarriage with contempt, despite his brief and therefore neutral account of her journey to the Holy Land.[36] Not only does Ralph choose the verb "repudiavit [cast off]" for the manner in which Louis divorced Eleanor, but he notes that she became Henry's wife "sine mora [without delay]," suggesting inappropriate haste.[37] Ralph notes Eleanor's death in 1204 by defining her as having wed first King Louis and then King Henry, probably to encourage readers to remember her as a sinful woman.[38] Certainly this chronicler did not shy away from expressing intolerance of any heretic or sinner, even a queen.[39] Like Ralph of Coggeshall, Gerald of Wales—who covers events to King John's death in 1216—does not hesitate to accuse Eleanor of moral wrongs. He reports that Henry and Eleanor had "adulterino concubito [adulterous intercourse]" before marriage,[40] and goes beyond previous chroniclers by asking how a union begun in lust could possibly produce good offspring.[41] Finally, writing in the mid-thirteenth century, Matthew Paris brands Eleanor an adulteress "qui genere fuit diaboli [who was engendered by the devil]," and whose crimes, along with consanguinity, caused Louis to divorce her.[42]

Accounts of the degree to which Eleanor encouraged her sons to rebel against Henry II vary among late twelfth- and early thirteenth-century chronicle histories, but a number of them blame her for the turbulent fifteen years preceding Henry's death in 1189. Many chroniclers impute to Philip II of France young Henry's first rebellion against his father in

1173–74, but they begin to blame Eleanor for the ongoing state of dynastic strife in England from 1173 until 1189. Robert of Torigni, covering events through 1186, states that after young Henry's death, Eleanor, Richard, and Geoffrey rebelled against Henry,[43] and seems to pun on the queen's name to suggest her turning her sons against their father.[44] The chronicle history ascribed to Benedict of Peterborough (covering 1169–92) also blames Eleanor, saying that Eleanor, Louis VII of France, and Radulph of Faia encouraged Henry's sons to rebel against him in 1173.[45] Some early thirteenth-century chroniclers make no negative comments about Eleanor, but this could be the result of their saying little about her at all. For example, Roger of Howden, whose chronicle history covers events up to 1201, does not connect her with her sons' rebellions against their father, but this is consistent with his neutral presentation of other events.[46] However, as we might expect given his sharp criticism of Eleanor's role in the Second Crusade, William of Newburgh blames the French king for advising young Henry to rebel, but makes Eleanor the primary culprit by stating that Richard and Geoffrey acted under the queen's influence by rebelling against their father in 1173 "connivente . . . matre" ([because of their] manipulative mother).[47] A quarter century later, Ralph of Coggeshall goes a step further: he brands Eleanor a co-conspirator with her sons and states that because she "cum filiis in eum insurgere voluit, per multos annos inclusam tenuit [wished to rise up with (her) sons against him (Henry II), he imprisoned (her) many years]."[48] Matthew Paris offers a slight variation on the claims of his predecessors by blaming King Louis for encouraging young Henry's first rebellion, and Eleanor for inciting Geoffrey and Richard to join their brothers in treason: "consilio matris suae, ut dicebatur, Alienor reginae, fratrem potius elegerunt sequi quam patrem [in consultation with or according to the plan of their mother Queen Eleanor, as it is said, they chose to follow (their) brother rather than (their) father]."[49] Such negative reports led to rumors that in 1175, Henry considered divorcing Eleanor.[50]

The chroniclers' assessments of Eleanor's character likewise take a turn for the worse in the late twelfth and early thirteenth centuries. Writing at the end of the twelfth century, Richard of Devizes offers a very positive portrait of Eleanor, probably to flatter the new king, Richard I.[51] But he does so in a very formulaic way, describing the queen in glowing if rather general terms, as "an incomparable woman, beautiful yet virtuous, powerful yet gentle, humble yet keen-witted, qualities which are most rarely found in women, who had lived long enough to have had two kings as husbands and two kings as sons, still tireless in all labours, at whose ability her age might marvel."[52] He undermines this portrait, however, with a marginal note—set off with an attention-grabbing wavy line surrounding it—about her supposed adultery on crusade.[53] In effect, Richard of Devizes draws attention to her alleged sin by claiming he should not discuss it, just as Geoffrey of Monmouth underscores Mordred and Guenevere's betrayal by saying he prefers to remain silent about it.[54] Gervase of Canterbury, who might have continued his work into the thirteenth century, takes a more direct approach when he defines Eleanor's character: "Erat enim prudens femina valde nobilibus orta natalibus, sed instabilis [She was a very wise woman, descended from noble stock, but fickle]"—an estimate many historians today accept unquestioningly.[55] Given some of her contemporaries' vehemently negative assessments of the queen, however, Gervase's characterization is hardly surprising. One example of such an opinion is Hugh of Lincoln's deathbed prophecy in 1200: because Eleanor insulted Louis VII by marrying Henry II so soon after her divorce, God's vengeance was to send Philip II of France to finish his work of ensuring that none of her four sons remained alive.[56] Given the serious weight accorded to deathbed prophecies at the time, and their function of expressing commonly held opinions, it is likely that others agreed with Hugh's assessment of the queen.[57] Of course, later chroniclers developed legends about Eleanor that had little or no basis in twelfth- and thirteenth-century chronicle histories: that she had an affair with Saladin, played at being an Amazon while on crusade, and murdered Henry II's mistress Rosamund Clifford.[58] Unfortunately, such legends still color historians' assessments of Eleanor.

What Has Eleanor to Do with Guenevere?
Eleanor and Wace's *Roman de Brut*

Circumstantial evidence connecting Eleanor of Aquitaine to Arthurian literature increases the likelihood that Eleanor provided the model for Wace's portrayal of Guenevere. First, some chroniclers connect events in Eleanor's life to Geoffrey of Monmouth's *Prophetiæ Merlini*. Roger of Howden connects the rebellion of the French and English nobles, young Henry, Richard, and Geoffrey against Henry II to one of the prophecies.[59] The 1189 entry in the Worcester annals associates Merlin's prophecy that the eagle will rejoice in her third nesting with Eleanor's divorce from Louis, her separation from Henry because incarceration, and the freedom Richard restored to her.[60] Wace's significance as an historian derives partly from the fact that he, John of Hexham, and John of Salisbury were the only historians of note writing during the first half of Henry II's reign. However, his significance also derives from his position as "Henry's official romance historian."[61] Although Gransden dismisses the strong tradition of the Norman romance historians whose work she feels offers only minor original contributions, I prefer to label these works as historiae in order to recognize, rather than dismiss, their blending of historical content with story or legend and the valuable information this mode of historiography yields.[62] This approach offers the benefit of revealing Wace as part of a historiographical tradition that includes his contemporaries as well as his predecessor Gaimar and his successor Benoît. By examining Wace in this context, we see not only that he and his colleagues created historiae that would please the Angevin kings but also, as Tamara O'Callaghan suggests in this volume, that Benoît might have designed his *Roman de Troie* to appeal to Eleanor as an "expected reader" by focusing on the disruption and final reestablishment of lineage, and by likening his Helen and Paris to Eleanor and Henry.[63]

Given this circumstantial evidence as well as Wace's own connections to Henry and Eleanor, it is not surprising that his portrait of Guenevere is more positive than Lawman's. Karen Broadhurst has confirmed that Wace's *Roman de Rou* "contains ample evidence of Henry's patronage," since he flatters Henry and, among other gifts, refers twice to a prebend in Bayeux the king gave him.[64] While there is no evidence of the royal couple's patronage of the *Roman de Brut,* Lawman's comment in the Caligula manuscript of the *Brut* that Eleanor received a copy of Wace's *Brut* "implies a relationship of potential patronage."[65] Despite the lack of an extant presentation copy, then, Wace's flattering portrait of Guenevere could represent an attempt to (re)gain the royal patronage and financial protection Wace thought he had when he began work on the *Roman de Rou* ca. 1160.[66] Wace, therefore, was in a position similar to that of Geoffrey of Monmouth ca. 1136 when the latter wrote the *Historia regum Britanniæ:* both were writing for a potential patron and probably shaped their portrayals of Guenevere to flatter a royal woman, respectively Empress Matilda and Eleanor of Aquitaine.

Given the *Roman de Brut*'s date of composition (1155), we would expect little if any negative coverage of Eleanor, whether stated in chronicle history or implied in *historiæ*. And, in fact, Wace's Guenevere receives the same kind of generalized emblematic praise that Eleanor did from some chroniclers.[67] Wace calls her "Une cuinte e noble meschine; / Bele esteit e curteise e gent, ... Mult fu de grant afaitement / E de noble cuntienement, / Mult fu large e buene parliere [a graceful and noble girl. She was beautiful, courteous and well-born, of a noble Roman family ... Her manners were perfect, her behaviour noble, and she talked freely and well" (vv. 9646–55)]. In addition, Wace adds to Geoffrey's account that "Artur l'ama mult e tint chiere; / Mais entr'els dous n'orent nul eir / Ne ne porent emfant aveir [Arthur loved her deeply and held her very dear; but the two of them produced no heir nor could they have any children" (vv. 9656–58)], perhaps to make his character resemble Eleanor, who suffered eight childless years with Louis VII and then had only daughters with him.[68] Wace makes Geoffrey of Monmouth's coronation scene more familiar and appealing to the royal couple by adding many lines about the wonderful finery at court—clothing, tapestries, and horses (vv. 10337–58). In addition, he changes Geoffrey's account of the knights' inability to choose between the king's and queen's processions because of the wonderful music to indecisiveness partly because of the music and partly because of ladies' presence at the ceremonies (v. 10428). Like Walter Map in *De Nugis Curialium* later in the twelfth century, Wace also comments on the evils of gambling, shifting from Geoffrey's focus on valorous tournament play inspired by the flirtatious damsels to one on the cheating and ensuing squabbles that come of dicing (vv. 10557–88).[69] More importantly, however, Wace claims that peasants and women in Arthur's realm are nobler than knights in other ones—"Neïs li povre païsant / Que chevalier en altres regnes, / E altresi erent les femes [vv. 10500–02]," and he expands the roles of female figures such as Lavinia and Tonuenne, mothers who help to build empires by producing heirs and, in Lavinia's case, by bringing dower land to her husband. Wace transforms Geoffrey's portrait of Lavinia the victim captured by Aeneas into a portrait of a potential ruler of Italy: as she becomes her father's only child and bears her son *after* Aeneas dies, she approaches the status of a cofounder of Rome.[70] Wace's comments on the sorrow and political danger of having one heir, no male heir, or no heir at all, as well as his flattering portraits of Marcia as qualified to rule by her intelligence and of Cordelia as reigning without her nephews' objections (as in Geoffrey's *Historia*), suggest that he translated his source with an eye to making his Guenevere a reflection of Eleanor.

Like the chroniclers who blame males for the rebellions of Henry's sons that created such turmoil, Wace places more blame on Mordred than on Guenevere as a betrayer of Arthur. Wace marks Mordred as disloyal from the outset, presages the damage he will do the realm, and describes his illicit love for the queen, which violates his feudal bond with his uncle as well as the laws against incest (vv. 11173–89). The poet then depicts Mordred as Arthur's betrayer when the king learns of the troubles at home (vv. 13013–46). Just as some annalists and chroniclers assume Eleanor had no role in her sons' rebellions and therefore do not mention her as a political actor, Wace makes Mordred the primary actor here, not Guenevere. Wace's depiction of a Mordred and Guenevere motivated by passion, moreover, resembles late-twelfth- and early-thirteenth-century chroniclers' portrayals of Eleanor and Raymond of Antioch, and of Henry and Eleanor at the time of their marriage. When Wace describes Arthur's queen as a tragic figure, he does so in ways that liken her to Eleanor. He notes that Arthur dotes upon her despite her inability to produce an heir (vv. 9657–58), as

Louis doted on Eleanor despite their lack of an heir. Though Wace impli-
cates Guenevere as Mordred's accomplice, he creates sympathy for her by
having her express remorse for tarnishing her honor and shaming the king,
and then withdraw to a nunnery (vv. 13206–22). Guenevere's conventual
retreat also likens her to Eleanor, who withdrew to the convent at
Fontevraud for much of her last ten years and became a nun before her
death.[71] Perhaps the poet's addition of Guenevere's guilt-ridden thoughts
and her desire to die reflects what Wace imagined Eleanor might have (or
should have) felt after her divorce from Louis.

Lawman's *Brut* as a Reflection of Eleanor of Aquitaine's Declining Reputation and as Historiography

Lawman's composition of his *Brut* at the turn of the thirteenth century or
soon thereafter,[72] his work as a priest or household chaplain,[73] and his
focus on national rather than Church history make him a pivotal figure in
English historiography. Antonia Gransden does not discuss his work, but
his production comes soon after what she calls the "golden age" of historiography in England in the 1180s and 1190s, years that witnessed the
composition of chronicles by such religious as William of Newburgh,
Richard of Devizes, and Gervase of Canterbury, and by secular clerks such
as Ralph of Diss and Roger of Howden.[74] The fervor with which Lawman recounts the glories of Arthur's campaigns abroad may therefore be
better understood if viewed as part of historians' larger tendency to shift
from a focus on governmental administration during Henry II's reign to
one on the king and Crusade during Richard's reign.[75] While Lawman focuses on a king we now treat as legendary, we should remember W.L. Warren's comment that "[t]he deeds of the legendary King Arthur were as
much a part of men's thinking in the twelfth century as the deeds (often
ill-understood) of the real King Henry II."[76] Lawman probably saw himself as part of larger trends in historiography, and scholars should do more
to position him in terms of those trends.

Lawman's streamlining of Wace's luxurious passages, some of which
dwell on female figures, results in a cursory treatment of Guenevere that
parallels the treatment of Eleanor in most annals and some chronicle histories.[77] Remembering chroniclers' harsher treatment of Eleanor as we
move into the thirteenth century, however, helps position Lawman's *Brut*
in the context of a larger pattern of English historiography. Writing at a
time when many chroniclers were harshly criticizing Eleanor, Lawman
transforms Wace's Guenevere in a way that suggests his awareness of contemporary responses to the queen-mother who threatened King Richard's
power by continuing to act as queen long after Henry II's death.[78] Like

Wace, Lawman chiefly blames Mordred for the kingdom's downfall—mourning that he was born (ll. 11084)—and praises Guenevere for her beauty and eloquence (ll. 11090–100). But he elaborates on Wace's statement that Arthur loved his queen dearly: perhaps to make her later betrayal all the more shocking, Lawman explains that the king remains in Cornwall all winter for love of her (ll. 11101–02), and will later return home to her with joy (ll. 11318–19). The poet also has Guenevere sit by the king's side at a feast (l. 11360), an intimation of her proper secondary role. In keeping with his strict adherence to gender hierarchy, when Lawman raises the issue of soldiers' idleness (l. 12426 ff.), he has Cador state bluntly Geoffrey of Monmouth and Wace's premise that peace makes men all but impotent, "nchal a-swunden" (l. 12450). Lawman thus defines feminine influence on men as a threat to political and even sexual potency. When Lawman foreshadows Mordred and Guenevere's betrayal for the second time, he says that Mordred was given Arthur's land to keep (l. 12709) and a few lines later states that *Mordred* was trusted with land, queen, and people (ll. 12735–36): the male figure is thus the controller of property. Yet Lawman demonizes Mordred and Guenevere equally, saying they were hated for destroying the land, and they both lost life and soul (ll. 12728–34). These revisions of Wace are consistent with Lawman's tendencies to categorize female figures either as useful to the system—as peace-weavers or tokens of exchange, noble partners who inspire men's bravery, and innocent victims—or as embodiments of evil that destroy the system. Just as Rowenne becomes a more calculating murderess in Lawman's translation of Wace's *Brut,* Guenevere becomes almost purely evil.[79]

Lawman develops a vehement account of Guenevere's crimes apparently because he felt that merely labelling her as evil was inadequate, just as William of Newburgh felt he had to offer a full account of Eleanor's misdeeds. The poet therefore adds Arthur's dream, in which Guenevere pulls down the hall roof on Arthur's head; Arthur responds by cutting her into pieces and throwing her into a black pit (ll. 14000–01). By thus disposing of Guenevere, Arthur eradicates her threat to his political and sexual potency. Certainly Arthur's vision of himself bestriding his hall as if it were a horse creates an image conflating political and sexual power (l. 13985), and his suffering from a fever indicates a visceral response to the threat Guenevere poses. His bemoaning her absence (l. 14021) again marks the queen as the root of the evil that destroys his kingdom. Lawman, then, creates a legend about Guenevere not unlike the chroniclers' tales about Eleanor. Not only does Lawman seem to relish the fact that Guenevere and Mordred do not expect Arthur to return to Britain and thereby expose their treachery (l. 14045), but he also has Arthur and Gawain pledge to kill the queen in spectacularly violent ways. Arthur will burn her, presumably as an adulteress (l. 14065), while Gawain will have her torn asunder by horses (l. 14083). All this venom cautions us against accepting Antonia Gransden's assessment of certain chronicle histories as "reliable" despite their male, clerical bias. Lawman reflects this bias when he ends his story of Guenevere with her despairing flight to the convent, calling her "kare-fullest wife [most sorrowful or most wretched of women (l. 14212)]"; the queen's mysterious disappearance could well suggest his feelings that a sinful woman might choose to absent herself from the world in shame or be executed for treason.[80] Through this suggestion, the poet completes the process of transforming Wace's noble queen who errs because of passion into a woman whom the reader should despise. Therefore, despite his legendary rather than historical content, Lawman participates in the same type of vehement woman-bashing prevalent in annals and chronicle histories from the late twelfth century on.

Conclusion

Lawman and Wace never state that they shape their versions of Guenevere according to their perceptions of Eleanor of Aquitaine. Nevertheless, given Wace's connections with Queen Eleanor and King Henry II and the composition of Lawman's text at a time when the historiographical tide was turning against Eleanor, an Eleanor-Guenevere connection is likely. Such a connection is all the more likely since, as others have noted, the divergent ways in which chroniclers treated Eleanor indicate that she was seen as representing women in general, just as Guenevere's character represents womankind in Wace's and Lawman's *Bruts*.[81] It should not surprise scholars, therefore, if Eleanor's declining reputation is the main cause of Guenevere's transformation from perfect courtly lady to dominion-destroying banshee; female figures, historical and literary, are often evaluated according to the extent to which they fit an author's ideal of womanhood, rather than by how they reflect the exigencies of their particular situations. Lawman's lashing out at Guenevere is not, then, fundamentally different from historians' harsh evaluations of King John's wife Isabella of Angoulême, who very soon after his death married a former fiancé in order to help her son Henry III, or of Henry III's wife Eleanor of Provence, who supposedly wielded excessive influence over him.[82] Since medieval chroniclers tend to depict feminine power as a threat to both Church and state, perhaps scholars should understand Eleanor's declining reputation from the turn of the thirteenth century onward as owing to increased clerical venom against women with political power as much as to the events of her life, and they should see the decay of Guenevere's reputation as a reflection of that decline.

Notes

I am grateful to Linda E. Mitchell of Alfred University for reading and commenting on an early draft of this article.

1. Twentieth-century biographies range from Rosenberg's *Eleanor of Aquitaine,* which both romanticizes Eleanor as a queen of the courts of love and vilifies her as a vengeful woman, to Meade's *Eleanor of Aquitaine,* which cites chronicle sources but creates a great deal of narrative out of these sources, to Weir's *Eleanor of Aquitaine* which provides documentation from chronicles and Pipe Rolls but often lacks references to specific passages or entries to support her interpretations.

2. Pappano, chapter 16 in this volume, cites Martin Aurell's "Aliénor d'Aquitaine (1124–1204) et ses historiens: la destruction d'un mythe?" pp. 43–49.

3. Broadhurst, "Henry II of England and Eleanor of Aquitaine" 53–84. Unlike Broadhurst, Owen, *Eleanor of Aquitaine,* p. 180, states as facts two assumptions about Eleanor: first, "If Henry saw himself as the neo-Arthur, then Eleanor was necessarily cast as the neo-Guenevere," and second, that Eleanor was "A known patron of this 'new wave' of courtly entertainment, [who] could not have failed to be aware of, and may well have relished, the role which it conferred on her."

4. I use the Latin term *historia* because its two main meanings, "history" and "story," embody the mixed content of twelfth- and thirteenth-century histories.

5. Pappano, chapter 16 in this volume, suggests that "The extent to which the chroniclers malign Eleanor may be related to her position as a woman who challenged the agnatic arrangement of power in the most far-reaching and fundamental way."

6. Pappano, chapter 16 in this volume.

7. Gransden, *Historical Writing* 1:320–21.

8. Gransden, *Historical Writing* 1:320–21.

9. Of course, Eleanor's marriage with Louis was annulled, so the term "divorce" is merely a convenient way of describing the separation of the royal couple with the Pope's blessing.

10. Gransden, *Historical Writing* 1:318.

11. See the Worcester annals and the *Chronicon Thomae Wykes,* ed. Luard, in *Annales Monastici,* respectively 4:380, 28. Except where indicated, English translations of passages from Latin annals and chronicle histories are my own.

12. Annals that do not allege Eleanor encouraged the rebellions of her sons include those of Waverley and Worcester, in *Annales Monastici,* respectively 2:240, 385; *Chronicon Thomae Wykes,* ed. Luard, in *Annales Monastici,* 4:34; and Roger of Wendover, *Flores Historiarum* 1:102. The Dunstable annals do mention her role (*Annales Monastici,* 3:201).

13. Waverley annals, in *Annales Monastici* 2:232.

14. One chronicle history that has little to say about Eleanor and presents her positively is *The Chronicle History of Jocelin of Brakelond*. Jocelin mentions Eleanor once (p. 46) because she returned the golden cup the abbey had given her since custom [*consuetudinem*] dictated that she receive one hundred marks when the king received a thousand. When Jocelin states that she returned it on behalf of the soul of King Henry, he makes no explicit editorial comment, but seems to include the incident to reveal the contrast between a greedy Richard I and his more caring, diplomatic mother.

15. *Chronicles of the Crusades*, p. 140. Hallam explains that, though Eleanor's presence on the Second Crusade was likely tolerated or encouraged because of her wealth, reasons given by contemporary writers included her overwhelming love for Louis, his for her, or jealousy that made him unable to leave her alone in France.

16. *Chronicles of the Crusades*, p. 140; Odo of Deuil, *De profectione Ludovici*. Berry explains at p. 16 that Eleanor "is mentioned only briefly" in Odo's chronicle history, and suggests at p. xxiii n67 that Odo might have revised his work after Eleanor's divorce and remarriage to remove most of his references to her; his few references to Eleanor appear in his text on pp. 55, 77, and 79.

17. Henry of Huntingdon, *Historia Anglorum*, ed. Arnold, p. 280.

18. Torigni, *Chronica*, ed. Howlett, 4:154, states they suffered "Quia de rapina pauperim et ecclesiarum spoliante."

19. John of Salisbury, *The Historia Pontificalis*, pp. 52–53, describes how Louis VII became suspicious of Raymond of Antioch's attentions to Eleanor and her desire to stay with Raymond when Louis traveled on; how Louis was upset at Eleanor's claim that her marriage to him should be dissolved due to consanguinity; and how Louis's forcing her to travel on with him only increased their anger at each other. Hallam, *Chronicles of the Crusades*, p. 140, explains that Eleanor's supposed affair with Raymond revived rumors about her relations with him when her father left her under his protection when she was about thirteen, rumors that later chroniclers exaggerated into a tale about Eleanor's romance with Saladin, who was actually about eleven years old in 1148.

20. Edbury and Rowe in *William of Tyre*, p. 55, state that William's information on the Second Crusade was relatively "thin."

21. William of Tyre, *Chronique*. For an English translation, see William of Tyre, *Deeds Done Beyond the Sea*.

22. William of Tyre, *Chronique*, p. 755. Pappano in chapter 16 in this volume argues that William connects Eleanor's supposed lack of chastity to a lack of national fidelity and depicts Raymond of Antioch's motivation as "purely political and then vengeful" while defining Eleanor's as "libidinous."

23. William of Tyre, *Chronique*, p. 755.

24. Monastic historians of the reigns of Henry II and Richard I included Robert of Torigni (wrote 1154–86), John of Hexham (fl. 1130–54), Gervase of Canterbury (ca. 1141–1210), and Richard of Devizes (fl. 1189–92).

Gransden, *Historical Writing,* p. 248, argues for grouping William of New-burgh (ca. 1135-ca. 1200) with the monastic historians, based on his Bene-dictine-influenced outlook, but for grouping Richard of Devizes with the secular historians because his outlook resembles that of secular clerks.

25. William of Newburgh, *Historia Rerum Anglicarum* 1:66.
26. William of Newburgh, *Historia Rerum Anglicarum* 1:92–93.
27. Howden, *Chronica* 1:210, 214.
28. Gerald of Wales [Giraldus Cambrensis], *De Principis Instructione Liber* 8:299.
29. Matthew Paris, *Chronica Majora* 2:182.
30. Henry of Huntingdon, *Historia Anglorum,* ed. Arnold, p. 283.
31. Torigni, *Chronique* 4:165.
32. Warren, *Henry II,* p. 42.
33. Gervase of Canterbury, *Opera Historica* 1:149; Pappano in chapter 16 in this volume.
34. Walter Map, *De nugis curialium,* p. 474.
35. Pappano, chapter 16 in this volume.
36. Ralph of Coggeshall, *Chronicon Anglicanum,* p. 12. Gransden, *Historical Writing,* pp. 323–24, notes that Ralph's contribution is hard to assess; probably he was the original author from 1187, but it is unlikely he continued the work to 1227, as the 1207 entry claims.
37. Ralph of Coggeshall, *Chronicon Anglicanum,* p. 13.
38. Ralph of Coggeshall, *Chronicon Anglicanum,* p. 144.
39. Gransden, *Historical Writing,* p. 328.
40. Gerald of Wales, [Giraldus Cambrensis], *De Principis Instructione Liber* 8:300. For other ramifications of Gerald's comments see Tamara F. O'Callaghan, chapter 14 in this volume.
41. Gerald of Wales [Giraldus Cambrensis], *De Principis Instructione Liber* 8:301.
42. Matthew Paris, *Chronica Majora,* 2:186: " . . .erant enim consanguinei in quarto gradu; praeterea diffamata est de [ad]ulterio, etiam cum infideli, et qui genere fuit diaboli [for they were related in the fourth degree; besides this she had been defamed on account of (her being) adulterous, also faith-less, and as having been engendered by the devil]."
43. Torigni, *Chronique* 4:256.
44. Torigni, *Chronique* 4:256: "similiter regina *Alienor* et filii sui, Ricardus comes Pictavensis et Gaufridus comes Britanniae *alienati* sunt ab eo [in like manner Queen Eleanor and her sons, Richard Count of Picardy and Ge-offrey Count of Brittany, were alienated from him (Henry)]," might be a pun on her name that reveals the "otherness through which [chroniclers] conflated representations of her foreignness, her sexual desire, her insubor-dination" (Pappano, chapter 16 in this volume).
45. Benedict of Peterborough, *Gesta Regis Henrici Secundi* 1:42. "Radulph de Faia" was Eleanor's maternal uncle Raoul de Châtelleraut, lord of Faye, her seneschal in Poitou.
46. Howden, *Chronica,* describes Young Henry's plot with Louis VII (2:46), the rebellion of Henry's sons in 1173 (2:48), the treaty between Henry and his

sons in 1174 (2:67), and notes Eleanor's presence at the peace made between Henry and his sons in 1184 (2:288). Roger's final description of
Eleanor (4:114) is of a hard-working, respectable queen who retires to
Fontevraud "senio et longi itineris labore fatigata [fatigued by old age and
the labor of a long journey]" serving the realm.

47. William of Newburgh, *Historia rerum anglicanum* 1:170–71.
48. Ralph of Coggeshall, *Chronicon Anglicanum*, p. 18.
49. Matthew Paris, *Chronica Majora* 2:286.
50. Gervase of Canterbury, *Opera Historica* 1:257.
51. Gransden, *Historical Writing*, p. 249, thinks Richard of Devizes romanticizes
    Eleanor, but this is an oversimplification. Richard of Devizes, *Chronicon*,
    notes at pp. 3 and 6 Eleanor's significance as Richard and John's mother,
    and at p. 14 as the possessor of Aquitaine, which she received as her dower
    so that she could live on her own income thenceforth. He describes at p.
    28 Richard I's affectionate and respectful treatment of his mother, and at
    p. 59 calls her "That matron, worthy of being mentioned so many times,
    Queen Eleanor." At p. 60, Devizes portrays her as a compassionate protec-
    tor of the people when the clergy's political wrangling caused them suf-
    fering and as a positive moral influence on her sons.
52. Richard of Devizes, *Chronicon*, p. 25.
53. Peggy McCracken, chapter 12 in this volume, citing Harvey, *Marcabru*, p.
    133.
54. Tolhurst, "The Britons as Hebrews, Romans, and Normans," 76–77.
55. Gervase of Canterbury, *Opera Historica* 1:242–3. Warren, *Henry II*, p. 120,
    cites this passage from Gervase of Canterbury as an accurate assessment of
    Eleanor's character.
56. Believing that the deaths of Eleanor's sons were God's vengeance for in-
    sulting Louis VII, Hugh prophesied: "this Frenchman, Philip, will wipe out
    the English royal stock, just as an ox plucks up grass by its roots, for already
    three of the sons [young Henry, Geoffrey of Brittany, and Richard I] have
    been eliminated and the fourth one [John] will only have a short respite"
    (Clanchy, *England and Its Rulers 1066–1272*, pp. 142–43, citing *The Life of
    St. Hugh of Lincoln* 2:185).
57. Clanchy, *England and Its Rulers*, p. 143. Evelyn Mullally, in chapter 11 in this
    volume, discusses one exception to the rule of Eleanor's declining reputa-
    tion, the *Histoire de Guillaume le Maréchal* (ca. 1226), which praises Eleanor
    as liberal in her gifts to William as his lord, as a wise counselor, and as a
    person who valued William's loyalty and rewarded it. However, this praise
    comes in a work that devotes little narrative space to Eleanor because its
    focus is William, and it may praise her to flatter Marshal, or as a function
    of his connection with Eleanor as young Henry's tutor.
58. For the development of these legends and others, see Chambers, "Some
    Legends Concerning Eleanor."
59. Roger of Howden, *Chronica* 2:47.
60. Worcester annals in *Annales Monastici* 4:162.

61. Grandsen, *Historical Writing*, pp. 219, 236.
62. Grandsen, *Historical Writing*, pp. 219, 236.
63. O'Callaghan, chapter 14 in this volume.
64. Broadhurst, "Henry II of England and Eleanor of Aquitaine," 56–57.
65. Broadhurst, "Henry II of England and Eleanor of Aquitaine," 72.
66. Broadhurst, "Henry II of England and Eleanor of Aquitaine," 55. Judith Weiss agrees with Broadhurst's assessment in the introduction to Wace's *Roman de Brut*, p. xiii.
67. All subsequent references are to Wace, *Roman de Brut*, ed. Weiss.
68. Brown, chapter 1 in this volume.
69. As Weiss points out (*Wace's Roman de Brut*, p. 266), several MSS omit lines 10543–88. Since we do not know what manuscript of the *Roman de Brut* Lawman used, however, we cannot know whether or not he knew these lines.
70. Tolhurst, "The Once and Future Queen," 277–80.
71. Brown, chapter 1 in this volume.
72. Le Saux in *Laȝamon's Brut*, pp. 9–10, argues persuasively for a *terminus ad quem* of 1216 (Henry III's accession).
73. *Laȝamon Brut*, ed. Barron and Weinberg p. xvii.
74. Gransden, *Historical Writing*, p. 219.
75. Gransden, *Historical Writing*, pp. 220–221.
76. Warren, *King John*, p. 4.
77. All subsequent references are to *Laȝamon*, ed. Brook and Leslie. I cite the Caligula MS because it gives a more complete account than the Otho MS. See Caligula, ll. 12211–341, 13982–14021, and 14203–16, versus the Otho account which, in these passages, tends to condense descriptive passages slightly without altering the main narrative line.
78. In chapter 1 of this volume, Brown notes that Eleanor continued to receive Queen's Gold long after she ceased to be queen.
79. Lawman was not the first to create an unpleasant Guenevere. Marie de France's twelfth-century *lai* "Lanval," creates a queen who first attempts to seduce Lanval, then claims he tried to seduce her (Marie de France, *Les Lais de Marie de France*, ed. Rychner, pp. 80–82).
80. *Laȝamon Brut*, ed. Barron and Weinberg, note for p. 729.
81. McCracken, chapter 12 in this volume.
82. My thanks to Linda E. Mitchell of Alfred University for bringing this pattern to my attention.

CHAPTER 16

MARIE DE FRANCE, ALIÉNOR D'AQUITAINE, AND THE ALIEN QUEEN

Margaret Aziza Pappano

This chapter argues for an historical connection between Eleanor of Aquitaine and the woman poet Marie de France. By contextualizing Marie's lay of Lanval within contemporary chronicle accounts of Eleanor's life, it proposes that Marie offers an alternative conceptualization of the dilemma of feminine sovereign desire and provides insight into a female understanding of Eleanor's position as distinct from that of male clerical chroniclers.

From the beginning of the twentieth century, there has been extensive speculation about the connection between the notorious French and English queen, Eleanor of Aquitaine, and the "anonymous" Franco-phone poet Marie de France, two women whose dates of activity and geographical localities amply justify such suggestion. Several scholars identified Marie as an illegitimate daughter of Geoffrey of Anjou, and thus a half-sister of Henry II and sister-in-law to Eleanor.[1] Other aristocratic identities were proposed—even that of Marie de Champagne, Eleanor's elder daughter with Louis VII.[2] In addition to such speculation on Marie's birth and possible kinship to the Angevin royal house, scholars have proposed close literary relations between Eleanor and Marie de France, suggesting that Marie was patronized by Eleanor and was perhaps even part of her "entourage."[3]

However unsubstantiated or even fantastic such relations may appear to contemporary scholars, such speculation testifies to the desire to link these two unusual women. Post-structuralists engaged in Marie scholarship in the 1980s and early 1990s—represented in the United States most famously by the work of Michelle Freeman and R. Howard Bloch[4]—dispensed with such historical speculation and contextualizing interpretation, however, in favor of purely textual analysis. Marie's gendered identity remained the only significant "empirical" characteristic in interpreting her works, accounting for a specifically feminine poetics (a "poetics of silence" in Freeman's analysis, or for Bloch evidence of [post-structuralist] "literary value") that critics identified in her writing. Yet, now that literary studies have taken a more historicist turn, Marie studies have been sparse, perhaps bearing witness to the difficulty in dating and locating her works precisely.[5] This chapter is intended as a corrective to that neglect. Given the paucity of biographical information about Marie, I seek to shape a more theoretical argument about the possibility of interpreting her literary work as historical engagement with, or intervention in, contemporary controversies surrounding Eleanor's career as queen of France and England. I will propose ways in which we may consider the reading and writing of literature itself, by its very function in court culture, as a self-documenting historical process in its own right.

Three works are ascribed to Marie de France: the *Lais,* a collection of twelve rhymed octosyllabic poems on courtly themes; the *Fables,* a collection of 103 beast fables; and a devotional treatise, the *Purgatory of St. Patrick,* a translation and adaptation of Henry of Saltrey's *Tractatus de Purgatorio sancti Patricii.*[6] While none of her works is definitively dated, they are generally located in the years 1160–1215, a period that converges with Eleanor of Aquitaine's lifespan (ca. 1124–1204). Although her dialect is not considered Anglo-Norman,[7] Marie uses place names from England and France in her *Lais,* indicating familiarity with regional localities in both countries. The *Lais* are dedicated to a "nobles reis," whom scholars have almost unanimously identified with Henry II. There is no evidence that the Angevin court actually patronized Marie, save a suggestive excerpt from Denis Piramus's *Vie Seint Edmund le Rei,* the only piece of external evidence that exists about Marie. Piramus complains of the English court's literary tastes:

> And likewise Lady Marie
> who made and assembled in rhyme
> and composed the verses of the lais,
> which are not at all true;
> and for this she is much praised
> and the rhyme loved by all,
> Because many like it, they have much joy,

country, barons, and knights;
and they are so enamoured of the writing
that they often have them read and recounted,
by which they have pleasure.
The lais are accustomed to please ladies,
with joy and pleasure they listen to those
things that are made according to their desire.[8]

Piramus's complaint perhaps reveals more about the circulation of manuscripts than it does about Marie's position vis-à-vis the Angevin court or
about Henry and Eleanor themselves.[9] But this disparaging passage evinces
an effort to displace Marie's works by convincing the court of the superiority of Denis's writing and his hagiographical subject matter. Hence, it appears that Piramus regards Marie as a competitor of sorts, if not for royal
favor then for courtly visibility. Even if it cannot be firmly established that
Marie wrote under Angevin patronage, or even in the courtly milieu, Piramus's testimony shows that her *lais* were well known at the court. Since
she very possibly dedicated the *Lais* to Henry II, those works at least may
have been intended specifically for that audience. On this basis, I believe it
is important to conjecture about Marie's relationship to Eleanor, how
Marie's writing may have been influenced by stories that circulated about
this notorious and powerful queen, and, albeit more speculatively, how
Marie's depictions of feminine desire may have provided the court with
another way to understand the particular contradictions of Eleanor's position—caught between two countries, kings, and allegiances, and maligned
by chroniclers for her "infidelities," both national and sexual. This chapter
concentrates on Marie's *lai* of *Lanval* as read through contemporary accounts of Eleanor of Aquitaine's life. I will argue that Marie's depictions
explicate the paradoxes endemic to feminine sovereign desire in con-
tradistinction to the chronicle tradition, which represents the queen's desire as a force of disorder and national destruction. In this regard, Marie's
works are of central importance to Eleanor scholarship, as they may represent the only surviving contemporary view of this controversial queen
written from a woman's perspective.

Aside from the chronicle tradition, which this paper will address, several scholars have recently examined a number of literary contexts that
demonstrate Eleanor's influence on twelfth-century vernacular writing.
Joan Ferrante has argued for a nexus of allusions to Eleanor in Benoît de
Sainte-Maure's *Roman de Troie* and the anonymous *Roman de Thebes*, which
she reads as compliments to the powerful queen, analyzing in particular
their embellished depictions of queen-mothers.[10] Roberta Kreuger agrees
that Benoît's address to a "riche dame de riche rei" alludes to Eleanor but

considers it "backhanded" as it occurs in the context of Briseida's betrayal of Troilus.[11] In this volume, Tamara O'Callaghan offers a convincing reading of Eleanor's influence on the representation of Helen in Benoît's *Roman*, suggesting that even if the poem is not dedicated to or commissioned by Eleanor, her presence as audience is evident in the compositional choices.[12] Ruth Warner has made a provocative case for allusions to Eleanor in the lyrics of Marcabru and Cercamon, both of whom were associated with the court of Eleanor's grandfather Guillaume IX of Aquitaine.[13] Warner suggests that these *canzones*, concerned as they are with moralizing about an unfaithful lady and written in the context of the Second Crusade, refer to the scandal involving Eleanor and her uncle, Raymond of Antioch, an incident whose frequent appearance bespeaks its effects in shaping popular opinion of Eleanor. Forty years ago Rita Lejeune proposed that much of the Francophone literature (and in particular the romance) of the twelfth century was shaped by Eleanor, the most powerful queen in western Europe for most of that century.[14] Yet with the exception of those named above, scholars have been wary of theorizing an influence where no precise documentation exists, given the fragmentary nature of twelfth-century records.[15] Literary reading needs to be taken more seriously as a form of evidence, or our historical analysis will endlessly replicate the documents and speak from only the perspective of scribes and their employers.[16]

I

From their ubiquity in chronicle accounts, we may assume that the events or rumors (as they may be) of Eleanor's life were notorious. In particular, the frequent representations of Eleanor as a *mal mariée*, a woman who seeks love outside the constraints of marriage, provide a suggestive model for Marie's heroines. By giving rein to their desires, these women break out of the most sturdy prisons and obdurate marriages to find adventure and worthy love.[17] In the *lai* of *Equitain*, a name that resonates provocatively with *Aquitaine*, the wife of a seneschal attempts to negotiate a better match for herself with the king. This tale is strikingly similar to Eleanor's life: she managed, within eight weeks in 1152, to annul her marriage to Louis VII of France and marry Henry Plantagenet, soon to be king of England, taking from one marriage to another her vast holdings, the largest duchy in western Europe. The English chronicler William of Newburgh describes the consequences of these events: "Thereafter the duchy of Aquitaine, which stretches from the borders of Anjou and Brittany to the Pyrenees which divide Gaul from Spain, gradually withdrew from the dominion of France and passed into the power of the Duke of Normandy by right of his wife.

The French began to waste away with envy but they could not block the progress of the duke."[18] William concisely expounds a far-reaching impact on the national imagination: but what does it mean for such an enormous amount of territory—one-third of France—to change allegiances as a consequence of the fluctuations of a woman's desire? Eleanor's singular position must be understood in relation to the enormous duchy over which she ruled due to the precipitous deaths of male heirs in her family. Marion Facinger has pointed out that until Eleanor's marriage to Louis VII, no royal bride in France brought any significant amount of land to the crown. After Eleanor, the acquisition of territory became an important consideration in choosing the king's wife.[19] From the outset, therefore, Eleanor was a different kind of queen, one whose power and value were closely linked to land, making her both enormously desirable as a commodity and threatening since she possessed personal resources and allegiances far exceeding those of earlier queens. As R. Howard Bloch succinctly states, "Eleanor of Aquitaine or Aliénor d' Aquitaine, is, as far as feudalism is concerned, the great alienator."[20]

Not only did Aliénor represent the ability to alienate land, to transform it from French to English, but she further represented the exemplary alien queen because of her sustained connection to her natal domain throughout her life. Facinger's study of Capetian queenship identifies significant transformations in regnal policy beginning with Eleanor's marriage to Louis, an analysis supported by more recent scholarship. In the twelfth century, it is argued, queens began to lose official status in their capacity as the king's partner and turned to cultivating unofficial forms of power.[21] In striking contrast to her predecessor, Queen Adelaide, Eleanor's name is markedly absent from Capetian royal charters and official documents such as writs, which bear the king's name alone. Facinger accounts for this change in royal policy in part by the fact that Eleanor brought the single largest inheritance ever with her to a royal marriage and retained some measure of control over the culturally distinct Aquitanian territory while wed to Louis. As Facinger notes, "Eleanor had probably a larger personal retinue and certainly a more formally organized group of functionaries than previous queens. This situation is accounted for by the fact that the queen of France was also the duchess of Aquitaine and required a more structured retinue for the administration and maintenance of liaison with her holdings."[22] This separation of powers favored the creation of distinct spheres, with the result that Eleanor and her personal household "tend to coalesce and to separate spatially at times from the royal household."[23] What Facinger thus traces is Aliénor's alien status within the Capetian court. She was not assimilated into a royal partnership like previous queens but retained separate powers and followers and perhaps cultivated separate networks and allegiances. During her reign, she sustained a double identity through her political identification with her territories in the south of France alongside her position as the Capetian queen.[24]

Aliénor's Occitan identity, moreover, marked her as a representative of cultural difference as well as foreign political allegiance in the royal domain. The historians Pauline Stafford and Robert Bartlett have discussed the constellation of political ambitions and anxieties surrounding the "foreign queen" in the Middle Ages: queens frequently came from foreign lands, entering royal marriages as outsiders and bringing different languages and customs into their husbands' courts.[25] Stafford notes that these foreign wives often became objects of suspicion and, though technically standing as a sign of resolution, might "generate tensions" by the mere fact that their presence represented a reminder of rivalry within the intimacy of the court.[26] Bartlett notes that queens might come from far away to avoid "polarizing tendencies within the native aristocracy,"[27] but this situation left the queen isolated in her husband's court and, as Stafford has shown, even mistreated as an outsider.[28]

Eleanor's position was particularly provocative and precarious because of Aquitaine's status in relation to Capetian France. As a southerner, Eleanor was perched on the border of familiar and alien, same and other— "almost the same, but not quite," in Homi Bhabha's formulation,[29] a position that troubles the very coherence of the dominant subjectivity. In the twelfth century, the southern territories were nominally under the suzerainty of the Capetians and owed them homage, but Occitania and France were considered different regions politically, genealogically, and culturally.[30] The differences between the royal domain and Occitania were marked not only linguistically (the *langue d'oil* and the *langue d'oc*),[31] but even more strongly by pronounced distinctions in customs. At the end of the twelfth century, Linda Paterson sees "a real cleavage of values; chivalric values and rituals were well-developed in France at this time, but made little impact in the south."[32] Paterson has shown how these ethnic differences are widely represented in the poetry of the period, demonstrating a concern with mapping regional differences in terms of cultural stereotypes and enacting cultural encounter and distinction through the use of bilingual poetry like the *partimen*. The characteristics most commonly associated with southerners have to do with their supposed warlike, passionate nature and interest in love, characteristics that are represented from the French point of view as both barbaric and overly cultivated to the point of being effeminizing. For example, when Constance of Arles married King Robert of France in the eleventh century, the chronicler Rudolph Glaber recorded the following effects of the clash of northern and southern cultures:

For her sake a great flood of strange men from Auvergne and Aquitaine began to flow into France and Burgundy; they were flippant and vain fellows with strange manners and clothes; their weapons and the equipment of their horses were curious, and they were close-shaven from half-way down their heads; they were beardless like actors, wore indecent hose and shoes, and were totally devoid of good faith and respect for agreed peace. Alas! Their evil example was seized upon avidly by the whole people of France, formerly the most honorable of nations . . .[33]

From Glaber's perspective, the southerners corrupt the decent and staunchly masculine values of the French, importing debauched manners and foppish clothing styles. Occitania is at once effeminate and warlike, frivolous and barbaric, overly refined and uncivilized. These extreme dichotomies point to Glaber's attempt to constitute French identity as a norm in opposition to the deviancy of her southern neighbors, neighbors who at this time far outstripped the Capetians in territory, wealth, and artistic achievement. Such accounts are typical of the discourses surrounding a foreign queen's influence; whatever cultural distinctions she might bring tend to be marked as corruptive rather than regenerative insofar as the court, within shifting national landscapes, stands as the locus of national identity in its purest and surest form. Glaber laments: "This life now produces tyrants with perverse bodies, / foolish men without peace or faith dressed in too-short clothes / the slack state groans under womanly counsel."[34] The queen's excessive influence on the king, her "womanly counsel," is associated with degeneration not only in French character and culture but also in French bodies, linking the royal marriage to the integrity of the realm physically, genealogically, and morally. The status of the queen's assimilation and accommodation—whether she is the king's partner or consort, his equal or subordinate—is thus a particularly critical way of representing national integrity in the Middle Ages. National coherence is often signified through the successful domestication of the queen and the management of her desire.

As a foreigner, the queen cannot represent national interest and identity in the same way as the king. Kingship and queenship bear different burdens of sovereign expression and impose different relations with the realm's subjects. Louise Fradenburg analyzes the queen's status in these terms:

> . . . queens are not only unlike their subjects in that they are queens but are frequently unlike them in that they are foreigners and are unlike the bearers of official power in that they are women; and they are like their subjects not only in that they are human but also in that, unless they are regnant, they owe fidelity and must dedicate their creativity, their bodies as well as their hearts, to the king.[35]

Fradenburg identifies a tension endemic to the structural relation between subject and queen: how does a queen express sovereignty if she is not allowed the same whimsical desires as the king? How does she display her difference from her subjects if her expressions of desire, like theirs, must find their object in the king? As we see in contemporary accounts of royal power, the king's desire is marked by whim. It is sovereign desire precisely because it cannot be accounted for; it cannot be interpreted but must be simply internalized by the subject as his own desire. In *De nugis curialium,* Walter Map compares the Angevin court to Fortuna, citing the indiscriminate and irrational fluctuations of favor and disfavor Henry II bestowed. While the king acts with the blindness of fortune, "constant only in inconstancy," the courtiers assign reason to the capriciousness of sovereign expression.[36] For even if the king acts indiscriminately, his actions must be made to bespeak a superintelligence beyond normal human modes of understanding. Hence, in Map's description, the court constantly reorders itself in relation to sovereign caprice, replicating the arbitrariness of the sovereign in its systems of punishments and rewards, justices and injustices, and likes and dislikes, thus creating its own logic based on illogic. Similarly, in Marie's *lai Lanval,* the king's whim works against Lanval when he is excluded from gifts that the other knights receive; he is simply expected to accept the abjection thrust upon him by the king's inexplicable decision. We are told by way of explanation only that "ne l' en sovint"—Arthur did not remember him in the crucial distribution of gifts patterning relations of fealty and service to the king.[37] There is no reason assigned to this sovereign gesture that has far-reaching repercussions for the loyal knight—for there is no reason, other than sovereign whim.

How is the queen's desire expressed, how is it different from the king's, and how does the subject relate to it? Marie's intimate concern with these questions makes her writings important sources for discussion of female sovereignty in the High Middle Ages. For all its claims to superhumanity, sovereignty does not transcend gender but, rather, exercises its power and symbolism through its prism. Recent scholarship on queenship identifies the twelfth century as an important moment of change in women's role in the regnal structure, a change perhaps related to the reorganization of French aristocratic families from kinship networks into agnatic lineages. This new organization promoted male primogeniture and removed women from inheritance, which then passed through a single and increasingly consolidated male line.[38] This was Georges Duby's influential model of the French nobility, which has recently been challenged by historians documenting the lives of aristocratic women in high-medieval France.[39] Evidence has now been brought forward that aristocratic women did control property and participate in alliances in both their natal and marital families, but queens during this period appear notably more subject than lesser noblewomen to restraints and imaginative models. Queenship, indeed, may be said to deploy models of feminine passivity that were, on a practicable basis, contested and reformed by other powerful women.[40] Tracing the growing emphasis on the purely maternal role of the queen during this period, André Poulet notes that the queen was "subject to the interests of lineage and inheritance, . . . confined in a genealogical vocation, passive yet indispensable to a system in which power was heredity's corollary."[41] Since continuity is figured as the father's replacement by the son, the queen becomes a "passive" vehicle through whom patrilineal power and property passed. Her body bears male heirs but her identity and contribution to offspring are erased as genealogies emphasize their uniformity and unbroken continuity in terms of sameness with paternal ancestry. Hence the woman's resistance to a purely genealogical role—precisely, her *desire*—is seen as imminently threatening to succession and, in the case of queens, to national stability. It is for this reason, Peggy McCracken conjectures, that queenly adultery becomes such a prominent theme in the literary production of the period.[42]

In *Lanval,* Guenevere's desire is a source of disharmony and possible rebellion that must be managed and ultimately resolved through the workings of the state. This is why the trial, the medium *par excellence* of national determination, is presented as the solution to the crisis of the state posed by the queen's desire. I propose that the dilemmas of female sovereignty Marie represents in this *lai* can be understood in relation to the contemporary Eleanor of Aquitaine, an obvious if controversial source for this literary depiction. As her contemporary and ancillary commentators claimed, Eleanor failed to be domesticated, to be subsumed into her role as "consort queen," as evidenced by her purported sexual liaisons, her divorce, and later, alleged participation in the 1173–74 revolt of her sons against Henry, which led to a fifteen-year imprisonment. Of that revolt, Robert of Torigni wrote: "similiter regina *Alienor* et filii sui Ricardu comes Pictavensis et Gaufridus comes Britanniae *alienati* sunt ab eo [at the same time, Queen Alienor and her two sons, Richard count of Picardy and Geoffrey, count of Brittany, were alienated from [Henry]."[43] Robert plays upon the doubleness in Alienor's name, displaying precisely what chroniclers saw as her irreducible otherness through which they conflated representations of her foreignness, her sexual desire, and her insubordination. But such representations are a corollary of the chroniclers' agenda of history writing, the terms of which position feminine desire as a disruption to the transmission of knowledge that the chroniclers arrange, as Gabrielle Spiegel has shown, along genealogical lines, precisely in relation to the patrilineal organization of family.[44] The extent to which the chroniclers malign Eleanor may be related to

her position as a woman who challenged the agnatic arrangement of power
in the most far-reaching and fundamental way. In Robert of Torigni's account, Eleanor's refusal of the position of "consort queen," passively subordinate to Henry II's power, results in the rupture of the lineage as the sons
are also "alienated" (or "aliénored").

In *Lanval,* Marie presents two "queens": Guenevere, who represents the
queen as king's consort, and the unnamed fairy lady, a regnant woman who
governs her own domain. I propose that the fairy lady too is related to the
figure of Eleanor, as an embodiment of sovereign femininity and sovereign
desire. By doubling the figure of the queen, Marie asks us to consider how
they are different, how their expressions of desire are split according to
their relations to territory and king.[45] She shows how the system of territorial passage upon which feudal and sovereign power depend has as its occluded, but essential, corollary the control of feminine desire, the eruption
of which threatens to disrupt the entire system. Through the figure of the
fairy lady, Marie holds out the alternative of female rule, control over property, and true and noble desire, perhaps even figuring Aquitaine as a sort
of Avalon. Though I consider Marie's *lai* in relation to chronicle records of
Eleanor's life, I will propose that literature itself may become "historical"
evidence whose truth-value competes with, and even outweighs, that of
the tendentious documentation of male and royalist chroniclers.

II

At the beginning of *Lanval,* Arthur is in Wales because the Scots and Picts
are destroying England. To retain his subjects' loyalty in this crisis, Arthur
distributes "wives and lands" to those who serve him—in Marie's words,
"femmes e terres departi," underscoring by her succinct syntax the dominant feudal arrangement whereby women and land are undifferentiated
from each other in value. This formulation suggests that woman are like
land, passively exchanged from sovereign to vassal, from father to husband,
from man to man, with no consideration of female desire.[46] While this was
clearly the situation in much of England and France, Aliénor was an exception to the rule. She controlled her own land and object choice, at least
at one crucial and notorious point, choosing to divorce one king and
marry another and in the process changing the political affiliations of a vast
amount of territory. Territory had become the preeminent means by
which the *lignage* defined itself, signifying the fixity that was one of the
chief strategies of twelfth-century aristocratic organization and representation.[47] The transfer of land through feminine desire thoroughly disrupted
and discredited the patrilineal system of territorial control, undoing all the
strategies of hereditary security that depended upon the invisibility of

women. The spectre of female power that Eleanor's remarriage raised is thus rendered by the chroniclers through the image of an errant libido, a feminine body whose uncontrollable sexuality imperils the nation. As Marie has pointed out, women were like land in the feudal imagination, passively exchanged from man to man; the rupture of the French territory is consequently figured as an open and desiring feminine body, a body whose national affinities are dangerously unstable. In *De nugis curialium,* Walter Map wrote of these events: "upon [Henry], Eleanor, queen of the French, wife of the most pious Louis, cast unchaste eyes [*oculos incestos*], contrived an unrighteous annulment, and married him, though she was secretly reputed to have shared Louis's couch with [Henry's] father Geoffrey [of Anjou]. That is why, it is presumed, their offspring, tainted at the source, came to nought."[48] Though Eleanor's marriage with Louis had failed to produce a male heir after fifteen years, Map depicts their divorce not as a decision of state but as a result of her uncontrollable desire, a desire that escalates to become polymorphous, adulterous, and incestuous, as it includes Henry's father as well. Eleanor's desire is here depicted, moreover, as corruptive of the lineage, though not in the strictly literal sense, for it was never suggested that any of her offspring were illegitimate products of an adulterous union. Instead, more revealingly, the threat depicted here is that the children are tainted by their mother's past. Since woman's passivity in the maternal role is the critical component to agnatic organization, Eleanor's maternity itself is rendered corrupt and corruptive; though legitimate, her children are marked by signs of the desiring queen.

Eleanor's marriage to Henry in 1152 is unlike most noble marriages in that it seemingly involved no patriarchal management of the alliance as an instrument of state or familial policy. There is no extant evidence that Eleanor consulted advisers or submitted to any authority in her decision to marry Henry.[49] Indeed, the marriage itself is the moment in which the *lignage,* a system defined through the singular and inclusive organization of its power (it is a line, after all), reveals its own limits. For the chroniclers, the circumstances of 1152 can only be assigned to the vagaries of feminine desire—and this desire is, in contrast to kingly desire, self-serving, capricious, sexual, and destructive of the national good. William of Newburgh explains that Eleanor was dissatisfied with Louis because of his "monkish habits," a term suggesting that it is the queen's libidinous nature, unfulfilled by her pious but sexually inadequate husband, that compels her to dissolve her royal marriage. According to William, she seeks a man "more congenial" (*congruas*) to her own character:

> Eleanor was extremely irritated by the habits of the king, and claimed that
> she had married a monk, not a king. It is also said that even during her

marriage to the king of France she longed to be wed to the duke of Normandy as one more congenial to her own character, and that therefore she desired and obtained a separation. So the pressures became heavier. Eleanor, we are told, was most insistent, while Louis's opposition was non-existent or fairly feeble; so the bond of conjugal unity between them was loosed by the force of ecclesiastical law. *Eleanor was now free from the legal authority of a husband and had the power to marry whom she wished. She left her two daughters with their father; he later made provisions for them, and they married Henry and Theobald, the two sons of the most renowned count Theobald. Eleanor eventually obtained the marriage which she desired* [emphasis added].[50]

William here acts as a typical twelfth-century chronicler, twice using the phrase "dicitur" (it is said; we are told) in this short passage to mark the authoritative accounts from which he obtained his information; he casts himself as a mere recorder and compiler of events that gain their value not from his narration so much as from their relation to a past source. Spiegel argues that the rise of this historical methodology converges with the reorganization of aristocratic families into agnatic lineages, and, in fact, agnatic genealogy became a model for the writing of history.[51] In this model, value is located in the past, and each generation enjoys its legitimacy in so far as it represents a manifestation of the past, an ancestor, or here, ancient source.[52] Consequently, it is striking that William casts himself in a similar role to that of Louis in this passage; both chronicler and king are passively placed as observers of the event. Dependent upon an organization of power that precedes and supercedes the present, they fail to raise significant protest against the abberration. Eleanor's "insistence" or "desire" creates a rupture in the genealogy (and the narrative) as she passes out of Louis's control.

The final section of this passage, italicized above, is especially striking. It consists of a single, heavily subordinated sentence in Latin that is awkward to translate into literal English: "Porro illa soluta a lege viri et habens potestatem cui vellet nubendi, duabus apud patrem filiabus relictis, quae postea duobus illustrissimi comitis Teobaldi filiis, Henrico scilicet et Teobaldo, paterna provisione nupserunt, desideratis tandem polita est nuptiis."[53] William begins the sentence by emphasizing the singularity of the moment by which Eleanor is free from legal bonds: she "now had the power to marry whomever she wished." He ends the sentence by writing that she "at last" or "finally" ["tandem"] obtained the marriage to Henry, a term that is surely pointedly sarcastic. What is enclosed between these two ends is extremely significant: William inserts several clauses, not only about Eleanor's abandonment of her daughters, for whom Louis provided, but also their subsequent marriages to Count Theobald's sons. Since the

participial constructions at the beginning of the sentence are grammati-
cally subordinate to the finite verb at the end, William's syntactical arrangement highlights the remarriage's swiftness—divorce and remarriage take
place in one sentence—and Eleanor's desire to marry Henry, which compelled her to free herself from Louis. By inserting the daughters' marriages
between her own, furthermore, William contrasts proper marriage, in
which the woman is given away by the father, to Eleanor's improper marriage, in which she makes her own choice. The syntactical subordination
of the daughters' marriages also serves to imply that Eleanor was guilty of
maternal disregard for them in her rush to marry Henry. By leaving them
with Louis, who arranges French marriages for them, Eleanor in William's
single sentence also rapidly alienates herself from her children by marrying the claimant to the English throne. By representing Eleanor's remarriage through the abandonment of her daughters, William subtly connects
her image as a bad mother, one of her chief roles as queen and consort,
with her shifting national allegiance and compulsive desire.[54]

Writing around 1188, approximately a decade before William, Gervase
of Canterbury also represents the divorce between Eleanor and Louis as
motivated by her sexual desire. In his account, Eleanor, "disgusted [fastidi-
ens]" by "worn-out Gallic embraces [gallicos amplexus decrepitos]," con-
trives to divorce Louis. At liberty, she returns to her lands, where she
arranges her marriage to Henry. In Gervase's words, "by means of a messenger sent secretly to the duke, she announced that she was free and dissolved [from marriage] and incited the duke's desire to contract
matrimony. It is said that even her contrived repudiation from Louis was
advanced by this design."[55] Like William, Gervase is captivated by the singularity of this moment in which Eleanor, a "domina," a woman with a
duchy of her own, arranges her own marriage. Gervase suggests that it is
scandalous that Eleanor should divorce Louis and that she should do so to
pursue Henry. He may see the plotted nature of Eleanor's desire as particularly objectionable as it suggests that a woman might organize marriage
alliances on her own terms, but he nevertheless assigns its cause to a restless libido that seeks new objects of satisfaction. Gervase's description of
the secret messenger, whose role is to incite [stimulat] desire in Henry, is
represented without any reference to its source and is found in no other
contemporary source; it appears that Gervase included it to embellish his
account. Certainly the use of messengers is an assumed part of political negotiation, but here the messenger functions much like a pander, a sexual
go-between, a trope common to romance and literary texts in the Ovid-
ian and, of course, courtly literary tradition.

It is striking that chroniclers consistently avoid any suggestion that
Eleanor could have been driven to divorce Louis and marry Henry by any

other motivation than sexual desire. It appears unthinkable to them that as
duchess of Aquitaine, she might have had political reason to align herself
with the ambitious Henry Plantagenet, whose royal destiny was imminent if
incomplete in 1152. In so failing, the chroniclers deny her the very terms
they would properly use in their chronicle histories to describe royal sovereignty's political logic. Rather, the chroniclers consistently sexualize women's
power to depict it as a disorderly, uncontrollable force and discredit it.[56]

One of the most notorious events ascribed to Eleanor's errant desire
occurred during the Second Crusade when the royal couple stayed in Antioch with the queen's uncle Raymond, after the devastation of the French
troops in 1147–48. Accounts suggest that Raymond seduced Eleanor to
the extent that she announced her desire to remain in Antioch and separate from Louis; this is usually considered the root of the dissension that
led to their divorce. In chapter 12 of this volume, Peggy McCracken discusses the various stories that evolved around this incident and, in particular, the later legends that add the tale of Eleanor's affair with Saladin,
accelerating the scandal to include interracial romance.[57] The two extended accounts roughly contemporary with Marie's *Lais* are found in
John of Salisbury's *Historia Pontificalis* and William of Tyre's *Historia rerum in
partibus transmarinis gestarum*. Although scholars have given credence to
John's version,[58] we can see that his manner of narrating the events is designed to portray Eleanor's desire as dangerous to the stability of the state
and indifferent to national image. As John describes it, Raymond paid excessive attentions to Eleanor, which were favorably received:

> But whilst [Eleanor and Louis] remained there to console, heal, and revive
> the survivors from the wreck of the army, the attentions paid by the prince
> to the queen, and his constant, indeed almost continuous, conversation with
> her, aroused the king's suspicions. These were greatly strengthened when the
> queen wished to remain behind although the king was preparing to leave,
> and the prince made every effort to keep her, if the king would give her
> consent. And when the king made haste to tear her away, she mentioned
> their kinship [*cognatio*], saying it was not lawful for them to remain together
> as man and wife, since they were related in the fourth and fifth degrees.[59]

John's narration of the events at Antioch juxtaposes Eleanor's dalliance
with Raymond with her apparent disregard for the French troops; he
pointedly suggests that when the king and queen were supposed to be attending to their devastated countrymen, Eleanor was enjoying conversation with her uncle. Both these representations produce an image of
Eleanor as heedless of her role as French queen, driven by her desire in
detriment to the national good.

John goes on to record that the king's counselor, Thierry Galeran, tells Louis that he must not allow Eleanor to remain in Antioch "because 'guilt under the guise of kinship [*cognato*] could lie concealed, [Ovid, *Heroides* iv.138]' suggesting that it would bring lasting shame to the kingdom of the Franks if, among the other disasters, it was reported that the king was deserted by his wife, or robbed of her."[60] This statement explicitly links the shame of the French defeat with that of Eleanor's conduct, establishing control over the queen's body as integral to national image. Scholars have failed to note the ambiguity in Thierry's statement: one reading suggests that the kinship to which he refers is Eleanor's relationship with her uncle. Yet following closely as it does upon the discussion of Louis and Eleanor's kinship [*cognatio*], it is also possible to read John's narrative as suggesting that Eleanor is using the kinship between herself and Louis to conceal her guilty relations with Raymond. John evokes Phaedra's letter to Hippolytus from Ovid's *Heroides* in which she urges her stepson into an affair, saying that they will be protected, even aided, by the protection that kinship affords. This is an explosive intertext, for it serves to compound Eleanor's guilt precisely in the matter of kinship since, according to John, this is the moment in which Eleanor first raises the issue of consanguinity between herself and Louis that eventually led to their divorce. Indeed, read another way, Eleanor's claiming of consanguinity [*cognatio*] with Louis is the "guilt" that Thierry evokes.

Recording these same events around 1179, William of Tyre renders even more explicit the fractious nature of Eleanor's national allegiances: in his account, her alliance with Raymond in part explains her behavior. Not only is she unchaste; her lack of sexual integrity is associated with her lack of national fidelity. William describes Raymond's wish to gain Louis's favor to aid him in a military expedition to enlarge his principality: "he greatly counted on the interest of the queen with the lord king"; she is described as Raymond's niece, daughter of his brother Count William X of Poitou, hence accentuating Raymond's investment in the familial connection. When Louis refuses his military assistance, Raymond begins his intrigues, according to William:

> Frustrated in his ambitious designs, he began to hate the king's ways; he openly plotted against him and took means to do him injury. He resolved also to deprive him of his wife, either by force or by secret intrigue. The queen readily assented to this design, for she was a foolish woman. Her conduct before and after this time showed her to be, as we have said, far from circumspect. Contrary to her royal dignity, she disregarded her marriage vows and was unfaithful to her husband.[61]

William's account represents Raymond's actions as purely political and then vengeful, but in any case unrelated to sexual desire, but he ascribes the motivations for Eleanor's actions to her libidinous nature. For William, the queen's uncontrollable sexuality makes her an easily manipulated pawn in Raymond's schemes, a position depicted as a threatening breach to national security as well as national honor. Eleanor's family ties to Raymond are constantly stressed so as to underscore her divided loyalties: we see that both John's and William's accounts depict Eleanor as an improper consort, cultivating personal and familial allegiances and resistant to her husband's command. Her ties to her uncle are depicted as superseding those to Louis and the kingdom, but even these family relations are ultimately of less explanatory value for the chronicler who concentrates on her causal sexual errancy. In the Antioch incident, we see a convergence of the alien queen, suspicious allegiance, and insubordinate desire.

In *Lanval,* Marie represents Guenevere's desire as similarly errant when she attempts to seduce Lanval, Arthur's vassal, and angrily accuses him of homosexual practice when he refuses her.[62] The crisis of state at the outset of the *lai,* the devastation wrought by the Scottish and Pictish invaders, is thus mirrored on a microlevel within the state by the queen's improper regulation of desire, her literal destruction of the domestic life of the court upon which Arthur depends for the stability of his realm. Arthur is in danger of losing his subjects' loyalty through Guenevere's transgressions, and indeed the nobility express great sympathy with Lanval. Yet in Marie's *lai,* unlike the chronicle depictions, we are made to understand that the queen's desire for Lanval is linked to an aristocratic marriage system that depends upon the negation of feminine desire. Women are passed from father to husband and from king to vassal to maintain the stability of family or state, just as queens are married to kings to strengthen alliances between kingdoms and, as in the case of Eleanor's youthful marriage to Louis, to secure territory for the crown. At the center of this system is the figure of the alien queen, a woman who functions as the supreme example of such exchanges between men. But *Lanval* shows that the queen's desire is inhabited by a paradox: as a sovereign she is expected to express desire, but as a foreigner, her desire, unlike Arthur's, is considered suspect, incommensurate with the dictates of the state. In the courtly system, the queen's desire is left unaccounted for, but this is precisely what produces the conflicts that threaten to disrupt the smooth operation of the entire system.

Lanval's inability to desire the queen marks him as a perverse subject, which is why Guenevere assumes that if she is not his object of desire, then he must not desire women at all. Guenevere's false accusation against him—that he first desired her but when rebuffed vengefully declared his desire for another—presents the very problem of the subject-queen relationship. He cannot desire her in the same way he desires another, for she is queen; but since she is queen, he cannot desire another more than her. Hence in this system it is necessary that the king legislate the object choice for his subjects, as Arthur does at the beginning of the *lai* when he distributes lands and wives, for how could they choose not to choose the queen herself? In the feudal system of managed relations, desiring the queen is a representation of desiring the king, and indeed it is the queen's responsibility to cultivate this desire and to play with the possibility of its transgression. Such transgressions ultimately magnify the king's power to forbid the desirable queen to his subjects. Yet, the realm is in trouble at the beginning of the *lai,* the court in exile from invaders, and Arthur unwisely seeks to establish stability by curtailing the circulation of desire through the queen. The gift-giving king becomes the exclusive focus of desire, and this ultimately leads to the eruption of the queen's desire.[63] Arthur, having failed in his responsibility to Lanval, then leaves the knight without a lady, without money, and consequently without a formal role, alienated from the life of the court.

When Arthur forgets Lanval in the system of rewards, the knight has no choice but to leave the court. As in Map's description, the court is represented as a closed system, organized around the sovereign's desire; disfavor by the sovereign literally propels the knight outside, into the natural world. While wandering alone in disaffectation and frustration, Lanval is relieved of his distressed condition by a mysterious lady who unexpectedly appears and grants him an astonishing bounty of gifts: her body, her love, and as much gold and silver as he can spend, as well as all that he desires. What is crucial about this fairy lady, as she has been called, is that she is unidentified, not part of the Arthurian court, and yet in wealth and beauty she exceeds any earthly sovereign. Marie describes this boundless wealth:

> They led him up to the tent,
> which was quite beautiful and well-placed.
> Queen Semiramis,
> however much more wealth,
> power or knowledge she had,
> or the Emperor Octavian
> could not have paid for one of the flaps.
> There was a golden eagle on top of it,
> whose value I could not tell,
> nor could I judge the value of the cords or the poles
> that held up the sides of the tent;
> there is no king on earth who could buy it,
> no matter what wealth he offered (ll. 80–92).[64]

The love that the fairy lady offers to Lanval is additionally represented as something unavailable to any earthly monarch—emperor, count, or king. She tells him:

> If you are brave and courtly
> no emperor or count or king
> will ever have known such joy or good;
> for I love you more than anything (ll. 113–16).[65]

What the fairy lady gives Lanval is beyond anything Arthur could give him, and it is precisely this excess that signifies the aristocratic patronage system's limitations. The fairy's love takes Lanval outside the system of courtly patronage and regulated desire; it is a different order of love entirely because it is not determined by material constraints characteristic of feudal policies and politics. It is fitting, therefore, that the gift she offers him is this: the more lavishly Lanval spends, the more gold and silver he will have. Desire is the determinant of property rather than the other way round, in which property regulates desire, the manifestation of which is rendered in the "femmes e terres" equation with which the *lai* begins. The lady's riches and availability to love are not coterminous, nor are they linked to the careful disposal of wealth according to the requirements of inheritance. Marie emphasizes that no sovereign could have such joy from love, for love in the system of feudal sovereignty depends upon the management of desire in relation to property: it is indeed no love at all. By this inversion of social and political realities, Marie exposes the anatomy of courtly power in a way unthinkable in the male discourse of chronicles or evidential documents.

The fairy lady is unnamed and unidentified with nation, but her excessive wealth, above that of any king or emperor, links her to Eleanor, whose lands made her the richest heiress in western Europe. The eagle on top of the tent may be an oblique reference to Eleanor. This was a symbol with which she was frequently associated through a prophesy attributed to Merlin, first recorded by Geoffrey of Monmouth and frequently repeated: "Aquila rupti foederis tertia nidificatione gaudebit [the eagle of the broken treaty shall rejoice in her third nesting]." As Ralph of Diss (Diceto) explains, "the queen is meant by the eagle, because she stretches out her wings over two kingdoms, France and England. She was separated from the king of the French on account of consanguinity, and from the king of the English by suspicion and imprisonment; . . .and so she was on both sides the eagle of a broken treaty."[66] I want to suggest that both the fairy lady and Guenevere refer to Eleanor, for they represent her dual identity: queen of England and duchess of Aquitaine, national and foreign, consort and ruler, English and Occitan. Guenevere is Eleanor as consort, subject to the king, trapped in a system of carefully regulated desire. The fairy lady exists outside feudal obligations, mistress of her own wealth, guided by her own laws of desire.

When assailed by Guinevere, Lanval rashly claims that his lady and her maidens are "better in body, face, beauty, learning, and goodness" than the queen. Such an insult tests the very myth of sovereignty; as Fradenburg argues, the claims of queenship depend upon those of heterogeneity as well as homogeneity: "the sovereign's need to be different from [her] subjects, to be extraordinary, excessive, and dangerous."[67] No one can be like the queen, much less more beautiful or good. The trial that concludes *Lanval* establishes the limits of female sovereignty, precisely its dependence on the machinations of male political alliances. The queen's desire is brought under control, her exclusivity sanctioned by the king's authority. Arthur tells Lanval that "You have made a foolish boast: / your love is much too noble / if her maid is more beautiful, / more worthy, than the queen (ll. 367–70)."[68] This statement establishes Lanval's insult as a transgression against the king, for if the vassal has a love object that does not ultimately refer to the king himself, he has stepped outside his function as monarchic cipher. The duke of Cornwall, who arrives at Arthur's court to participate in the trial, voices the contradiction at the heart of the courtly system:

> If one were to speak the truth
> there should be no need for defense,
> except that a man owes his lord honor
> in every circumstance (ll. 445–48).[69]

Ultimately, the insult is to the king, who guarantees that the queen remain ascendant; the subject must speak whatever lies the king demands, including that of the queen's supremacy. This importantly demonstrates that in the court of Arthur and Guenevere the queen's power is dependent on, or more exactly, subordinate to, that of the king. Hence the queen, a dangerous alien to the state whose desire threatens domestic stability, uses the apparatus of the state—the trial—to become domesticated, to show that her sovereignty is coextensive with that of the state. Guenevere undergoes the trial, assuming that her exemplarity and exclusivity will be proved by the dictates of law. Yet the consequence of this process and its judgment are damning, for she will henceforth function under the authority of the law. While sovereignty is by definition beyond the law, the foreign queen bears burdens different from that of the king: she must prove not only that she is different from her subjects—exemplary—but that she is the same as well: she can take on national identity and serve national interests. Hence, in the end, she must be willing to enact her subordination to the king and to be subsumed as consort-queen into his identity.

Guenevere's increasing powerlessness is displayed as the trial progresses: the narrative is twice interrupted to report that the queen is waiting for the verdict, but her command does not seem to matter. It merely locates her as trapped in the time of the state's legal apparatus. She is paralyzed until the decision is made; one manuscript of the poem even suggests that she must fast until the verdict is reached.[70] We no longer have a queen who desires; we have a queen who waits. Subject to state time, subject to the mechanisms of evidence and judgment, Guenevere is now a mere shadow of a queen. Thus it is hardly surprising that when the maidens of the fairy lady arrive they are pronounced "more impressive / than the queen had ever been (ll. 31–32)."[71] The trial produces the arena whereby subjects may comment on the queen's beauty, which is to say queenship itself: once her beauty is the subject for interpretation, her exclusivity is lost. Her power is now entirely dependent on that of the king.

The narrative of the trial is trisected by the slow procession of the fairy lady's entourage, which arrives in three different stages, each time breaking off the legal proceedings. During all this commotion, Guenevere does nothing but wait for the trial to resume, but the trial waits for the fairy lady. Nothing could be more clearly indicative of the split in forms of regnal power: the domestic and foreign queen, the queen as subject to the state and legal time and the queen with her own domain, for whom the resolute time of legal inquiry stands still. Finally, Lanval's lady arrives on a white palfrey, an image of inexpressible wealth and sumptuousness. The text indulges in lengthy descriptions of her beauty and the elegance and costliness of her trappings, holding the reader captive as the palfrey winds through the town: "she proceeded at a slow pace [ele veneit meins que le pas]" (l. 580). Marie's narrative likewise slows to follow the pace of the fairy lady as the reader and textual audience viewing her become coterminous. Narrative time cedes to the fairy lady as well. Marie here takes on the role of courtly poet, subordinating the narrative's temporality to the *topos* of ornate description, signaling sovereignty's power to alter the pace of human movement and the linear demands of narrative. The fairy lady's beauty remakes the world, and, in seeking to represent the transcendence of sovereign perfection, the poet can only mark a rupture with the real.

The lady displays herself to the court just long enough to free Lanval, displaying her body as "evidence" but refusing to be contained. The text twice states that "she didn't want to wait" (l. 614), and "The king could not detain her, / though there were enough people to serve her" (ll. 631–32).[72] The fairy lady's disappearance also marks the narrative's end, for after an encounter with "the most beautiful woman in the world," a return to the world of the everyday, even the world of Camelot, would inevitably appear faded and dull. The encounter with the fairy lady inscribes the Arthurian court's limits, circumscribing too the judges' power to contain feminine desire in their failed attempt to render judgment—and, also, allusively, historical judgment of the type aligned with the chronicle tradition. Guenevere might be a much diminished queen, but so too is the court. The solution offered in *Lanval* to the paradox of the queen's desire is Avalon, the quintessential site of feminine rule in medieval legend. In an ironic reversal of the ubiquitous folktale motif, the *lai* ends with Lanval's leaping on the fairy lady's horse behind her, to be carried off to Avalon, a place like Aquitaine, where the queen is not foreign but her king is.[73]

III

While other studies have suggested Eleanor's importance to Marie's *lais* in general terms, to my knowledge none has claimed the level of historical referentiality that I am proposing. I believe that Marie prepares us to read her text this way by presenting herself as a type of historian who records circulating oral adventures, preserving the truth in writing for posterity. Yet, not only does Marie evince a particular perspective on Eleanor, a unique understanding of the paradox endemic to feminine sovereign desire, but she develops a distinctive angle on the process of writing history. The system of citation in medieval chronicle writing meant that rumors never faded or were challenged, for each chronicler incorporated the works of his predecessor into his own narrative, utilizing old material to lend his account authority. One sees this process at work in the chronicle of Richard of Devizes, who wrote in England in the last decade of the twelfth century, during Richard I's reign. While relating Eleanor's journey to Navarre to fetch Berengaria as a wife for Richard, Devizes pauses to sketch a portrait of the aged queen that can only be described as encomiastic. Yet, after praising Eleanor as "femina incomparabilis," beautiful and virtuous, powerful yet modest, humble and clever, tireless in her labors for national prosperity, he adds: "Many know what is better that none of us should know. This same queen, during the time of her first husband, was at Jerusalem [*sic,* for Antioch]. Let no one say any more about it. I too know it well. Keep silent!"[74] Richard has written about Eleanor at several other points in his chronicle, but it is intriguingly in the context of bringing a new queen to England that he recalls the Antioch scandal. Perhaps he makes his suggestive aside at this point in his narrative to express anxiety about Eleanor's influence on succession, recognizing uncomfortably that one foreign queen was bringing another to England. Does Berengaria's arrival raise the spectre of queenly desire that proved so troubling to previous historians? Given the national concerns that produced such extensive commentary around Eleanor, Richard may unwittingly express concern for the new queen's assimilation into the regnal relation.

Richard of Devizes's reference to the scandal at Antioch indicates, moreover, that no matter how much has changed in England, how many exemplary duties she has performed for the nation, the representation of Eleanor will remain riven with scandal, subject to clerkly chroniclers' judgments and license. For the chroniclers, Eleanor evokes a number of anxieties: crossing from French to English and charged with inciting her sons' rebellion against her husband, she represents the insecurity of national boundaries and generational succession. For the clerkly producers of history, Eleanor poses the problems and contradictions of the gendered image of power, for she sought to exercise authority in her own right and was able to do so increasingly after Henry II's death. By way of contrast to the chronicle depictions, Marie ends her *lai* with the following lines:

> When the girl came through the gate
> Lanval lept, in one bound,
> onto the palfrey, behind her.
> With her he went to Avalun,
> so the Bretons tell us,
> to a very beautiful island;
> there the youth was carried off.
> No one heard of him again,
> And I have no more to tell (ll. 638–46).[75]

Subsumed into a feminine lineage, Lanval disappears with the fairy lady, beyond the boundaries of historical representation.[76] By emphasizing that he knows more than he tells, Devizes positions himself as the authority behind his text and a controller of Eleanor's historical representation, but Marie creates her text as an autonomous authority. She vows, ironically, in the *lai*'s opening lines, "I shall tell you the adventure of another *lai*, / just as it happened" (ll. 1–2).[77] Her knowledge is bounded by the story just as the story is bounded by the fairy's disappearance with Lanval: "No man heard of him again, / and I have no more to tell," she insists (ll. 645–46).[78] Her declaration that there is nothing more to talk about marks the moment when feminine history vanishes into the beyond, simultaneously implying that clerkly history, the chronicle tradition that continues, is mere speculation. Rather than offer "Avalon/Aquitaine" as the "solution," therefore, it would be more accurate to say that there is no real solution beyond the aporia of feminine desire itself. Marie herself hints that this is indeed the case, for "Avalon" is a "virtual anagram" of "Lanval," the title of the *lai* as well as its male hero.[79] Unlike the male chroniclers, Marie is not interested in the interpretation or containment of feminine sovereign desire in her writing. "Avalon" marks a rupture with the narrative more than an actual place, and by making it refer to her *lai* itself as well as to the vassal who becomes the object of the queen's desire, Marie represents a circularity that reveals the text's inability to reduce Aliénor's otherness to its mechanisms.

Notes

I wish to thank Martin Aurell, Joan Ferrante, Adnan Husain, and Eugene Vance for generous and invaluable comments on drafts of this essay. I dedicate it to my grandmother, Eleanor D. Svehla, the alia aliénor.

1. Fox, "Mary Abbess of Shaftesbury"; A. Ewert, "Introduction," to Marie de France, *Lais;* Wind, "L' idéologie courtoise."

2. E. Winkler, *Marie de France.* For a summary of conjectures about Marie's biographical identity, see the introduction to *The Lais,* trans. Hanning and Ferrante.

3. Kelly, *Eleanor and the Four Kings;* Dronke, "Peter of Blois"; Rita Lejeune, "Rôle littéraire d' Aliénor." For a critique of the conjectural patronage relations between Eleanor and Marie, Broadhurst, "Henry II and Eleanor of Aquitaine."

4. Michelle Freeman, "Marie de France's Poetics of Silence" and "The Power of Sisterhood." Also, R. Howard Bloch, "The Lay and the Law" and "The Medieval Text—'Guigemar'—As a Provocation to the Discipline of Medieval Studies."

5. Several notable collections and works from the early 1990s that offer more historicizing interpretations of Marie include *In Quest of Marie de France, a Twelfth-Century Poet,* ed. Chantal E. Marechal; Bruckner, *Shaping Romance;* and the essay that comes closest to my own concerns, Kinoshita, "Cherchez La Femme"; the beginning of Kinoshita's essay offers a more thorough review of trends of literary analysis in Marie studies than I offer here. A recent essay representing an important innovation in historicizing Marie's *lais* that came to my attention after this chapter was completed is Finke and Schichtman's "Magical Mistress Tour: Patronage, Intellectual Property, and the Dissemination of Wealth in the *Lais* of Marie de France."

6. All French quotations in this essay are from Marie de France, *Lais,* ed. Karl Warnke, and will appear with parenthetical citations. All English translations are from *The Lais of Marie de France,* trans. Hanning and Ferrante; line numbers from this edition will be cited parenthetically in the text.

7. Ian Short argues that "none of Marie's works passes the conventional dialect test that would admit her into the Anglo-Norman court." He proposes that she was originally from the Ile-de-France and "worked at the Anglo-Norman court, probably in the 1170s." See his "Patrons and Polyglots: French Literature in Twelfth-Century England," 240.

8.   E dame Marie autresi,
     Ki en rime fist e basti
     E compassa les vers de lai,
     Ke ne sunt pas del tut verais;
     E si en est ele mult loée
     E la rime par tut amée,
     Kar mult l' aiment, si l' unt mult cher
     Cunte, barun e chivaler;
     E si enaiment mult l' escrit
     E lire le funt, si unt delit,
     E si les funt sovent retreire.
     Les lais solent as dames pleire,
     De joie les oient e de gré,
     Qu' il sunt sulun lur volunté (ll. 35–48).

     Author's translation from Denis Piramus, *La Vie Seint Edmund le Rei*. While
     the dating of this work is also uncertain, scholars have tended to locate it
     around 1190–1200. For an abbreviated discussion of various conjectures
     about the text's date, see Fourrier, *Le courant réaliste dans le roman courtois en
     France au moyen âge*, p. 441 n390.

9.   For discussion of the *lais*' possible circulation separately and in a collection,
     see Bruckner, "Textual Identity and the Name of a Collection in Marie de
     France's *Lais*," in *Shaping Romance*, pp. 157–206.

10. For thorough discussion of Eleanor's role as a patron of and influence on
     romance literature, including that of Chretien de Troyes, see Ferrante, *Glory
     of Her Sex*, pp. 112–19.

11. Krueger, *Women Readers*, pp. 4–7.

12. Tamara O' Callaghan, chapter 14 in this volume.

13. Harvey, *Marcabru*, pp. 122–39.

14. Lejeune, "Rôle littéraire d' Aliénor," 1–57.

15. A case in point is Broadhurst's article, "Henry II and Eleanor of Aquitaine."
     Using only the most definitive documentary evidence of commissions and
     working with a restrictive and ahistorical definition of patronage, Broad-
     hurst (83) asserts that "the vision of [Eleanor's] powerful influence on the
     production of this literature—courtly, lyric, or otherwise—is not at all sus-
     tainable by the available evidence." While Broadhurst asserts that others
     have confused "flashes of inspiration" and "allusions" with actual patron-
     age, her privileging of documented commissions as the most important as-
     pect of literary production is problematic in the context of twelfth-century
     literary culture. Not only must one challenge what is considered "available
     evidence" but further, a more nuanced idea of patronage is necessary to
     take into account the various roles that powerful women played in literary
     culture. For discussion of different sorts of "patronage" relations powerful
     women might play in the composition of texts, see Ferrante, "Women's
     Role in Latin Letters." In the same volume, Caviness, "Anchoress, Abbess,
     and Queen," discusses the "constant blurring of boundaries among patrons,

donors, recipients, and users" endemic to medieval artistic production (p. 113). Parsons, "Of Queens, Courts, and Books," in the same volume, provides a good example of how evidence from one courtly context and set of regnal patronage relations might illuminate those of other queens and courts for which less "documentary" evidence exists. While actual evidence of commissions for texts by Eleanor of Aquitaine may be scarce, the literary production and testimony of active literary life at her courts is not.

16. I take this important formulation from Steven Justice, "Inquisition, Speech, and Writing: A Case from Late-Medieval Norwich," 10: "the act of verbal production *as an act of meaning* locates itself in the hierarchy that controls meaning as it controls other things. And since, in Medieval and Early Modern Studies at least, no matter whose words we are trying to examine, we receive them through the filter of clerical privilege, imagining that writing always first of all *means* that we may hear only clerics and their bosses." In a recent article, Martin Aurell discusses the extent to which recent scholarship has been wary of according Eleanor any influence in affairs of state because of the absence of her name from charters and other forms of official documentation. The "meticulous" attention to "empirical" documentation as historicist methodology in and of itself has thus led to an equally inaccurate portrayal of Eleanor's role as sovereign (Aurell, "Aliénor d'Aquitaine et ses historiens"). In her 1992 article, Jane Martindale calls for the importance of utilizing a great variety of sources in discussing Eleanor, asserting that "vernacular writing cannot simply be discounted because historians may not be trained to read or interpret it" (Martindale, "Eleanor of Aquitaine," p. 37).

17. Important discussions of the motif of the *"mal mariée"* include the introduction to *Lais,* trans. Hanning and Ferrante, pp. 1–27; Stephen G. Nichols, "Marie de France's Commonplaces," *Yale French Studies* 44 (1991):134–48; and Bloch, *Medieval Misogyny,* chap. 7. Henry II's fifteen-year imprisonment of Eleanor may have provided the impetus behind the images of imprisoned women in *Guigemar* and *Yonec;* this would mean that these *lais* should be dated after 1174, but I think such a dating scheme is feasible.

18. " . . . mox ducatus Aquitaniae, qui a finibus Andegavensium et Britonum ad Pyranaeos usque montes Galliam Hispaniamque dirimentes extenditur, Francorum se ditioni paulatim subducens ratione conjugis in ducis Normannici potestatem transivit, Francis quidem invidia tabescentibus sed impedire non valentibus ejusdem ducis provectum" (William of Newburgh, *History of English Affairs,* ed. Walsh and Kennedy, pp. 130–31 [I have slightly modified the translation to make it more literal]).

19. Facinger, "Medieval Queenship," 12.

20. Bloch, *Medieval Misogyny,* p. 190; see also his chap. 7, "Heiresses and Dowagers: The Power of Women to Dispose," for a discussion of *Lanval* in terms different from mine.

21. Facinger, "Medieval Queenship." For more recent scholarship on transformations in regnal policy, see Parsons, "Mothers, Daughters, Marriage,

Power," and "The Queen's Intercession"; Poulet, "Capetian Women and the Regency"; and Huneycutt, "Intercession."

22. Facinger, "Medieval Queenship," 36.

23. Facinger, "Medieval Queenship," 36.

24. For Eleanor's close identification with Aquitaine during her marriage to Louis, see Marie Hivergneaux, chapter 2 in this volume. Louis in fact exploited Eleanor's position in Aquitaine as part of his policy to legitimize Capetian authority in the autonomous territory.

25. Stafford, *Queens, Concubines, and Dowagers;* Bartlett, *Making of Europe,* pp. 230–32.

26. Stafford, *Queens, Concubines, and Dowagers,* p. 44.

27. Bartlett, *Making of Europe,* pp. 230–31, notes that the choice of a foreign queen was encouraged by the Church's emphasis on exogamous marriages for the aristocracy and also served to avoid "polarizing alliances within the native aristocracy," but brought with it "the danger of cultural alienation."

28. Stafford, *Queens, Concubines, and Dowagers,* p. 46, describes the position of the Merovingian princess Clotild, who "became a subject for revenge when she went as a foreign princess to the court of her husband Amalaric the Visigoth. She found herself ill-treated and defenseless in a distant court."

29. Homi K. Bhabha, "Of Mimicry and Man: The Ambivalence of Colonial Discourse," in Bhabha, *The Location of Culture,* p. 86.

30. See Martindale, "Eleanor of Aquitaine," 17–58, for discussion of the political status of the duchy of Aquitaine in relation to Capetian France. Eleanor's grandfather Duke William IX refused to render homage for Aquitaine to the king of France and it is unclear whether and to what extent royal power actually extended into the duchy, which had been passed down intact in a single lineage since the ninth century. Martindale, p. 31, points out that during his marriage to Eleanor, Louis used the double title "rex Francorum" and "dux Aquitanorum," suggesting that Aquitaine continued to be seen as "an autonomous political entity."

31. Dante is credited with the first use of these terms, but linguistic difference between the North and South is described much earlier. See Paterson, *World of the Troubadours,* p. 3. The term "Occitania" has been adopted by scholars to refer to the regional identity of southern France since "Languedoc" is historically anomalous for the Early Middle Ages.

32. Paterson, *World of the Troubadours,* p. 5.

33. " . . . [cum rex Rotbertus accepisset sibi reginam Constaniam a partibus Aquitanie in coniugium], coeperunt confluere gratia eiusdem reginae in Franciam atque Burgundiam ab Aruernia at Aquitania homines omni leuitate uanissimi, moribus et ueste distorti, armis et equorum faleris incompositi, a medio capitis comis nudati, histrionum more barbis rasi, caligis et ocreis turpissimi, fidei et pacis foedere omni uacui" (Glaber, *Five Books of Histories,* pp. 166–67). I am indebted to Paterson's *World of the Troubadours* for directing me to this source.

34. These lines are from the "heroic verse" Glaber composed on the subject of France's corruption and includes in the chronicle: "Corpore peruerson creat haec nunc uita tyrannos, / Trunca ueste uiros sine federe pacis ineptos; / Consilio muliebre gemit republica laxa" (Glaber, *Five Books of Histories*, pp. 166–69; I have slightly modified the editor's translation.)

35. Fradenburg, *City, Marriage, Tournament*, p. 79.

36. Walter Map, *De nugis curialium*. See especially the beginning of the text, "A Comparison of the Court with the Infernal Regions," pp. 1–9, and the very end, "A Recapitulation of the Beginning of This Book, Differing in Expression but Not in Substance," pp. 499–513.

37. E as cuntes e as baruns,
    a cels de la table rounde
    (n' ot tant de tels en tut le munde!)
    femmes e terres departi,
    fors a un sul ki l' ot servi.
    Ceo fu Lanval; ne l' en sovint,
    ne nuls des soens bien ne li tint (ll. 14–20).

38. The classic discussion of transformations in aristocratic family organization and inheritance patterns in twelfth-century France is Duby, *The Chivalrous Society*. For the specific impacts on women's power and status, see Gold, *The Lady and the Virgin*.

39. See the recent collection *Aristocratic Women*, ed. Evergates, particularly the introduction by Evergates and LoPrete, and the essays by Amy Livingstone, "Aristocratic Women in the Chartrain," Evergates, "Aristocratic Women in the County of Champagne," and Cheyette, "Women, Poets, and Politics."

40. This is an example of how sovereignty might be said not to "transcend gender" but to utilize the particular powers and symbols of gender to shore up regnal authority. The emphasis on the queen as consort and, hence, her maternal nature, becomes an important part of royal ceremonial in the twelfth century while, as Amy Livingstone illustrates, the model of marriage as a partnership appears to remain current in aristocratic families, where women might be styled "domina" or "female lord" (Livingstone, "Aristocratic Women in the Chartrain," p. 66). The distinction noted here may be a result of the queen's "foreign" status; while aristocratic women often married within local power dynamics and participated in their functioning, the queen was usually cut off from family and was supposed to represent national interests alone. Eleanor's dilemma is that she is both "foreign" and "local," "regina" and "domina."

41. Poulet, "Capetian Women and the Regency," p. 103.

42. McCracken, *Romance of Adultery*.

43. Torigni, *Chronica*, ed. Howlett, 4:256. Emphasis mine.

44. Spiegel, "Genealogy." See below for further discussion of Spiegel's theory of twelfth-century historiography.

45. In a later version of *Lanval*, the fourteenth-century *Sir Launfal*, the doubleness of the fairy lady and Guenevere is made especially clear in another

way. When the fairy lady comes to the Arthurian court at the end of the romance, she confronts and blinds Guenevere, displaying the phobic reaction that attends the meeting with the doppelgänger Freud discusses in "The Uncanny." See "Sir Launfal" in *Middle English Verse Romances,* ed. Sands, pp. 201–32.

46. As an especially pertinent example of this mechanism, Roger of Howden describes how the 1161 dispute between Henry II and Louis VII over territories and castles in Gisors and Néaufle was settled by giving Louis's daughters, Margaret and Alice, in marriage to Henry the Younger and Richard. Though still young children, the girls were sent to live at the English court (Howden, *Chronica* 1:257).

47. Bloch, *Etymologies and Genealogies,* pp. 73–75, 85. For current rethinking of the "feudal" system, see Reynolds, *Fiefs and Vassals.*

48. " . . . in quem iniecit oculos incestos Alienor Francorum regina, Lodovici piisimi coniux, et iniustum machinata divorcium nupsit ei, cum tamen haberet(ur) in fama privata quod Gaufrido patri suo lectum Lodovici participasset. Presumitur autem inde quod eorum soboles in excelsis suis intercepta devenit ad nichilum" (Map, *De Nugis Curialium,* pp. 474–77).

49. William of Newburgh, *History of English Affairs,* ed. Walsh and Kennedy, pp. 128–29, writes that they sealed the marriage pact "less solemnly [i.e., with less ceremony] than their status justified."

50. " . . . illa maxime moribus regiis offensa et causante se monacho non regi nupsisse, dicitur etiam quod in ipso regis Francorum conjugio ac ducis Normannici nuptias suis magis moribus congruas aspiraverit, atque ideo praeoptaveritque procuraveritque discidium, itaque causis ingravescentibus et illa quidem, ut dicitur, multum instante, illo vero vel non vel remissius oblucante, per ecclesiasticae legis vigorem solutum est inter eos vinculum copulae conjugalis, porro illa soluta a lege viri et habens potestatem cui vellet nubendi, duabus apud patrem filiabus relictis, quae postea duobus illustrissimi comitis Teobaldi filiis, Henrico scilicet et Teobaldo, paterna provisione nupserunt, desideratis tandem potita est nuptiis" (William of Newburgh, *History of English Affairs,* ed. Walsh and Kennedy, pp. 128–29 [emphasis mine]).

51. Spiegel, "Genealogy," p. 109, discusses how this historiographic structure "replicate[s] the patrilineal origin of mankind itself": "Historical myth and historiographical mythos are one and the same expression of an underlying Christian metaphysics which explains the generation of mankind in patriarchal terms, and which thereby seeks a supernatural foundation for the continuance of patriarchy as an exemplary structure of social order."

52. Bloch's formulation of the relation of agnatic lineage to textual sign systems remains useful. See in particular *Etymologies and Genealogies,* ch. 2, "Kinship," pp. 64–91.

53. William of Newburgh, *History of English Affairs,* ed. Walsh and Kennedy, p. 128.

54. Eleanor's maternal image has been the subject of some interest and controversy. For a highly circumstantial view of her as a negligent mother, Turner, "Eleanor of Aquitaine and her Children," and in response to Turner, Huneycutt, "Public Lives, Private Ties." An alternative viewpoint that concentrates specifically on Eleanor's relations with her daughter Marie de Champagne is McCash, "Marie de Champagne and Eleanor of Aquitaine."

55. My translation from Gervase of Canterbury, *Opera Historica* 1:149: "Alianor autem, iam repudiata et propriae libertati eddita, terram suam, Aquitaniam, scilicet et Pictaviam, aliasque terras suas quae eam jure contingebant haereditario, ut domina possidebat. Quae, missis clanculo ad ducem nuntiis, liberam et absolutam se nuntiat esse, et ad matrimonium contrahendum ducis animum stimulat. Dicebatur enim artificiosam repudiationem illam ex ipsius processisse ingenio."

56. Martindale, "Eleanor of Aquitaine," pp. 39–45, discusses the accounts' gendered bias against Eleanor, noting for example that Louis VII's third marriage just five weeks after the death of his second wife rarely receives the type of commentary accorded Eleanor's swift remarriage in 1152.

57. Peggy McCracken, chapter 12 in this volume.

58. Owen, *Eleanor of Aquitaine,* p. 104, writes for instance, after quoting the passage detailing the events in Antioch, that the chronicler "seems to have kept an open mind." Owen offers no evidence to suggest why he believes this to be the case.

59. "Sed dum ibi morarentur ad naufragi exercitus reliquias consolandas, fovendas et reparandas, familiaritas principis ad reginam et assidua fere sine intermissione colloquia regi suspicionem dederunt. Que quidem ex eo magis invaluit quod regina ibi voluit remanere, rege preparante recessum" (John of Salisbury, *Historia Pontificalis,* pp. 52–53).

60. "Is ei persuasit audentius ne ipsam Antiochie morari diutius pateretur, tum quia 'cognato poterat nomine culpa tegi,' tum quia regno Francorum perpetuum opprobrium imminebat si inter cetera infortunia rex diceretur spoliatus coniuge vel relictus" (John of Salisbury, *Historia Pontificalis,* p. 53).

61. William of Tyre, *Historia rerum,* pp. 752–53: "Ubi videt se non proficere, cum rex Hierosolymam votis ardentibus irrevocabiliter ire proposuisset, spe frustratus, mutato studio, regis vias abominari, et ei praestruere patenter insidias et in eius laesionem armari coepit; uxorem enim eius in idipsum consentientem, quae una erat de fatuis mulieribus, aut violenter aut occultis machinationibus, ab eo rapere proposuit. Erat, ut praemisimus, sicut et prius et postmodum manifestis edocuit indiciis, mulier imprudens, et contra dignitatem regiam negligens maritalem, thori conjugalis fidem oblita"; translation from William of Tyre, *Deeds Done Beyond the Sea* 2:179–81.

62. The queen got angry;
    in her wrath she insulted him:
    "Lanval," she said, "I am sure
    you don' t care for such pleasure;
    people have often told me
    that you have no interest in women.
    You have fine-looking boys
    with whom you enjoy yourself (ll. 275–81)."

63. It is interesting that Arthur alone is given the role of distributing gifts, since gift-giving was a practice in which the queen was usually engaged, as one sees for instance in the fourteenth-century *Sir Launfal*. There, Guenevere's failure to bestow a gift on the knight precipitates the tale's action. That Arthur is in sole control of the gifts in Marie's *lai* also demonstrates the foreclosure of the circulation of desire through and around the queen that usually characterizes the medieval court. On the queen's critical role in forging relations between lord and followers, see Michael J. Enright, *Lady with a Mead Cup: Ritual, Prophesy, and Lordship in the European Warband from La Tene to the Viking Age.*

64. De si qu' al tref l' unt amené
    ki mult fu beals e bien asis.
    La reïne Semiramis,
    quant ele ot unkes plus aveir
    e plus puissance e plus saveir,
    ne l' emperere Octavian
    n' eslijassant le destre pan.
    Un aigle d' or or ot desus mis;
    de cel ne sai dire le pris
    ne des corded ne des pessuns
    ki del tref teinent les giruns:
    suz ciel n' a rei kis eslijast
    pur nul aveir qu' il i donast. (ll. 80–92)

65. Se vus estes pruz e curteis,
    emperere ne quens ne reis
    n' ot unkes tant joie ne bien;
    kar jo vus aim sur tute rien. (ll. 113–16)

66. "Aquila siquidem appellata quoniam duas alas expandit super duo regna, tam Francorum quam Anglorum. Sed a Francia propter consanguinitatem disjuncta fuit per divortium, ab Anglis vero per custodiam carceralem a thoro viri segregata fuit; . . .Sic 'Aquila rupti foederis' utrobique." Ralph of Diss (Diceto) explains the "third nestling" as a reference to Richard, Eleanor's third and favorite son, who released her from imprisonment (Ralph of Diss, *Opera Historica* 2:67).

67. Louise Olga Fradenburg, "Introduction: Rethinking Queenship," in *Women and Sovereignty*, ed. Fradenburg, p. 3.

68. Trop par est noble vostre amie,

quant plus est bele sa meschine
e plus vaillanz que la reine. (ll. 370–72)

69. "... ki bien en vuelt dire le veir,
ja n' i deüst respuns aveir,
se pur ceo nun qu' a sun seignur
deit um par tut porter honur." (ll. 447–50)

70. *Lais,* ed. Hanning and Ferrante, trans., p. 120.

71. "... n' i ot cele mielz ne valsist / qu' unkes la reïne ne fist" (ll. 535–36).

72. "... ele parla en tel mesure, / kar de demurer nen ot cure" (ll. 629–30);
"... e la pucele s' en depart. / Ne la pot li reis retenir; / asez ot gent a li servir" (ll. 648–50.")

73. Aquitaine's proximity to France and England allowed Eleanor to be both alien and queen but also meant that she was never fully assimilated into the national identity of her regnal body. The chroniclers produce this conflict in their records of her numerous crossings between England and France, marking her ceaseless mobility as a sign of the unstable national identity, threatened through her equally wandering sexual desire. For them, Aliénor remained irreducibly alien everywhere except Aquitaine. For an overview of the national policies of Louis and Henry that at times cultivated and other times severed Eleanor's relation with Aquitaine, see Hivergneaux, chapter 2 in this volume.

74. "Multi nouerunt quod utinam nemo nostrum nosset. Hec ipsa regina tempore prioris mariti fuit Ierosolimis. Nemo plus inde loquatur. Et ego beni noui, Silete!" (Richard of Devizes, *Chronicon,* pp. 25–26).

75. "Quant la pucele ist fors de l' us,
sur le palefrei detriers li
de plein eslais Lanval sailli.
Od li s' en vait en Avalun,
ceo nus recuntent li Bretun,
en un isle qui mult est beals;
la fu raviz li dameiseals.
Nuls n' en oï puis plus parler,
ne jeo n' en sai avant cunter" (ll. 656–64).

76. This representation was apparently disturbing to later writers for its emasculating indications. In the fourteenth-century version noted above, Thomas Chestre depicts Sir Launfal departing on his own palfrey, which is led out to him by a servant. Chestre, moreover, makes it clear than Lanval maintains his own knightly identity by establishing a subsequent history for him in Avalon: Lanval sets himself up as a knight there, challenging anyone who comes to joust with him ("Sir Launfal," in *Middle English Verse Romances,* ed. Sands, pp. 201–32).

77. "L' aventure d' un alter lai, / cum ele avint, vus cunterai" (ll. 1–2).

78. "Nuls n' en oï puis plus parler, / ne jeo n' en sai avant cunter" (ll. 663–64).

79. Burgess, *The Lais of Marie de France: Text and Context,* p. 18.

Fig. 17.1 The Eleanor Vase

CHAPTER 17

THE ELEANOR OF AQUITAINE VASE

George T. Beech

> *The Eleanor vase, a spectacular survival of the Spanish Reconquest, belonged in the twelfth century to two kings, Queen Eleanor, the first troubadour poet, and a great abbot.*

A rare, if not unique, example of a surviving personal possession of the best-known English queen of the twelfth century is the so-called Eleanor of Aquitaine vase, in the Louvre Museum in Paris.[1] This pear-shaped vessel of rock crystal (a semi-precious form of quartz), 37.3 cm in height, is mounted on a circular base of silver and gold on which has been carved a semi-abstract floral design encrusted with jewels. Topping the vase is a second metallic mounting that gradually tapers in three distinct stages of similar design to a narrow opening at the top. A projecting hinge indicates that originally it could be closed by a cap, now lost.

That Eleanor once owned this vase has been known ever since the mid-twelfth century, thanks to an inscription entered on the bottom of the base and that dates from the 1140s. Suger, the distinguished abbot of the monastery of Saint-Denis outside Paris, at that time possessed the vase and, in order to identify the four owners prior to himself, had this inscription added in preparation for its permanent entry into the treasury he was then constituting for his abbey. He evidently wished all subsequent viewers to know the pedigree of famous people to whom this object had once belonged. Late medieval inventory catalogues and book engravings of the eighteenth century show that the vase remained on display in the abbey treasury until the French Revolution. Though the rock crystal body was then damaged, it survived and was somehow transferred to the Convention and later incorporated into the collection of royal memorabilia on display until recently in the Galerie Apollon of the Louvre. Today it is on permanent exhibit in the newly established early medieval section of that Museum.

The vase's luxurious mounting alone reveals that Abbot Suger looked upon this vase as one of the finest pieces in his abbey's treasury, subsequently one of the most famous collections of the medieval monastic world. In his treatise *De Administratione,* Suger himself tells of having the vase mounted and the inscription added:

> Vas quoque aliud, quod instar justae berilli aut cristalli videtur, cum in primo itinere Aquitanae regina noviter desponsata domino regi Ludovico dedisset, pro magno amoris munere nobis rex, nos vero sanctis Martyribus dominis nostris ad libandum divinae mensae affectuousissime contulimus. Cujus donationis seriem in eodem vase, gemmis auroque ornato, versiculis quibusdam intitulavimus: Hoc vas sponsa dedit Aanor regi Ludovico, Mitadolus avo, mihi rex, Sanctisque Sugerus.[2]

> [Still another vase, looking like a pint bottle of beryl or crystal, which the Queen of Aquitaine had presented to our Lord King Louis as a newlywed bride on their first voyage, and the King to us as a tribute of his great love, we offered most affectionately to the Divine Table for libation. We have recorded the sequence of these gifts on the vase itself, after it had been adorned with gems and gold, in some little verses: As a bride, Eleanor gave this vase to King Louis, Mitadolus to her grandfather, the King to me, and Suger to the Saints.]

In this last line Suger has repeated word for word the inscription on the base, and the central position he gives the queen in it explains why the object came to be known as the Eleanor of Aquitaine vase instead of, for instance, the King Louis, or the Suger, vase. Due to its precise association with such a famous personality, as well as its own inherent beauty, this vase has long been celebrated among art historians. Curiously enough, modern historians and the queen's biographers appear to have been unaware of it, a consequence perhaps of compartmentalization among academic disciplines in modern times. But two basic problems concerning the vase baffled the art historians who took an interest in it at the beginning of the twentieth century, and until recently it received little attention. Those problems were, first, to whom did the vase belong originally, and second, when and where was it made?

Suger himself knew who the first owner was, and indeed he named that person in his inscription: "As a bride, Eleanor gave this vase to King Louis,

Mitadolus to her grandfather. . . ." Mitadolus had given the vase to Eleanor's grandfather, who in turn gave it to her. Identification of this Mitadolus promised to solve the problem, but to the earliest scholars addressing the question in the late nineteenth and early twentieth centuries, the name was completely unknown. Its juxtaposition with names of royalty, Eleanor herself and King Louis, seemed to suggest that Mitadolus was a person of similar status and consequence, even renown, whose name alone would have been recognized by alert observers in mid-twelfth-century France. No one, however, could find anyone with a name remotely resembling it among political or religious dignitaries of the Latin Christian West at that time, or among any elements of the population for that matter. Several possibilities were suggested, including a Muslim emir from Spain, a fictional name made up of Greek elements, and the wife of Eleanor's paternal grandfather, William IX of Aquitaine (d. 1126), but no corroborating evidence could be found, and these hypotheses were abandoned.

My own work on William IX of Aquitaine brought me into the question several years ago, and led me to propose the following solution, which appears to have persuaded those interested in the vase even though it remains not absolutely certain.[3] "Mitadolus" was the title (of office) of the last Muslim king of Saragossa in northeastern Spain (Aragon today) early in the twelfth century, a man named (Imad al-dawla) Abd al-Malik ibn Hud (1110–30). "Mitadolus" was Suger's latinization of the Arabic title "Imad al-dawla." A Latin chronicle of the First Crusade provided the clue to this identification. In the course of his chronicle, the anonymous author wrote that the son of the Turkish emir of Antioch in Syria in 1098 was named "Sensadolus," a name with a suffix, "dolus," identical to that of Mitadolus. Arabic sources of the time also speak of this man, whose name in that language reads al-dawla. Thus "dolus" was the Latin equivalent for "al-dawla." This was not a name, but part of a title of office meaning column of the dynasty (or state), rule or term of office. Contemporary Arabic dynasties commonly preceded it with another term also having a meaning, and the two together made a full title. "Amid al-dawla," for instance, meant "supporter of the dynasty" and "Walid al-dawla," "friend of the dynasty." None of the ruling dynasties of the Arab states of the Middle East at this time had a king named with a prefix that could have given "Mit-" in Latin, but several of the dozen or so Taifa or party kingdoms of eleventh-century Muslim Spain did have monarchs called "Imad al-dawla" (pillar or column of the dynasty). If "Mit-" was Suger's equivalent for the Arabic Imad, then Mitadolus could well have been his Latin rendering of "Imad al-dawla." Only in Saragossa, however, did an Imad al-dawla hold royal office early in the twelfth century (1110–30), at about the time when Eleanor's grandfather acquired the vase.

There is no evidence that her maternal grandfather, Viscount Aimeri of Châtellerault (1101–51), ever visited Spain. But her paternal "avus" (the term used in the vase inscription), Duke William IX of Aquitaine (1086–1126), the earliest known troubadour poet, did have close Spanish connections. His daughter Agnes's marriage made him the father-in-law of King Pedro I of Aragon (r. 1094–1104); and on June 17, 1120, William led a contingent of several hundred Aquitanian knights as part of King Alfonso I of Aragon's army, which won a great victory over the North African Almoravids at Cutanda, south of Saragossa. Thus Duke William IX contributed to the Aragonese Reconquista, which had begun late in the eleventh century, and in which his father, Duke Guy-Geoffrey-William, had also fought (at the battle of Barbastro in 1065). The target of the Aragonese and their allies was the wealthy, cultivated Muslim city and kingdom of Saragossa, on their southern frontier along the Ebro river.

At the same time, in the later eleventh and early twelfth centuries, the Muslim Almoravids were invading from the south in the process of imposing their rule on what they considered the decadent Taifa kingdoms left over from the Caliphate period. They reached the city of Saragossa in 1110, ahead of the Aragonese Christians. Threatened simultaneously by the latter from the north, and the Almoravids from the south, Imad al-dawla, enthroned only a few months earlier, chose to abandon his capital and ally with the Christians rather than submit to the Almoravids. Ruling what remained of his kingdom from a castle to the west, he then collaborated with Alfonso I of Aragon in an effort to regain the city.

Though he did not participate in the Aragonese conquest of Saragossa in 1118, the recent discovery of a previously lost segment of a history by the thirteenth-century Arab writer Ibn Idari shows that Imad al-dawla commanded Saragossan soldiers under the leadership of King Alfonso I at the battle of Cutanda on June 17, 1120. Since Duke William IX led Aquitanian knights under Alfonso's generalship on the same battlefield, the two men must have known each other as allies in the same army. This does not prove that Imad al-dawla gave William IX the vase at this time nor does it explain why he might have done so. But it does provide an occasion for such a gift (the use of the word "dedit," gave, in Suger's inscription implies that the vase was a gift and not booty seized from a defeated enemy). Moreover, Imad al-dawla's need for allies to support his continued governance of what now amounted to a Muslim island surrounded by a Christian sea makes perfectly comprehensible a gift of this nature to a foreign prince who had influence with the king of Aragon. Nor would this have been the only time Imad al-dawla sought to purchase Christian favors. In 1112, he paid gold and silver to King Alfonso's queen, Urraca, to persuade her to release some of his soldiers then being held in custody.[4]

A Christian narrative, the chronicle of the monastery of Sahagún in Castile, tells of Imad al-dawla's gift of gold and silver to Urraca in 1112; the Latin original is lost, but a sixteenth-century Castilian translation exists. Because this is the only surviving Christian source to name the Saragossan king (all other references to him are in Arabic texts), it provides important evidence for the rendering of his Arabic title into Latin at the time. The author of this chronicle twice named the Saragossan king in connection with the 1112 gift, and in the Castilian of his day, the sixteenth-century translator wrote his name as "Amidolan" and "Midadolan." Presumably he read something like "Amidolanus" and "Midadolanus" in the original Latin, with the variants resulting from the original author's uncertainty about how best to render the Arabic into Latin. In any case both variants, particularly the second, are reasonably close to the "Mitadolus" of Suger's vase inscription. And this reinforces, even though it does not prove, the hypothesis that the Sahagún chronicler and the abbot of Saint-Denis were striving to find the best Latin form for Imad al-dawla.

The arguments advanced above can be summarized as follows. Linguistic and historical evidence support the high probability that King Imad al-dawla of Saragossa was the "Mitadolus" whom Suger named as the first owner of the Eleanor vase. To win Duke William IX of Aquitaine's support in his struggle to preserve his Muslim kingdom, Imad al-dawla bestowed the vase on William when they fought together in the same army at Cutanda in June 1120. The vase thus commemorates a most unusual act of collaboration between Muslims and Christians at a time in the Reconquista when their relations were normally characterized by hatred and violence.

Inevitably, the realization that the Eleanor vase came into early twelfth-century France from Muslim Spain reopens the second question with which this chapter began, that of the vase's origins. Ignorant of Mitadolus's identity, earlier scholars—above all the art historians who specialized in the study of hardstone vessels—understandably hesitated to pronounce on this point. For many years the most authoritative view was that of C. J. Lamm, who in 1930 called it Egyptian and dated it to the period of the late Empire.[5] Duke William IX, Eleanor, and Abbot Suger almost certainly assumed that since it had come from Saragossa, it must be a product of Muslim Spain, but the study of the production of this type of carved hardstone vessel rules out this possibility. Nothing of this kind of Spanish manufacture has come down to the present, nor could it have come from any other western European country, where the techniques used in the vase were unknown at that time. At present, there is no certainty on the place and date of the Eleanor vase's creation. Studying it from the perspectives of its material (rock crystal), and its size, shape, and decoration greatly limits the geographical and chronological possibilities, however, and has led me to a tentative conclusion that it was made in Persia during the Sassanian period, sometime in the third to the seventh centuries.[6]

Craftsmen first began to carve rock crystal into containers and art objects in antiquity, mainly in the eastern Mediterranean. This art form flourished in Egypt, Persia, and parts of the Roman Empire, and in late Antiquity, in Byzantium.[7] Nothing comparable existed in the northwestern provinces either at that time or in the early Middle Ages. A study of size and shape yields little, since craftsmen in Antiquity produced pear-shaped vases of the same dimensions throughout the Mediterranean world. But this did not hold true for the form of decoration chosen by the Eleanor vase's anonymous artist. The entire surface of the exposed rock crystal is carved into small, circular concave depressions, a form of decoration known as honeycomb facetting dues to its resemblance to the honeycomb of bees. A few examples of honeycomb facetting have survived from Egypt during the period of the Empire and from Byzantium at the beginning of the Middle Ages, but in both cases in the medium of glass, not in rock crystal. The latter material, known in Egypt since the second millennium B.C., came into particular favor there after the end of antiquity. The Fatimid period, in the tenth and eleventh centuries, was one of the greatest ages in the art of carved rock crystal vessels, but facetting for decoration is utterly lacking in Egypt during those centuries. In Persia, on the other hand, facetting came to be preferred over all other forms of decoration during the Sassanian period, and it is the only country or region prior to the twelfth century that furnishes specimens comparable to the Eleanor vase. The only reason for hesitation about Persia as the place of origin for the vase is the fact that all surviving examples are of glass, not of rock crystal. This need not rule out a Sassanian origin for the vase, however, for specialists believe that ancient artists used the same techniques almost interchangeably in the two different mediums. Still, this means that at the present time, the Eleanor vase stands as a unique specimen, with no precise counterpart from Persia, Egypt, or any other country prior to the twelfth century.

Equally problematic is the purpose for which the artist made this vase. Lacking either a handle or spout, it cannot have served as a pitcher. It may have been used for drinking, if not initially in its place of origin, then during its sojourn in Muslim Spain; eleventh-century Arabic love poetry from that country refers to rock crystal containers used for wine drinking. Or the very great value and high prices attached to rock crystal vessels in ancient and medieval times may mean that owners kept them simply for display.

How and when the vase made its way from its place of origin in the Middle East to Saragossa its unknown. During this time, all sorts of ties—religious, commercial, and intellectual—kept Muslim Spain in constant contact with the Arabic peoples of the eastern Mediterranean. The Andalusis took much of their scientific, literary, and artistic culture from their ancestors in the East, and a good many eastern artifacts and objets d'art survive in Spain today to witness the amplitude of the exchanges taking place then. In all probability one of the Hudid kings (the ruling dynasty) of Saragossa bought the vase from a merchant from the Middle East, and it passed down in the royal family until Imad al-dawla's time.

The inscription Suger added to the vase in the 1140s leaves no doubt about its itinerary after Mitadolus gave it to the duke of Aquitaine. William IX must have taken it with him when he returned to his capital at Poitiers in 1120. Then it somehow came into the possession of his granddaughter Eleanor, who was born either in 1122 or 1124. Suger's inscription does not state explicitly that William gave it to her, whereas he is precise about this with regard to the others: Eleanor gave it to Louis, Louis to Suger, and Suger himself to the saints. Nor does Suger name William as he does the others; he calls him simply "avus," grandfather.[8] One explanation for this could be that the limited space available for the inscription—the circumference of the vase's mounting—forced Suger to economize and eliminate all but essential words. However that may be, the inscription clearly implies that the "avus" gave her the vase.

It is tempting to speculate that William IX, then just over fifty, gave the vase as a baptismal gift to his granddaughter who, as an adult, would have had only dim memories of him; he died in 1126, when she was at most four years old. In any case, Eleanor attached extraordinary value to the vase, for she then chose it as her wedding gift to Louis VII of France in 1137. As she was then the heiress to the duchy of Aquitaine, the vase thus symbolized the unification of her huge province with the kingdom of France. Their marriage ended in 1152, however, and subsequent bad memories might explain why Louis VII willingly parted with the vase shortly thereafter. In his account in *De Administratione,* Suger writes that Louis gave him the vase as "a tribute of his great love." Then in the process of assembling works of art for his abbey's treasury, knowing the vase and aware of the unhappy divorce, Suger could well have prevailed on Louis to make it a gift to the royal abbey. After this, he tells us in the same passage, he adorned the vase with gems and gold and added an inscription to identify four owners prior to himself and the abbey. All of this was in preparation for offering the vase to "the Divine Table for libation," for use as a communion vessel, presumably after it was blessed to erase any possible stains from its pagan past. Perhaps it was subsequently used in the liturgy at Saint-Denis, but ultimately it became a museum piece and countless visitors must have seen it over the centuries as one of the prize possessions of the abbey's treasury.

As well as being an objet d'art of exquisite beauty, the Eleanor vase has an exceptional historical interest from several different perspectives. It is a prime example of the spread of Spanish Muslim influences into Latin Christendom in northwestern Europe, in science, philosophy, the arts, and perhaps literature, in the twelfth century. What is most unusual is that the time, places, and manner of this vase's itinerary are precisely known and dated. As one of the earliest pieces of rock crystal to become known in northern Europe, it may have played a role in the development of techniques of hardstone carving by local craftsmen toward the end of the twelfth century. Finally, rare are the works of art that have come down to us from the Middle Ages through direct association with so many famous people: a king from a Muslim city celebrated in the Chanson de Roland, the first known troubadour poet in the history of European vernacular literature, a king of France, the distinguished abbot of a great royal monastery, and a queen who is counted among the most renowned women of the age.

Notes

1. What follows is based on Beech, "Eleanor Vase"; Beech, "Eleanor Vase: Its Origins"; and Beech, "The 'Eleanor Vase': Witness."
2. Cited in *Abbot Suger on St.-Denis,* ed. Panofsky, pp. 78–79.
3. See Beech, "Eleanor Vase."
4. Beech, "The Eleanor Vase," 7.
5. Lamm, *Mittelalterliche Gläser,* 1:187 and 2: pl. 64.
6. Beech, "Eleanor Vase: Its Origins," 69–79.
7. Vickers, "Rock Crystal."
8. A further curiosity about Suger's inscription is its spelling of Eleanor's name: "Aanor." I have not verified it systematically in all twelfth-century references to Eleanor of Aquitaine, but I believe this is the only instance of someone calling her "Aanor." The name Ainor, Anor, Aynor, is well attested in twelfth- and thirteenth-century sources, and was in fact that of Eleanor's maternal ancestors. But in her own charters Eleanor always called herself "Alienor," as did others when referring to her. Though close and obviously related, the two forms are not identical, and it is not clear why Suger chose "Aanor."

CHAPTER 18

THE QUEEN'S CHOICE:
ELEANOR OF AQUITAINE
AND THE TOMBS AT FONTEVRAUD

Kathleen Nolan

Eleanor of Aquitaine, in the tradition of queens controlling burial sites and monuments, commissioned her family tombs at Fontevraud, drawing from a lifetime of experience with royal funerary customs.

For all that she is the most famous woman of the medieval period, Eleanor of Aquitaine remains an historically elusive figure. Much earlier scholarly literature was preoccupied with her personal life, casting her as the unfaithful wife of her first husband, Louis VII of France, or the jealous and scheming wife of her second, Henry II of England.[1] Recent studies, like those in this volume, suggest a new image of Eleanor of Aquitaine as a politically astute woman, an image independent of romance novels or memories of the magnificently aging Katharine Hepburn. This new work has come chiefly from historians who have examined the whole range of extant documents for Eleanor's career, not only the chronicles of the day or Louis and Henry's official charters, in which she figures very little.[2] To join these unsentimentalizing reappraisals, I will reconsider here Eleanor of Aquitaine's relationships to the Angevin/Aquitanian tombs at Fontevraud Abbey: those of Henry II (d. 1189), their son Richard I (d. 1199), and Eleanor herself (d. 1204).

With Alain Erlande-Brandenburg, the master scholar of French tomb sculpture, and others, I argue that Eleanor commissioned the kings' effigies soon after her son's death, and ordered her own tomb at a slightly later date.[3] My project is thus to situate Eleanor within the discourse of queens and funerary sites or monuments. In this regard, I draw on what we know of women's roles as preservers of family memory and the caretakers of souls as well as queens' roles, in France especially, as creators of memorial monuments. In support of the theory that Eleanor commissioned the effigies, I argue that her personal and royal ties, and her travels in youth and old age, exposed her to royal burial practices and memorials that at least partly underlie the innovative Fontevraud tombs. Finally, I argue that the tombs' character corresponds to what we know of Eleanor's tastes and concerns as a patron of art.

Why Fontevraud?

I bring to Eleanor's tomb perspectives informed by my work on royal women's burial customs and monuments, and on relationships established or perpetuated by royal women's choices about where and how they would be interred. I argue elsewhere that twelfth- and thirteenth-century French queens' absence or near-absence from the Capetian necropolis at Saint-Denis need not be viewed solely an exclusion from the most desirable burial site. Rather, queens who were not buried at Saint-Denis often deliberately chose burial at other houses with which they had forged privileged relationships as founders or patrons.[4] The Angevin/Aquitanian tombs at Fontevraud also involved choices, and we must consider who made them.

The first choice is that of Fontevraud as a burial site. The abbey's history is well known: the reforming priest and itinerant preacher Robert of Arbrissel founded a community at a deserted spot called Fons Evraldi, on the boundaries of Anjou, Poitou, and Touraine. There he welcomed men and women, including reformed prostitutes; as the community grew, the women assumed a life of prayer in the cloister, and the men worked to support them. It became the Fontevrist model that the brothers served the nuns, and the order had an abbess at its head. As an aristocratic women's order, Fontevraud grew in stature and popularity through the twelfth century, soon established daughter houses, and enjoyed the patronage of noble families in the region.[5]

The first royal burial at Fontevraud was that of Eleanor's husband Henry II, who died in 1189 at nearby Chinon. At first, Henry had meant to be buried at Grandmont, a severely ascetic house in the diocese of Limoges, which had come to him through his marriage to Eleanor and which he had actively patronized.[6] Medieval and modern historians disagree as to why Henry was ultimately buried at Fontevraud. If his death

Fig. 18.1: Fontevrault Abbey, Interior of Nave and Choir from West (Editions Gaud).

Fig. 18.2: Fontevrault Abbey, Tombs of Henry II and Eleanor of Aquitaine (Nolan).

was as prolonged as the chroniclers suggest, it is hard to imagine he would not have made his own decision on a matter so important to a king. But Gerald of Wales thought it not his choice and saw divine retribution in Henry's burial in the house to which he had tried to consign Eleanor after her revolt.[7] It has been suggested that Eleanor made the decision, but she was in England when Henry died and could not have directed his burial at Fontevraud only days later. Elizabeth A. R. Brown sees his burial there as a convenience; Erlande-Brandenburg, as a way to cement Henry's political claims to territories north and south of Fontevraud.[8]

Fontevraud does not, however, evoke Henry's spheres of influence alone. The place is in fact liminal, on the edges of Henry and Eleanor's natal regions. If his Angevin forebears had traditionally endowed the house, and if he generously granted lands and incomes, she too had ancestral ties to Fontevraud: her paternal grandmother founded and later entered a Fontevrist priory, her maternal grandfather made concessions and gifts to Fontevraud, and her father greatly enriched the house.[9] For Jane Martindale, to whom I owe my understanding of Eleanor in the context of her natal region, Fontevraud was an obvious place of retreat and a base of power for her; Henry's burial there was coincidental. Before 1199, however, we

Fig. 18.3: Fontevrault Abbey, Tomb of Eleanor of Aquitaine (Art Resource).

have few indications of Eleanor's devotion to the house, though their number need not prove disinterest: her first known visit to the monastery was in 1152, her earliest recorded grant to the house in 1185. We do not, however, know what independent wealth she enjoyed early in life, and in captivity she presumably had few means to patronize any institution. The 1185 gift was thus significant: though her liberty was still restricted, Eleanor was allowed to accompany her daughter Matilda and son-in-law Henry of Saxony to France, where she made the grant to Fontevraud. In the same period of relative liberty, when she must have controlled some financial resources, she founded and endowed a Fontevrist priory at La Rochelle, a port city clearly of some significance to her.[10]

What is clear is that as a free woman after Henry's death, Eleanor chose Fontevraud as a base that reflected her political identity, and she enhanced her spiritual authority through her ties to the nuns, whose prayers might ensure the eventual repose of her family's souls and her own.[11] The next royal choice touching Fontevraud was made by Eleanor's son Richard, who when dying at Châlus in 1199 requested burial at Fontevraud with his father. Later that year, Eleanor and Henry's daughter Joan, dowager queen of Sicily and briefly the unhappy wife of Raymond VI of Toulouse, took the veil on her deathbed and was buried among the nuns. In 1204, Eleanor joined Henry and Richard in the abbey choir.[12]

Why Effigies?

As everyone familiar with the abbey church of Notre-Dame at Fontevraud knows, the royal effigies now in the nave represent pivotal innovations in the evolution of tomb sculpture.[13] The effigies of Henry II, Richard I, and Eleanor were later joined by that of Henry and Eleanor's daughter-in-law Isabelle of Angoulême (d. 1246, the effigy was ordered in 1254). The three earlier tombs are among the first fully sculptural, life-sized effigies of contemporary or recently deceased monarchs, a very unusual phenomenon in northern Europe at the time the effigies were made, ca. 1200 (See Figs. 18.2–18.3). The kings' effigies, moreover, offer iconographically novel evocations of the dead rulers' ritual lying in state in regalia that recalls their coronations; the effigies thus reenact the funerary tribute and recall the inauguration of kingship.[14]

Nothing in Henry II's English or Angevin backgrounds offers a precedent for this cluster of dynastic sculptured tombs. The English monarchy did not yet have a single place of burial; various monasteries were in favor at different times, and not until the late thirteenth century did Westminster Abbey emerge as the chief contender as a burial site among royally endowed houses. Nor was any royal tomb in England before 1200 marked by

Fig. 18.4: Fontevrault Tombs, Tomb of Eleanor of Aquitaine, detail of head and torso (Editions Gaud).

large-scale figural sculpture.[15] The only significant association on Henry's side of the family was on French soil. His father, Geoffrey V of Anjou, died at the age of thirty-seven in 1151, and was buried in the choir of Le Mans cathedral. His tomb was marked by a noteworthy enamel plaque that depicts Geoffrey as a handsome and valiant warrior, with a sword and a large shield emblazoned with the earliest known representation of a personal armorial device.

Marie-Madeleine Gautier argues that Empress Matilda, Geoffrey's widow and Henry II's mother, ordered this sumptuous and imposing image and that it reflects Matilda's concerns with lineage. This same concern is reflected in Matilda's tomb at Bec-Hellouin, an abbey she had richly endowed and where she was buried in a place of honor in 1167. Her tomb had no figural imagery, but its well-known epitaph situated her within a male lineage of power.[16]

At twenty-five by thirteen inches, Geoffrey's plaque is large for enamel work but is still well under lifesize and could have supplied only a partial precedent for the sculptures at Fontevraud, which impersonate living beings in their scale and three-dimensionality. We must rather look to Eleanor of Aquitaine herself and her connections. Through travel or family ties, Eleanor had knowledge of all then-existing traditions of Christian

Fig. 18.5: Tomb Plaque of Geoffrey of Anjou, Le Mans, Musée de Tessé (Art Resource).

dynastic burial sites and of figural funerary monuments that may be seen as precedents for the commanding and individualized figures at Fontevraud.

As a woman of twenty-five, Eleanor in 1147 traveled with Louis VII to the Holy Land. They spent a month in Constantinople, where their tours of local shrines surely included the church of the Holy Apostles, now lost but known from Procopius's *De Aedificiis* and from a late-twelfth-century description. At the time of Eleanor's visit, the Holy Apostles complex included the mausolea of Constantine and Justinian, which housed the tombs of most Eastern emperors from the fourth to the eleventh centuries. These massive sarcophagi of porphyry, or occasionally marble, were apparently unadorned with figural sculpture. With their imposing monuments, however, the mausolea exemplified a royal burial site in which successive rulers were individually commemorated. Often their wives were included as well, for it was not unknown for a wife to share her husband's sarcophagus: of thirty-nine rulers buried at Holy Apostles (and elsewhere), at least ten lay in the same tomb with their wives, and an equal number of empresses had their own tombs at Holy Apostles. Thus the Byzantine tradition, unlike Saint-Denis in Eleanor's day, absorbed the female royal body at the chief burial site almost as readily as the male.[17]

Eleanor and Louis VII arrived in the Holy Land in 1148. Writing decades later, William of Tyre noted that to fulfill his pilgrim's obligations, Louis visited the holy sites, including the church of the Holy Sepulcher in Jerusalem. While William does not mention Eleanor in this regard, she had also taken pilgrim's vows and likely visited the same sites.[18] Reconstruction of the church of the Holy Sepulcher was probably nearly complete when Louis and Eleanor were there, though they did not remain in Jerusalem for its consecration on July 15, 1149. At that time, the tombs of four crusader kings stood inside the church's southern door, before the chapel of Adam; the earliest was that of Godfrey of Bouillon (d. 1100), the most recent that of Fulk of Anjou (d. 1142). Known from descriptions and engravings, these tombs were impressive freestanding stone structures with austere foliate carving, but they did not include images of the dead. The two earlier tombs were surmounted by stone canopies supported by short columns.[19]

The rulers buried at Holy Sepulcher were all male. At the time of Eleanor's visit, however, a burial site of great spiritual resonance was evolving for crusader queens. Queen Morphia, Baldwin II's Armenian wife, died some time before 1129 and was buried in the Church of Our Lady, built in the valley of Jehoshaphat east of Jerusalem, over the Virgin's (empty) tomb. A Danish queen who died on pilgrimage in 1106 had also been buried at this revered site, which would later house the tomb of Morphia's

Fig. 18.6: Sarcophagus of Blanca of Navarre, Santa Maria del Real, Nájera, detail of front (C. and E. del Alamo).

daughter Queen Melisende (d. 1161), a political strategist and art patron.[20] By 1148, then, the city most venerated by medieval Christians offered well-established traditions of marking male rulers' tombs at a sacred site with individual aboveground monuments positioned in relationship to one another, and also of interring queens at a site of spiritual significance.

A third tradition of impressive royal funerary monuments existed in Sicily, where Eleanor visited in 1149 on her return voyage from the Holy Land and in 1191 to collect her widowed daughter Joan.[21] Sicilian rulers' long tradition of dynastic burial memorials began with the monumental tombs and mausolea of the first Norman rulers on the mainland. Later rulers promoted three churches as privileged burial sites, at Cefalù, Palermo, and Monreale, though beginning with Roger II's first wife, Elvira, queens and princes were usually buried not with kings but in a chapel dedicated to Mary Magdalene that Elvira founded at Cefalù. Monreale was chosen as a dynastic burial site by Joan's husband, William II, who buried his mother there in 1183 and moved his father's body to a new tomb ordered for Monreale. William I's tomb represents one form favored by the Norman kings: a massive porphyry urn, derived from Roman porphyry troughs.[22] In 1191, Eleanor probably did not visit Monreale; she apparently stopped only at Messina.[23] But Joan doubtless told her of William II's plans for his father's tomb and his own wish, ultimately fulfilled, to rest in the church he saw as a dynastic necropolis. Thus, while these tombs included no images of the dead, Sicily provided another example of individual tombs at a site specifically chosen for dynastic burials.

Eleanor must also have known of a fourth, extremely rich, royal burial tradition through another daughter. In 1170, her daughter Leonor (1162–1214) married Alphonso VIII of Castile (1156–1214), and through her Eleanor surely knew of Las Huelgas, a Cistercian women's convent Leonor and Alphonso founded near Burgos in 1187 as a burial site for the Castilian royal house.[24] Given Aquitanian and northern Spanish nobles' cultural and political ties, Eleanor might have been familiar with Spanish royal burial customs even before 1190, and her contacts with northern Spain in 1189–90 while negotiating Richard's marriage to Berengaria of Navarre might have informed her of Las Huelgas's founding. Then, soon after Richard and Joan died, but presumably before the Fontevraud effigies were commissioned, Eleanor in 1200 visited Castile to escort Leonor's daughter Blanche to marry the future Louis VIII of France, and she surely became aware then of Las Huelgas's dynastic functions.[25]

As an aristocratic female house Queen Leonor had known from childhood, Fontevraud must have influenced her wish to found a women's monastery in Castile. But as Leonor founded Las Huelgas in 1187, two years before Henry II was buried at Fontevraud, the latter could not have

Fig. 18.7: Tomb Slab of Adelaide of Maurienne, Saint-Pierre-de-Montmartre, Paris (Arch. Phot. Paris/CNMHS).

been her model for a family mausoleum, as has sometimes been argued.[26] The catalyst was the strong Iberian tradition of religious houses founded as royal necropoli; eleventh- and twelfth-century power struggles among the various kingdoms of northern Spain meant there were several such royal burial sites. Las Huelgas in fact blended two well-established northern Spanish traditions, for the royal custom of endowing unmarried infantas with wealthy convents meant that Las Huelgas was one of many aristocratic women's houses.[27]

Las Huelgas also suggests links to a Spanish tradition of figural, narrative tomb sculpture. Alphonso VIII's mother, Sancho III's wife Blanca of Navarre, died at Alphonso's birth in 1156 and was buried in the Navarrese royal pantheon at the church of Santa Maria del Real at Nájera. Blanca's remarkable sculpted sarcophagus, brilliantly analyzed by Elizabeth Valdez del Alamo, depicted Christological narratives appropriate to a woman who died in childbirth, as well as scenes representing Blanca's death and Sancho's grief.

This tomb is not unique; other Spanish noble tombs before and after Blanca's include depictions of the individual in death and, at times, in life.[28] While not effigies, these notably elaborate and personalized monuments marked the graves of both male and female rulers.

None of these royal burial traditions—Constantinople, Jerusalem, Sicily, or Spain—can, however, be thought of as the inspiration for life-sized sculptural funerary images. It was rather in France that a tradition of figural royal effigies first developed. Here we must think not only of Eleanor's own French roots but of the doubtless still-powerful associations of her dissolved Capetian first marriage. The Capetian dynastic burial site par excellence was Saint-Denis, but individualized burial monuments were not part of the dionysian tradition until Louis IX's time; the grave of Louis VI (d. 1137), for example, was marked only by an inscribed slab.[29] But directly connected with Eleanor's personal past, and with her sense of identity as a queen, was the first full-figure effigy of a contemporary monarch: the tomb slab of Adelaide of Maurienne, Eleanor's first mother-in-law.

Adelaide died in 1154 after entering the female Benedictine convent of Saint-Pierre-de-Montmartre in the north of Paris, which at her instigation she and Louis VI had restored and converted to a house of nuns. Adelaide had actively patronized Saint-Pierre and apparently ordered a tomb sculpture to be placed over her grave in the choir of Saint-Pierre.[30]

Adelaide's tomb slab is all the more exceptional because of its technique. Now in fragmentary condition, it must have resembled closely the nearly contemporary cenotaph made for the remains of the Merovingian queen Frédégonde (d. 597).

Frédégonde's monument was created for the Merovingian tombs' reinstallation at Saint-Germain des Prés, a project completed by 1163. The

Figure 18.8: Tomb Slab of Fredegonde, from Saint-Germain des Prés, now Saint-Denis (Zodiaque).

tomb slabs of both queens were originally set with multi-colored stones, like a large-scale mosaic. This technique was extremely unusual in the mid-twelfth century and must have been a deliberate evocation of antiquity.[31] Eleanor likely had no great love for Adelaide, whose political activism perhaps marginalized Eleanor in governmental affairs.[32] Adelaide was, however, a queen whose personal history determined her burial site, a monastery where her soul would be appropriately commemorated and where she chose a distinctive, indeed uniquely personal grave monument.

Adelaide herself may have followed the example of an earlier French queen. Philip I's widow, Bertrade de Montfort, had joined the order of Fontevraud and was buried in 1128 in the priory at Haute-Bruyère, which had been founded on her dower lands. She rested in the choir under a copper plaque, destroyed in the Revolution, which apparently bore her image. Bertrade's tomb may thus provide a precedent, perhaps known to Adelaide and the nuns at Montmartre, of a queen who joined a convent she had patronized, and was buried in a place of honor in the choir, where her tomb exceptionally bore the founder-queen's image. For Eleanor, Bertrade was a link to Fontevraud and, as Henry II's paternal great-grandmother and Louis VII's step-grandmother, a relative through both Eleanor's marriages.[33]

Another French royal connection concerns the tomb of Eleanor's first husband, Louis VII. Louis broke with Capetian tradition and was buried in 1180 not at Saint-Denis but at the monastery of Fleury, where he enjoyed founder's status as well as the benefits of Cistercian prayers for the dead.[34] Some time after his death, his widow Adela of Champagne—another queen who took charge of funerary imagery—commissioned for his tomb a lifesized stone effigy, destroyed in the Revolution. Known from engravings, this effigy was the first fully sculptural effigy of a contemporary or lately deceased monarch in France. It depicted Louis robed for his coronation, with crown and scepter.[35] Eleanor must have known of this effigy by the time of Henry II's death, and when Richard died she may have been moved to outdo her former husband's funerary splendor.

In considering Eleanor's motivations for commissioning the effigies that mark the graves of her husband and son, we should avoid the pitfall of applying modern norms of familial ties to medieval monarchs and should not see the Angevins/Aquitanians as dysfunctional, nor view Eleanor as estranged from her marital family.[36] Despite years of enforced captivity, Eleanor had the moral and political responsibility to care for Henry II's soul as well as her children's. Patrick Geary and others have discussed medieval women's role as keepers of family memory and providers of perpetual care for the soul.[37] These concerns, together with Eleanor's desire to affirm her own status as queen, shape the 1199 document with which Jane Martindale begins her study of Eleanor: the queen gave revenues to the nuns of Fontevraud not only to observe in perpetuity the anniversary of her death but also to commemorate the souls of Henry II, her sons Henry and Richard, and her other children.[38]

Further support for the belief that Eleanor commissioned the Fontevraud tomb sculptures comes from what we know of her patronage in years when her financial and political resources allowed it. The Eleanor vase, her gift to Louis VII, is an explicit example of her interest in exceptional art objects.[39] Another significant work is the Crucifixion window in Poitiers cathedral. It has been suggested that she promoted the construction of Poitiers cathedral itself, and at the window's base, Eleanor's image and Henry II's offer Christ a miniature window.[40] Madeline Caviness cogently argues, moreover, that Eleanor sponsored Saint-Denis's Jesse Tree window, and may have commissioned other examples of this new iconography in stained glass, at York Minster and Canterbury Cathedral. If Caviness is correct, as I believe she is, and if she is right that the windows depict not the usual patriliny for Christ but a matriliny, these windows are evidence well before the Fontevraud effigies of Eleanor's patronal originality and of a concern for reginal imagery in her commissions.[41]

The Tomb Sculptures

The three effigies at Fontevraud now stand in the western bay of the abbey church's nave. Roger of Howden wrote that the royal burials were originally within the church's choir, but the twelfth-century choir's extent and the tombs' location within it are not altogether clear.[42] [See Fig. 18.1]

The earlier effigies, those of Henry II and Richard I, are the work of one artist and thus date from after Richard's death in 1199. [See Fig. 18.2] On stylistic grounds they are usually dated ca. 1200.[43] As we have seen, they are among the first fully sculptural effigies of contemporary rulers in France, preceded only by Louis VII's Barbeaux effigy. While stylistically similar to the kings' effigies, Eleanor's is by another artist. [See Figs. 18.3 and 18.4] All three are of painted *tuffeau,* a chalky limestone from the Loire Valley.[44] The fourth effigy is that of Eleanor's daughter-in-law Isabelle of Angoulême, who first lay in an unadorned grave in the nuns' cemetery. In 1254, her son Henry III of England had her body moved to the choir and ordered her wooden effigy to match the earlier stone sculptures, a case of sophisticated medieval sensitivity to the resonances of formal character.[45]

As scholars have noted, the two kings' effigies are similar in style, while Eleanor's stands apart from them. Most scholars compare them with well-known late twelfth- and early thirteenth-century French portal sculpture at Saint-Denis, Chartres, Laon, and Bourges.[46] Such comparisons are useful in that they generally confirm the dating suggested by historical circumstances, but they fail to address the central issue of why the effigies look the way they do. With funerary sculpture as loaded with political and religious freight as the Fontevraud effigies, it is not enough merely to ask whether the artists had seen Chartres or trained with carvers who worked at Saint-Denis. There are obvious issues of intentionality—of what these sculptures, with their carefully constructed symbolism and ritualistic locus, were meant to evoke in the viewer's eyes.

In this regard, Erlande-Brandenburg suggests links between the Fontevraud figures and a tradition of metal tomb sculpture now largely lost in France, noting details in the kings' garments reminiscent of metalwork techniques, such as extremely regularized drapery folds and nesting V-folds.[47] [See Fig. 18.2] While metalwork from ca. 1200 is as likely to be sinuous as geometric, the kings' effigies have a compressed quality, a lack of volume curiously at odds with their monumental scale and possibly meant to evoke metalwork. A tradition of lifesized metalwork tombs in bronze and gilt copper for saints and eminent clerics seems to have flourished in Germany; several surviving examples predate the Fontevraud effigies. Erlande-Brandenburg posited large-scale tombs of goldsmiths' work in France that predated the thirteenth-century tombs from Limoges that are known to have existed.[48] Such metalwork tombs would have had great prestige because of their expensive medium, and because they were associated with the eminent clerics frequently buried in privileged sites near the high altar, where their souls might benefit from the nearby celebration of mass.[49] If Erlande-Brandenburg is right, then, in addition to the dynastic burial monuments Eleanor knew of, the Fontevraud tombs were perhaps inspired by another burial tradition of which little is known.

The flattened, arid style of the kings' effigies was also effective in that it was especially suited to the representation of death. As noted, the two male figures at Fontevraud are not images of living kings but specific recreations of the lying-in-state of the king's body. Beginning with the death of Eleanor's son Henry in 1183, Angevin funerary rites specifically recalled the coronation. Described by Benedict of Peterborough when this funerary rite was repeated for Henry II, the ceremonial displayed the king's body, face uncovered, dressed in full royal regalia—crown, scepter, sword, spurs, gloves. The gloves bore gold medallions, recreated in stone on the effigies in apparent reference to the fact that English kings, like bishops, were anointed on the hands. As Erlande-Brandenburg notes, Eleanor's purpose in ordering funerary monuments with this novel and deliberate iconography was no doubt political, affirming the dynasty's legitimacy and authority through its coronation.[50] Eleanor was not present at the lying-in-state of the young king Henry nor of Henry II, since she was in captivity during those years, but she doubtless was aware of the rituals performed and presumably orchestrated Richard's, as she was present at his death.[51] The kings' effigies speak of a desire to perpetuate the memory of their secular authority and ensure its continuation through Eleanor's surviving son John, just as her burial in the choir and her gifts for perpetual memorial prayers speak of her concern for the care of the family's souls.

The Eleanor statue itself is a different matter. While Erlande-Brandenburg suggested a reference to metalwork for her effigy as well, the overall impression is one of vitality.[52] The Eleanor figure is more robustly three-dimensional than those of the kings, and lacks their mannered, angular drapery folds. The most significant difference between Eleanor's statue and those of the kings is, of course, that while they are shown in death, her image is manifestly alive, holding an open book and engaged in the act of reading. [See Fig 18.4] The book apart, her only attribute is a crown. Historians tend to assume that her lack of other royal insignia would have signaled to medieval eyes that she was less powerful than her male relatives. Erlande-Brandenburg thought she was entitled only to a crown since she was evidently never crowned queen of England, and as queen of France was perhaps only crowned, not anointed.[53]

In any event, the image of reading signifies to feminist eyes not an absence of authority but a claim to a different kind of power. A complex and nuanced discourse surrounds women and the book in contemporary scholarship.[54] On one hand, as Madeline Caviness notes, the open book was so much associated with noblewomen that it became virtually an attribute for "queen"; but on the other, mere possession of a book did not necessarily indicate a woman's control over its text or images.[55] Nonetheless, at this final and independent stage of her life, there is every reason to suppose that the book Eleanor's effigy holds would have been for her a sign of autonomy and self-identification, perhaps even evoking her own literary patronage. In this context, the most obvious significance of the open book is the perpetual study of a devotional book.[56] The act linked Eleanor to her place of retreat, political retrenchment, and burial, in a community of devout women. More important, it affirmed her devotion and so her passage to Heaven, the most significant reference that could be made in the funerary context for which these sculptures were produced. If Eleanor commissioned the tombs and took charge of their imagery, as I believe, it is telling that she chose to isolate herself from the insignia of secular power Henry and Richard's monuments claimed for them. She could have requested representation with a scepter, a symbol widely associated with the visual imagery of queens as well as kings, as demonstrated by the scepter held by the effigy of the Merovingian queen Frédégonde executed for Saint-Germain-des-Prés in the 1150s, and perhaps too in the now-effaced left hand of Queen Adelaide's effigy.[57] [See Figs. 18.7 and 18.8] Instead, ever pragmatic, Eleanor claimed for herself the iconography of the ultimate Christian victory. Her effigy evokes not a royal lying-in-state, but the activity of a living queen. [See Fig. 18.4]

Conclusion

I believe the tombs at Fontevraud articulate issues of women, death, and power. By this, I mean that controlling the locus of death or burial, and their lasting manifestations, gave medieval royal women a potent authority outside modern notions of power.[58] Thus we should enlarge our understanding of Eleanor of Aquitaine to include a woman who, free of Henry II's control, exercised political power in the immediate sense, but also manipulated the potent imagery of death: drawing from a lifetime of experience with royal funerary functions, she created a memorial to herself and her family at a site guaranteed to benefit their souls.

We should also situate Eleanor within the tradition of twelfth- and thirteenth-century queens in France who exercised autonomy in matters of death and commemoration. Queens' or empresses' commissions dominate rulers' extant memorial imagery in France from the late twelfth and early thirteenth centuries. There is every reason to think Adelaide of Maurienne ordered her own tomb; Empress Matilda probably ordered Geoffrey V's enamel tomb plaque soon after 1151, and Adela of Champagne ordered Louis VII's effigy after 1180. Thus Eleanor, who styled herself "Anglie regina" even when her sons' wives could claim that title, followed a precedent set by other queens of her era and, like her mother-in-law and her ex-husband's widow, took charge of the memorial imagery of kings and queens.[59]

Notes

This essay was written with the encouragement and guidance of Bonnie Wheeler and John Carmi Parsons. To John Parsons I owe a special debt for sharing with me his insights into queenship and the culture of death in the Middle Ages. Lois Huneycutt, Whitney Leesom, Jane Long, Christina Salowey, and Elizabeth Valdez del Alamo generously contributed further ideas and bibliographic support to this study.

1. Of a vast bibliography, many studies not noted below are cited in Labande, "Pour une image véridique," a title reflecting the elusiveness of a "true" image of Eleanor. Romance colors Kelly's *Eleanor and the Four Kings* which uncritically uses twelfth-century chronicles and vernacular literature. As Martindale notes ("Eleanor of Aquitaine," pp. 35–36), historians who write of Eleanor as her husbands' pendant reveal more of their attitudes toward women's social roles than of Eleanor herself.

2. Martindale's "Eleanor of Aquitaine" is especially useful on Eleanor's identification with her native Aquitaine. Also helpful is *Eleanor of Aquitaine: Patron and Politician,* ed. Kibler, esp. Brown, "Eleanor of Aquitaine: Parent, Queen and Duchess" (revised as chapter 1 in this volume), and Greenhill, "Eleanor, Abbot Suger, and Saint-Denis." William W. Clark's entry, "Fontevrault Abbey," is a handy overview of questions raised by the Fontevraud tombs.

3. I rely on Erlande-Brandenburg's study of French royal funerary practice, *Le roi est mort* and his works on the Fontevraud tombs: "Le 'cimitière des rois' à Fontevrault"; "La sculpture funéraire"; and "Les gisants de Fontevrault." Others who believe Eleanor ordered the tombs are Clark, "Fontevrault Abbey," p. 290; Caviness, "Anchoress, Abbess, and Queen," suggesting at p. 130 that the effigies were executed after Eleanor's death; and Parsons, "Burials and Posthumous Commemorations of English Queens," p. 326, citing Erlande-Brandenburg, "La sculpture funéraire," pp. 563–64.

4. These ideas were presented in "The Queen's Body and Institutional Memory: The Tomb of Adelaide of Maurienne," at the Thirtieth International Congress on Medieval Studies, Western Michigan University, May 1995; and "La reine Est Morte: The Tomb of Queen Adelaide of Maurienne and Reginal Burial Practice in Twelfth-Century France," read to the University of Virginia' s Medieval Circle, February 1997; see my "The Queen's Body." Arguments for independent choice can be made for Suzanne, first wife of Robert II; Adelaide of Maurienne, wife of Louis VI; Ingeborg, repudiated wife of Philip II, Blanche of Castille, wife of Louis VIII and mother of Louis IX; and, with less certainty, for Bertrade of Montfort, wife of Philip I, and Anne of Russia, wife of Henry I (Nolan, "Queen's Body and Institutional Memory"); see also Erlande-Brandenburg, *Le roi est mort,* pp. 75, 77, 122–23, 159, 160, 160–61, 162–63, 165.

5. The community included "mulieres . . . meretrices et masculorum aspernatrices" (Migne, PL 162: col. 1053). See Gold, *The Lady and the Virgin,* pp. 93–113, with ample Fontevraud bibliography; Bienvenu, *Robert d'Arbrissel;* Bezzola, *Origines,* pp. 278–92; J. Daoust, "Fontevrault"; Boase, "Fontevrault and the Plantagenets"; Bienvenu, "Aliénor et Fontevraud."

6. Howden, *Chronica* 2:367. When Henry said in 1170 that he would seek burial at Grandmont, his barons argued that its severe asceticism was unsuited to his dignity; Henry then funded new works there, perhaps to make it a more splendid setting for his tomb (Hallam, "Royal Burial and the Cult of Kingship," 369). He perhaps finally abandoned Grandmont as a burial site because of discord within the house (Hallam, "Henry II, Richard I and the Order of Grandmont," 167–68).

7. Giraldus Cambrensis, *De Principis Instructione Liber* 8:306, discussed by Brown, "Eleanor as Parent, Queen and Duchess," pp. 30–31 n95, and Hallam, "Royal Burial and the Cult of Kingship," 371.

8. Erlande-Brandenburg, "Le 'cimetière des rois' à Fontevraud," 483, implied Eleanor decided Henry's burial at Fontevraud; Bienvenu, "Aliénor et

Fontevraud," 22, showed the choice could not have been hers. Erlande-Brandenburg modified his position, and his arguments for a politically motivated choice of Fontevrault seem compelling ("Les gisants de Fontevrault," 4–5). Brown, "Eleanor of Aquitaine: Parent, Queen, and Duchess," p. 20, had seen no proof Henry chose Fontevraud and thought his burial there a likely convenience, concluding it represented Eleanor's "final triumph over him."

9. I owe this characterization to Whitney Leesom. The concept of liminality was evolved by the sociologist Arnold van Gennep to describe the transitional phase of rites of passage, as discussed in the introduction to V. Turner, *Image and Pilgrimage*, pp. 2–4. On Angevin links to Fontevraud, Bienvenu, "Aliénor et Fontevraud" 18–19, and Boase, "Fontevrault and the Plantagenets," 2–3. Henry II's great-grandmother Bertrade de Montfort left her Angevin husband for Philip I of France, after whose death (1108) she entered a Fontevrist priory founded on her dower lands at Haute-Bruyère (Boase, "Fontevrault and the Plantagenets," 3; Bezzola, *Origines*, pp. 288–90; Bienvenu, "Aliénor et Fontevraud," 18; Erlande-Brandenburg, *Le roi est mort*, p. 89; Rabourdin, *Le prieuré royal*, pp. 15–23; and discussion of Bertrade's tomb, below in this chapter). For Henry's gifts to Fontevraud, see CDF 1:375, 377 *ter*, 378; and *Recueil des actes de Henry II* 1:385–86, 390–91, 540–41, 554–55, and 2:157–58. For Eleanor's and her ancestors' grants, see Bienvenu, "Aliénor et Fontevraud" 16–17; Martindale, "Eleanor of Aquitaine," 19–21.

10. Martindale, "Eleanor of Aquitaine," 20–21. On the 1152 visit, see Bienvenu, "Aliénor et Fontevraud" 19, and *Recueil des actes de Henri II* 1: no. 24 at pp. 31–32. On the 1185 grant, Bienvenu, "Aliénor et Fontevraud," 21; CDF, no. 1080 at p. 318; Boase, "Fontevrault and the Plantagenets," 5–6, and Bienvenu, "Aliénor et Fontevraud," 21–22.

11. Just after Richard's death in 1199, Eleanor granted the nuns of Fontevraud 100 pounds Poitevin yearly in perpetuity so they would observe her anniversary after her death and care for the souls of Henry II, Richard I, and her other children. The text is in Marchegay, "Chartes de Fontevraud," 337–38; see also Martindale, "Eleanor of Aquitaine," pp. 17–18. Clearly by 1199 Eleanor was thinking of Fontevraud as a family burial site and source of spiritual support as well as a politically strategic site.

12. For Richard and Eleanor, see Matthew Paris, *Chronica Majora* 2:451–52, 488. On Joanna, Boase, "Fontevrault and the Plantagenets," 6; the text of her will, with bequests to Fontevraud, is in CDF 1:392.

13. The evolution of tomb memorials that represent the human figure, especially the effigy's formal evolution from a flat object to a three-dimensional impersonation of the deceased, is the subject of Panofsky's classic *Tomb Sculpture*. Similar discussion forms part of Philippe Ariès, *L' Homme devant la mort* [Hour of Our Death], which seeks to incorporate attitudes toward death and rituals of passage as well as the monuments. Binski's *Medieval Death* also seeks to integrate visual memorials with the mentality and cultic practices of the period.

14. For the chronology, Erlande-Brandenburg, "La sculpture funéraire," p. 561. As visual representations, the Fontevraud effigies are preceded by the tomb of Adelaide of Maurienne—not a fully sculptural monument but an inlaid slab, as discussed below. The earliest known sculptural effigy was that of Louis VII at Barbeaux, also noted below. As Panofsky notes (*Tomb Sculpture,* p. 57), the Fontevraud effigies are perhaps the first true *gisants*—tomb sculptures conceived as recumbent figures, not standing figures seen horizontally. For Angevin kings' funerary rites, see below, n50.

15. For English royal burial sites, see Hallam, "Royal Burial and the Cult of Kingship," 359–80, and Mason, "Royal Monastic Patronage," Hallam, "Royal Burial," 367–68, usefully observes that a wish for individual intercession played a large role in a king's choice of burial site; Suger thus excused Philip I's burial elsewhere than at Saint-Denis.

16. Gauthier, "Naissance," pp. 101–03, seems to link Geoffrey's plaque to that of Bishop Ulger (d. 1148), originally in Angers cathedral. On the plaque, see Panofsky, *Tomb Sculpture,* p. 50, pl. 190, and Petzold, *Romanesque Art,* pp. 79–80, pl. 55. On Matilda's tomb, see Chibnall, *The Empress Matilda,* pp. 190–91, a reference I owe Lois Huneycutt.

17. On Louis's visit to churches in Constantinople, see Odo of Deuil, *De profectione Ludovici VII,* pp. 64–66; Odo does not note Eleanor's visit, but Berry (Odo of Deuil, *De profectione Ludovici VII,* p. xxiii n67) thinks references to her were cut from the work. Reports of the tombs at Holy Apostles were compiled by Constantine VII (d. 959) and amended in later copies (Grierson, "Tombs and Obits," 3–6, 38–60, also using at 7–9 and 10–12, the *Necrologium Imperatorum,* a list of obits, lengths of reigns, and tombs for every emperor from Constantine I [d. 337] to Michael V [d. 1042]).

18. William of Tyre, *Deeds Done Beyond the Sea* 2:183; writing after Eleanor and Louis divorced, William is critical of her. She took the cross at Vézelay on March 31, 1146 (Berry, "The Second Crusade" 2:469; Kelly, *Eleanor and the Four Kings,* p. 34; William of Newburgh, *Historia Rerum Anglicarum,* 1:66, 82).

19. Jaroslav Folda, *Art of the Crusaders,* pp. 177–78; noting Louis's party left Jerusalem before Holy Sepulcher's dedication, Folda infers the Western crusaders had little to do with the project. For the royal tombs, see Folda, *Art of the Crusaders,* pp. 38–39, fig. 1; Baldwin II's and Fulk of Anjou's were rectangular and lacked canopies (Folda, *Art of the Crusaders,* pp. 114, 174). On Baldwin V's tomb (d. 1186), its figural ornamentation limited to busts of Christ and two angels, see Jacoby, "The Tomb of Baldwin V."

20. Folda, *Art of the Crusaders,* p. 113, thinks Morphia's burial reflects a decision not to bury queens at Holy Sepulcher; nothing is known of her tomb. At p. 516 n134, Folda cites the 1106 burial as precedent for queens' burials at Jehoshaphat. He examines at pp. 324–28 Melisende's career and tomb, which he assumes was ordered before her death. Undoubtedly she chose her burial site, though Folda implies at p. 324 that she perhaps wished for burial at the Templum Domini as her grants there exceeded

those to Jehoshaphat. See also Mayer, "Queen Melisende"; Hamilton, "Women in the Crusader States," pp. 148–57; Folda, "Images of Queen Melisende"; Lambert, "Queen or Consort."

21. Kelly, *Eleanor and the Four Kings,* pp. 70, 262–65; Landon, *Itinerary of King Richard I,* pp. 47–48.

22. Déer, *Dynastic Porphyry Tombs,* pp. 28–31; for William's promotion of Monreale, see Déer, *Dynastic Porphyry Tombs,* pp. 14–15, for porphyry troughs, pp. 42–45, and for Sicilian queens' burials, see pp. 2–3.

23. Landon, *Itinerary of Richard I,* pp. 47–48.

24. Elizabeth Valdez del Alamo offered bibliographical help and shared with me her insights into Spanish sepulchral monuments and traditions of patronage among Spanish royal women. On Las Huelgas, see Miriam Shadis, "Piety, Politics and Power"; Gómez Moreno, *El Panteón Real de las Huelgas;* Elorza, *El Panteón Real de Las Huelgas de Burgo;* Gómez Barcena, *Escultura Gótica Funeraria en Burgos,* pp. 187–201. Plans for founding Las Huelgas may have been in hand by 1179 (Gómez Barcena, *Escultura Gótica,* p. 194).

25. For the marriage, see Richardson, "The Letters and Charters," 201; Landon, *Itinerary of Richard I,* p. 227 n6, assumes Eleanor arranged the marriage and escorted Berengaria to her wedding. On northern Spanish and Aquitanian cultural ties, del Alamo, "Lament for a Lost Queen," esp. 321 n53.

26. Many points in Shadis's study of Leonor of England's patronage are persuasive, but I disagree on the direction of influence between Las Huelgas and Fontevraud ("Piety, Politics and Power," pp. 203–204).

27. The tumultuous history of medieval Spain is summarized in Reilly, "Medieval Spain." On northern Spanish dynasties' ritual character, see Ruiz, "Unsacred Monarchy," pp. 109–44, a reference I owe to John Parsons. Royal burial traditions were established in northern Spain well before Las Huelgas was founded. San Isidoro in León, founded in the early eleventh century, served as a pantheon for the Leonese dynasty, and after Sancha of León wed Fernando of Castile, functioned for a time as the Castilian royal burial site. For chronological and stylistic issues raised by this complex monument, see del Alamo, "Ortodoxia y heterodoxia." Del Alamo generously shared excerpts from this study, still in press. On endowing infantas with wealthy convents, see Havens Caldwell, "Urraca," 119. Wright, "Royal Tomb Program," 231, thinks Las Huelgas inspired Blanche of Castile and Louis IX' s foundation at Royaumont as a burial site. For Las Huelgas's influence on Portuguese royal burials at Alcobaça, on Royaumont and, later, on Westminster Abbey, see Parsons, "Mothers, Daughters, Marriage, Power," p. 75.

28. Del Alamo, "Lament," 311–33, esp. 314–15 and fig. 5, citing historiated queens' tombs including the well-known sarcophagus of Sancha (d. 1096), daughter of Ramiro I of Aragon in Jaca, originally in the women's monastery of Santa Cruz de la Séros. In addition to depictions of Sancha's

funeral, the sarcophagus contains a scene del Alamo interprets as Sancha with her sisters, patrons of the chapel at Santa Cruz where they were buried. See also Panofsky, *Tomb Sculpture*, p. 59 and figs. 235–36; Simon, "Le Sarcophage de Doña Sancha à Jaca" and "Sarcophagus of Doña Sancha," fig. 105.

29. Erlande-Brandenburg, *Le roi est mort,* pp. 68–80, discusses Saint-Denis's evolution as a royal mausoleum through the twelfth and thirteenth centuries. A useful overview of royal burial practices is Hallam, "Royal Burial and the Cult of Kingship," 359–80; for burials at Saint-Denis before the thirteenth century, see Wright, "Royal Tomb Program," 227–29, and Brown, "Burying and Unburying." Erlande-Brandenburg, *Le roi est mort,* p. 109, notes no evidence for pre-thirteenth-century elaboration of royal graves at Saint-Denis save Dagobert's; a statue of Dagobert enthroned, known from Montfaucon's engraving, was carved ca. 1160 but came from another context in the church (Wright, "Royal Tomb Program," 229–30, figs. 4–5).

30. The effigy is the subject of my study, "The Queen's Body and Institutional Memory," noted above. Erlande-Brandenburg, *Le roi est mort,* pp. 89–90, 122–23, 160–61 also discusses Adelaide's tomb; Brown notes it briefly in "Burying and Unburying," pp. 243–44. The chief published sources for the church are: *Recueil des chartes de Montmartre,* ed. de Barthélemy; Francis Deshoulières, "L'église Saint-Pierre de Montmartre"; M. Dumolin, "Notes sur l'abbaye de Montmartre"; Fossard, "L'église Saint-Pierre"; Erlande-Brandenburg, "Eglise Saint-Pierre-de-Montmartre." The abbey's foundation charter states that the house was reformed "[E]t prece et consilio karissime uxoris nostre Adelidis regine" (*Recueil des chartes de l'abbaye royale de Montmartre,* pp. 60–61).

31. For the chronology of rebuilding at Saint-Germain, see Clark, "Spatial Innovations," 360 n36, and "Defining National Historical Memory," forthcoming. See also discussion of Saint-Germain in Brown, "Burying and Unburying," p. 243. Frédégonde's tomb slab is noted in Panofsky, *Tomb Sculpture,* p. 50; Erlande-Brandenburg, *Le roi est mort,* pp. 114, 122–23, 130–40; and Nolan, "Queen's Body and Institutional Memory." For the implications of this historicizing technique that recalled, e.g., Suger's lost mosaic in the south tympanum of Saint-Denis's west portal, see Nolan, "Queen's Body and Institutional Memory."

32. As Huneycutt observed in a paper presented May 10, 1997, "Alone of All Her Sex? Eleanor of Aquitaine and Her 12th-Century Predecessors," at the Thirty-Second International Congress on Medieval Studies, Western Michigan University; Huneycutt deals with the activism of Eleanor's English predecessors in chapter 5 of this volume. On the French contexts of Eleanor's career, see the collected papers in *Aristocratic Women in Medieval France,* ed. Evergates, especially LoPrete, "Adela of Blois," which demonstrates the wide range of power exercised by Adela throughout her career.

33. For Bertrade's life and ties to Fontevraud, see above, n9. No description of her tomb survives, but Erlande-Brandenburg, *Le roi est mort,* p. 89, implies the plaque must have had some sort of representation of the queen.

34. For Louis's burial at Barbeau, see Erlande-Brandenburg, *Le roi est mort,* pp. 75–77, 87–88; Hallam, "Royal Burial," 369; Brown, "Burying and Unburying," pp. 243–44, notes that Louis thus gained the Cistercian order's prayers. For the efficacy of Cistercian prayers for the dead and their cultivation of royal burials, see Binski, *Medieval Death,* pp. 58–60, another reference I owe to John Carmi Parsons.

35. On Adela and Louis's tomb sculpture, see Erlande-Brandenburg, *Le roi est mort,* p. 161 n161. See also *Le roi est mort,* pp. 111–12, 161–62, and figs. 37, 38; Brown, "Burying and Unburying," pp. 243–44, fig. 1. Unlike the Fontevraud tombs, Louis's did not evoke the royal burial rite. As far as can be determined from contemporary sources, French kings' funerals were less elaborate than their English colleagues' until the death of Philip II (d. 1223); even then, Philip's burial attire seemingly did not imitate that of his coronation (*Le roi est mort,* pp. 12–14, 18–19). Adelaide's and Louis's tombs were preceded by commemorative tomb statues of much earlier kings, executed in the 1140s. Known from engravings and extant fragments, enthroned statues of the Carolingians Louis IV and Lothair, carved in the round, marked their graves at Saint-Rémi in Reims (Sauerländer, *Gothic Sculpture,* pp. 395, fig. 15, pl. 28; Erlande-Brandenburg, *Le roi est mort,* pl. 16 at pp. 119–20). Two Merovingian kings were similarly commemorated at Saint-Médard in Soissons by apparently wooden sculptures, now lost, that like the Reims statues evoked Carolingian ruler portraits (Erlande-Brandenburg, *Le roi est mort,* pp. 119–20). The Dagobert sculpture from Saint-Denis, noted above, n29, probably dated from the same period but was not associated with his tomb.

36. Those who apply modern family norms to this medieval queen include Kelly, *Eleanor and the Four Kings,* and Simon Schama in a *New Yorker* magazine column (September 15, 1997, p. 62), comparing Eleanor to the Diana, the late princess of Wales, as a royal wife betrayed and belittled by an errant husband. While speculating on emotional damage Eleanor's young children perhaps suffered when parted from her, Brown, "Eleanor of Aquitaine: Parent, Queen, and Duchess," warns against judging medieval relationships against modern norms of domestic life; Martindale, "Eleanor of Aquitaine," pp. 38–44, criticizes estimates based on assumptions of romantic love and jealousy. Turner, "Eleanor of Aquitaine and Her Children" assumes Eleanor's physical absence from her children proves a lack of maternal care. Huneycutt, "Public Lives, Private Ties" balances such views, noting at pp. 297–98 that in the Middle Ages as today, time spent in a child's presence is not the only gauge of parental involvement, and that the non-survival of relevant documents is a significantly limiting factor. Parsons, "'Que nos lactauit in infancia,'" notes royal parents' intense and sustained involvement with those

who helped rear their children. I am grateful to Dr. Parsons for sharing this
stimulating essay with me while it was in press.

37. Contemporary historians' work on memory has deepened art historians'
understanding of the functions of memorial rituals and monuments. This
work rests upon such studies as Carruthers's *The Book of Memory*. Especially relevant to my project are Geary's *Living with the Dead* and *Phantoms
of Remembrance;* in the latter, see especially "Men, Women, and Family
Memory," pp. 48–80. On the distinct character of women' s memory, see
Laura A. Smoller, "Miracle, Memory and Meaning in the Canonization of
Vincent Ferrer, 1453–1454," *Speculum* 73 (1998):429–54. In both ancient
and medieval cultures, women were closely associated with mourning and
preparation of the body for burial; see my "'Ploratus et Ululatus'" and del
Alamo, "Lament for a Lost Queen," 317–19. That women' s associations
with death are transcultural is demonstrated by anthropologists, e.g., Maurice Bloch, "Death, Women, and Power." Anthropologists also note that
ties between women and death could imply both power and contamina-
tion; for ideas of pollution in many cultures, see Mary Douglas, *Purity and
Danger.*

38. Martindale, "Eleanor of Aquitaine," pp. 17–18; for the charter's text, see
Marchegay, "Chartes de Fontevraud," 337–38. Made urgent by the developing concept of Purgatory, anniversary commemorations were well established by the late twelfth century (Erlande-Brandenburg, *Le roi est mort,*
pp. 99–100; Hallam, "Royal Burial," 371; Ariès, *Hour of Our Death,* pp.
152–54; Binski, *Medieval Death,* pp. 115–16, 181–88). The standard study of
the evolving doctrine of Purgatory is Le Goff, *The Birth of Purgatory.*

39. In addition to George T. Beech's essay in this volume, see his "Eleanor
Vase"; Gaborit-Chopin, "Suger's Liturgical Vessels," p. 289 and " Le Vase d'
Aliénor," pp. 170–72.

40. Lozinski, "Henri II," examines the traditional attribution of the cathedral's
construction to Henry and Eleanor; noting a lack of evidence, Lozinski
links the building's architectural character to military structures built for
Henry. Caviness, "Anchoress, Abbess, and Queen," p. 126, notes, however,
that Poitiers was Eleanor's ancestral territory, not Henry's, and that in the
Crucifixion window Eleanor is in the place of honor on Christ's right. Erlande-Brandenburg, *Gothic Art,* p. 519, states that "The identity of the ar-
chitect remains a mystery . . . Eleanor of Aquitaine, whose illustrious court
was the focal point of Poitiers at the time, may have had a hand in the project. Work on this colossal monument probably began during the episco-
pate of Jean Belmain (1162–82)."

41. Caviness, "Anchoress, Abbess, and Queen," p. 129, and "Suger's Glass," p.
267, notes that the three windows, widely separate in date (Saint-Denis,
1144; York, 1170; Canterbury, 1195), are very similar in composition, and
that particular circumstances in Eleanor' s life may have prompted each donation. On matriliny, see Caviness, "Anchoress, Abbess, and Queen," pp.
129–30.

42. Howden, *Chronica* 2:367. For interpretations of Roger' s text and the archeological evidence, see Erlande-Brandenburg, "Le 'cimetière des rois' à Fontevraud,"p. 485; Clark, "Fontevrault Abbey," p. 291.
43. Sauerländer, *Gothic Sculpture,* pp. 448–49.
44. Erlande-Brandenburg, "La sculpture funéraire," p. 566; on *tuffeau,* see *Gothic Sculpture in America,* ed. Gillerman, pp. xvii, 310.
45. Erlande-Brandenburg, "Le 'cimetière des rois' à Fontevraud," 486–90.
46. Gardner, *Medieval Sculpture in France,* pp. 348–49, links the effigies to the Coronation of the Virgin portal at Chartres. Schreiner, *Die frühgotische,* pp. 71–75, looks to the Coronation portal at Laon and the north portal at Bourges. Sauerländer, *Gothic Sculpture,* pp. 448–49, sees similarities between the kings' effigies, Saint-Denis's north portal and the Childebert *gisant* now at Saint-Denis. Erlande-Brandenburg, "La sculpture funéraire," 565–66, notes that use of *tuffeau* suggests a Loire Valley artist familiar with that stone and affirms general similarities to portal sculptures from Saint-Martin at Angers dated 1175–80, now in the Yale University Gallery.
47. Erlande-Brandenburg, "La sculpture funéraire," pp. 564–65.
48. Erlande-Brandenburg, "La sculpture funéraire," p. 29, citing Rudolph of Swabia's surviving bronze tomb in Merseburg Cathedral and Frederick of Wettin's in Magdeburg Cathedral; for these figures, see Panofsky, *Tomb Sculpture,* pp. 51–52, figs. 197, 200.
49. The privilege of lay burial within a church was restricted in principle to the house's founders (Durandus, *Rationale,* p. 370). Ariès, *Hour of Our Death,* pp. 45–51, 71–73, surveys evolution of the Christian desire for burial within churches, initially to enjoy the protection of saints buried there, but by the twelfth century to rest near the altar, locus of the celebration of mass, with its intercessory benefits for the deceased's soul. Canonical prohibitions of lay burial in churches, especially near altars, only slowly gave way in the face of lay disregard for such sanctions (Ariès, *Hour of Our Death,* pp. 45–47). By 1240, even Cistercians allowed royal burials in their churches (Binski, *Medieval Death,* pp. 59–60). For these developments' impact on fifteenth-century tomb sculpture, Johnson, "Activating the Effigy."
50. Young Henry's funeral is described in Matthew Paris, *Chronica Majora* 2:319, discussed in Erlande-Brandenburg, "La sculpture funéraire," pp. 562–63. For Henry II's lying in state, see *Gesta Regis Henrici Secundi* 2:71; discussion in Erlande-Brandenburg, "La sculpture funéraire," 562–63 (citing descriptions by Paris and Roger of Wendover), and *Le roi est mort,* pp. 15–16. For links between funerary rites and theories of kingship, see Kantorowicz, *King's Two Bodies,* pp. 383–450, which, however, does not mention the Angevin rites and, at p. 431 n383, makes only passing reference to the Fontevraud tombs. A. Martindale, "Patrons and Minders," considers late-medieval aristocratic women's creation of monuments to the males of their families, a tradition Eleanor of Aquitaine may have helped to inaugurate at the turn of the thirteenth century.

51. Eleanor's April 1199, charter states she was present at Richard' s death (CDF 1:473 [no. 1304]).

52. Erlande-Brandenburg, "La sculpture funéraire," p. 567.

53. Erlande-Brandenburg, "La sculpture funéraire," p. 564 n19, citing de Pange, p. 320, without citation: Eleanor "semble juger définitive la consécration qu' elle a reçue comme reine de France, car il ne semble pas que, plus tard, elle se fera couronner reine d' Angleterre." John Parsons has suggested to me that Eleanor may not have shared Henry II' s December 1154 coronation because of advanced pregnancy; her son Henry was born early in 1155. Parsons notes the pregnant queen's special, often intercessory role in late medieval romance and chronicle in England ("The Pregnant Queen"). Eleanor was not certainly anointed at her wedding and coronation at Bordeaux in 1137, when Louis was still king-designate. Suger was present, but stated only that she received a crown (Suger, *Vie de Louis VI le Gros,* trans. Cusimano and Moorhead, pp. 150, 157). By the mid-twelfth century queens were generally anointed at their coronations, as documented for Louis's second wife, Constance of Castile (Facinger, "Medieval Queenship":17–20). Useful on French reginal coronations is Sherman, "The Queen in Charles V's 'Coronation Book,'" 268–70. Jackson's *Ordines Coronationis Franciae* includes many references to earlier sources. For the *ordo* perhaps used for Eleanor's 1137 coronation, see Brown, *"Franks, Burgundians, and Aquitanians,"* which, however, sheds no light on the question of her unction at that time.

54. Bell, "Medieval Women Book Owners," raises a range of issues related to late medieval women and the production, possession, and use of books. Recent contributions include Sheingorn, "'The Wise Mother'"; the essays in *The Cultural Patronage of Medieval Women,* ed. McCash; and *Women and the Book,* ed. Taylor and Smith.

55. Caviness, "Anchoress, Abbess, and Queen," p. 130, and "Patron or Matron?" both explore complex issues of female patronage. Another illuminating study of this richly encoded MS is Holladay, "The Education of Jeanne d'Evreux." For links between an intended female reader and distinctive iconography, see my "'Ploratus et Ululatus,'" 103–05.

56. It is obviously unclear what sort of book Eleanor' s effigy was meant to hold. A growing body of evidence links women and books of hours in the later Middle Ages, but in the early thirteenth century Eleanor would more likely have read a psalter, a book often associated with French royal women in that century (for psalters associated with Queens Ingeborg and Blanche of Castile, see Caviness, "Anchoress, Abbess, and Queen," pp. 133–36). Eleanor of Aquitaine's literary patronage is under renewed debate; see Owen, *Eleanor of Aquitaine;* Broadhurst, "Henry II of England and Eleanor of Aquitaine"; and Brown, chapter 1 in this volume.

57. In addition to the Frédégonde and Adelaide effigies, the lost marble tomb slab of Philip II' s first wife, Isabelle of Hainaut, which survived in Notre-Dame in Paris until the eighteenth century, displayed a scepter (Erlande-

Brandenburg, *Le roi est mort,* pp. 42–43, 163, 181–182); her seal, found in her tomb in 1858, also shows her with a scepter (*Le roi est mort,* pp. 42–43, fig. 20; Bedos Rezak, "Women, Seals, and Power," p. 75 fig. 2). Eleanor herself may have chosen a scepter as a visual sign in a context more secular than her tomb. In an effaced seal from 1199, the dowager queen appears to hold a branch-like scepter in her right hand, and an orb in her left; Eygun, *Sigillographie,* pp. 159–160, pl. 1, fig. 4.; and Douët d'Arcq, *Collection de sceaux,* 3:263. We cannot be sure that queens of Eleanor's era actually received a scepter at their coronations. Sherman, "The Queen in Charles V's 'Coronation Book,'" 269–70, notes that the *ordines* indicate that thirteenth- and fourteenth-century French queens received a scepter smaller than those of kings; Parsons, "Ritual and Symbol," pp. 62–63, concludes that at least by 1330 English queens received scepters, though not necessarily with solemn ritual.

58. Historians have lately evolved new concepts of what constituted power for women. An important early study in this regard is Sherman, "Taking a Second Look." Essays in *Women and Power in the Middle Ages,* ed. Erler and Kowaleski, continue this re-evaluation; see especially the introduction, pp. 1–17. See also Parsons "'Never was a body buried,'" suggesting at pp. 333–34 that queens, like other noblewomen, "manipulat[ed] . . . the imagery of their tombs" for reasons that link temporal and spiritual authority. Parsons calls attention to A. Martindale's "Patrons and Minders," dealing with women's importation of secular imagery into late medieval sacred spaces, especially through the iconography of tombs. Clearly, in a society absorbed with preparation for the afterlife, a queen's ability to determine both visual and liturgical commemorations constituted power of a very real sort.

59. Eleanor styled herself "queen of England" in (among other documents) her Fontevraud charters between 1192 and 1200 (CDF, pp. 387–91, 394).

CHAPTER 19

FONTEVRAUD, DYNASTICISM,
AND ELEANOR OF AQUITAINE

Charles T. Wood

> *How Eleanor of Aquitaine, Henry II, and so many of their relatives came to be buried at Fontevraud is the story of chance coupled with a growing sense of dynasticism. Henry II had made other plans, but they came to nought when those in charge of his funeral found Fontevraud much more convenient. Eleanor chose to bury her children Jeanne and Richard there, and before she joined them in death, she probably planned the way in which all of their tombs should be clustered as a family grouping. Nevertheless, the burial wishes of later Plantagenets suggest that the dynastic thinking that drew them to Fontevraud involved Eleanor's family as much as Henry's, if not more so.*

In 1204, when Eleanor of Aquitaine died, she was interred at Fontevraud, the double monastery in which three members of her immediate family already lay buried: her husband Henry II, her daughter Jeanne of Toulouse, and her son Richard the Lionheart. Before the century was out, these three and Eleanor were joined by Isabelle of Angoulême, countess of La Marche and former wife of Eleanor's son John; by Raymond VII of Toulouse, Eleanor's grandson via Jeanne; and by the heart of John's son— her grandson—Henry III. Small wonder, then, that this final resting place of so many Plantagenets has long been known as the Royal Abbey of Fontevraud.[1]

In order to understand the nature and purpose of these burials at the abbey, it may first be useful to know some of the ways in which Fontevraud differed from other monasteries. Founded in 1101, it owed many of its unusual features to Robert d'Arbrissel, a widely celebrated preacher-reformer much admired by Eleanor's poet grandfather, William IX of Aquitaine. Robert as founder was, moreover, a man uniquely committed to what Kevin Brownlee calls "a new and exalted conception of the status of women."[2] In proof of the point, he envisioned Fontevraud as a monastery not just for both sexes, but also as a place of seclusion in which the women would be contemplatives while the men did all the manual labor. As confirmed by Pope Paschal II, its rule provided for a double hierarchy in which, at the express wish of the whole community, the monks were subordinated to the nuns in temporal and spiritual matters, with both sexes under the authority of an abbess who was preferably to be a widow, not a virgin. Whether lay or clerical, the men were Augustinians and the women, Benedictines though they followed a modified rule.

In this form Fontevraud prospered down to the time of the French Revolution, its wealth and stature sustained by the fact that its abbesses frequently came from the French royal family. In 1793, however, revolutionaries sacked the abbey, effectively bringing its religious life to a close, but eleven years later Napoleon came up with an innovative plan for renewal. Never a man to let good buildings go to waste, he decided to give new scope to Robert d'Arbrissel's penitential vision by transforming the monastic fabric into a penitentiary. Only in 1963 did Fontevraud's life as a prison end. Happily, soon thereafter the Ministry of Culture (or, more precisely, various bodies under its jurisdiction, notably the Musées de France) decided that, insofar as possible, the abbey should be restored to its original condition, with bars left on the windows of only a few outbuildings in order to testify to more recent alternative use.[3]

Renovation proved surprisingly complex. In the abbey church, for example, prison authorities had added a second floor to the nave, making it into a two-story cell block, and here restoration necessarily involved not just removal of the additions, but also reconstruction of the walls, work that could be done only after determining their original configuration. Unexpectedly, however, as restoration neared its completion, a much smaller physical challenge exploded into a much greater intellectual debate: what to do with the *gisants* of Eleanor, Henry II, Richard I, and Isabelle, the four such tomb effigies that were believed to have survived—or so the restorers assumed until, late in the game, the badly damaged recumbent image of Raymond VII turned up under the nave's paving stones. How were these effigies to be displayed? Where were they to be placed? And in what relationship to each other? French intellectual life being what it is, by June 1987 the Centre Culturel de l'Ouest was complaining: "Arguments have been exchanged not only on the esthetic and historical plane, but on the philosophic and religious one as well," the point being that while nearly everyone opposed the restorers' original plan, all parties were united in wanting the effigies so arranged that viewers would be able to grasp something of their symbolism as that symbolism would have been understood at the time that the effigies had been made.

Although no one is ever likely to resolve these disputes to everyone's satisfaction, in so far as historians may have a better understanding of people within their historical contexts than do philosophers, students of religion, and estheticians, there is something to be said for examining a few of the family realities that may help to explain the tomb effigies at Fontevraud, their purpose, and meaning. And prime among those realities is dynasticism, a topic of great concern for the Plantagenets as well as their French rivals the Capetians. In so far as both families had taken over kingships that were in principle surprisingly elective, early generations were quick to see that hereditary succession based on strict dynasticism might well provide a less contentious way of transmitting the crown from one person to the next. Still, as this new approach gained increasing support on both sides of the Channel, the evidence suggests that while the Norman and Angevin kings of England initially followed French leads, in later years the Capetians began to imitate precedents first developed by the English. Nevertheless, if the Capetians achieved most of their goals, the Plantagenets did not: a family long on ambition, they proved short on luck.

In an immediate sense, the story begins on October 25, 1154, with the death of Stephen of Blois, king of England. If the crown then passed to Henry Plantagenet, count of Anjou and duke of Normandy, it was not because Henry was Stephen's immediate blood heir. That honor belonged to Stephen's son William, who might well have become king himself had it not been for the Treaty of Winchester of November 1153 in which Stephen had, with William's concurrence, designated Henry "as my successor in the kingdom of England, and as my heir by hereditary right."[4] Whatever Stephen's motives here—and Henry's political strength, not to say his military might, had not a little to do with the treaty's provisions— the use of designation to name an heir was far from new in post-Conquest England, and the practice did not end with Henry's accession. William the Conqueror himself (r. 1066–87) was the first to designate successors, naming his first son, Robert, duke of Normandy, and his second, William Rufus, king of England. The third son, Henry I (r. 1100–35), continued the precedent. In 1119, for example, a royal charter informed its readers that Henry's one legitimate son, William Audelin, was properly to be styled *Dei gratia rex designatus*,[5] and after William's death by drowning the following year, Henry turned with remarkable persistence to his daughter Matilda, at least three times—in 1127, 1131, and 1133—recognizing her as his heir and demanding that his barons pledge her their fealty.[6] In much the same way, Stephen many times recognized his elder son Eustace as heir, unsuccessfully trying (though not quite so often) to persuade the archbishop of Canterbury to anoint and crown him during Stephen's own lifetime.[7] With these attempts to crown Eustace, moreover, Stephen was clearly trying to bring English practice into full conformity with French precedents that went back to 987 and Hugh Capet's decision to designate and crown his eldest son Robert within months of his own accession.[8] Only Eustace's premature death on August 17, 1153, tipped the scales in favor of Henry Plantagenet, though as the eldest son of the thrice-designated Matilda, Henry himself had a plausible hereditary claim.[9]

Even more to the point, once on the throne Henry II followed the same precedents. In 1169–70, his attempts to impose a land settlement on his sons were clearly part of a complex plan of designated succession,[10] one that culminated in two English coronations of his eldest son, also named Henry: first at Westminster Abbey on May 24, 1170, and then again at Winchester in August 1172.[11] In much the same way, just over a year after becoming king, Richard the Lionheart reported to Pope Clement III that "should it happen that we die without issue," he wanted the crown to pass to Arthur, "our nephew and heir."[12] Nine years later, Arthur failed to become king at Richard's death, and at least part of the explanation lies in the fact that supporters of the successful claimant, John, found it expedient to insist that at the last possible moment the dying Richard had changed his designation from nephew to brother. That switch helped to pave the way for John's formal election by speaking to the doubts of those who may have shared the view of Henry II's justiciar Ranulf Glanvill that the hereditary rights of the son of a deceased older brother (Arthur's position) were at least slightly stronger than those of a living younger one like John.[13]

Although historians have long recognized that royal succession in twelfth-century England remained ungoverned by principles of strict heredity or primogeniture, they have failed to note the extent to which attempts to gain recognition for such principles were based on the Capetian model or, more cautiously, on the practice of designation as it had come increasingly to be observed by the noble families of northern France.[14] Nevertheless, this failure is understandable. After all, few of those so designated in England ever became king (or, in Matilda's case, queen), and the prevalence of the practice has been further obscured by the fact that so many of the chosen—for example, Rufus, Matilda, Henry II, Arthur, and John—were people other than the oldest son of a reigning king.

On the other hand, these practices provide a key to the family grouping at Fontevraud. Centrally important are, first, the prevalence of designation and, second, the extent to which kings of England and France showed a marked preference for their oldest legitimate son or, in Arthur's case, the eldest living branch of the family. The twelfth-century rulers of both countries pursued dynastic policies that were profoundly shaped by a growing emphasis on the nuclear family and on children born of a canonical union or, more generally, by an increasing sensitivity to long-term questions of genealogy. Furthermore, in these tendencies they were undoubtedly responding to the specifics of Gregorian reform, notably its stress on the sacrament of marriage and its insistence on observing the Levitican incest taboos.[15] Nevertheless, if the Plantagenets ultimately failed as a dynasty, everything suggests that the Capetians learned from what they had attempted to do—or at least from what the Capetians thought they had been trying to do, which may or may not be entirely the same thing.

Initially, however, borrowings went in the other direction and were far from limited to the practice of designation alone. For example, because Hugh Capet's accession in 987 marked a sharp break from the Carolingian line of descent that Pope Stephen II had enjoined upon the Franks in 754, many of his immediate successors found it expedient to marry women of at least arguably Carolingian blood. In much the same way, when William the Conqueror ended Anglo-Saxon rule at the battle of Hastings, his son Henry I sought to restore continuity within three months of his own coronation by marrying a daughter of St. Margaret of Scotland, granddaughter of England's King Edmund Ironside, a man who had lost his life and his realm to the conquering Cnut of Denmark.[16]

The connection with Anglo-Saxon royalty was thereby reaffirmed in somewhat attenuated form, but Henry II, the grandson of that union, tried to enhance the link in new and more fruitful ways. He apparently believed that descent alone did not adequately convey the familial debt to the house of Wessex, so from the moment of coronation he began to press for the canonization of Edward the Confessor, last of the Wessex line and younger half-brother of Henry's own ancestor, Edmund Ironside. Thus, when Alexander III proclaimed the Confessor's sainthood in 1161,[17] it appeared not only that the first of the Plantagenet kings had successfully forged a new link to the Anglo-Saxon past, but also that with this achievement he had sanctified the whole of Edward's subsequent family. By successfully urging the canonization of yet another ancestor, Henry II laid the foundations for what might have become a sacred dynasty potentially similar to the one that, a half-century later, the Capetians began attempting to create, possibly because of the Plantagenet precedents. Whatever the case, though, French efforts were initially hindered by the awkward fact that the sanctity of their principal saint, Charlemagne, had been proclaimed by a mere anti-pope, Alexander III's rival Paschal III, and never by one of St. Peter's legitimate successors. Because attempts to canonize Philip Augustus proved unavailing,[18] the Capetians had to wait until the canonization of Louis IX in 1297 before they could achieve full parity with the English.

If this new approach proved ultimately fruitful for the Capetians, for Henry II it did not. Unhappily for him, if the canonization of the Confessor came in 1161, nine years later the martyrdom of Becket tended to suggest a somewhat different relationship between Henry and saints. In fact, it seemed to confirm the story, allegedly popular with King John, that the Planagenets owed their origins to the marriage of an early count of Anjou to Melusine, the daughter of Satan. As the author of that story, the ever-inventive Gerald of Wales, has St. Bernard putting the case at a time before the Angevins had reached England: "From the Devil they came, and to the Devil they will return."[19]

Over the longer term, Henry found that during the 1170s and 1180s his dynastic policies were undermined first by the murder of Becket; then by the continental revolts of his sons that Eleanor of Aquitaine may herself have inspired;[20] and, finally, by the death in 1183 of his son Henry, the heir whom he had designated and then twice had had crowned. Despite all, however, Henry II remained a great king, and a part of that greatness lay in his capacity to see opportunity even in the worst of circumstances. For example, adversity struck again in 1186 when his third son, Geoffrey, died while his wife Constance of Brittany was pregnant. On March 29, 1187, she gave birth to a son, potentially the heir after Richard not just to England and Henry's continental possessions, but also to the vast domains of his grandmother Eleanor. Since that birth came, moreover, at a time when authors like Geoffrey of Monmouth, Wace, and Chrétien de Troyes had succeeded in making King Arthur the hero of the age, Constance quickly decided that her child, too, should be named Arthur. Finding herself living in the midst of potentially restless Bretons, she had no better way of buttressing her own uncertain position than by reminding them of the noble roots from which they had sprung—and from which, in continuing obedience, they could take renewed pride.

Although Henry II would doubtless have preferred a first grandson bearing his own name,[21] for what appear to be dynastically suggestive reasons he never challenged his daughter-in-law's decision. As Henry was apt to have viewed the situation, if Richard his heir were to remain childless— a not unlikely prospect insofar as marital negotiations on his behalf seemed to be going nowhere—then upon the Lionheart's death England would become Britain once more, a land in which Arthur's return would provide Plantagenet dynasticism with Trojan foundations of such awesome proportions that French dynasts would never be able to rival them even if, as happened in the next century, they were to trot out their own Trojan ancestor, King Pharamond. To put the case in terms first used in Geoffrey of

Monmouth's "Prophecies of Merlin," red dragon would prevail over white, while the island itself would "be called by the name of Brutus and the title given to it by foreigners [would] be done away with."[22] Here again, though, disaster ensued. Just two when Henry died, the boy Arthur was to find ten years later that his rights as confirmed by Richard were thwarted by John's accession. Not content with imprisoning his nephew, the new king soon saw to it that his sleep would forever remain uninterrupted.[23]

Still, if Arthur's passing led almost immediately to serious repercussions at Fontevraud, it is important to realize that before that point the abbey had long enjoyed a steady stream of Angevin benefactions, notably from Henry II, a donor whose gifts culminated in a bequest of 2,000 marks promised in his will of 1182.[24] Subsequently, when refounding the nunnery at Amesbury, he showed his continuing approval of Fontevraud by insisting that Amesbury adopt its rule, including obedience to its abbess. Both king and abbess then attended Amesbury's rededication in 1186, and soon thereafter Fontevraud sent twenty-four of its nuns to England to replenish the depleted ranks of its new daughter house.[25]

Nevertheless, nothing in these repeated marks of favor suggests that Henry II ever intended Fontevraud to be his final resting place. On the contrary, because he greatly admired the austerities of Grandmont, he had long been planning his burial there, sending it English workmen as early as 1170 to make the structural changes needed for his future tomb. Even though the project temporarily came to an end because of Grandmont's outrage over Becket's fate, the monks' wrath diminished and work started again after papal legates absolved Henry in 1172—especially after he performed public penance at Canterbury in 1174. By 1175–76, Henry's accounts show him purchasing large quantities of lead at Carlisle, shipping it to La Rochelle, and transporting it in 800 carts to Grandmont for use in building the new roof needed to replace the one lost during the alterations undertaken to create a space suitable for his tomb.[26] Henry's will of 1182 again specified that he was to be buried at Grandmont, a house that was also to receive a bequest of 3,000 marks, half again as much as he left to Fontevraud.[27] According to Gerald of Wales, in fact, the one time that Henry II ever tried to put Fontevraud to practical family use, his efforts failed when Eleanor of Aquitaine refused to entertain the idea of becoming a nun there.[28] Twice burned as a bride already, she was not about to risk it a third time—even when the groom would have been Christ and even when, as things turned out, the alternative proved to be just over a decade and a half as Henry's prisoner.

In the end, though, Henry's own post mortem plans were no more successful. He died at Chinon on July 6, 1189, and because Grandmont, in the Limousin, lay farther away than anyone cared to take his body in a summer that was proving exceptionally hot,[29] nearby Fontevraud became his final resting place. Nevertheless, insofar as his death seemed to fulfill one of Becket's prophecies—that Henry would die badly only after two of his sons had predeceased him[30]—it is perhaps unsurprising that his first burial was far from elaborate. Hoping for more gifts during his lifetime, the abbey may have found it expedient to call him a "magnificent benefactor" and "father of Fontevraud's church,"[31] but doubts must still have existed, for how could any religious establishment honor even the unwitting destroyer of Blessed Thomas? As Gervase of Canterbury put the more negative case when finishing his tale of Becket's prophecies: "The father died within seven days of being cursed by a monk and was ignominiously [and] miserably buried at Fontevrault."[32]

Henry II's burial at Fontevraud was thus no more than a product of chance, not of dynastic planning. But the situation was far different in 1199 when the deaths of Richard and Jeanne brought their bodies to the abbey after funereal journeys of considerable length: Richard from the Limousin in mid-April and Jeanne from Rouen in late September.[33] Admittedly, spring and fall do not pose the kind of heat hazards that prevented Henry from reaching Grandmont, but the effort made for his children suggests that someone was now beginning to think dynastically, undoubtedly Eleanor of Aquitaine.[34] By 1204, when she herself joined husband, daughter, and son, Fontevraud was well on its way to becoming not just a genuine royal abbey, but also a royal necropolis, one in which the shrewd placement of tombs could help the living to foster a dynastic cult by demonstrating their own line of descent from the dead.

Further to illustrate the point, when Henry III twice visited the abbey, in 1254 and 1256, he found these four members of his family grouped together in the nuns' part of the choir.[35] Henry II and Eleanor, side by side, were closest to the altar, their tombs topped by painted stone effigies. Almost 750 years later the effigies continue to show Henry lying crowned, both hands clasping a scepter and Eleanor holding an open book, apparently one from which she has just been reading. On her head she wears a small crown over a simple headdress not unlike that of a nun.[36] The children's tombs lay at their feet, Jeanne's topped only by an inscribed slab and Richard's by an effigy similar to his father's, though its scepter has long since gone missing. At the time of Henry III's visits, neither Isabelle of Angoulême, his mother, nor Raymond VII, his cousin, was a part of this grouping, though in 1256 he finally asked that his mother be moved and added to it.

Just as the evidence suggests that Eleanor had Richard and Jeanne buried at Fontevraud, so too is she likely to have ordered their effigies and determined how all the tombs were to be arranged—including her own.

Because she stayed at Fontevraud many times, often for extended periods after Henry's death and her own liberation,[37] she had frequent opportunities for making these decisions. Initially, too, her visits appear to have had little to do with her late husband's presence there. After all, the abbey had been founded by a man much admired by her grandfather William IX, and for her the preeminent place it granted to all women, not just its abbess, would have had an obvious further appeal. In this context, moreover, a final point is worth pondering. Although Fontevraud is usually described as being in the border region between Anjou and Poitou, most people probably think of it as Angevin. Yet its location places it in the diocese of Poitiers,[38] not in Henry's lands but in Eleanor's, another circumstance she must have found pleasing.

That is not to say, however, that Eleanor was also responsible for Henry's original burial, a decision clearly made on the spot by William Marshal.[39] On the other hand, during her initial stays at the abbey after regaining her own freedom, Robert d'Arbrissel's contemplative ideal could well have led her to ponder the ironies of a role reversal in which she was now keeping an eye on Henry, unexpectedly become the unwilling sojourner in her lands, from which he would never escape. Still, whatever her thoughts regarding Henry, ten years later her reaction to the deaths of Jeanne and Richard had to have been different. Then well past her biblical allotment of three score years and ten,[40] she had seen far more of life than had most of her contemporaries, and her children's deaths must inevitably have led her to ponder the meaning of family and family life. In her own case, for example, from the time of her father's decision to provide for her security by marrying her to the future Louis VII, her life had seemingly involved little more than the unceasing struggles of families trying to preserve themselves from the twin dangers of external enemies and internal dissidence, and toward the end of her life that experience was likely to have influenced the ways in which she thought about the future as well.

Thus, as Eleanor might have viewed the deaths of 1199, her daughter Jeanne could not possibly be returned to Toulouse, far away and already a hotbed of heresy. Rather, she would have to be brought to Fontevraud, a monastery to which she had long been devoted and one that she alone selected as her place of interment as a nun when she realized just how close to death she was.[41] Similarly, in the case of Richard, formerly count of Poitiers, his mother would have seen his burial at the abbey almost as a homecoming. After that, though, other family considerations came into play. First, Eleanor's periods of residence at Fontevraud began to increase both in length and in frequency.[42] Secondly, longer stays encouraged her to recognize that, with son and daughter now present for eternity, long-term burial plans would have to be made, ones that included parents too, mother as well as father. Far from being parted by death, Eleanor and Henry found it finally reuniting them after their lengthy estrangement in life.

Planner of Fontevraud's Plantagenet tombs, their arrangement and effigies, Eleanor was also not just the great-grandmother of St. Louis but the person who decided which of her Castilian granddaughters should become the wife of Louis VIII[43] and hence mother of that Capetian whose own sanctity gave his dynasty the same kind of sacred luster that Henry II had sought for the Plantagenets with the canonization of Edward the Confessor. As a result, it may be appropriate to note that Louis IX and his advisors were no less appreciative than Eleanor of the symbolic force that tombs and tomb effigies could have, for those responsible for rearranging the royal tombs at Saint-Denis during his reign clearly understood the genealogical power that their proper placement could have.[44] As a result, it might initially appear that Saint-Denis's ancestral display was little more than a vast elaboration of the one that Louis's great-grandmother had earlier begun to make at Fontevraud with only four tombs and two generations.

Yet that view rests on the assumption that Eleanor intended her tomb arrangement to honor just Henry's family, not her own, and such an interpretation of her purposes may not be right. After all, matrilineal descent continued to determine the inheritance practices of some families well into the twelfth century, and widespread familiarity with its basic principles survived long thereafter, thanks to all the romances that told of how nephews like Tristan and Mordred were thought, or thought of themselves as being, the true heirs of uncles like Mark and Arthur, kings who were in every case the brothers of their nephews' mothers. In that context, and especially given Eleanor's own high status—twice a queen by marriage and in her own right duchess of Aquitaine—it seems entirely plausible that what we know as the Plantagenet tombs were in her mind equally intended to be monuments to her own greatness and that of her ancestral family, something that would help to explain why she had them placed in the nuns' part of the choir.

Because Eleanor remained as silent on these matters as her book-holding effigy, the only way to test the hypothesis is by exploring the views of others, the most promising of whom are Isabelle of Angoulême and Raymond VII of Toulouse, members of the family who were buried at Fontevraud more than forty years after Eleanor's death. Because their burial wishes are known and appear to have been freely made, they carry weight. Evidence suggests, however, that both decisions were complex. As John's wife, Isabelle had been queen of England and, though after his death she had quickly married an earlier suitor, Hugh the Brown, count of La Marche, she, like the so-called Empress Matilda, never forgot the high royal station that her first marriage had brought her. In 1241, for example, an otherwise unknown royal agent sent an apparently secret report to Blanche of Castile, regent for her young son Louis IX, in which the agent alleged that the regent's recent failure to grant Isabelle the deference due her queenly status had so enraged the countess that her subsequent tear-filled temper tantrums had finally persuaded Hugh to rise in rebellion.[45] Unlike Hugh's first revolt, against John, this one ended in disaster, but the agent's report about its origins would certainly suggest that when Isabelle chose burial at Fontevraud, it was so that in death she would finally receive the honors she deserved as a former queen. In turn, since her queenship depended on John's patrilineal descent, this interpretation of events would mean that the family she thought she was joining was Henry II's, not Eleanor's.

Unfortunately, like other such secret reports, this one seems off the mark. In particular, its assessment of Isabelle is at variance with what is known about her actual conduct while in residence at Fontevraud. In 1243, with Hugh's uprising heading for defeat, Isabelle sought refuge at the abbey. She may have done so because of its Plantagenet associations, but nothing suggests that she there made a great show of her own place in the family or that she ever expected a queenly burial in its company. Rather, for the next three years she lived quietly with the sisters. When she died on June 4, 1246, she was buried in the *salle capitulaire,* the nuns' burial place. That her fortunes ultimately took a different turn was entirely a decision of her son Henry III. During his second visit in 1256, he asked that her tomb be moved into the choir next to her four in-laws and that it be surmounted with a recumbent regal figure.[46] Made of wood, it is one of the four effigies that survive intact.

These facts make Isabelle's own intentions much more difficult to discern. Initially she may have decided to come to Fontevraud because of its status as a nascent royal necropolis, but once there she appears contentedly to have lived the life of an ordinary nun, wholly without royal pretensions. Her activities and simple first burial suggest that, like her former mother-in-law, she had become increasingly attracted to the ideals of Fontevraud and to its way of life. If so, her real preferences on the question of a matrilineal versus a patrilineal family remain unknown.

In the case of Raymond VII, however, the evidence is much more certain. By the time of his death in 1249, the Albigensian Crusade had effectively made Toulouse into a conquered land. With Raymond's decease, the terms imposed by the 1229 Treaty of Paris provided that the county was to pass into the hands of his son-in-law, St. Louis's brother Alfonse of Poitiers.[47] Under these circumstances, the family stance taken by Raymond's last will and testament seems unusually revealing. For example, after its opening salutation first titles him "by the grace of God count of Toulouse [and] marquis of Provence," it further identifies him as "the son of the former lady Queen Jeanne" without once mentioning his paternity. Indeed, the slight thereby accorded to Raymond VI goes even deeper, for Jeanne had acquired her queenly title only by virtue of her first marriage to King William of Sicily. It had nothing to do with either her Plantagenet birth or her second marriage into the house of Toulouse. Raymond VII's first wish, moreover, was not just that he wanted to be buried "at the monastery of Fontevrault, where King Henry of England our grandfather, and King Richard our uncle, and Queen Jeanne our mother" had already been laid to rest: he asked specifically that his tomb be placed "at the feet of our same mother."[48] In this way, then, he continued to underscore the extent to which matrilineal descent alone tied his ancestry to kings and queens alike, Eleanor and Jeanne as well as Henry and Richard.

Unhappily, the count of Toulouse never got his wish, for his tomb and effigy were placed on the south side of the northwest pillar of the crossing, not with his relatives in the choir.[49] No one knows why the site was picked or who chose it and why,[50] but Raymond's misfortune was far from being the greatest disaster that he and the Plantagenets experienced in their relationship with Fontevraud. That distinction clearly belongs to John, reputedly Eleanor's favorite son but also the man chiefly responsible for Fontevraud's failure to become a full-fledged dynastic necropolis. John's murder of Arthur had consequences, after all, one of which was its disastrous impact on further development of a royal funerary cult centered on the abbey.

By the time of Eleanor's death, rumors of Arthur's passing had already begun to increase John's difficulties, the origins of which went back to Hugh the Brown's angry reaction to his marriage with Isabelle of Angoulême. Moreover, insofar as that reaction was ultimately responsible for Philip Augustus's condemnation of John as a contumacious vassal, the latter soon found Hugh's revolt being superseded by royal French conquest that made Fontevraud a part of Capetian France. Even though Isabella and Raymond VII later received burial there, John himself did not.[51] Only his heart and that of his son Henry III later made it to Fontevraud,[52] and after that no physical remains of later English kings ever entered the abbey in any form. Indeed, even their obituary notices came to an end with the one for Edward I.[53] As far as France was concerned, the potential threat of Plantagenet dynasticism had ended, and its failure is nowhere better suggested than in the tomb effigy that Henry III had made for Isabelle his mother: plain, severe, and totally different in style from those of her in-laws, it is an image of death pure and simple. As such, it surely does not symbolize that dynastic immortality about which, possibly, Eleanor of Aquitaine continues to dream as she gazes out over her book.

Nevertheless, the very presence of Isabelle of Angoulême and Raymond VII of Toulouse encourages a different view of family, a view far richer than the one suggested by the term "Plantagenet dynasticism." Their reasons for being at Fontevraud transcend those of mere royal descent, and in Raymond's case they evoke not only a time in French history that was increasingly dominated by Capetian dynastic success, but also a period and a sacred setting in which tombs offered an opportunity for both the living and the dead to pay homage to families of women as well as men. It seems unlikely, then, that modern restorers will ever find the proper esthetic, religious, philosophical, or even historical way to arrange the Plantagenet tombs satisfactorily. That would require the skills of Eleanor of Aquitaine, but she's already resting in eternity, otherwise engaged.

Notes

1. This article is a revised and expanded version of "Les gisants de Fontevraud et la politique dynastique des Plantagenêts," a paper given at a conference at Fontevraud on May 28, 1988, and published in *La figuration des morts dans la chrétienté médiévale justqu' à la fin du premier quartier du XIVe siècle* (Fontevraud: Centre Culturel de l'Ouest, 1989), pp. 195–208. For further information on those buried at Fontevraud, see the piece in the same collection by the person most responsible for the abbey's restoration: Alain Erlande-Brandenburg, "Les gisants de Fontevrault," 3–15. I am grateful to the late Roger Grégoire, then vice president of the Centre Culturel de l'Ouest, for inviting me to participate in this conference and to the American Council of Learned Societies for a travel grant that made participation possible. Lastly, I am especially indebted to Elizabeth A.R. Brown for her comments and for sharing with me her transcriptions of Fontevraud obituary notices as published in Pavillon, *La vie dv Bien-hevrevx Robert d'Arbrissel.*
2. "Robert d'Arbrissel," in *Dictionary of the Middle Ages,* ed. Joseph R. Strayer et al. (New York, 1982–89) 10:429a [429a–431a] [hereafter: *DMA*]. For the relationship between Robert d'Arbrissel and William IX, see Reto R. Bezzola, "Guillaume IX, le premier troubadour, et Robert d'Arbrissel, le fondateur de Fontevrault," in Bezzola, *Origines,* pp. 275–316.
3. The specifics found in this and the following paragraph are based on memoranda and news releases of the Centre Culturel de l'Ouest, all dating from 1986 or 1987, which Roger Grégoire sent to me at the time he invited me to speak. The center is headquartered at the abbey and is dedicated to diffusing knowledge of Fontevraud's history.
4. Rymer, *Foedera* 1:18.
5. *RRAN2: Regesta Henrici Primi 1100–1135,* no. 1204. The precise date on which Henry I named William Audelin *rex designatus* remains uncertain, but it must have been in 1116 or 1117.

6. Warren, *Henry II*, pp. 11, 18–19.

7. Warren, *Henry II*, pp. 32, 34, 38, 41, 42, 226.

8. On Capetian practice see Wood, *Apanages*, pp. 2–9.

9. Warren, *Henry II*, p. 51.

10. Warren, *Henry II*, pp. 108–11.

11. Warren, *Henry II*, p. 111.

12. Rymer, *Foedera* 1:53.

13. Glanvill, *De Legibus*, pp. 101–104.

14. Wood, *Apanages*, pp. 4–6; Lewis, *Royal Succession*, pp. 28–77. Warren, *Henry II*, p. 34, is one of the few historians who has ever appreciated the extent of this borrowing.

15. In general, the impact of Gregorian reform is well analyzed in Herlihy, *Medieval Households*, pp. 79–111. For a discussion of its effects on the royal families of England and France, see Wood, "Queens, Queans and Kingship," in Wood, *Joan of Arc and Richard III*, pp. 18–28.

16. Upon marriage Henry's wife dropped her original name, Edith, and became known as Matilda. Since that was the name of Henry's mother, the wife of William the Conqueror—and also the name Henry and the new Matilda gave their own daughter—some sort of matrilineal dynasticism seems to have been involved, though no one has yet explained how it was supposed to function.

17. Warren, *Henry II*, p. 223, and n2. In Westminster Abbey a sanctuary for Edward's relics was then constructed, and consecrated in October 1163.

18. Wood, *Joan of Arc and Richard III*, p. 21.

19. Giraldus Cambrensis, *De Principis Instructione Liber* 8:301–302, 309.

20. In the present volume, this view of Eleanor's likely complicity is more forcefully stated in Brown, chapter 1.

21. On this preference and the context for Constance's decision, see Warren, *King John*, pp. 81–82.

22. Geoffrey of Monmouth, trans. Thorpe, pp. 171, 175.

23. Warren, *King John*, pp. 79–84.

24. Rymer, *Foedera* 1:47.

25. Colvin, *History of the King's Works* 1:87–89.

26. I discuss Henry's plans for burial at Grandmont in "La mort et les funérailles d'Henri II," 120.

27. Rymer, *Foedera* 1:47.

28. Giraldus Cambrensis, *De Principis Instructione Liber* 8:306. But see n36 below on Eleanor becoming a nun after Henry's death.

29. Warren, *Henry II*, p. 625.

30. Gervase of Canterbury, *Opera Historica* 1:449.

31. Pavillon, *La vie dv Bien-hevrevx Robert d'Arbrissel*, no. 89 at p. 583; also quoted in translation in Bienvenu, "Aliénor et Fontevraud," 22.

32. Gervase of Canterbury, *Opera Historica* 1:449.

33. *DMA* 10:384a (Richard I); Erlande-Brandenburg, "Les gisants de Fontevrault," 5 (Jeanne). Jeanne, pregnant, left Toulouse to have her baby at

Rouen, and apparently died of complications following a Caesarian birth. In general, the best sources in both instances are the obituary notices in Pavillon, *La vie dv Bien-hevrevx Robert d'Arbrissel*, no. 90 at pp. 584–85 (Richard), and no. 96 at 588 (Jeanne).

34. Erlande-Brandenburg, "Les gisants de Fontevrault," 5, subscribes to this view and, realistically, there is no other viable candidate. The dying Richard may well have requested burial at Fontevraud, as Kathleen Nolan points out in chapter 18 in this volume, but only someone like Eleanor had the power to ensure that his wish was carried out. She was, in fact, with him when he died and accompanied his body to the abbey (Brown, chapter 1 in this volume). I should stress, though, that while my language in what follows is more cautious than Nolan's, I agree with her that Eleanor was responsible for Fontevraud's first three effigies and for arranging the tombs.

35. For all details in this paragraph except Eleanor's headdress, Erlande-Brandenburg, "Les gisants de Fontevrault," 3, 5–6.

36. As Brown points out (chapter 1 in this volume), Fontevraud recognized that Eleanor and Jeanne of Toulouse had become nuns before their deaths, so the headdress is appropriate.

37. Bienvenu, "Aliénor et Fontevraud," 15–27, records most of her known stays, but see also Brown, chapter one above.

38. *DMA* 10:429b.

39. Wood, "La mort et les funérailles d'Henri II," 122.

40. For persuasive proof that Eleanor was born ca. 1124, two years later than commonly assumed, see Lewis, chapter 7 in this volume.

41. For Jeanne's personal devotion to Fontevraud and her decision to be buried there, see her obituary notice in Pavillon, *La vie dv Bien-hevrevx Robert d'Arbrissel*, no. 96 at p. 588.

42. Wood, "Les gisants de Fontevraud et la politique dynastique des Plantagenêts," 203; the increasing length of her stays shows up clearly in Brown, chapter one above.

43. Brown, "Eleanor of Aquitaine: Parent, Queen, and Duchess," pp. 33–34. These facts are more starkly presented above in Brown, chapter one above.

44. Wood, *Joan of Arc and Richard III*, p. 21; Wright, "Royal Tombs at St. Denis," pp. 94–100; Brown, "Burying and Unburying."

45. Delisle, "Mémoire sur une lettre inédite," 525–29.

46. Erlande-Brandenburg, "Les gisants de Fontevrault," 3.

47. Wood, *Apanages*, pp. 40, 72.

48. *Histoire générale de Languedoc* 8: col. 1255: "In primis sepulturam nostram eligimus apud monasterium Fontisebraudi, ubi jacet rex Henricus Anglie avus noster, & rex Richardus avunculus noster, & regina Johanna mater nostra, ad pedes scilicet ejusdem matris nostre." For more direct but tantalizingly inconclusive evidence on the possibility that Eleanor herself had a matrilineal view of family, see Nolan, chapter 18 in this volume.

49. Erlande-Brandenburg, "Les gisants de Fontevrault," 6.

50. Strikingly, Raymond's obituary notice (Pavillon, *La vie dv Bien-hevrevx Robert d'Arbrissel*, no. 94 at p. 587) also claims that he "elegisset sepeliri ad pedes matris suae," and that when his body arrived at the abbey, "ad pedes matris suae, sicut in vita sua petierat sepultus est." This repeated claim is bothersome, for while it's possible that Raymond was first buried at his mother's feet and only later moved to the spot identified by Erlande-Brandenburg, it's at least modestly surprising that such a change in location attracted no notice in his obituary notice. It looks as though obituary notices were either written very early and then remained unchanged or, at the opposite extreme, as though they were written so long after the event (at least in the form that we now have them) that their authors had long forgotten many of the specifics, assuming that they had ever known them. Either alternative strikes me as entirely possible.

51. Since John died in England, it might be thought that burial at Fontevraud was never a real possibility. I disagree. If John had not lost his continental possessions and if Fontevraud had truly become the new royal necropolis, his body would have been sent there even from England. After all, doing so would have been little different from what happened in reverse when Henry V died at Vincennes in 1422: his remains were shipped back to England immediately.

52. Erlande-Brandenburg, "Les gisants de Fontevrault," 5, believes that Henry probably pledged his heart to the abbey during his visit in 1254 but notes that even though he died in 1272, the heart arrived only twenty years later, in 1292. Since Eleanor of Provence, Henry's widow, died only in 1291, John Carmi Parsons has informed me in a personal communication that he has always assumed that she kept the heart during her lifetime, allowing it to be sent to Fontevraud only after her death. On the other hand, I wonder whether this delay resulted less from a widow's devotion than from French doubts about the desirability of allowing Fontevraud to have the heart at all. That is, if the abbey continued to receive even body parts left to it by English kings, that could enhance the dynastic cult of a monarchy that might at any time decide to renew its claims to the French lands it once had ruled—and of which Fontevraud could be made a powerful symbol. Since Poitiers, Angers, and Le Mans remained Capetian royal bishoprics even after John's formerly Plantagenet lands were ceded in apanage to St. Louis's brothers Alfonse and Charles (Wood, "Regnum Francie," 119 esp. n11), I believe that, operating through the bishop of Poitiers, the kings of France had the power to prevent such gifts from continuing, though I have no evidence that any king ever tried to do so. In the absence of evidence, this difference in interpretation cannot be resolved, but it surely illustrates why both Parsons and I believe that, when fully understood, burial practices can shed an enormous amount of light on the basic beliefs of the society in which they occur (cf. Parsons, "Burials and Posthumous Commemorations of English Queens").

53. Pavillon, *La vie dv Bien-hevrevx Robert d'Arbrissel*, no. 92 at pp. 586–87.

EPILOGUE

ELEANOR OF AQUITAINE
AND A "QUEENLY COURT"?

Jane Martindale

Eleanor of Aquitaine's personality and career have been the object of an extraordinarily wide range of interpretations over the centuries. Recently Martin Aurell has argued that these ought to be distinguished with care and that the different historical methods and historiographical approaches applied to discussion of Eleanor's life should be disentangled, and related to the intellectual and historical context of the times in which their various authors lived. In particular, he suggests that twentieth-century historians' use of interpretations based on psychoanalytical methods has meant that the traditional portrait of the "queen of the troubadours," president and judge in courts of love, and patron of the arts became that of "a possessive mother, responsible for all her sons' traumas, complexes, and hatreds." Aurell concluded that such startling transformations in Eleanor's reputation have induced a deep skepticism in scholars, who now seem content to record legends and images transmitted by the sources "without trying to understand what these may have taken from historical reality from beyond the outlook of scribes, chroniclers and writers."[1]

The legends that clustered like moss around medieval figures have their own historical interest and value since, especially where these legends have a contemporary origin, they often transmit the dominant features of an individual's reputation, which contributed to the formation of more elaborate legends. The commemoration of Eleanor's most renowned son demonstrates this point. The Occitan *planh* that commemorated King Richard I's death already compared him to the legendary King Arthur, to Alexander, "the king who conquered Darius," and to the more recent "historical" figure Emperor

Charles the Great (in this poem simply called "Carles" without any title). Even to modern historians, that must convey something of Richard's fearsome but also heroic reputation as a warrior for his contemporaries. Furthermore, because of the language in which it was composed, this song by the troubadour Gaucelm Faidit must surely have been designed to reach a secular audience throughout the romance-speaking world.[2] In this particular case, praise composed in the vernaculars of the world in which King Richard had lived was certainly related to what Aurell describes as "des réalités historiques," as historians can tell from other sources of widely differing character and outlook, for instance the narratives of Richard's exploits on the Third Crusade.[3] The poetic lament understandably accentuated Richard's military prowess and the renewed vigor that his death would engender in "Sarrazin, Turc, Paian e Persan [Saracens, Turks, Pagans and Persians]."[4] This is not so irrelevant to a volume focused on Richard's mother, Eleanor, as it might first appear to be. I introduce it to draw attention to the hypothesis that there are far more difficulties involved in reconciling a woman's "legend" with "historical realities" than there are in the case of a man who, like King Richard, was renowned as a great warrior and defender of Christendom during his own lifetime. By contrast, the terms in which a woman's achievements could be presented were far more restricted than those available for a man. A woman's activities that did not fit into the received frame of reference might not be recorded at all, or only remembered and interpreted in an extremely harsh light. That contrast is surely borne out by the way in which Eleanor's mother-in-law, the Empress Matilda, was commemorated: "Great by birth, greater by marriage, greatest in her offspring / Here lies the daughter, wife and mother of Henry." There is no reference to her struggles in aiding her son to succeed to his Anglo-Norman inheritance, though those occupied nearly twenty years of her adult life. Or else that activity was seen as secondary to her birth, marriages (presumably in particular the renown and status she acquired through her childless marriage to Emperor Henry V), and her mothering of the son who eventually became the English king Henry II, Eleanor's second husband. Matilda's political role is only allusively mentioned in another epitaph, asserting that she surpassed women in "having nothing womanly." In other words, despite the "historical realities" of conflict and war in which she engaged personally to achieve the aim that either she or her son Henry would displace King Stephen and his descendants in the Anglo-Norman kingdom, Matilda's actual contribution to that end would only be grudgingly recognized. Indeed, it seems unlikely that her son would have succeeded to his grandfather's kingdom without his mother's active participation in this political conflict; and yet, she was primarily remembered as the instrument by which the right of succession to that kingdom was transmitted to King Henry II.[5]

In many respects, the territorial and political background to Eleanor's life and her experiences as queen—first as wife of the Capetian Louis VII, then as "regina Anglorum" and wife of Henry II of the English—were different from those of the Anglo-Norman Empress Matilda. Nevertheless, a valid comparison can still be made between them as queens and "women of power." In particular, they were both deeply involved in the political affairs of their times, and both played an important part in the government of their own and their husbands' territories.[6] Eleanor, however, did not really become involved in the bitter politics of succession until the very end of her life, during the dispute between her son John and her grandson Arthur of Brittany, whereas her mother-in-law was almost continuously engaged in such conflict after her father, King Henry I's, death in 1135.[7] The significance of Queen Eleanor's activity at different stages of her life has too often been obscured by the lure of a legend that was essentially constructed out of rumors, or perhaps memories, of her alleged sexual indiscretions with her uncle Prince Raymond in distant Antioch. That episode supposedly occurred during the long journey to Jerusalem she made with her first husband, King Louis VII, on the Second Crusade. By the later twelfth century, however, she was even presented as a queen who had indulged in "serial adultery," and that charge, leveled against her by the prolific writer Gerald of Wales (Giraldus Cambrensis), has often been accepted without critical examination by modern commentators.[8] Few modern historians treat these anecdotes with the reserve and discretion shown by John of Salisbury, whose *Historia Pontificalis* alludes to suspicions about a liaison between Eleanor and Raymond by means of a glancing reference to Ovid's *Heroides*.[9] In the collection of rather less censorious *Vidas* of the troubadours, Eleanor was also portrayed only as a lover of the great lyric poet Bernard de Ventadour, whom she supposedly received at her court in Aquitaine, though that romantic vision is not supported by any other source. In any case, it does not fit with the known chronology of the queen's life. Alfred Richard, the historian of Poitou, converted this into the hypothesis that the poet could have acted as the queen's chancellor in her native country.[10] Furthermore, Queen Eleanor's role as the focus of erotic adventures and the arbiter of amatory etiquette appears to be confirmed by the part she plays in that enigmatic treatise, Andreas Capellanus's *De Amore*. The "judgments" on such matters attributed to her in that text also undoubtedly contributed to her legend as a woman chiefly concerned with "courtly love."[11]

Some modern reconstructions of the legends associated with Queen Eleanor have been fantastically developed. Her presumed liaisons have even been interpreted as showing the survival of "la Prostituée Royale . . . l'image historicisée de la grande Déesse," according to which, in undefined

Celtic times, there was a supposed symbiosis between a queen's sexual activity and male royal supremacy achieved through military success.[12] Even the more moderately phrased assertion, found in the introduction to an interesting literary study, that "Eleanor of Aquitaine's story provides a provocative starting point for a study of the prominent representation of adulterous queens in medieval romances," seems to beg a number of questions about the problematic connections between legend and "des réalités historiques."[13]

Certainly any biography or study based essentially on the matter and interpretation of Queen Eleanor's legends will be seriously unbalanced if the sources for the legends are, in Martin Aurell's words, "dégagés de leur cadre historique."[14] But while there is still a need for studies of the historiography and development of Eleanor's legend, and though it seemed necessary to consider some aspects of the outlines of those legends, this epilogue will be chiefly concerned with her position as a "woman of power." Within the setting of important twelfth-century developments, the full extent of Eleanor's contribution to the politics and government of the Angevin empire has often been undervalued,[15] and it deserves more critical attention than it has often received.

Power Exercised by Queen Eleanor

I will be chiefly concerned here with the years after Henry II's death in 1189 which led to the queen's definitive release from the imprisonment and supervision she had endured since the revolt of the year 1173. The range of the authority that would be confided to Queen Eleanor, and the extent of her competence, become especially visible within the English kingdom during the summer of 1189. But the power she then wielded must be considered against the background of the affairs of the Angevin empire as a whole. The death in July 1189 of King Henry II at the great castle of Chinon occurred during a time of acute crisis for the Angevin dynasty. The political conflicts that preceded Henry's death, together with the problems that immediately confronted his heir, bear out observations that had been made some decades earlier by Abbot Suger of Saint-Denis that "disorders, scandals, and rebellions are liable to occur . . . at the deaths of kings."[16] After his father's funeral and burial at the abbey of Fontevraud, the primary aim of the new king, Richard—still officially known as "the Poitevin count"—was to secure possession of Normandy. He formally became its duke when he received "the sword of the duchy [gladium ducatus Normanniae]" in Rouen cathedral on Saint Margaret's Day (July 20), a reminder that the elaborate inauguration liturgy entailed ritual and the performance of gestures in which a woman could not appropriately participate.[17] The dynastic conflicts that had preceded King Henry's death also meant that some sort of settlement would have to be patched up with the Capetian king Philip II over issues that had probably helped to precipitate the Angevin king's death.

At this stage of the transmission of power to Richard, it was also apparently regarded as imperative to review the affairs of all the continental territories within the Angevin empire. That involved a show of punishing or rewarding—according to what Richard regarded as their just deserts— those who had been prominent in his father's government or in the recent political conflicts. For instance, King Henry's treasure and castles were demanded from Stephen of Tours, seneschal of Anjou, who was arbitrarily thrown into prison heavily chained; at Richard's orders he was also separated from his wife because it was considered that, as a "noble girl," she had been disparaged by this marriage. A number of powerful men from Normandy's borders with Brittany and Maine were also deprived of their castles and lands. In contrast, however, great heiresses from throughout the Angevin lands were bestowed in marriage on some of those who (like William Marshal) had remained faithful to the king during the time of war.

All this activity was reported at length by historical writers within the English kingdom.[18] The people of that kingdom, on the other hand, would not be able to welcome their new ruler, or see him consecrated king, until he had disposed of the apparently more pressing affairs of duchies and counties beyond the Channel. During these months, the government of England could not, of course, be wholly neglected, but even authors with strong English interests who wrote within the kingdom show that for some time after his father's death, Richard's priorities lay "beyond the sea." The significance of the prominent role allotted to Queen Eleanor at this time can only be properly appreciated if it is considered against the wider background of the political problems that beset Richard as Henry II's successor throughout the territories ruled by the Angevin dynasty.

Richard's solution was to entrust the conduct of affairs in England to his mother, Queen Eleanor. According to the historian Ralph de Diceto, she was to have "the power of doing whatever she wished in the kingdom" in which she had (for better of worse) been King Henry's queen-consort since their coronation in 1154. During this late phase of her life, Eleanor was most prominently occupied with English political and administrative matters; but in modern studies the significance of her involvement has frequently been treated rather summarily or even inaccurately. In some general discussions of queenship, moreover, these active aspects of this one queen's role have often been neglected in favor of a more extended discussion of the "family values" royal women transmitted from one generation to the next—for instance, in the education of their daughters and in training them for marriage.[19] Twelfth-century writers as well as modern historians have often shown greater interest in the story of Queen Eleanor's release from custody and in the dramatic change in her fortunes brought about by Richard's succession to his father. Ralph de Diceto again commented allusively on her release in words he adapted from the "Prophecies of Merlin":"the eagle of the broken agreement will rejoice in her third nestling." Ralph contrasted Eleanor's new freedom with the many years in which, by Henry II's orders, she had been "consigned to close custody."[20]

Detailed accounts of Queen Eleanor's activity in England during the months before Richard I's consecration as king reveal how extensive were the powers that she exercised during this interregnum. She herself, it was alleged, dispatched "a body of trustworthy men, both clergy and laity . . . throughout all the counties of England" to deal with the most pressing judicial matters outstanding at the time of Henry's death. But though some outlawries and penalties that were remitted were surely intended to benefit her dead husband's soul, the queen was also credited with aims of a more secular character.[21] She tried to curb the "rapacity" of sheriffs and royal foresters by threatening them with heavy punishments if they did not cease oppressing those within their jurisdictions. She was also credited with the abolition of Henry II's practice of sending his horses to be stabled in English monastic houses; and, even if it is not altogether clear why this was singled out as one of the more deplorable offenses committed at the late king's command, in general the correction of abuses and the meting out of justice were, of course, seen as essentially royal tasks.[22] The description of Eleanor's performance of these tasks shows that she was no mere puppet being manipulated by her dead husband's former officials or *familiares,* or by her son's supporters. The chronicler Roger of Howden, a secular clerk experienced in ecclesiastical and royal administration, portrayed her "circulating with a queenly court: she set out from city to city and castle to castle just as it pleased her [et reginalem curiam circumducens, de civitate in civitatem et de castello in castellum sicut ei placuit profecta est]." Roger adds that she was concerned with the oath that "all freemen of the whole kingdom" were to swear to be faithful to their future king "for life and limbs and earthly honor just as [they would be] to their liege lord, against all men and women living and dead."[23]

The term "reginalis curia" is an arresting one, though its importance seems largely to have been overlooked by historians of Angevin politics and government. (Bishop Stubbs, for example, editor of the *Gesta Ricardi,* merely glossed the adjective "reginalis" as "royal.") Nevertheless, Howden must have been deliberately insisting that the authority he attributed to Eleanor in 1189 should be interpreted as power that was gendered; linguistically, he surely chose the adjective "reginalis" with care. Descriptive terms such as "regius" or "regalis," for instance, could have conveyed the sense of "royal" or "regal" just as well as "reginalis"; but those Latin terms are more neutral and would not in themselves have indicated the sex of the royal personage presiding over the court. Educated contemporaries who read Howden's historical work would have recognized that attention was being drawn to the fact that as woman and as queen, Eleanor was exercising a form of authority that was scarcely ever confided to a woman alone, even if she were a consecrated queen. In writing of Eleanor's "queenly court," Howden, moreover, chose an adjective that is extremely rare in sources of the twelfth century and earlier. A "reginalis curia" could, after all, refer only to a court presided over by a woman, albeit one exercising royal office.[24] Howden must have been emphasizing the autonomy of Eleanor's position after she had received her son's mandate *de ultra mare:* she was free to organize her own itinerary and agenda for pacifying the kingdom. It is also surely implied that she was free to enter whatever cities and castles she wished.[25] Since constant itineration was a characteristic feature of early medieval kingship, these references too would show the extent of the authority entrusted to the queen-mother. Additionally, Howden was also making a dramatic contrast between this freedom of action and the years of captivity Eleanor had endured by her late husband's orders after the revolt of 1173—years when she played no political role in the kingdom, even though she was still officially queen-consort.

Queen Eleanor continued to play a prominent part in the affairs of the English kingdom and the Norman duchy even after Richard's coronation. In November 1189, for instance, it was she who ordered the papal legate, John of Anagni, not to advance beyond the port of Dover unless he received the king's permission to do so. This seems to have meant that the papal legate was unable to secure an entirely ecclesiastical solution to the long-running dispute between Archbishop Baldwin of Canterbury and the monks of his cathedral priory. At any rate, the "final peace and concord" was witnessed by "King Richard and his mother Queen Eleanor" with "almost all the bishops, abbots and priors of England."[26] One of Eleanor's most recent biographers has concluded that, after her release from custody and her reception of her son's "mandate" "from beyond the sea," the queen mother "displayed all her old energy and dispatch." There could be little disagreement with that point of view. But it still seems that such an assessment ought to be accompanied by detailed analysis of the way in which her "energy" was deployed in fulfilling governmental and political functions entrusted to her in the absence of either husband or son(s). Though particular aspects of her activity are mentioned by her modern biographers, in general this involvement in government and administration is regarded as marginal, as though it cannot be seriously compared with the power wielded by the kings of the Angevin dynasty.[27]

Eleanor's exercise of authority was even more crucial to the maintenance of King Richard's cause during his crusade, particularly when he was imprisoned after his capture by the duke of Austria, and then transferred to Emperor Henry VI's prison. A similar pattern can be traced during the period between Richard's premature death in 1199 and Eleanor's own death in the year 1204. During this very last phase of her life, however, Eleanor scarcely intervened directly in the affairs of the English kingdom, though her primary political aim appears to have been to ensure that her son John's succession should be preferred to that of her grandson Arthur (son of John's elder brother, Geoffrey) throughout all the Angevin-held territories.[28] Nevertheless, a reconstruction of Eleanor's activity during the years after Richard's departure for Sicily and Syria demonstrates without the shadow of a doubt that she played a critical role in the politics and diplomacy of the Angevin dynasty. Many of the most important issues could only be resolved outside the English kingdom, and in these too Eleanor's role often seems to have been of vital significance. Her long journeys to Sicily and to Castile provide the most obvious examples of Eleanor's involvement in Angevin political and matrimonial diplomacy. Unfortunately, however, these have too often been interpreted as though she were acting as little more than a glorified chaperone—successively to Richard's future wife Berengaria of Navarre, and then to her own granddaughter Blanche of Castile, chosen for marriage to the heir to the Capetian throne.[29]

The whole episode of Richard's captivity reveals how crucial Eleanor's political contribution was to her son's release and to the prevention of open revolt in the English kingdom. She played a central part in the collection of the king's ransom and was engaged politically in making sure that the future King John did not usurp his brother's power either in England or in Normandy. Richard's release, too, seems to have been eventually speeded up by his mother's journey to the imperial court and by her counsel to the captive king that he should perform homage to Henry VI.[30] Whatever adverse criticisms might be passed by historians on that "queenly" counsel, it successfully achieved the object of gaining Richard's liberation. Eleanor also dominated the final incident in this disastrous episode, for she was credited with the difficult task of reconciling Richard and John, whose betrayal of the king had become known through the damning and treacherous agreements he had made with the Capetian King Philip II. Richard did not, therefore, need to hold a formal hearing nor to pass judgment on John, though the younger brother had been summoned to appear before a great council in the English kingdom in May.[31]

Eleanor's role as conciliator and peacemaker is once more revealed in the measures she took after Richard's death in 1199. From the abbey of Fontevraud, to which she had by then retired, she attempted to detach the Poitevin barons from their intrigues with the Capetian king and Arthur of Brittany, but she warned her son King John that he was in danger of losing the regional castles, and therefore some of his most important political bases, in her ancestral county.[32]

All these instances of authority attributed to, and power wielded by, Queen Eleanor were not, of course, exercised without the support of many officials and the machinery of Angevin government and administration. As far as it is possible to tell, she could rely on the personnel of royal government in the kingdom, but also on regional officials (e.g., in Aquitaine) and on her own household or court. She certainly became involved in details of royal administration and finance: Richard's ransom, for instance, was guarded "under the seal of the lady queen, the king's mother, and the seal of the lord archbishop of Rouen." Sources from the abbey of Bury Saint Edmunds, moreover, show that on at least one occasion Eleanor intervened personally with the officials of the Exchequer since, when Bury's abbot had to offer a great gold chalice as the abbey's contribution to the huge sum the emperor demanded for Richard's ransom, the queen made sure that the chalice was eventually restored to the abbey, which had lacked enough ready cash to make a payment in coin.[33] On the other hand, her order to increase the fortifications of Canterbury, which was also related to the political crises that erupted during Richard's absence on crusade, are known only from the concessions she later made to the monks of Canterbury, whose men had been obliged to work on those fortifications. The monks considered that their men's labor had been exacted "contrary to law and custom," though the queen had justified her orders "on account of the disturbance of the land."[34] It seems to have been at about this time, too, when Richard's position as king was threatened, that Eleanor's power and responsibility were first emphatically accentuated in royal documents through her use of the phrase *teste me ipsa* ("witness myself"—note the use of the feminine *ipsa*). That was a relative novelty at this date in the diplomatic of any royal documents; it is especially significant to find a queen making use of a phrase that has been interpreted as proving the ruler's personal interest in the matter of the document (probably including its close scrutiny).[35]

This survey of the power wielded by Queen Eleanor has obvious limitations in terms of her total life span. It does not take into account the extent to which her conduct of government after 1189 arose out of experience gained during the years before the "great revolt" in which she was an active queen-consort in the English kingdom (1154–73). Questions relating to the amount of patronage at Queen Eleanor's disposal are of great importance but likewise cannot be considered in this epilogue, nor can the crucial topic of the economic foundations upon which her power rested. But what this queen did, over a number of years, far exceeded the scope of what is normally associated with concepts of queenship or the actual activity of medieval queens. It has seemed worthwhile, therefore, to add to previous discussions of the general problem of whether medieval queens "exercised any real power"[36] this chronologically selective but topically detailed account of Eleanor's involvement in the politics and government of the Angevin empire.

The significance of women's influence on issues relating to family and dynasty has become central to recent accounts of medieval queenship. Recognition of the importance of what John Carmi Parsons has called "matrimonial diplomacy" has added a new dimension to discussions of royal women's involvement in the politics and government of their husbands and kin, though in the past, many historians treated these topics as marginal compared with "serious" problems like, say, the growth of royal government and bureaucracy.[37] How to make a good royal match was clearly of great concern to Eleanor, even if it is less clear whether political and territorial interests took precedence for her over individuals' wishes or personal attraction for each other. Eleanor of Aquitaine's journey through the length of Italy with Berengaria of Navarre seems to prove that she attached much importance to female participation in the achievement of such a dynastic alliance. As it is now virtually certain that Richard must have been responsible for negotiating his own marriage with the Navarrese king's daughter during a journey to Gascony, however, it can no longer be accepted that Eleanor was principally responsible for the "matrimonial diplomacy" that created the Anglo-Navarrese alliance.[38] The close links between kinship, the planning of royal marriages, and political policy are more certainly illustrated by Eleanor's journey, this time down the length of Aquitaine, to choose her granddaughter, Blanche of Castile, as a bride for the son and heir of the Capetian King Philip Augustus.[39] How far at an earlier stage in her life Eleanor was responsible for preparing her daughters for marriage cannot be easily established; but, certainly her daughters Joanna and Matilda were received back into the Angevin court or household at times of personal crisis or political upheaval. Indeed, Queen Eleanor was the executor of Joanna's testament after that unfortunate pregnant daughter fled from her second husband, the count of Toulouse, and then died in childbirth at Rouen.[40] References to Eleanor surrounded by her *puellae* at Richard's second coronation suggest that she did have in her care a number of unmarried girls whose education and training had been confided to her.[41] But if we ask how far the queen herself was able to promote their marriages, we stumble straight into one of the most dangerous minefields of Angevin politics: the king's financial interests were deeply bound up with his control of aristocratic marriages. In 1189, for example, Queen Eleanor was present at what must have been a very grand celebration, the marriage of Andrew de Chauvigny and the widowed heiress of Déols; but it was King Richard who "gave" the bride to Andrew, his knight and close military companion.[42]

In essence and detail, Queen Eleanor's exercise of authority differed little from the way a king conducted government, whether Henry II, Richard I, or John, though within the Anglo-Norman kingdom (at least during the reigns of Henry and Richard) her power depended on holding the king's "mandate."[43] But the power she came to wield in her own inheritance, Aquitaine, strengthens the impression that she was conscious of the extent of the princely power that should be at her disposal in the counties and duchy her ancestors had ruled before 1137. Her most notable activity in the duchy, however, came even later than her remarkable exertions in England: after Richard's death, during the very last years of her life. In Aquitaine, she then bestowed economic and communal privileges on towns, other urban settlements, and agglomerations such as the Ile d'Oléron and employed ducal resources to divert the regional aristocracy from the blandishments of the Capetian king and his candidate for the Angevin inheritance, Arthur of Brittany. She sought to placate the viscount of Thouars, the lords of Mauléon and Mauzé, and also Andrew de Chauvigny; but while she thus had to alienate a number of domains that had long been in her predecessors' possession, she was adamant that the flourishing town of La Rochelle should remain in the hands of the ruler of Poitou.[44] The documents issued in her name for this region drew on the expertise of the English chancery (e.g., the phrase *teste me ipsa,* noted above), and she employed the imperious language characteristic of Angevin kings' government.[45]

Whether individual medievalists are primarily interested in the politics or social history of the twelfth century, or in its literature and cultural changes, we may suggest a number of explanations for their failure to recognize the importance of the power Eleanor of Aquitaine wielded during different phases of her life. As Martin Aurell implies, the investigation of "des réalités historiques" may seem less enticing than legends constructed out of rumors of sexual misconduct and perhaps decorated with different authors' own social or psychological preconceptions. Another rather different problem seems to be that Queen Eleanor is a woman of such towering stature that it is difficult to appraise her career within the context of generalizations on medieval queenship. The queen-consorts who followed her in England were pale figures by comparison and never wielded similar political power. Nobody, for example, seems to have proposed in 1216 that King John's widow, Queen Isabella, should act as potential ruler on behalf of her young son King Henry III. For very different reasons, Queen Berengaria never appears to have had the opportunity to act as queen-consort to Richard during the few years of their marriage.[46] Better comparisons can be made between Eleanor and more "heroic" women of the earlier twelfth century: the forceful Queen Urraca of Castile, a woman who ruled in her own right, did direct the affairs of her own kingdom after the deaths of brother, husband, and father; so did Queen Melisende of Jerusalem. Furthermore, even though their legendary reputations are wholly dissimilar, as far as "historical reality" goes the careers of the Empress Matilda and Queen Eleanor do have a certain amount in common. That probably derives from the fact that both women were great heiresses—and the implications of that fact cannot be overlooked, notwithstanding that they only intermittently exercised power directly.[47] A third reason for underestimating the significance of Queen Eleanor's career might be rather tendentiously described as "geopolitical" since, whereas anglophone historians at any rate have ceaselessly discussed the contribution made by Normandy to the establishment and success of the Anglo-Norman *regnum,* Aquitaine was often regarded as a liability by historians of the Angevin empire. Despite revisionist interpretations by John Gillingham, the prestige of the ruler of Aquitaine and the resources and power associated with that duchy have too often been underestimated in the context of medieval political affairs.[48]

Finally, because there was no contemporary concept of "queenship" to which Eleanor's actions as a "woman of power" could be related, the authority and power she wielded at the end of her life have not been adequately represented in discussions of Angevin political and governmental developments. In particular, a female ruler had no place in the treatises on law and "financial management" composed in the English kingdom toward the end of Henry II's reign. By the last decades of the twelfth century, as Eleanor was growing into her extraordinary old age, the accounts of royal power in these treatises are expressed in forcibly masculine terms. Richard Fitz Nigel's *Dialogue of the Exchequer,* for instance, elaborated arguments that justified (or perhaps excused) the part clerics (*ecclesiastici viri*) played in serving kings as "supreme" under God. But Fitz Nigel's ulterior motive appears to have been to link his description of the Exchequer's workings with the proposition that "money is no less indispensable in peace than in war," and that "the glory of princes consists in noble actions in war and peace alike." Those expressions are familiar to all historians of twelfth-century government, but perhaps there has never been any need to consider some of their implications on the view that equal emphasis should be

laid on military affairs and on government in time of peace. Even
Glanville's treatise *On the Laws and Customs of England* begins with the assertion that for the king, "royal power . . . must be furnished with arms
against rebels and nations which rise up against him and the kingdom."[49]
Such an ideal of *regia potestas*—and those are the first words of Glanvill's
treatise—could not easily be adapted as a theoretical model for "queenly
power," though it has been established that during King Richard's absence
from England, Queen Eleanor oversaw problems connected with the fortification and control of castles, a source of expense specifically noted in
the *Dialogue of the Exchequer.*[50] Eleanor's intervention in such matters both
in England and Aquitaine was obviously related to the "royal" duty to sup-
press rebellion; nevertheless, in Eleanor's case, as a woman, her "castle
policy" was not allied to the "noble actions in war" around which the legend of her son Richard was formed. On one occasion she is admittedly
recorded as leading a military expedition, but that was in the desperate circumstances of Arthur of Brittany's campaigns in Anjou.[51] Unlike her husband or sons, she played no part in seasonal warfare: on the whole, she
seems to have been more concerned with pacification than with the promotion of political aims through war. She was prepared to advise Richard
to perform homage to the emperor to secure his release and avert future
conflict in England or other Angevin territories. Unusually, after Richard's
death she herself did homage to the Capetian King Philip II in the town
of Tours.[52] It seems, then, that there was no clear formulation of what
Roger of Howden might have called *reginalis potestas* had he wished to attribute gendered activities to *regia potestas* exercised by a woman.

This brief review is not intended to provide a comprehensive account of Eleanor's activity as queen, still less as duchess of Aquitaine. I
have hoped to show that in her old age, Eleanor fulfilled most political
and governmental functions that her late-twelfth-century contemporaries would have regarded as characteristically royal. On the other
hand, even when her royal authority was at its most extensive, it was
never clearly defined or analyzed. Soon after his accession, and his acceptance by his mother as her *rectus hæres* [rightful heir], for example,
King John made a grant of overarching power to her: he ordained that
"we wish that she shall be lady [*domina*] over us and all our lands and
affairs."[53] Compared to the expansive declarations by FitzNigel or
Glanvill, with their discussions of the nature of royal power, the authority assigned to Queen Eleanor is remarkably vague. That, it seems to me,
remains a major problem for all investigations of the power medieval
women exercised, and—in broader general terms—for the study of medieval queenship.

Notes

1. A free translation of part of the following passage: "De tels avatars ont peut-être rendu sceptiques les chercheurs qui se contentent désormais de décrire les légendes, thèmes et images véhiculés par les sources, sans essayer de comprendre ce qu'elles auraient pu emprunter à des réalités historiques extérieures à la conscience des scribes, chroniqueurs et écrivains" (Aurell, "Aliénor d'Aquitaine et ses historiens," p. 49). For an extensive review of recent bibliography, see Brown, chapter 1 in this volume.

2. *Les poèmes de Gaucelm Faidit,* no. 50, ll. 10–18; Gillingham, *Richard I,* pp. 332–34.

3. Gillingham, *Richard I,* pp. 123–221,"Roger of Howden on Crusade" and "Legends of Richard the Lion Heart."

4. The poet also asserts that the recapture of "the Sepulchre" will be set back because of Richard's death (*Les poèmes de Gaucelm Faidit,* no. 50, stanza V, esp. ll. 37–42).

5. For all citations, see Chibnall, *The Empress Matilda,* p. 191 nn57–58; cf. Stafford, "The Portrayal of Royal Women," pp. 143–49, 157–61. See also Holt, "Feudal Society and the Family."

6. Though Matilda was more actively involved in her father's territories (Chibnall, *Empress Matilda,* pp. 57–62, 118–51). My biography of Eleanor (now in course of preparation) will contain an extended account of her involvement before 1189.

7. Chibnall, *Empress Matilda,* pp. 64–121. There can be few doubts that the "politics of succession" helped shape the reputations of many women in positions of power during the twelfth century; see Stafford, "Portrayal of Royal Women," p. 154, and cf. Parsons, "Family, Sex and Power," pp. 2–3.

8. For some skeptical comments (with which I would still agree), see Martindale, "Eleanor of Aquitaine," pp. 17–50, repr. in Martindale, *Status, Authority,* pp. 40–41, esp. nn49–51.

9. John of Salisbury, *Historia Pontificalis,* pp. 52–53. Eleanor's own reference to the possibility that she and the king were related within the prohibited degrees is first mentioned in this passage.

10. One version of these later lives referred to Ventadour as "the lord and master of all her court" (Martindale, "Eleanor of Aquitaine" [1997], p. 37 n52).

11. *Andreas Capellanus On Love,* pp. 92–93, 252–53, 256–57; cf. remarks in Martindale, "Eleanor of Aquitaine" (1997), pp. 38–39. Further work is surely needed on this difficult text, and it is not intended here to return to the much-debated topic of courtly love.

12. " . . . the royal prostitute . . . the historicised image of the great goddess" (Jean Markale, *La vie, la légende, l'influence d'Aliénor,* p. 215). Markale also suggests (pp. 219–26) that the legend of Yseult may have had an influence on Eleanor, who might have served as a model for Arthur's adulterous queen Guenevere. Rather more nuanced suggestions are made by Owen, *Eleanor of Aquitaine,* pp. 40, 166–67; and see Fiona Tolhurst, chapter 15 in this volume.

13. McCracken, *The Romance of Adultery,* pp. 1–2, 12, 19–22.

14. Aurell, "Aliénor d'Aquitaine et ses historiens," p. 49.

15. In the most monumental modern work on Henry II (with the exception of references to her role in the revolt of 1173–74) Boussard, *Le gouvernement d'Henry II,* pp. 28–29, 31, 113–15, and cf. pp. 471–87, mentions Eleanor chiefly in terms of the "domaine" or "domaines" she brought to her two husbands. But see also Turner, chapter 3 in this volume.

16. Suger, *Vie de Louis VI le Gros,* ed. Molinier, p. 149, cited in Martindale, "Succession and Politics," no.V, p. 20 and nn1–4. On the political situation in 1189, see Gillingham, *Angevin Empire,* pp. 36–40; and cf. Gillingham, *Richard I,* pp. 76–101. See also Warren, *Henry II,* pp. 618–26.

17. Roger of Howden, *Gesta Ricardi* 2:73. For comments on the place of the sword in a ruler's consecration (as king rather than duke, however), see Martindale, "The Sword on the Stone," 226–30.

18. Ralph of Diss, [de Diceto] *Opera Historica* 2:66–67; Roger of Howden, *Gesta Ricardi,* 2:71–73; Gillingham, *Richard I,* pp. 101–04.

19. For the citation, see the original Latin, below next note, and below, nn. 37–40.

20. "Alienor regina, quae per annos plurimos artae fuerat deputata custodiae, statuendi quae vellet in regno potestatem accepit a filio . . .Aquila rupti foederis . . . tertia nidificatione gaudebit [this followed by the explanation that Richard was her third son]" (Ralph of Diss, [Diceto] *Opera Historica* 2:67). See also Martindale, "Eleanor of Aquitaine: The Last Years," pp. 141–42 and, for the prophecy, p. 143 n19.

21. Martindale, "Eleanor of Aquitaine: The Last Years," pp. 142–43.

22. "Equos Henrici regis, quos in stabulis abbatiarum Alienor regina deputatos audivit, erogatione pia distribuit [then follow references to the curbing of the oppression of sheriffs and foresters]" (Ralph of Diss, [de Diceto] *Opera Historica* 2:68; Roger of Howden, *Gesta Ricardi* 2:74–75).

23. Roger of Howden, *Gesta Ricardi* 2:74–75; Martindale, "Eleanor of Aquitaine: The Last Years," pp. 142 n16 (for references to Howden). A valuable assessment of Howden's attitudes to history, his sources of information, and his judgment is provided by Gillingham, "Historians without Hindsight," pp. 9–13.

24. No particular significance was earlier attached to the phrase, though it was literally translated by Martindale, "Eleanor of Aquitaine: The Last Years," pp. 142–43 (see Roger of Howden, *Gesta Ricardi* 2:74). Early editions of DuCange's *Glossarium* list no occurrences of the adjective "reginalis" before the fourteenth century; but the early and isolated reference to a "queenly throne [reginali solio]" in Asser's *Life of Alfred* is recorded in Niermeyer's *Lexicon.* (My thanks to Janet Nelson for assistance on this point.) Further work is needed on the gendering of the language of power; cf., e.g., Stafford, "Portrayal of Royal Women," p. 150, and for ninth-century western condemnations of the exercise of *femineum imperium,* Nelson, "Women at the Court of Charlemagne," pp. 43–61.

25. Interestingly, Howden is less precise about the nature of Richard's movements after his return to England, stating merely "Deinde perrexit de loco ad locum [then he travelled from place to place]" (Roger of Howden, *Gesta Ricardi* 2:97, and 2:98 for the Canterbury settlement). According to Warren, *Henry II,* p. 626, ceaseless travel involved far more than a sign that the ruler wished to impose his will on his kingdom.

26. "Eodem anno, mense Novembris Johannes cardinalis applicuit in Angliam apud Dover; et prohibitum fuit ei ex parte Alienor reginae, ne ulterius procederet, nisi per mandatum regis filii sui; et ita factum est" (Roger of Howden, *Gesta Ricardi* 2:97). Cf. Ralph of Diss [Diceto], *Opera Historica,* 2:72: "Johannes Anagniensis, tituli Sancti Marci presbiter cardinalis, apostolicae sedis legatus, applicuit apud Doveriam xii° kalendas Decembris. Interdictum est ei die sequenti per reginam Alienor ne procederet, quoniam citra conscientiam regis regnum suum entraverat."

27. Owen, *Eleanor of Aquitaine,* citation at p. 79. Cf. Kelly, *Eleanor and the Four Kings,* p. 149:" . . . Eleanor at once assumed the regency. Gathering a retinue with that sudden urgency to which Henry's vassals were accustomed . . . "

28. Martindale, "Eleanor of Aquitaine: The Last Years," pp. 144–54. Specific references to the queen's activity are documented in that article, which will be used to support the following notes.

29. Martindale, "Eleanor of Aquitaine: The Last Years," pp. 144–45. On the outward journey, she paused for a meeting with Emperor Henry VI, and on the way back met the newly elected Pope Celestine III, both of which involved more than mere courtesy visits.

30. Martindale, "Eleanor of Aquitaine: The Last Years," p. 145 and n28.

31. John had been summoned to appear in May by the Nottingham council of March 1194, but before that date the brothers became "friends" again, "mediante Alienor regina matre eorum" (Martindale, "Eleanor of Aquitaine," p. 147 n35). Richard must have been aware of the extent of John's betrayal, for he had been shown the *conventiones* that his brother had made with King Philip; see Gillingham, *Richard I,* pp. 239–40, 270–71.

32. Martindale, "Eleanor of Aquitaine: The Last Years," p. 151 n52.

33. Martindale, "Eleanor of Aquitaine: The Last Years," p. 147 n38.

34. Martindale, "Eleanor of Aquitaine: The Last Years," pp. 147–48 and n40.

35. Martindale, "Eleanor of Aquitaine: The Last Years," pp. 147–52 (with a general reference at p. 147 n45). This diplomatic usage was a relative novelty in the late twelfth century. For Eleanor's seals, see Brown, chapter 1 in this volume.

36. Holt drew the distinction between accounts referring to a "concept of monarchy" and the way in which power was actually wielded (Holt, "Ricardus rex Anglorum" repr. in Holt, *Magna Carta,* p. 67). Cf. Stafford, "Emma: The Powers of the Queen," pp. 11–12 [3–26]; and references in Martindale, "Eleanor of Aquitaine: The Last Years," p. 148 n4.

37. Parsons, "Mothers, Daughters, Marriage, Power," p. 65; but for the description of power in exclusively masculine terms by, e.g., Saint Bernard, see

Huneycutt, "Female Succession," pp. 189–201, and Sarah Lambert, "Queen or Consort," pp. 153–69.

38. It seems likely that Richard was already involved in negotiations for this marriage while in Gascony in early February 1190 (Gillingham, *Richard I,* pp. 124–27.

39. Martindale, "Eleanor of Aquitaine: the Last Years," pp. 140–41.

40. Parsons, "Mothers, Daughters, Marriage, Power," pp. 73–74. For a brief reference to Joanna's situation, see Martindale, "Eleanor of Aquitaine," (1997), p. 18 n4. The political fall of Matilda of Saxony's husband Duke Henry the Lion forced her to return to England during the period of Eleanor's imprisonment (Warren, *Henry II,* pp. 223, 278, 497, 603).

41. For the reference, see Martindale, "Eleanor of Aquitaine: The Last Years," p. 142 n8.

42. On Richard's arrival in England, "venit Wintoniam; deinde ad civitatem Sarisbiriensiem, ubi dedit cuidam militi suo, Andreae de Chavenni, filiam Radulfi de Dols, cum castro Radulfi et honore de Berri ad illum castrum pertinente . . .et fecit eos desponari . . . in presencia Alienor reginae . . . " (Roger of Howden, *Gesta Ricardi,* ed. Stubbs, 2:76, and cf. 2:75 for other examples). On Déols and Andrew de Chauvigny, see Gillingham, *Richard I,* pp. 102, 104, 138, 235. The classic discussion of the workings of Angevin marriage policy can be found in J.C. Holt, *Magna Carta,* 2nd ed., pp. 52–55.

43. "Datum . . . in mandatis regni principibus, et quasi sub edicto generali statutum . . . " Ralph of Diss [Diceto], *Opera Historica* 2:67.

44. Martindale, "Eleanor of Aquitaine: The Last Years," pp. 161–62.

45. Martindale, "Eleanor of Aquitaine: The Last Years," pp. 149–52 (discussion of these documents as a group); cf. Martindale, "Eleanor of Aquitaine" (1997), pp. 44–46, 46–50.

46. John begged William Marshal to take over the guardianship of his young son (Carpenter, *Minority of Henry III,* p. 14 nn6–7); Gillingham, "Richard I and Berengaria of Navarre," pp. 113–37.

47. These cases are referred to by Martindale, "Succession and Politics," pp. 38–39; see also Chibnall, *The Empress Matilda,* pp. 50–54; Gillingham, *Angevin Empire,* pp. 9–12.

48. On the significance of Henry's acquisition of Aquitaine for the making of the "Angevin empire," see Gillingham, *Angevin Empire,* p. 17–21, and Martindale, "Eleanor of Aquitaine" (1997), pp. 24–29.

49. *Dialogus de Scaccario,* pp. 1–3; *Tractatus de legibus et consuetudinibus regni Angliae qui Glanvilla vocatur,* p. 1.

50. *Dialogu de Scaccario,* pp. 2, 20, 89 (the last specifically referring to the use of the king's writ to command his sheriffs to fortify castles).

51. Martindale, "Eleanor of Aquitaine: The Last Years," p. 154 and n60.

52. Martindale, "Eleanor of Aquitaine: The Last Years," pp. 140–41.

53. For discussion of the context of this grant and some of the problems associated with it, see Martindale, "Eleanor of Aquitaine: The Last Years," pp. 155–57 and esp. nn67–69.

CONTRIBUTORS

GEORGE T. BEECH, professor emeritus of medieval history at Western Michigan University, has written on various aspects of Aquitanian history in the eleventh and twelfth centuries: rural society, aristocracy (studies of Duke William IX, the troubadour), monasticism, personal names, relations with England, Spain, and the crusader East, and the Conventum narrative of ca. 1030. He is presently completing a biography of William IX and a history of the eleventh-century Muslim kingdom of Zaragoza in Spain.

CONSTANCE HOFFMAN BERMAN (Ph.D., University of Wisconsin) is a professor of History at the University of Iowa. She has published four books: *Medieval Agriculture, the Southern-French Countryside, and the Early Cistercians* (1986), *The Cistercian Evolution: The Invention of a Religious Order in Twelfth-Century Europe* (2000), *Women and Monasticism in Medieval Europe: Sisters and Patrons of the Cistercian Order* (2002), and with Judith Rice Rothschild and Charles W. Connell, *The Worlds of Medieval Women: Creativity, Influence, Imagination* (1985), as well as numerous articles, most recently "How Much Space did Medieval Nuns Have or Need?" in *Shaping Community: The Art and Archaeology of Monasticism,* ed. Sheila McNally (2001). She is currently at work on a number of projects including one on nuns and economic development in medieval Rome inspired by a recent NEH seminar in which she was a participant.

CONSTANCE BRITTAIN BOUCHARD received her BA from Middlebury College, and her MA (1973) and Ph.D. (1976) from the University of Chicago. She is professor of medieval history at the University of Akron and has received fellowships from the National Endowment for the Humanities and the John Simon Guggenheim Memorial Foundation. She is the author of eight books on the medieval nobility and the church, including *Sword, Miter, and Cloister: Nobility and the Church in Burgundy, 980–1198* (Ithaca: Cornell University Press, 1987); *"Strong of Body, Brave and Noble": Chivalry and Society in Medieval France* (Ithaca: Cornell University, 1998); and *"Those of My Blood": Constructing Noble Families in Medieval Francia* (Philadelphia: University of Pennsylvania Press, 2001).

ELIZABETH A.R. BROWN is professor emeritus of history of the City University of New York (Brooklyn College and the Graduate School). She has also taught at the École des Hautes Études en Sciences Sociales, Harvard University, New York University, and Yale University. She is a specialist in medieval and early modern French history, and her publications include works on French legal and institutional history, and the French monarchy and royal ceremonial. She is completing a book on the abbey church of Saint–Denis from the time of Abbot Suger through the present.

JAMES A. BRUNDAGE, Ahmanson-Murphy Distinguished Professor of History and Courtesy Professor of Law at the University of Kansas, is the author of ten books, including *Law, Sex and Christian Society in Medieval Europe* (Chicago: University of Chicago Press, 1987), and *Medieval Canon Law* (London: Longman, 1995), in addition to more than 250 scholarly articles and reviews.

RÁGENA C. DEARAGON, associate professor of history at Gonzaga University in Spokane, Washington, holds her doctorate from the University of California at Santa Barbara. She has published several articles on Anglo-Norman social and prosopographical history, and is completing a monograph on the Vere earls of Oxford.

MARIE HIVERGNEAUX, a former student of the Ecole Normale Superieure (E.N.S.) de Fontenay-Saint-Cloud, *agrégée* in history, is finishing under the supervision of Professor Martin Aurell a doctoral thesis at the Université de Poitiers (C.E.S.C.M.) about twelfth-century princesses in Northern France and in Aquitaine. She has given papers on Eleanor of Aquitaine at international colloquia held at Thouars and Montpellier in 1999; her Montpellier paper is published in the Acts of the colloquium (2001).

LOIS L. HUNEYCUTT holds her doctorate in medieval history from the University of California at Santa Barbara and is associate professor of history at the University of Missouri, Columbia. She has published a series of articles on twelfth-century Anglo-Scottish queenship and is completing a monograph on Queen Matilda II of England (d. 1118).

ANDREW W. LEWIS is professor of history at Southwest Missouri State University. He is the author of *Royal Succession in Capetian France: Studies on Fa-*

milial Order and the State (Cambridge, MA: Harvard University Press, 1981; French edn., Paris: Gallimard, 1986), and numerous articles. He is currently completing an edition and translation of the chronicle and historical notes of Bernard Itier.

JANE MARTINDALE is a life member of Clare Hall Cambridge. She taught English medieval history in the department of English and American studies at the University of East Anglia, Norwich, although her research was always focused on early medieval France. She has published papers ranging on topics from the eighth to the thirteenth century and some of these papers are collected in the volume *Status, Authority and Regional Power: Aquitaine and France Ninth to Twelfth Centuries* [London:Variorum, 1997].

PEGGY MCCRACKEN is associate professor of French at the University of Michigan. She is the author of *The Romance of Adultery: Queenship and Sexual Transgression in Old French Literature* (Philadelphia: University of Pennsylvania Press, 1998), and co-editor, with Karma Lochrie and James A. Schultz, of *Constructing Medieval Sexuality* (Minneapolis: University of Minnesota Press, 1997).

EVELYN MULLALLY is an honorary senior research fellow in medieval French at the Queen's University of Belfast. Her current research interests are in Anglo-Norman, particularly in the type of French used in Ireland in the Middle Ages. She has recently completed a new edition and translation of a chronicle for the Anglo-Norman Text Society, "La Geste des Engleis enYrlande" (previously called "The Song of Dermot and the Earl"), which is an account of the colonization of Ireland by Strongbow and Henry II, composed ca. 1190–1200.

KATHLEEN NOLAN received her Ph.D. from Columbia University and is associate professor of art history at Hollins University. She has published articles on narrative in public sculpture in twelfth-century Ile-de-France in *The Art Bulletin, Gazette des Beaux-Arts,* and *Studies in Iconography,* as well as an essay on the tomb of Adelaide of Maurienne in *Memory and the Medieval Tomb,* edited by ElizabethValdez del Alamo. She is currently working on a book about tombs of queens in France in the twelfth and early thirteenth centuries.

TAMARA F. O'CALLAGHAN holds a Ph.D. in medieval studies from the University of Toronto and is assistant professor in the Department of Literature and Language at Northern Kentucky University, where she teaches English literature and Latin. She is completing a modern English translation of Benoît de Sainte-Maure's *Roman de Troie.*

MARGARET AZIZA PAPPANO, assistant professor in the Department of English and Comparative Literature at Columbia University, is currently completing a book-length study entitled *The Priest's Body in Performance: Clerical Playing and Theatrical Space in the Medieval England.*

JOHN CARMI PARSONS holds a Ph.D. in medieval studies from the University of Toronto. He is the author of *Eleanor of Castile: Queen and Society in Thirteenth-Century England* (New York: St. Martin's, 1995), and articles on medieval queenship and prosopography. He has edited *Medieval Queenship* (New York: St. Martin's, 1993) and, with Bonnie Wheeler, *Medieval Mothering* (New York: Garland, 1996). He is preparing, with Kathleen Nolan, *Capetian Women,* to appear in the series The New Middle Ages, and *Queens and Queenship in Medieval Europe* (London: London Books, 2003).

MIRIAM SHADIS (Ph.D., Duke University) has written essays including "Piety, Politics, and Power: the Patronage of Leonor of England and her Daughters Berenguela of Leon and Blanche of Castile," in *The Cultural Patronage of Medieval Women,* ed. June Hall McCash (Athens:University of Georgia Press, 1996), and "Berenguela of Castile's Political Motherhood: the management of sexuality, marriage, and succession," in *Medieval Mothering,* ed. John Carmi Parsons and Bonnie Wheeler (New York: Garland,1996.) She currently teaches at Ohio University. She is preparing for publication her study, *Berenguela of Castile (1180–1246) and Her Family: Political Women in the High Middle Ages.*

HEATHER J. TANNER holds her doctorate in medieval history from the University of California at Santa Barbara. Her publications include articles on King Stephen's reign that have appeared in *Medievalia et Humanistica, Majestas,* and *Anglo-Norman Studies,* and she is a contributor to the *New Dictionary of National Biography.* She has completed a book on early medieval politics and governance, entitled *Families, Friends and Allies: Boulogne and Politics in northern France and England, c. 879-c.1162.*

FIONA TOLHURST, associate professor of English at Alfred University, teaches medieval and renaissance literature. She has published articles on English and French Arthurian literature in *Arthuriana* and *BBIAS,* has edited a special issue of *Arthuriana* on Geoffrey of Monmouth, and co-edited with Bonnie Wheeler *On Arthurian Women: Essays in Memory of Maureen Fries* (Dallas: Scriptorium, 2001).

RALPH V. TURNER is retired Distinguished Research Professor, Department of History, the Florida State University, Tallahassee. He took his doctorate in medieval history at the Johns Hopkins University and is a former Fulbright Scholar to France, a Fellow of the Royal Historical Society, and former vice–president of the Charles Homer Haskins Society. His books include *The King and his Courts: the Role of King John and Henry III in the Administration of Justice, 1199–1240* (Ithaca: Cornell University Press, 1968); *The English Judiciary in the Age of Glanvill and Bracton c. 1176–1239* (Cambridge, UK: Cambridge University Press, 1985); *Men Raised from the Dust: Administrative Service and Upward Mobility in Angevin England* (Philadelphia: University of Pennsylvania Press, 1988); *King John* (Longman, 1994); and co-author of *The Reign of Richard Lionheart: Ruler of the Angevin Empire, 1189–1199* (New York: Longman, 2000). He has published articles and reviews in *Albion, American Historical Review, American Journal of Legal History, French Historical Studies, Journal of British Studies, Speculum* and other scholarly journals.

BONNIE WHEELER teaches English and Medieval Studies at Southern Methodist University (Dallas). She has written articles on a wide range of medieval topics and she has edited or co-edited several volumes, including *On Arthurian Women: Essays in Memory of Maureen Fries* (2001), *The Malory Debate: The Texts of Le Morte Darthur* (2000), *Listening to Heloise: The Voice of a Twelfth-Century Woman* (2000), *Becoming Male in the Middle Ages* (1997), and *Fresh Verdicts on Joan of Arc* (1996). She is the editor of the *Arthuriana,* the journal for the International Arthurian Society/North American Branch, and she is series editor of Palgrave Macmillan's The New Middle Ages, in which this book appears.

CHARLES T. WOOD is Daniel Webster Professor of History, emeritus, at Dartmouth College where he was also a Professor of Comparative Literature. He is a Fellow of the Medieval Academy of America and is presently working on Arthurian frauds of Glastonbury Abbey.

BIBLIOGRAPHY

Unpublished Sources

Angers, Archives départementales du Maine-et-Loire, 101 H 225 bis, pp. 90–91 (seventeenth-century copy of the Grand cartulaire of Fontevraud).

Colchester, Essex County Record Office, D/Du 102/28 (charter issued by King Stephen of England, n.d., London).

London, British Library, MS Cotton Vespasian E 14 (cartulary of Premonstratensian monastery of Leestun, Norfolk).

Oxford, Bodleian Library, MS Tanner 425 (thirteenth-century cartulary of the Priory of Hickling, Norfolk).

Paris, Archives nationales, J628, no. 5 (original charter of Eleanor of Aquitaine, 1199).

Paris, Archives nationales, S*4386 (cartulary of Saint-Antoine, grants by John and Isabelle).

Paris BnF, Fonteneau (lat. 18376–18404), vol. 18, p. 48 (charter issued by Mirable, wife of Robert de Sillé at Chinon, 1172), and vol. 15, p. 779 (charter issued by Louis VII at Étampes, 1146); vol. 25, pp. 287–88 (charter issued by Louis VII and Eleanor at Lorris, 1139).

Paris BnF, Moreau, vol. 31, fol. 81r-v.

Paris BnF, Baluze 375, vol. 375, fols. 27v–28r. (charter issued by Eleanor at Périgueux, 1169 X 1173).

Paris BnF, Clairambault, vol. 1188, fol. 5r (a copy of a charter issued by Eleanor at Poitiers, 1169 X 1172 made for Roger de Gaignières).

Paris, BnF, Picardie vol. 250, fol. 268r-v (charter issued by Queen Matilda in 1136).

Paris BnF, fr. 9222 ("chronique abrégée").

Paris BnF, lat. 5419 (copy of the cartulary of La Trinité of Vendôme, made for Roger de Gaignières).

Paris BnF, lat. 5480 (seventeenth-century manuscript copy of the cartulary of Fontevraud, made for Roger de Gaignières).

Paris BnF, lat. 5452 (early fourteenth-century manuscript from Saint-Martin of Limoges containing copies of earlier materials from Saint-Martial of Limoges).

Paris BnF, lat. 13892 (cartulary of the abbey of Le Lys, compiled in the fourteenth century).

Poitiers, BM MS Fonteneau 14, fols. 251–52 (18th-century copy by Dom Fonteneau of charter issued by Eleanor of Aquitaine at Chizé, 1156–57).

Pontoise, Archives départementales du Val-d'Oise, sér. 72H12 (register for Blanche of Castile's construction of the abbey).

Pontoise, Archives départementales du Val-d'Oise, sér. 58 H, 1–58 (building records for Blanche of Castile's Notre-Dame-la-Royale at Maubuisson).

Published Sources

L'abbaye de Maubuisson (Notre-Dame-la-Royale): histoire et cartulaire; publiés d'après des documents entiérement inédits, ed. Adolphe Dutilleux and Joseph Depoin, 2 vols. (Pontoise: A. Paris, 1882–90). [Dutilleux and Depoin, *L'abbaye de Maubuisson*]

L'abbaye royale de Notre-Dame-des-Clairets, histoire et cartulaire (1202–1290), ed. Vicomte de Souancé (Vannes, n.p., 1894). [*L'abbaye royale de Notre-Dame-des-Clairets*]

Les abbayes Caennaises, ed. Musset. See *Les actes de Guillaume le Conquérant et la reine Mathilde pour les abbayes Caennaises.*

Abbot Suger on St.-Denis, ed. Panofsky. See Suger, Abbot of St.-Denis.

Acta sanctorum quotquot toto orbe coluntur, vel a catholicis scriptoribus celebrantur, ed. John van Bolland et al. (1646–1887; repr. Brussels: Culture et Civilisation, 1965–1970). [AASS]

Actes des comtes de Flandre, 1071–1128, ed. Ferdinand Vercauteren (Brussels: Palais des académies, 1928). [*Actes des comtes de Flandres*]

Les actes de Guillaume le Conquérant et la reine Mathilde pour les abbayes Caennaises, ed. Lucien Musset (Caen: Société des Antiquaires de Normandie, 1967). [*Les abbayes Caennaises,* ed. Musset]

Adalbero of Laon. "Rythmus satyricus," ed. Claude Hohl in "Le comte Landri de Nevers dans l'histoire et dans la Geste de *Girart de Roussillon,*" in *La chanson de geste et le mythe carolingien. Mélanges René Louis publiés par ses collègues, ses amis et ses élèves à l'occasion de son 75ᵉ anniversaire,* ed. Comité de publication des Mélanges René Louis (Saint-Père-sous-Vézelay [Mayenne]: Musée archéologique régional, 1982), pp. 781–800. [Adalbero of Laon, "Rythmus satyricus"]

Aelred of Rievaulx. "Genealogia regum anglorum," Migne PL 195: cols. 711–58.

Alberic of Trois-Fontaines. *Chronica,* MGH SS 23.

Alfonso X [king of Castile and León]. *Primera Crónica General de España,* ed. Ramón Menéndez Pidal, 2 vols. (Madrid: Gredos, 1955). [Alfonso X, *Primera Crónica General*]

Alger von Lüttichs Traktat "De misericordia et iustitia": ein kanonistischer Konkordanzversuch aus der Zeit des Investiturstreits: Untersuchungen und Edition, ed. Robert Kretzschmar (Sigmaringen: Jan Thorbecke, 1985).

Andreas Capellanus On Love, ed. and trans. Patrick Gerard Walsh (London: Duckworth, 1982). [*Andreas Capellanus On Love*]

Anecdotes historiques, légendes et apologues tirés du recueil inédit d'Etienne de Bourbon, ed. A. Lecoy de la Marche (Paris: Librairie Renouard, 1877). [*Anecdotes historiques*]

The Anglo-Saxon Chronicle, ed. and trans. Dorothy Whitlock, David C. Douglas, and Susie I. Tucker (London: Eyre and Spottiswoode, 1961). [*Anglo-Saxon Chronicle*]

Annales de Burton, ed. Henry Richards Luard, in vol. 1 of *Annales Monastici*, 5 vols., Rerum Britannicarum medii aevi scriptores 36 (London: H.M. Stationery Office, 1864–69).

Annales de Margan, ed. Henry Richards Luard, in vol. 1 of *Annales Monastici*, 5 vols., Rerum Britannicarum medii aevi scriptores 36 (London: H.M. Stationery Office, 1864–69).

Les Annales de Saint-Pierre de Gand et de Saint-Amand, ed. Philip Grierson (Brussels: Palais des académies, 1937). [*Annales de Saint-Pierre de Gand*]

Annales Monasterii de Bermundseia, ed. Henry Richards Luard, in vol. 3 of *Annales Monastici*, 5 vols., Rerum Britannicarum medii aevi scriptores 36 (London: H.M. Stationery Office, 1864–69). [*Annales Monasterii de Bermundseia*]

Annales Monasterii de Osneia, ed. Henry Richards Luard, in vol. 4 of *Annales Monastici*, 5 vols., Rerum Britannicarum medii aevi scriptores 36 (London: H.M. Stationery Office, 1864–69).

Annales Monasterii de Waverleia, ed. Henry Richard Luard, in vol. 2 of *Annales Monastici*, 5 vols., Rerum Britannicarum medii aevi scriptores 36 (London: H.M. Stationery Office, 1864–69).

Annales Monasterii de Wintonia, ed. Henry Richards Luard, in vol. 2 of *Annales Monastici*, 5 vols., Rerum Britannicarum medii aevi scriptores 36 (London: H.M. Stationery Office, 1864–69).

Annales Monastici, ed. Henry Richards Luard, 4 vols., Rerum Britannicarum medii aevi scriptores 36 (London: H.M. Stationery Office, 1864–69). [*Annales Monastici*]

Annales Prioratus de Dunstaplia, ed. Henry Richards Luard, in vol. 3 of *Annales Monastici*, 5 vols., Rerum Britannicarum medii aevi scriptores 36 (London: H.M. Stationery Office, 1864–69).

Annales Prioratus de Wigornia, ed. Henry Richards Luard, in vol. 4 of *Annales Monastici*, 5 vols., Rerum Britannicarum medii aevi scriptores 36 (London: H.M. Stationery Office, 1864–69).

Annales de Theokesberia, ed. Henry Richards Luard, in vol. 1 of *Annales Monastici*, 5 vols., Rerum Britannicarum medii aevi scriptores 36 (London: H.M. Stationery Office, 1864–69).

Anselme de la Vierge Marie, le Père (Pierre Guibours). *Histoire généalogique et chronologique de la Maison Royale de France*, 3rd edn., ed. Honoré Caille, lord of Le Fourny, and les Pères Ange de Sainte Rosalie (François Raffard) and Simplicien, 9 vols. (Paris: La Compagnie des libraires, 1726–33; repr. Paris: Éditions du Palais Royal, 1967). [Anselme, *Histoire généalogique*]

Bede. *Historica ecclesiastica gentis Anglorum*, ed. Charles Plummer (Oxford: Clarendon Press, 1896).

Benedict of Peterborough. *Gesta Regis Henrici Secundi Benedicti Abbatis*, ed. William Stubbs, 2 vols., Rerum Britannicarum medii aevi scriptores 49 (London: Longmans, Green, Reader, and Dyer, 1867; repr. Wiesbaden: Kraus, 1965), includes *Gesta Ricardi* in vol. 2. [*Gesta Regis Henrici Secundi*]

Benoît de Sainte-Maure. *Le Roman de Troie,* ed. Léopold Constans, 6 vols. (Paris: Firmin Didot, 1904–12). [Benoît, *Le Roman de Troie*]

———. *Chronique des ducs de Normandie (ca. 1174–89),* ed. Carin Fahlin, 3 vols. (Uppsala: Almqvist & Wiksells, 1951–67).

Bernard of Clairvaux. *Sancti Bernardi Opera,* ed. Jean Leclercq, Charles H. Talbot, and Henri M. Rochais, 8 vols. in 9 (Rome: Editiones Cistercienses, 1957–77). [Bernard, *Sancti Bernardi Opera*]

———. *Letters of St. Bernard of Clairvaux,* trans. Bruno Scott James (London: Burns Oates, 1953; repr. New York: AMS Press, 1980). [Bernard of Clairvaux, *Letters*]

Bouvet, Jean. "Le récit de la fondation de Mortemer," *Collectanea Ordinis Cisterciensium reformatorum* 22 (1960):149–58.

Burchard of Worms. *Decretum,* in Migne PL, vol. 140.

Buzelin, Johan. *Annales Gallo-Flandrie* (Douai, 1624).

CDF, ed. Round. See *Calendar of Documents Preserved in France Illustrative of the History of Great Britain and Ireland, Vol. 1: A.D. 918–1206.*

Calendar of Ancient Correspondence concerning Wales, ed. J. Goronwy Edwards (Cardiff: Board of Celtic Studies, 1935).

Calendar of Documents Preserved in France Illustrative of the History of Great Britain and Ireland, Vol. 1: A.D. 918–1206, ed. J. Horace Round (London: H.M. Stationery Office, 1899; repr. Nedeln: Kraus, 1967). [CDF, ed. Round]

Calendar of the Patent Rolls, A.D. 1232–1247 (London: H.M. Stationery Office, 1906).

Cartae Antiquae, Rolls 1–10, ed. Lionel Landon, Pipe Roll Society, n.s. 17 (London: The Pipe Roll Society, 1939). [*Cartae Antiquae Rolls*]

"Cartulaire de l'abbaye de la Grace Notre-Dame ou de Charonen Aunis (Abbatia. Gratiae E.M. de Carente)," ed. L[ouis].[Marie Meschinet] de Richemond in *Archives historiques de la Saintonge et de l'Aunis* 11 (Paris: Société des archives historiques de la Saintonge et d'aunis, 1883). ["Cartulaire de l'abbaye de la Grace Notre-Dame ou de Charon"]

Cartulaire de l'abbaye de la Madeleine de Châteaudun, ed. Lucien Merlet and Louis Jarry (Châteaudun: Pouillier, 1896). [*Cartulaire de Châteaudun*]

"Cartulaire de l'abbaye de la Merci-Dieu, autrement dite de Bécheron au diocèse de Poitiers," ed. Etienne Clouzot in *Archives historiques du Poitou* 34 [1905]. ["Cartulaire de l'abbaye de la Merci-Dieu"]

Cartulaire de l'abbaye de la Sainte-Trinité de Tiron, ed. Lucien Merlet (Chartres: Garnier, 1883). [*Cartulaire de Tiron*]

Cartulaire de l'abbaye de Notre-Dame de l'Eau (Chartres: Charles Métais, 1908). [*Cartulaire de l'abbaye de Notre-Dame de l'Eau*]

Cartulaire de l'abbaye de Notre-Dame de la Trappe, ed. Hyacinthe Charencey (Alençon: Renart de Broise, 1889). [*Cartulaire de la Trappe*]

Cartulaire de l'abbaye de Notre-Dame des Vaux-de-Cernay, ed. Lucien Merlet and Auguste Moutié (Paris: Plon, 1857). [*Cartulaire des Vaux-de-Cernay*]

"Cartulaire de l'abbaye de Sainte-Croix," ed. Aristide Ducaunnès-Duval in *Archives historiques de la Gironde* 27 (1892). ["Cartulaire de l'abbaye de Sainte-Croix"]

Cartulaire de l'abbaye royale du Lieu-Notre-Dame-lez-Romorantin, ed. Ernest Prat (Romorantin: n.p., 1881). [*Cartulaire de l'abbaye royale du Lieu*]

Cartulaire de l'église collégiale Saint-Seurin de Bordeaux, ed. [Elie] J[ean].-A[uguste]. Brutails, Académie nationale des sciences, belles-lettres et arts de Bordeaux (Bordeaux: G. Gounouilhou, 1897). [*Cartulaire de l'église collégiale Saint-Seurin*]

Cartulaire de la Léproserie de Grand-Beaulieu et du prieuré de Notre-Dame de la Bourdinière, Archives départementales d'Euré et Loir. *Collection de Cartulaires Chartrains,* ed. René Merlet and Maurice Jusselin, 2 vols (Chartres: Garnier, 1906–09). [*Cartulaire de la Léproserie de Grand-Beaulieu*]

Cartulaire de Notre-Dame de Chartres, no. 294 [1249], ed. Eugène de Buchère de Lépinois and Luc Merlet. 3 vols. Société archéologique d'Euré et Loir (Chartres: Garnier, 1862–65).

Cartulaire de Notre-Dame de Voisins de l'Ordre de Cîteaux, ed. Jules Doinel (Orléans: Herluison, 1887). [*Cartulaire de Voisin*]

Cartulaire du Bas-Poitou (département de la Vendée), ed. Paul Marchegay (Les Roches-Baritaud:Vendée, 1877). [*Cartulaire du Bas-Poitou*]

Cartulaire saintongeais de la Trinité-de-Vendôme, ed. Charles Métais, *Archives Historiques de la Saintonge et de l'Aunis* 22 (1893). [Métais, "Cartulaire saintongeais"]

Cartulaires de l'abbaye royale de Notre-Dame de Saintes, de l'ordre de Saint-Benoît. 2. Cartulaires inédits de la Saintonge, ed. Pierre-Théodore Grasilier (Niort: L. Clouzot, 1871).

Cartularium monasterii Sancti Johannis Baptiste de Colecestria, ed. Stuart A. Moore (London: Roxburgh Club, 1897). [*Cartularium monasterii Sancti Johannis Baptiste de Colecestria*]

Cartularium Prioratus de Colne, ed. John L. Fisher (Colchester, UK: Essex Archaeological Society, 1946). [*Cartularium Prioratus de Colne*]

The Cartulary of Blythe Priory, ed. Reginald Thomas Timson, 2 vols. (London: Thoroton Society Record Series, 1973).

The Cartulary of Holy Trinity Aldgate, ed. Gerald A.J. Hodgett, London Record Society Publications 7 (London: London Record Society, 1971).

The Cartulary of the Knights of St John of Jerusalem in England. Secunda Camera Essex, ed. Michael Gervers (Oxford-New York: Oxford University Press for the British Academy, 1982–1996). [*The Cartulary of the Knights of St John*]

Chansons de Guillaume. See William IX, duke of Aquitaine.

"Chartes," ed. Eugène Frédéric Ferdinand Hucher, *Revue des sociétés savantes* 5th ser. 3 (1872):53–544. [Hucher, "Chartes"]

"Chartes de la Commanderie magistrale du Temple de La Rochelle (1139–1268)," ed. L[ouis].[Marie Meschinet] de Richemond, *Archives historiques de la Saintonge et de l'Aunis* 1 (1874):25–26. [Richemond, "Chartes"]

"Chartes de Fontevraud concernant l'Aunis et La Rochelle," ed. Paul Marchegay, *Bibliothèque de l'Ecole des Chartes,* 4th ser. 19 (1858):132–70, 321–47. [Marchegay, "Chartes de Fontevraud"]

"Chartes et documents de l'abbaye de Saint-Maixent," ed. Alfred Richard, *Archives historiques du Poitou* 1 (1886). ["Chartes de Saint-Maixent"]

La châtelaine de Vergi, ed. Gaston Raynaud, rev. Lucien Foulet (Paris: Champion, 1921).

Le Chevalier au Cygne et Godefroid de Bouillon. Poème historique, ed. le Baron de Reiffenberg and Adolphe Borgnet, 3 vols., Monuments pour servir à l'histoire des provinces de Namur, de Hainaut et de Luxembourg, 4–6 (Brussels: M. Hayez, 1846–54). [*Chevalier au Cygne et Godefroid de Bouillon*]

Child, Francis J. *The English and Scottish Popular Ballads*, 10 vols. (Boston, 1882–98). [Child, *Ballads*]

Chrétien de Troyes. *Erec and Enide*, trans. D[ouglas] D[avid] R[oy] Owen in *Arthurian Romances: Chrétien de Troyes*, Everyman Classics (London: J.M. Dent, 1988, rev. ed. 1993).

"Chronica de gestis consulum Andegavorum," in *Chroniques des comtes d'Anjou et des seigneurs d'Amboise*, ed. Louis Halphen and Réne Poupardin. ["Chronica de gestis consulum Andegavorum"]

Chronica Monasterii de Melsa, ed. Edward Augustus Bond, 3 vols., Rerum Britannicarum medii aevi scriptores 43 (London: Longmans, Green, Reader, and Dyer, 1866–68).

The Chronicle of Jocelin of Brakelond. See *Jocelini de Brakelond Cronica*, trans. Butler.

Chronicles of the Crusades: Nine Crusades and Two Hundred Years of Bitter Conflict for the Holy Land Brought to Life through the Words of Those Who Were Actually There, ed. Elizabeth Hallam (New York: Weidenfeld and Nicolson, 1989). [*Chronicles of the Crusades*]

Chronicles and Memorials of the Reign of Richard I, ed. William Stubbs, 2 vols., Rerum Britannicarum medii aevi scriptores 38 (London: H.M. Stationery Office, 1864–65). [*Chronicles and Memorials of the Reign of Richard I*]

Chronicles of the Reigns of Stephen, Henry II and Richard I, ed. Richard Howlett, 4 vols., Rerum Britannicarum medii aevi scriptores 82 (London: Longman, 1884–89; repr. Wiesbaden: Kraus, 1964).

Chronicon comitum Pictaviae, in RHF, ed. Bouquet, vol. 12.

Chronicicon Dolensis coenobi, in RHF, ed. Bouquet, vol. 12.

Chronicon monasterii de Abingdon, ed. Joseph Stevenson, 2 vols., Rerum Britannicarum medii aevi scriptores 2 (London: H.M. Stationery Office, 1858). [*Chronicon monasterii de Abingdon*]

Chronicon Turonensi, in in RHF, ed. Bouquet, vol. 12.

Chronicon Vulgo Dictum Chronicon Thomae Wykes, ed. Henry Richards Luard, in vol. 4 of *Annales Monastici*, 5 vols., Rerum Britannicarum medii aevi scriptores 36 (London: H.M. Stationery Office, 1864–69). [*Chronicon Thomae Wykes*, ed. Luard]

La chronique de Saint-Maixent, ed. and trans. Jean Verdon, Les classiques de l'histoire de France au moyen âge, 33 (Paris: Éditions Belles-Lettres, 1979). [*Chronique de Saint-Maixent*, ed. Verdon]

Chronique latine de Guillaume de Nangis de 1113 à 1300 avec les continuations de cette chronique de 1300 à 1368, ed. Hercule Géraud, 2 vols., Société de l'Histoire de France, Publication no. 33, 35 (Paris: Jules Renouard, 1843). [*Chronique latine de Guillaume de Nangis*]

Chroniques anglo-normandes, ed. Francisque Michel, 3 vols. printed as one (Rouen: F. Michel, 1836).

Chroniques de Saint-Martial de Limoges, ed. Henri Duplès-Agier, Société de l'histoire de France, Publications in octavo (Paris: Librairie Renouard, 1874). [*Chroniques de Saint-Martial de Limoges*]

Chroniques des comtes d'Anjou et des seigneurs d'Amboise, ed. Louis Halphen and René Poupardin, Collection de texts pour servir à l'étude et à l'enseignement de l'histoire . . . 48 (Paris: A. Picard, 1913).

Chroniques des églises d'Anjou, ed. Paul Marchegay and Emile Mabille, Société de l'Histoire de France, Publications in octavo (Paris: Renouard, 1869; repr. New York: Johnson, 1968). [*Chroniques des églises d'Anjou,* ed. Marchegay and Mabille]

"Codex Udalrici," ed. Philipp Jaffé, Monumenta Bamburgensia, *Monumenta Germaniae Historica* Bibliotheca rerum germanicarum 5 (Berlin: Wiedmann, 1869; repr. Aalen: Scientia Verlag Aalen, 1964).

Colker, M[arvin].L[eonard]. "Latin Texts concerning Gilbert, Founder of Merton Priory," *Studia monastica* 12 (1970):241–72.

A Collection of All the Wills, Now Known to be Extant, of the Kings and Queens of England, Princes and Princesses of Wales, and Every Branch of the Blood Royal, from the Reign of William the Conqueror, to that of Henry the Seventh Exclusive. With Explanatory Notes, and a Glossary, ed. John Nichols (London: J. Nichols, 1780). [*Collection of All the Wills,* ed. Nichols]

Constitutiones Concilii Quarti Lateranensis una cum commentariis glossatorum, ed. Antonio García y García, Monumenta iuris canonici, corpus glossatorum, vol. 2 (Vatican City: Biblioteca Apostolica Vaticana, 1981). [*Constitutiones Concilii Quarti Lateranensis*]

Corpus iuris canonici, ed. Emil Friedberg (Leipzig: B. Tauchnitz, 1879; repr. Graz: Akademische Druck-u. Verlagsanstalt, 1959).

Cox, David C. "Two Unpublished Charters of King Stephen for Wenlock Priory," *Shropshire History and Archaeology* 66 (1989):56–59.

Crónica Latina de los Reyes de Castilla, ed. Luis Charlo Brea (Cádiz: Universidad de Cádiz, 1984). [*Crónica Latina*]

Daretis Phrygii De excidio Troiae historia, ed. Ferdinand Meister (Leipzig: B.G. Teubner, 1873). [*Daretis Phrygii*]

"De B. Ida vidua, Comitissa Boloniae in Gallo Belgica," *AASS,* April 13, cols. 139–50.

Decrees of the Ecumenical Councils, ed. Giuseppe Albiergo, trans. Norman P. Tanner, 2 vols. (London: Sheed and Ward, 1990). [*Decrees of the Ecumenical Councils,* ed. Albiergo]

Delisle, Léopold. "Mémoire sur une lettre inédite adressée à la Reine Blanche par un habitant de la Rochelle," *Bibliothèque de l'École des Chartes* 4th ser. 2 (1856):513–55. [Delisle, "Mémoire sur une lettre inédite"]

Denis Piramus. *La Vie Seint Edmund le Rei,* ed. Hilding Kjellman (Geneva: Slatkine, 1935, repr. 1974).

Deux rédactions du roman des sept sages de Rome, ed. Gaston Paris (Paris: Firmin Didot, 1876).

Dialogus de Scaccario (The course of the Exchequer) by Richard fitz Nigel and Constitutio Domus Regis (The Establishment of the Royal Household), [both] ed. and trans. Charles Johnson, rev. edn. F.E.L. Carter and Diana E. Greenway (Oxford: Clarendon Press, and New York: Oxford University Press, 1983). [*Dialogus de Scaccario*]

Documentación del Monasterio de las Huelgas de Burgos, ed. José Manuel Lizoain Garrido, 4 vols. of 8 (Burgos: Ediciones J.M. Garrido Garrido, 1985–1990). [*Documentación del Monasterio de las Huelgas*]

"Documents pour l'histoire de l'église Saint-Hilaire de Poitiers," ed. Louis Redet, *Mémoires de la Société des Antiquaires de l'Ouest,* 1st ser. 14 [1848]. [Redet, "Saint-Hilaire de Poitiers"]

Douët d'Arcq, Louis. *Collection de sceaux,* 3 vols., Archives de l'Empire, Inventaires et documents (Paris: Henri Plon, 1863–68).

Monasticon Anglicanum, ed. William Dugdale, 6 vols. (London: Longman, Hurt, Rees, Orme & Brown, 1817–30); 2nd edn., ed. J. Caley, 6 vols. in 8 (London: H.M. Record Commissioners, 1816–46). [Dugdale, *Monasticon*]

Durandus of Mende. *Rationale divinorum officiorum* (Naples: J. Dura, 1859). [Durandus, *Rationale*]

Eadmer. *Historia novorum in Anglia,* ed. Martin Rule, Rerum Britannicarum medii aevi scriptores 81 (London: H.M. Stationery Office, 1884; repr. London: Longman, 1965). [Eadmer, *Historia*]

The Early Charters of the Augustinian Canons of Waltham Abbey, Essex (1062–1230), ed. Rosalind Ransford (Woodbridge: Boydell and Brewer, 1989). [*Waltham Abbey,* ed. Ransford]

Early Charters of the Cathedral Church of St Paul, London, ed. Marion Gibbs (London: Offices of the Royal Historical Society, 1939). [*Early Charters of the Cathedral Church of St Paul*]

English Historical Documents 1042–1189, vol. 2, ed. David C. Douglas and George W. Greenway (London: Oxford University Press, 1968).

Essai d'itinéraire et regestes d'Aliénor reine d'Angleterre, duchesse d'Aquitaine 1189–1204, ed. Irène Baldet, typescript deposited in the library of the CSEM, Poitiers.

"Ex chronico anonymi canonici, ut videtur, Laudunensis," in RHF, ed. Bouquet, 13.

"Extrait d'un abrégé de l'histoire des rois de France," in RHF, ed. Bouquet, 12.

Feudal Society in Medieval France. Documents from the County of Champagne, ed. and trans. Theodore Evergates (Philadelphia: University of Pennsylvania Press, 1993).

La fille du comte de Pontieu, conte en prose, versions du XIIIᵉ et du XVᵉ siècle, ed. Clovis Félix Brunel, Société des anciens texts français lxxv (Paris: H. Champion, 1923). [*La fille du comte de Pontieu, conte en prose*]

Florence of Worcester. *Florentii Wigorniensis monachi Chronicon ex Chronicis.* ed. Benjamin Thorpe. 2 vols. (London: English Historical Society, 1848–49). [Florence of Worcester, *Chronicon ex Chronicis*]

Flores Historiarum. See Roger of Wendover.

Foedera, conventiones et cujuscunque generis acta publica inter reges Angliæ, et alios quosvis imperatores, reges, pontifices, principes, vel communitates, ab ineunte sæculo duodecimo, ed. Thomas Rymer and Robert Sanderson, 20 vols. (London: J. Tonson, 1704–35); rev. edn., ed. Adam Clarke, Frederic Holbrooke, John Caley, 4 vols. in 7 (London: H.M. Record Commission, 1816–69). [Rymer, *Foedera*]

"Fragmentum genealogicum ducum Normanniae et Angliae regum," in RHF, ed. Bouquet, 18.

Gallia Christiana in provincias ecclesiasticas distributa, ed. Denis de Sainte-Marthe and Pierre Piolin, new edn. 16 vols. (Paris: J.B. Coignard, 1715–1865; repr. Farnborough, UK: Gregg, 1970). [*Gallia Christiana*]

"Genealogiae comitum Andegavensium" in *Chroniques des comtes d'Anjou et des seigneurs d'Amboise,* ed. Louis Halphen and René Poupardin (Paris: A. Picard, 1913). ["Genealogiae comitum Andegavensium"]

Geoffrey of Monmouth. *The Historia regum Britannie of Geoffrey of Monmouth I: Bern, Bürgerbibliothek MS 568,* ed. Neil Wright (Cambridge, UK: D.S. Brewer, 1984).

———. *The History of the Kings of Britain,* trans. Lewis Thorpe (Harmondsworth: Penguin Books, 1966). [Geoffrey of Monmouth, trans. Thorpe]

Geoffroi de Vigeois. *Chronica,* in vol. 2 of *Nova bibliotheca mss. librorum,* ed. Philippe Labbe (Paris: Cramoisy, 1657).

———. *Chronique,* in RHF 12, ed. Bouquet.

Gerald of Wales. See Giraldus Cambrensis.

Gerbert of Aurillac (Gerberts von Reims). *Die Briefsammlung Gerberts von Reims,* ed. Fritz Weigle (Weimar: Böhlaus, 1966). [*Die Briefsammlung Gerberts*]

Gervase of Canterbury. *Opera Historica,* ed. William Stubbs, 2 vols., Rerum Britannicarum medii aevi scriptores 73 (London: H.M. Stationery Office, 1879–80; repr. Wiesbaden: Kraus, 1965). [Gervase of Canterbury, *Opera Historica*]

Gesta Regis Henrici Secundi. See Benedict of Peterborough.

Gesta Stephani: The Deeds of Stephen. ed. Kenneth Reginald Potter and Ralph Henry Carless Davis (Oxford: Clarendon Press, 1976). [*Gesta Stephani*]

Geschichte der deutschen Kaiserzeit, ed. Wilhelm von Giesebrecht, 5th edn., 6 vols. in 8. (Braunschweig: C.A. Schwetschke/Leipzig: Duncker and Humblot, 1875–90). [*Geschichte der deutschen Kaiserzeit*]

Giraldus Cambrensis [Gerald of Wales]. *De Principis Instructione Liber,* ed. George Frederick Warner in vol. 8 of *Giraldi Cambrensis Opera,* ed. John Sherren Brewer, James Francis Dimock, and George Frederic Warner, 8 vols., Rerum Britannicarum medii aevi scriptores 21 (London: H.M. Stationery Office, 1861–91). [Giraldus Cambrensis, *De Principis Instructione Liber*]

Gislebert of Mons. *Chronicon Hanoniense,* MGH SS 21. [Gislebert of Mons, *Chronicon Hanoniense*]

Glaber, *Five Books of Histories. See* Rodulfus Glaber.

Glanvill, Ranulf. *De legibus et consuetudinibus Angliae,* ed. George Edward Woodbine (Oxford: Clarendon Press as Oxford University Press, 1932). [Glanvill, *De Legibus*]

———. *Tractatus de Legibus et Consuetudinibus regni Angliae qui Glanvilla vocatur,* ed. G.D.G. Hall, Nelson's Medieval Texts (London: Thomas Nelson, 1965).

Grand Cartulaire de Fontevraud (Pancarta et cartularium abbatissae et ordinis Fontis Ebraldi), ed. Jean-Marc Bienvenu (Poitiers: Société des antiquaires de l'ouest, 2000). [*Grand Cartulaire de Fontevraud*]

The Great Roll of the Pipe for the First Year of the Reign of King Richard I, ed. J. Hunter. Publications of the Pipe Roll Society (London: The Pipe Roll Society, 1844). [Pipe 1 Richard I]

The Great Roll of the Pipe . . .[5 Henry II-17 John], Publications of the Pipe Roll Society, vols. 1–38 (London: Pipe Roll Society, 1884–1925), new series, vols. 1–37 (London: The Pipe Roll Society, 1926–64).

Gregory of Tours. *The History of the Franks,* trans. Lewis Thorpe (Harmondsworth: Penguin Books, 1982).

Helgaud of Fleury. *Epitoma regis Rotberti pii,* in *Vie de Robert le Pieux,* ed. Robert-Henri Bautier and Gillette Labory (Paris: Centre National de la Recherche Scientifique, 1965). [Helgaud of Fleury, *Epitoma*]

Helinand de Froidmont. *Chronicon,* in Migne PL, 212:cols. 1057–58.

Henry of Huntingdon. *Henrici Huntingdonensis Historia Anglorum,* ed. Thomas Arnold, Rerum Britannicarum medii aevi scriptores 74 (London: H.M. Stationery Office, 1879). [Henry of Huntingdon, *Historia Anglorum,* ed. Arnold]

———. *Historia Anglorum,* ed. Diana Greenway (Oxford: Oxford University Press, 1996). [Henry of Huntingdon, *Historia Anglorum,* ed. Greenway]

Herman of Tournai. *De Restauratione Sancti Martini Tornacensis,* ed. Georg Friedrich Waitz, MGH SS 14.

Hildebert of Lavardin. *Opera omnia,* in Migne PL, vol. 171.

L'histoire de Guillaume le Maréchal, comte de Striguil et de Pembroke, régent d'Angleterre de 1216 à 1219, ed. Paul Meyer, 3 vols., Société de l'histoire de France, octavo 61; publications 255, 268, and 304 (Paris: Librairie Renouard, H. Laurens successeur, 1891–1901). [*L'histoire de Guillaume le Maréchal*]

Historia gloriosi regis Ludovici VII, in RHF, vol. 12.

Howden [Hoveden]. *See* Roger of Howden.

Hugh the Chanter. *The History of the Church of York, 1066–1127,* ed. and trans. Charles Johnson, 2nd edn. rev., ed. M. Brett, C[hristopher]. N[ugent] L[awrence]. Brooke, and M. Winterbottom (Oxford: Clarendon Press, 1990). [Hugh the Chanter, *The History of the Church of York*]

Hugh of Fleury. "Modernum regum Francorum Acta," MGH SS 9.

L'Huillier, J. "Inventaire des titres concernant la seigneurie que les religieuses de l'abbaye royale de Notre-Dame du Lys possédaient à Malay-le-Roi," *Bulletin de la société historique de Sens* 10 (1882):345–47. [L'Huillier, "Inventaire de Notre-Dame du Lys"]

Ingulph of Crowland. *Chronicle of the Abbey of Crowland,* trans. H.T. Riley (London: Bohn, 1854).

"Inventaire de La-Royale-de-Maubuisson-lez-Pontoise (1483–1538)," ed. A. Dutilleux and J. Depoin, *Recueil d'anciens inventaires publié sous les auspices de Comités des travaux historiques* (Paris: Comité des travaux historiques, 1896). [Dutilleux and Depoin, "Inventaire de Maubuisson"]

L'ystoire des sept sages, in *Deux rédactions du roman des sept sages de Rome* or *Le roman des sept sages de Rome.*

Istoire et chroniques de Flandres d'après les textes de divers manuscrits, ed. Kervyn de Lettenhove, 2 vols. (Brussels: F. Hayez, 1879). [*Istoire et chroniques de Flandres*]

The Itinerary of John Leland in or about the Years 1535–1545, ed. Lucy T. Smith, 4 vols. (London: G. Bell, 1907–10).

The Itinerary of Richard I, ed. Lionel Landon, Publications of the Pipe Roll Society, 47, n.s. 13 (London:The Pipe Roll Society, 1935). [Landon, *Itinerary of Richard I*]

Ivo of Chartres, *Decretum*, in PL, vol. 161.

Ivo of Chartres, *Prologue*, ed. and trans. Bruce C. Brasington, in *Preface to Canon Law Books in Latin Christianity*, ed. and trans. Robert Somerville and Bruce C. Brasington (New Haven:Yale University Press, 1998).

Jocelini de Brakelonde Cronica, ed.Thomas Arnold in *Memorials of St. Edmund's Abbey*, Rerum Britannicarum medii aevi scriptores, or, Chronicles and memorials of Great Britain and Ireland during the Middle Ages, in vol. 1 of 3 vols., no. 96 (London: H.M. Stationery Office, 1890–96). [*Jocelini de Brakelonde Cronica*]

Jocelini de Brakelond Cronica. The chronicle of Jocelin of Brakelond, concerning the acts of Samson, abbot of the monastery of St. Edmund, trans. with intro., notes, and appendices by H[arold].E[dgeworth]. Butler in *Memorials of St. Edmund's Abbey* (London-New York:Thomas Nelson & Son, 1949; New York: Oxford University Press, 1949). [*Jocelini de Brakelond Cronica*, trans. Butler].

John of Hexham. *Continuation of the* Historia Regum *of Symeon of Durham*, in *Symeon of Durham: Historical Works*, ed.T.Arnold, 2 vols., Rerum Britannicarum medii aevi scriptores 75 (London: H.M. Stationery Office, 1882–85). [John of Hexham, *Continuation*]

John of Salisbury. *The Historia Pontificalis of John of Salisbury*, ed. and trans. Marjorie Chibnall, Oxford Medieval texts 1 (London:Thomas Nelson, 1956; repr. Oxford: Clarendon Press, New York: Oxford University Press, 1986). [John of Salisbury, *Historia Pontificalis*]

———. *The Letters of John of Salisbury*, ed. and trans.W.J. Millor, Harold Edgeworth Butler, and C[hristopher]. N[ugent] L[awrence]. Brooke, vol. 2 (Oxford: Clarendon Press, 1979). [John of Salisbury, *Letters*]

Johannes de Oxenedes, *Chronica*, ed. Henry Ellis, Chronicles and Memorials of Great Britain and Ireland during the Middle Ages, no. 13 (London: Longman, Brown, Green, Longmans & Roberts, 1859).

Jordan Fantosme's Chronicle, ed. R[onald].C[arlyle]. Johnston (Oxford: Clarendon Press, 1981).

Joseph of Exeter. *Trojan War I-III*, ed. A[lan].K[eith]. Bates (Bristol: Bolchazy-Carducci;Warminster:Aris & Phillips;Atlantic Highlands, NJ: Humanities Press, 1986).

Lambert of Ardres, *Historia Comitum Ghisnensium*, ed. G.H. Pertz in MGH SS 24 (Hannover: A. Hahn, 1879; repr. New York: Kraus, 1963–65).

The Lancashire Pipe Rolls and Early Lancashire Charters, ed.William Farrer (Liverpool: H.Young and Sons, 1902). [*Lancashire Pipe Rolls*]

Laȝamon: Brut Edited from British Museum MS Cotton Caligula A.IX and British Museum MS. Cotton Otho C.xiii, ed. G[eorge].L[eslie]. Brook and R[oy].F[rancis]. Leslie, 2 vols. (London: Oxford University Press for EETS, 1963–78). [*Laȝamon*, ed. Brook and Leslie]

Laȝamon Brut or Hystoria Brutonum, ed. and trans. W[illiam].R.J. and S.C[arole].Weinberg (Essex-New York: Longman, 1995). [*Laȝamon Brut*, ed. Barron and Weinberg]

Layettes du Trésor des chartes, ed. Alexandre Teulet, 6 vols. (Paris: Imprimeries Impériale et Nationale, 1863–1909). [*Layettes*, ed. Teulet]

L'Épinois, Henri de. "Comptes relatifs à la fondation de l'abbaye de Maubuisson, d'après les originaux des archives de Versailles," *Bibliothèque de l'École des chartes* 19 (1858):550–69. [L'Épinois, "La fondation de Maubuisson"]

The Letters and Charters of Gilbert Foliot, ed. [Robert] A. Morey and C[hristopher].N[ugent].L[awrence]. Brooke (Cambridge: Cambridge University Press, 1965). [*Letters and Charters of Gilbert Foliot*]

Letters of the Queens of England, 1100–1547, ed. Anne Crawford (Stroud, UK/Dover, NH: Alan Sutton, 1994). [*Letters*, ed. Crawford]

The Life of St. Hugh of Lincoln, ed. Decima Longworthy Douie and Hugh Farmer, 2 vols., Medieval Texts (London: Thomas Nelson, 1961–62).

Llibre dels fets del Rei En Jaume, ed. Jordi Bruguera (Barcelona: Editorial Barcino, 1991). [*Llibre dels fet*]

Madox, Thomas, ed., *Formulare Anglicanum: or, A Collection of Ancient Charters and Instruments of Divers Kinds, Taken from the Originals, Placed under Several Heads, and Deduced (in a Series according to the Order of Time from the Norman Conquest, to the End of the Reign of King Henry the VIII* (London: Jacob Tonson and R. Knaplock, 1702). [Madox, *Formulare Anglicanum*]

Malory, Sir Thomas. *Works*, ed. Eugène Vinaver, 3rd. edn., rev. P[eter]. J.C. Field (Oxford: Clarendon Press, 1990).

Map, Walter. See Walter Map.

Marie de France. *Lais*, ed. Alfred Ewert (Oxford: Blackwell, 1947).

———. *Les Lais de Marie de France*, ed. Jean Rychner (Paris: Honoré Champion, 1966).

———. *The Lais of Marie de France*, trans. Robert Hanning and Joan Ferrante (Durham, NC: Labyrinth, 1987). [*Lais*, trans. Hanning and Ferrante]

———. *Lais*, ed. Karl Warnke (Paris: Le Livre de Poche, 1990). [*Lais*, ed. Warnke]

Materials for the History of Thomas Becket, ed. J[ames].C[raigie]. Robertson, 7 vols., Rerum Britannicarum medii aevi scriptores 67 (London: H.M. Stationery Office, 1875–85). [*Materials for Becket*, ed. Robertson]

Matthew Paris. *Chronica Majora*, ed. Henry Richard Luard, 7 vols., Rerum Britannicarum medii aevi scriptores 57 (London: H.M. Stationery Office, 1872–1884). [Matthew Paris, *Chronica Majora*]

The Memoranda Roll for the Michaelmas Term of the First year of the Reign of King John (1199–1200), ed. H[enry] G[erald]. Richardson, Publications of the Pipe Roll Society, 59, n.s. 21 (London: Pipe Roll Society, 1943). [*Memoranda Roll for the Michaelmas Term of the First year of the Reign of King John*]

Middle English Verse Romances, ed. Donald B. Sands (Exeter, UK: University of Exeter Press, 1986).

Migne, PL. See *Patrologiae cursus completus*.

Des Minnesangs Frühling, Nach Karl Lachmann, Moriz Haupt und Friedrich Vogt, ed. Carl von Kraus, 33 Aufläge (Stuttgart: Hirzel Verlag, 1962).

"The Miracles of St. Ithamar," ed. Denis Bethell, *Analecta Bollandiana* 89 (1971):421–37. ["Miracles of St. Ithamar"]

Monumenta Germaniae Historica. Electronic Monumenta Germaniae Historica [computer file]. Release 2. (Munich: Monumenta Germaniae Historica; Brepols: Turnhout, 1996-).

La Mort le roi Artu: roman du XIIIe siècle, ed. Jean Frappier, 3rd. edn. (Geneva: Droz; Paris: Minard, 1964).

Nova bibliotheca mss. librorum, ed. Philippe Labbe (Paris: Cramoisy, 1657).

Obituaires de la province de Sens, ed. Armand Boutillier du Retail and Pierre Piétresson de Saint-Aubin, vol. 4, *Diocèses de Meaux et de Troyes,* Receueil des historiens de la France (Paris: Imprimerie nationale, 1923). [*Obituaires de la province de Sens*]

Odo of Deuil. *De profectione Ludovici VII in Orientem,* ed. and trans. Virginia Gingerick Berry, Records of Civilization, Sources and Studies 42 (New York: Columbia University Press, 1948). [Odo of Deuil. *De profectione Ludovici VII*]

Orderic Vitalis. *Historia Æcclesiastica (The Ecclesiastical History of Orderic Vitalis).* Ed. and trans. Marjorie Chibnall, 6 vols, Oxford Medieval Texts (Oxford: Clarendon Press, 1969–80; repr. Oxford: Clarendon Press, and New York: Oxford University Press, 1990-). [Orderic Vitalis, *Historia Æcclesiastica*]

Ordines Coronationis Franciae: Texts and Ordines for the Coronation of Frankish and French Kings and Queens in the Middle Ages, ed. Richard A. Jackson, 2 vols. The Middle Ages Series (Philadelphia: University of Pennsylvania Press, 1995). [Jackson, *Ordines Coronationis Franciae*]

Patrologiae cursus completus. Series Latina, ed. J[acques].-P[aul]. Migne and A[dalbert].-G[autier]. Hamman, 221 vols. (Paris: Garnier, 1844–64). [Migne, PL]

Percy, Thomas. *Reliques of Ancient English Poetry: Consisting of Old Heroic Ballads, Songs, and other Pieces of our earlier Poets . . . Together with some few of later Date,* 3 vols. (London, 1765). [Percy, Thomas, *Reliques of Ancient English Poetry*]

Peter of Blois. *Petri Blesensis epistola,* in Migne PL, vol. 207.

Pierre Cochon. *Chronique normande,* ed. Charles de Robillard de Beaurepaire (Rouen: A. Le Brument, 1870). [Cochon, *Chronique normande*]

Les poèmes de Gaucelm Faidit, troubadour du XII siècle, ed. Jean Mouzat, Les classiques d'Oc (Paris: A.G. Nizet, 1965). [*Les poèmes de Gaucelm Faidit*]

Portugaliae Monumenta Historica: Leges et Consuetudines 1 (Lisbon: Typis Academicis, 1881; repr. Nedeln: Kraus, 1967). [*Portugaliae Monumenta Historica*]

La Queste del saint Graal: roman du XIIIe siècle, ed. Albert Pauphilet (Paris: Champion, 1923). [*Queste del saint Graal*]

RHF. See *Recueil des historiens des Gaules et de la France.*

RRAN. See *Regesta Regum Anglo Normannorum.*

Ralph of Coggeshall. *Radulfi de Coggeshall Chronicon Anglicanum,* ed. Joseph Stephenson, Rerum Britannicarum medii aevi scriptores 66 (London: H.M. Stationery Office, 1875). [Ralph of Coggeshall, *Chronicon Anglicanum*]

Ralph of Diss [Diceto]. *Radulfi de Diceto decani Lundoniensis Opera Historica,* ed. William Stubbs, 2 vols., Rerum Britannicarum medii aevi scriptores 68 (London: H.M. Stationery Office, 1876). [Ralph of Diss, *Opera Historica*]

Reading Abbey Cartularies, ed. Brian R. Kemp, 2 vols. (London: The Royal Historical Society, 1986–87). [*Reading Abbey Cartularies*]

Récits d'un Ménestrel de Reims au treizième siècle, ed. Natalis de Wailly (Paris: Renouard, 1876). [*Récits d'un Ménestrel de Reims*]

Records of the Templars in England in the Twelfth Century, ed. B[eatrice].A[cklin]. Lees (London: Oxford University Press, for the British Academy, 1935). [*Records of the Templars in England*]

Recueil d'annales angevines et vendômoises. Annales de Saint-Aubin, ed. Louis Halphen, Collection de textes pour servir à l'étude et à l'enseignement de l'histoire 37 (Paris: A. Picard, 1903). [*Recueil d'annales angevines et vendômoises*]

"Recueil de documents concernant la commune et la ville de Poitiers," ed. Edouard Audouin, *Archives historiques du Poitou* 44 (1923):49–52. ["Recueil de documents concernant la commune et la ville de Poitiers"]

"Recueil des documents de l'abbaye de Fontaine-le-Comte (XIIᵉ-XIIIᵉ s.)," ed. Georges Pon, *Archives historiques du Poitou* 61 (1982). [Pon, "Fontaine-le-Comte"]

Recueil des actes de Henri II, roi d'Angleterre et duc de Normandie, concernant les provinces françaises et les affaires de France, ed. Léopold Delisle and Élie Berger, 4 vols., Chartes et diplômes relatifs à l'histoire de France, 4, 7.1–3 (Paris: Imprimerie nationale, Librairie C. Klincksieck, 1909–27). [*Recueil des actes de Henri II*]

Recueil des actes de Lothaire et de Louis V, rois de France (954–87), ed. H. d'Arbois de Jubainville, Louis Halphen and Ferdinand Lot, Chartes et diplômes relatifs à l'histoire de France (Paris: Imprimerie nationale, Librairie C. Klincksieck, 1908). [*Recueil des actes de Lothaire*]

Recueil des chartes de l'abbaye royale de Montmartre, ed. Édouard de Barthélemy (Paris: H. Champion, 1883). [*Recueil des chartes de l'abbaye royale de Montmartre*]

"Recueil des documents de l'abbaye de Fontaine-le-Comte (XIIᵉ-XIIIᵉ s.)," ed. Georges Pon, *Archives historiques du Poitou* 61 (1982). [Pon, "Fontaine-le-Comte"]

"Recueil des documents relatifs à l'abbaye de Montierneuf de Poitiers," ed. François Villard, *Archives historiques du Poitou* 59 (1973). ["Recueil des documents relatifs à l'abbaye de Montierneuf de Poitiers"]

Recueil des historiens des croisades. Historiens occidentaux, 5 vols. (Paris: Imprimerie royale, Académie des Inscriptions et Belles-Lettres, 1844 95; repr. Farnborough, UK: Gregg, 1967).

Recueil des historiens des Gaules et de la France [RHF], ed. Martin Bouquet et al., 24 vols. (Paris: Aux dépens des libraires associés, 1738–1904; repr. Paris: Victor Palmé, 1869–1904). [RHF]

Regesta Regum Anglo Normannorum [RRAN], ed. Charles Johnson, Henry W.C. Davis, R[obert].J[owitt].Whitwell, Henry A. Cronne, and Ralph Henry Carless Davis, 4 vols. (Oxford: Clarendon Press, 1913–69). [RRAN]

Répertoire des documents nécrologiques français, 2, ed. Jean-Loup Lemaître, Recueil des Historiens de la France publié par l'Académie des Inscriptions et Belles-Lettres, Obituaires 7 (Paris: Imperimerie Nationale, 1980). [*Répertoire,* ed. Lemaître]

Richard Coeur de Lion, ed. Karl Brunner, *Die Mittellenglische Versroman Über Richard Löwenherz*, Wiener Beiträge zur Englische Philologie 42 (Vienna and Leipzig: Wilhelm Braumüller, 1913). [*Richard Coeur de Lion*, ed. Brunner]

Richard of Devizes [Devises]. *Chronicon Ricardi Divisensis de Tempore Regis Ricardi Primi. The Chronicle of Richard of Devizes of the Time of King Richard the First*, ed. and trans. John T. Appleby, Nelson's Medieval Texts (London: Thomas Nelson, 1963). [Richard of Devizes, *Chronicon*]

Richard, Prior of Hexham. *Chronicle*, ed. Richard Howlett in vol. 3 of *Chronicles of the Reigns of Stephen, Henry II and Richard I*. [Richard of Hexham, *Chronicle*]

Richer. *Historia*, ed. Robert Latouche as *Histoire de France (888–995)*, 2 vols. (Paris: H. Champion, 1930–37). [Richer, *Historia*, ed. Latouche]

Robert of Gloucester. *Robert of Gloucester's Chronicle*, ed. Thomas Hearne, in *The Works of Thomas Hearne, M.A.*, 2 vols. (1724; repr. London: S. Bagster, 1810). [Robert of Gloucester, *Chronicle*]

Robert of Torigni. [Torigny]. *Chronique de Robert de Torigni*, ed. Léopold Delisle, 2 vols., Société de l'Histoire de Normandie, Publications 3 (Rouen: Brumont, 1872–73). [Torigni, *Chronique*]

———. *Chronica Roberti de Torigneio, Abbatis Monasterii Sancti Michaelis in Periculo Maris*, ed. Richard Howlett in vol. 4 of *Chronicles of the Reigns of Stephen, Henry II, and Richard I*. [Torigni, *Chronica*, ed. Howlett]

Rodrigo Jiménez de Rada. *Historia de rebus hispanie sive historia Gothica*, ed. Juan Fernandez Valverde (Turnhout: Brepols, 1987). [Rodrigo Jiménez de Rada, *De rebus hispanie*]

Rodulfus Glaber. *Rodulfi Glaber Historiarum Libri Quinque. The Five Books of the Histories*, ed. and trans. John France (Oxford: Clarendon Press; New York: Oxford University Press, 1989). [Glaber, *Five Books of Histories*]

Roger of Howden. *Chronica magistri Rogeri de Houeden*, ed. William Stubbs, 4 vols., Rerum Britannicarum medii aevi scriptores 51 (London: H.M. Stationery Office, 1868–71). [Howden, *Chronica*]

———. *Gesta Ricardi*, ed. Stubbs, in vol. 2 of *Gesta Regis Henrici Secundi*. [Roger of Howden, *Gesta Ricardi*]

Roger of Wendover. *Liber qui dicitur Flores Historiarum*, ed. Henry G[ay]. Hewlett, 3 vols., Rerum Britannicarum medii aevi scriptores 84 (London: H.M. Stationery Office, 1886–89). [Roger of Wendover, *Flores Historiarum*]

Le Roman de Mélusine ou Histoire de Lusignan par Coudrette, ed. Eleanor Roach (Paris: C. Klincksieck, 1982). [*Roman de Mélusine*]

Le roman des sept sages de Rome: A Critical Edition of the Two Verse Redactions of a Twelfth-Century Romance, ed. Mary Blakely Speer (Lexington, KY: French Forum, 1989). [*Le roman des sept sages de Roms*] Also see *Deux rédactions du roman des sept sages de Rome*, ed. Gaston Paris (Paris: Firmin Didot, 1876).

Rotuli Chartarum in Turri Londoniensi Asservati, ed. Thomas Duffus Hardy, vol. 1. part 1, *Ab Anno MCXCIX ad Annum MCCXVI* (London: Eyre and Spottiswoode, for H.M. Record Commissioners, 1837). [*Rotuli Chartarum*]

Rotuli de Dominabus et Pueris et Puellis de XII comitatibus <1185>, ed. John Horace Round, Pipe Roll 35 (London: Publications of the Pipe Roll Society, published for the Society by St. Catherine Press, 1913).

Rotuli Litterarum Patentium, ed. T. Duffus Hardy (London: H.M. Record Commissioners, 1835). [*Rotuli Litterarum Patentium*]

Royal Writs in England from the Conquest to Glanvill, ed. R[aoul].C. van Caenegem, Selden Society Publications, 77 (London: The Selden Society, 1959). [Caeneghem, *Royal Writs*]

S. Bernardi Vita Secunda, in Migne, PL 185.

Sacrorum Conciliorum Nova et Amplissima Collectio, ed. Joannes Dominus Mansi, 54 vols. in 60 (Paris: H. Welter, 1960–61). [*Sacrorum Conciliorum*, ed. Mansi]

"Saint-Eutrope et son prieuré," ed. Louis Audiat, *Archives historiques de la Saintonge et de l'Aunis* 2 (1877). [Audiat, "Saint-Eutrope et son prieuré"]

Saladin: Suite et fin du deuxième cycle de la croisade, ed. Larry Stuart Crist (Geneva: Droz, 1972). [*Saladin*, ed. Crist]

Sir Christopher Hatton's Book of Seals, ed. Lewis C. Lloyd and Doris Mary Stenton (Oxford: Clarendon Press, 1950). [*Sir Christopher Hatton's Book of Seals*]

Statuta capitulorum generalium ordinis cisterciensis ab anno 1116 ad annum 1786, ed. J.-M. Canivez, 8 vols. (Louvain: Bureaux de la Revue, 1933). [*Statuta capitulorum generalium*]

Suger, Abbot of St.-Denis. *Abbot Suger on the Abbey Church of St.-Denis and its Art Treasures*, ed. and trans. Erwin Panofsky, 2nd edn. (Princeton: Princeton University Press, 1979). [*Abbot Suger on St.-Denis*, ed. Panofsky]

———. *Epistolae*, in Migne, PL, vol. 186. [Suger, *Epistolae*]

———. *Œuvres*, in *Écrits sur la consécration de Saint-Denis ; L'oeuvre administrative de l'abbé Suger de Saint-Denis; Histoire de Louis VII*, ed. Françoise Gasparri, Les classiques series de l'histoire de France au Moyen Age 37 (Paris: les Belles Lettres, 1996). [Suger, *Œuvres*, ed. Gasparri]

———. *Œuvres complètes de Suger, recueillies, annotées et publiées d'après les manuscrits pour la Société de l'histoire de France*, ed. Albert Lecoy de la Marche, Société de l'Histoire de France, Publications in octavo, 139 (Paris: Veuve J. Renouard, 1867) [Suger, *Œuvres complètes*]

———. *Vie de Louis VI le Gros par Suger suivie de l'histoire de Louis VII*, ed. Auguste Molinier (Paris: A. Picard, 1887). [Suger, *Vie de Louis VI le Gros*, ed. Molinier]

———. *Vie de Louis VI le Gros*, ed. Henri Waquet, Les classiques de l'histoire de France au moyen âge (Paris: H. Champion, 1929, repr. 1964), trans. Richard Cusimano and John Moorhead as *The Deeds of Louis the Fat* (Washington, D.C.: Catholic University of America Press, 1992). [Suger, *Vie de Louis VI le Gros*]

"Tabula Ottonorum," MGH SS 3:215.

Thietmar of Merseburg, *Chronicon* 4.38, MGH SS 3:785.

Three Coronation Orders, ed. Johane G. Wickham Legg, Henry Bradshaw Society 19 (London: Harrision and Sons, 1900).

Torigni. [Torigny]. See Robert of Torigni. [Torigny].

Vic, Claude de and Jean-Joseph Vaissete. *Histoire générale de Languedoc avec des notes et les pièces justificatives,* ed. Auguste Molinier, 2nd. edn., 15 vols. (Toulouse: E. Privat, 1872–92). [*Histoire générale de Languedoc*]

Vincent, Nicholas. "Six New Charters of King Stephen: The Royal Forest During the Anarchy," *English Historical Review* 114 (1998):899–928.

Vitae Henrici et Cunegundis Imperatorum, ed. Georg Waitz, MGH SS 4 (Hannover: Hahn, 1841).

Vita Sancti Bernardi, in Bouquet, RHF 14. [*Vita Sancti Bernardi*]

Wace. *Roman de Rou,* ed. A.J. Holden, 3 vols. Société des anciens textes français (Paris: A. and J. Picard, 1970).

———. *Wace's Roman de Brut A History of the British: Text and Translation,* ed. and trans. Judith Weiss (Exeter: University of Exeter Press, 1999). [Wace, *Roman de Brut,* ed. Weiss]

Walter of Coventry. *Memoriale Fratris Walteri de Coventria,* ed. William Stubbs, 2 vols., Rerum Britannicarum medii aevi scriptores 58 (London: H.M. Stationery Office, 1872; repr. Wiesbaden: Kraus, 1965). [Walter of Coventry, *Memoriale*]

Walter Map. *De nugis curialium: Courtiers' Trifles,* ed. and trans. Montague Rhodes James, rev. ed. C[hristopher]. N[ugent] L[awrence]. Brooke and Roger Aubrey Baskerville Mynors (Oxford: Clarendon Press; New York: Oxford University Press, 1983). [Walter Map, *De nugis curialium*]

Waltham Abbey, ed. Ransford. See *The Early Charters of the Augustinian Canons of Waltham Abbey, Essex (1062–1230).*

William IX, duke of Aquitaine, *Les chansons de Guillaume IX, duc d'Aquitaine (1071–1127),* ed. Alfred Jeanroy (Paris: H. Champion, 1913). [*Les chansons de Guillaume IX*]

William of Malmesbury. *Willelmi Malmesbiriensis monachi De gestis regum Anglorum libri quinque; Historiæ novellæ libri tres,* ed. William Stubbs, 2 vols., Rerum Britannicarum medii aevi scriptores 90 (London: H.M. Stationery Office, 1887–80; repr. [Wiesbaden]: Kraus, 1964). [Malmesbury, *De gestis regum anglorum*]

———. *Historia Novella,* ed. and trans. Kenneth R[eginald]. Potter (London: Thomas Nelson, 1955). [Malmesbury. *Historia Novella*]

William of Newburgh. *Historia rerum anglicarum,* ed. Richard Howlett in vol. 1 of *Chronicles of the Reigns of Stephen, Henry II and Richard I.* [William of Newburgh. *Historia rerum anglicarum*]

———. *The History of English Affairs,* ed. and trans. P[atrick].G[erald]. Walsh and M.J. Kennedy (Wiltshire: Aris and Phillips Ltd., 1988). [William of Newburgh, *History of English Affairs*]

William of St.-Denis. *Vita Sugerii,* in RHF, vol. 12.

William [Archbishop] of Tyre. *Historia rerum in partibus transmarinis gestarum,* in *Recueil des historiens des croisades. Historiens occidentaux,* vol. 1 (Paris: Imprimerie Royale, 1844). [William of Tyre, *Historia rerum*]

———. *A History of Deeds Done Beyond the Sea,* trans. Emily Atwater Babcock and A.C. Krey, 2 vols. (New York: Columbia University Press, 1943). [William of Tyre, *Deeds Done Beyond the Sea*]

————. *Chronique*, ed. R.B.C. Huygens with dating by H.W. Maher and Gerhard Rösch, 2 vols. (Turnhout: Brepols, 1986). [William of Tyre, *Chronique*]

Secondary Works

Abbot Suger and Saint-Denis: A Symposium, ed. Paula Lieber Gerson (New York: The Metropolitan Museum of Art, 1986). [*Abbot Suger and Saint-Denis*, ed. Gerson]

Abulafia, David. *Frederick II. A Medieval Emperor* (London: Allen Lane, 1988).

Abu-Lughod, Lila. "The Romance of Resistance: Tracing Transformations of Power Through Bedouin Women," in *Beyond the Second Sex*, ed. Sanday and Goodenoughr, pp. 311–38.

Acton, Harold. *The Last Medicis*, rev. ed. (London: Methuen, 1958).

Adair, Penny. "Constance of Arles," forthcoming in *Capetian Women*, ed. Parsons and Nolan.

Adhémar, Jean, et al. "Les tombeaux de la Collection Gaignières: dessins d'archéologie du XVIIe siècle," *Gazette des Beaux-Arts*, 6th per., 116th year, vol. 84 (July–September 1974); 6th per., 118th year, vol. 88 (July–August 1976); 6th per., 119th year, vol. 90 (July–August 1977). [Adhémar et al., "Les tombeaux"]

Age of Chivalry: Art in Plantagenet England 1200–1400, exhibition catalogue, ed. Jonathan Alexander and Paul Binski (London: Royal Academy of Arts, 1987). [*Age of Chivalry*]

Airlie, Stuart. "Private Bodies and the Body Politic in the Divorce Case of Lothar II," *Past and Present* 161 (1988):3–38.

Alexander, James W. "Medieval Biography: Clio Lo Volt," *The Historian* 35 (1973):355–64.

The Anarchy of Stephen's Reign, ed. Edmund King (Oxford-New York: Clarendon Press at Oxford University Press, 1994).

Anglo-Norman Political Culture and the Twelfth-Century Renaissance, ed. C. Warren Hollister (Woodbridge: Boydell and Brewer, 1997).

Appleby, John T. *England without Richard, 1189–1199* (Ithaca: Cornell University Press, 1965). [Appleby, *England without Richard*]

Arbellot, François. "Étude historique et bibliographique sur Geoffroy de Vigeois," *Bulletin de la Société archéologique et historique du Limousin*, 2nd ser. 14, vol. 36 (1888):135–61. [Arbellot, "Étude sur Geoffroy de Vigeois."]

Ariès, Philippe. *L'Homme devant la mort* (Paris: Editions du Seuil, 1977); trans. Helen Weaver as *The Hour of Our Death* (London-New York: Oxford University Press, 1981). [Ariès, *L'Homme devant la mort*]

Aristocratic Women in Medieval France, ed. Theodore Evergates (Philadelphia: University of Pennsylvania Press, 1999). [*Aristocratic Women*, ed. Evergates]

The Art of Medieval Spain, A.D. 500–1200, Exhibition Catalogue (New York: The Metropolitan Museum of Art, 1993).

Aubert, Marcel. *Suger, Figures monastiques* (Fontenelle: Abbaye Saint-Wandrille, 1950).

Audin, Maurice. *Les chartes communales de Poitiers et les établissements de Rouen* (Paris, 1913).

Audoin, Edouard. "La commune et la ville de Poitiers (1063–1327)," *Archives historiques du Poitou* 44 [1923]. [Audoin, "Poitiers"]

Aurell, Martin. "Aliénor d'Aquitaine (1124–1204) et ses historiens: la destruction d'un mythe?" in *Guerre, pouvoir et noblesse au Moyen Age. Mélanges en l'honneur de Philippe Contamine,* ed. Jacques Paviot and Jacques Verger (Paris: Presses de l'Université de Paris-Sorbonne, 2001), pp. 43–49. [Aurell, "Aliénor d'Aquitaine et ses historiens"]

———. "Richard Coeur de Lion, le roi chevalier," *L'Histoire* 230 (March 1999): 62–67. [Aurell, "Richard Coeur de Lion."]

Auteur, Hillary (aka Ted Gottfried). *The Scarlet Raptures of Eleanor of Aquitaine,* The Courtesans Series (New York: Pinnacle, 1984).

Auvry, Claude. *Histoire de la Congrégation de Savigny,* 3 vols., Publications de la Société de l'Histoire de Normandie (Paris: A. Lestringant, A. Picard et fils, 1869–99). [Auvry, *Histoire de la Congrégation de Savigny*]

Baccque, Antoine de. *The Body Politic: Corporeal Metaphor in Revolutionary France, 1770–1800,* trans. Charlotte Mandel (Stanford, CA: Stanford University Press, 1993). [Baccque, *Body Politic*]

Bachrach, Bernard S. *Fulk Nerra, the Neo-Roman Consul, 987–1040: A Political Biography of the Angevin Count* (Berkeley-Los Angeles: University of California Press, 1993). [Bachrach, *Fulk Nerra*]

Bak, János M. "Queens as Scapegoats in Medieval Hungary," in *Queens and Queenship in Medieval Europe,* ed. Duggan, pp. 223–33.

Baldwin, John W. *The Government of Philip Augustus: The Beginnings of French Royal Power in the Middle Ages* (Berkeley: University of California Press, 1986). [Baldwin, *Philip Augustus*]

———. *Masters, Princes, and Merchants: The Social Views of Peter the Chanter and His Circle,* 2 vols. (Princeton: Princeton University Press, 1970). [Baldwin, *Masters, Princes, and Merchants*]

Bardonnet, A[uguste], "Les comptes et enquêtes d'Alphonse, comte de Poitou (1253–1269)," *Archives historiques du Poitou* 8 (1879).

Barlow, Frank. *Thomas Becket* (London: Weidenfeld and Nicolson, 1986).

———. *William Rufus* (Berkeley-Los Angeles: University of California Press, 1983).

Barnes, Patricia M. "The Anstey Case," in *A Medieval Miscellany for Doris M. Stenton,* ed. P.M. Barnes and C.F. Slade (London: Pipe Roll Society, 1962), pp. 1–24. [Barnes, "The Anstey Case"]

Barrière, Bernadette. "Le Limousin et Limoges au temps de l'émail champlevé," in *L'œuvre de Limoges: émaux limousins du Moyen Âge,* exhibition catalogue, Musée du Louvre, Metropolitan Museum of Art (Paris: Réunion des musées nationaux, 1995), pp. 22–29. [Barrière, "Le Limousin et Limoges au temps de l'émail champlevé"]

Barron, W[illiam].R.J. and S.C[arole]. Weinberg. "Introduction." *Laʒamon's Brut or Hystoria Brutunum* (Essex-New York: Longman, 1995), pp. ix-xxi.

Barthélemy, Dominique. "Note sur le '*maritagium*' dans le grand Anjou des XIᵉ et XIIᵉ siècles," in *Femmes, mariages, lignages (XIIᵉ-XIVᵉ siècles): Mélanges offerts en hommage à Georges Duby,* Bibliothèque du Moyen Age, 1 (Brussels: De Boeck-Université, 1992), pp. 9–24. [Barthélemy, "Note sur le *maritagium*"]

Bartlett, Robert. *The Making of Europe: Conquest, Colonization and Cultural Change 950–1350* (Princeton: Princeton University Press, 1993). [Bartlett, *Making of Europe*]

Bascher, Jacques de. "Robert d'Arbrissel, Bernard de Tiron, Vital de Savigny, Raoul de la Futaie et l'expansion érémitique de Fontgombault (11e–12e siècles)," *La Province du Maine* 85 (1993):121–38. [Bascher, "Robert d'Arbrissel"]

Bates, David. "The Origins of the Justiciarship," *Anglo-Norman Studies* 4 (1981):1–12. [Bates, "Origins of the Justiciarship"]

———. *William the Conqueror* (London: Philip, 1989).

Baumgartner, Emmanuèle. "La Très Belle Ville de Troie de Benoît de Sainte-Maure," in *Hommage à Jean-Charles Payen: farai chansoneta novele. Essais sur la liberté créatrice au Moyen Âge* (Caen: Centre de Publications de l'Université de Caen, 1989), pp. 47–52. [Baumgartner, "La Très Belle Ville de Troie"]

———. "Repères," intro. to *Le Roman de Troie par Benoît de Sainte-Maure*, ed. and trans. Baumgartner (Paris: Union Générale d'éditions, 1987), pp. 11–31. [Baumgartner, "Repères"]

Bautier, Robert-Henri. *Chartes, sceaux, et chancelleries. Études de diplomatique et de sigillographie médiévales*, 2 vols., Mémoires et documents de l'École des chartes, 34 (Paris: École des chartes, 1990). [Bautier, *Chartes, sceaux, et chancelleries*]

———. "Échanges d'influences dans les chancelleries souveraines du Moyen Âge d'après les types de sceaux de majesté," *Académie des Inscriptions et Belles-Lettres, comptes rendus des séances de l'année 1968 (avril-juin)*, pp. 192–220; repr. in Bautier, *Chartes, sceaux et chancelleries*, 2:563–92. [Bautier, "Échanges d'influences"]

———. "Empire Plantagenêt *ou* espace Plantagenêt? Y eut-il une civilisation du monde Plantagenêt?," *Cahiers de civilisation médiévale* 1–2 (1986):139–47. [Bautier, "Empire Plantagenêt ou espace Plantagenêt?"]

Becquet, Jean. "La vie religieuse en Limousin aux XIIe et XIIIe siècles," in *L'oeuvre de Limoges: émaux limousins du Moyen Âge*, exhibition catalogue, Musée du Louvre and the Metropolitan Museum of Art (Paris: Réunion des musées nationaux, 1995), pp. 30–32. [Becquet, "La vie religieuse en Limousin"]

Bedos Rezak [also published as Bedos-Rezak], Brigitte. *Form and Order in Medieval France: Studies in Social and Quantitative Sigillography*, Variorum Collected Studies Series 424. (Aldershot: Variorum, 1993). [Bedos-Rezak, *Form and Order in Medieval France*]

———. "The King Enthroned, a New Theme in Anglo-Saxon Royal Iconography: The Seal of Edward the Confessor and its Political Implications," in *Kings and Kingship*, ed. Rosenthal, pp. 53–88; repr. as no. IV in Bedos-Rezak, *Form and Order in Medieval France*. [Bedos-Rezak, "The King Enthroned"]

———. "Medieval Women in French Sigillographic Sources," in *Medieval Women and the Sources of Medieval History*, ed. Rosenthal, pp. 1–36; repr. as no. X in Bedos-Rezak, *Form and Order in Medieval France*. [Bedos-Rezak, "Medieval Women"]

———. "Women, Seals, and Power in Medieval France, 1150–1350," In *Women and Power in the Middle Ages*, ed. Erler and Kowaleski, pp. 61–82; repr. as no. IX in Bedos-Rezak, *Form and Order in Medieval France*. [Bedos Rezak, "Women, Seals"]

Beech, George T. "The Eleanor of Aquitaine Vase: Its Origins and Its History to the Early Twelfth Century," *Ars Orientalis* 22 (1994):69–79. [Beech, "Eleanor Vase: Its Origins"]

———. "The Eleanor of Aquitaine Vase, William IX of Aquitaine, and Muslim Spain," *Gesta* 32.1 (1993):3–10. [Beech, "Eleanor Vase"]

———. "The 'Eleanor Vase': Witness to Christian-Muslim Collaboration in Early Twelfth-Century Spain," *Medieval Life: A New Magazine of the Middle Ages* 3 (1995):12–16. [Beech, "The 'Eleanor Vase': Witness"]

Beitscher, Jane. "'As the Twig is Bent . . .': Children and Their Parents in an Aristocratic Society," *Journal of Medieval History* 2 (1976):181–91.

Bell, Susan Groag. "Medieval Women Book Owners: Arbiters of Lay Piety and Ambassadors of Culture," *Signs* 7 (1982):742–68; repr. in *Women and Power in the Middle Ages,* ed. Erler and Kowaleski, 1988), pp. 149–87, and in *Sisters and Workers in the Middle Ages,* ed. Bennett, Clark, O'Barr, Vilen, and Westphal-Wihl, pp. 135–161. [Bell, "Medieval Women Book Owners"]

Belloc, Hillaire. *Marie Antoinette* (London: G.P. Putnam's Sons, 1909).

Belperron, Pierre. *La "joie d'amour," contribution à l'étude des troubadours et de l'amour courtois* (Paris: Plon, 1948). [Belperron, *La "joie d'amour"*]

Bennett, Judith M. "Confronting Continuity," *Journal of Women's History* 9 (1997): 73–94. [Bennett, "Confronting Continuity"]

Benton, John F. "The Court of Champagne as a Literary Center," *Speculum* 36 (1961):551–91; repr. in *Culture, Power and Personality in Medieval France,* ed. Bisson, pp. 3–43. [Benton, "The Court of Champagne"]

Berger, Élie. *Histoire de Blanche de Castille, reine de France,* Bibliothèque des Écoles françaises d'Athènes et de Rome 70 (Paris: Thorin et fils, 1895). [Berger, *Blanche de Castille*]

———. "La formule 'Rex Francorum et dux Aquitanorum' dans les actes de Louis VII," *Bibliothèque de l'École des chartes* 45 (1884):305–13. [Berger, "La formule 'Rex Francorum'"]

Berman, Constance. "Abbeys for Cistercian Nuns in the Ecclesiastical Province of Sens. Foundation, Endowment and Economic Activities of the Earlier Foundations," *Revue Mabillon* 73 (1997):83–113. [Berman, "Abbeys for Cistercian Nuns"]

———. *The Cistercian Evolution. The Invention of a Religious Order in Twelfth-Century Europe* (Philadelphia: University of Pennsylvania Press, 2000). [Berman, *The Cistercian Evolution*]

———. "How Much Space Did Medieval Nuns Need?" in *Shaping Community,* ed. McNally, pp. 100–116.

———. "The Labors of Hercules, the Cartulary, Church and Abbey for Nuns of La-Cour-Notre-Dame-de-Michery," *Journal of Medieval History* 50 (1991):30–70. [Berman, "The Labors of Hercules"]

Bernard of Clairvaux, *Bernard de Clairvaux: Histoire, Mentalités, Spiritualité,* Colloque de Lyon-Cîteaux-Dijon, Sources chrétiennes 380 (Paris: Éditions du Cerf, 1992).

Bernier, Olivier. *Secrets of Marie Antoinette* (Garden City, NY: Doubleday, 1985).

————. *Words of Fire, Deeds of Blood: The Mob, The Monarchy and The French Revolution* (Boston: Little, Brown and Company, 1989).

Berry, André. *Florilège des troubadours* (Paris: Firmin-Didot, 1930).

Berry, Virginia G. "The Second Crusade," in *The First Hundred Years*, ed. Marshall W. Baldwin, vol. 1 of *A History of the Crusades*, gen. ed. Kenneth M. Setton, pp. 463–512. [Berry, "The Second Crusade"]

Between the Living and the Dead: Strategies for Commemoration in the Middle Ages, ed. Elizabeth Valdez del Alamo and Carole Pendergast (Aldershot, UK: Ashgate Press, 1999).

Beyond the Second Sex: New Directions in the Anthropology of Gender, ed. Peggy Reeves Sanday and Ruth Gallagher Goodenough (Philadelphia: University of Pennsylvania Press, 1990).

Bezzola, Reto R[adoulf]. *Les origines et la formation de la littérature courtoise en Occident (500–1200)*, 3 vols., Bibliothèque de l'École des Hautes Études, Sciences historiques et philologiques 286, 313, 319–320 (Paris, É. Champion, 1944–1963). Vol. 2, *La société féodale et la transformation de la littérature de cour*, part 2 of *Les grandes maisons féodales après la chute des Carolingiens et leur influence sur les lettres jusqu'au XIIe siècle*, Paris: H. Champion, 1960). [Bezzola, *Origines*]

Bhabha, Homi K. *The Location of Culture* (New York: Routledge, 1994).

Biddle, Martin. "Seasonal Festivals and Residence: Winchester, Westminster and Gloucester in the Tenth to Twelfth Centuries," *Anglo-Norman Studies* 8 (1986):51–63. [Biddle, "Seasonal Festivals"]

Bienvenu, Jean-Marc. "Aliénor d'Aquitaine et Fontevraud," *Cahiers de civilisation médiévale* 29 (1986):15–27. [Bienvenu, "Aliénor et Fontevraud"]

————. *L'étonnant fondateur de Fontevrault: Robert d'Arbrissel* (Paris: Nouvelles Éditions Latines, 1981). [Bienvenu, *Robert d'Arbrissel*]

Binski, Paul. *Medieval Death: Ritual and Representation* (Ithaca: Cornell University Press, 1996). [Binski, *Medieval Death*]

————. *Westminster Abbey and the Plantagenets: Kingship and the Representation of Power 1200–1400* (New Haven, CT: Yale University Press for the Paul Mellon Centre for Studies in British Art, 1995). [Binski, *Westminster Abbey*]

Birch, Walter de Gray. "A Fasciculus of the Charters of Mathildis, Empress of the Romans, and an Account of her Great Seal," *Journal of the British Archaeological Association* 31 (1875):376–98. [Birch, "A Fasciculus of the Charters of Mathildis"]

————. *Catalogue of Seals in the Department of Manuscripts in the British Museum*, 6 vols. (London: British Museum, 1887–1900). [Birch, *Catalogue of Seals in the British Museum*]

Birns, Nicholas. "The Trojan Myth: Postmodern Reverberations," *Exemplaria* 5.1 (March 1993):45–78.

Bisson, Thomas N. *The Medieval Crown of Aragon: A Short History* (Oxford: Clarendon Press, 1986). [Bisson, *Crown of Aragon*]

Black, Antony. *Political Thought in Europe, 1250–1450*, Cambridge Medieval Textbooks (Cambridge: Cambridge University Press, 1992).

Blackburn, M[ark]. "Coinage and Currency," in *The Anarchy of Stephen's Reign,* ed. Edmund King, pp. 145–206. [Blackburn, "Coinage and Currency"]

Bloch, Marc. *La société féodale* (Paris: Albin Michel, 1939; repr. Paris: Bibliothèque de l'Humanité, 1994). [Bloch, *La société féodale*]

Bloch, Maurice. "Death, Women, and Power," in *Death and the Regeneration of Life,* ed. Maurice Bloch and Jonathan Parry (Cambridge, UK: Cambridge University Press, 1982), pp. 211–30.

Bloch, R. Howard. *Etymologies and Genealogies: A Literary Anthropology of the French Middle Ages* (Chicago: University of Chicago Press, 1983). [Bloch, *Etymologies and Genealogies*]

———. "The Lay and the Law: Sexual/Textual Transgression in *La Chastelaine de Vergi, the Lai d'Ignaure,* and the *Lais* of Marie de France," *Stanford French Review* 14 (1990):181–210.

———. *Medieval Misogyny and the Invention of Western Romantic Love* (Chicago: University of Chicago Press, 1991). [Bloch, *Medieval Misogyny*]

———. "The Medieval Text-'Guigemar'-As a Provocation to the Discipline of Medieval Studies," in *The New Medievalism,* ed. Brownlee, Brownlee, and Nichols, pp. 100–12.

Blomme, Yves. *Poitou gothique* (Paris: Picard, 1993).

Boase, Thomas S.R. "Fontevrault and the Plantagenets," *Journal of the British Archaeological Association,* 3rd ser. 34 (1971):1–10. [Boase, "Fontevrault and the Plantagenets"]

Boaventura, San. *Historia chronologica, e critica da Real Abbadia de Alcobaça* (Lisbon: Impresao Regia, 1827). [Boaventura, *Abbadia de Alcobaça*]

Boehm, Barbara Drake. "*Opus lemovicense.* La diffusion des émaux limousins," in *L'oeuvre de Limoges: émaux limousins du Moyen Âge,* exhibition catalogue, Musée du Louvre and the Metropolitan Museum of Art (Paris: Réunion des musées nationaux, 1995), pp. 40–47. [Boehm, "*Opus lemovicense.* La diffusion des émaux limousins"]

Boissonnade, Pierre. "Administrateurs laïques et ecclésiastiques anglo-normands en Poitou à l'époque d'Henri II Plantagenêt," *Bulletin de la Société des antiquaires de l'Ouest* 3rd ser. 5 (1919):156–90. [Boissonnade, "Administrateurs laïques"]

Bondéelle-Souchier, Anne. "Les moniales cisterciennes et leurs livres manuscrits dans la France d'ancien régime," *Cîteaux* 45 (1994):193–336. [Bondéelle-Souchier, "Les moniales cisterciennes et leurs livres manuscrits"]

Bonis, Armelle. *Abbaye cistercienne de Maubuisson* (Pontoise, 1990). [Bonis, *Maubuisson*]

Bonnard, Jean. *Les traductions de la Bible en vers français au moyen âge* (Paris: Imprimerie Nationale, 1884).

Bonnardot, Hippolyte. *L'abbaye royale de Saint-Antoine-des-Champs de l'Ordre de Cîteaux. Étude topographique et historique* (Paris: Letouzey, 1882). [Bonnardot, *L'Abbaye royale de Saint-Antoine-des-Champs*]

Bouchard, Constance Brittain. "Consanguinity and Noble Marriages in the Tenth and Eleventh Centuries," *Speculum* 56 (1981):269–71. [Bouchard, "Consanguinity"]

————. "The Migration of Women's Names in the Upper Nobility, Ninth-Twelfth Centuries," *Medieval Prosopography* 9.2 (1988):1–19. [Bouchard, "Migration of Women's Names"]

————. "Patterns of Women's Names in Royal Lineages, Ninth-Eleventh Centuries," *Medieval Prosopography* 9.1 (1988):1–32. [Bouchard, "Patterns of Women's Names"]

————. *"Strong of Body, Brave and Noble": Chivalry and Society in Medieval France* (Ithaca: Cornell University Press, 1998). [Bouchard, *"Strong of Body, Brave and Noble"*]

————. *Sword, Miter and Cloister: Nobility and the Church in Burgundy, 980–1198* (Ithaca: Cornell University Press, 1987). [Bouchard, *Sword, Miter and Cloister*]

————. *Those of My Blood: Constructing Noble Families in Medieval Francia,* The Middle Ages (Philadelphia: University of Pennsylvania Press, 2001). [Bouchard, *Those of My Blood*]

Bourgain, Pascale. "Aliénor d'Aquitaine et Marie de Champagne mises en cause par André le Chapelain," *Cahiers de civilisation médiévale* 29 (1986):29–36. [Bourgain, "Aliénor d'Aquitaine et Marie de Champagne"]

Bournazel, Eric. *Le gouvernement capétien au XIIᵉ siècle (1108–1180): Structures sociales et mutations institutionelles* (Paris: Presses Universitaires de France, 1975). [Bournazel, *Le gouvernement capétien*]

Boussard, Jacques. *Le gouvernement d'Henri II Plantagenêt* (Paris: Librarie d'Argences, 1956). [Boussard, *Le gouvernement d'Henri II*]

Bouvet, Jean. "Le récit de la fondation de Mortemer," *Collectanea Ordinis Cisterciensium reformatorum* 22 (1960):149–58. [Bouvet, "Le récit de la fondation de Mortemer"]

Bradley, Marion Zimmer. *The Mists of Avalon* (New York: Knopf, 1982; New York: Ballentine Books, 1982).

Brandenburg, Erich. *Die Nachkommen Karls des Grossen (I-XIV. Generation)* (Leipzig: Zentralstelle für Deutsche Personen- und Familiengeschichte, 1935). [Brandenburg, *Die Nachkommen Karls des Grossen*]

Brandes, Stanley. "Like Wounded Stags: Male Sexual Ideology in an Andalusian Town," in *Sexual Meanings,* ed. Ortner and Whitehead, pp. 216–39.

Broadhurst, Karen M. "Henry II of England and Eleanor of Aquitaine: Patrons of Literature in French?" *Viator* 27 (1996):53–84. [Broadhurst, "Henry II and Eleanor of Aquitaine"]

Brooke, C[hristopher].N[ugent].L[awrence]. and G[illian]. Keir. *London 800–1216: The Shaping of a City* (Berkeley-Los Angeles: University of California Press, 1975). [Brooke and Keir. *London 800–1216*]

Brooke, Z[achary].N[ugent]. and C[hristopher].N[ugent].L[awrence]. Brooke. "Henry II, Duke of Normandy and Aquitaine," *English Historical Review* 61 (1946):81–89. [Brooke and Brooke. "Henry II, Duke of Normandy and Aquitaine"]

Brown, E[lizabeth] A.R. "Burying and Unburying the Kings of France," in *Persons in Groups,* ed. Trexler, pp. 41–66; repr. in Brown, *The Monarchy of Capetian France and Royal Ceremonial,* no. IX. [Brown, "Burying and Unburying"]

————. "Eleanor of Aquitaine: Parent, Queen, and Duchess," in *Eleanor of Aquitaine: Patron and Politician,* ed. Kibler, pp. 9–23. [Brown, "Eleanor of Aquitaine: Parent, Queen, and Duchess"]

————. *"Franks, Burgundians, and Aquitanians" and the Royal Coronation Ceremony in France,* Transactions of the American Philosophical Society 82.7 (Philadelphia: American Philosophical Society, 1992). [Brown, *"Franks, Burgundians, and Aquitanians"*]

————. *The Monarchy of Capetian France and Royal Ceremonial.* Variorum Collected Studies Series 345 (Aldershot, UK: Variorum, 1991). [Brown, *Capetian France and Royal Ceremonial*]

————. "La notion de la légitimité et la prophétie à la cour de Philippe Auguste," in *La France de Philippe Auguste,* ed. Bautier, pp. 77–110; repr. as no. I in Brown, *The Monarchy of Capetian France and Royal Ceremonial.* [Brown, "La notion de la légitimité et la prophétie à la cour de Philippe Auguste"]

————. *The Oxford Collection of the Drawings of Roger de Gaignières and the Royal Tombs of Saint-Denis,* Transactions of the American Philosophical Society, 78.5 (Philadelphia: American Philosophical Society, 1988). [Brown, *The Oxford Collection*]

————. "Ritual Brotherhood in Western Medieval Europe," *Traditio* 52 (1997):357–81. [Brown, 'Ritual Brotherhood']

————. "Saint-Denis and the Turpin Legend," in *The* Codex Calixtinus *and the Shrine of St. James,* eds. Williams and Stones, pp. 51–88. [Brown, "Saint-Denis and the Turpin Legend"]

————. "The Tyranny of a Construct: Feudalism and Historians of Medieval Europe," *The American Historical Review* 79 (1974):1063–78. [Brown, "The Tyranny of a Construct"]

————. and Michael W. Cothren. "The Twelfth-Century Crusading Window of the Abbey of Saint-Denis: *Praeteritorum enim Recordatio Futurorum est Exhibitio,"* *The Journal of the Warburg and Courtauld Institutes* 49 (1986): 1–40. [Brown and Cothren, "The Twelfth-Century Crusading Window"]

Brownlee, Kevin. "Robert d'Arbrissel," in *Dictionary of the Middle Ages,* ed. Strayer, 10:429a–431a.

Bruckner, Matilda Tomaryn. *Shaping Romance: Interpretation, Truth, and Closure in Twelfth-Century French Fictions* (Philadelphia: University of Pennsylvania Press, 1993). [Bruckner, *Shaping Romance*]

Brundage, James A. *Law, Sex and Christian Society in Medieval Europe* (Chicago: University of Chicago Press, 1987). [Brundage, *Law, Sex and Christian Society*]

————. *Medieval Canon Law* (London: Longman, 1995). [Brundage, *Medieval Canon Law*]

————. "The Rise of Professional Canonists and Development of the Ius Commune," *Zeitschrift der Savigny-Stiftung für Rechtsgeschichte, kanonistische Abteilung* 81 (1995):26–63. [Brundage, "The Rise of Professional Canonists"]

————. "St. Bernard and the Jurists," in *The Second Crusade and the Cistercians,* ed. Gervers, pp. 25–33. [Brundage, "St. Bernard and the Jurists"]

Bruzelius, Caroline A. "*Ad modum franciae*. Charles of Anjou and Gothic Architecture in the Kingdom of Sicily," *Journal of the Society of Architectural Historians* 50 (1991):402–20. [Bruzelius, "*ad modum franciae*"]

———. "Seeing is Believing: Clarissan Architecture ca. 1213–1340," in *Monastic Women's Architecture*, special issue of *Gesta* 31 (1992):83–91. [Bruzelius, "Seeing is Believing"]

Bührer-Thierry, Geneviève. "La reine adultère," *Cahiers de civilisation médiévale* 35 (1992):299–312.

Bullough, Vern L. "Medieval Medical and Scientific Views of Women," *Viator* 4 (1973):485–501.

Bur, Michel. "Les comtes de Champagne et la 'Normanitas': sémiologie d'un tombeau," *Proceedings of the Battle Conference on Anglo-Norman Studies* 3 (1980):22–32, 202–303. [Bur, "Les comtes"]

———."L'image de la parenté chez les comtes de Champagne," *Annales: Économies, Sociétés, Civilisations* 5 (1983):1016–30. [Bur, "L'image de la parenté"]

Burgess, Glyn S. *The Lais of Marie de France: Text and Context* (Athens: The University of Georgia Press, 1987).

Burke's Guide to the Royal Family, ed. J. Burke (London: Burke's Peerage, 1973). [*Burke's Guide*]

Burton, Janet. *Monastic and Religious Orders in Britain, 1000–1300* (Cambridge, UK: Cambridge University Press, 1994). [Burton, *Monastic and Religious Orders*]

The Cambridge History of Medieval Political Thought, c. 350–c. 1450, ed. J.H. Burns (Cambridge, UK: Cambridge University Press, 1988).

Campan, Jeanne-Louise-Henriette Genest. *Memoirs of Marie Antoinette: Queen of France and Wife of Louis XVI by Madame Campan, her Lady-in-Waiting*, n. trans., Memoirs of the courts of Europe, vol. 3 (New York: Collier and Sons, 1910). [Campan, *Memoirs*]

Cantor, Norman. *Medieval Lives: Eight Charismatic Men and Women of the Middle Ages* (New York: Harper Perennial Library, 1994, repr. 1995).

Capetian Women, ed. John Carmi Parsons and Kathleen Nolan, The New Middle Ages (New York: Palgrave Macmillian, forthcoming).

Carney, Elizabeth. "Fact and Fiction in 'Queen Eleanor's Confession,'" *Folklore* 95 (1984):167–70.

Carpenter, David. "The Burial of King Henry III, the *Regalia* and Royal Ideology," in Carpenter, *The Reign of Henry III*, pp. 427–61. [Carpenter, "Burial of King Henry III"]

———. *The Minority of Henry III* (London: Methuen, 1990). [Carpenter, *Minority of Henry III*]

———. *The Reign of Henry III* (London: Hambledon, 1996).

Carruthers, Mary. *The Book of Memory: A Study of Memory in Medieval Culture* (Cambridge, UK: Cambridge University Press, 1990). [Carruthers, *The Book of Memory*]

Carter, Kathy P. "Arthur I, Duke of Brittany, in History and Literature," Ph.D. dissertation, Florida State University, 1996. [Carter, "Arthur I"]

Castelot, André. *Queen of France: A Biography of Marie Antoinette*, trans. Denise Folliot (New York: Harper and Row, 1957).

Caviness, Madeline. "Anchoress, Abbess, and Queen: Donors and Patrons or Intercessors and Matrons?" in *The Cultural Patronage of Medieval Women*, ed. McCash, pp. 105–54. [Caviness, "Anchoress, Abbess, and Queen"]

———. "Patron or Matron? A Capetian Bride and a Vade Mecum for her Marriage Bed," *Speculum* 68 (1993):333–62. [Caviness, "Patron or Matron?"]

———. "Suger's Glass at Saint-Denis: The State of Research," in *Abbot Suger and Saint-Denis*, ed. Gerson, pp. 256–72. [Caviness, "Suger's Glass"]

Chamberlayne, Joanna L. "Crowns and Virgins: Queenmaking During the Wars of the Roses," in *Young Medieval Women*, ed. Lewis, Menuge, and Phillips, pp. 47–68.

———. "Margaret of Anjou, Queen Consort of Henry VI: A Reassessment of her Role, 1445–53," in *Crown, Government and People in the Fifteenth Century*, ed. Archer, pp. 107–43.

Chambers, Frank McMinn. "Some Legends Concerning Eleanor of Aquitaine," *Speculum* 16 (1941):459–68. [Chambers, "Some Legends Concerning Eleanor"]

Chaplais, Pierre. *Essays in Medieval Diplomacy and Administration* (London: Hambledon, 1981).

———. "Le traité de Paris de 1259 et l'inféodation de la Gascogne allodiale," *Le Moyen Âge* 61 (1955): 121–37; repr. as no. II in Chaplais, *Essays in Medieval Diplomacy and Administration*. [Chaplais, "Le traité de Paris"]

Chapters in the Administrative History of Medieval England, ed. Thomas Frederick Tout. 6 vols. (Manchester: University of Manchester Press, 1929–33).

Chartier, Roger. *The Cultural Origins of the French Revolution*, trans. Lydia G. Cochrane (Durham, NC: Duke University Press, 1991).

Chassel, Jean-Luc. "L'usage de sceau au XIIᵉ siècle," in *Le XIIᵉ siècle. Mutations et renouveau en France dans la première moitié du XIIᵉ siècle*, Cahiers du Léopard d'Or, 3. (Paris: Le Léopard d'Or, 1994), pp. 61–102. [Chassel, "L'usage de sceau"]

Chédeville, André. *Chartres et ses campagnes (XIᵉ-XIIIᵉ siècle)* (Paris: Klincksiek, 1973).

Cheney, C[hristopher].R[obert]. *English Synodalia of the Thirteenth Century*, 2nd. edn. (London: Oxford University Press, 1968). [Cheney, *English Synodalia*]

———. *Hubert Walter* (London: Nelson, 1967).

Cheyette, Fredric L. "Women, Poets and Politics in Occitania," in *Aristocratic Women in Medieval France*, ed. Evergates, pp. 138–77. [Cheyette, "Women, Poets and Politics"]

Chibnall, Marjorie. *The Empress Matilda: Queen Consort, Queen Mother and Lady of the English* (Oxford: Blackwell, 1991). [Chibnall, *The Empress Matilda*]

Choffel, Jacques. *Louis VIII, le Lion, roi de France méconnu, roi d'Angleterre ignoré* (Paris: Lanore, 1983). [Choffel, *Louis VIII*]

Civitatum Communitas. Studien zum Europäischen Städtewesen. Festschrift Heinz Stoob zum 65. Geburtstag, eds. Helmut Jäger, Franz Petri, and Heinz Quirin, 2 vols. (Cologne: Böhlau, 1984).

Clanchy, Michael T. *England and Its Rulers, 1066–1272*, 2nd edn. (Oxford: Blackwell, 1998).

Clark, William W. "Defining National Historical Memory," (forthcoming).

————. "Fontevrault Abbey," in *The Dictionary of Art,* ed. Jane Shoaf Turner (New York: Grove's Dictionaries, 1996), pp. 290–91. [Clark, "Fontevrault Abbey"]

————. "Spatial Innovations in the chevet of Saint-Germain-des-Prés," *Journal of the Society of Architectural Historians* 39 (1979):348–65. [Clark, "Spatial Innovations"]

Cleve, Thomas Curtis van. *The Emperor Frederick II of Hohenstaufen: Immutator Mundi* (Oxford: Clarendon Press, 1972).

The Codex Calixtinus *and the Shrine of Saint James,* ed. John Williams and Alison Stones, Jakobus-Studien, 3 (Tübingen: Gunter Narr, 1992). [*The* Codex Calixtinus ed. Williams and Stones]

Cokayne, George Edward. *The Complete Peerage,* 2d edn., ed. Vicary Gibbs, 13 vols. in 14 (London: The Saint Catherine Press, 1910–59).

Colvin, H[oward]. M[ontagu], R. Allen Brown and A[lfred]. J[ohn]. Taylor. *The History of the King's Works,* 6 vols. (London: H.M. Stationery Office, 1963–82). [*History of the King's Works*]

Conflicted Identities and Multiple Masculinities: Men in the Medieval World, ed. Jacqueline Murray, Garland Medieval Casebooks (New York: Garland Publishing, 1999).

Constable, Giles. "The Second Crusade as Seen by Contemporaries," *Traditio* 9 (1953):213–79. [Constable, "Second Crusade"]

Cottineau, Laurent. *Répertoire topo-bibliographique des abbayes et prieurés* (Mâcon: Protat, 1939). [Cottineau, *Repertoire topo-bibliographique*]

Courajod, Louis. "Les sépultures des Plantagenets à Fontevrault (1187–1867)," *Gazette des Beaux-Arts* 23 (1867): 537–58. [Courajod, "Sépultures"]

Cowdrey, Herbert Edward John. "The Anglo-Norman *Laudes regiae,*" *Viator* 12 (1981):37–78.

Cowney, Emma. *Religious Patronage in Anglo-Norman England 1066–1135* (Woodbridge: Boydell Press, 1998).

Cowper, F[rederick]. A[ndries]. deG[raaf]. "Date and Dedication of the Roman de Troie," *Modern Philology* 27 (1929–30):379–82.

Cronin, Vincent. *Louis and Antoinette* (New York: William Morrow, 1975).

Cronne, H[enry]. A[lfred]. *The Reign of Stephen* (London: Weidenfeld and Nicolson, 1970). [Cronne, *Reign of Stephen*]

Crouch, David. *William Marshal: Court, Career and Chivalry in the Angevin Empire, 1147–1219* (London: Longman, 1990). [Crouch, *William Marshal*]

Crown, Government and People in the Fifteenth Century, ed. R[owena]. E. Archer (Stroud: Alan Sutton, 1995; New York: St, Martin's Press 1995).

Crozet, René. "Fontevrault," *Congrès archéologique de France* 122 (1964) (*Anjou*):426–77. [Crozet, "Fontevrault"]

————. "Lanternes des morts du Centre et de l'Ouest," in *La grand' Goule* (Poitiers, 1936).

The Cultural Patronage of Medieval Women, ed. June Hall McCash (Athens: University of Georgia Press, 1996).

The Culture of Christendom: Essays in Medieval History in Memory of Denis L. T. Bethell, ed. Marc A. Meyer (London: Hambledon, 1993).

Culture, Power and Personality in Medieval France, ed. Thomas N. Bisson (London: Hambledon Press, 1991).

Cultures of Power: Lordship, Status, and Process in Twelfth-Century Europe, ed. Thomas N. Bisson (Philadelphia: University of Pennsylvania Press, 1995).

Dalarun, Jacques. *L'impossible sainteté. La vie retrouvée de Robert d'Arbrissel (v. 1045–1116), fondateur de Fontevraud* (Paris: Éditions du Cerf, 1985). [Dalarun, *L'impossible sainteté*]

Daniell, Christopher. *Death and Burial in Medieval England, 1066–1550* (London: Routledge, 1997).

Daoust, J[oseph]. "Fontevrault," in *Dictionnaire d'histoire et de géographie ecclésiastiques,* ed. Alfred Baudrillant (Paris: Letouzey et Ané, 1971), cols. 961–71. [Daoust, "Fontevrault"]

Daudet, Pierre. *Les origines carolingiennes de la compétence exclusive de l'église en France et en Germanie en matière de juridiction matrimoniale* (Paris: Sirey, 1933). [Daudet, *Les origines carolingiennes*]

Davis, Judith. "Guillaume IX d'Aquitaine, *Homo ludens* and Uncourtly Lover," in *Abstracts of Papers,* Eighth Conference on Medieval Studies (Kalamazoo: Medieval Institute, Western Michigan University, 1973), pp. 94–95. [Davis, "Guillaume IX d'Aquitaine"]

Davis, Natalie Zemon. "Women on Top: Symbolic Sexual Inversion and Political Disorder in Early Modern Europe," in *The Reversible World,* ed. Babcock, pp. 147–90.

Davis, R[alph].H.C. "The College of St Martin-Le-Grand and the Anarchy, 1135–1154," *London Topographical Record* 23 (1972):9–26. [R.H.C. Davis, "The College of St Martin-Le-Grand"]

———. *King Stephen.* 2nd edn. (London: Longman, 1977); 3rd edn. (London: Longman, 1990).

DeAragon, RáGena. "Dowager Countesses, 1066–1230," *Anglo-Norman Studies* 17 (1995):87–100.

Dectot, Xavier. "Ou périr ou régner? Les tombeaux des comtes de Champagne à Saint-Étienne de Troyes," in *Splendeurs de la cour de Champagne au temps de Chrétien de Troyes,* exhibition catalogue, special number of *La vie en Champagne* (Troyes: Bibliothèque municipale, 1999), pp. 22–27. [Dectot, "Ou périr ou régner?"]

Déer, Joseph. *The Dynastic Porphyry Tombs of the Norman Period in Sicily* (Cambridge, MA: Harvard University Press, 1959). [Déer, *Dynastic Porphyry Tombs*]

Deshoulières, Francis. "L'église Saint-Pierre de Montmartre," *Bulletin monumental* 77 (1913):5–13.

Devailly, Guy. *Le Berry du XIIe au milieu du XIIIe siècle* (Paris: Mouton, 1973). [Devailly, *Le Berry*]

Dhondt, Jean. "Sept femmes et un trio de rois," *Contributions à l'histoire économique et sociale* 3 (1964–65):35–70. [Dhondt, "Sept femmes"]

Dictionary of the Middle Ages, ed. Joseph R. Strayer, 13 vols. (New York: Charles Scribner, 1982–89).

Dictionnaire des églises de France, ed. Jacques Brosse, 5 vols. in 17 (Paris: Laffont, 1966–71).

Dictionnaire d'histoire et de géographie ecclésiastiques, ed. Alfred Baudrillant, 26 vols. to date (Paris: Letouzey et Ané, 1971–).

Didron, Alphonse-Napoléon [*sic,* for Adolphe-Napoléon] *Christian Iconography: The History of Christian Art in the Middle Ages,* trans. E.J. Millington and Margaret Stokes from the French *Iconographie chrétienne-Histoire de Dieu* (1843), 2 vols. (London: Henry G. Bohn and G. Bell, 1851–86; repr. New York: Frederick Ungar, 1965). [Didron, *Christian Iconography*]

Dillard, Heath. *Daughters of the Reconquest: Women in Castilian Town Society, 1100–1300* (Cambridge, UK: Cambridge University Press, 1984). [Dillard, *Daughters of the Reconquest*]

Dimier, Anselme. *Saint Louis et Cîteaux* (Paris: Letouzey, 1953). [Dimier, *Saint Louis et Cîteaux*]

———, and Delabrouille, R.-H. *Notre-Dame-du-Lys* (Paris, 1960). [Dimier and Delabrouille, *Notre-Dame-du-Lys*]

Dockray-Miller, Mary. *Mothering and Motherhood in Anglo-Saxon England,* The New Middle Ages (New York: Palgrave, 2000).

Donahue, Charles Jr. "English and French Marriage Cases in the Later Middle Ages: Might the Differences be Explained by Differences in the Property Systems in *Marriage, Property, and Succession,* ed. Bonfield, pp. 339–66; repr. in *Miscellanea Domenico Maffei dicata,* ed. Garcia y Garcia and Weimar. [Donahue, "English and French Marriage Cases"]

———. "What Causes Fundamental Legal Ideas? Marital Property in England and France in the Thirteenth Century," *Michigan Law Review* 78 (1979):59–88. [Donahue, "What Causes Fundamental Legal Ideas?"]

Douglas, David C. *William the Conqueror: The Norman Impact upon England* (Berkeley-Los Angeles: University of California Press, 1964). [Douglas, *William the Conqueror*]

———. *William Rufus* (Berkeley-Los Angeles: University of California Press, 1983).

Douglas, Mary. *Purity and Danger: An Analysis of the Concepts of Pollution and Taboo* (London: Routledge, 1966).

Dronke, Peter. "Peter of Blois and Poetry at the Court of Henry II," *Mediaeval Studies* 38 (1976):185–235. [Dronke, "Peter of Blois"]

Duby, Georges. *The Chivalrous Society,* trans. Cynthia Postan (Berkeley-Los Angeles: University of California Press, 1977). [Duby, *The Chivalrous Society*]

———. *Le Chevalier, la Femme et le Prêtre* (Paris: Hachetter, 1981); trans. Barbara Bray as *The Knight, The Lady, and The Priest: The Making of Modern Marriage in Medieval France* (New York: Pantheon Books, 1983). [Duby, *The Knight, The Lady, and The Priest*]

———. *Dames du XIIᵉ siècle,* 1: *Héloïse, Aliénor, Iseut et quelques autres,* Bibliothèque des Histoires (Paris: Gallimard, 1995–96); incompletely trans. Jean Birrell in 3 vols. as *Women of the Twelfth Century,* 1: *Eleanor of Aquitaine and Six Others;* 2: *Remembering the dead;* 3: *Eve and the Church* (Chicago: University of Chicago Press, 1997). [Duby, *Women of the Twelfth Century*]

————. *France in the Middle Ages, 987–1460,* trans. Juliet Vale (Oxford: Blackwell, 1991). [Duby, *France in the Middle Ages*]

————. *Guillaume le Maréchal, ou le meilleur chevalier du monde* (Paris: Librairie Arthème Fayard, 1984); trans. Richard Howard as *William Marshal, Flower of Chivalry* (London: Faber, 1986). [Duby, *Guillaume le Maréchal,* trans. as *William Marshal*]

————. *Medieval Marriage: Two Models from Twelfth-Century France,* trans. Elborg Forster, Johns Hopkins Symposia in Comparative History 11 (Baltimore: Johns Hopkins University Press, 1978). [Duby, *Medieval Marriage*]

————. *Rural Economy and Country Life in the Medieval West,* trans. Cynthia Postan (Columbia, SC: University of South Carolina Press, 1968). [Duby, *Rural Economy*]

————. "Women and Power," in *Cultures of Power,* ed. Bisson, pp. 69–85. [Duby, "Women and Power"]

Dumas, Françoise. "La monnaie dans les domaines Plantagenêt," *Cahiers de civilisation médiévale* 29 (1986):53–59. [Dumas, "La monnaie dans les domaines Plantagenêt"]

Dumolin, Maurice. "Notes sur l'abbaye de Montmartre," *Bulletin de la Société de l'histoire de Paris et de l'Ile-de-France* 58 (1931):145–238, 244–325.

Dumontier, Michel, with Georges Bernage. *L'empire des Plantagenêts: Aliénor d'Aquitaine et son temps.* (Paris: Copernic, 1980). [Dumontier, with Bernage, *L'empire des Plantagenêts*]

Dunbabin, Jean. "What's in a Name? Philip, King of France," *Speculum* 68 (1993):949–68. [Dunbabin, "What's in a Name?"]

Dunn, Douglas. "Margaret of Anjou: Monster-Queen, or Dutiful Wife?," *Medieval History* 4 (1994):199–217.

Dupré, Alexandre. "Les comtesses de Chartres et de Blois. Etude historique," *Mémoires de la société archéologique d'Eure-et-Loir* 5 (1872):198–236. [Dupré, "Les comtesses de Chartres"]

Early Medieval Kingship, ed. P[eter].H. Sawyer and I[an].N. Wood (Leeds: Institute for Medieval Studies, 1977).

Edbury, Peter W. *The Kingdom of Cyprus and the Crusades, 1191–1374* (Cambridge, UK: Cambridge University Press, 1991). [Edbury, *The Kingdom of Cyprus*]

————, and John Gordon Rowe. *William of Tyre: Historian of the Latin East* (Cambridge, UK: Cambridge University Press, 1988).

Eleanor of Aquitaine, Patron and Politician, ed. William W. Kibler, Symposia in the Arts and Humanities 3 (Austin, TX: University of Texas Press, 1976). [*Eleanor of Aquitaine, Patron and Politician,* ed. Kibler]

Eley, Penny. [aka Penny Sullivan]. "The Myth of Trojan Descent and Perceptions of National Identity: The Case of *Eneas* and the *Roman de Troie,*" *Nottingham Medieval Studies* 35 (1991):27–40. [Eley, "Myth of Trojan Descent"]

Elkins, Sharon K. *Holy Women of Twelfth-Century England* (Chapel Hill-London: University of North Carolina Press, 1988).

Elliott, Dyan. *Spiritual Marriage: Sexual Abstinence in Medieval Wedlock* (Princeton, NJ: Princeton University Press, 1993).

Elorza, Juan C. *El Panteón real de las Huelgas de Burgos: Los Enterramientos de los Reyes de Castilla* (Valladolid: Junta de Castilla y León, 1988). [Elorza, *El Panteón real de las Huelgas*]

Enguehard, Henri. "Les travaux de l'abbaye de Fontevrault aux XIXe et XXe siècles," *Congrès archéologique de France* 122 (1964) (*Anjou*):478–81. [Enguehard, "Les travaux"]

Ennen, Edith. "Zur Städtepolitik der Eleonore von Aquitanien," in *Civitatum Communitas,* eds. Jäger, Petri, and Quirin, 1:42–55. [Ennen, "Zur Städtepolitik der Eleonore"]

Enright, Michael J. *Lady With a Mead Cup: Ritual, Prophesy, and Lordship in the European Warband from La Tene to the Viking Age* (Dublin: Four Courts Press, 1996).

Erlande-Brandenburg, Alain. "Le 'cimetière des rois' à Fontevraud," *Congrés archéologique de France, Anjou* 122 (1964):481–92. [Erlande-Brandenburg, "Le 'cimetière des rois' à Fontevraud"]

———. "Église Saint-Pierre-de-Montmartre," *Dictionnaire des églises de France, 4c: Paris et ses environs,* ed. Jacques Brosse (Paris: R. Laffont, 1968), pp. 103–04. [Erlande-Brandenburg, "Église Saint-Pierre-de-Montmartre"]

———. "Les gisants de Fontevrault," in *La figuration des morts dans la chrétienté médiévale,* pp. 3–15. [Erlande-Brandenburg, "Les gisants de Fontevrault"]

———. *Gothic Art,* trans. I. Mark Paris (New York: Abrams, 1989). [Erlande-Brandenburg, *Gothic Art*]

———. *Le roi est mort: étude sur les funérailles, les sépultures et les tombeaux des rois de France jusqu'à la fin du XIIIe siècle,* Bibliothèque de la Société française d'archéologie 7 (Geneva: Droz, 1975). [Erlande-Brandenburg, *Le roi est mort*]

———. "La sculpture funéraire vers les années 1200: les gisants de Fontevrault," in *The Year 1200: A Symposium,* pp. 561–77. [Erlande-Brandenburg, "La sculpture funéraire"]

Eroticism and the Body Politic, ed. Lynn Hunt (Baltimore: Johns Hopkins University Press, 1991).

Esmein, Adhémar. *Le mariage en droit canonique,* 2 vols. (Paris: Larose et Forcel, 1891; repr. New York: Burt Franklin, 1968). [Esmein, *Le mariage en droit canonique*]

Essays in Medieval History presented to Thomas Frederick Tout, ed. A[ndrew].G[eorge]. Little and F[rederick].M[aurice]. Powicke (Manchester: n.p., 1925; Freeport, NY: Books for Libraries Press, 1967).

Evergates, Theodore. "Aristocratic Women in the County of Champagne," in *Aristocratic Women in Medieval France,* ed. Evergates, pp. 74–110. [Evergates, "Aristocratic Women in Champagne"]

———. *Feudal Society in the Bailliage of Troyes under the Counts of Champagne, 1152–1284* (Baltimore: Johns Hopkins University Press, 1975). [Evergates, *Feudal Society*]

Eygun, François. *Sigillographie du Poitou jusqu'en 1515: étude sur les institutions, les arts et la civilisation d'après les sceaux* (Mâcon and Poitiers: Protat Frères and Société des antiquaires de l'Ouest, 1938). [Eygun, *Sigillographie*]

Eyton, R[obert].W[illiam]. *Court, Household and Itinerary of King Henry II* (London: Holborn, 1878; repr. Hildesheim: Olms, 1974). [Eyton, *Henry II*]

Facinger Marion F. *See* Meade, Marion (Facinger). "A Study of Medieval Queenship: Capetian France (987–1237)," *Studies in Medieval and Renaissance History* 5 (1968):1–47. [Facinger, "Medieval Queenship"]

Faris, Janice. "Alice, Queen of Cyprus," unpublished M.A. paper, University of Iowa, 1993.

Farmer, Sharon A. "Persuasive Voices: Clerical Images of Medieval Wives," *Speculum* 61 (1986):517–43. [Farmer, "Persuasive Voices"]

Favreau, Robert. "Les débuts de la ville de la Rochelle," *Cahiers de civilisation médiévale* 30 (1978):3–32. [Favreau, "Les débuts de la ville de La Rochelle"]

Fawtier, Robert. *Les Capétiens et la France; leur role dans sa construction* (Paris: Presses Universitaires de France, 1942), trans. Lionel Butler and R.J. Adam as *The Capetian Kings of France: Monarchy and Nation (987–1328)* (London: Macmillan, 1960; New York: St. Martin's Press, 1960, repr. 1965). [Fawtier, *Les Capétiens*]

Feminism and Art History: Questioning the Litany, ed. Norma Broude and M[ary].D. Garrard (Boulder, CO: Westview Press; New York: Harper & Row, 1982).

Ferrante, Joan M. "*Cortes' Amor* in Medieval Texts," *Speculum* 55 (1980):686–95. [Ferrante, "*Cortes' Amor*"]

———. *To the Glory of Her Sex: Women's Roles in the Composition of Medieval Texts* (Bloomington: Indiana University Press, 1997). [Ferrante, *Glory of Her Sex*]

———. "Women's Role in Latin Letters from the Fourth to the Early Twelfth Century," in *The Cultural Patronage of Medieval Women,* ed. McCash, pp. 73–104. [Ferrante, "Women's Role in Latin Letters"]

La figuration des morts dans la chrétienté médiévale jusqu'à la fin du premier quart du XIVe siècle, ed. Roger Grégoire (Fontevraud: Centre culturel de l'Ouest, 1988).

Finke, Laurie, and Martin B. Shichtman. "Magical Mistress Tour: Patronage, Intellectual Property, and the Dissemination of Wealth in the *Lais* of Marie de France," *Signs* 25.2 (2000):479–503.

Flandrin, Jean-Louis. *Familles: parente, maison, sexualite dans l'ancienne societe* (Paris: Hachette, 1976). Trans. Richard Southern as *Families in Former Times: Kinship, Household and Sexuality,* (Cambridge, UK: Cambridge University Press, 1979). [Flandrin, *Families in Former Times*]

Fliche, Augustin. *Le règne de Philippe Ier, roi de France (1060–1108)* (Paris: Société française d'imprimerie et de librairie, 1912; repr. Geneva: Slatkine, 1975). [Fliche, *Philippe I*]

Florez, Enrique. *Memorias de las Reinas católicas de España,* 2 vols. (Madrid: Antonio Marin, 1761; 3rd edn., Madrid: Aguilar, 1959). [Florez, *Reinas Católicas*]

Flori, Jean. *Richard Coeur de Lion* (Paris: Payot, 1999). [Flori, *Richard Coeur de Lion*]

Flutre, Louis-Fernand, and Francine Mora. "Benoît de Sainte-Maure," in *Dictionnaire des lettres françaises: le Moyen Age,* Encyclopédies d'Aujourd'hui, ed. Robert Bossuat, Louis Pichard, and Guy Raynaud de Lage (Paris: Fayard, 1964), rev. ed. Geneviève Hasenohr and Michel Zink (Paris: Fayard, 1992), pp. 139a–141a. [Flutre and Mora, "Benoît"]

Folda, Jaroslav. *The Art of the Crusaders in the Holy Land, 1098–1187* (Cambridge, UK: Cambridge University Press, 1995). [Folda, *Art of the Crusaders*]

————. "Images of Queen Melisende in Manuscripts of William of Tyre's *History of Outremer:* 1250–1300," *Gesta* 32 (1993):97–111. [Folda, "Images of Queen Melisende"]

Fossard, Denis. "L'église Saint-Pierre, anciennement Saint-Denis," in *Les anciennes églises suburbaines de Paris (IVe-Xe siècles)*. *Mémoires de la Fédération des Sociétés historiques et archéologiques de Paris et de l'Ile-de-France* 11 (1961):208–25. [Fossard, "L'église Saint-Pierre"]

Foucault, Michel. *Power/Knowledge: Selected Interviews and Other Writings 1972–77*, ed. and trans. Colin Gordon (New York: Pantheon Book, 1980).

Fourrier, Anthime. *Le courant réaliste dans le roman courtois en France au moyen âge* (Paris: A.G. Nizet, 1960).

Fox, J[ohn].C[harles]. "Mary Abbess of Shaftesbury," *English Historical Review* 26 (1911):317–26.

Fradenburg, Louise Olga. *City, Marriage, Tournament: Arts of Rule in Late Medieval Scotland* (Madison: University of Wisconsin Press, 1991). [Fradenburg, *City, Marriage, Tournament*]

————. "Introduction: Rethinking Queenship," in *Women and Sovereignty*, ed. Fradenburg, pp. 1–13.

La France de Philippe Auguste: le temps des mutations. Actes du Colloque international organisé par le Centre National de la Recherche Scientifique (Paris, 29 septembre–4 octobre 1980), ed. Robert-Henri Bautier (Paris: Éditions du CNRS, 1982).

François-Souchal, Geneviève. "Les émaux de Grandmont au XIIe siècle," *Bulletin monumental* 120 (1962):339–57; 121 (1963):41–64, 123–50, 219–35, 307–29; and 122 (1964):7–35, 129–59. [François-Souchal, "Les émaux"]

Fraser, Antonia. *Mary, Queen of Scots* (London: Weidenfeld and Nicolson, 1969).

Freccero, Carla. "Marguerite de Navarre and the Politics of Maternal Sovereignty," in *Women and Sovereignty*, ed. Fradenburg, pp. 132–49.

Freeman, Michelle. "Marie de France's Poetics of Silence: The Implications for a Feminine *Translatio*," *PMLA* 99 (1984):860–83.

————. "The Power of Sisterhood: Marie de France's 'Le Fresne,'" *French Forum* 12 (1987):5–26, repr. in *Women and Power in the Middle Ages*, ed. Erler and Kowaleski, pp. 250–264.

Freisen, Joseph. *Geschichte des canonischen Eherechts bis zum Verfall der Glossenlitteratur*, 2nd edn. (Paderborn: Ferdinand Schöningh, 1893). [Freisen, *Geschichte des canonischen Eherechts*]

Freud, Sigmund. "The Uncanny," in *The Standard Edition of the Complete Psychological Works of Sigmund Freud*, ed. James Strachey, vol. 17 (London: Hogarth Press, 1953–74), pp. 219–56.

Fuhrmann, Horst. Deutsche Geschichte im hohen Mittelalter: von der Mitte des 11.bis zum Ende des 12. Jahrhunderts, 2nd. edn. (Gottingen: Vandenhoeck & Ruprecht, 1983). Trans. Timothy Reuter as *Germany in the High Middle Ages, c. 1050–1200*, Cambridge Medieval Textbooks (Cambridge, UK: Cambridge University Press, 1986). [Fuhrmann, *Germany in the High Middle Ages*]

Gaborit-Chopin, Danielle. *Regalia. Les instruments du sacre des rois de France, les "Honneurs de Charlemagne,"* Monographies des musées de France (Paris: Ministère de la Culture et de la Communication, Éditions de la Réunion des musées nationaux, 1987). [Gaborit-Chopin, *Regalia*]

———. "Suger's Liturgical Vessels," in *Abbot Suger and Saint-Denis,* ed. Gerson, pp. 283–93. [Gaborit-Chopin, "Suger's Liturgical Vessels"]

———. "Le Vase d'Aliénor," In *Le trésor de Saint-Denis,* ed. Montesquiou-Fezensac and Gaborit-Chopin, pp. 170–72. [Gaborit-Chopin, "Le Vase d'Aliénor"]

Gaiffier, Baudouin de. "Sainte Ide de Boulogne et l'Espagne," *Analecta Bollandiana* 86 (1968):67–82. [de Gaiffier, "Sainte Ide"]

Galbraith, Vivian H. "Good Kings and Bad Kings in English History," *History* 30 (1945):119–32, repr. in Galbraith, *Kings and Chroniclers* (London: Hambledon, 1982). [Galbraith, "Good Kings and Bad Kings"]

Galloway, Penelope. "Discreet and Devout Maidens: Women's Involvement in Beguine Communities in Northern France, 1200–1500," in *Medieval Women in their Communities,* ed. Watt, pp. 92–115. [Galloway, "Discreet and Devout Maidens"]

Gardelles, Jacques. "La sculpture monumentale en Bordelais et en Bazadais à la fin du XIIe et au début du XIIIe siècle," *Bulletin monumental* 132 (1974):29–48. [Gardelles, "La sculpture monumentale en Bordelais"]

Gardner, Arthur. *Medieval Sculpture in France* (Cambridge, UK: Cambridge University Press, 1931). [Gardner, *Medieval Sculpture in France*]

Gaudemet, Jean. *Le mariage en occident: les moeurs et le droit* (Paris: Éditions du Cerf, 1987). [Gaudemet, *Le mariage en occident*]

Gaussin, Pierre-Roger. "Y a-t-il eu une politique monastique des Plantagenêt?" *Cahiers de civilisation médiévale* 29 (1986):83–94. [Gaussin, "Politique monastique"]

Gauthier, Marie-Madeleine. "Les chapiteaux de Notre-Dame du Bourg de Langon," in *Langon-Sauternais-Cernès. Fédération historique du Sud-Ouest. Actes du XXIIe Congrès d'études régionales tenu à Langon les 2 et 3 mai 1970* (Périgueux: P. Fanlac, 1973), pp. 18–47. [Gauthier, "Les chapiteaux de Notre-Dame du Bourg"]

———. *Émaux du moyen âge occidental* (Fribourg: Office du Livre, 1972). [Gauthier, *Émaux*]

———. "La légende de sainte Valérie et les émaux champlevés de Limoges," *Bulletin de la Société archéologique et historique du Limousin* 86 (1955):35–80. [Gauthier, "La légende de sainte Valérie"]

———. "Naissance du défunt à la vie éternelle: les tombeaux d'émaux de Limoges aux XIIe et XIIIe siècles," in *La figuration des morts dans la chrétienté médiévale,* ed. Grégoire, pp. 101–103. [Gauthier, "Naissance"]

Gayoso, Andrea. "The 'Lady' of Las Huelgas: A Royal Abbey and Its Patronage," *Cîteaux* 51 (2000):95–115. [Gayoso, "The 'Lady' of Las Huelgas"]

Geary, Patrick J. *Living with the Dead in the Middle Ages* (Ithaca, NY: Cornell University Press, 1994). [Geary, *Living with the Dead*]

———. *Phantoms of Remembrance: Memory and Oblivion at the End of the First Millennium* (Princeton, NJ: Princeton University Press, 1994). [Geary, *Phantoms of Remembrance*]

Gescher, Franz. "Synodales: Studie zur kirchliche Gerichtsverfassung und zum deutschen Ständewesen des Mittelalters," *Zeitschrift der Savigny-Stiftung für Rechtsgeschichte, kanonistische Abteilung* 29 (1940): 358–446. [Gescher, "Synodales"]

Gierke, Otto. *Political Theories of the Middle Ages,* trans. Frederic William Maitland (Cambridge: Cambridge University Press, 1900).

Giesebrecht, Wilhelm von. *Geschichte der deutschen Kaiserzeit,* 5th edn., 6 vols. in 8 (Brunswick: C.A. Schwetschke/ Leipzig: Duncker and Humblot, 1875–90).

Giesey, Ralph E. "Models of Rulership in French Royal Ceremonial," in *Rites of Power,* ed. Wilentz, pp. 41–64.

Gilissen, John. *La coutume,* Typologie des sources du moyen âge, fasc. 41 (Turnhout: Brepols, 1982). [Gilissen, *La coutume*]

Gillingham, John. *The Angevin Empire,* 2d. edn. (London: Arnold, 2001). [Gillingham, *Angevin Empire*]

——. "Historians without Hindsight: Coggeshall, Diceto and Howden on the Early Years of John's Reign," in *King John: New Interpretations,* ed. Church, pp. 1–26. [Gillingham, "Historians without Hindsight"]

——. "Love, Marriage and Politics in the Twelfth Century," *Forum for Modern Language Studies* 25 (1989):292–303; repr. in Gillingham, *Richard Coeur de Lion,* part 2, no. 12, pp. 243–55. [Gillingham, "Love, Marriage and Politics"]

——. *Richard Coeur de Lion. Kingship, Chivalry and War in the Twelfth Century* (London: Hambledon Press, 1994). [Gillingham, *Richard Coeur de Lion*]

——. *Richard I,* Yale English Monarchs (New Haven: Yale University Press, 1999). [Gillingham, *Richard I*]

——. *Richard the Lionheart* (London: Weidenfeld and Nicolson, 1978).

——. "Richard I and Berengaria of Navarre," *Bulletin of the Institute of Historical Research* 53 (1980):157–73; repr. in Gillingham, *Richard Coeur de Lion,* part 2, no. 4, pp. 119–40. [Gillingham, "Richard I and Berengaria of Navarre"]

——. "The Unromantic Death of Richard I," *Speculum,* 54 (1979):18–41; repr. in Gillingham, *Richard Coeur de Lion,* part 2, no. 6, pp. 155–80. [Gillingham, "The Unromantic Death of Richard I"]

——. "Roger of Howden on Crusade," in *Medieval Historical Writing in the Christian and Islamic Worlds,* ed. D.O. Morgan (London: University of London School of Oriental and African Studies, 1982), pp. 60–75, repr. in Gillingham, *Richard Coeur de Lion,* part 2, no. 5, pp. 141–53. [Gillingham, "Roger of Howden on Crusade"]

——. "Some Legends of Richard the Lion Heart: Their Development and their Influence," in *Ricardo Cuor di Leone nella storia e nella leggenda,* Accademia Nazionale dei Lincei, problemi attuali di Scienza e di cultura 253 (1981):35–50; repr. in Gillingham, *Richard Coeur de Lion,* part 2, no. 7, pp. 181–92. [Gillingham, "Legends of Richard the Lion Heart"]

Giry, Arthur. "Les Établissements de Rouen. Études sur l'histoire des institutions municipales de Rouen, Falaise, Pont-Audemer, Verneuil, La Rochelle, Saintes, Oléron, Bayonne, Tours, Niort, Cognac, Saint-Jean d'Angély, Angoulême, Poitiers, etc.," *Bibliothèque de l'École des Chartes* 59.2 (1885). [Giry, "Les Établissements de Rouen"]

Godefroy, Theodore, and Denys Godefroy. *Le ceremonial francois,* 2 vols. (Paris: Sebastien and Gabriel Cramoisy, 1649). [Godefroy and Godefroy, *Le ceremonial francois*]

Gold, Penny Schine. *The Lady and the Virgin: Image, Attitude and Experience in Twelfth-Century France* (Chicago: University of Chicago Press, 1985). [Gold, *The Lady and the Virgin*]

Golding, Brian. "Burials and Benefactions: an Aspect of Monastic Patronage in Thirteenth-Century England," in *England in the Thirteenth Century: Proceedings of the 1984 Harlaxton Symposium,* ed. W.M. Ormrod (Woodbridge: Boydell, 1985), pp. 64–75.

Gómez Barcena, Maria Jesús. *Escultura gótica funeraria en Burgos* (Burgos: Excelentísima Diputación Provincial de Burgos, 1988). [Gómez Barcena, *Escultura gótica funeraria en Burgos*]

Gómez Moreno, Manuel *El Panteón real de las Huelgas de Burgos* (Madrid: Consejo Superior de Investigaciones Cientificas, Instituto Diego Velazquez, 1946). [Gómez Moreno, *El Panteón real de las Huelgas*]

González, Julio. *Alfonso IX,* 2 vols. (Madrid: Consejo Superior de Investigaciones Cientificas, 1944). [Gonzalez, *Alfonso IX*]

———. *El Reino de Castilla en la epoca de Alfonso VIII,* 3 vols. (Madrid: Consejo Superior de Investigaciones Cientificas, 1960). [Gonzalez, *Alfonso VIII*]

———. *Reinado y diplomas de Fernando III,* 3 vols. (Cordoba: Monte de Piedad y Caja de Ahorros de Córdoba, 1980–86).

Goody, Jack. *The Development of the Family and Marriage in Europe* (Cambridge: University of Cambridge Press, 1983). [Goody, *The Development of the Family and Marriage*]

Gothic Sculpture in America, I: The New England Museums, ed. Dorothy Gillerman (New York: Garland, 1989). [*Gothic Sculpture in America,* ed. Gillerman]

Gramont, Sanche de [aka Ted Morgan]. *Epitaph for Kings* by Sanche de Gramont (London: Hamish Hamilton, 1967).

Gransden, Antonia. *Historical Writing in England c. 550 to c. 1307* (Ithaca: Cornell University Press, 1974).

Grant, Lindy. *Abbot Suger of St-Denis: Church and State in Early Twelfth-Century France,* The Medieval World (London: Longman, 1998). [Grant, *Abbot Suger*]

———. "Suger and the Anglo-Norman World," *Anglo-Norman Studies* 10 (1988):50–67. [Grant, "Suger and the Anglo-Norman World"]

A Great Effusion of Blood: Varieties of Violence in Medieval Society, ed. Mark Meyerson, Daniel Thiery, and Oren Falk (Toronto: University of Toronto Press, forthcoming).

Green, Judith. "Aristocratic Women in Twelfth-Century England," in *Anglo-Norman Political Culture and the Twelfth-Century Renaissance,* ed. Hollister, pp. 59–82. [Green, "Aristocratic Women"]

———. "Financing Stephen's War," *Anglo-Norman Studies* 14 (1992):91–114. [Green, "Financing Stephen's War"]

Green, Mary Anne Everett. *Lives of the Princesses of England from the Norman Conquest,* 6 vols. (London: Henry Colburn, 1849–55). [Green, *Lives of the Princesses*]

Greenhill, Eleanor S. "Eleanor, Abbot Suger, and Saint-Denis," in *Eleanor of Aquitaine, Patron and Politician*, ed. Kibler, pp. 81–114. [Greenhill, "Eleanor, Abbot Suger, and Saint-Denis"]

Grierson, Philip. "Tombs and Obits of the Byzantine Emperors (337–1042)," *Dumbarton Oaks Papers* 16 (1942):3–8, 38–60. [Grierson, "Tombs and Obits"]

Grodecki, Louis with Catherine Brisac and Claudine Lautier. *Le vitrail roman* (Fribourg and Paris: Office du Livre and Vilo, 1977). [Grodecki et al., *Le vitrail roman*]

Gronier-Prieur, Armande. *L'abbaye Notre-Dame-du Lys à Dammarie-les-Lys*, Monuments historiques de Seine-et-Marne, no 4 (Verneuil-l'Etang [Seine-et-Marne]: Amis des monuments et des sites de Seine-et-Marne, 1971).

Guerreau-Jalabert, Anita. "Note critique sur les structures de parenté dans l'Europe médiévale," *Annales E.S.C.* 6 (1981):1028–49. [Guerreau-Jalabert, "Note critique"]

Guibert, Louis. "Des formules de date et de l'epoque du commencement de l'annee en Limousin," *Bulletin de la Société des Lettres, Sciences, et Arts de la Corréze* 8 (1886):159–211. [Guibert, Louis. "Les formules de date"]

Guilloreau, Léon. "Les fondations anglaises de l'abbaye de Savigny," *Revue Mabillon* 5 (1909):290–335. [Guilloreau, "Les fondations anglaises"]

Hale, Rosemary Drage. "Joseph as Mother: Adaptation and Appropriation in the Construction of Male Virtue," in *Medieval Mothering*, ed. Parsons and Wheeler, pp. 101–16.

Hallam, Elizabeth M. "Henry II, Richard I and the Order of Grandmont," *Journal of Medieval History* 1 (1975):165–86. [Hallam, "Henry II, Richard I and the Order of Grandmont"]

———. "Royal Burial and the Cult of Kingship in France and England, 1060–1330," *Journal of Medieval History* 8 (1982):339–80. [Hallam, "Royal Burial and the Cult of Kingship"]

Hallett, Cecil. "The Last Resting-Place of our Angevin Kings," *The Nineteenth Century and After* 52 (1902):265–81. [Hallett, "Last Resting-Place"]

Hamburger, Jeffrey F. *Nuns as Artists: The Visual Culture of a Medieval Convent* (Berkeley: University of California Press, 1997). [Hamburger, *Nuns as Artists*]

Hamilton, Bernard. "Women in the Crusader States: The Queens of Jerusalem (1100–1190)," in *Medieval Women*, ed. Baker, pp. 143–74. [Hamilton, "Women in the Crusader States"]

Hardegen, Friedrich. *Imperialpolitik König Heinrichs II. von England*, Heidelberger Abhandlungen zur mittleren und neueren Geschichte, 12 (Heidelberg: Carl Winter, 1905). [Hardegen, *Imperialpolitik König Heinrichs II*]

Harding, Wendy. "Medieval Women's Unwritten Discourse on Motherhood: A Reading of Two Fifteenth-Century Texts," *Women's Studies* 21 (1992):197–209.

Hardwick, Julie. *The Practice of Patriarchy: Gender and the Practice of Household Authority in Early Modern France* (University Park, PA: Pennsylvania State University Press, 1998). [Hardwick, *The Practice of Patriarchy*]

Harris, Barbara J. "A New Look at the Reformation: Aristocratic Women and Nunneries, 1450–1540," *Journal of British Studies* 32 (1993):89–113. [Harris, "A New Look"]

Harvey, Ruth E. *The Troubadour Marcabru and Love* (Westfield College, University of London: Committee for Medieval Studies, 1989). [Harvey, *Marcabru*]

Haskins, Charles Homer. "Henry II as a Patron of Literature," in *Essays in Medieval History presented to Thomas Frederick Tout*, ed. Little and Powicke, pp. 71–77. [Haskins, "Henry II as a Patron of Literature"]

Haslip, Joan. *Madame du Barry: The Wages of Beauty* (New York: Grove and Weidenfeld, 1991).

Havens Caldwell, Susan. "Urraca of Zamora and San Isidoro in Léon: Fulfillment of a Legacy," *Woman's Art Journal* 7 (1986):119–25. [Havens Caldwell, "Urraca"]

Hayward, Jane, and Louis Grodecki. "Les vitraux de la cathédrale d'Angers," *Bulletin monumental* 124 (1966):7–10.

Hefele, Karl-Josef von [Charles-Joseph Héfélé] *Conciliengeschichte. Nach den Quellen bearbeitete*, ed. Joseph Hergenröther and Alois Knöpfler, 7 vols. (Freiburg in Breisgau: Herder, 1855–74). [Hefele, *Conciliengeschichte*]

———. *Conciliengeschichte. Nach den Quellen bearbeitete*, ed. and trans. H. Leclercq as *Histoire des conciles d'après les documents originaux*, 11 vols. in 22 (Paris: Letouzey et Ané, 1907–52). [Hefele, *Histoire des conciles*, ed. Leclercq]

———. *Histoire des conciles* d'après les documents originaux, ed. and aug. H. Leclerq, 11 vols. in 22 (Paris: Letouzey et Ané, 1913). [Hefele, *Histoire des conciles*]

———. *A History of the Christian Councils from the original documents*, ed. and trans. William R. Clark; rev. 2nd. edn., 5 vols. (Edinburgh: T. and T. Clark, 1872–96; repr. New York: AMS Press, 1972). [Hefele, *History of the Christian Councils*, ed. Clark]

Helmholz, Richard H. *Marriage Litigation in Medieval England* (Cambridge: Cambridge University Press, 1974). [Helmholz, *Marriage Litigation*]

Herlihy, David. "'Did Women Have a Renaissance?' A Reconsideration," *Medievalia et Humanistica* n.s. 13 (1985):1–22. [Herlihy, "'Did Women Have a Renaissance?'"]

———. "Land, Family, and Women in Continental Europe, 701–1200," *Traditio* 1 (1962):89–120.

———. *Medieval Households* (Cambridge, MA: Harvard University Press, 1985). [Herlihy, *Medieval Households*]

———. *Women, Family, and Society in Medieval Europe. Historical Essays, 1978–1991*, ed. Anthony Molho (Providence, RI: Berghahn Books, 1995) [Herlihy, *Women, Family, and Society*]

Héron, A. "La chapelle Ste. Radegonde de Chinon," *Touraine Romane, Zodiaque* 19 (1977):327–35.

———. "La châsse royale de la chapelle Ste. Radegonde à Chinon," *Archéologia* 2 (1965):81–96.

Hillion, Yannick. "La Bretagne et la rivalité capétiens-plantagenêts. Un exemple: la duchesse Constance," *Annales de Bretagne* 92 (1985):111–44. [Hillion, "La Bretagne et la rivalité capétiens-plantagenêts"]

Hinschius, Paul. *Das Kirchenrecht der Katholiken und Protestanten in Deutschland: System des katholischen Kirchenrechts mit besonderer Rücksicht auf Deutschland*. 6 vols. in 7 (Berlin: J. Guttentag, 1869–97). [Hinschius, *Das Kirchenrecht*]

A History of the Crusades, ed. Kenneth M. Setton, 6 vols. (Madison: University of Wisconsin Press, 1969–89).

Hivergneaux, Marie. "Recherches sur la reine Aliénor: Rôle et pouvoir d'une femme au XIIᵉ siècle," unpublished *Mémoire de maîtrise* 2 vols. (University of Paris XII-Val de Marne, 1995). [Hivergneaux, "Recherches sur la reine Aliénor"]

Hohl, Claude. "Le comte Landri de Nevers dans l'histoire et dans la Geste de Girart de Roussillon," in *La chanson de geste et le mythe carolingien. Mélanges René Louis publiés par ses collègues, ses amis et ses élèves,* ed. Comité de publication des Mélanges René Louis (Saint-Père-sous-Vézelay [Mayenne]: Musée archéologique régional, 1982), pp. 781–800.

Holdsworth, Christopher "The Church," in *The Anarchy of Stephen's Reign,* ed. King, pp. 216–28. [Holdsworth, "The Church"]

Holladay, Joan. "The Education of Jeanne d'Evreux: Personal Piety and Dynastic Salvation in her Book of Hours at the Cloisters," *Art History* 17 (1994):585–611. [Holladay, "The Education of Jeanne d'Evreux"]

Hollister, C. Warren. "Magnates and 'Curiales' in Early Norman England," *Viator* 4 (1973):115–122, repr. in Hollister, *Monarchy, Magnates and Institutions,* pp. 97–115. [Hollister, "Magnates and 'Curiales'"]

———. *Monarchy, Magnates and Institutions in the Anglo-Norman World* (London: Variorum, 1986).

———. "The Rise of Administrative Kingship: Henry I," *The American Historical Review* 83 (1978):868–91, repr. in Hollister, *Monarchy Magnates and Institutions,* pp. 223–45. [Hollister, "Administrative Kingship"]

Holt, J[ames].C. "Ricardus rex Anglorum et dux Normannorum," in *Riccardo Cuor di Leone nella storia e nella leggenda,* Accademia Nazionale dei Lincei, problemi attuali di scienza e di cultura 253 (1981):17–33, repr. in Holt, *Magna Carta and Medieval Government* (London: Hambledon, 1985), pp. 67–83. [Holt, "Ricardus rex Anglorum"]

———. *Magna Carta and Medieval Government,* 2nd edn. (Cambridge, UK: Cambridge University Press, 1992). [Holt, *Magna Carta*]

———. "Aliénor d'Aquitaine, Jean sans Terre et la succession de 1199," *Cahiers de civilisation médiévale* 29 (1986):95–100. [Holt, "Aliénor"]

———. "Feudal Society and the Family in Early Medieval England: IV. The Heiress and the Alien," *Transactions of the Royal Historical Society* 5th ser. 35 (1985):1–28; repr. in Holt, *Colonial England, 1066–1215* (London: Variorum, 1997), pp. 245–69. [Holt, "Feudal Society and the Family"]

Horrent, Jules. "Chroniques espagnoles et chansons de geste," *Le Moyen Age,* 4th ser. 2, vol. 53 (1947):271–302. [Horrent, "Chroniques espagnoles et chansons de geste"]

———. "Matilda of Flanders," in the *New Dictionary of National Biography* (Oxford: Oxford University Press, forthcoming 2004).

Howe, Nicholas. *Migration and Mythmaking in Anglo-Saxon England* (New Haven, CT: Yale University Press, 1989). [Howe, *Migration and Mythmaking*]

Howell, Margaret. *Eleanor of Provence. Queenship in Thirteenth-Century England* (Oxford: Blackwell, 1998). [Howell, *Eleanor of Provence*]

———. "The Resources of Eleanor of Provence as Queen Consort," *The English Historical Review* 102 (1987):373–93.

Hudson, J[ohn]. *Land, Law and Lordship in Anglo-Norman England* (Oxford: Clarendon Press, 1994). [Hudson, *Land, Law and Lordship*]

Huneycutt, Lois L. "Alone of All Her Sex? Eleanor of Aquitaine and her Twelfth-century Predecessors," paper presented at the Thirty-Second International Congress on Medieval Studies, Western Michigan University, May 10, 1997.

———. *Another Esther in Our Times: Matilda II and the Formation of a Queenly Ideal in Anglo-Norman England* (Ph.D. dissertation, University of California at Santa Barbara, 1992). [Huneycutt, *Another Esther*]

———. "Female Succession and the Language of Power in the Writings of Twelfth-Century Churchmen," in *Medieval Queenship*, ed. Parsons, pp. 189–201. [Huneycutt, "Female Succession"]

———. "The Idea of the Perfect Princess: The *Life of St Margaret* in the Reign of Matilda II (1100–1118)," *Anglo-Norman Studies* 12 (1990):81–97. [Huneycutt, "Perfect Princess"]

———. "Images of Queenship in the High Middle Ages," *The Haskins Society Journal* 1 (1989):65–79. [Huneycutt, "Images of Queenship"]

———. "Intercession and the High-Medieval Queen: The Esther Topos," in *Power of the Weak*, ed. Carpenter and MacLean, pp. 126–46. [Huneycutt, "Intercession"]

———. "Proclaiming Her Dignity Abroad: The Literary and Artistic Network of Matilda of Scotland, Queen of England 1100–1118," in *The Cultural Patronage of Medieval Women*, ed. McCash, pp. 155–74. [Huneycutt, "Proclaiming Her Dignity Abroad"]

———. "Public Lives, Private Ties: Royal Mothers in England and Scotland, the Responsibilities of Queenship and the Success of Royal Mothers in England and Scotland, ca. 1070–1204," in *Medieval Mothering*, ed. Parsons and Wheeler, pp. 293–310. [Huneycutt, "Public Lives, Private Ties"]

Hunt, Lynn. "The Many Bodies of Marie Antoinette: Political Pornography and the Problem of the Feminine in the French Revolution," in *Eroticism and the Body Politic*, ed. Hunt, pp. 118–30.

Hutchison, Carole. *The Hermit Monks of Grandmont*, Cistercian Studies Series, 118 (Kalamazoo: Cistercian Publications, 1989). [Hutchison, *The Hermit Monks of Grandmont*]

Huyghebaert, N[icolas]. "La mère de Godefroid de Bouillon: la comtesse Ide de Boulogne," *Publications de la section historique de l'Institut grand-ducal de Luxembourg* 95 (1981):43–63. [Huyghebaert, "La mère de Godefroid de Bouillon"]

In Quest of Marie de France, a Twelfth-Century Poet, ed. Chantal E. Marechal (Lewiston: Edwin Mellen Press, 1992).

Isabelle, comtesse de Paris. *Moi, Marie-Antoinette* (Paris: Robert Laffont, 1999).

Isenburg-Büdingen, Wilhelm Karl von, and Frank Freytag von Loringhoven. *Stammtafeln zur Geschichte der Europäischen Staaten*, 2nd edn., 3 vols. in 2 (Marburg: J.A. Stargardt Verlag, 1953–56).

Jackman, Donald C. *The Konradiner: A Study in Genealogical Methodology* (Frankfurt am Main: V. Klostermann, 1990). [Jackman, *The Konradiner*]

Jackson, Richard A. "Manuscripts, Texts, and Enigmas of Medieval French Coronation Ordines," *Viator* 23 (1992):35–70. [Jackson, "Manuscripts, Texts, and Enigmas"]

Jacoby, Zehava. "The Tomb of Baldwin V, King of Jerusalem (1185–86), and the Workshop of the Temple Area," *Gesta* 17 (1979):3–14. [Jacoby, "The Tomb of Baldwin V"]

Jarrett, Bede. *The English Dominicans,* ed. Walter Gumbley (London: Burns, Oates & Washbourne Ltd., 1937).

Jeffreys, Elizabeth M. "The Comnenian Background to the *Romans d'Antiquité,*" *Byzantion* 50 (1980):455–86. [Jeffreys, "The Comnenian Background"]

Johns, Susan. "The Wives and Widows of the Earls of Chester, 1100–1252: The Charter Evidence," *The Haskins Society Journal* 7 (1995):117–32.

Johnson, Geraldine A. "Activating the Effigy: Donatello's Pecci Tomb in Siena Cathedral," *Art Bulletin* 77 (1995):445–59; repr. in *Between the Living and the Dead,* ed. Valdez del Alamo and Pendergast, pp. 99–117. [Johnson, "Activating the Effigy"]

Johnson, Penelope D. *Equal in Monastic Profession: Religious Women in Medieval France* (Chicago: University of Chicago Press, 1991).

Johnstone, Hilda. "The Queen's Household," in *Chapters in the Administrative History of Medieval England,* ed. T.F. Tout, 6 vols. of Manchester Historical Studies, vols. 34–35, 48–49, 57, 64 (Manchester: University of Manchester Press, 1929–33), 5:231–39. [Johnstone, "The Queen's Household"]

Joly, Aristide. *Benoît de Sainte-More et le Roman de Troie, ou les métamorphoses d'Homère et de l'épopée gréco-latine au Moyen Age* (Paris: Extrait des Mémoires de la Société des Antiquaires de Normandie, 1869). [Joly, *Benoît*]

Jones, Rosemarie. *Theme of Love in the Romans d'Antiquité* (New York-London: M.H.R.A, 1972). [Jones, *Theme of Love in the Romans d'Antiquité*]

Jordan, Erin. "'For the Safety of my Soul': The Religious Patronage of Jeanne and Marguerite of Constantinople, Sisters and Successive Countesses of Flanders and Hainaut, 1206–1280," Ph.D. diss., University of Iowa, 2000. [Erin Jordan, "'For the Safety of my Soul'"]

Jordan, William Chester. *Louis IX and the Challenge of the Crusade* (Princeton: Princeton University Press, 1979). [Jordan, *Louis IX*]

———. "Isabelle d'Angoulême, by the Grace of God, Queen," *Revue belge de philologie et d'histoire* 69 (1991):821–52. [Jordan, "Isabelle d'Angoulême"]

Justice, Steven. "Inquisition, Speech, and Writing: A Case from Late-Medieval Norwich," *Representations* 48 (1994):1–29.

Kantorowicz, Ernst H. *Frederick the Second, 1194–1250,* trans. E.O. Lorimer (London: Constable, 1931; repr. New York: Frederick Ungar, 1957). [Kantorowicz, *Frederick the Second*]

———. *The King's Two Bodies: A Study in Medieval Political Theology* (Princeton: Princeton University Press, 1957). [Kantorowicz, *King's Two Bodies*]

Karnein, Alfred. "Auf der Suche nach einem Autor: Andreas, Verfasser von *De Amore*," *Germanisch-Romanische Monatsschrift*, n.s. 28, vol. 59 (1978):1–20. [Karnein, "Auf der Suche nach einem Autor"]

Katzenellenbogen, A[dolf]. *Allegories of the Virtues and Vices in Medieval Art* (London; The Warburg Institute, 1939; repr., Medieval Academy Reprints for Teaching, Toronto: The University of Toronto Press, 1989).

Kelly, Amy. "Eleanor of Aquitaine and Her Courts of Love," *Speculum* 12 (1937):3–19. [Kelly, "Eleanor of Aquitaine and Her Courts of Love"]

————. *Eleanor of Aquitaine and the Four Kings* (Cambridge, MA: Harvard University Press, 1950). [Kelly, *Eleanor and the Four Kings*]

Kelly, Douglas. "The Invention of Briseida's Story in Benoît de Sainte-Maure's *Troie*," *Romance Philology* 48.3 (1995):221–41. [D. Kelly, "The Invention of Briseida's Story"]

Kelly (-Gadol), Joan. "Did Women Have a Renaissance?" In *Becoming Visible: Women in European History*, ed. Renate Bridenthal and Claudia Koonz, 1st edn. (Boston: Houghton Mifflin, 1977), pp. 175–201; repr. in Joan Kelly, *Women, History and Theory: The Essays of Joan Kelly* (Chicago: University of Chicago Press, 1984), pp. 19–50. [Kelly, "Did Women Have a Renaissance?"]

Kenaan-Kedar, Nurith. "Aliénor d'Aquitaine conduite en captivité. Les peintures murales commémoratives de Sainte-Radegonde de Chinon," *Cahiers de civilisation médiévale* 41 (1998):317–30. [Kenaan-Kedar, "Aliénor d'Aquitaine conduite en captivité"]

Kertesz, Christopher. "The *De Arte (Honeste) Amandi* of Andreas Capellanus," *Texas Studies in Literature and Language: A Journal of the Humanities* 13 (1971):5–16. [Kertesz, "The *De Arte (Honeste) Amandi*"]

Kessler, Ulrike. *Richard I. Löwenherz: König, Kreuzritter, Abenteurer* (Graz: Verlag Styria, 1995).

Kinder, Terryl. "Blanche of Castile and the Cistercians: An Architectural Re-evaluation of Maubuisson Abbey," *Cîteaux* 22 (1969):161–88. [Kinder, "Blanche of Castile and the Cistercians"]

King John: New Interpretations, ed. S.D. Church (Woodbridge: Boydell, 1999).

Kings and Kingship, ed. Joel T. Rosenthal (Binghamton: Center for Medieval and Early Renaissance Studies, 1986).

Kinoshita, Sharon. "Cherchez La Femme: Feminist Criticism and Marie de France's *Lai de Lanval*," *Romance Notes* 34 (1993–94):263–73. [Kinoshita, "Cherchez La Femme"]

Klauser, Renate. *Der Heinrichs-und Kunigundenkult im mittelalterlichen Bistum Bamberg* (Bamberg: Selbstverlag des Historischen Vereins, 1957). [Klauser, *Der Heinrichs-und Kunigundenkult*]

Knowles, David, and R.N. Hadcock. *Religious Houses, England and Wales.* 2nd. edn. (London: Longman, 1971). [Knowles and Hadcock, *Religious Houses*]

Krueger, Roberta L. *Women Readers and the Ideology of Gender in the Old French Verse Romance* (Cambridge, UK: Cambridge University Press, 1993). [Krueger, *Women Readers*]

Kuttner, Stephan. "Les débuts de l'école canoniste française," *Studia et documenta historiae et iuris* 4 (1938):193–204; repr. in Kuttner, *Gratian and the Schools of Law* (London: Variorum, 1983), no.VI. [Kuttner, "Débuts de l'école canoniste française"]

———. "Harmony from Dissonance," originally published as a lecture (Latrobe, PA: Archabbey Press, 1960); repr. in Kuttner, *History of Ideas and Doctrines of Canon Law in the Middle Ages,* 2nd edn. (Aldershot:Variorum, 1980), no. I. [Kuttner, "Harmony from Dissonance"]

La Monte, J[ohn].L[ife]. *The World of the Middle Ages. A Reorientation of Medieval History* (New York: Appleton Century Crofts, 1949).

Labande, Edmond-René. "Les filles d'Aliénor d'Aquitaine: étude comparative," *Cahiers de civilisation médiévale* 29 (1986):101–12. [Labande, "Filles"]

———. "Les liens entre l'Angleterre médiévale et la France de l'Ouest," *Actes du Colloque de Poitiers 1976* (Poitiers: CSEM, 1977):5–11.

———. "Pour une image véridique d'Aliénor d'Aquitaine," *Bulletin de la Société des antiquaires de l'Ouest* 4th ser. 2 (1951):175–234; repr. in Labande, *Histoire de l'Europe Occidentale XF-XIV* s. (London:Variorum, 1973), no.V. [Labande, "Pour une image véridique"]

Labarge, Margaret Wade. *A Small Sound of the Trumpet: Women in Medieval Life* (Boston: Beacon Press, 1986).

Lacurie, J.-L. *Histoire de l'abbaye de Maillezais, depuis sa fondation jusqu'à nos jours, suivie de pièces justificatives la plupart inédites* (Fontenay-le-Comte: E. Fillon, 1852). [Lacurie, *Histoire de l'abbaye de Maillezais*]

Lambert, Sarah. "Queen or Consort: Rulership and Politics in the Latin East, 1118–1228," in *Queens and Queenship in Medieval Europe,* ed. Duggan, pp. 153–72. [Lambert, "Queen or Consort"]

Lamm, Carl Johan. *Mittelalterliche Gläser und Steinschnittarbeiten aus dem Nahen Osten,* 2 vols. (Berlin: D. Reimer, 1930). [Lamm, *Mittelalterliche Gläser*]

Landau, Peter. *Die Entstehung des kanonischen Infamiebegriffs von Gratian bis zur Glossa Ordinaria, Forschungen zur kirchlichen Rechtsgeschichte und zum Kirchenrecht,* vol. 5 (Cologne: Bohlau, 1966). [Landau, *Die Entstehung des kanonischen Infamiebegriffs*]

Larrainzar, Carlos. "El decreto de Graciano del Códice Fd 9 (= Firenze, Biblioteca Nazionale Centrale, Conventi Soppressi A.I.402)," *Ius Ecclesiae* 10 (1998):421–89. [Larrainzar, "El decreto de Graciano del Códice Fd 9"]

Laski, Philip M. *The Trial and Execution of Madame du Barry* (London: Constable, 1969).

Lassner, Jacob. *Demonizing the Queen of Sheba: Boundaries of Gender and Culture in Postbiblical Judaism and Medieval Islam* (Chicago: University of Chicago Press, 1993). [Lassner, *Demonizing the Queen of Sheba*]

Laube, Daniela. *Zehn Kapitel zur Geschichte der Eleonore von Aquitanien,* Geist und Werk der Zeiten, Historisches Seminar Zurich, 68 (Bern: Peter Lang, 1984). [Laube, *Zehn Kapitel*]

Lazar, Moshé. *Amour courtois et fin'amors dans la littérature du XIF siècle,* Bibliothèque française et romane, Section C, Études littéraires, 8 (Paris: C. Klincksieck, 1964). [Lazar, *Amour courtois*]

Le Goff, Jacques. *La naissance du Purgatoire, Bibliotheque des histoires* (Paris: Gallimard, 1981); trans. Arthur Goldhammer as *The Birth of Purgatory* (Chicago: University of Chicago Press, 1984). [Le Goff, *The Birth of Purgatory*]

———. *Saint Louis* (Paris: Gallimard, 1996). [Le Goff, *Saint Louis*]

Le Jan, Régine. *Famille et pouvoir dans le monde franc (VIIe-Xe siècles): Essai d'anthropologie sociale* (Paris: Publications de la Sorbonne, 1995). [Le Jan, *Famille et pouvoir*]

Le Saux, Françoise H.M. *Laȝamon's Brut: The Poem and Its Sources* (Cambridge: D.S. Brewer, 1989).

Leclercq, Jean. "Il Monachesimo femminile nei secoli XIIe-XIIIe," in *Movimenti religiosi femminile e francescanesimo nel secoli XIII. Atti del Convegno internazionale della Società internazionale di Studi Francescani* (Assisi: La Società, 1980), pp. 61–99. [Leclercq, "Il Monachesimo femminile"]

Lee, Patricia-Ann. "Reflections of Power: Margaret of Anjou and the Dark Side of Queenship," *Renaissance Quarterly* 29 (1986):183–217.

Lees, B[eatrice]. "The Letters of Queen Eleanor of Aquitaine to Pope Clement III," *English Historical Review* 21 (1906):73–93. [Lees, "Letters of Eleanor to Pope Clement III"]

Legge, Mary Dominica. *Anglo-Norman Literature and its Background* (Oxford: Oxford University Press, 1963). [Legge, *Anglo-Norman Literature*]

———. "La littérature anglo-normande au temps d'Aliénor d'Aquitaine," *Cahiers de civilisation médiévale* 29 (1986):113–18. [Legge, "La littérature anglo-normande au temps d'Aliénor"]

Leicester, H. Marshall, Jr. "Of a Fire in the Dark: Public and Private Feminism in the *Wife of Bath's Tale*," *Women's Studies* 2 [1984]:152–78.

Lejeune, Rita. "Rôle littéraire d'Aliénor d'Aquitaine et de sa famille," *Cultura neolatina. Bollettino dell'Istituto di Filogia Romanza* 14 (1954):5–57. [Lejeune, "Rôle littéraire d'Aliénor"]

———. "Rôle littéraire de la famille d'Aliénor d'Aquitaine," *Cahiers de civilisation mediévale* 1 (1958):319–36. [Lejeune, Rita. "Rôle littéraire de la famille d'Aliénor"]

Lever, Evelyne. *Marie-Antoinette: The Last Queen of France*, trans. Catherine Temerson (New York: Farrar, Straus, Giroux, 2000).

Lewis, Andrew W. "The Career of Philip the Cleric, Younger Brother of Louis VII: Apropos of an Unpublished Charter," *Traditio* 50 (1995):111–28. [Lewis, "Philip the Cleric"]

———. *Royal Succession in Capetian France: Studies on Familial Order and the State* (Cambridge, MA: Harvard University Press, 1981). [Lewis, *Royal Succession*]

———. "Successions ottoniennes et robertiniennes: un essai de comparaison," in *Le roi de France et son royaume autour de l'an Mil*, ed. Michel Parisse and Xavier Barral i Altet, Actes du Colloque Hughes Capet, 987–1987 (Paris: Picard, 1992), pp. 47–53. [Lewis, "Successions ottoniennes et robertiniennes"]

Lewis, C[harlton].T[homas]. *An Elementary Latin Dictionary* (Oxford: Oxford University Press, 1891; repr. Oxford: Oxford University Press, 1981).

Leyser, Henrietta. *Medieval Women: A Social History of Women in England 450–1500* (New York: Saint Martin's, 1995).

Linehan, Peter. *The History and Historians of Medieval Spain* (Oxford: Clarendon Press, 1993). [Linehan, *History and Historians*]

Livermore, H[arold].V[ictor]. *A History of Portugal* (Cambridge, UK: Cambridge University Press, 1947).

Livingstone, Amy. "Aristocratic Women in the Chartrain," in *Aristocratic Women in Medieval France,* ed. Evergates, pp. 44–73. [Livingstone, "Aristocratic Women in the Chartrain"]

L'œuvre de Limoges: émaux limousins du Moyen Âge, exhibition catalogue, Musée du Louvre and the Metropolitan Museum of Art (Paris: Réunion des musées nationaux, 1995).

Lomenec'h, Gérard. *Aliénor d'Aquitaine et les troubadours* (Luçon: Sud Ouest, 1997).

Longford, Elizabeth. *Queen Victoria: Born to Succeed* (New York: Harper and Row, 1964).

Loomis, Stanley. *The Fatal Friendship: Marie Antoinette, Count Fersen and the Flight to Varennes* (New York: Doubleday, 1972). [Loomis, *Fatal Friendship*]

LoPrete, Kimberley. "Adela of Blois: Familial Alliances and Female Lordship," in *Aristocratic Women in Medieval France,* ed. Evergates, pp. 7–43.

―――. "Adela of Blois as Mother and Countess," in *Medieval Mothering,* ed. Parsons and Wheeler, pp. 313–33.

―――. "The Anglo-Norman Card of Adela of Blois," *Albion* 22 (1990):569–89.

Lot, Ferdinand. "La chanson de Landri," *Romania* 32 (1903):1–17. [Lot, "La chanson de Landri"]

―――. *Les derniers Carolingiens* (Paris: É. Bouillon, 1891). [Lot, *Derniers Carolingiens*]

Lozinski, Jean Louis. "Henri II, Aliénor d'Aquitaine et la cathédrale d'Angers," *Cahiers de civilisation médiévale* 37 (1994):91–100. [Lozinski, "Henri II"]

Luchaire, Achille. *Études sur les actes de Louis VII* (Paris: Picard, 1885). [Luchaire, *Louis VII*]

Lumiansky, R[obert].M. "Structural Unity in Benoît's *Roman de Troie,*" *Romania* 79 (1958):410–24.

Maddicott, John R. *Simon de Montfort* (Cambridge, UK: Cambridge University Press, 1994). [Maddicott, *Simon de Montfort*]

Makowski, Elizabeth. *Canon Law and Cloistered Women: Periculoso and its Commentators, 1298–1545* (Washington, D.C.: Catholic University of America Press, 1997). [Makowski, *Canon Law and Cloistered Women*]

Mandach, André de. *Naissance et développement de la chanson de geste en Europe,* vol. 1, *La geste de Charlemagne et de Roland,* Publications romanes et françaises, 69 (Geneva: Droz, 1961). [Mandach, *Naissance et développement de la chanson de geste*]

Mareille, Vital. *La vie ardente d'Eléonore d'Aquitaine* (Paris, 1931). [Mareille, *La vie ardente d'Eléonore*]

Markale, Jean. *Aliénor d'Aquitaine. La vie, la légende, l'influence d'Aliénor, comtesse de Poitou, duchesse d'Aquitaine, reine de France, puis d'Angleterre, dame des troubadours et des bardes bretons* (Paris: Payot, 1979). [Markale, *La vie, la légende, l'influence d'Aliénor*]

Marriage, Property, and Succession, ed. Lloyd Bonfield, Comparative Studies in Continental and Anglo-American Legal History, 10 (Berlin: Duncker and Humblot, 1992).

Martin, Georges. "L'escarboucle de Saint-Denis, le roi de France et l'empereur des Espagnes," in *Saint-Denis et la royauté. Études offertes à Bernard Guenée, Membre de l'Institut,* ed. Françoise Autrand, Claude Gauvard, and Jean-Marie Moeglin, Histoire ancienne et médiévale 59 (Paris: Publications de la Sorbonne, 1999), pp. 439–62. [Martin, "L'escarboucle de Saint-Denis"]

Martindale, Andrew. "Patrons and Minders: The Intrusion of the Secular into Sacred Spaces in the Late Middle Ages," in *The Church and the Arts,* ed. Diana Wood, Studies in Church History 28 (Oxford: Blackwell, 1992), pp. 143–78. [A. Martindale, "Patrons and Minders"]

Martindale, Jane. "'Cavalaria et Orgueill': Duke William IX of Aquitaine and the Historian," in *The Ideals and Practice of Medieval Knighthood, 2,* ed. Christopher Harper-Bell and Ruth Harvey (Woodbridge: Boydell & Brewer, 1988), pp. 87–116; repr. as no. 10 in Martindale, *Status, Authority.* [Martindale, "'Cavalaria et Orgueill'"]

———. "Eleanor of Aquitaine," in *Richard Coeur de Lion in History and Myth,* ed. Janet L. Nelson, King's College London Medieval Studies 7 (London: King's College London Centre for Late Antique and Medieval Studies, 1992), pp. 17–50; repr. as no. 11 in Martindale, *Status, Authority.* [Martindale, "Eleanor of Aquitaine"]

———. "Eleanor of Aquitaine: The Last Years," in *King John: New Interpretations,* ed. S.D. Church (Woodbridge: Boydell, 1999), pp. 137–64. [Martindale, "Eleanor of Aquitaine: The Last Years"]

———. *Status, Authority and Regional Power. Aquitaine and France, 9th to 12th Centuries,* Variorum Collected Studies Series, 488 (Aldershot, UK: Variorum, 1997).

———. "Succession and Politics in the Romance-Speaking World, ca. 1000–1140," in *England and her Neighbours, 1066–1485: Essays in Honour of Pierre Chaplais,* ed. Michael Jones and Malcolm Vale. (London: Hambledon Press, 1989), pp. 19–41, repr. as no. 5 in Martindale, *Status, Authority.* [Martindale, "Succession and Politics"]

———. "The Sword on the Stone: Some Resonances of a Medieval Symbol of Power (the Tomb of King John in Worcester Cathedral)," *Anglo-Norman Studies* 15 (1993):226–30. [Martindale, "The Sword on the Stone"]

Mason, Emma. "'Pro statu et incolumitate regni mei': Royal Monastic Patronage, 1066–1154," in *Religion and National Identity,* ed. S. Mews, Studies in Church History, 18 (Oxford: Blackwell, 1982), pp. 99–117. [Mason, "Royal Monastic Patronage"]

Maurer, Helen Estelle. "Margaret of Anjou: Queenship and Power in Late Medieval England, 1445–61," Ph.D. diss., University of California at Irvine, 1999.

Mayer, H[ans].E[berhard]. "Studies in the History of Queen Melisende of Jerusalem," *Dumbarton Oaks Papers* 26 (1972):93–182. [Mayer, "Queen Melisende"]

Maza, Sarah. "The Diamond Necklace Affair Revisited (1785–1786): The Case of the Missing Queen," in *Eroticism and the Body Politic,* ed. Hunt, pp. 62–89.

————. *Private Lives and Public Affairs: The Causes Célèbres of Prerevolutionary France* (Berkeley-Los Angeles: University of California Press, 1993).

McCartney, Elizabeth. "Ceremonies and Privileges of Office: Queenship in Late Medieval France," in *Power of the Weak: Studies on Medieval Women*, ed. Carpenter and McLean, pp. 178–219. [McCartney, "Ceremonies and Privileges of Office"]

McCash, June Hall Martin. "Marie de Champagne and Eleanor of Aquitaine: A Relationship Reexamined," *Speculum* 54 (1979):698–711. [McCash, "Marie de Champagne and Eleanor of Aquitaine"]

McCracken, Peggy. *The Romance of Adultery: Queenship and Sexual Transgression in Old French Literature* (Philadelphia: University of Pennsylvania Press, 1998). [McCracken, *Romance of Adultery*]

McGrew, Roderick E. *Paul I of Russia, 1754–1801* (Oxford: Clarendon Press, 1992).

Meade, Marion [Facinger]. *Eleanor of Aquitaine: A Biography* (New York: Hawthorn Books, 1977). [Meade, *Eleanor of Aquitaine*]

Medieval Mothering, ed. John Carmi Parsons and Bonnie Wheeler, Garland Reference Library of the Humanities, The New Middle Ages 3 (New York: Garland Press, 1996). [*Medieval Mothering*, ed. Parsons and Wheeler]

Medieval Queenship, ed. John Carmi Parsons (New York: St. Martins Press, 1993).

Medieval Women, ed. Derek Baker, Studies in Church History, Subsidia 1 (Oxford: Blackwell, 1978). [*Medieval Women*, ed. Baker]

Medieval Women and the Sources of Medieval History, ed. Joel T. Rosenthal (Athens: University of Georgia Press, 1990).

Medieval Women in Their Communities, ed. Diane Watt (Toronto: University of Toronto Press, 1997).

Meyer, Marc A. "The Queen's 'Demesne' in Later Anglo-Saxon England," in *The Culture of Christendom*, ed. Meyer, pp. 75–113. [Meyer, "The Queen's 'Demesne'"]

Migliorino, Francisco. *Fama e infamia: Problemi della società medievale nel pensiero giuridico nei secoli XII e XIII* (Catania: Giannotta, 1985). [Migliorino, *Fama e infamia*]

Milsom, S[troud].F.C. "Inheritance by Women in the Twelfth and Early Thirteenth Centuries," in *On the Laws and Customs of England: Essays in Honour of S.E. Thorne*, ed. Morris S. Arnold (Chapel Hill: University of North Carolina Press, 1981), pp. 60–89. [Milsom, "Inheritance by Women"]

Miscellanea Domenico Maffei dicata, ed. Antonio Garcia y Garcia and Peter Weimar, 4 vols. (Goldbach: Keip, 1995).

Mitchell, Linda E. "The Lady is a Lord: Noble Widows and Land in Thirteenth-Century Britain," *Historical Reflections/Reflexions Historiques* 18.1 (1992):71–97.

Mitford, Nancy. *Madame de Pompadour* (London: Hamish Hamilton, 1954).

Montfaucon, Bernard de. *Les monumens de la monarchie françoise*, 5 vols. (Paris: Julien-Michel Gandouin et Pierre-François Giffart, 1729–33). [Montfaucon, *Les monumens de la monarchie françoise*]

Moore, John S. "The Anglo-Norman Family: Size and Structure," *Anglo-Norman Studies* 14 (1992):153–96.

Le Moyen Age. Dictionnaire des Lettres Françaises, ed. Georges Grente, Robert Bossuat, Louis Pichard, and Guy Raynaud de Lage (Paris: Fayard, 1964).

Mullally, Evelyn. "La colonisation de l'Irlande au XIIᵉ siècle d'après une chronique anglo-normande," *Cahiers de civilisation médiévale* 37 (1994):365–70. [Mullally, "La colonisation de l'Irlande"]

———. "Did John of Earley write the *Histoire de Guillaume le Maréchal?*" in *The Court Reconvenes: Selected Proceedings of the Ninth Triennial Congress of the International Courtly Literature Society* (Cambridge, UK: Boydell and Brewer, 2001). [Mullally, "Did John of Earley write the *Histoire de Guillaume le Maréchal?*"]

———. "The Portrayal of Women in the *Histoire de Guillaume le Maréchal,*" *Peritia: Journal of the Medieval History of Ireland* 10 (1996):351–62. [Mullally, "The Portrayal of Women"]

Murray, Jacqueline. *Women in the Middle Ages,* video recording (Toronto: University of Toronto, 1992). [Murray, *Women in the Middle Ages*]

Musto, Ronald G. "Queen Sanchia of Naples (1286–1345) and the Spiritual Franciscans," in *Women of the Medieval World,* ed. Kirshner and Wemple, pp. 179–214.

Nelson, Janet L. "Inauguration Rituals," in *Early Medieval Kingship,* ed. Sawyer and Wood, pp. 50–71.

———. "Women at the Court of Charlemagne: A Case of Monstrous Regiment?" in *Medieval Queenship,* ed. Parsons, pp. 43–61. [Nelson, "Women at the Court of Charlemagne"]

———. "Medieval Queenship," in *Women in Medieval Western European Culture,* ed. Mitchell, pp. 179–207.

Nelson, Mary. "Why Witches Were Women," in *Women: A Feminist Perspective,* ed. Freeman, pp. 335–50.

The New Medievalism, ed. Marina S. Brownlee, Kevin Brownlee, Stephen G. Nichols (Baltimore: Johns Hopkins University Press, 1991).

Nicholas, Karen S. "Countesses as Rulers in Flanders," in *Aristocratic Women in Medieval France,* ed. Evergates, pp. 111–37. [Nicholas, "Countesses as Rulers in Flanders"]

Nichols, Stephen G. "Marie de France's Commonplaces," *Yale French Studies* 44 (1991):138–48.

Nip, Renée. "Godelieve of Gistel and Ida of Boulogne," in *Sanctity and Motherhood,* ed. Mulder-Bakker, pp. 191–223. [Nip, "Godelieve"]

Nolan, Barbara. *Chaucer and the Tradition of the Roman Antique* (Cambridge and New York: Cambridge University Press, 1992). [B. Nolan, *Chaucer and the Tradition of the Roman Antique*]

Nolan, Kathleen. "The Queen's Body and Institutional Memory: The Tomb of Adelaide of Maurienne," in *Between the Living and the Dead,* ed. Valdez del Alamo and Pendergast, pp. 249–67. [Nolan, "The Queen's Body and Institutional Memory"]

————. "La reine est morte: The Tomb of Queen Adelaide of Maurienne and Reginal Burial Practice in Twelfth-Century France," paper presented to the University of Virginia's Medieval Circle, February 1997.

————. "'Ploratus et Ululatus': The Mothers in the Massacre of the Innocents at Chartres Cathedral," *Studies in Iconography* 17 (1996):125–26. [Nolan, "'Ploratus et Ululatus'"]

Noonan, John T., Jr. "Gratian Slept Here: The Changing Identity of the Father in the Systematic Study of Canon Law," *Traditio* 35 (1979):145–72. [Noonan, "Gratian Slept Here"]

Norgate, Kate. *England Under the Angevin Kings,* 2 vols. (London-New York: MacMillan, 1886–87; repr. New York: Haskell House, 1969). [Norgate, *England Under the Angevin Kings*]

————. *John Lackland* (London-New York: MacMillan, 1902; repr. New York: AMS Press, 1970). [Norgate, *John Lackland*]

O'Callaghan, Joseph. *The Cortes of Castile-León, 1188–1350* (Philadelphia: University of Pennsylvania Press, 1989). [O'Callaghan, *Cortes of Castile-León*]

————. *History of Medieval Spain* (Ithaca: Cornell University Press, 1975). [O'Callaghan, *Medieval Spain*]

Oliva, Marilyn. *The Convent and the Community in Late Medieval England: Female Monasteries in the Diocese of Norwich, 1350–1450* (Woodbridge, UK: Boydell, 1998). [Oliva, *The Convent and the Community*]

Ortner, Sherry B. "Gender and Sexuality in Hierarchical Societies: the Case of Polynesia and Some Comparative Implications," in *Sexual Meanings,* ed. Ortner and Whitehead, pp. 359–409.

Owen, D[ouglas].D[avid].R[oy]. *Eleanor of Aquitaine: Queen and Legend* (Oxford-Cambridge, MA: Blackwell, 1993). [Owen, *Eleanor of Aquitaine*]

Pange, Jean de. *Le roi très chrétien* (Paris: Fayard, 1949). [Pange]

Painter, Sidney. "Castellans of the Plain of Poitou in the eleventh and twelfth centuries," in Painter, *Feudalism and Liberty,* pp. 17–40. [Painter, "Castellans of the Plain of Poitou"]

————. *Feudalism and Liberty: Articles and Addresses of Sidney Painter,* ed. Fred A. Cazel, Jr. (Baltimore: Johns Hopkins University Press, 1961).

————. "The Lords of Lusignan in the eleventh and twelfth centuries," in Painter, *Feudalism and Liberty,* pp. 41–89. [Painter, "The Lords of Lusignan"]

————. *William Marshal: Knight-Errant, Baron and Regent of England* (Baltimore: Johns Hopkins University Press, 1933). [Painter, *William Marshal*]

Panofsky, Erwin. *Tomb Sculpture: Four Lectures on Its Changing Aspects from Ancient Egypt to Bernini,* ed. H.W. Janson (New York: Harry N. Abrams, 1964). [Panofsky, *Tomb Sculpture*]

Paris, Gaston. "La légende de Saladin," *Journal des savants* (1893):284–99, 354–65, 428–58, 486–98. [Paris, "La légende de Saladin"]

Parsons, John Carmi. *Eleanor of Castile: Queen and Society in Thirteenth-Century England* (New York: St. Martins Press, 1995). [Parsons, *Eleanor of Castile*]

————. "Family, Sex, and Power: the Rhythms of Medieval Queenship," in *Medieval Queenship,* ed. Parsons, pp. 1–11. [Parsons, "Family, Sex, and Power"]

————. "The Intercessionary Patronage of Queens Margaret and Isabella of France," in *Thirteenth Century England VI: Proceedings of the Durham Conference 1995*, ed. Michael Prestwich, R.H. Britnell and Robin Frame (Woodbridge, UK: Boydell, 1997), pp. 145–56.

————. "'Loved Him, Hated Her': Honor and Shame at the Medieval Court," in *Conflicted Identities and Multiple Masculinities*, ed. Murray, pp. 279–98. [Parsons, "'Loved Him, Hated Her'"]

————. "Mothers, Daughters, Marriage, Power: Some Plantagenet Evidence, 1150–1500," in *Medieval Queenship*, ed. Parsons, pp. 63–78. [Parsons, "Mothers, Daughters, Marriage, Power"]

————. "'Never was a body buried in England with such solemnity and honor': The Burials and Posthumous Commemorations of English Queens to 1500," in *Queens and Queenship in Medieval Europe*, ed. Duggan, pp. 317–37. [Parsons, "Burials and Posthumous Commemorations of English Queens"]

————. "Of Queens, Courts, and Books: Reflections on the Literary Patronage of Thirteenth-Century Plantagenet Queens," in *The Cultural Patronage of Medieval Women*, ed. McCash, pp. 175–201. [Parsons, "Of Queens, Courts, and Books"]

————. "The Pregnant Queen as Counsellor and the Medieval Construction of Motherhood," in *Medieval Mothering*, ed. Parsons and Wheeler, pp. 39–61. [Parsons, "The Pregnant Queen"]

————. "The Queen's Intercession in Thirteenth-Century England," in *Power of the Weak*, ed. Carpenter and MacLean, pp. 144–77. [Parsons, "Queen's Intercession"]

————. "'Que nos lactauit in infancia': The Impact of Childhood Caregivers on Plantagenet Family Relationships in the Thirteenth and Early Fourteenth Centuries," in *Women, Marriage, and Family in Medieval Christendom*, ed. Rosenthal and Rousseau, pp. 289–324. [Parsons, "'Que nos lactauit in infancia'"]

————. "Ritual and Symbol in the English Medieval Queenship to 1500," in *Women and Sovereignty*, ed. Fradenburg, pp. 61–78. [Parsons, "Ritual and Symbol"]

————. "Violence, the Queen's Body and the Medieval Body Politic," forthcoming in *A Great Effusion of Blood*, ed. Meyerson, Thiery, and Falk.

————. "The Year of Eleanor of Castile's Birth and Her Children by Edward I," *Mediaeval Studies* 46 (1984): 245–65. [Parsons, "The Year of Eleanor of Castile's Birth"]

Pastoureau, Michel. *Traité d'héraldique*. Grands manuels Picard, Bibliothèque de la sauvegarde de l'art français (Paris: Picard, 1979). [Pastoureau, *Traité d'héraldique*]

Paterson, Linda M. *The World of the Troubadours: Medieval Occitan Society, ca. 1100-ca. 1300* (Cambridge, UK: Cambridge University Press, 1993). [Paterson, *World of the Troubadours*]

Patterson, Lee. *Chaucer and the Subject of History* (Madison, WI: University of Wisconsin Press, 1991). [Patterson, *Chaucer and the Subject of History*]

Pavillon, B. *La vie dv Bien-hevrevx Robert d'Arbrissel; Patriarche des Solitaires de la France, et Institvtevr de l'ordre de Font-Evravd. Divisée en Devx parties Et justifiée par Tîtres rares, tirez de divers Monasteres de France, d'Espagne, & d'Angleterre* (Saumur: François Ernou, 1667). [Pavillon, *La vie dv Bien-hevrevx Robert d'Arbrissel*]

Pernoud, Régine. *Aliénor d'Aquitaine,* 2nd. edn. (Paris: Albin Michel, 1965). [Pernoud, *Aliénor d'Aquitaine*]

Perrier, Antoine. "De nouvelles précisions sur la mort de Richard Coeur de Lion," *Bulletin philologique et historique (jusqu'à 1610) du Comité des travaux historiques et scientifiques* (1959):159–69. [Perrier, "De nouvelles précisions sur la mort de Richard Coeur de Lion"]

Persons in Groups: Social Behavior as Identity Formation in Medieval and Renaissance Europe, ed. Richard C. Trexler, Medieval and Renaissance Texts and Studies 36 (Binghamton, NY: Center for Medieval and Early Renaissance Studies, 1985).

Peters, Edward. *The Shadow King: Rex Inutilis in Medieval Law and Literature, 751–1327* (New Haven, CT: Yale University Press, 1970). [Peters, *The Shadow King*]

Petit, Aimé. "L'Anachronisme dans les romans antiques du XIIe siècle," in *Relire le Roman d'Eneas,* ed. Jean Dufournet (Geneva: Slatkine, 1985), pp. 105–48. [A. Petit, "L'Anachronisme"]

Petit, Ernest. *Histoire des ducs de Bourgogne de la race capétienne,* 6 vols. (Dijon: Imprimerie Darantière, 1885–1905). [Petit, *Histoire des ducs de Bourgogne*]

Petit-Dutaillis, Charles. *Étude sur la vie et le règne de Louis VIII (1187–1226)* (Paris: Bouillon, 1894). [Petit-Dutaillis, *Louis VIII*]

Petzold, Andreas. *Romanesque Art* (New York: Harry N. Abrams, 1995). [Petzold, *Romanesque Art*]

Pfister, Charles. *Études sur le règne de Robert le Pieux* (Paris: F. Vieweg, 1885). [Pfister, *Robert le Pieux*]

Philip, Brian. *Excavations at Faversham, 1965* (Kent Archaeological Research Group, 1968). [Philip, *Excavations at Faversham*]

Pibrac, Anatole du Faur, comte de, "Histoire de l'abbaye de Voisins," *Mémoires de la Société d'Agriculture, Sciences, Belles-Lettres, et Arts d'Orléans* 22 (1881):177–224. [Pibrac, "l'abbaye de Voisins"]

Pinches, John Harvey, and R[osemary].V. Pinches. *The Royal Heraldry of England* (London: Heraldry Today, 1974). [Pinches and Pinches, *Royal Heraldry*]

Plaidy, Jean. *The Plantagenet Prelude* (London: Robert Hale, 1976). [Plaidy, *The Plantagenet Prelude*]

Poey d'Avant, Faustin. *Monnaies féodales de France,* 3 vols. (Paris: Rollin, 1858–62). [Poey d'Avant, *Monnaies féodales de France*]

Pollock, Frederic W. and Frederic William Maitland. *The History of English Law before the Time of Edward I,* 2nd. edn., 2 vols. (Cambridge: Cambridge University Press, 1898, repr. 1968). [Pollock and Maitland, *The History of English Law*]

Poole, A[ustin].L[ane]. *From Domesday Book to Magna Carta, 1087–1216,* Oxford History of England 3, 2nd. edn. (Oxford: Clarendon Press, 1955). [Poole, *Domesday Book to Magna Carta*]

Posse, Otto. *Die Siegel der deutschen Kaiser und Könige von 751 bis 1806,* 5 vols. (Dresden: W. Baensch, 1909–13). [Posse, *Siegel*]

Poulet, André. "Capetian Women and the Regency: The Genesis of a Vocation," in *Medieval Queenship,* ed. Parsons, pp. 93–116. [Poulet, "Capetian Women and the Regency"]

Power of the Weak: Studies on Medieval Women. ed. Jennifer Carpenter and Sally-Beth MacLean (Urbana: University of Illinois Press, 1995).

Powicke, Frederick Maurice. "Loretta, Countess of Leicester," in *Historical Essays in Honour of James Tait*, ed. J. Goronwy Edwards (Manchester; Manchester University Press, 1933), pp. 247–72.

———. *The Loss of Normandy: Studies in the History of the Angevin Empire*, 2nd edn. (Manchester: University of Manchester Press, 1961). [Powicke, *The Loss of Normandy*]

Prestwich, Michael. *Edward I* (Berkeley-Los Angeles: University of California Press, 1988).

Prynne, William. *Aurum reginae: Or a compendious tractate and Chronological Collection of Records in the Tower and Court of Exchequer Concerning Queen's Gold. Evidencing the Quiddity, Quantity, Quality, Antiquity, and Legality of this Golden Prerogative, Duty, and Revenue of the Queen-Consorts of England . . .* (London, n.p.: 1668). [Prynne, *Aurum reginae*]

Queens and Queenship in Medieval Europe, ed. Anne J. Duggan (Woodbridge: Boydell, 1997). [*Queens and Queenship*, ed. Duggan]

Queens, Regents and Potentates, ed. Teresa M. Vann (Cambridge, UK: Academia, 1993).

Rabourdin, A[ndré-Nicolas]. *Le prieuré royal de Haute-Bruyère de l'ordre de Fontevrault* (Rambouillet: Société archéologique de Saint-Alban, 1948). [Rabourdin, *Le prieuré royal*]

Reilly, Bernard F. *The Kingdom of León-Castilla Under Alfonso VII, 1126–1157* (Philadelphia: University of Pennsylvania Press, 1998). [Reilly, *Alfonso VII*]

———. "Medieval Spain, A.D. 500–1200," in *The Art of Medieval Spain, A.D. 500–1200*, exhibition catalogue (New York: The Metropolitan Museum of Art, 1993), pp. 2–11. [Reilly, "Medieval Spain"]

Reimagining Women: Representations of Women in Culture, ed. S[hirley].C. Neuman and G[lennis Byron]. Stephenson (Toronto: University of Toronto Press, 1993).

Rémy, Paul. "Les 'cours d'amour': légende et réalité," *Revue de l'université de Bruxelles* n.s. 7 (1955):179–97. [Rémy, "Les 'cours d'amour'"]

Renart, Jean. *Galeran de Bretagne, roman du XIIIᵉ siècle*, ed. Lucien Foulet (Paris: E. Champion, 1925). [Renart, *Galeran de Bretagne*]

The Reversible World. Symbolic Inversion in Art and Society, ed. Barbara Babcock (Ithaca: Cornell University Press, 1978).

Reynolds, Susan. *Fiefs and Vassals: The Medieval Evidence Reinterpreted* (Oxford: Oxford University Press, 1994). [Reynolds, *Fiefs and Vassals*]

———. "Medieval *Origines Gentium* and the Community of the Realm," *History* 68 (1983):375–90. [Reynolds, "Medieval *Origines Gentium*"]

Richard, Alfred. *Histoire des comtes de Poitou, 778–1204*, 2 vols. (Paris: A. Picard, 1903). [Richard, *Histoire des comtes de Poitou*]

Richard, Jean. *Les ducs de Bourgogne et la formation du duché au XIVᵉ siècle* (Dijon: Imprimerie Bernigaud et Privat, 1954). [Richard, *Les ducs de Bourgogne*]

Richardson, H[enry] G[erald]. "The Marriage and Coronation of Isabelle of Angoulême," *English Historical Review* 61 (1946):289–324. [Richardson, "The Marriage and Coronation of Isabelle of Angoulême"]

————. "The Letters and Charters of Eleanor of Aquitaine," *English Historical Review* 74 (1959):193–213. [Richardson, "Letters and Charters"]

————. "The Coronation in Medieval England: The Evolution of the Office and the Oath," *Traditio* 16 (1960):126–31. [Richardson, "Coronation in Medieval England"]

————. and G[eorge].O[sbourne]. Sayles. *The Governance of Mediaeval England from the Conquest to Magna Carta* (Edinburgh: Edinburgh University Press, 1963). [Richardson and Sayles, *Governance*]

Riley-Smith, Jonathan. *The First Crusaders, 1095–1131* (Cambridge, UK: Cambridge University Press, 1998). [Riley-Smith, *The First Crusaders*]

Rites of Power: Symbolism, Ritual, and Politics since the Middle Ages, ed. Sean E. Wilentz (Philadelphia: University of Pennsylvania Press, 1985).

Robertson, D[urant].W., Jr. "The Subject of the *De Amore* of Andreas Capellanus," *Modern Philology* 50 (1953):145–61. [Robertson, "The Subject of the *De Amore*"]

Roman, Joseph-Hippolyte. *Manuel de sigillographie française* (Paris: Picard, 1912). [Roman, *Manuel de sigillographie française*]

Rosenberg, Melrich V. *Eleanor of Aquitaine: Queen of the Troubadours and of the Courts of Love* (Boston: Houghton Mifflin, 1937). [Rosenberg, *Eleanor of Aquitaine*]

Rossignol, M. "Une charte d'Aliénor d'Aquitaine de l'an 1172," *Revue d'Aquitaine* (1861). [Rossignol, "Une charte d'Aliénor"]

Round, John Horace. "Who Was Alice of Essex?" *Transactions of the Essex Archaeological Society*, n.s. 3 (1889):242–51.

————. "Pharamus of Boulogne," *The Genealogist* 12 (1896):145–151.

Rucqoi, Adeline. *Histoire médiévale de la Péninsule ibérique* (Paris: Seuil, 1993). [Rucqoi, *Histoire médivale de la Péninsule ibérique*]

Ruiz, Teofilo F. "Unsacred Monarchy: The Kings of Castile in the Late Middle Ages," in *Rites of Power*, ed. Wilentz, pp. 109–44. [Ruiz, "Unsacred Monarchy"]

Saltman, Avril. *Theobald, Archbishop of Canterbury*. University of London Historical Studies, 2 (London: Athlone Press, 1956). [Saltman, *Theobald*]

Sample, Dana. "Joanna, Queen of Sicily," *Anglo-Norman Anonymous* 18.1 (January 2000):5.

San Juan, Rose Marie. "The Queen's Body and Its Slipping Mask: Contesting Portraits of Queen Christina of Sweden," in *Reimagining Women*, ed. Neuman and Stephenson, pp. 19–44.

Sanctity and Motherhood: Essays on Holy Mothers in the Middle Ages, ed. Anneke B. Mulder-Bakker (New York: Garland Publishing, 1995).

Sanders, I[von].J[ohn]. *English Baronies: A Study of Their Origin and Descent to 1327* (Oxford: Oxford University Press, 1960). [Sanders, *English Baronies*]

Sandford, Francis. *A Genealogical History of the Kings of England, and Monarchs of Great Britain, &c.* (London: Thomas Newcomb for Sandford, 1677); 2nd. edn., ed. Samuel Stebbing (London: M. Jenour, 1707). [Sandford, *Genealogical History*]

Sauerlander, Willibald. *Gotische Skulptur in Frankreich. 1140–1270*, Ill. von Max Hirmer (Munich: Hirmer (1970); trans. J. Sondheimer as *Gothic Sculpture in France, 1140–1270* (New York: Harry N. Abrams, 1973). [Sauerländer, *Gothic Sculpture*]

————. *Das Jahrhundert der grossen Kathedralen 1140–1260*, Universum der Kunst 36 (Munich: C.H. Beck, 1990).

Sayles, George O. *The Medieval Foundations of England*, rev. edn. (London: Methuen, 1964).

Schabel, Chris. "Frankish Pyrgos and the Cistercians," *Report of the Department of Antiquities of Cyprus* (2000), pp. 349–60. [Schabel, "Frankish Pyrgos"]

Schama, Simon. *Citizens: A Cultural History of the French Revolution* (New York: Alfred A. Knopf, 1989).

Schirmer, Walter F., and Ulrich Broich. *Studien zum literarischen Patronat im England des 12. Jahrhunderts* (Cologne: Westdeutscher Verlag, 1962). [Schirmer and Broich, *Studien*]

Schneider, Reinhard. *Vom Klosteraushalt zum Stadt- und Staatshaushalt der Zisterziensiche Beitrag* (Stuttgart: Anton Hiersemann, 1994). [Schneider, *Vom Klosteraushalt*]

Schramm, Percy Ernst. *Der König von Frankreich: Das Wesen der Monarchie vom 9. zum 16. Jahrhundert. Ein Kapitel aus der Geschichte des abendländischen Staates.* 2nd. edn., 2 vols. (Weimar: Hermann Bohlaus, 1960). [Schramm, *Der König von Frankreich*]

———. *A History of the English Coronation*, trans. Leopold G. Wickham Legg (Oxford: Clarendon Press, 1937). [Schramm, *History of the English Coronation*]

Schreiner, Ludwig. *Die frühgotische Plastik Südwestfrankreichs* (Cologne: Böhlau Verlag, 1963). [Schreiner, *Die frühgotische*]

Sears, Elizabeth. *The Ages of Man: Medieval Interpretations of the Life Cycle* (Princeton: Princeton University Press, 1986). [Sears, *The Ages of Man*]

The Second Crusade and the Cistercians, ed. Michael Gervers (New York: St. Martin's Press, 1992).

Settipani, Christian. *La préhistoire des Capétiens, part 1* (Villeneuve d'Ascq: P. van Kerrebrouck, 1993). [Settipani, *La préhistoire des Capétiens*]

Seward, Desmond. *Eleanor of Aquitaine: The Mother Queen* (Newton Abbott, UK: David and Charles, 1978); reissued as *Eleanor of Aquitaine* (New York: Times Books, 1979). [Seward, *Eleanor of Aquitaine*]

Sexual Meanings: The Cultural Construction of Gender and Sexuality, ed. Sherry B. Ortner and Harriet Whitehead (Cambridge, UK: Cambridge University Press, 1981).

Shadis, Miriam. *Berenguela of Castile and her Family: Political Women in the High Middle Ages*, The New Middle Ages (New York: Palgrave, forthcoming). [Shadis, *Berenguela of Castile*]

———. "Berenguela of Castile's Political Motherhood: The Management of Sexuality, Marriage, and Succession," in *Medieval Mothering*, ed. Parsons and Wheeler, pp. 335–358. [Shadis, "Political Motherhood"]

———. "Blanche of Castile and Facinger's 'Medieval Queenship': Reassessing the Argument," in *Capetian Women*, ed. Parsons and Nolan. [Shadis, "Blanche of Castile"]

———. "Piety, Politics and Power: The Patronage of Eleanor of England and her Daughters Berenguela of León and Blanche of Castile," in *The Cultural Patronage of Medieval Women*, ed. McCash, pp. 202–27. [Shadis, "Piety, Politics and Power"]

Shaping Community: The Art and Archaeology of Monasticism, ed. Sheila McNally, papers from a Symposium held at the Frederick R. Weisman Museum at the University of Minnesota, March 10–12, 2000 (BAR International Series 941, 2001).

Sheingorn, Pamela. "The Maternal Behavior of God: Divine Father as Fantasy Husband," in *Medieval Mothering*, ed. Parsons and Wheeler, pp. 77–100. [Sheingorn, "The Maternal Behavior of God"]

———. "'The Wise Mother': The Image of St. Anne Teaching the Virgin Mary," *Gesta* 32 (1993):69–80. [Sheingorn, "'The Wise Mother'"]

Sherman, Claire Richter. "The Queen in Charles V's 'Coronation Book': Jeanne de Bourbon and the 'Ordo ad Reginam Benedicendam,'" *Viator* 8 (1977):255–98. [Sherman, "The Queen in Charles V's 'Coronation Book'"]

———. "Taking a Second Look: Observations on the Iconography of a French Queen, Jeanne de Bourbon (1338–1378)," in *Feminism and Art History: Questioning the Litany*, ed. N. Broude and M.G. Garrard (New York: Harper and Row, 1982), pp. 100–117. [Sherman, "Taking a Second Look"]

Short, Ian. "Patrons and Polyglots: French Literature in Twelfth-Century England," *Anglo-Norman Studies* 14 (1991):229–49.

Simon, David. "Le sarcophage de Doña Sancha à Jaca," *Les cahiers de Saint-Michel de Cuxa* 10 (1979):107–24. [Simon, "Le sarcophage"]

———. "Sarcophagus of Doña Sancha," in *The Art of Medieval Spain, A.D. 500–1200*, pp. 229–32. [Simon, "Sarcophagus of Doña Sancha"]

Sisters and Workers in the Middle Ages, ed. Judith Bennett, Elizabeth A. Clark, Jean F. O'Barr, B. Anne Vilen, and Sarah Westphal-Wihl (Chicago: University of Chicago Press, 1989).

Sivéry, Gérard. *Blanche de Castille* (Paris: Fayard, 1990). [Sivéry, *Blanche de Castille*]

———. *Louis VIII, le Lion* (Paris: Fayard, 1995). [Sivéry, *Louis VIII*]

Smith, Jacqueline. "Robert of Arbrissel's Relations with Women," in *Medieval Women*, ed. Baker, pp. 175–84. [Smith, "Robert of Arbrissel's Relations with Women"]

Smoller, Laura A. "Miracle, Memory and Meaning in the Canonization of Vincent Ferrer, 1453–1454," *Speculum* 73 (1998):29–54.

Spiegel, Gabrielle. "Genealogy: Form and Function in Medieval Historical Narrative," *History and Theory* 22 (1983):43–53, repr. in Spiegel, *The Past as Text*, pp. 99–110. [Spiegel, "Genealogy"]

———. "History, Historicism and the Social Logic of the Text in the Middle Ages," *Speculum* 65 (1990):59–86. [Spiegel, "Social Logic"]

———. *The Past as Text: The Theory and Practice of Medieval Historiography* (Baltimore: Johns Hopkins University Press, 1997).

Stafford, Pauline. "Emma: the Powers of the Queen," in *Queens and Queenship in Medieval Europe*, ed. Duggan, pp. 3–26. [Stafford, "Emma: the Powers of the Queen"]

———. *Queens, Concubines and Dowagers: The King's Wife in the Early Middle Ages* (Athens, GA: University of Georgia Press, 1983).

———. *Queen Emma and Queen Edith: Queenship and Women's Power in Eleventh-Century England* (Oxford: Blackwell, 1997). [Stafford, *Queen Emma and Queen Edith*]

————. "The Portrayal of Royal Women in England, Mid-tenth to Mid-twelfth Centuries," in *Medieval Queenship*, ed. Parsons, pp. 143–67. [Stafford, "The Portrayal of Royal Women"]

Stahl, Alan. "Coinage in the Name of Medieval Women," in *Medieval Women*, ed. Rosenthal, pp. 321–41. [Stahl, "Coinage"]

Stenton, Doris Mary. *The English Woman in History* (London: Allen and Unwin, 1957).

Stothard, Charles Alfred. *The Monumental Effigies of Great Britain*, 2 vols. (London: J. M'Creery, 1817). [Stothard, *Effigies*]

Strickland, Agnes. *Lives of the Queens of England, from the Norman Conquest*, 6 vols. (London: Bell and Daldy, 1864–65). [Strickland, *Lives of the Queens*]

Stringer, Keith J. *The Reign of King Stephen: Kingship, Warfare and Government in Twelfth-Century England* (London: Routledge, 1993). [Stringer, *Reign of King Stephen*]

Stuard, Susan Mosher. "Fashion's Captives: Medieval Women in French Historiography," in *Women in Medieval History and Historiography*, ed. Stuard, pp. 59–80. [Stuard, "Fashion's Captives"]

Stubbs, William. *Historical Introductions to the Rolls Series*, ed. Arthur Hassall (London: Longman, Green and Company, 1902; repr. New York: Haskell Press, 1968, and New York: AMS Press, 1971). [Stubbs, *Historical Introductions to the Rolls Series*]

Taburet-Delahaye, Élisabeth. Entries in *L'oeuvre de Limoges: émaux limousins du Moyen Âge*, exhibition catalogue, Musée du Louvre and the Metropolitan Museum of Art (Paris: Réunion des musées nationaux, 1995). [Taburet-Delahaye, in *L'oeuvre de Limoges*]

Tachau, Katherine. "God's Compass," *Art Bulletin* 80 (1998):7–33. [Tachau, "God's Compass"]

Tanner, Heather. "Between Scylla and Charybdis: The Political Role of the Comital Family of Boulogne in Northern France and England (879–1159)," (Ph.D. diss., University of California at Santa Barbara, 1993). [Tanner, "Between Scylla and Charybdis"]

————. "Trial by Chronicle: Assessing the Failures of Three Rulers of England and Normandy, 1070–1300," *Majestas* 4 (1996):39–60. [Tanner, "Trial by Chronicle"]

Taylor, Craig. "'Le royaume ne peut tomber en fille': The Salic Law and French Queenship," in *Capetian Women*, ed. Parsons and Nolan.

Tefler, Canon W. "Faversham Reconsidered," *Archaeologia Cantiana* 80 (1965):215–220. [Tefler, "Faversham Reconsidered"]

Thibout, Marc. "Peinture murale. À propos des peintures de la chapelle Sainte-Radegonde de Chinon," *Bulletin monumental* 125 (1967):95–96. [Thibout, "Peinture murale"]

Thompson, Sally. *Women Religious: The Founding of English Nunneries after the Norman Conquest* (Oxford: Clarendon Press, 1991). [Thompson, *Women Religious*]

Tolhurst, Fiona. "Lawman's Virgilian and Exodial Heritage: The Process of Translation from Geoffrey, to Wace, to Lawman," paper presented at the International

Congress on Laʒamon's *Brut,* The University of New Brunswick, Saint John, New Brunswick, July 1997.

———. "The Britons as Hebrews, Romans, and Normans: Geoffrey of Monmouth's British Epic and Reflections of Empress Matilda," *Arthuriana* 8.4 (Winter 1998):69–87.

———. "The Once and Future Queen: The Development of Guenevere from Geoffrey of Monmouth to Malory," *BBIAS* 50 (1998):272–308.

Toman, Rolf. *Romanesque Architecture, Sculpture, Painting* (Cologne: Könemann, 1997).

Le trésor de Saint-Denis, ed. Blaise, comte de Montesquiou-Fezensac and Danielle Gaborit-Chopin, 3 vols. (Paris: A. et J. Picard, 1973–77). [*Le trésor de Saint-Denis,* ed. Montesquiou-Fezensac and Gaborit-Chopin]

Trindale, Ann. *Berengaria: In Search of Richard the Lionheart's Queen* (Dublin: Four Courts Press, 1999). [Trindale, *Berengaria*]

Trouncer, Margaret. *Eleanor: The Two Marriages of a Queen* (London: Heinemann, 1967). [Trouncer, *Eleanor: The Two Marriages*]

Turner, Ralph V. "Eleanor of Aquitaine in the Reign of her Son Richard Lionheart," paper presented at the Charles Homer Haskins Society Conference, Cornell University, November 1999.

———. "Eleanor of Aquitaine and Her Children: An Inquiry into Medieval Family Attachment," *Journal of Medieval History* 14 (1988):325–26. [Turner, "Eleanor and Her Children"]

———. *King John* (London: Longman, 1994). [Turner, *King John*]

———. "The Mandeville Inheritance, 1189–1236: Its Legal, Political and Social Context," *The Haskins Society Journal* 1 (1989):147–72.

———. "Richard Lionheart and English Episcopal Elections," *Albion* 29 (1997):1–13. [Turner, "Richard Lionheart"]

Turner, Victor. *Image and Pilgrimage in Christian Culture: Anthropological Perspectives* (New York: Columbia University Press, 1978). [V. Turner, *Image and Pilgrimage*]

Ullmann, Walter. *A History of Political Thought: The Middle Ages* (Harmondsworth: Penguin Books, 1965).

Valdez del Alamo, Elizabeth. "Lament for a Lost Queen: The Sarcophagus of Doña Blanca in Nájera," *The Art Bulletin* 78 (1996):311–33. [Valdez del Alamo, "Lament for a Lost Queen"]

———. "Ortodoxia y heterodoxia en el estudio de la escultura románica española: estado de la cuestión," *Anuario del Departamento de Historia y Teoría del Arte* (Madrid: Universidad Autónoma de Madrid, forthcoming). [Valdez del Alamo, "Ortodoxia y heterodoxia"]

Van Houts, Elisabeth M.C. "Matilda of Flanders," in the *New Dictionary of National Biography* (Oxford: Oxford University Press, forthcoming 2004). [van Houts, "Matilda of Flanders"]

———. *Memory and Gender in Medieval Europe 900–1200* (Toronto: University of Toronto Press, 1999). [van Houts, *Memory and Gender*]

Vann, Theresa M. "The Theory and Practice of Medieval Castilian Queenship," in *Queens, Regents and Potentates,* ed. Vann, pp. 125–47. [Vann, "Medieval Castilian Queenship"]

Venarde, Bruce. *Women's Monasticism and Medieval Society: Nunneries in France and England, 890–1215* (Ithaca: Cornell University Press, 1997). [Venarde, *Women's Monasticism*]

Vernadsky, George. *Kievan Russia,* A History of Russia 2 (New Haven, CT: Yale University Press, 1948). [Vernadsky, *Kievan Russia*]

Vickers, Michael. "Rock Crystal: The Key to Cut Glass and *diatreta* in Persia and Rome," *Journal of Roman Archaeology* 8 (1996):49–65. [Vickers, "Rock Crystal"]

Victoria County Histories: as cited in chapter notes.

Vincent, Nicholas. "Isabella of Angoulême; John's Jezebel," in *King John: New Interpretations,* ed. Church, pp. 166–219. [Vincent, "Isabella of Angoulême"]

Vodola, Elizabeth. *Excommunication in the Middle Ages* (Berkeley: University of California Press, 1986). [Vodola, *Excommunication*]

Wakefield, Walter E. *Heresy, Crusade and Inquisition in Southern France, 1100–1250* (Berkeley-Los Angeles: University of California Press, 1974). [Wakefield, *Heresy, Crusade and Inquisition*]

Walker, Curtis Howe. *Eleanor of Aquitaine* (Chapel Hill: University of North Carolina Press, 1950).

———. "Eleanor of Aquitaine and the Disaster of Cadmos Mountain on the Second Crusade," *American Historical Review* 55 (1950):847–61. [Walker, "Eleanor and the Disaster of Cadmos Mountain"]

Warnecke, Retha M. *Anne Boleyn: Family Politics at the Court of Henry VIII* (Cambridge, UK: Cambridge University Press, 1989).

Warner, Marina. *Alone of All Her Sex: The Myth and the Cult of the Virgin Mary* (New York: Wiedenfeld and Nicolson, 1976).

Warren, W[ilfred].L[ewis]. *Henry II* (Berkeley-Los Angeles: University of California Press; London: Eyre Methuen, 1973; repr. New Haven, CT: Yale University Press, 2000). [Warren, *Henry II*]

———. *King John* (Berkeley-Los Angeles: University of California Press, 1961; New York: Norton, 1961, repr. 1978).

Weigand, Rudolf. "Zur künftigen Edition des Dekrets Gratians," *Zeitschrift der Savigny-Stiftung für Rechtsgeschichte, kanonistische Abteilung* 83 (1997):32–51. [Weigand, "Zur künftigen Edition des Dekrets Gratians"]

Weir, Alison. *Eleanor of Aquitaine: By the Wrath of God, Queen of England* (London: Cape, 1999). [Weir, *Eleanor of Aquitaine*]

Weiss, Judith. "Introduction" to *Wace's Roman de Brut A History of the British: Text and Translation,* ed. and trans. Judith Weiss (Exeter: University of Exeter Press, 1999), pp. xi–xxix. [Wace, *Roman de Brut,* ed. Weiss]

Wertheimer, Laura. "Adeliza of Louvain and Anglo-Norman Queenship," *Haskins Society Journal* 7 (1995):101–15. [Wertheimer, "Adeliza of Louvain"]

West, Francis J. *The Justiciarship in England, 1066–1232* (Cambridge, UK: Cambridge University Press, 1966). [West, *Justiciarship*]

White, Graeme. "Continuity in Government," in *The Anarchy of Stephen's Reign*, ed. King, pp. 117–44. [White, "Continuity in Government"]

White, T[erence].H[anbury]. *The Once and Future King* (New York: Ace Books. 1996).

Wind, Bartina H. "L'idéologie courtoise dans les lais de Marie de France," in *Mélanges de linguistique romane et de philologie médiévale offerts à M. Maurice Delbouleville*, ed. Madeleine Tyssens (Gembloux: J. Duclot, 1964). [Wind, "L'idéologie courtoise"]

Winkler, Emil. *Marie de France* (Vienna: A. Holder, 1918).

Winroth, Anders. "The Two Recensions of Gratian's Decretum," *Zeitschrift der Savigny-Stiftung für Rechtsgeschichte, kanonistische Abteilung* 83 (1997):22–31. [Winroth, "The Two Recensions of Gratian's Decretum"]

Wolffe, B.P. *The Royal Demesne in English History: The Crown Estate in the Governance of the Realm from the Conquest to 1509* (London: Allen and Unwin/Ohio University Press, 1971). [Wolffe, *The Royal Demesne*]

Women: A Feminist Perspective, ed. Jo Freeman (Palo Alto, CA: Mayfield Publishing, 1975).

Women and Power in the Middle Ages, ed. Mary Erler and Maryanne Kowaleski (Athens: University of Georgia Press, 1988). [*Women and Power*, ed. Erler and Kowaleski]

Women and Sovereignty, ed. Louise Olga Fradenburg, special number of *Cosmo*, 7 (Edinburgh: University of Edinburgh Press, 1992).

Women and the Book: Assessing the Visual Evidence, ed. Jane H.M. Taylor and Lesley Smith, British Library Studies in Medieval Culture (London and Toronto: British Library and University of Toronto Press, 1997). [*Women and the Book*, ed. Taylor and Smith]

Women in Medieval History and Historiography, ed. Susan Mosher Stuard (Philadelphia: University of Pennsylvania Press, 1987).

Women in Medieval Western European Culture, ed. Linda E. Mitchell (London-New York: Garland Publishing, 1991).

Women in the Middle Ages and the Renaissance, ed. Mary Beth Rose (Syracuse, NY: Syracuse University Press, 1986). [*Women in the Middle Ages and the Renaissance*, ed. Rose]

Women, Marriage, and Family in Medieval Christendom: Essays in Memory of Michael M. Sheehan, CSB, ed. Joel T. Rosenthal and Constance Rousseau (Kalamazoo, MI: Medieval Institute Press, 1998).

Women of the English Nobility and Gentry, 1066–1500, comp., ed. and trans. Jennifer C. Ward (Manchester: Manchester University Press, 1995).

Women of the Medieval World, ed. Julius Kirshner and Suzanne Fonay Wemple (Oxford: Blackwell, 1985).

Wood, Charles T. "The First Two Queens Elizabeth," in *Women and Sovereignty*, ed. Fradenburg, pp. 121–32. [Wood, "The First Two Queens Elizabeth"]

———. *The French Apanages and the Capetian Monarchy 1224–1328* (Cambridge, MA: Harvard University Press, 1966). [Wood, *Apanages*]

Printed in the United States
202522BV00005B/7-57/P